Evolutionary Economics and Social Complexity Science

Volume 11

The Japanese Association for Evolutionary Economics (JAFEE) always has adhered to its original aim of taking an explicit "integrated" approach. This path has been followed steadfastly since the Association's establishment in 1997 and, as well, since the inauguration of our international journal in 2004. We have deployed an agenda encompassing a contemporary array of subjects including but not limited to: foundations of institutional and evolutionary economics, criticism of mainstream views in the social sciences, knowledge and learning in socio-economic life, development and innovation of technologies, transformation of industrial organizations and economic systems, experimental studies in economics, agent-based modeling of socio-economic systems, evolution of the governance structure of firms and other organizations, comparison of dynamically changing institutions of the world, and policy proposals in the transformational process of economic life. In short, our starting point is an "integrative science" of evolutionary and institutional views. Furthermore, we always endeavor to stay abreast of newly established methods such as agent-based modeling, socio/econo-physics, and network analysis as part of our integrative links.

More fundamentally, "evolution" in social science is interpreted as an essential key word, i.e., an integrative and /or communicative link to understand and re-domain various preceding dichotomies in the sciences: ontological or epistemological, subjective or objective, homogeneous or heterogeneous, natural or artificial, selfish or altruistic, individualistic or collective, rational or irrational, axiomatic or psychological-based, causal nexus or cyclic networked, optimal or adaptive, micro- or macroscopic, deterministic or stochastic, historical or theoretical, mathematical or computational, experimental or empirical, agent-based or socio/econo-physical, institutional or evolutionary, regional or global, and so on. The conventional meanings adhering to various traditional dichotomies may be more or less obsolete, to be replaced with more current ones vis-à-vis contemporary academic trends. Thus we are strongly encouraged to integrate some of the conventional dichotomies.

These attempts are not limited to the field of economic sciences, including management sciences, but also include social science in general. In that way, understanding the social profiles of complex science may then be within our reach. In the meantime, contemporary society appears to be evolving into a newly emerging phase, chiefly characterized by an information and communication technology (ICT) mode of production and a service network system replacing the earlier established factory system with a new one that is suited to actual observations. In the face of these changes we are urgently compelled to explore a set of new properties for a new socio/economic system by implementing new ideas. We thus are keen to look for "integrated principles" common to the above-mentioned dichotomies throughout our serial compilation of publications. We are also encouraged to create a new, broader spectrum for establishing a specific method positively integrated in our own original way.

More information about this series at http://www.springer.com/series/11930

Robert Boyer • Hiroyasu Uemura
Toshio Yamada • Lei Song
Editors

Evolving Diversity and Interdependence of Capitalisms

Transformations of Regional Integration in EU and Asia

Springer

Editors
Robert Boyer
Institut des Amériques
Vanves, France

Hiroyasu Uemura
Yokohama National University
Yokohama, Japan

Toshio Yamada
Nagoya University
Nagoya, Japan

Lei Song
Peking University
Beijing, China

ISSN 2198-4204 ISSN 2198-4212 (electronic)
Evolutionary Economics and Social Complexity Science
ISBN 978-4-431-55000-6 ISBN 978-4-431-55001-3 (eBook)
https://doi.org/10.1007/978-4-431-55001-3

Library of Congress Control Number: 2018959102

This Springer imprint is published by the registered company Springer Japan KK part of Springer Nature.
The registered company address is: Shiroyama Trust Tower, 4-3-1 Toranomon, Minato-ku, Tokyo 105-6005, Japan

Acknowledgments

The authors gratefully acknowledge financial support from the project, "The Diversity of Economic Institutions and the Interdependence of Growth Regimes in Regional Integration: EU-Asia Comparative Analysis" (No. 18K01564), funded by Japan Society for the Promotion of Science. Lei Song and other authors are also grateful to the research project, "Development Strategy of Modern National Governance" (17JJD810003) in China.

This book is the result of international collaborative research that has been supported by many French, Japanese, Chinese, and Korean colleagues for about 30 years. Since the publication of the book, Boyer, R. and Yamada, T. (eds.) *Japanese Capitalism in Crisis: A Régulationist Interpretation* (Routledge 2000), this international collegial network has developed extensively, leading us to various collaborations in which not only the Japanese but also Chinese and Korean economies have been studied. As the result of the extending collaborations, Boyer, R., Uemura, H., and Isogai, A. (eds.) *Diversity and Transformations of Asian Capitalisms* (Routledge 2012) and Boyer, R., Uemura, H. and Isogai, A. (dir.) *Capitalismes asiatiques: Diversité et transformations* (Presses Universitaires de Rennes 2015) were published. During the same period in Europe, the Euro crisis happened, and European integration had a severe trouble in the early 2000s. Responding to this transformation and crisis, Boyer, R. *The Euro Crisis: History and Polices of European Integration* (Fujiwara Shoten 2013) was also published. In this situation, these extending collaborative researches led us to the comparative analysis of regional integration in Europe and East Asia. Especially, it was very helpful for our Europe-Asia collaborative researches to have active academic discussions in Recherche et Régulation 2015, Colloque international, "La théorie de la régulation à l'épreuve des crises," 9–12 June 2015, Université Paris-Diderot-Inalco, Paris.

On many occasions, the contributors have received useful comments and helpful suggestions from Bruno Amable, Benjamin Coriat, Yasuo Inoue, Akinori Isogai, Midori Kizaki, Sebastien Lechevalier, Wooseok Ok, Kazuhiro Okuma, Kengo Uchihashi, Hiroki Yokota, and other members of the European Association for Evolutionary Political Economy and the Japan Association for Evolutionary

Economics. We are grateful for the interest they have shown and would like to declare the usual caveat that none of them is held responsible for the final content of the book, or any errors that remain. We must also thank Jacqueline Jean sincerely, who has supported our international collaboration wholeheartedly since we started it at the Centre pour La Recherche Economique et ses Applications (CEPREMAP), Paris, a quarter of a century ago.

Contents

About the Authors

Robert Boyer is a French economist trained at Ecole Polytechnique, Sciences-Po Paris and Université Paris 1 Panthéon Sorbonne. He was a senior researcher at CNRS and a professor at EHESS, and is now a fellow at Institut des Amériques, Paris. He has developed an historical and comparative analysis of the transformations of capitalisms, under the label of the *régulation* theory. His publications include R. Boyer and Y. Saillard, *Régulation Theory: The State of the Art*, Routledge, 2001; R. Boyer, *The Future of Economic Growth*, Edward Elgar, 2004; R. Boyer, *Les financiers détruiront-ils le capitalisme?* Economica, 2011; and R. Boyer, *Economie politique des capitalismes*, La Découverte, 2015. He is also an editor of *Revue de la Régulation*.

Nicolas Canry is an assistant professor of economics at Université Paris 1 Panthéon Sorbonne in France. His main topics of research are the macroeconomic analysis of growth and distribution, especially, the relations between income distribution, inequality, and economic growth. His recent research also focuses on global imbalances in the international economy.

Yuji Harada is an associate professor of economics at Setsunan University in Japan. His research focuses on the diversity of capitalisms and economic dynamics from the perspective of institutional economics. His publications include "The Diversity of the "Neoliberal Policy Regime" and Income Distribution," in H. Magara (ed.) *Policy Change Under New Democratic Capitalism*, 2016.

Hitoshi Hirakawa is a professor of international economy at Kokushikan University and an emeritus professor at Nagoya University. He published books and articles on Asian development from the viewpoint of the world economy, including Hirakawa et al. (eds.) *Innovative ICT Industrial Architecture in East Asia,* Springer, 2017, and Hirakawa et al. (eds.) *Servitization, IT-ization, and Innovation Models*, Routledge, 2013.

Yasuro Hirano is an emeritus professor at Fukuoka Prefectural University in Japan. He has published books and articles on the contemporary Japanese economy from the viewpoint of labor and social policy. These include *The Japanese Institutions and Economic Growth,* Fujiwara Shoten, 1996. Furthermore, he contributed to a chapter in R. Boyer, H. Uemura, and A. Isogai (eds.) *Diversity and Transformation of Asian Capitalisms*, Routledge, 2012.

Jacques Mazier is an emeritus professor of economics at University Paris 13 Sorbonne Paris Cité. He has published books and articles in the field of macroeconomic modeling and the *régulation* theory, including J. Mazier, V. Duwicquet, and M. Clévenot, *Quand les crises reviennent*, Economica, 2015. He has participated in the Augur project of the European Commission, "Europe in the World of 2030."

Hiroshi Nishi is a professor of economics at Hannan University in Japan. His research interests include analytical political economy based on post-Keynesian economics and empirical study using econometric analysis. His recent publication is "Sources of Productivity Growth Dynamics: Is Japan Suffering from Baumol's Growth Disease?," *Review of Income and Wealth* (https://doi.org/10.1111/roiw.12363).

Myoung-keun On is a PhD course student at University Paris 13 Sorbonne Paris Cité. He studies the Korean and Asian economies from the international perspective.

Pascal Petit is a French economist and an emeritus research officer at CNRS (Centre National de la Recherche Scientifique), attached to the Centre d'Economie de Paris Nord CEPN, University Paris 13 Sorbonne Paris Cité. He has published books and articles on economic growth, innovation and employment, structural changes, and institutional dynamics. These include B. Coriat, P. Petit, and G. Schmeder (eds.) *The Hardship of Nations: Exploring the Paths of Modern Capitalism*, Edward Elgar, 2006, and J. Eatwell, T. Mckinly, and P. Petit (eds.) *Challenges for Europe in the World, 2030*, Sage Publications, 2014.

Dominique Plihon is an emeritus professor at the Department of Economics of Paris-Nord University in France. He was in charge of a Master Program in Banking and Finance. He was the dean of the Department of Economics from 1995 to 1997. He graduated from Paris University (MA) and from the State University of New York at Albany (US) (PhD). He worked at the Banque de France (1974–1983) and at the Commissariat du Plan (1983–1988). He published books in the fields of banking, international finance, European economics: *The banks, New Strategies* (in French) in 1998 by the Documentation Française; *Central Banks and the Financial Crisis*, Documentation Française, 2011; *Exchange Rates* (in French), La Découverte, 2017.

Lei Song is a professor of comparative political economy at Peking University in China. His research interests range from the diversity of capitalisms to the business-government relations. He is working on book-length projects about the political economy of China's mode of production and policy transfer between China and the Western countries.

Shinji Tahara is an assistant professor of economics at Chiba University of Commerce. He participated in annual estimates of the SNA and the compilation of the Input-Output Table for Japan at Cabinet Office. His main research themes in economics are industrial structural change and de-industrialization. His work appears in *Revue de la régulation*, among others.

Norio Tokumaru is an associate professor of economics at Nagoya Institute of Technology in Japan. He has published books and articles on innovation systems in Nordic countries and East Asia from the comparative institutionalist and evolutionary perspectives.

Hironori Tohyama is a professor of economics at Shizuoka University in Japan. He has published books and articles in the field of the comparative political economy, including "Varieties of Asian Welfare Capitalisms and the Influence of Globalization," *Journal of International and Comparative Social Policy*, Vol. 31, No.1, 2014.

Hiroyasu Uemura is a professor of economics at Yokohama National University in Japan. He published books and articles widely in the field of comparative institutional analysis and macroeconomic analysis from the perspective of the *régulation* theory. These include R. Boyer, H. Uemura, and A. Isogai (eds.) *Diversity and Transformations of Asian Capitalisms*, Routledge, 2012.

Mitsuru Uemura is a doctoral course student at the University of Tokyo in Japan. He studies international relations in the EU. He published articles on migration policies of the EU and France. These include Mitsuru Uemura "Europeanization in EU Immigration Policies – European Integration and the Transformation of French Immigration Politics," *Sophia Journal of European Studies*, Vol. 8, 2015.

Hiroyuki Uni is a professor at the Graduate School of Economics, Kyoto University, Japan. His research interests encompass political economy, institutional economics, and comparative analysis of capitalism. He is the editor of *Contemporary Meanings of John R. Commons's Institutional Economics: An Analysis Using a Newly Discovered Manuscript*, Springer, 2017.

Sebastian Valdecantos holds the title of "Docteur en Sciènces Économiques" from the Université Paris 13 Sorbonne Paris Cité, 2015. His main field of research is macroeconomic modeling. Most of his work has been done at the United Nations Economic Commission for Latin America and the Caribbean, where he has studied the main challenges that Latin American economies face in their quest for development.

Toshio Yamada is an emeritus professor at Nagoya University in Japan. He is a main contributor to the *régulation* theory in Japan. He has published books and articles on economic theories, Japanese capitalism, and varieties of capitalism in the world. These include R. Boyer and T. Yamada (eds.) *Japanese Capitalism in Crisis: A Regulationist Interpretation*, Routledge, 2000, and T. Yamada, *Contemporary Capitalism and Civil Society: The Japanese Experience*, Springer, 2018.

Chengnan Yan is a professor of economics at Rikkyo University in Japan. He published books and articles wildly on the changes of economic growth regime and institutional reforms in China and East Asian economies, including C. Yan, *The Economic Development and Institutional Changes in China*, in Japanese, Kyoto University Press, 2011.

Chapter 1
Introduction

Robert Boyer, Hiroyasu Uemura, Toshio Yamada, and Lei Song

The last two decades have been described as the epoch of fast technical change and globalization. The first attribute is not self-evident since innovation may be seen in business and economic policy but not in productivity statistics: Solow's paradox was based on the emergence of new information and communication technologies, but it is also relevant for biotechnologies and artificial intelligence breakthroughs. Concerning the second attribute, globalization, it is too broad a concept to be useful in any analytical study. Frequently considered to belong to a single mechanism, there are numerous and contrasting conceptions of globalization: the *emergence of multinationals* as key actors in the domestic and world economy, the creation of *global value chains*, the complete *mobility of financial capital* from one country to another, the generalization of *export-led growth regimes*, the domination of economic policy by *competitiveness* concerns, the *attractiveness of domestic territory* for highly mobile productive and financial capital, the *loss of autonomy* by the national state, the diffusion of *American lifestyle and technical norms*, the separation of *global cities* from their hinterland, and the *social polarization* between winners and losers.

R. Boyer (✉)
Institut des Amériques, Vanves, France
e-mail: r.boyer2@orange.fr

H. Uemura (✉)
Yokohama National University, Yokohama, Japan
e-mail: huemura@ynu.ac.jp

T. Yamada
Nagoya University, Nagoya, Japan
e-mail: tyamada@rainbow.plala.or.jp

L. Song
Peking University, Beijing, China
e-mail: slei@pku.edu.cn

R. Boyer et al. (eds.), *Evolving Diversity and Interdependence of Capitalisms*,
Evolutionary Economics and Social Complexity Science 11,
https://doi.org/10.1007/978-4-431-55001-3_1

Last but not least, some economists define globalization as the *primacy of competition* at the world level, namely, the equivalent of the law of gravity for physics.

1.1 Complex Contemporary Transformations in the Search of Theorization

This book adopts a very different approach: over the past three decades, *complex dynamic processes* have been transforming the dividing line between a territory and the world's international regions.

1.1.1 The Interweaving of Economics and Politics

A definite set of political decisions has put into motion the opening for trade, then for foreign direct investment, and finally for financial capital in general. This has not been a smooth evolution since recurring financial and economic crises have erupted and destabilized many national economies. In retrospect, the rise and maturation of Asian new industrialized economies have become the most relevant force affecting the world system. Therefore, it is crucial to understand how political strategic decisions interact with the evolution of the institutional forms that shape evolution and growth regimes. The juncture of the social forces that have promoted the opening of the world to competition can enter a crisis, either through brutal economic collapse (e.g., the 2008 American financial crisis) or through the demise of a political coalition promoting internationalization (e.g., the Brexit vote and the subsequent political fallout). This concern for *mixing political and economic analyses* is common in all the chapters.

1.1.2 The Nation-State Balancing International, Regional, and Local Demands

The image of a single large market operating at the global level is quite misleading indeed, contrary to the title of a world best seller, *The Earth Is Not Flat*, as there are various industry levels that interact. In some sectors, such as electronics and pharmaceuticals, the productive processes operate at *the world level*. By contrast, other sectors (construction, healthcare, education, everyday consumption) are *nationally embedded* in response to idiosyncratic demand and an intrinsic connection with the domestic territory. Under the post-WWII Bretton Woods system, the national and international levels used to be the two relevant levels. Since its collapse, the importance of the nation-state has been challenged by a *double shift*. On the one hand, in Europe, national governments have agreed to delegate and pool some of their sovereignty attributes at the regional level; in other zones, international trade treaties have been negotiated and implemented at the regional level. On the other hand, the shift in the productive paradigm away from Fordism mass production techniques implies a redeployment of economic activity across *localities*.

Consequently, the observed dynamics cannot be captured by the extreme simplification of a unique level analysis but has to take into account the complexity of the *nested four levels*: international, regional, national, and local.

1.1.3 Innovation Systems and Exchange-Rate Regimes Matter

International markets are organizing competition among different production areas. This so-called competitiveness is the outcome of the interaction among a series of social systems of production and innovation and a specialization of external trade in commodities, standardized consumer goods, highly sophisticated intermediate components, and, finally, equipment goods and high value-added services to businesses. This *complementarity between the domestic and the international spheres* contradicts the conventional vision of a uniform and homogeneous distribution of production at the world level. The fact that *many national currencies* coexist defines a second reason why the world is split into different monetary zones linked by the choice of an exchange rate regime.

Within the eurozone, irreversible parities have been established with the adoption of a unique currency, whereas in East Asia, more or less perfect flexible exchange rates have preserved a degree of freedom in adjusting diverging production costs and prices across national economies. Therefore, the division of labor and specialization among members do not follow the same patterns in East Asia and in Europe. Thus, the concept of globalization does not capture this essential feature of the contemporary world. The international flows of capital today tend to set exchange rates that differ from the purchasing power parity theory that used to be valid when trade balances were the main drivers of exchange rate adjustments. This explains why various chapters of this book investigate the economic outcomes of a whole *spectrum of exchange rate regimes.*

1.1.4 Still the Century of Capitalism Diversity

This is the core of the comparison of the regional integration processes in the EU and East Asia. Each capitalist type is defined by an ad hoc complementarity/compatibility among a wage labor nexus, a domestic form of competition, and a degree of integration into the international regime. There are a few reasons why they should converge toward a common and "best" model of capitalism. First, economic history shows that emulating a leading and hegemonic capitalism (England in the nineteenth century, the USA in the twentieth century) has triggered a hybridization that ends up as a genuine brand (e.g., German capitalism is not at all a replica of the English, and Japan has not converged toward the USA). Second, these *different complementarities* among institutional forms derive from the political and social domination of a *hegemonic bloc*. It is itself the outcome of the layering of past political struggles and compromises among key social groups. Third, some forms of capitalism appear to be unable to sustain lifestyle progress and imply an *economic decline*; however, symmetrically *new forms can emerge* that are not mere variants of existing configurations when domestic political changes encounter the opportunity brought by the international economy. The two chapters on China are a good illustration of the innovative capabilities of capitalism.

1.1.5 A World of Interdependent National Growth Regimes

The concept of globalization is too broad, and it raises many criticisms that converge toward an alternative analytical framework. The tensions and limits of world value chains point toward the *processes of economic regional integration*, but an apparent paradox has to be overcome: the more advanced European integration via the progressive construction of supranational institutions has been facing a systemic crisis, whereas the more silent de facto economy-led integration of East Asia is still progressing. The book proposes an interpretation: the *interdependence of contrasting national growth regimes* has to be overcome either by the flexibility of the exchange rate (Asia) or by compensating transfers when a unique currency is created as this is one source of the eurozone crisis of the 2010s.

These themes are elaborated on in the three parts of this book. First, regional integration in Europe and Asia is analyzed in the context of evolving diversity and interdependence of capitalisms, where the interactions between the economy and polity are crucial in determining the dynamics of the integration processes. Second, the transformation of European integration is analyzed from the viewpoint of the coexistence of diverse capitalisms and growth regimes, within the monetary union. Brexit might mean a tipping point in a six-decade-long European integration process. Third, China and Japan are analyzed in the context of the diversity and interdependence of Asian capitalisms. The international division of labor is being reorganized drastically due to the rapidly growing Chinese economy. New growth regimes are emerging in the context of unprecedented interdependence.

1.2 Comparing Europe and East Asia: The Conditions for Successful Regional Economic Integration

The first part of the book analyzes regional integration in Europe and East Asia from the viewpoint of the evolving diversity and interdependence of capitalisms and considers the conditions for successful regional economic integration.

1.2.1 The Dialectic between Supranational Institution Building and Economic Dynamism

Robert Boyer (Chap. 2) adopts a comparative analysis of two different regional integration processes in Europe and East Asia and derives some general conditions about the viability of regional economic integration. The core argument is that economic logic and political legitimacy have to be combined into viable configurations, largely path dependent. The EU has made progress via supranational institution building in anticipation of economic growth stimulus, whereas the soft coordination within the ASEAN is conceived as accompanying the growing interdependence created by business strategies. The euro has aggravated the divergence of macroeconomic trajectories between the north and the south while removing a key adjustment mechanism via exchange rates. In the absence of transfers within the eurozone, the integration hits structural and political obstacles, whereas the pragmatic choice of exchange-rate regimes allows the ASEAN to cope with the rise of China and its impact on the regional division of labor. In the EU, heterogeneous growth models—finance led, innovation and export based, or consumption led—would be compatible only with either adjustable/flexible exchange rates and, thus, a form of national sovereignty is maintained or with fiscal solidarity that assumes that member states agree to a fully fledged and explicit federalist pact. This framework explains why since the 2010s, the EU and ASEAN have been trading places as possible benchmarks concerning the ingredients of successful regional economic integration. Nevertheless, geopolitical potential conflicts point to a crucial weakness in East Asian integration, and the jury is still out concerning the future of the EU.

Hitoshi Hirakawa (Chap. 3) considers the institutionalization of the East Asian region in the transforming world economy, focusing on the mechanism that causes this structural shift and its effect on the region and the world economy. East Asia has recently grown to surpass the current economic size of Europe and America, and is displaying the concomitant dramatic changes in regional economic structure. International institutions, such as the World Bank, Asian Development Bank, and OECD, among others, have predicted that Asia will continue to grow and become a major economic power. However, this study investigates the mechanism causing this structural shift and the effects of the structural shift on the region and the world economy. This study discusses a shift in the development mechanism in emerging economies from the export-led model of newly industrializing economies (NIEs model) to the potentially bigger market-oriented model of development (PoBMEs model) and also sees East Asia's institutionalization proceeding mainly through the ASEAN. The author calls it a "reverse," "spontaneous" institutionalization compared with European and/or American institutionalization. The objective of this chapter is to examine East Asia's economic growth and associated issues from the two perspectives of, first, its development mechanism and, second, regional institutionalization through a cooperation regime focusing on East Asia.

1.2.2 How Contrasting Growth Regimes Imply Trade Imbalances

Hiroyuki Uni (Chap. 4) conducts a comparative analysis of regional trade imbalance in the eurozone and East Asia. He analyzes the structures and actors of intra-regional trade imbalances in East Asia and the eurozone after 1995, using mainly the World Input-Output Database (WIOD). In China, Korea, and Taiwan, export competitiveness in machinery products improved, and the trade surplus expanded significantly. Their intermediate goods trade in this field also turned into a surplus. The basic cause of this expanding regional trade imbalance is the success of the export-led growth through export-biased productivity growth, currency depreciation, and wage suppression in East Asia. In East Asia, however, some necessary conditions for export-led growth have already been eroded, and the governments are seeking a shift to domestic demand-led growth. Some problems need to be solved for the transformation from export-led growth to domestic demand-led growth. In Spain, Portugal, Greece, and other countries, the wage growth rate exceeded the growth rate of labor productivity of export goods, and in Germany, it was the opposite. In the monetary integration, it was impossible to adjust for these differences through changes in exchange rates. Unequal changes in unit labor costs under monetary integration are the fundamental causes of the expanding trade gap in the eurozone.

1.2.3 Consequence of Growing Interdependence among Heterogeneous Growth Regimes

Hiroyasu Uemura and Shinji Tahara (Chap. 5) analyze the evolving diversity and interdependence of growth regimes and the patterns of de-industrialization in Germany, France, Italy, and the UK in the context of the European integration and Japan in the context of Asian economic integration, using the World Input-Output Database (WIOD). De-industrialization is usually defined as the relative decline in output and employment in the manufacturing industry, which is observed universally in all the advanced economies. The transformations and interdependence of growth regimes and industrial structural changes are analyzed to understand the structural characteristics of de-industrialization in the European countries and Japan. This study attempts to extend the theoretical framework of "growth regime" in the *régulation*[1] theory, taking account of long-term industrial structural changes in the open economy framework. In Europe, Germany, France, Italy, and the UK exhibit different growth regimes and different patterns of de-industrialization with their diversified

[1]This spelling, "*régulation*," relates to the French *régulation* theory that analyzes the dynamic processes to channel capital accumulation and the long-term evolution and diversity of capitalisms. In the following text, the wording, "regulation," can also (rarely) be used to refer to the American meaning of delegated legislation.

positions as EU member states, faced with the subprime crisis, trade imbalance within the EU, and the euro crisis. In the Japanese case, de-industrialization has accelerated very rapidly since the early 1990s, faced with institutional changes in the domestic economy and dramatic changes in international economic interdependence, especially with China and other Asian countries.

1.2.4 The Choice of an Exchange-Rate Regime Is Important

Jacques Mazier, Myoung-keun On, and Sebastian Valdecantos (Chap. 6) take into account new issues generated by the 2008 financial crisis and the increasing role of China at the world level in order to evaluate alternative monetary regimes for East Asia; the authors compare these with the European regime. The tool used is stock-flow consistent (SFC) modeling. The first model, based on a simple structure of China, East Asia, the USA, and rest of the world, gives a rough description of the East Asian monetary regimes as they have been observed in the past: the dollar-pegged regime during the middle of the 1990s, the hybrid regime of the end of the 1990s and the beginning of the 2000s, and the more flexible regime of the 2010s. Two regimes corresponding to rather long-term scenarios are also examined, the yuan zone, where the East Asian currency is anchored to the yuan, which is floating or managed against the dollar, and the yuan block, where the East Asia/yuan parity is managed and not fixed. The second set of models separates out China, Japan, and East Asia countries and analyzes the consequences of exchange-rate regimes like the ACU regimes, the Asian Bancor regimes based on a clearing union, and finally, global ACU regime, which implies the launching of a new international currency. Some lessons are also drawn from the failures of the European experience with monetary integration.

1.3 Origins and Ways Out of the EU Crisis

The second part of the book considers origins and possible ways out of the EU crisis with analyses of growth regimes in Germany and France, multi-layered migration governance in the EU and France, innovation systems in Finland as a Nordic model, and the ongoing process in Brexit that will determine the future of European integration.

1.3.1 Common Environment, Contrasting National Responses

Nicolas Canry (Chap. 7) explains German and French trajectories in the 2000s in terms of their institutional settings. A common explanation for German economic success for 10 years has been its ability to reform its labor institutions: the emblematic example is the Hartz laws (2003–2005), which strengthened labor market flexibility by reducing the reservation wage and implementing active labor market policies, among others. The author does not try to minimize the importance of institutional change in Germany. Nevertheless, he shows that beyond the deep reforms and institutional transformations implemented by Germany for two decades, the economic success that this country has been currently experiencing rests fundamentally on the same devices and macroeconomic tools as before. To support this analysis, the author compares France and Germany growth regimes since 2000: he asserts that France and Germany have actually been facing pretty similar macroeconomic constraints, particularly a significant excess of private saving with respect to domestic private investment (by firms). Then, he characterizes the means by which the two countries managed to face this potentially destabilizing gap: in Germany, wage bargaining focusing on unemployment and weak public intervention but with export-led growth to compensate for the deficit in domestic demand; in France, stronger importance was given to government spending to stabilize demand and activity. This difference reflects long-term patterns followed by German versus French capitalism.

1.3.2 Migration Policies between National and Integrated Governance

Mitsuru Uemura (Chap. 8) considers the EU multi-layered migration governance and the externalization of French migration management from the perspective of polity, policies, and politics. The nature of the EU multi-layered governance of external migration management is analyzed, focusing on France, and the political dynamics is investigated based on what intention France and third countries have in constructing migration management systems. In the multi-layered migration governance in the EU that consists of the EU, EU member states, and third countries, there is a conflicting configuration among these actors. While the EU tries to establish effective migration policies on the basis of the harmonization of policies among the member states as well as cooperation by third countries, the member states and third countries try to maximize their own interests. Therefore, the EU Readmission Agreement and the Mobility Partnership between the EU and third countries were not effective at the beginning due to the insufficient bargaining power of the EU; the pursuit of member states, such as France, in keeping strong ties with third countries, for example, Senegal, Cape Verde, and Tunisia; and the lack of cooperativeness of third countries. This may have caused the serious migration problem in the EU recently. In this situation, it is important to establish complementary institutions at different levels of governance.

1.3.3 Innovation Systems: Dynamism in the North But No Catching Up in the South

Norio Tokumaru (Chap. 9) analyzes the transformations in the role of public policies for innovation in Finland from the viewpoint of the role of institutional foundations as a Nordic state. While the role of the public sector in innovation has been downplayed in the dominant, market-centered view, advanced economies are facing challenges to develop novel approaches to innovation policies. The reasons behind this include the changing focus of innovation and the catch-up by the latecomer countries. Based on a detailed case study of the implementation of a novel approach to innovation policy, demand- and user-driven innovation (DUI) policy in the EU and Finland, this study examines how the role of the public sector has been transformed in implementing innovation policies and argues that the novel role of the public and semipublic sectors in a DUI policy can be understood as the governance of the evolutionary process of innovation, where the public and semipublic sectors should be deeply involved in the innovation process. This is contrary to the conventional role of the public sector as the provider of useful complementary resources, such as institutional frameworks, funding, and education, while standing outside the innovation process. From the institutionalist perspectives, the Nordic welfare and corporatist institutions, including the active third-sector organizations, might play a key role in implementing DUI policies. Nevertheless, the dynamic Nordic innovation systems have not emulated the catch-up of Southern Europe, and this discrepancy plays an important role in the EU crisis.

1.3.4 Brexit and the Future of the EU

Robert Boyer (Chap. 10) analyzes the process leading to Brexit and draws some general lessons for the viability of the European Union. Brexit is the unintended consequence of the irruption of the UK's Independence Party on the agenda of the Conservative Party, and it shows the disconnection of the political elite from the rest of society. The distribution of the votes by education level, age, and localities brutally reveals a great social divide that has silently deepened with the internationalization of the British economy in the context of welfare decreases. The inflow of foreign workers, the consequence of the British economic success, feeds the anger of those left behind who expressed the rejection of the loss of national sovereignty, personified by Brussels regulations. Thus, economic liberalization, social fragmentation, and an anti-European political offer coalesced into a major threat to the very principles of European integration. The EU is facing a perilous dilemma. Can different national interests agree on a strategy to overcome the triple perils of the EU simultaneously, namely, the dysfunctional institutional setting of the eurozone, the primacy of international finance over citizen demands, and the rise of xenophobia and nationalism in response to the inflow of political refugees and economic migrants? Is there a sustainable isolationist economic strategy that could appease demands for more national sovereignty?

1.3.5 Alternative European Scenarios

Jacques Mazier, Pascal Petit, and Dominique Plihon (Chap. 11) analyze possible ways out of the eurozone crisis. One example is given by the role of the European Central Bank (ECB), which was at first severely constrained in its power to deal with the debt crisis. Progress has been made, however, enabling the initiatives of the ECB to cope with the legal constraints of its statute and allowing some easing of its ability to manage the Euro crisis. A second example mainly concerns the functioning of the euro. The creation of the euro has left open the issue of ensuring the convergence of member states, although it was a crucial issue for the sustainability of a currency union. If divergence trends occur, some institutional mechanisms should be available to set the union back on a sustainable track. Flexible exchange rate mechanisms could have helped, providing that a multiple euro system would have received sufficient political support to facilitate a delicate transition. A third example of ways out could be in taking advantage of the momentum of the climate policies decided at the Paris COP21 conference to launch targeted investment schemes that would reverse the diverging trends and set the EU on a transition path toward an economically, socially, and environmentally sustainable development path. The EU is clearly at a crossroad, and drastic choices have to be made.

1.4 China and Japan in Asian Diversity of Capitalisms

The third part of the book considers the development pattern of Chinese capitalism and the transformation and dysfunction of Japanese capitalism in the context of the evolving diversity and interdependence of Asian capitalisms in Asian economic integration.

1.4.1 How Institutions Shape Asian Innovation Systems

Hironori Tohyama and Yuji Harada (Chap. 12) analyze the institutional diversity and technological systems of Asian capitalisms. This study examines whether the coherence among macro-institutional diversity, innovative capabilities, and industrial specialization exists in Asian capitalism. This empirical analysis reveals the coherence of five types of Asian capitalism through institutional environments at the macro-level, the relative strength and composition of different industries at the meso-level, and firm behaviors engaging in innovation at the microlevel. This means that institutional configurations provide companies with better capacities to advance in certain types of technologies, resulting in cross-national patterns of innovative specialization and, then, in patterns of industrial specialization. The authors argue that technological progress is path dependent because it seems to proceed along the technological and industrial trajectories defined by the diversity of Asian capitalisms. What matters more for Asian economies is not closing their technological gaps with the frontier but rather finding the technological trajectories available to them.

1.4.2 China: Political Reforms, Development State, and Partial Technical Upgrading

Lei Song and Chengnan Yan (Chap. 13) aim to provide a self-consistent analytical framework to understand China's previous high-speed growth and the emergence of the "new normal" from the point of view of the mode of *régulation*. The authors use the term Chinese-style "developmentalism" to label China's mode of *régulation*. Economic flexibility and political rigidity coexist in this model, but their relative relationship changes from time to time. The variations of the relationship between economic flexibility and political rigidity shape the dynamics of the Chinese-style development. Before the second decade of the twenty-first century, Chinese economic development had no obvious confrontation with its political system. In that period, the Chinese-style developmentalism manifested as flexible rigidity with which high-speed economic growth was achieved by successive economic reform policies, and, in turn, economic growth supported political stability. However, as economic reforms entered the deepwater zone, political reforms became the prerequisite of sustainable economic development. Seen in this light, flexible regidity has been weakened, and the redesign of the relation between the economic and political systems is necessary.

Lei Song (Chap. 14) analyzes, from the viewpoint of the diversity of capitalism approach including the *régulation* school, the mode of production within the diversity of regions and industries. In addition, inspired by the tradition of the Schumpeter School, this chapter investigates the origin and evolution of dominant modes of production in China's two leading industries, the automobile and the ICT industries, by paying special attention to the link between technology and organization. Two modes of production exist that share similarities yet differ in some respects. Both modes of production of the two leading industries relate to the modularity of product architecture and can be termed a modular mode of production. However, these modular modes of production differ from each other in ownership structure, generation mechanism of modularity, degree of modularity of product architecture, interfirm relationships, and in the possibility of technical advance. This study also finds that in the foreseeable future, the modes of production of the two leading industries will remain modular, although automobile manufacturers are more likely to upgrade their technological capabilities than their counterparts in the ICT industry.

1.4.3 Japan: The Rise of Heterogeneity and the Crisis of the Companyist Compromise

Hiroshi Nishi (Chap. 15) empirically analyzes the relationship among structural change, sector disparity, and economic growth in Japan over the past 40 years. He defines growth in terms of real value added and labor productivity as a measure of economic growth, and he assumes that the structural change in value added measures the structural change in output and that in capital and labor, growth is defined as the structural change in inputs. The use of the Japan Industrial Productivity Database of 2014 (compiled by the Research Institute of Economy, Trade and Industry) shows the pace of the structural change in inputs and outputs, the evolution of the sector dispersion of economic performance, the changing distribution of the sector contributing to aggregate economic growth, and empirical evidence of the relationship between structural change and economic growth. The Japanese growth process since the 1990s has been transformed from a regime combining a decreasing heterogeneity with an overall growth process to another where an increasing heterogeneity goes along with an uneven growth process. Furthermore, the impact of structural change in output on economic growth has been positive, although its magnitude has been weakening over time.

Yasuro Hirano and Toshio Yamada (Chap. 16) consider the multinationalization process of Japanese firms and its consequence over the dysfunction of companyist *régulation* in Japan. Most Japanese large-scale manufacturing firms have reduced their debt loads and have accumulated profits since the late 1990s, and many have directed the resulting internal reserves to foreign direct investment. By virtue of the creation of the East Asian production networks and the multinationalization of manufacturing, Japanese firms have managed to survive in the face of global competition. Nonetheless, this transformation has been realized at workers' expense, with labor's relative share decreasing and the proportion of non-regular workers increasing. The "companyist" compromise, namely, the system of Japanese socioeconomic coordination among workers, managers, and banks, used to support the Japanese postwar economic growth. In the 2010s, its two pillars—employment security in return for workers' loyalty to the company and management security by the main bank system—have almost broken down, except in some particular cases. The decoupling of continuously expanding multinationals from the stagnant domestic economy suggests that Japan is no longer an export-led growth regime. A new nationwide compromise is needed for overcoming low economic activities and widening inequalities.

A conclusion wraps up the main findings and develops themes that cross the successive chapters as shown by Fig. 1.1.

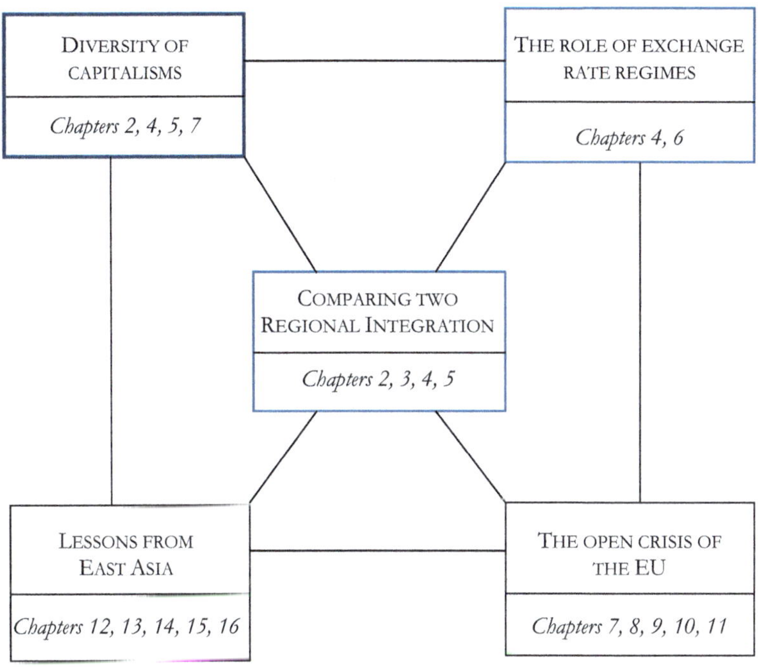

Fig. 1.1 The themes of the present book: a synoptic view

Part I
Regional Integration in the Context of Evolving Diversity of Capitalisms in Europe and Asia

Chapter 2
Two Dialectics Between Polity and Economy: European and Asian Integration Processes Compared

Robert Boyer

2.1 Introduction

Since the 1990s, the concept of globalization has brought the implicit vision of a progressive constitution of a prosperous world economy, featuring a rapid effort by lagging economies to catch up. The rise of Asia seemed to confirm this diagnosis, but Africa was still suffering from many illnesses, whereas Latin America had learned to cope with financial and economic crises. The 2008 world crisis was the key turning point in the representation of economists and the programs of policy-makers. Governments tried to recover control over international flows of capital, the volume of world trade decelerated, and in China the authorities aimed at a new domestic consumption-led growth regime. These strategies demonstrated the failure of the negotiations of a new multilateral trade regime within the World Trade Organization and opened a new epoch. The second turning point came after June 2016 when British citizens voted for Brexit (The Economist 2016), in other words, the first withdrawal from the European Union. In March 2017, the Trump Presidency's "America First" strategy explicitly called for protectionist measures and made the renegotiation of the North American Free Trade Agreement (NAFTA) rather uncertain. This could well be a tipping point in the history of international relations: the hegemonic nation abandons multilateralism and free trade (The Economist 2018).

Do these shifts mean that the time for regional economic integration is over and that the era of extended free-trade agreements has come to an end? This chapter investigates the factors that shape the re-centering of economic transactions within territories large enough to sustain an efficient division of labor. On one side, the world has become so heterogeneous and conflicted, and the international institutions

R. Boyer (✉)
Institut des Amériques, Vanves, France
e-mail: r.boyer2@orange.fr

R. Boyer et al. (eds.), *Evolving Diversity and Interdependence of Capitalisms*,
Evolutionary Economics and Social Complexity Science 11,
https://doi.org/10.1007/978-4-431-55001-3_2

built after World War II are unable to design and implement new compromises on the global commons. On the other side, most national territories had become too small compared with the size and power of multinationals and the flow of financial short-term capital movements. Pooling some attributes of national sovereignty opened a third strategy between a full-fledged international order required for globalization to continue, on one side, and a purely nationalistic/protectionist retreat from the headwinds unleashed by cutthroat competition among all nation-states, on the other side. Two key objections could immediately be addressed.

This reasoning may be relevant only for medium-sized economies such as Germany, France, and Italy. At one extreme of size distribution, continental economies, such as the United States, China, India, and to some extent Brazil and Russia, could aim at large autonomy with respect to the world economy or at least negotiate separately with a strong bargaining power. China is a good example of asymmetric integration into international relations. At the other extreme, small economies are necessarily open to trade and investment since they thrive on international intermediation – the Netherlands, for instance – or by exploiting niche markets, Denmark, Sweden, and Finland. These last countries have joined the European Community (EC), which became the European Union (EU), but Switzerland has not. Regional integration is not exclusively an economic issue: politics matters since it converts a series of private interests and ideological orientations into collective decisions, in particular, concerning the degree and modalities of international integration. The title of this chapter captures this interplay between polity and economy, hence, between politics and economics.

A second caveat is still more important. If we actually live in the epoch of regional economic integration, how do we explain the following paradox: the European integration that started 60 years ago and that used to be taken as an (implicit) benchmark by some experts and governments in Latin America and Asia is currently in turmoil so severe that some anticipate its complete disintegration? Symmetrically, the quite fuzzy superposition of many free-trade agreements in Asia has proven to be more resilient in the 2010s: is not the bad pupil of regional integration outperforming the "master"? Comparing integration in Europe with East Asian integration is a method for progressing toward a more relevant theorizing that might overcome the limit of a methodology based upon a unique and specific territory, be it the nation-state or a supranational entity.

The following analysis is built upon four core hypotheses.

- Regional integration deals with trade, production, investment, and employment, but as soon as tariffs are reduced, countries experience transformations in the relative position of sectors, social groups, and individuals. Conflicts frequently emerge, which are to be overcome by collective deliberation in the political arena, and many noneconomic factors are involved in the design of rules and institutions required to cope with the opening up to international competition. The search for an optimal solution by the economic discipline has to be complemented if not replaced by *a political-economic approach.*

- Opening up to foreign competition is not an easy transition from an economic equilibrium to another, expected to be Pareto-superior in response to the gains of trade. Regional integration is *an evolving process* that takes time, the outcomes of which cannot be totally anticipated by conventional modeling. *Crises* are usually part of the process, when policy-makers and actors have to reassess their expectations and strategies. They can be *minor*, in other words, limited to a precise domain, or they are *systemic or structural*, because they put at risk the whole architecture of the supranational rules elaborated through time.
- Any relevant analysis has to cross *various disciplines of social sciences* and recombine them. The traditional opposition between the national and the international has to be replaced by a dialectical analysis of their interweaving and nesting according to a two-directional causality. Similarly, the economic analysis cannot consider that the choice of the governments about the style of integration is totally exogenous. A third dimension relates to the interaction between private interests and public concern in the direction of regional integration. It is a *multifaceted complex process.*
- *The end point of any regional integration strategy is largely unknown* because each is the outcome of an idiosyncratic interplay between economic constraints and opportunities on the one hand and strategic political decisions at some bifurcation points on the other. The *Zollverein* customs union led to the political unification of Germany, whereas the Council of Mutual Assistance broke down with the collapse of the Soviet Union. The euro that was supposed in 2000 to irreversibly seal the destiny of the old continent of nation-states is since 2016 perceived as a threat to continental solidarity. Regional integration studies rarely show a steady state and easily predictable trajectories, nor do they detect any one best way that could be used as a benchmark by other regions.

It is thus crucial to sketch out the different steps of European and Asian integration before looking for any explanation of their success or failure (Sect. 2.2). The objective is then to analyze the interplay between economic factors and political strategies. The present state of the European Union is the (unintended) outcome of the pursuit of a political objective by the means of organized economic competition among former enemies. The creation of a web of supranational institutions changes both the domestic political arena and firms' behavior (Sect. 2.3). East Asia displays a quite different trajectory: the economic dynamism of some economies and the strategy of multinationals, both Asian and foreign, drives a boom in intraregional trade and FDI. These new interdependencies call for some (modest) coordination principles among the nation-states (Sect. 2.4). Thus, the two entities react quite differently to the successive international crises that reveal the contrasting patterns of regional integration. Nevertheless, common factors, differently combined, can be diagnosed and could be the starting point for a political economy of regional integration based on the ability of supranational negotiations to work out rules of the game that allow the long-run coexistence of different socioeconomic and/or accumulation regimes. When these conditions are not fulfilled, the risk of regional integration reversing is very high, as evidenced by the EU crisis since 2010 (Sect. 2.5).

2.2 Supranational Building in Europe Versus a Variable Geometry of Free-Trade Agreements in East Asia

Far from defining a stable configuration, these two forms of regional integration are the outcome of a series of processes that have to be described and then analyzed with the lenses of various theorizing.

2.2.1 From the Rome Treaty to Lisbon Treaty: More Than Half a Century of Efforts and a Major Crisis

At the very beginning of the present-day European Union, the issue was essentially *geopolitical*: how to prevent a new conflict between Germany and France, the source of the two devastating world wars that have meant the end of the old European hegemony. In 1950, six countries agreed to "make war not only unthinkable but materially impossible," as stated by the French Foreign Minister, Robert Schuman. The method belonged to the *economic domain* and consisted in coordinating modernization of steel and coal production, more through collective intervention than market mechanisms. A light transnational body was created and proved to be successful in organizing these two core sectors. In a parallel effort, the project of a Community of European Defense (CED) aimed at pooling national armies as a step toward a future *political integration*. The French parliament's rejection of CED in 1954 closed this embryonic path for explicit European federalism.

The European governments have thus embarked along the avenue of *economic integration*. The Rome Treaty created in 1958 a European Economic Community (EEC) that extends the strategy adopted for steel and coal to manufactured goods. The Treaty in its preamble stated that signatory states were "determined to lay the foundations of an ever closer union among the peoples of Europe." Nevertheless, the EEC was the de facto embryo of a customs union. This sets into motion a series of processes. Firstly, since markets are social constructions, directives by the European Commission have to define common norms to appease trade conflicts between members: this is a regulatory role that will unfold at each stage of economic integration (Fligstein and Stone 2002). Secondly, when this is extended to agriculture, common prices are set at the European level, and modest funds are allocated to countries that face structural problems in adjusting to competition. Thirdly, recurring crises that oppose conflicting national interests occur, but they are interpreted as an incentive for new compromises favoring more integration: since economies become more interdependent, they should perceive that they have to agree on common rules

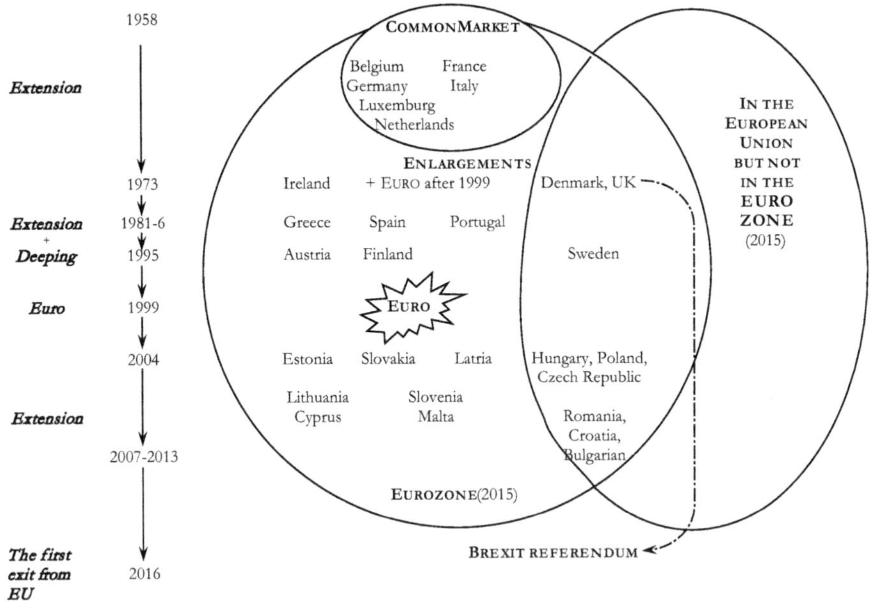

Fig. 2.1 The European integration: a cumulative process of supranational institution building among core members until Brexit

of the game. This is the origin of the neo-functionalist paradigm, at the core of the European project (Monnet 1976). Fourthly, the dynamism of the EEC attracted new members that had to agree on an *acquis communautaire*, in other words, to implement the whole body of Brussels regulations. This builds an increasingly sophisticated common institutional architecture (Fig. 2.1).

Two major world events gave a new direction to integration. On the one side, the *collapse of the Soviet bloc* after 1989 raised the challenging political issue of European reunification, which is especially important for Germany. Joining the European Union appeared quite attractive to many Central and Eastern European governments. This has increased the heterogeneity of members and complicated compliance with the strict economic criteria required for the deepening of the single market decided among core founders of European integration. Implicitly, a political rationale has won out over a cold economic analysis about the viability of such a rapid extension of the EU. On the other side, during the 1990s, the *recurring exchange-rate crises* among partners were the consequences of unequal competitiveness exacerbated by international capital mobility. They were perceived as putting at risk the very existence of the single market. Facing the limits of a managed exchange rate system, the governments of the core members decided to irreversibly set them by adopting a common currency, the euro, to be monitored by an independent European Central Bank.

This ambitious architecture is challenged when the 2008 collapse of Lehmann Brothers reverberated into a *eurozone crisis*. National governments did not submit to the straitjacket of the Lisbon Treaty, and the European Commission did not have the tools to respond to the dire financial situation. This strengthens the analysis of EU members that had refused to join the euro: they feared losing the autonomy of their economic and welfare policies with few and uncertain benefits (Calmfors 1997). Basically, eurozone governance has proven to be dysfunctional as many foreign observers had pointed out (Stiglitz 2016). Simple statistical data confirm that the contribution of the euro to economic integration has been exhausted. The launching of the single market did increase the intra-European share of total exports; then the euro proved beneficial during the early 2000s, but afterward the degree of integration steadily declined within the eurozone (Schmitter and Lefkofridi 2015). Paradoxically, this integration is higher for non-members of the euro, but the euro crisis finally reverberated to the rest of the EU. The abandonment of monetary sovereignty necessary for economic integration was thus severely challenged.

Another unexpected crisis has been caused since 2015 by the consequence of the mass inflows of *economic migrants and political refugees*. In the absence of a previously agreed common immigration policy (see Chap. 8), many Eastern European governments were opposed to the quota proposed by the European Commission. They argued that migration policy had to be decided by the national government and parliament elected by citizens, not by a supranational administrative body, far from the feelings and perceptions of public opinion (Armingeon and Ceka 2013). Both the euro and migration crises show the limits of the *economic-neo-functionalist* strategy of European integration and the brutal return of long-neglected political debates.

2.2.2 East Asia: An Open Method and Reactivity to International Context and Crises

The autonomy of the exchange rate allows for coping with the heterogeneity of national development patterns, and governments keep their tax, public spending, and monetary policy levers. No major political issue is implicit in the process of economic integration: members want to reap the economic benefits of the emerging international division of labor. A new stage began with the 1997 Asian financial crisis: the quick inflow of foreign financial capital generated an unbalanced and speculative boom, and the reversal of confidence in the future of Asian countries triggered a major economic crisis. This was a watershed moment for Asian countries, both domestically and in terms of regional integration. At home, governments decided to prevent the repetition of the 1997 crisis by the constitution of important reserves in order to get rid of the painful IMF adjustment programs, and some dared to implement capital controls. The contagion of the crisis across Asian countries, however different, showed the relevance of coordination among them in order to stabilize their exchange rates. The proposal for an Asian Currency Unit (ACU) was taken more seriously; the idea of a regional alternative to the IMF/World Bank was

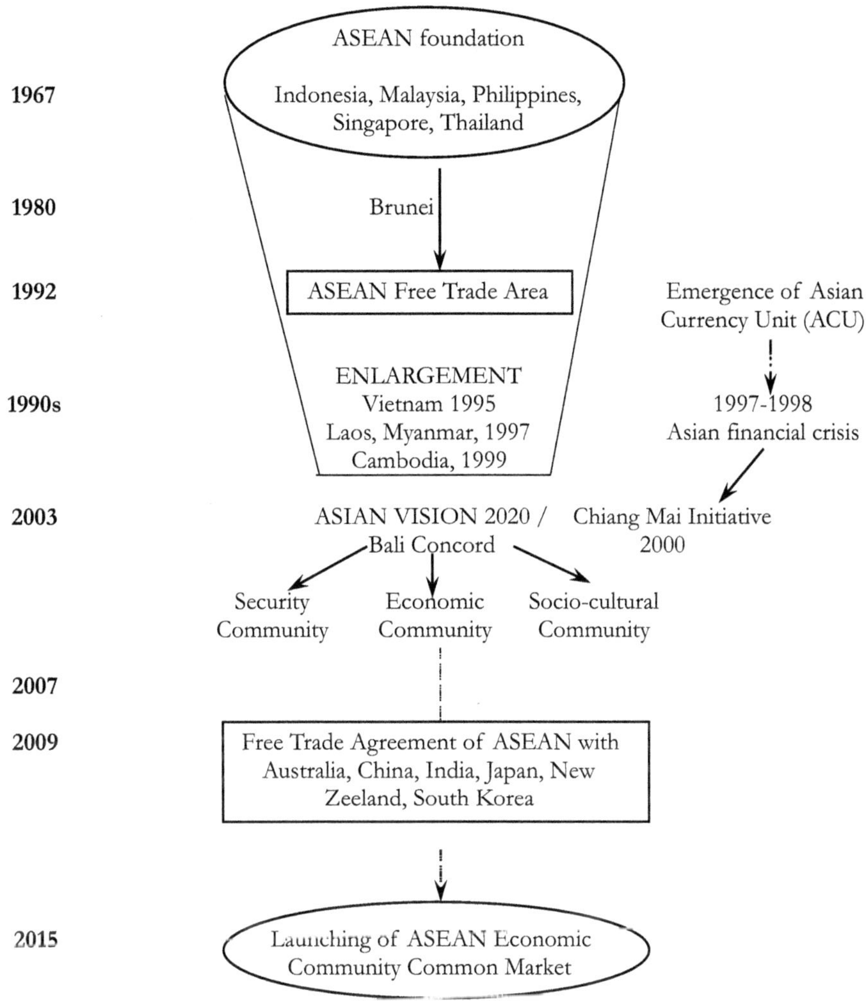

Fig. 2.2 A brief history of ASEAN foundation: soft integration but no common currency

floated but blocked by Washington; and in 2000 some Asian central bankers decide to cooperate in the defense of financial stability (Fig. 2.2).

The evolution of intraregional trade suggests a counterintuitive observation: neither intensive supranational institution building nor monetary integration is a necessary condition for the deepening of regional integration processes. For instance, NAFTA intraregional trade grew from 33.8% to 45% from 1980 to 2005, and during the same period, ASEAN +3 intraregional trade increased from 34.6% to 54.5%. By comparison, the strengthening of intraregional trade has been more modest in the EU, from 61.3% to 66.2% (World Bank 2016). This is an invitation to investigate the relationship between supranational institution building and regional economic integration (Sect. 2.5).

2.2.3 The Transpacific and Transatlantic Partnerships: Foregone Alternative to Past Regional Integration?

At this stage, economic integration appears quite different indeed in Europe and Asia, but both Europe and Asia are threatened by the same peril, in other words, the negotiation of new ambitious treaties across the Atlantic and Pacific. There is a core distinction between Europe and Asia. The emergence of an economic entity – the European Commission under the ex post control of the European Council and European Parliament – that negotiates with partners outside the region in the name of members is a distinctive feature of the EU (Hall 1997). This means the search for FTAs benefits a majority, if not all countries. Centrifugal forces are thus contained. In Asia, each government keeps its autonomy and is entitled to develop its own strategy without any explicit concertation with other partners. During recent years, Asian countries have been very active in multiplying FTAs with ad hoc partnerships (4 FTAs in 2012, 11 in 2013, 12 in 2014, and 10 in 2015 (World Bank 2016)). These vibrant negotiations do not favor the coherence of the division of labor within Asia. This is a distinctive feature of the economic approach adopted by Asian countries.

Nevertheless, geopolitical motives are not absent since most of these FTAs exclude China and can be analyzed as a reply to the Trans-Pacific Partnership (TPP) among selected countries across the Pacific Ocean, largely at the initiative of the United States. In 2017, the Trump administration's withdrawal from the TPP opened a new phase of Asian integration excluding the United States. This was a quite clever method for slowing down – if not stopping – regional integration in both Asia and Europe, because its implementation would have meant institutionalizing the superiority of privately generated norms over public regulations in response to citizens' demands (Boyer 2014).

Multilateral trade negotiations had failed to make any significant progress during the last decade. Taking into account the collapse of the OECD's Multilateral Agreement on Investment (MAI) initiative in 1998, the governments have engaged in a multiplicity of Bilateral Investment Treaties (BITs), so numerous and intertwined that the final outcome is quite messy indeed. In a sense, both the Transatlantic Trade and Investment Partnership (TTIP) and TPP play a tentative role in overcoming these two failures by exploring a middle ground: the strategy aims at involving the members of both regions in the design of a multilateral investment and trade agreement that may or may not pave the way to diffusion to the rest of the world. Nevertheless, this is less an autonomous decision by governments than their response to the relentless pressures from multinational firms to adopt common and transparent rules that would allow them to redeploy their investment within a safe and predictable environment. Of course, pooling the resources of various national states might help the EU resist the most daring demands of mobile capital, but in any case the name of the game is to upgrade the status and protection of foreign investment over the defense of regional and local interests. Clearly, the motto "leveling off the playing field" expresses this superiority of economic competition to the possible but not inevitable detriment of regional arrangements. This danger is very clear in Asia: at least three mega-regional trade agreements did coexist until 2016, the Trans-Pacific Partnership, Regional Comprehensive Economic Partnership, and the Free Trade Area of the Asia-Pacific (World Bank 2016: 221).

2.2.4 Economics, Politics, and Geopolitics: From One Discipline to Another

From one period to another and when the analysis shifts from Europe to Asia, different concepts and tools are required since a single approach cannot capture the evolving patterns of regional integration. The Asian case can be understood largely through the tools of international trade, finance, and investment theory, but it is useful to look at international relations to capture some key features of the current tensions, frictions, and risks of military conflicts. By contrast, nearly all the analytical tools have to be used to explain the cumulative nature of European integration and how the interplay between polity and economy is evolving, especially during the crisis periods. In the 2010s, the dysfunctional institutional architecture of the eurozone and EU informs the federalist theorizing about some dead-end facing constructivism based on the observance of strict legal rules incompatible with diverging growth regimes shaped by powerful economic and financial forces. In passing, the macroeconomists have to reassess the role of the state and the necessity of financial stability, and they should abandon the illusion of an austerity-led boom, as general configuration. Finally, international political economy is enlightening the fragility of continental/regional integration when multinational enterprises struggle to become the actors that define the rules of the game that nation-states have to comply with. This opens a stimulating research agenda for *regulation theory* and an allied research program (Table 2.1).

2.3 European Integration: From Synergy Between Polity and Economy to an Open Crisis

Let us explain how the euro has dramatically challenged half a century of careful supranational institution building and falsified the premise that economic logic finally shapes political choices.

Table 2.1 Regional integrations: from economics to political economy

	Free-trade zone	Custom Union	Common market	Single market	Economic Union	...	Form of Federalism
Trade							
Lower tariff	*1	*	*	*	*		*
Common external tariff		*2	*	*	*		*
Capital, labor mobility			*3	*	*		*
Competition policy							
Domestic institutions affecting trade				*4	*		*
Taxation					*5		*
Subsidies					*		*
Credit					*		
Federal Institutions							
Common currency							*6
Federal budget							*
Political representations							*

2.3.1 European Public Good Creation as the Response to Successive Crises

As already pointed out, the project of the founding fathers was to prevent the repetition of the two world wars that had meant European self-destruction and the subsequent decline of the old continent. *Peace* was the primary public good to be sought: if it was impossible to get it by a "Europe of the Defense," the other road was the organization of orderly economic relations between Germany, France, and all other nations involved in these recurring conflicts. However, a common market with supposed rules of the game in order to maintain *fair competition* was elevated to the status of a European public good (Boyer and Dehove 2001).

With adoption of a flexible exchange rate and the high international mobility of capital, the process has to be relaunched in response to the intra-European exchange-rate volatility and its impact on the competitiveness of national economies. After a long period of experimentation, a growing share of European elites became convinced that a *common currency* was necessary to continue to benefit from the deepening of intra-European exchange. Some were conscious that it could be a jump into a radically new configuration. It was the merit and the strength of the Germans to propose to extend the approach of *ordo-liberalism* into the relations

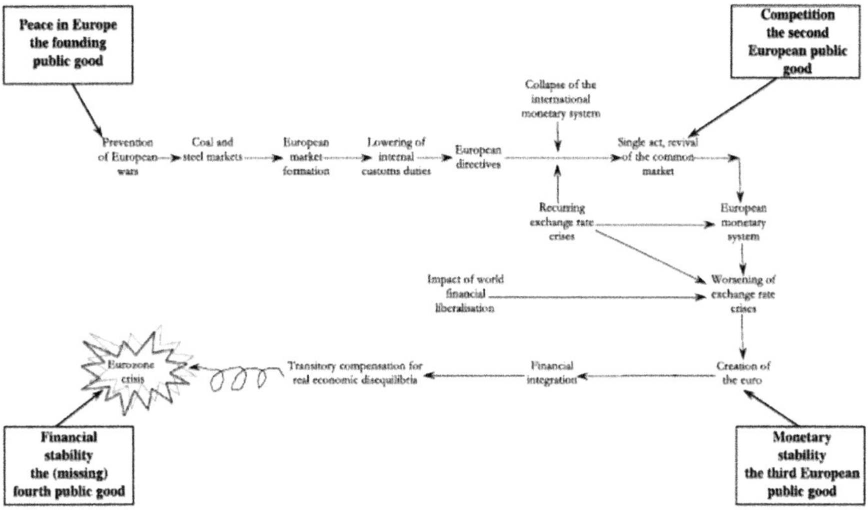

Fig. 2.3 The European economic integration

between Brussels and national entities: the viability of monetary integration, without fiscal solidarity and political union, could be warranted by the respect for common rules in order to prevent any opportunistic national behavior to bankrupt the eurozone.

This was the victory of German conceptions for organizing the European Union, but not at all a transposition of German federalism, since an institutionalized redistributive system, equivalent to the one created among the *Länder*, was not proposed. Actually, this genuine *prudential federalism* was supposed to make fiscal, financial, and political federalism unnecessary. However, when unanticipated sources of fragility appear – for instance, if the rules are not followed by all and financial speculation bets on the collapse of the euro – should policy-makers accept a financial meltdown just to better enforce the rules that have been violated and thus prevent moral hazard to generate another crisis? Europeans had to recognize painfully what was evident for North American scholars: it is difficult to defend the euro in the absence of a lender of last resort, with a tiny European budget and a clear lack of political leadership. The dangerous path followed from March 2010 to July 2012 shows *financial stability* was the next public good in order to preserve the cohesion of the EU, but it was quite late (Fig. 2.3).

2.3.2 A Neglected Issue: The Euro Was Polarizing Domestic Societies

By reducing transaction costs, removing uncertainty inherent in exchange rate volatility, and preventing inflation that otherwise erodes competitiveness, it was thought that the euro would bring general improvements to the wellbeing of citizens. The existence of powerful mechanisms of redistribution among possible losers and a majority of winners – via taxation and welfare transfers – was thought to suffice in alleviating opposition as voiced by a portion of the population that could be negatively affected by fiercer competition and the restructuring of firms and jobs.

Public opinion surveys conducted while preparing the euro actually showed generally positive appraisals of the common currency. For example, in April 1997, 70% of the French population had a positive evaluation of its likely consequences, and, with the exception of the UK, a majority of Europeans expressed positive expectations. Nonetheless, the distribution of opinions was not at all uniform across socioeconomic groups within each nation. In France, surveys detected a clear heterogeneity among social groups (SOFRES 1997: 110).

Large firms anticipated few and only transitory difficulties because their transnational operations were largely facilitated by the launch of the euro, which allowed them to redeploy their production sites in line with their performance and, for some products, to be closer to areas of greater demand. This feeling was not shared by small- and medium-sized enterprises (SMEs) and retailers, who are generally less export-led and are more likely to be linked to domestic and local markets. Unlike their German counterparts, French SMEs and subcontractors especially suffered from pressures applied to their costs, as exerted by large multinational firms. This difference in perception is reflected in statements by various business organizations among these two business categories, *vis-à-vis* the euro.

Young people did not expect many problems as a result of the euro; they were also right to imagine that the euro could facilitate their mobility, since most but not all of them had acquired the education and competence needed to succeed in an arena that featured more open competition. On the other hand, low-skilled, low-income groups expected long-lasting problems to arise from their adaptation – or lack thereof – to the epochal change of the euro. They were largely right to expect such things, since internationalization and "Europeanization" forced them to compete with workers who were earning lower wages and were devoid of any extensive welfare. Finally, the most pessimistic tended to be the elderly citizens, since they feared a negative impact on the generosity of their pensions and their deindexing from current wages and ultimately higher consumer prices.

The potential sources of destabilization of both past social compromises and equilibria were thus clearly diagnosed by all the actors. This was a source of early political opposition, under the banner of "national sovereignty defense," with which governments were forced to cope. This polarization between large and small firms and young, educated, and low-skilled workers would be brutally revealed in the 2010s when populist movements and anti-European parties experienced great success in parliamentary or presidential elections. The great divide between Brexiters and Remainers is a vivid confirmation of this creeping social polarization (see Chap. 10).

2.3.3 *The Euro Has Boosted Diverging Macroeconomic Trajectories*

The euro has been victim of a second underestimation, the illusion of continuity between the phase of progressive stabilization of internal exchange rates and their irreversible fixation with the euro. All members lost two key instruments: the rate of interest and the exchange rate. In the past, periodic reevaluations and devaluations allowed unequal structural competitiveness to be overcome while organizing a relative convergence of standards of living. To the contrary, the same monetary policy and external exchange rate implied that real economic activity was now the basic adjustment mechanism. The countries that used to reevaluate would grow faster than those with a weak currency in the past. In other words, the euro led to *economic divergence* between Northern and Southern Europe.

Statistical observations confirm this prognosis (Artus 2011). Northern economies (e.g., the Netherlands, Finland, and Germany) enjoy a good fit with the evolution of the world economy, with an effective and reactive State, and relative (if even imperfect) financial control. They thrive relatively well in terms of external surplus and ability to reduce the public deficit; thus, they can comply quite readily with EU and eurozone rules. Successful northern economies ask their partners to do the same because they represent the benchmark of most European policies.

Unfortunately, southern economies do not have the same configuration, since they tend to suffer from a structural lack of competitiveness with the inability to devaluate, and the State tends to have a limited ability to intervene efficiently in order to curb public deficits. Some of them have suffered from speculative real-estate bubbles generated by financial liberalization. Given the persistence of public deficits and the deterioration of external trade, a surge in international debt has been, transitorily, a stabilizing mechanism.

The heterogeneity of the eurozone is found to be still larger when one takes into account three hybrid configurations: France is the intermediate case between north and south; Greece is an exceptional case of clear and largely irreversible insolvency; and Ireland is a failed Celtic "tiger" perverted by careless financial liberalization but with a large capacity to rebound to a viable export-led regime.

2.3.4 *Contrasting Economic Situations Not Correlated with Support for the EU and the Euro*

The euro was assumed to foster economic convergence among members, and this prognosis contributed to the positive welcome by a majority of members. This is no longer the case since 2010, and public opinion surveys confirm this wide gap between rather prosperous northern economies and ailing southern ones (Eurobarometer 2016: 22). In between, Central European countries exhibit intermediate outcomes. Nevertheless, the relative ranking of EU and euro approval is not correlated with national economic performance (Eurobarometer 2016: 20). For instance, Denmark, Sweden, and the UK are the most opposed to European integration despite the positive assessment of the economic situation by their public opinion. None of them has joined the euro, and the UK has been the first to decide by referendum to leave the supranational institutions of the old continent. Conversely, for the more ailing economies (Greece, Spain, Portugal, and France), a majority of citizens agree to the present configuration of the EU. All eurozone members have a positive opinion.

Thus, some economies that are able to succeed economically within the EU have an anti-EU majority public opinion, whereas in some others pro-European public opinion goes along with the structural economic obstacles that make their belonging problematic in the long run. Such a paradox deserves some explanation. One may question the accuracy of comparing surveys across various cultures for which the European project has different meanings. For instance, for Spain, Portugal, and Greece, the adhesion to Europe was part of the will of citizens to be reintegrated within the club of democracies and for the elite to provide a program of economic and social modernization. For the UK, the EU should be limited to a regional free-trade zone, the first step before its fusion into a globalized world. Clearly, for public opinion in other nations, economic gains are not the unique issue at stake: the ability to move across former borders (Eurobarometer 2016: 18) and to share the same currency are rather important for young generations and are perceived as impressive achievements by older generations. Greece is a paradigmatic case for this disconnection between the imposition of an inefficient and unfair austerity plan by the European Commission, the European Central Bank, and the IMF and the will expressed by citizens to remain within Europe.

2.3.5 A Crisis of Democracy at the European Level?

A second paradox emerges from comparing the distribution of judgments over the EU (Eurobarometer 2016: 22) and that of the ability of citizens to influence its decisions (Eurobarometer 2016: 18). Most of the more pro-EU members admit that their voices are not heard. Again, Greece is one of the most striking examples of this divorce between adhesion to the EU and fulfillment of democracy (Scharpf 2011), quite surprising indeed for a project based upon the diffusion of democratic principles.

The sense of exclusion from Brussels decisions is especially acute for newly integrated members, but it is also present in the founders of European integration: neither German nor French citizens feel that they are EU actors, despite the traditional role attributed to the joint leadership of their governments in periodically relaunching the integration process. More generally, the extreme heterogeneity of perceptions and expectations about the EU makes quite difficult the elaboration of any common strategy. Since the 2010 euro crisis, diversity has become an obstacle to unity.

Is there a domain in which the convergence of public opinion legitimizes common policies? An overwhelming majority of all 28 EU members expressed support in 2016 for the free movement of citizens anywhere in the EU (Eurobarometer 2016). The European barometer shows 63% support for intra-European mobility even in the UK, but this figure has been contested by the proponents of Brexit, whereas this issue was seen as a key benefit for the Remain camp. This shows how determinant media are in forging the links between objective evolutions, individual perceptions, and policies: this arena continues to be essentially domestic and rarely European. A complex mix of personal economic interests, appreciation of national prosperity, and defense of national identity, emotions, and affects shapes attitudes toward the EU. The 2016 Brexit Referendum confirms this statement (Clarke et al. 2017: 153–174). This is a major objection to the theory of median voters based upon a continuum of citizens ranked according to a single variable, for instance, income (Downs 1957).

2.3.6 Immigration and Security: The New Demands Addressed to the EU

The 2010s have opened a new period for European policy-makers. Their priority has first been to prevent the collapse of the euro by the creation of new tools concerning the Central Bank, the financial system, and the surveillance of macroeconomic imbalances that led to the climax of the crisis in 2012. Since then, the relaxation of credit has been buying time, and de facto for EU public opinion, the urgency of economic issues has constantly declined since mid 2016 (Eurobarometer 2016: 5). With a 2-year lag in unemployment, what was the main concern for most public opinions during the last decade is not more at the top of the agenda, as perceived by the majority of citizens. Since 2013, immigration has become a major source of anxiety for nearly half of the European population, and in 2016 terrorism was a concern for at least a third of the population.

According to the treaties that govern the EU, immigration is typically the responsibility of each nation-state. The massive flows coming from the Middle East and Africa have made this subsidiarity principle obsolete, since once admitted by one entry country, economic migrants and political refugees can move within the EU, and they try to settle in quite a few countries, those offering the best economic opportunity and welcome. The European Commission has proposed criteria for setting national quotas, but these have been refused by nearly all Central and Northern European members. This is a major crisis for European governance that was not designed to tackle the difficult issue of immigration and nationality. Similarly, the terrorist threat raises the long-neglected issue of a common defense and security. This should become the next European public good (see Sect. 2.2 *supra*), but perceptions and interests differ considerably across the EU. Actually, survey data suggest the *polarization of public opinion* around two different priorities (Eurobarometer 2016:11).

- Unemployment remains the first issue facing Greece, Spain, France, Italy, and Portugal, and the redesign of economic governance should be the priority, but their demands are blocked by the hegemony of German conceptions. One could say, "European economic integration as usual," but the EU authorities are facing a dead end in the emergence of a more balanced approach to the economic policy mix, given the domination of the German legal approach to the implementation of the treaties.
- For most Central and Eastern European countries, such as Hungary, the Czech Republic, Poland, and Romania, the issue of immigration has become crucial, since these countries were traditionally affected by emigration, and the populations are not used to welcoming migrants. Nevertheless, after 2015, this preoccupation has also been shared by the Netherlands, Denmark, Sweden, the United Kingdom, and Italy, in other words, the more attractive countries for migrants and refugees. This is an unprecedented challenge addressed to the EU. The nationalistic movements that used to fight against the pooling of national sovereignty and the single currency are then at the forefront of anti-immigration policies.

These two series of contradictions cannot be overcome by a purely technocratic approach that is typical of the community method: a form of political deliberation is required, and it appears easier at the national level than in Brussels.

2.3.7 Enter (Or Not), Remain, or Exit? The Political Regime Matters

The typical method of economists is to undertake an overall analysis within their favorite (and highly simplified) model. Thus, the proponents of the euro concluded that its launch would enhance national welfare; they then lobbied civil servants and policy-makers to convince them to adopt their vision and finally decide to join the euro. If they perceived opposition from a portion of society, they proposed that renewed pedagogical efforts be undertaken to disseminate their solution. They could say that their viewpoint had been informed by rigorous and scientific analysis far removed from ideology and passionate politically oriented debates. From the start, the euro suffered from a *democratic legitimacy gap* in many countries.

Nevertheless, this was not inevitable: some societies are more democratic than others, and this feature has had definite consequences. For example, after intensive, pluralistic, and decentralized debates, the *Swedish government* decided not to join the euro, since some gains were certain but minor, whereas some adverse and highly uncertain consequences might be quite detrimental to Swedish social cohesion and Sweden's ability to decide its economic fate autonomously. In an expert report

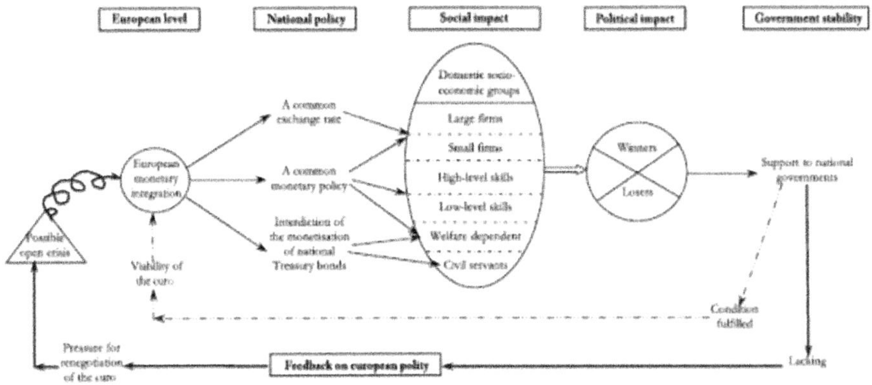

Fig. 2.4 The social and political viability of member states adhesion to the Euro

released prior to the Swedish government's decision (Calmfors 1997), at least 14 different criteria were analyzed; for each of them, the assessment was quite balanced and contained no aggregate monetary evaluations, because they could not capture the complexity of the expected changes in Swedish society. The reduced democratic sphere of deliberation implied by joining the euro was found to be a cost that might be incommensurate with Sweden's larger influence within the EU. Finally, the report focused on the large amount of uncertainty surrounding the consequences of the euro, with acute problems in the case of failure. The UK government, too, decided that it was not in the interest of the country to join the euro. Nonetheless, 11 other governments made the opposite choice.

From where does this opposition come? Basically, the intricacies of each national political system have played a role, because it is the sphere where various interests, visions, and strategies struggle to set a final decision. Political scientists have the task of disentangling the contribution of a complex web comprising those economic, social, and ideological processes, but they are far from agreeing on common conclusions. Nevertheless, the average voter hypothesis here appears to resemble a drastic and probably misleading fiction (Fig. 2.4).

Europe exhibits a large variety of electoral and political systems, and this characteristic has played a specific role, besides those related to the aforementioned purely economic and institutional differences: parliamentary versus more presidential regimes, proportional or majority-based electoral systems, possible or compulsory appeals to referendums, the frequency of elections, and the average terms of governments are all factors to be taken into account. The *French case* is a good illustration of this complexity: in 2005, a referendum on the approval of the European Constitution was called, and the answer by a clear majority was "No." Nevertheless, the government decided to present a slightly amended treaty to its parliament, and it was approved. All these differences in the political systems continue to play a significant role, in the midst of a major systemic eurozone crisis. In Germany, every agreement made in Brussels with regard to financial funds for bailing out other governments or banks has had to pass through the domestic political and legal system (i.e., the Federal Constitutional Court of Germany). In France, however, these agreements were automatically translated into French legislation, without real parliamentary deliberation.

Clearly, *polity matters*: in response to the same challenges (adhere or not, remain or exit, bail out the banks or not), member states take different options, and some of them shape the long-run trajectory of society.

2.3.8 A Turning Point for the EU: Toward a Return to Nationalism?

If one accepts the core argument presented to date, the euro is *not* failing because any constructivism is bound to fail, but because the crisis is a consequence of various flaws in the design of its governance, many of which could have been prevented. The relief provided by the unambiguous and full support of the ECB to the euro can be used to build the required European procedures and institutions (e.g., in the direction of a common financial supervision, a banking union, and a fiscal compact open to clauses of exception), but it might not be sufficient because political legitimacy does not derive mechanically from technical solutions.

The jury is still out, so to speak: will private actors and, especially, financiers be convinced that a genuine European federalism is in the process of being made, or will any bad news trigger a "domino effect" toward a more or less complete renationalization of economic policies (Fig. 2.5)?

There may be many reasons for this polarization of a wide variety of interests across only two options.

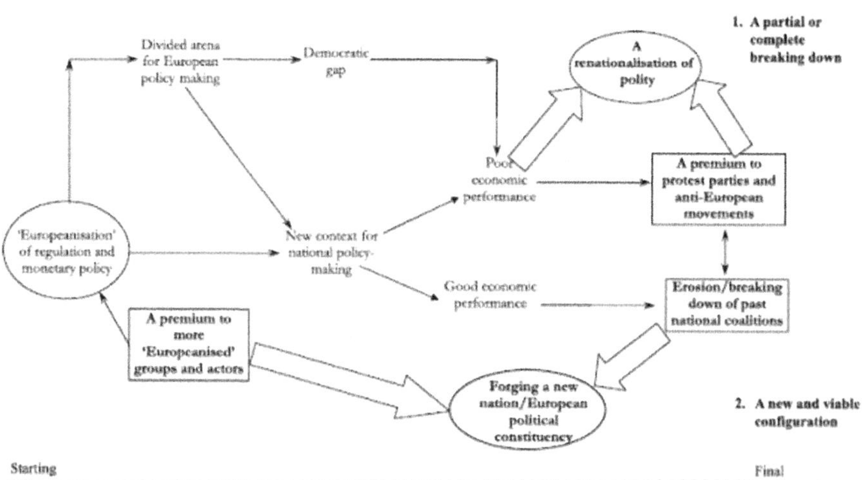

Fig. 2.5 The contemporary bifurcation of the EU: a radical redesign or renationalization?

- First, nostalgia for a "Golden Age" persists: some actors still dream of returning to a period when wage increases had the wonderful consequence of higher employment and a lower public deficit while preserving the dynamism of investment. If austerity measures fail, then the opposite should succeed, correct? Let us return to the past socioeconomic regime. Clearly, this slogan assumes a complete reversibility of two decades of internationalization and financial globalization, and it neglects the consequence of the productive paradigm shift out of Fordism and the transformation of European societies.
- Second, if the EU has not been able to implement more democratic control in Brussels and Frankfurt, public opinion is entitled to ask for a return to tighter government control by citizens; until now, the nation-state has been the only territory whose polity is organized and where democracy can be exerted, however, imperfectly. The enforcement of drastic adjustment programs, run jointly by the EC, the ECB, and IMF, has proven unable to restore either growth or public finance, especially in Greece, and this feeds the feeling that a form of technocratic logic has replaced democratic principles.
- Third, the fact that the EU was and is still based on the cornerstone of unfettered competition and its relentless extension – from manufacturing to services, from labor and finance to collective services – calls for a return to more cooperative strategies: if they are blocked at the European level, a nation, region, or local community can favor them.
- Fourth, facing the limits of the generalization of export-led growth and the hegemony of finance, anti-globalization movements may convince a growing proportion of public opinion to abandon unfettered free trade. In contrast, the appeal of European institutions is quite low, which plays a role in the nature of the likely bifurcation of European integration. Will it serve as a "high road" out of the crisis or signal the collapse of the very ideal of European integration?

2.4 Asia: From an International to a Flexible Regional Division of Labor at the Initiative of Firms

The juncture is quite different in Asia, since the key actors are quite different, and a de facto integration emerges out of a specific process, which is much less institutionalized. The domestic dynamics of high investment and technological catching up in a series of newly industrialized economies (NIEs) first responds to the evolution of the rest of the world, but the 1997 Asian crisis and 2008 world crisis call for a redeployment of division of labor within the region, just to reduce dependency on financial volatility and the uncertainty of international trade generated by North America and Europe. Nevertheless, geopolitical rivalry conflicts with the progressive building of economic complementarities, and thus a monetary and financial coordination is made difficult, not only because of diverging trends in prices and unit costs but also for political reasons. Fortunately, the various forms of flexible exchange rates adopted by each country have made possible the adjustments of heterogeneous growth regimes.

2.4.1 Neither North America nor the European Union

In contrast to the EU, the Asian approach to integration has been primarily market-driven, as opposed to functionally and institutionally driven. The Asian Development Bank summarized the Asian approach to integration in the following manner:

> The evolving approach to integration in Asia is **market-friendly, multitrack, and multispeed**, allowing for a healthy dose of **pragmatism** among a collegial group of economies. This approach is workable for a region of such size and **diversity,** and holds several advantages. First, any group of territories, economies, or sub-regions can integrate according to its **particular levels of development** and the specific opportunities that regionalism offers. Second, as partnerships strengthen, smaller groups are more likely to **merge into larger ones**, leading to wider and deeper relations across an ever-growing swathe of Asia. Third, this approach ensures that Asia's economic integration remains market-friendly – that its framework continues to be **responsive to private sector needs** as expanding business and open markets power Asian economies ahead. (Asian Development Bank 2008: v. quoted by Morten Hansen 2011).

The international crises have prompted European leaders to push the directives, rules, and regulations a step further in order to guide markets in the name of a progressive convergence. In some cases, they have removed uncertainty and were helpful; in others, they distracted from an efficient adjustment to world competition and the increase of productive capacities in Europe. In Asia, the heterogeneity of development and the unpredictability of brutal reversal of trade and finance have validated an experimental and step-by-step regional integration on the basis of voluntary adhesion to the construction of a trading zone (Fig. 2.6). In a sense, it is very similar to the "flexible Europe" or "Europe *à la carte*" promoted since the 1990s by some British think tanks. Finally, the Lehman Brothers collapse triggered on the one hand the euro crisis and on the other simply a progressive slowdown in Asia that calls into question the investment and/or export-led growth regimes and makes possible more inward-looking strategies that reduce economic dependence on the United States and Europe.

Consequently, the share of intra-Asian trade among total trade continues to grow, and the progress of regional integration is larger than in NAFTA, probably due to the dynamics of increasing returns to scale in Asia and the delocalization of some North American firms to Asia, including China. The degree of regional integration remains higher in the EU, but the euro does not bring the extra stimulus expected, since the EU is unable to capture the benefits of information and communication technologies and does not move its specialization upwards (Asian Development Bank 2016).

A closer look at intra-subregional Asian trade confirms the extreme heterogeneity of such a vast region. That integration is more advanced in East and South Asia than in other subregions is not surprising given the geographical dispersion of the

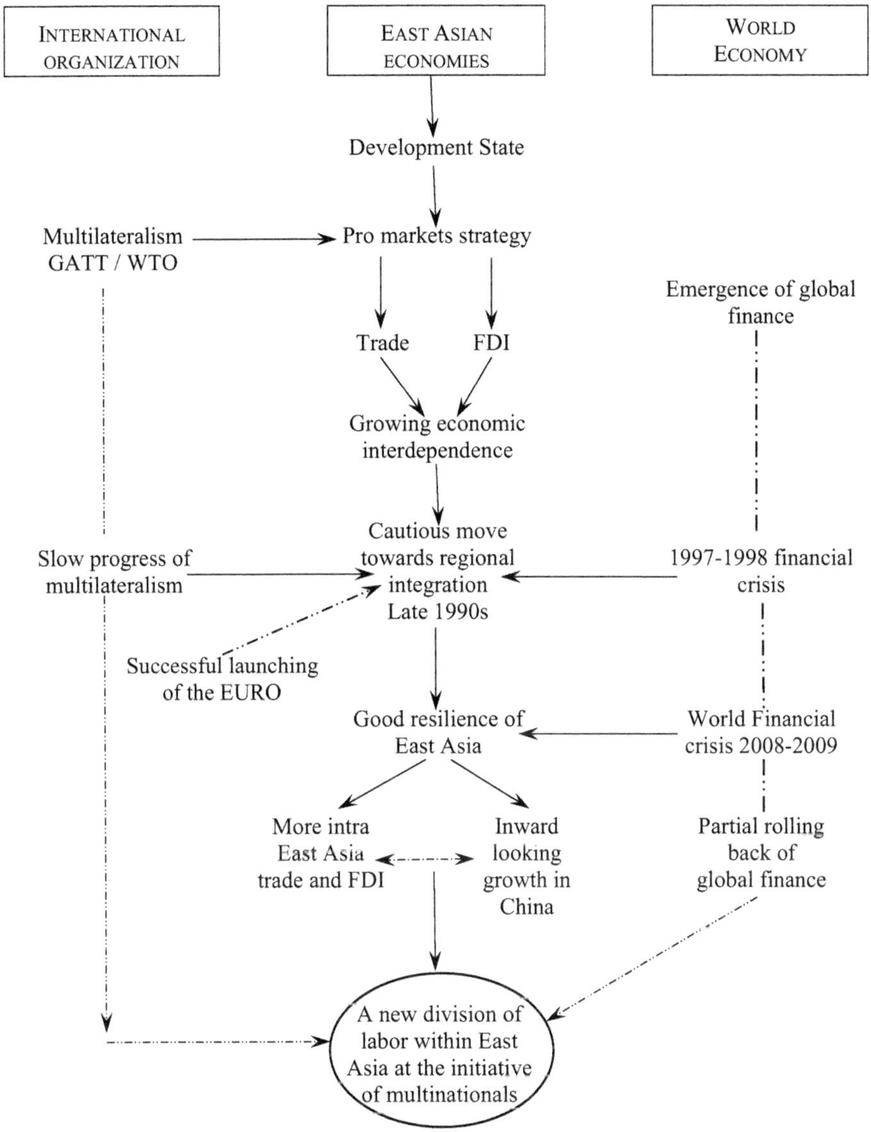

Fig. 2.6 East Asian integration: multinationals led with diverse international agreements and flexible exchange rates

economies. Internationalization may continue to organize the external orientation of those countries that are highly specialized or unable to cooperate with their neighbors (Asian Development Bank 2016).

2.4.2 Building Regional Productive Links and the Upgrading of Specialization

Previous collective research has already diagnosed some characteristics of Asian economic integration (Yan 2012; Wang et al. 2012). First, the "flying geese" model does not fit any more the patterns observed: the same productive model does not migrate from a leading to a lagging country, since on the contrary the hierarchy of technological sophistication remains, but the more advanced countries export intermediate and capital goods to other countries that specialize in assembling consumption goods (Chap. 5). Second, multinational corporations from the United States and Japan and recently from Korea are key actors in the construction of these backward and forward linkages via their FDI and trade, but the patterns differ quite a lot across sectors and subsectors (textiles, electronics, transport, equipment, etc.). Third, this interdependency is the outcome of a complex, but still limited, division of labor across East Asia, and the 2008 world crisis has shown how dependent on demand for consumer goods from the rest of the world the region was. Fourth, the export sector has been an engine of growth for China during the 1990s, and this has expanded international linkages via import of intermediate goods. Since 2008, infrastructure and housing investments have been used to foster growth and pave the way for consumption and a service-led economy. This implies a redirection of China's linkage with East Asia.

East Asian regional integration is also evolving under the impact of the ambitious and steady innovation policy of China. On one side, the upscaling of the production system toward advanced technologies and high value-added affects the import of similar goods from Japan and Korea. In the long term, this could erode one of the rare growth engines for Japan. On the other side, new countries such as Indonesia or Vietnam could replace China as the platform for the production of consumer goods and their export to Asia and the rest of the world. India seems quite apart from this process of re-localization.

Consequently, the 2010s seem to open a new epoch for Asian integration. Not only is world trade slowing down and inducing a more inward-looking strategy, but Asian trade itself also undergoes a structural change, whereby consumption goods become more dynamic than intermediate and capital goods (Asian Development Bank 2016: 11).

2.4.3 Better Resilience with Respect to the World Economy's Ups and Downs

One of the objectives of regional integration is to reduce the disturbances associated with world trade volatility and capital "sudden stops" by the promotion of internal engines of growth and the creation of contracyclical economic policy tools. In this respect, the EU dramatically failed to protect members from the repercussions of the

American financial and economic crisis (see *supra* 3.3). The Asians have learned from their 1997 crisis, and they decided to pile up large currency reserves, to add capital controls to their tool box, to coordinate the defense of their national currencies, and last but not least to push further their economic integration by redirecting their growth from export to domestic demand.

An econometric study does confirm that these efforts have borne fruit. Before 2008, Asian output variance was mainly explained by external shocks, then by internal ones, and finally by a financial risk factor measured at the international level. In the post-crisis period, the proportion of Asian output explained by external shock factors declined from 41% to 24%; the risk factor remained stable, and, therefore, domestic impulses have become overwhelmingly dominant (Asian Development Bank 2016: 6).

2.4.4 The Impact of China on Other Asian Countries

This rebalancing of regional integration is enhanced by the growing importance of China and its repercussions for the rest of Asia. The "new normal" growth is the direct consequence of the world economic turmoil that blocks net exports as a mechanism for adjusting a structural overcapacity typical of the acute competition among so many local State corporatism. Therefore, productive investment has to slow down too. The building of infrastructure becomes a key growth engine after 2009 until it reaches the limits of local public finances. The long-term decline of consumption share in GDP has to stop, which opens the possibility of a long-awaited domestic demand-led regime, which was the official objective of the past and present governmental plans. Whereas nearly all countries experienced a form or another of deindustrialization, China had become the center of world manufacturing, serving both domestic and international markets. This trend concluded in 2011 because services tend to outrun manufacturing as share of GDP, just to respond to new demands linked to urbanization and welfare (Asian Development Bank 2016: 12).

One may thus expect new macroeconomic regularities in China and a different contribution to Asian integration: less dependence on foreign intermediate products and equipment, a progressive reduction in imported energy and natural resource content of GDP, a reorientation of the innovation system, and the need to adopt another exchange-rate regime. All these structural changes are bound to affect the present division of labor in Asia. Such a transformation can be detected by the estimated response of Asian GDP to an exogenous change in Chinese GDP, supposed to be independent from the rest of Asia, but influenced by lagging US growth (Asian Development Bank 2016: 6).

- Before 2008, higher Chinese growth had a positive impact on Asia for 1 year, but it turned negative during the next 3 years before being again positive. One possible interpretation is the following: in the short run, Chinese imports feed Asian growth, but the extra demand for natural resources triggers an inflation that hurts most Asian economies that are poor in natural resources (Asian Development Bank 2016: 7).

- After the 2008 international crisis, Chinese growth has had a higher and always positive impact upon Asia, but it has declined as time elapses. The first mechanism appears stronger than the second because the relative size of Chinese imports has grown, and the price formation of oil and natural resources may have changed. If so, Asian economic regional integration is a positive-sum game, possibly threatened by territorial/maritime conflicts. Clearly, once more, economic logic does not coincide with political and geopolitical motives.

A variant of the VAR model delivers two more results. After 2008, the United States and China are trading places concerning the forces that shape Asian evolution: the US factor has decreased, but the share of the China growth factor has increased from 16% to 24%. The reduction of American influence is common to all Asian countries, but the increase is asymmetric for China: Singapore, Indonesia, Korea, and Taipei are more dependent and the Philippines, Malaysia, and Vietnam less so.

2.4.5 *Evidence About the Speed of Asian Integration: From Import to Net Export of Capital*

When one compares these rapid changes in Asia with the slower moves observed in the EU, a hypothesis emerges: the two integration processes do not obey the same logic, and they actually belong to two distinct historical periods. As China's industrialization does not replicate the British industrial revolution, relations between development and internationalization are different. The wide opening up of world markets and construction of global value chains have both created a space for compressed development:

> . . .the label 'compressed development,' recognize(s) that all late development is compressed in the sense that it accelerated, but that new development paths through engagement with global value chains introduces levels of simultaneity and international engagement that is qualitatively different from those of archetypical late developers. (Whittaker et al. 2007)

In retrospect, the EU was implicitly conceived as a copy of the *Zollverein* of the 19th century, whereby a customs union unfolds until a nation-state is formed. Asian regionalism aims at fostering the development of each nation-state using as leverage the interests of multinationals and requiring minimal regional coordination. This is why catching up and internationalization have been so fast. Far removed from the product-cycle theory of the post-World War II era, Asian tigers such as Taiwan or Singapore have been the first economies to shift from being massive importers of FDI and technologies to exporters of capital and technological expertise. This is now observed at the level of Asia (UNCTAD 2014).

Nevertheless, China plays a determinant role in this evolution of FDI flows. It is closely related to the transformation of its domestic growth regime. First, FDI brings new technologies and knowledge of world markets (textiles and ICT); then it follows the rise of the domestic market (transport equipment) and the progress of the national innovation system. Consequently, the dynamism of Chinese firms makes foreign capital in (e-commerce, for instance) less necessary. Since the mid-2010s, FDI outflows look for the security of the natural resources required by long-term growth, and Chinese multinationals try to acquire promising high-tech industries. Moreover, the huge overcapacity in the infrastructure sectors is planned to be reduced by the launching of an ambitious program of continental and maritime transport infrastructure linking Asia to the rest of the world (Sum 2016).

2.5 Comparing Europe and Asia: Theorizing Regional Integration

Clearly, the patterns of these two forms of regional integration are quite different. One may conclude that each region has developed an idiosyncratic trajectory, which resists any generalization. Nevertheless, a number of common mechanisms and processes are present in both regions and more generally in all other continents: their interactions discriminate between progress and resilience on one side and progress and then crisis on the other. Analyzing the balance between economy and polity allows us to deal with a large variety of forms of regional integration. Régulation theory favors such a comparative approach (Boyer 2003) and proposes three lessons.

- First, *the more heterogeneous* the socioeconomic regimes, *the more problematic* an economic integration based upon strict enforcement of rules is.
- Second, the governments of the most dynamic socioeconomic regime tend to impose a supranational order, in which their economies thrive. The *unequal economic performance* is converted into *asymmetric power* to define and enforce the rules of the game that govern regional integration.
- Third, *the more numerous and rigidly asymmetric the rules* of the game are, *the more likely* regional integration is to enter *a systemic crisis* affecting both the supranational architecture and the modes of development of all the member states.

2.5.1 Limited Size and Power Differences: A Precondition for Supranational Institution Building

Many episodes of European and Asian integration have shown that heterogeneity of size, power, and socioeconomic regimes is a major obstacle to the pooling of national sovereignty even for simple customs unions.

- Europe is a good example since it provides contrasting configurations. After World War II, nearly all countries had lost a large part of their systems of production; their infrastructure had been destroyed, and the basic needs of their populations curbed. All governments faced the same problems: how to use reconstruction for modernizing their society, and public intervention was perceived as necessary, which was very different from the past debates between free marketeers and interventionists. Neither France nor Germany had clear superiority, and smaller countries were eager to join the Marshall Plan proposed by the United States. For at least four decades, this balance of power between the two countries launched the process of Europeanization. Since the end of the 1990s, the economic success of Germany and the inability of the French government to restore rapid growth and full employment have built a structural asymmetry in the decision process of supranational institution building. Ironically, France proposed the creation of the euro, but the Germans accepted abandoning the Deutsche Mark only on their own very strict conditions, largely inspired by principles of ordo-liberalism. The rejection of any permanent transfer among members and the idea that legal and constitutional rules would be sufficient to prevent any economic or financial crisis have been imposed on reluctant partners, too weak economically and politically to impose more balanced European treaties. The economic health of Germany has been a shield for the euro in the short to medium term, but it is also the source of the present systemic crisis of the EU (see Chap. 10).
- When ASEAN took off at the end of the 1960s, no member had the capacity to play a hegemonic role, which explains the emergence of soft compromises and the slow progression toward voluntary-based economic cooperation. With the emergence of newly industrialized countries, and the impressive technological catching up by China, Asian regional integration exhibits major imbalances. First, the stagnation of the Japanese economy in the face of the continuous rise of China is an obstacle to governmental cooperation in managing the growing economic interdependence of the domestic productive system via multinational activities. Second, the ascension of China as a regional and even world power challenges the security of many other East Asian countries. Last but not least, the TPP, abandoned in 2017 by the United States, was initially perceived as a geopolitical device to circumvent the de facto redesign of labor division at the Asian level under the aegis of China. For this reason, the pooling of sovereignty associated with the construction of Asian currency coordination is far away. Many other structural divergences explain the obstacles toward a common currency (see Chaps. 4 and 6).
- Why has the North American share of intraregional trade grown in the first phase of NAFTA and then declined? Basically, the treaty has been largely imposed to the Mexican and Canadian governments, given the huge gap in bargaining power both at the level of technology and economic performance and in terms of geopolitical power. By the way, most of the conditions are asymmetric; they are valid for the United States but not for Mexico and Canada. Similarly, Mexico joined TPP not through a deliberate national strategic decision but merely to follow and extend the economic specialization and institutional complementarities created by NAFTA. Nevertheless, exchange-rate variations

give some room for maneuver, and Canadian financial regulations have prevented a Lehmann Brothers-type crisis. Thus, a trade-off exists between an ambitious regional integration and the resilience to the ups and downs of world trade and the bursting of financial bubbles.

- MERCOSUR is a fourth confirmation of the perverse link between size heterogeneity and incentives to adhere to regional integration. Basically, the economies involved have seen their industrialization processes blocked by the unfavorable terms of trade imposed by already developed economies. Thus, it would be logical to institute a customs union in order to reap the benefits of a larger market and to trigger a process of technological catch-up, favorable to all members. Alas, if one excludes the special treaty on the car industry, these expectations have been falsified: Brazil's size and power are so much greater than those of Argentina that the Brazilian government has no clear interest in cooperating, for example, in stabilizing the exchange rate between the *peso* and the *real*. Uruguay and Paraguay are dependent on this duopoly, without any clear bargaining power.

Again, the central issue is about the links between the economy and polity. In many cases, a large and dynamic economy may convert its superiority into a trump for internationalizing: why to pool sovereignty if the gains are limited or even nonexistent? To the contrary, the weaker members in terms of size and economic performance may have very good proposals for more efficient and fair integration but insufficient economic and financial ammunition to impose a compromise.

2.5.2 Contrasting Growth Regimes Cannot Coexist Within a Fixed Exchange-Rate System Without Fiscal Solidarity

Size heterogeneity is not the only obstacle to regional integration: the diversity of the growth regimes and régulation modes is still more important. Either this diversity is recognized by the supranational rules that organize their coexistence or even their complementarity, or the unfolding of integration reveals and exacerbates their incompatibility via diverging national trajectories. A political crisis may then challenge the benefits of economic regionalism. These two configurations are observed, respectively, in the East Asia and the EU.

2.5.2.1 The Four Basic Growth Regimes Within the EU

Most macroeconomic theories frequently state that the same model – be it Keynesian, classic, Walrasian, new classic, or Schumpeterian – is representative of all (developed) economies with minor second-order differences due to various imperfections or frictions. The possibility of economic integration boils down to the balance between symmetric and asymmetric shocks. Comparative research inspired by régulation theory has shown that contrasting socioeconomic regimes coexist in the long term (Amable 2003; Boyer et al. 2012). Then the implementation of a common rule – this is

Table 2.2 The growing heterogeneity of accumulation regimes: the structural origin of the euro crisis

	Features		Compatibility with	
Growth Regimes	Key feature	Hierarchical institutional form	Competition on the single market	Euro
Finance-led accumulation United Kingdom	Stock market key macro-variable	Financial system	Poor due to deindustrialization	Difficult, need for an autonomous monetary policy
Export and innovation-led Germany, Sweden, Denmark	Price maker sector, engine of growth	Integration into the world economy via exports	High The implicit benchmark of the euro zone	Good in theory, problematic due to the euro zone heterogeneity
Consumption-led France, Italy, Greece	Real wage rigidity and wage led demand	Wage labor nexus	Poor: deindustrialization, unemployment	Mediocre: loss of economic policy autonomy
Foreign investment-led Poland, Czech Republic, Hungary	Technological catching up	Integration into EU economy via FDI	Good, linked to price competitiveness	Not evident in the transition period
Hybrid regimes • Price takers, export-led, and consumption Spain • FDI and finance-led Ireland	Shift triggered by speculative boom and burst	Dual institutional architecture	Good if no real estate bubble	Mitigated: incentive to re-localization, but loss of economic policy autonomy

Source: Personal elaboration from Baccaro and Howell (2015), Baccaro and Pontusson (2016) and Myant and Drahokoupil (2010), Stockhammer (2015)

not at all the equivalent of a stochastic shock – may have opposite effects on various socioeconomic regimes, far from a real convergence assumed to sustain regional integration. This is precisely what has happened with the implementation of the euro. It could have been anticipated by Tinbergen's (1956) rule (the loss of two instruments makes it impossible for past national trajectories to continue), and the difference among various accumulation regimes is converted into growing tensions between the respect for European rules and national economic performance (Table 2.2).

- Finance-led regime
  The *finance-led regime* typical of the United Kingdom is governed by the requisites of shareholder value and not at all by the primacy of competition in the single market: deindustrialization and a large trade deficit are the direct consequences of belonging to the EU. Massive inflows of capital sustain growth in high value-added jobs but not growth in low-paid ones. The autonomy of monetary

policy is crucial to monitor such a crisis-prone financial system, which is why successive governments have refused to join the euro. *Brexit* is the outcome of this UK exceptionalism (see Chap. 10).

- Export- and innovaton-led regime
  An *export- and innovation-led regime* is built upon the advances and resilience of a strong price-maker sector able to sell everywhere in the world due to the top quality of the goods and services produced. The integration into world trade is the a hierarchical institutional form: it is thus easy to comply with the EU's "free and unfettered competition" principle. Germany is emblematic of this configuration that has become the implicit benchmark for other EU members. This is the reason for the euro crisis (unsustainable competitive pressures on weaker EU economies) but also for the resilience of the old continent (trade surplus at the European level and ability to extend public credit to ailing economies).
- Consumption-led regime
  The *consumption-led regimes* are an inheritance of the Fordist epoch, when mass production and mass consumption were in synergy within each national territory. The hysteresis of past social and political compromise with respect to technological change and internationalization implies that the wage-labor nexus is still the dominant institutional form: real wage rigidity boosts a wage-led demand regime at the cost of a deterioration of the trade balance, hence a stagnation of domestic production and high employment. The euro is first an analgesic because it allows the relaxation of credit constraint in response to financial deregulation and then a major obstacle to the response to domestic social demands. France and Italy belong to this category.
- Foreign direct investment-led regime
  A *foreign direct investment-led regime* is still different: typically, Ireland and new Central European members enjoy a rapid catching up that is organized by the decentralization of production by American and European multinationals. Integration into the European economy is the hierarchical institutional form. Capital and labor mobility is crucial in conformity with the very objective of the EU. The ability to join the euro is problematic when the issue of national sovereignty is important for public opinion, in countries once under Soviet domination.

The panorama is not complete without the *hybrid regimes* torn between two opposite regimes: between an export-led regime and a consumption-led one (Spain) or between an FDI- and finance-led regime (Ireland). These configurations show the complexity of the processes operating in the EU, at odds with the convergence hypothesis.

2.5.2.2 A Common Rule Discriminates Among These Regimes

Simply stated, new and binding *common supranational rules*, badly designed, may generate *unprecedented economic divergences* across members. The euro is a striking example of this apparent paradox (see 3.3). Consumption-led regimes cannot prosper anymore when they lose the exchange-rate adjustments that used to be their traditional tools to restore their price competitiveness: wage austerity is a difficult and unpopular substitute, the more so, the more the demand regime is wage- and consumption-led.

Where do these supranational rules come from? In theory, one could imagine that an open and fair negotiation looks for a configuration compatible with the long-term coexistence of all the domestic regimes, however different they might be. Actually, some members are "more equal" than others, and they are able to convert their strong economic positions into the power to set the rules according to their interests and representations of the world. Why not adopt at the EU level the equivalent of the rules that explain success at home: stability of the rules of the game, opposition to discretionary policies, permanent search for competitiveness, and subsidiarity as long as local decisions do not exert negative externalities over the competition on the single market and on monetary stability?

These common principles are easy for Germany to comply with, difficult for France and Spain, impossible for Greece, and irrelevant for the United Kingdom where national autonomy is the primary concern of citizens and policy-makers. For German public opinion, the euro crisis is seen as the exclusive consequence of the violation of European treaties: they have thus to be strengthened, no matter how counterproductive they have been for growth, job-creation recovery, and the decomposition of the domestic regimes other than export- and innovation-led.

Simply said, the unequal distribution of power to decide EU rules and policies is a direct threat to the economic viability of nearly six decades worth of efforts to unite the old continent. The ambitious motto "United in Diversity" is in the process of becoming its opposite: "Diversity against Unity."

2.5.2.3 The Heterogeneity of Asian Socioeconomic Regimes

Still larger diversity is observed in East Asia, but the coexistence of regimes is easier due to more modest ambitions and the adoption of a pragmatic method without too much institutionalization (Table 2.3).

- Insular semi-agrarian capitalism
  Insular semi-agrarian regimes were essentially built on an inward-looking strategy that gives the *state/economy nexus* primacy among institutional forms. The ability to join regional integration is not evident, especially when the population is large and the modernity of the productive system limited. Joining a common currency is a still more distant horizon.
- Trade-led industrialization capitalism
  Trade-led industrialization relates to the typical export-led strategy to which is the success of newly industrialized countries by opposition to the import substitution typical of Latin American development after World War II. This regime becomes possible with trade opening and liberalization. The domination of

Table 2.3 The large heterogeneity of socioeconomic regimes in East Asia: an obstacle to deep regional integration

Socioeconomic regimes	Key feature	Hierarchical institutional form	Impact on regional integration	
			Common Market	Monetary integration
Insular semi-agrarian Indonesia, Philippines	Inward looking	Clientelist state	Limited	Marginal
Traded-led industrializing Malaysia, Thailand	Export and FDI led	Competition	Significant	Marginal
City capitalism Hong Kong, Singapore	Trade and financial intermediation	Finance/integration into world economy	Marginal	Marginal
Mature industrial Japan, South Korea, Taiwan	Export and innovation	Integration into world economy	Limited: bilateral trade/part of ASEAN +3	Early stage (ACU)
Continental mixed economy China	Investment and export led	Competition	Spill overs from China to neighbor economies	Proposition of an alternative International Monetary System

Source: Elaborated from Harada and Toyhama (2012)

competition is a priori compatible with regional integration, but the link with monetary integration is more problematic, since the exchange rate is a crucial tool for adjusting the competitiveness of each country.

- City capitalism
  City capitalisms exploit agglomeration effects in order to promote an attractive and efficient international intermediation for trade and finance. The state can play a role in designing the institutions that fit with the requirements of world competition. Regionalism is not a crucial issue since intermediation can concern the world and not only a regional integration zone.
- Mature industrial capitalism
  Mature industrial capitalisms display features very similar to export- and innovation-led regimes. The centrality of foreign competition makes adhesion to a regional integration zone relatively easy since most other institutional forms are already coherent with the competitiveness imperative. Pooling monetary policy is less evident since the speed of innovation is unequal and the wage-labor nexuses differ significantly (Chap. 3), not to mention geopolitical rivalry inherited from World War II that remains between China and Japan, for instance.
- Continental mixed capitalism
  A continental mixed economy defines a fifth regime that features a huge domestic prospective market and the capacity for the public authorities to nurture acute competition among a myriad of local corporatist states. Intensive investment is the driver of growth, and the productive capacity serves both the domestic

and the world market. China has this unique configuration. Beyond the multiplicity of formal free-trade agreements that do not include China, Beijing is becoming the key actor in East Asian integration and the proponent of an alternative international monetary system no longer based on the dollar.

The diversity of these regimes explains why ASEAN and its progressive extensions have not mimicked the European trajectory, *because they adopted a variety of exchange-rate regimes and flexible international arrangements.*

First, Asian policy-makers have not adopted the objective of unifying their economies but simply that of reducing the conflicts emerging from their growing interdependence. Second, they have not anticipated that the rising economic complementarity would imply monetary and then political integration. The neo-functionalism at the origin of the contemporary EU has not been exported to Asia. Third, the diversity of political regimes and the defense of national identities have put aside the issue of future political integration.

Moreover, from a strict macroeconomic standpoint, Asian governments have not abandoned their autonomy in the use of the domestic policy instruments that allow them to react to the vagaries of international finance and to respond to domestic social demands and crises. The choice of an exchange-rate regime is crucial: any regional integration is either possible and viable or unbalanced and bound to fail (Chap. 5). In a sense, the realism of Tinbergen's rule – as many instruments as national objectives (Tinbergen 1956) – has been taken seriously in Asia (Moon et al. 2000). By contrast, in Europe, the conditions for the success of the neo-functionalism bet are no longer fulfilled (Hooghe and Marks 2008), and they unleash the forces of disintegration (Schmitter and Lefkofridi 2015).

2.5.3 Supranational Institution Building Is Challenged by Complete Financial Capital Mobility

There is a third limit to contemporary regional integration: it has to be compatible with the relentless, impatient, and powerful assessment by international financiers. This was not the case in the first stages of European integration because financial intermediation was under the control of the State and the international flows were essentially public and limited compared with production and value created. The pooling of central bank reserves to limit the volatility of international capital is a very imperfect substitute. The present international system has dramatically eroded the balance of power between public authorities and private capital. The former exert their prerogatives over a given political territory; they have limited fiscal resources compared with the rapid accumulation of wealth allowed by the success of globalization, and politicians must comply with the rules set by a constitutional order and take into account the slow process of democratic deliberation. The latter has access to all territories, instruments, and maturities; it can develop totally obscure financial innovations for the regulators, and it can trade anywhere at any moment and invest a large volume of resources by leveraging, using options, and futures loosely related to value creation.

Consequently, at any moment, a strategy of regional integration has to cope with the expectations of financiers. For instance, previously, the periodic exchange-rate crises of the euro derailed or slowed down the ongoing economic integration process. The euro was conceived as a mechanism for irreversible setting of fixed exchange rates among members. Hence, the speculation shifted to other assets and bets about sustainability of public finance and the resilience of commercial banks. If governments do not react quickly enough, powerful financiers think that the euro is bound to collapse, and their speculation sets into motion a self-fulfilling prophecy. They would have succeeded, had not the ECB solemnly stated that it would do anything to rescue the euro. The plans adopted, including austerity programs, were intended to rebuild trust but not necessarily to foster the integration process.

The extreme flexibility of credit and liquidity creation exacerbates pro-cyclical economic policies. In good times, financiers are eager to buy treasury bonds even if doing so is an incentive to postpone the necessary adjustments in terms of tax, public spending, and competitiveness. When public debt reaches unprecedented levels, a reversal of trust triggers a recession or even a depression. Both the boom and the crisis destabilize regional integration. The short-termism associated with the search for high profits thus erodes the pillars of the EU. In this context, credit is about buying time and not all about strengthening the premises for long-term growth, the implicit objective of European integration (Streeck 2014).

2.5.4 *Regulation Theory and Regional Integration in Comparative Perspective*

The previous developments have revealed the complexity of the evolutions observed in Europe and East Asia. The régulation approach has proposed a series of interpretations and hypotheses. It is time to review how alternative theorizing analyzes the various phases of regional integration and the succession of successes and failures. Each of them captures a fraction of the stylized facts. This chapter suggests an overarching framework that helps select the most relevant processes.

2.5.4.1 Europe: No General Theory Copes with All the Phases of Integration

- The functionalist theory
  The functionalist theory is crucial for the early beginnings of European integration (Schimmelfennig and Rittberge 2006). Actually, the idea that growing economic interdependence creates the need for common rules embedded in supranational institutions has motivated the actors themselves (Monnet 1976). Until the 1980s, this vision has been effective in the genesis of the instruments to

Table 2.4 A brief comparison of regional integration theories applied to the EU

		Interpretations	
Theories	Core Hypothesis	Emergency and maturation	Post-2011 Crisis
1. Neo-functionalism	Interdependence as incentives for supranational institution building	Relevant until the 1980	No mechanical spill over from economic crisis to political innovation
2. Intergovernmentalism	The outcome of bargaining among national politicians	Relevant until the 1990	Conflicts upon the viability of the euro
3. Federalism	Multilevel governance (political, economic)	A *sui genesis* federalism inspired by ordo-liberalism	An unbalanced distribution of power
4. International relations	Emergence of an international organization	More than expertise a delegation of national sovereignty	Intricacy of domestic and international levels
5. International trade theory	Regional integration promotes efficiency and growth	A declining relevance after the single market	A dramatic neglect of polity
6. New economic geography	Agglomeration effects and increasing returns to scale shape regional division of labor	Relatively moderate impact within flexible exchange rate regimes	A polarization of industry in the North, services in the South
7. Neo-corporatist political economy	Trans-nationalization of economic interests	Construction of a continental market	Limit of the European political process
8. Régulation theory	Interdependent accumulation regimes interacting within a multilevel governance	Major macroeconomic incoherencies generated by the euro transitorily compensated by financial liberalization	An open political crisis due to unequal power distribution (labor/capital; Northern-Southern and Eastern Europe)

govern the march to the single market. It enters into crisis with the euro: the pooling of monetary sovereignty was supposed to be governed by purely technical rules embedded within formal treaties. This was a dramatic error because it meant that no European political power was required to deal with the conflicts and crises (Boyer 1999). The ECB had to enter the arena and replace, transitorily and partially, divided national governments in the rescue of the euro (Table 2.4).

- Intergovernmentalism
  Intergovernmentalism seems thus to replace the promotion and defense of the successive European public goods that have been designed and implemented by policy-makers and civil servants dedicated to the progressive construction of a form of European federalism (Moravcsik 1993, 1998). The blockage of the process originates in the contradictory objectives pursued by governments: they

agree that a common policy is necessary, but they want to keep the full autonomy of their own policies (Goulard and Monti 2012). This dilemma has not been overcome, and it points to the absence of a viable compromise between political legitimacy and a renewed economic dynamism.

- Federalism theories
  The theories of *federalism* also give an interpretation of the present state of European integration. Many experts have pointed out that its failure originates from the neglect of the lessons of American federalism: no common currency is viable without fiscal solidarity among members (Crouch 2000; Stiglitz 2016). The bailing out of financial systems has de facto mobilized public finance at the level of national governments; a European regulatory agency has been created and the principle of a banking union has been adopted. Nevertheless, the illusion of a slow march to federalism that can be engineered by compliance with formal rules but without pooling political sovereignty is still present in Germany and is an obstacle to understanding how and why the EU is a new brand of federalism in search of adequate theorizing (Theret 2001, 2012).
- International relations theories
  International relations theories put into perspective regional integration (Palan 2000). How is the EU to be located with respect to other international organizations such as the OECD, World Trade Organization, and International Monetary Fund? Is not the invention by the EU of an Open Method of Coordinatiom (OMC) the recognition of this proximity and the role of soft coordination as opposed to formal supranational institutions? In any case, this literature emphasizes how international relations have been shaping the design of most domestic institutions (Chavagneux 2010). This interdependence operates at various levels: the world, regions such as the EU or East Asia, nation-states, and localities.
- International trade theories
  International trade theories restrict their analyses to the impact of regionalism upon the intensity and direction of trade, growth, productivity, employment, wages, and inequality (Balassa 1961). For most economists, these are central issues because free-trade agreements, customs unions, and common markets are justified as improving economic efficiency. The complex and sophisticated models have delivered rather optimistic estimates of the benefits of the single market that have not been confirmed by ex post evolution (Commission of the European Communities 1988). This weakness is reiterated by the studies anticipating the impact of TTIP or TPP, whereas public opinion is concerned with more diverse issues such as the deterioration of product-quality norms and their imposition by powerful transnational lobbies (Boyer 2014). This economistic approach has downplayed the social transformations brought about by regional competition and the issue of political legitimacy with the widening of the gap between European policy-makers and grass-roots citizens (see Chap. 10).
- New economic geography
  New economic geography is interesting because it provides predictions about the spatial distribution of economic activity in response to economies or

dis-economies associated with agglomeration effects (Krugman, 1991). It has proven especially relevant when the euro has eliminated exchange-rate volatility: the concentration of industrial production in Northern Europe and non-tradable services elsewhere is the underlying cause of the diverging macroeconomic trajectories after 2000 (see 3.3 *supra*).

- Neo-corporatist political economy
  Neo-corporatist political economy addresses a different issue: the building of an integrated European market requires agreement about nomenclatures and norms of quality and building procedures to settle conflicts about the fairness of competition that now transcends national borders (Fligstein 2008). What are the forces that finally contribute to the norms and regulations (in the American meaning of this term) over this new economic space? The bargaining power of large transnational firms comes first because they are entitled to lobby the European Commission and the Parliament, and they deploy more efforts and financial resources than the NGOs that defend consumers, workers, and citizens. This could represent a new form of corporatism translated at the supranational level with the caveat that the triangle business-workers' union-state civil servants is now a dialogue over the governance of competition, which largely excludes the workers (Schmitter 1974).
- *Régulation* theory
  Régulation theory starts from the transformations of post-World War II socioeconomic regimes under the internationalization of production and the globalization of finance (Bieling et al. 2016). Can various accumulation regimes coexist and thrive within an emergent new regional order (Boyer 2000b)? Everything depends on the degree of compromise embedded within the supranational rules of the game and/or the sufficient degrees of freedom granted to members to warrant the long-run viability of their economic systems and the social and political legitimacy of the delegation of sovereignty to the supranational entities. These conditions were more or less fulfilled until the 1990s, but the euro has implied their breach: the 2008 world crisis brutally revealed this dysfunctionality in the distribution of competences that could be detected at an early stage (Dehove 1997; Boyer 2000a). This meta-theory can thus be oriented toward a more balanced analysis of economic dynamics and political evolutions. The precise analysis has to take into account space and time specificities of each form of regional integration.

2.5.4.2 Asia: From the "Flying Geese" Hypothesis to the Development State-Promoted Internationalization

The Asian trajectory is quite different, but the previous general proposition applies: the heterogeneity of socioeconomic regimes, sizes, and political organizations is still larger than in Europe, but the growing interdependence via FDI and trade has been accommodated through the preservation of national autonomy in terms of taxation, while public spending has been maintained via the choice of an ad hoc exchange-rate regime and sometimes capital controls.

Table 2.5 Alternative theories of regional integration applied to East Asia integration

Theories	Core hypothesis	Interpretations of emergence and maturation	Post-2008 Crisis
International trade theory	Benefits from FTA within East-Asia and the rest of the world	Pragmatic adjustment, soft coordination	The slowdown of world trade pushes to regional integration
Optimum currency area theory	Heterogeneity of development, balance of asymmetric / symmetric shocks does not justify in the 1990s a common currency	The 1997–1998 Asian crisis favors a coordination around a Asian Common Union	An incentive for more financial intermediation at the Asian level
Development State theory	The domestic strategy is key in capturing economies of scale domestically and then internationally	This calls for a market driven, competition led integration	First a consolidation by opposition to liberal capitalisms, then an emerging crisis (China)
"Flying geese" theory	The Japanese development mode migrates to other East-Asian economies, step by step	Partial until the 1990s, overcome by multinationals strategies	Less and less relevant: Korea challenges Japan, China becomes dominant
International political economy	The international prerequisites of Asian miracles • American geopolitical role • Early trade and FDI liberalization	Financial globalization destabilizes Asian integration	Emerging tensions between Japan and China
Network theory	The interconnection of private and public networks in the design of regional soft integration	Few top-down approaches to integration	Flexibility of international integration
Régulation theory	Contrasted development modes made interdependent by FDI and trade but compatible via ad hoc exchange rate regimes	A step-by-step cautious coordination, no institutional nor political big bang	Resilience but contradictions: economic complementarity, geopolitical rivalry (Japan, China, United States)

Many interpretations have been elaborated (Park 2002; Dieter and Higgott 2003; Beeson 2004; Pradumna 2006): some are inspired by the international literature, while others are home-grown, in other words, invented to explain typically Asian features, not observed elsewhere, for instance, in Latin America. Let us recall that in the social disciplines, any theory is born locally and has to test its generality by its progressive extension to other societies and/or historical epochs. Both local and foreign interpretations are listed and compared (Table 2.5). Only a few observations will be detailed.

- The optimum currency area theory
  The same standard theory can be used quite differently in Asia and Europe. For instance, back in the 1990s, none of the two configurations fulfilled the very demanding conditions for defining an *Optimum Currency Area* (OCA) (Mundell

1961). Nevertheless, the Europeans made the prognosis that rational actors would take seriously the irreversibility of the euro and that their new strategies would finally create an OCA. The Asians were not so confident about the impact of voluntarism and the relevance of the rational expectation hypothesis: they considered it too risky to go from an ACU to complete monetary integration (Eichengreen and Bayoumi 1999).

- International political economy
  International political economy applies differently in Asia: the rivalry between the United States, Japan, and China is multifaceted and introduces tensions that make the delegation of some components of national autonomy quite difficult. An integrated Europe was first favored by the United States and then perceived as a rival in the conception of a post-Bretton Woods international system.
- The flying geese theory
  Two forms of local theorizing are quite specific to Asia. According to the *Flying Geese* theory, the Japanese development style is supposed to progressively diffuse to the NIEs and then to China (Kojima 2000). Japanese multinationals have no doubt brought modern productive organization to many Asian countries (Wang et al. 2012; Hirakawa 2016). In so doing, they have not reproduced the original inward-looking development of Japan before 1973. Quite to the contrary, they organized an unprecedented complementarity among East Asian economies.
- The development state theory
  The *development state theory* emerged out of the atypical nature of the Asian trajectory. In the American (populist) tradition, state and market are opposing coordination mechanisms; the first one is structurally inefficient; the second is the driver of prosperity. In Asia, such an opposition is not observed, since public authorities govern the market (Wade 1990), and they decide pro-market reforms while preserving some control under the supervision of the State. International organizations had to admit the relevance of this paradigm (World Bank 1993), and this has led to rigorous theorizing about how American and Japanese firms and forms of capitalism differ (Aoki, 2001). In a sense, the pro-market and pro-firm Asian integration is a new expression of the development State in the era of globalization (Asian Development Bank 2008).

Clearly, the differences in the national modes of development matter, and they shape quite distinct forms of regional integration.

2.5.4.3 Internal and External Tensions in Regionalisms: The Contradictions of New International Relations

Let us turn to our central theme: what is the interplay between polity and the economy in the process of creation of transnational order? Actually, the EU and Asia are part of the reconfiguration of the world economy, and their respective roles are quite asymmetric. China is polarizing not only the Asian division of labor but also the evolution of nearly all other regions. In fact, the Middle Kingdom is the

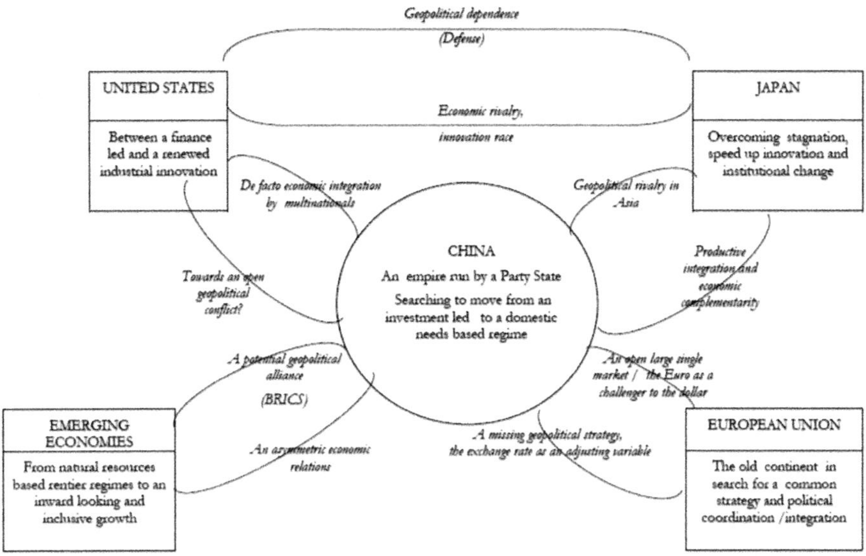

Fig. 2.7 A peril for regional integrations: China torn between economic complementarity and geopolitical rivalry

center of a web of contradictions that operate in the contemporary world: between economic complementarity and geopolitical rivalry in Asia, especially with Japan; between reluctant cooperation and open conflict with the United States; between an alliance for rebuilding international institutions and asymmetrical integration with Latin America and Africa; and between the need to maintain with the euro a currency that may compete with the dollar and the pressure to turn the yuan into an international currency, so that the autonomy of monetary and exchange-rate policy continues to be the essential tool for governing and controlling the Chinese economy. In this global game, the European Union occupies an even less enviable position than Japan: dominated by American finance, open to the winds of Asian competition, Europe is an aggregate of old nations that have given up the exercise of any geopolitical power in the reconfiguring of the coming world through the defense and diffusion of their welfare capitalism and a multilateral approach to international conflict resolution (Fig. 2.7).

2.6 Conclusion

The interaction between economic, financial, and political processes is the thread that allows the following provisional lessons.

1. The failure of the ambitious multilateral negotiations under the aegis of the World Trade Organization is not so surprising given the present state of international relations: the world has become so heterogeneous and contradictory, and

simultaneously most nation–states appear too small to exert any influence upon the redesign of international institutions. This blockage has renewed the interest of politicians, firms, and experts in *regional integration as a third way to be explored*. Until the 2000s, European integration attracted a lot of interest, and sometimes it was defined as a benchmark, whereas East Asian integration was perceived as lagging and quite imperfect. This implicit hierarchy is now dramatically challenged by a cluster of structural changes: the open crisis of the euro and then of the European Union after 2010. These are incentives for a fresh approach in terms of comparative analysis of European and Asian forms of integration in the light of the most recent experience.

2. Contemporary regional forms of integration are quite diverse since they entail *more than purely technical economic issues* about the impact of tariff removal upon domestic growth and employment in trying to build a cumulative process. They start with trade liberalization, but they may unfold into a customs union, the success of which opens a new phase, that of a common market built upon the mobility of goods, services, capital, and labor. In turn, the consolidation of a single market may call for a coordination of exchange rates and possibly the creation of a common, and ultimately, a single currency, by the pooling of monetary sovereignty. Thus, the process becomes *a political issue*, and a whole spectrum of disciplines has a say: macroeconomics, political economy, political science, theory of federalism, and international political economy. Instead of juxtaposing these disciplines that usually deliver different and even contradictory appraisals of European or Asian integration, *régulation theory* proposes an integrated analysis around a central issue: does regional integration contribute to the long-run viability of a domestic economic growth regime, and is it legitimized by a stable political coalition? The answer might be positive, and the integration process goes on and unfolds to a new frontier, but it might enter a crisis either from economic imbalances or by the breaking down of past domestic political alliances. Relevant theorizing has to fulfill two requisites: first, provide a balanced analysis of polity and economy; second, open the issue of success or failure up to empirical analysis. It is especially important when comparing European and Asian trajectories that do not coincide.

3. This analytical framework enlightens us on the *difference between Europe and East Asia*, which are not minor imperfect variants of a typical economic regionalism. They differ on three counts. First, they emerged out of *contrasting world contexts*: in Europe, a reconstruction and modernization period features a strong belief in efficient public intervention, possibly given limited private capital mobility. In East Asia, the liberalization of trade and capital movements but a weak defense of intellectual property rights gives an unprecedented chance to an industrialization built upon the import of equipment and intermediate goods and the export of mass-produced final consumption goods. Second, and still more fundamentally, *the rationales of integration* are not the same. The march to a common market is conceived in Europe as a tool to rebuild the political unity of divided and conflicting nation-states; therefore, supranational institution building

precedes private-actor strategies, and the new continental division of labor is the expression of a political will to monitor economic activity. By contrast, in East Asia, the impulse originates in the dynamism of firms that develop new international flows; hence, more interdependencies across nations call for a minimal form of coordination: supranational rules are reactions to financial crises, and in a sense the national governments basically provide support for leading private economic interests. Third, *the tool kit available for promoting regional* integration is not the same. A cumulative set of formal treaties, directives organizing a form or another of supranational sovereignty (enforcement of competition, negotiation of external tariffs, monetary and budgetary policy), make possible a dysfunctional multilevel governance, when economic activity is more hurt than helped by the political initiatives in favor of integration. The European Union has been undergoing such a crisis since the 2010s. Given the light-touch regulatory approach of ASEAN (peer review, naming and blaming, degrees of freedom in negotiating bilateral free-trade treaties, and strategic use of exchange regime choice), the possible divergences among members can be accommodated within the existing treaties. This explains *why Europe and Asia traded places in the 2010*s: Europe, the benchmark of the 1990s, has become a dramatic counterexample, and conversely the resilient dynamism of division of labor among East Asian countries is now scrutinized by experts and policy-makers.

4. The search for the factors that enhance or on the contrary inhibit regional integration processes delivers some provisional hypotheses to be tested more systematically. One could detect *four obstacles to the emergence of a supranational economic and political order.*

   - First of all, *the heterogeneity of development* makes difficult the soft and mutually beneficial coexistence within a free-trade agreement in the absence of explicit transfers to help the lagging economies with industrialization. The joining of Greece, and to a certain extent Portugal, to the euro was quite perilous. De facto the irreversibility of the single currency implied on the one hand a strengthening of the agglomeration effects linked to scale economics in the manufacturing sector in the north and on the other hand the reallocation of financial portfolios in search of diversification in the south/periphery. The logical outcome has been an unsustainable polarization of trade surplus and credit in Germany and trade deficit and debt (private and then public) in Greece, Portugal, and even Spain. An equivalent danger could emerge, should ASEAN+3 push a step forward in economic integration.
   - A second, somehow related, brake to supranational order building is *the dissymmetry of geopolitical power* among member states. If so, the leaders of a dominant economy might impose supranational rules of the game that are beneficial to their country but detrimental to the long-run viability of regional integration. This is one source of the euro crisis: the extension of German ordo-liberalism principles to the design of the successive European treaties that aim at a rule-based federalism that excludes any permanent transfer or long-term solidarity (Issing 2012). This principle has been reinforced after

the euro and Greek crisis with the imposition on very weak partners of a "fiscal compact" that puts all the burden of adjustment on deficit countries. An equivalent danger looms within East Asia: is not the rising economic and geopolitical power of China an obstacle to the negotiation of a mutually beneficial deepening of regional integration?

- The declining but still strong *power of international finance* makes regional integration quite difficult. Any public decision is immediately converted into a stock-market valuation, a move in the national currency, and its long-term assessment by futures markets. This asymmetry between the loss of autonomy of national governments in response to the demands of citizens and the opportunistic flexibility of finance makes the patient elaboration of supranational institutions quite problematic. The configuration was totally different when European integration was launched. Today, the permanent and instantaneous arbitrage between national treasury bonds, currencies, and quoted firms is shaping the political agenda: powerful private actors interacting via markets set expectations the governments have to comply with. Intergovernmental coordination becomes more a reaction to crises than the promotion of an anticipatory redesign of supranational institutions.
- A successful regional integration is supposed to navigate between *two opposite risks*. If political motives play a leading or exclusive role, rigid supranational institutions might turn out to be incompatible with the related economic incentives: a financial and economic crisis means the dead end and the blocking of a polity-led regional integration. On the contrary, a purely economic approach might encounter another limit: the confrontation of private interests is unable to generate the public goods or the commons required for the deepening of regional integration. The contemporary European Union explores the first limit, and the uncertainty about East Asian integration is evidence for the second limit.

5. *Regional integration is an ongoing process* that transforms itself via internal crises but also the unexpected impact of the structural transformation of international relations: it is not the outcome of a once-and-for-all "big bang," since polity and economy interact according to ever-changing patterns. Six decades of European integration confirm this feature: a first step is successful, and it suggests an extension from coal and steel to manufactured goods. Nevertheless, conflicting national interests can block the process and open a political crisis that is afterwards overcome by a new compromise. Another stage is explored, and it might unfold and finally generate conflict about a quite different issue: should governments put the single market at risk in accepting the volatility of intra-European exchange rates, or should they decide their irreversibility by adopting the euro? The present challenges addressed to European political leaders have to take into account the historicity of the successive bifurcations. In this respect, East Asia and the European Union differ dramatically.

   - The *crisis is systemic and far-reaching in the EU*, threatening its very survival. First, the primacy of an institutional constructivism has created a currency managed by the European Central Bank but without the guarantee of a

European State: the remarkable innovations spurred by the euro crisis are not a substitute for a political foundation of this new currency. Second, the Lisbon Treaty has formalized a set of economic policy rules that prevent delivery of satisfactory macroeconomic outcomes for the weaker countries. This is the origin of public opinion reversal about the benefits of the EU and the rise of anti-European movements and parties. The nationalistic protests are exacerbated by the surge of migration: internally within the EU, they derive from the divergence of standards of living since 2009; externally, they derive from the flow of refugees from the Middle East. Last but not least, the Brexit vote directly challenges the purpose of the EU "to promote an ever closer integration among peoples." This is not at all a case of repetition of the previous crises, including the near "Grexit": the very existence of the EU is at stake. Within *régulation* theory taxonomy, this is a *major (great) crisis* by comparison with a minor one. Existing multilevel governance cannot survive intact.

- In East Asia, two different patterns are operating. On the one side, *the crises coming from the world economy* – respectively, 1997 and 2008 – are occasions to redirect the regional integration first toward the accumulation of reserves by central banks and their cooperation to limit the consequences of "sudden stops" in the inflows of financial capital and second toward more inward-looking domestic growth strategies and a deepening of the Asian division of labor. None of the mechanisms is rigidly codified in conformity with the DNA of the ASEAN project. Actually, on the other side, the new strategies continue to rely upon *the same principles*: a flexible geometry of FTA; a multilayered juxtaposition of general agreements concerning security, the economy, or culture; and a low degree of institutionalization of supranational entities in charge of monitoring the treaties, without the creation of any supranational agora involving the citizens. Therefore, the member states keep sufficient tools to deal with the specific properties of their economic and social systems. *Different exchange regimes* coexist among members and allow for coping with asymmetric shocks, quite a breach with respect to the EU. Of course, many tensions emerge within East Asia: unsolved post-World War II conflict between China and Japan, the geopolitical role of the United States in the region, and growing asymmetric power relations due to the breakthrough of the Chinese economy. However, for the time being, they do not imply a structural crisis of Asian integration led by the dynamism of firms that develop new productive complementarities among countries.

6. *The 2010s are the decade of reckoning for the European Union.* Contrary to most interpretations that single out a unique factor and thus consider that the crisis has an easy solution, the long maturation of the integration process has generated a web of disequilibria and contradictions that now spill over from one domain to another. They have now to be overcome simultaneously.

   - The intellectual epistemological foundation of the EU, *neo-functionalism*, has not simply been defeated by the victory of intergovernmentalism. It was built on the dubious premise that politics is the servant of economics: roughly admissible during the reconstruction phase, it becomes dangerous when it sustains the idea of a complete continuity between a common market and a single currency.

- Money is not a veil because it is the cornerstone of market economies and capitalism. Credit is the source of money creation, and these two entities can be organized according to a significant variety of monetary and financial systems. The euro system, which was conceived to forbid any monetization of national treasury bonds, could not resist the 2010 public debt crisis. The crucial role of lender of last resort reminds us that *any viable monetary system has to be backed by a political authority.*
- Besides the refinancing of the public debt by the central bank, *the loss of two economic policy instruments*, the rate of interest and exchange rate, should have been replaced by others. For instance, an active income policy should warrant a parallelism between nominal wages and productivity increases, and an innovation/industrial policy would keep domestic competitiveness in line with the transformations of the world economy. This was not decided in most Southern European member states, whereas Germany enjoyed the benefits of wage moderation: the divergence of a productive systems was the direct consequence of the blocking of exchange-rate adjustments.
- In this context, with the enforcement of competition and full liberalization by the European Commission and jurisdiction, the slimming down of welfare generosity and supply of collective goods such as education and health, and finally the reduction in the progressivity of personal income taxation, the EU has been perceived as slowly moving toward *a winner-take-all society.* The losers have been prone to join in nationalist/protectionist demands, whereas the winners were unaware of the danger of such *a social polarization.* The 2016 Brexit referendum makes evident this dividing line among citizens, even if globalization and the power of finance, more than rigid regulations from Brussels, have generated this open conflict about the EU.
- Another erroneous prognosis has been also dissipating: a federalism built upon the eradication by an international treaty of any negative externality from one member to the whole Union could weather the internally and externally generated crises. The structural economic imbalances among members and the reactivity of governments to the demands of citizens have made the rules, such as the Stability and Growth Pact, impossible to fulfill permanently, even for the best pupils preaching ordo-liberalism. The rebuttal by northern members of a federalism embedding a principle of solidarity has sealed *the mirage of this legal rule-based federalism.* The defense of national interests has basically prevailed upon the search for a common and general interest.
- The *Grexit* threat episode points out another major dilemma for the EU. Membership in the euro has been finally maintained but paid for by the strengthening of a disastrous cut in public services, wages, and tax rises. Why has such a plan proven to be based upon erroneous estimates of public spending multipliers? Actually, it was imposed by a multinational troika (ECB, the European Commission, and the IMF) in the name of macroeconomic orthodoxy against the will of Greek citizens in response to an ambiguous referendum. Thus, *the interest of creditors* has prevailed upon the

principles of *democratic sovereignty*. In a sense, *Brexit* affirms the supremacy of the voice of the people: this is good news for democracy, but bad news for the future of Europe, perceived as the defender of vested interests of a transnational elite.

- The refugee and immigration crisis in 2016 puts the emphasis upon the widening gap between the core *European principles* (democracy, prevention of wars by diplomatic negotiation, superiority of welfare capitalism, and openness to political and economic refugees...) and *the policies implemented since 2010*. Far from exporting its model to the rest of the world and redesigning a more peaceful international system, Europe, handicapped by poor and unequal economic performance and unprecedented political turmoil, has become the spectator of a historical transformation of the world.

7. *Régulation theory* proposes one synthetic criterion concerning the dividing line between the success and failure of a regional integration project: everything is up to *the compatibility of various national accumulation regimes with the rules of the game* that result from intergovernmental bargaining. Therefore, a dynamic process is set into motion with uncertain outcomes: either a self-sustaining deepening of labor division along with supranational institutional innovation or a dead end and/or open crisis with the abandonment of regional integration.

   - The *European Union crisis of the 2010s* is usually attributed to the divergence of unit-labor costs that reveal macro-imbalances among member states, which makes the euro unsustainable. However, this divergence originates in the problematic coexistence of different growth regimes: *innovation- and export-led* in Germany and the Netherlands and *consumption-led* in France and Italy. Since the Lisbon Treaty follows the way opened by the Rome Treaty and makes competition the driving force of economic integration, the irreversibility of internal exchange rates favors the first regime and erodes the second. With the crisis of public debts, bargaining power brutally shifts from debtor to creditor countries. The latter impose austerity plans that depress economic activity and make the public debt of southern countries still more unsustainable. The extension of the euro to some Central European members and Baltic states, eager to benefit from the protection against exchange-rate volatility, is also quite problematic, since they explore a still different growth regime, namely, *FDI-led*. The adhesion to the euro may push growth in an early phase, but it can be transformed into an obstacle by reducing the degree of maneuver of national economic policy. This analytical framework explains also why successive British governments have refused to join the euro: the *finance-led growth regime* of the UK displays distinctive macroeconomic cyclical patterns that are incompatible with a monetary policy in charge of monitoring the contradiction between export- and consumption-led regimes.
   - *East Asian integration* has also to deal with the *heterogeneity of contrasting socioeconomic regimes*: insular semi-agrarian, trade-led industrializing, and innovation–/export-led. Nevertheless, the choice of an exchange-rate regime, complementary with the domestic growth regime as well as the full

autonomy of tax and public spending policies, allows flexible responses to the stiffening of competition associated with regional integration. Of course, brutal inflows and then outflows of capital may provoke some volatility, but the legacy of the 1997 Asian crisis has promoted new instruments such as large central bank reserves and capital controls, recently rehabilitated by the IMF as a short-term useful tool. Consequently, until 2017, no cyclical crisis has announced the arrival of a systemic crisis of East Asian integration. Nevertheless, two major contradictions confront East Asia. First, whereas multinationals and the spillovers from China's dynamism are silently constructing economic complementarities between members, geopolitical rivalry around maritime frontiers and security issues oppose them. This divorce between polity and economy is a potential source of crisis. A second danger looms in East Asia: both the new Silk Road strategy and the surge of Chinese Foreign Direct Investment out of Asia bring the risk of a deceleration of East Asian integration.

Here are some building blocks for a renewed theorizing of international relations: they can be analyzed as the process by which interdependent socioeconomic regimes search for imposition and/or compromise over supranational coordinating mechanisms.

References

Amable B (2003) The diversity of capitalism. Oxford University Press, Oxford

Aoki M (2001) Toward a comparative institutional analysis. MIT Press, Cambridge

Armingeon K, Ceka B (2013) The loose of trust in the European Union during the great recession since 2007: the role of heuristics from the national political system. European Union Politics.

Artus P (2011) « L'introduction du fédéralisme dans la zone euro: les avantages et les risques ». *Flash économie*. 18 avril. no 284. p. 7

Asian Development Bank (2008) Emerging Asian regionalism: a partnership for shared prosperity. Asian Development Bank, Mandaluyong City

Asian Development Bank (2016) Asian economic integration report 2015: how can special economic zones catalyze economic development. Asian Development Bank, Mandaluyong City

Baccaro L, Howell C (2015) European industrial relations since the 1970s: trajectories of neoliberal transformation, concluding chapter. Oxford University Press, Oxford

Baccaro L, Pontusson HJ (2016) Rethinking Comparative Political Economy: The Growth Model Perspective. Polit Soc 44(2):175

Balassa B (1961) The theory of economic integration. Richard D. Irwin, Inc., Homewood

Beeson M (2004) Political and economic integration in East Asia. Encyclopaedia of public policy: governance in a global age. Routledge, London

Bieling H-J, Jäger J, Ryner M (2016) Regulation theory and the political economy of the European Union. JCMS 54(1):53–69. https://doi.org/10.1111/jcms.12331

Boyer R (1999) Le gouvernement de la zone Euro. La Documentation Française, Paris

Boyer R (2000a) The political in the era of globalization and finance; focus on some *Régulation* School Research. Intl J Urban Reg Res 24(2):274–322 (en Japonais: Comp Econ Stud: 61–83)

Boyer R (2000b) The unanticipated fallout of European Monetary Union: the political and institutional deficits of the Euro. In Crouch C (ed) After the Euro. Oxford: Oxford University Press, pp 24–88

Boyer R (2003) European integration and its implication for Asia, Chapter 5. In Moon Wosik (2000)

Boyer R (2014) The transatlantic trade and investment partnership: the end of European regulatory distinctiveness and consecration of the US regulatory model? Mimeograph
Boyer R, Dehove M (2001) « Du 'gouvernement économique' au gouvernement tout court », Critique internationale, n° 11, avril, pp 179–195
Boyer R, Uemura H, Isogai A (eds) (2012) Diversity and transformations of Asian capitalisms. Routledge, London
Calmfors L (1997) EMU: a Swedish perspective. Kluwer Academic Publishers, Boston
Chavagneux C (2010) L'économie politique internationale. Repères. La Découverte, Paris
Clarke D, Goodwin M, Whiteley P (2017) Brexit why Britain voted to leave the European Union. University of Essex Publication, Cambridge
Commission of the European Communities (1988) Europe 1992: the overall challenge. European archives
Crouch C (2000) After the Euro. Oxford University Press, Oxford
Dehove M (1997) L'union européenne inaugure-t-elle un nouveau grand régime d'organisation des pouvoirs publics et de la société internationale? In: L'Année de la Régulation 1. La Découverte, Paris
Dieter H, Higgott RA (2003) Exploring alternative theories of economic regionalism: From trade to finance in Asian cooperation. Rev Int Polit Econ 10(3):430–454
Downs A (1957) An Economic Theory of Political Action in a Democracy. J Polit Econ 65:135–150
Eichengreen, B., Bayoumi T (1999) Is Asia an optimum currency area? Can it become one. In Collignon S, Ferry JP, Park YC (eds) Exchange rate policies in emerging Asian countries. Routledge, London
European Community (2016) Eurobarometer. Brussels, July
Fligstein N (2008) Euroclash, The EU, European identity, and the future of Europe. Oxford University Press, Oxford
Fligstein N, Stone SA (2002) Constructing polities and markets: an institutionalist account of European integration, Am J Sociol 107(5):1206–1243
Goulard S, Monti M (2012) De la démocratie en Europe. Flammarion, Paris
Hall P (1997) The political challenges facing regional trade regimes. La Lettre de la Régulation n° 22 https://theorie-regulation.org/revues/publications/lettres-de-la-regulation/
Harada Y, Tohyama H (2012) Asian capitalisms: institutional configurations and firm heterogeneity. In Boyer R, Uemura H, Isogai A (eds) Diversity and transformations of Asian capitalisms. Routledge, London, pp 243–263
Hirakawa H (2016) Structural shift of global economy and East Asia's regional institutionalization, with a focus on ASEAN (This volume)
Hooghe L, Marks G (2008) A post-functionalist theory of European integration: from permissive consensus to constraining dissensus. Br J Polit Sci 39:1–23
Issing O (2012) Europe's political union is an idea worthy of satire. Financial Times, July 29
Kojima K (2000) The 'flying geese' model of Asian economic development: origin, theoretical extensions, and regional policy implications. J Asian Econ 11:375–401
Krugman P (1991) Increasing Returns and Economic Geography. J Polit Econ 99(1):483–499
Monnet J (1976) Mémoires. Fayard, Paris
Moon W, Yeogseop R, Ryong YD (2000) Asian monetary cooperation: a search for regional monetary stability in the Post Euro and Post Asian crisis era. Econ Pap 3(1):159–193
Moravcsik A (1993) Preferences and power in the European Community: a liberal intergovernmental approach. J Common Mark Stud 31:473
Moravcsik A (1998) The choice of Europe. Cornell University Press, Ithaca
Morten H (2011) Regional integration in Europe and East Asia: differences in degree, not in kind. Korea Rev Intl Stud 27–37
Mundell RA (1961) A theory of optimum currency areas. Am Econ Rev 51(4):657–665
Myant M, Drahokoupil J (2010) Transition economies: Political economy in Russia, Eastern Europe, and Central Asia. Wiley, New York

Palan R (2000) Global Political Economy: Contemporary Theories. Psychology Press
Park S-H (2002) East Asian economic integration – finding a balance between regionalism and multilateralism. EIAS briefing paper
Pradumna RB (2006) Economic integration in East Asia: trends, prospects, and a possible roadmap. Office of Regional Economic Integration. Asian Development Bank, Manila
Scharpf F (2011) Monetary Union, Fiscal crisis and the preemption of democracy. Max-Planck-Institute Köln working paper
Schimmelfennig F, Rittberge B (2006) Theories of European integration. Assumptions and hypotheses. In Richardson J (ed) European Union. Power and policy-making, 3rd edn. Routledge, London, pp 3–95
Schmitter P (1974) Still the century of corporatism? In: Pike FB, Stritch T (eds) The new corporatism. Notre Dame University Press, Notre Dame, pp 85–131
Schmitter P, Lefkofridi Z (2015) Neo-functionalism as a theory of disintegration. In European disintegration – a blind spot of integration theory? 22nd CES conference, Paris
SOFRES (1997) L'opinion publique française, Paris
Stiglitz J (2016) A split euro is the solution for the single currency. Financial Times, August 17
Stockhammer E (2015) Neoliberal growth models, monetary union and the Euro crisis. A post-Keynesian perspective. New Polit Econ 21(4)
Streeck W (2014) Buying time: The delayed crisis of democratic capitalism. Verso, London
Sum N-L (2016) A regulationist and variegated capitalism approach to China since 1978: four stages of complex exportism in the world economy. In Boyer R (ed) China and regulation theory. Beijing University (Forthcoming)
The Economist (2016) The start of the break-up, what do other countries make of Brexit? August, 6th page
The Economist (2018) America is undermining the rules based system of world trade. March 10–16, pp 19–22
Theret B (2001) Economie politique du fédéralisme. Critique internationale. 11:128–130
Theret B (2012) Dettes et crise de confiance dans l'euro. Analyse et voies possibles de sortie par le haut. IRISSO – Université Paris Dauphine, CNRS
Tinbergen J (1956) Economic policy: principles and design. Elsevier Science Publishing, Amsterdam
UNCTAD (2014) Bilateral FDI statistics. UNCTAD, Genova
Wade R (1990) Governing the market: economic theory and the role of government in East Asian industrialization. Princeton University Press, Princeton
Wang J, Nagendra S, Uemura H (2012) Chinese international production linkages and Japanese multinationals: evolving industrial interdependence and coordination. In: Boyer R, Uemura H, Isogai A (eds) *Diversity and transformations of Asian capitalisms*. Routledge, London, pp 143–164
Whittaker H, Tianbiao Zhu TJ Sturgeon MHT, Okita T (2007) Compressed development in East Asia. ITEC working paper series 07–29 December
World Bank (1993) The East Asian miracle: economic growth and public policy. World Bank, Washington, DC
World Bank (2016) Potential macroeconomic implications of the trans-Pacific partnership. Chapter 4, Global economic prospects, January, pp 219–233
Yan C (2012) Analysis of the linkage effect in Chinese export-led growth: according to the subdivisions of Asian international input–output tables. In: Boyer R, Uemura H, Isogai A (eds) *Diversity and transformations of Asian capitalisms*. Routledge, London

Chapter 3
Transformation of the World Economy and Institutionalization of East Asian Region

Hitoshi Hirakawa

3.1 Introduction

It has been half a century since the start of the economic growth of East Asia. During this period, we saw high economic growth and industrialization of Japan starting in the 1960s, followed by the newly industrialized economies (NIEs) since the late 1960s, the advanced economies of the Association of Southeast Asian Nations (ASEAN) from the second half of the 1980s, and China and the latecomer ASEAN economies since the 1990s. By the end of the twentieth century, East Asia has achieved the indisputable position as the world's manufacturing base.

By coining the term BRICs in 2001, Jim O'Neill of the US investment bank Goldman Sachs directed the interest of investors to the possibility of development in highly populated countries, such as China and India, that would have a large influence on the global economy in the next 10 years or so (O'Neill 2001). An ensuing report from the same bank showed a shocking simulation that in 2050 the only countries remaining in the G6, in terms of economic size, would only be the USA and Japan (Wilson and Purushothaman 2003). In 2007, the World Bank predicted that by 2025 East Asia would account for 40% of the global economy should the current growth continue (Gill and Kharas 2007). In the following year of 2008, America's National Intelligence Council (NIC) publicized its view that China, India, and Russia will develop under a model of "state capitalism" that is different from democracy and may become one of the major economic zones of the world by 2025 (NIC 2008). A 2011 report of the Asian Development Bank has even predicted the possibility that East Asia will exceed half of the global GDP, restoring Asia to the

H. Hirakawa (✉)
School of Asia 21, Kokushikan University, Machida, Japan
e-mail: hhirakaw@kokushikan.ac.jp

R. Boyer et al. (eds.), *Evolving Diversity and Interdependence of Capitalisms*, Evolutionary Economics and Social Complexity Science 11,
https://doi.org/10.1007/978-4-431-55001-3_3

dominant position in the global economy, which it held 300 years before the industrial revolution.

Actually, East Asia has grown to surpass the current economic size of Europe and America and is displaying concomitant dramatic changes in regional economic structure. However, what is the mechanism that caused this structural shift? What has this structural shift brought about to the region? Ironically, this structural shift is one consequence of the globalization promoted by market fundamentalist ideology at the end of the twentieth century, giving birth to the possibility of greatly changing the current international order.

The objective of this chapter is to examine the East Asia's economic growth and associated issues from the two perspectives of its growth mechanism and the regional institutionalization through cooperation regime based on the ASEAN.

3.2 The Global Economy's Structural Transformation and East Asia

Let us start by confirming the structural shift of global economy using the IMF statistics. Some interesting facts could be gleaned from Fig. 3.1, which shows changes in the economic size, with respect to that of the USA, European Union, East Asia (Japan, China, NIEs, ASEAN5[1]), and India.

Firstly, in 1980, the EU and East Asia were 1.3 times and 0.6 times the size of the USA, respectively. At the time of the Plaza Accord of 1985, the EU and East Asia's economies shrank but recovered toward 1995 and at one time overtook the USA. East Asia and the EU shrank during the time of the Asian currency crisis in 1997–1998 and rebounded. The growth of the EU, however, once again halted as a result of the global financial crisis. On the other hand, East Asia steadily followed in the footsteps of the USA from 2004 to 2005, overcame the USA in 2010, and in the 2012 surpassed the EU. East Asia, at present, has grown to be the largest economic zone in the world.

How has the structure within the East Asian region changed? Through its relationship with America, Japan was able to expand its share, peaking to 69% in 1995 and declining to 31% in 2007. On the other hand, China increased its share from 7% in 1980 to 41% in 2010, surpassing Japan's 38% for the same year. Japan yielded the position of second world's largest GDP to China, and in 2014 Japan's GDP was half of China. The gap would steadily widen from hereon.

It is not clear from this figure, but the NIEs and ASEAN have pursued a catch-up orbit of smooth growth, though they show a drop due to the Asian currency crisis and

[1]East Asia consists of China, Japan, the NIEs (Korea, Taiwan, Hong Kong, and Singapore), ASEAN5 (Indonesia, Malaysia, Philippines, Thailand, and Vietnam), Brunei, Cambodia, Laos, Myanmar, Mongolia, and East Timor.

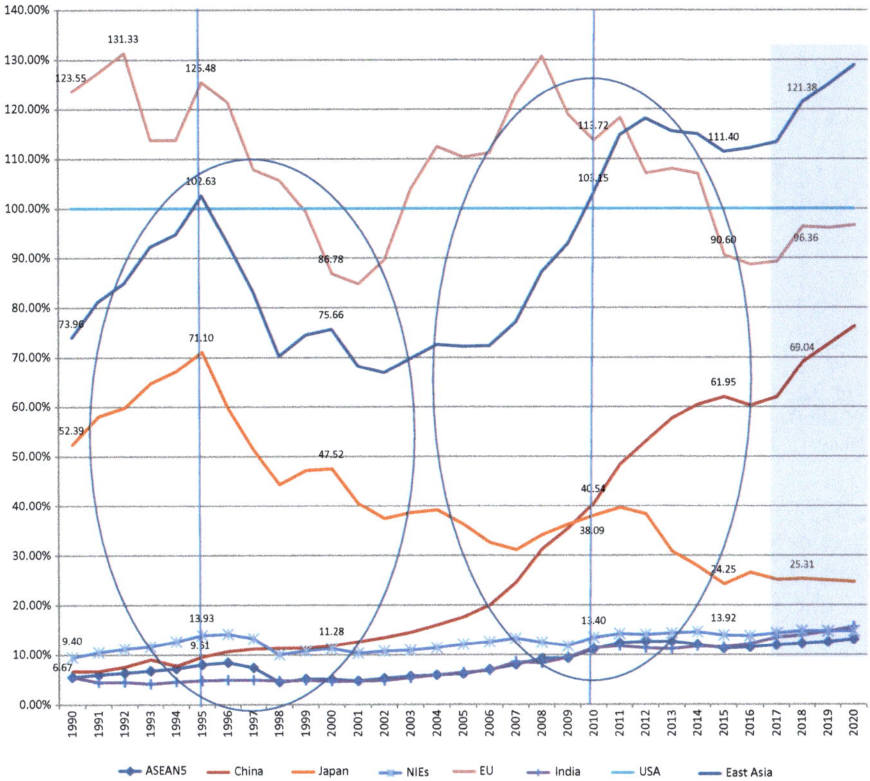

Fig. 3.1 Catch-up GDP ratio with respect to the USA, by major country and region. (Source: The data of Hirakawa 2014 was updated)
Note: Estimates start after 2017. NIEs: Korea, Taiwan, Hong Kong, and Singapore. ASEAN5: Indonesia, Malaysia, the Philippines, Thailand, and Vietnam. East Asia: ASEAN5, NIEs, China, and Janan. The USA's GDP is 100. GDP is in a nominal base

global financial crisis. In East Asia, it is only Japan that structurally had a declining share due to stagnated Japanese economy.

From Fig. 3.1, another important fact can be confirmed. The driving force of East Asia's growth dramatically changed from Japan to China. Up to the beginning of this century, the economy of East Asia more or less moved together with that of Japan but around 2005–2006 came to move together with that of China. The main actor in East Asia is now China.

Here let us make a simple check of export values of the EU and East Asia. Reflecting on market integration, the scale of EU export rapidly increased from the second half of the 1980s. This was followed by the increase in US exports, then by that of the NIEs in the 1990s, and by a dramatic increase of China's exports entering this century. Comparing the total export value of East Asia, consisting of Japan, the NIEs, ASEAN5, and China, with that of America and the EU, East Asia's total exports made up \$345.0 billion in 1985, surpassing \$289.0 billion of the USA, and

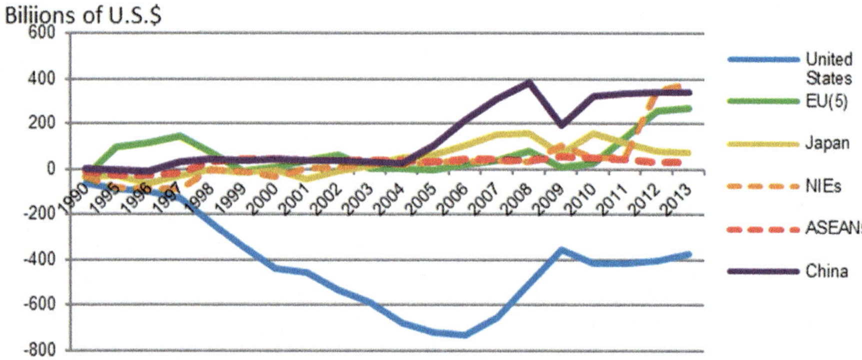

Fig. 3.2 Trade balance of goods and services by major economy and nation 1990–2013 (Source: World Bank 2015 and Taiwan Statistical Data Book 2012)
Note: Taiwan's data is not available for 2012–2013

became \$3.609 trillion in 2006, surpassing \$3.537 trillion of the EU. Thereafter, East Asia has become the world's largest export zone.

Checking the goods/services trade balance of the three economic zones of EU, NAFTA, and East Asia gives us Fig. 3.2. The biggest feature is that, since the second half of the 1990s, the US deficit has rapidly ballooned, while, entering this century, the surplus of China has caused a rapid increase and the EU's trade surplus remained more or less at equilibrium. In general, the trade surpluses of the NIEs and ASEAN5 have also been increasing. This has rapidly increased the foreign exchange reserves of East Asia, especially China, and prompted a rise in the political economic position of East Asia in the world economy.

Let us again check the structural change within the East Asian region, including India. Figure 3.3 looks at the catch-up rate of China, the NIEs, ASEAN4, as well as India, with Japan's GDP as reference. It could be seen that, entering this century, China unwaveringly pursued Japan, overtaking her in 2010. China expanded to two times Japan in 2014. The NIEs and ASEAN had temporary setbacks due to effects of the global financial crisis but have been steadily closing the gap with Japan since then. In short, the structure of East Asia's development is one where only Japan has reduced its share within the region. The table does not show it, but, from the IMF's GDP statistics, Japan's share in the combined GPD of East Asia and India dropped from 66.5% in 1990 to 33.2% in 2010. In contrast, China's share rose from 8.4% to 35.9%, while the NIEs and ASEAN countries basically maintained their shares (IMF 2012).

Incidentally, in terms of current GDP per capita in 2014, Singapore and Hong Kong have \$56,009 and \$40,078, respectively, surpassing Japan's \$36,156, followed by South Korea with \$27,970, Taiwan with \$22,618, Malaysia with \$11,050, China with \$7625, Thailand with \$5889, and Indonesia, the Philippines,

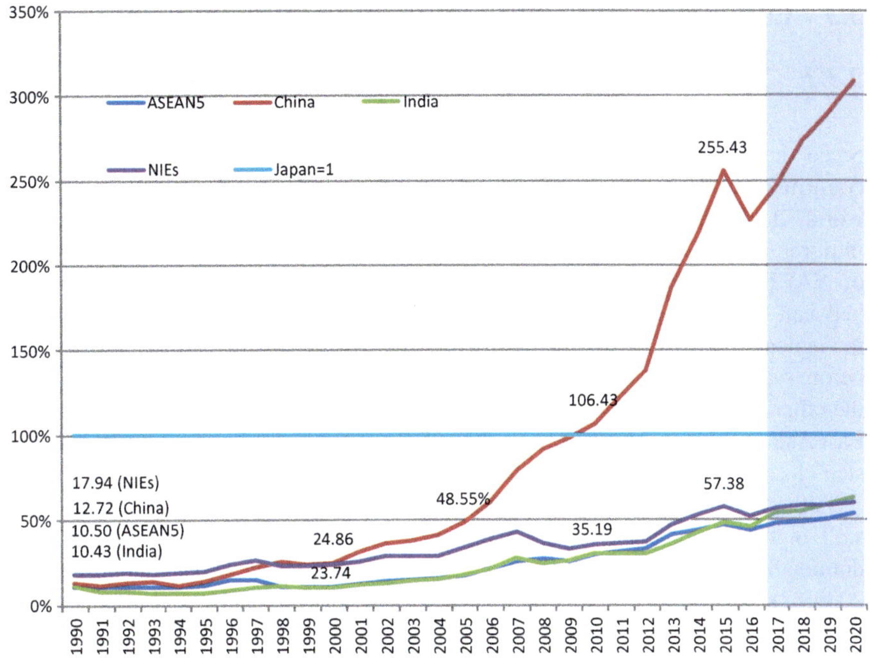

Fig. 3.3 GDP trends of China, the NIEs, and ASEAN with respect to Japan 1980–2020 (Source: IMF 2018)
Note: Estimates start from 2017

India, and Vietnam (IMF 2016). China's growth has been spectacular, but in terms of GDP per capita rankings, smaller-population countries are at the top, while larger-population emerging countries successfully try to catch up. In short, East Asia as a region has a big leeway for growth and an extremely huge development potential. This structure will give rise to the possibility for a large change in political economy of the East Asian region and the world economy. The huge growth potential held by China, which has become the second largest economy in the world, holds an unfathomable influence in the international political economy, and, of course, in international society as well as regional society, resources, energy, and global climate issues. In December 2012, the National Intelligence Council, which oversees US intelligence institutions, announced in their predictions for 2030 an increase in instability due to the spread of power in the international society. In Asia, this is especially serious in the middle and south, but in East Asia it is predicted that, due to the decline in the status of the USA and the growing nationalism in China, "regional trends probably will continue to pull countries in two directions: toward China economically but toward the USA and each other for security" (NIC 2012, 76–77).

3.3 East Asian Integration and its Driving Mechanism

3.3.1 The De Facto Market–Led Integration in East Asia

Since the 1980s, economic integration has proceeded in East Asia. Figure 3.4 confirms the intra-regional export shares of major regional economies of the world. It can be seen that, from the 1980s up to 1990s, irrespective of region, intra-region has advanced with EU leading the way. The intra-regional export shares of NAFTA and East Asia were 43.9% and 34.3%, respectively. There is a gap between the two, with both shares increasing in the 1990s and showing similar movements. However, after stalling for nearly 10 years at the start of this century before reaching 50%, East Asia finally was able to surpass the 50% wall in 2010. On the other hand, NAFTA has been reducing its intra-regional share peaking in 2005. East Asia still lags behind at two thirds of EU's intra-regional export but has come a step closer to the possibility of a higher degree of integration.

Although the ASEAN intra-regional share rose in the 1990s, it ran into the 25% wall in this century. Moreover, the ASEAN intra-regional trade is traditionally dominated by Singapore and the ASEAN 4, particularly Malaysia, trade (Yun 2009:82). According to the ASEAN statistics collated by JETRO, the share of the Singapore-ASEAN 4 trade tends to decline, reaching 70.4% in 2000 and dropping to 59.3% in 2009 (JETRO 2010), but the share is still quite high. This means that the main axis of intra-regional trade of East Asia is not within the ASEAN region, but rather that the East Asian integration is advancing with the ASEAN being included in the intra-region centering China, Japan, and the NIEs.

This intra-regional economic integration in East Asia has a remarkable feature, compared with NAFTA and EU. The 2007 White Paper published by the Japanese Ministry of Economy, Trade, and Industry (METI) reports that intermediate goods

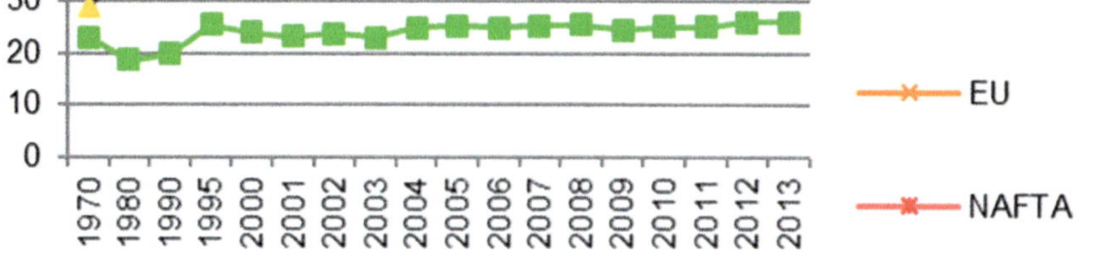

Fig. 3.4 Intra-regional export ratio by major economic zone 1970–2013. (Source: World Bank 2005. The data after 2004 are UNCTAD statistics, and the data for East Asia since 2004 was computed from the JETRO World Trade Matrix)

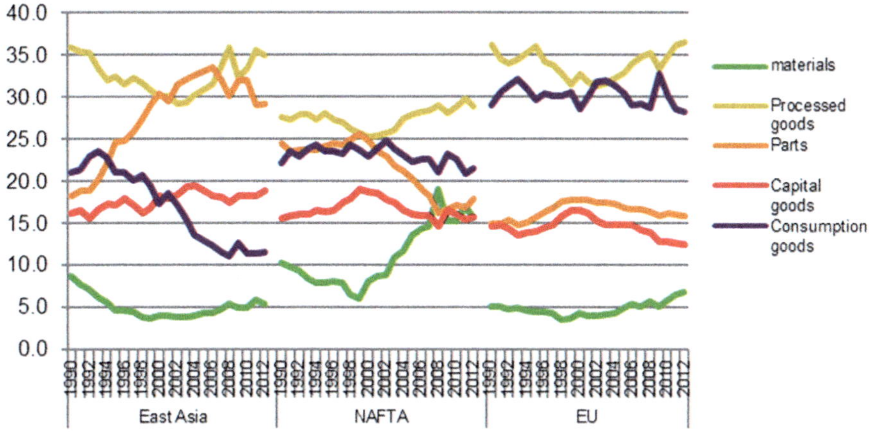

Fig. 3.5 Trade structure of major economic zones by goods 1990–2012. (Source: Data of METI 2014: Fig. II-3-1-5)

(consisting of parts and processed goods) trade has been flourishing in East Asia, compared to the EU and NAFTA, where there are a lot of domestically completing type industries. East Asia is an "economic zone having chained base industries" "which achieved an organic connection among industries in the region" (METI 2007:108–19). Figure 3.5 is created from the data of the "METI White Paper 2013" on the structure of trade by commodities of East Asia, NAFTA, and EU from 1990 to 2012. East Asia had a rapid increase of parts trade from 18.3% to 29.0% during this period. In contrast, NAFTA's dropped from 23.5% to 18.0%, while the EU's stayed more or less in the neighborhood of 15%. On the other hand, during the same period, the trade in consumer goods dropped by about half in East Asia from 21.0% to 11.5% but did not change much in NAFTA (22.1% to 21.6%) and the EU (29.1% to 28.2%). Processed goods occupy the highest shares in all regions, and it is only in East Asia where a trade structure centered on parts and processed goods can be clearly seen. However, facts do not support the assertion that the intermediate goods trade is distributed equally across all intra-regional countries by all industries. Depending on the industry, there is a push for a restructuring among countries in the region. It is necessary to deal with the fact that there are countries that tend to be excluded from this international division of labor (Maquito and Hirakawa 2010).

Incidentally, the late 1960s up to the 1980s period was extolled as the age of development of the NIEs through an export-led model of growth. The NIEs grew under the so-called triangular structure, importing raw materials from Japan, processing, assembling, and then exporting to the US market. In addition, yen appreciation triggered by the Plaza Accord of 1985 pushes Japanese firms, in the form of FDI, to head toward the NIEs, advanced ASEAN countries, and then China. This became the core that created a complicated international division of labor in East Asia. It was the NIEs that were able to get a chance to develop their local

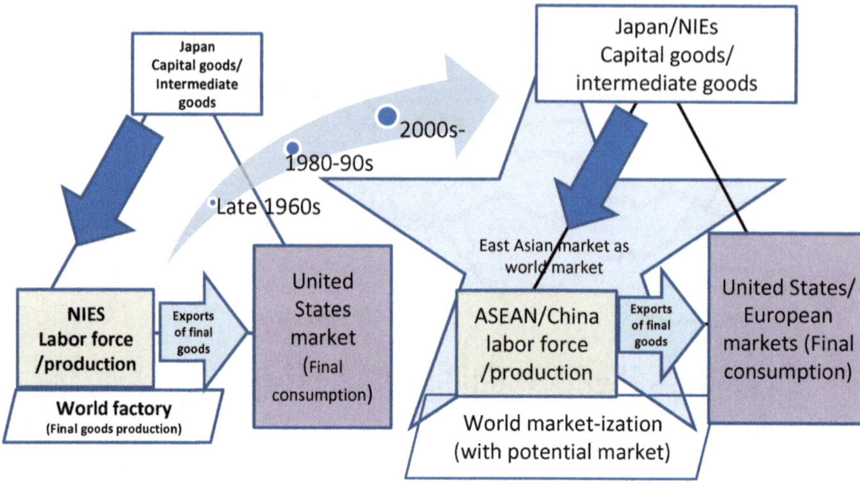

Fig. 3.6 Advancement of the triangular structure of high-growth East Asia. (Source: Author's creation, referring to METI 2005 and others)

industries in this structure. In this manner, the international division of labor led mainly by Japanese firms was upgraded with the participation of the NIEs since the 1990s.

This structure maintains existing triangular structure that places advanced economies as the main market. It is under this structure that the process of creating the advanced Asian intra-regional trade proceeded as is shown in Fig. 3.6; the position of intermediate goods production, which Japan occupied in the past, now includes the NIEs; and the position held then by the NIEs of assembling for final goods using an abundant labor force now includes China and ASEAN. The final goods made here are exported to the American and European markets. This forms a development mechanism, the upgrading of which can be confirmed from the rise of traded goods prices (METI 2005:167).

East Asia's share of the global machinery and equipment exports was 37.1% in 2007, 53.8% of which was ICT-related goods. East Asia's share in this ICT-related goods reached 56.7% of world exports (ITI 2008). East Asia is the production base for hi-tech goods, the export structure for which is shown Table 3.1. In 2007, the intra-regional trade in IT parts was 72.9%, but that of final goods was merely 39.1%. In contrast, the share of exports to the USA and the EU was, respectively, 10.0% and 11.4% for parts and 24.8% and 22.3% for final goods. Entering this century, one remarkable thing was the rise in the intra-regional share and the decrease in export share to the USA and EU. Even in the final goods, the intra-regional export share surpassed the export share to the USA.

This triangular structure enables, through upgrading, the accumulation of value added within the region. The 2008 version of the "METI White Paper" states that, based on the UN data, the real value added of the manufactured goods exports of the ASEAN+6 (Japan, China, South Korea, Australia, India, and New Zealand) was

Table 3.1 Intra-regional export ratio of IT-related goods (total, parts, final goods) by East Asian main country/region 2000, 2007

%, $100m

Export \ Import	Japan		East Asia 10		U.S.A.		EU		**World**		
	2000	2007	2000	2007	2000	2007	2000	2007		2000	2007
	IT-related Goods (Total)										
China	12.9	5.9	52.4	44.8	22.3	21.2	19.1	22.1	100	**50,525**	**378,800**
Hong Kong	5.3	3.8	61.9	75.4	17.8	8.4	14.0	9.9	100	**60,461**	**162,114**
Korea	11.3	7.0	46.2	59.4	28.6	12.5	16.7	16.4	100	**61,719**	**102,003**
Taiwan	13.3	8.6	46.3	66.4	26.8	15.4	20.6	12.5	100	**68,029**	**81,180**
ASEAN 5	10.0	7.7	51.9	61.1	24.7	17.0	17.1	13.6	100	**191,729**	**253,324**
Japan	-	-	44.8	61.5	29.3	16.4	20.4	14.6	100	**141,366**	**142,983**
East Asia 10	7.8	5.5	50.0	57.9	25.6	16.6	18.1	16.2	100	**573,830**	**1,120,402**
	IT-related Goods (Parts)										
China	15.7	7.2	68.7	63.9	12.8	12.4	13.5	15.8	100	**24,888**	**130,095**
Hong Kong	5.2	3.2	69.3	84.8	14.0	5.5	11.8	6.2	100	**42,274**	**114,833**
Korea	12.2	8.9	55.7	74.8	24.3	8.2	13.9	10.4	100	**41,618**	**56,525**
Taiwan	11.4	9.2	54.4	76.0	22.4	9.6	17.0	9.7	100	**45,850**	**67,080**
ASEAN 5	9.0	7.8	58.9	70.8	20.9	11.5	15.4	12.4	100	**133,827**	**170,926**
Japan	-	-	59.5	70.8	21.0	11.0	15.5	12.0	100	**82,474**	**85,013**
East Asia 10	7.7	6.0	60.0	72.9	20.2	10.0	14.9	11.4	100	**370,931**	**624,472**
	IT-related Goods (Final Goods)										
China	10.2	5.2	36.5	34.7	31.6	25.8	24.5	25.4	100	**25,637**	**248,704**
Hong Kong	5.5	5.3	44.7	52.8	26.6	15.2	19.0	18.8	100	**18,187**	**47,281**
Korea	9.5	4.6	26.4	40.2	37.5	17.8	22.5	23.8	100	**20,101**	**45,478**
Taiwan	17.2	5.7	29.5	20.8	36.0	43.3	28.1	25.9	100	**22,179**	**14,099**
ASEAN 5	12.3	7.3	35.7	41.0	33.3	28.4	20.8	16.0	100	**57,903**	**82,397**
Japan	-	-	24.2	47.7	41.0	24.4	27.3	18.4	100	**58,892**	**57,970**
East Asia 10	8.1	4.9	31.7	39.1	35.4	24.8	24.0	22.3	100	**202,899**	**495,930**

Source: Calculated from Institute for International Trade and Investment (2008)
Note: ASEAN5: Indonesia, Malaysia, the Philippines, Singapore, and Thailand. East Asia 10: ASEAN5, China, Hong Kong, Korea, Taiwan, and Japan

1 trillion and 86 million dollars in 2001, surpassing the 1 trillion and 64 million dollars of NAFTA. In the following year of 2002, it became 1 trillion and 93 million dollars, surpassing the 1 trillion and 88 million dollars of EU27. The gross value added of 2006 was 2 trillion and 55 million for ASEAN+6, 1 trillion and 83 million for NAFTA, and 2 trillion and five million for EU27. It can be seen that the difference has been increasing (METI 2009:145).

The 2011 version of the "METI White Paper" studied "rising affluence of emerging nations." It observed that the middle class[2] of the Asian emerging nations rose more than six times from 0.24 billion people in 2000 to 1.46 billion in 2010. It is predicted to further increase to 2.31 billion people by 2020 (METI 2011:153). In thc 2012 predictions made by the real estate large corporation, Knight Frank and CITI bank, by 2050, the NIE economies of South Korea, Taiwan, Hong Kong, and Singapore would become the most affluent economies in the world. According to this prediction, based on Internet information, the present centa-millionaires, in the Asian region including ASEAN, China, and Japan, number 18,000 people, surpassing the 17,000 people in the USA and the 14,000 in Western Europe. By 2016, this

[2]The lower middle-income class is defined as those having more than $5000 and less than $15,000 in average disposable income of households, while upper middle-income is between $15,000 and less than $35,000. Wealthy class is $35,000 or above.

will rise to 26,000 people in the abovementioned Asian region, 21,000 people in Northern America, and 15,000 people in Western Europe. Should Asia's deca-millionaires are those with more than 10 billion dollars in assets, their number would already be very much surpassing that of Europe and in the next 10 years that of the USA (http://business.inquirer.net/77117/asian-economies-to-top-richest-list-by-2050-study).

The economic integration of Asia until around 2000 has one more feature. Often mentioned is the de facto market-led type of integration. In Europe, there is the institutional process starting from the European Market White Paper announcement of the European Economic Community of 1985, the signing of the Maastricht Treaty of 1992, the complete market integration in 1993, and the creation of the EU. In Northern America, the US-Canadian Free Trade Agreement was signed in 1989, and NAFTA was formed in 1992. However, in East Asia, there has been a moved toward the ASEAN Free Trade Area (AFTA) in the Fourth ASEAN Summit Meeting of 1992, but this has not spread to the whole East Asian region. Moreover, as shown in Fig 3.4, AFTA has not exhibited any results. Nevertheless, the regional integration of East Asia, at the same time, has advanced as in other economic zones. This was achieved mainly by the wave of Japanese FDI in the NIEs, ASEAN, and China, following the appreciation of the yen.

3.3.2 The Mechanism for Forming Emerging Economies: From a NIEs Model to PoBMEs Model of Development

Development of the East Asian economy for the past half century has proven wrong predictions of a lot of economists. East Asia, without exception, has achieved a "compressed style" of high growth once it started to grow. Confronted with a global recession of the 1970s, that time, the NIEs were thought to have been blocked off from the development path based on an export-led growth. Even during the Asian currency crisis of 1997 and the global financial crisis of 2008, pessimistic predictions were rampant. However, the region went through a V-type of recovery despite severe economic crises. The East Asian economy's toughness instead came to be cited.

In the context of development theory up to the 1970s, developing regions were faced with solution of important issues of poverty, lack of capital, and excess population. Today, however, the issue lies in the management of large influxes of short-term capital, and large labor population has even come to be viewed as a growth bonus. Until recent times, recession of advanced economies has immediately brought about a severe recession in the developing economies. Now, however, East Asian nations have shown a V-shape type of ability to recover even as it is greatly affected in the short term. There is even the feeling that the crisis has become an opportunity to rise to the next and higher step in the development process. How are we to make of this phenomenon? In general, there is attention on the internal development capability of East Asian nations, but it is the understanding of this author that, even more so, we should focus on the changes of the international environment during this period.

The development strategy of the current developing economies should be export-led. This is a conventional wisdom in economics. We cannot deny development of East Asia under globalization. Looking back, a socialist type of development strategy and an import substitution development strategy tried in the developing regions at the second half of the twentieth century ended up in failure. It was only the export-led development seen in the NIEs that succeeded (Hirakawa 1999). This development was initiated by the direct investments of multinational firms, creating the development of an international division of labor.

Figure 3.7 shows the share of received foreign direct investment (FDI) by region. It is confirmed that from the 1980s up to now, there has been a significant change in

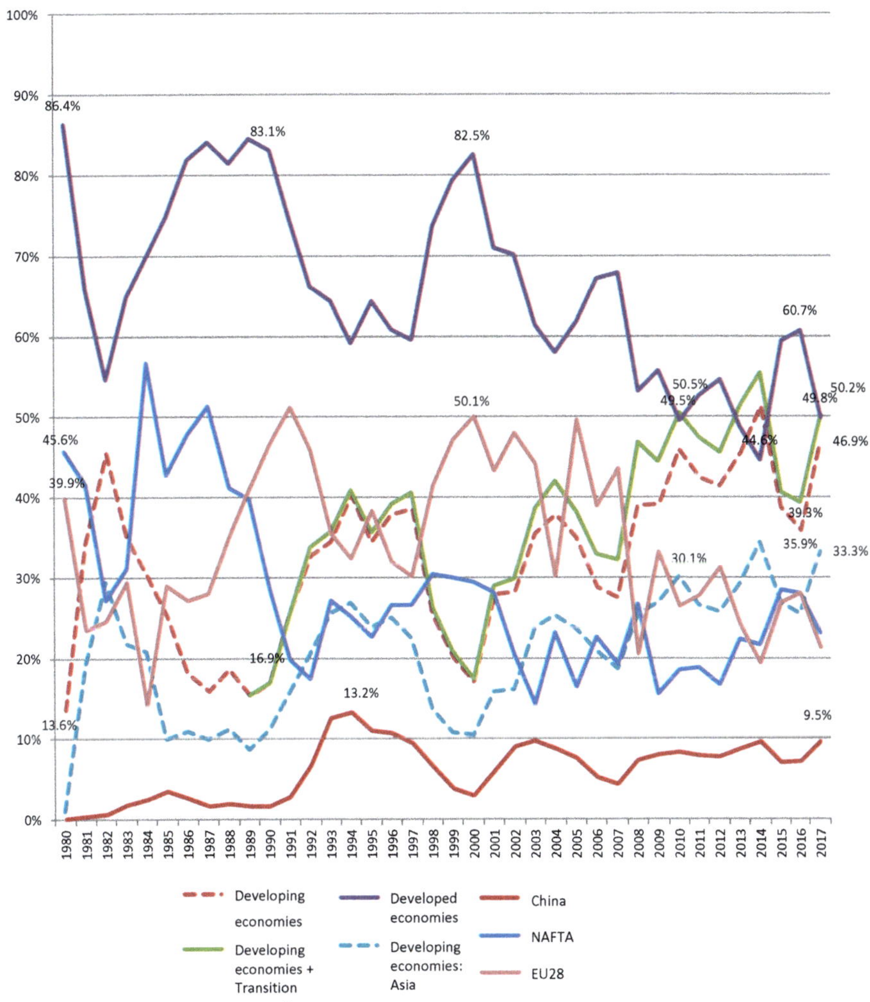

Fig. 3.7 Share of inward FDI flows (annual) by group 1980–2017. (Source: Created from UNCTADstat. Accessed on Aug. 20, 2018)

the geographical proportion of FDI. The share of developed economies in 1980 was 86.4%, with its half (45.6%) headed for NAFTA, especially the USA. However, since then, the share went up and down with a tendency to decline. Entering this century, the share significantly declined, going below half in 2010 and 49.8% in 2017. In contrast, the developing economies became new destinations for FDI. The share of the developing economies is 13.6% in 1980, 45.8% in 2010, and 46.9% in 2017. Adding transitional economies, the share of developing and transitional economies increased from 50.5% in 2010 to 50.2% in 2017. Of which, the developing world of Asia saw the share increase to 30.1% in 2010 and 33.3% in 2017 (UNCTADstat). Why did the FDI, which has been heading toward advanced economies, headed toward Asia? The NIEs grew due to an export-led policy and, needless to say, is running at the head of today's emerging economies. This is the development of the labor-intensive industries and processes, based on abundant and cheap labor. In short, multinational firms in search of low wages moved their manufacturing sections to the NIEs.

Entering this century, Goldman Sachs selected countries that held a growth possibility following of course the BRICs. It called these countries the Next 11 (O'Neill 2001; Wilson and Purushothaman 2003; O'Neill et al., 2005; Wilson and Stupnytska 2007). What is so special about these countries? According to the survey, undertaken by the Japan Bank for International Cooperation (JBIC) since the 1990s, of Japanese firms operating abroad, since entering this century, the most promising countries for business development over medium term (the next 3 years) include China, India, Thailand, Vietnam, Indonesia, Brazil, and Russia. The number of firms, which once viewed the USA as a promising investment destination, is clearly on a downward trend. The first reason for the emerging countries including the BRICs and the Next 11 to be promising countries was "the future growth potential of local market," replacing the "low wages" reason for investments to the NIEs (JBIC, various surveys).

This change in conceptual distinction has become possible through reconsideration of the industrialization of the developing East Asian economies from the factors of capital (including technology), labor, and markets to a spatial dimension. Figure 3.8 is a conceptualization of this. The first stage is the period wherein the developing economy adopts an import substitution policy after its dependence. Of course, a disparity in adoption timing could be seen among the countries, but we could identify this stage as roughly the 1950s to the 1960s. The second stage is the development stage of the NIEs and is the period from the second half of the 1960s up to the 1990s. The third stage is the stage from the end of the 1990s to the present, wherein there has been a rise in interest on China and the other emerging economies/markets, and the BRICs term was coined. The author would like to call this stage as potentially bigger market economies (PoBMEs). At this stage, the potential existence of a market is a critical factor in a firm's decision to enter a country (Hirakawa 2011; Hirakawa and Aung 2011).

In the first stage, the developing country was poor and domestic market is limited in scale. There is excess population causing people to look for jobs. Capital from advanced countries flowed in, aiming at the markets of these countries. However,

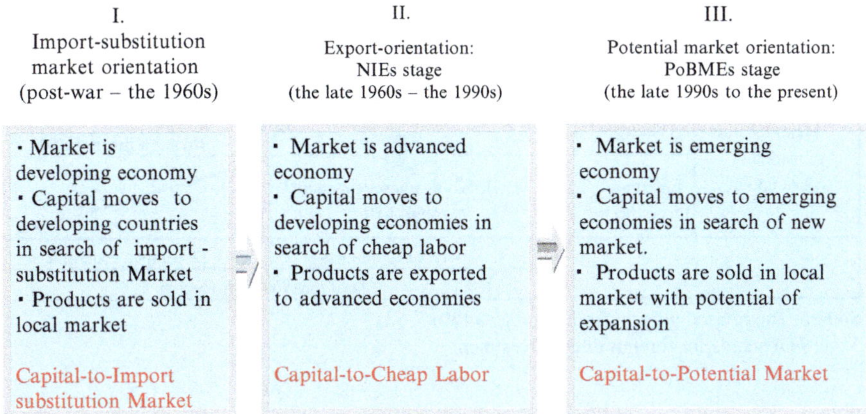

Fig. 3.8 Changes in spatial relationships of capital, labor, and market in development process of emerging economies: A conceptual diagram. (Source: Revised version of Hirakawa 2013: 283)
Note: To be more precise, there is traditionally the entry of capital in developing countries aimed at the natural resources

developing countries faced the problems of foreign currency, which accompanies importation of capital goods, while foreign firms also faced a lack of market. On the whole, these problems have promoted neither industrialization nor employment.

At the NIEs stage, capital and technology flow into the NIEs from advanced economies, and industrialization is achieved in combination with the abundant low-cost labor force. This is due to the acquisition of the external market in the advanced economies. In Asia, the Japan-NIEs-US growth triangle structure is created. Advanced country multinational firms, centering on Japanese firms, actualized industrialization in the NIEs by utilizing the inexpensive labor and land, for processing/assembling of goods exported to advanced economies. This transfer of international production base caused the NIEs model of development to succeed and gave the opportunity for development to the local firms of the NIEs.

The third stage is the period wherein capital head toward developing economies in search of potential markets due to affluent but limited markets in the advanced economies. Industrialization and growth of developing economies needs capital and technology, which are mainly brought in by external firms. In short, firms of advanced countries enter countries that have a large potential market due to a large population. These firms are interested in large population countries, such as China, where the NIEs model of export-oriented development is occurring in the coastal area, Russia, with its resource exports, and India, where there is rapid growth of exports of ICT-based services.

Incidentally, since the NIEs could make development successful through abundant supply of labor, it becomes possible to consider that growth of developing economies could rely on supply of working population, instead of supply of capital, and eventually on the population size itself. In short, there was now awareness that the size of population itself is a condition for achieving growth or a potential force for growth. Actually, East Asian development has given birth to the "population bonus" discussion. In 2001, the term BRICs was coined, from such an interest in

Table 3.2 Emerging economy model of development through foreign direct investment in the global economy

Major location of market or consumption	Advanced economies	**NIEs development model through FDI**	**Intra-advanced-region development model through mutual FDI**
	Emerging economies	**PoBMEs development model through FDI**	
		Emerging economies	Developed economies
		Major location of production	

Source: The revised version from Hirakawa (2017, 53)
Note: FDI stands for foreign direct investment

population, by the investment bank Goldman Sachs (O'Neill 2001). BRICs created a 180 degree reversal of the traditional negative attitude toward population and poverty. A huge poor population is not a shackle. It is rather considered as an indicator of a potential for growth. Since the very end of the twentieth century, such countries have already been displaying their ability for rapid growth (Hirakawa and Aung 2011).

East Asia's development stages are also shown in Table 3.2, which is a matrix of advanced and emerging economies with locations of market on the one axis and location of production on the other axis. In this table, NIEs development data are located in the second quadrant, and PoBMEs development is in the third quadrant. Until very recently, major destination of FDI was that of toward advanced economies, where major locations of production and market were both inside advanced economies. This is the intra-advanced-region mutual development model located in the first quadrant. However, since the late 1960s, multinational firms in advanced economies headed for NIEs to manufacture their products, based on applying cheap labor, that were exported back to advanced economies' market. Production and market were spatially divided. Since late 1990s, especially entering this century, production coincides with market in location again. As market grows bigger, firms come to invest and sell their products in emerging economies in search of a big potential market.

3.4 East Asia's Economic Integration and "Reverse" Institutionalization: From ASEAN to East Asia

3.4.1 Regional Cooperation and the "Reverse" Institutionalization of ASEAN

The first attempt to institutionalize economic integration in East Asia is the Association of Southeast Asian Nations (ASEAN). Despite being a gathering of small nations, ASEAN has exhibited initiative in institutionalization of the East Asian region for nearly half a century. Its role since the end of the 1990s has been particularly large. Moreover, ASEAN has adopted the so-called ASEAN way of consultation and consensus, wherein there is mutual respect of sovereignty and nonintervention among the member countries. Even with regard to regional diplomatic policy, a special framework has been created called "conference diplomacy," with several overlapping layers such the ASEAN+3, East Asia Summit (EAS), and the Asia-Pacific Economic Cooperation (APEC) (Sato 2003; Suzuki 2004). This is a process which is not bound by rules, but rather rules are formed from the building of trusting relationships. The author calls this ASEAN's "reverse," "spontaneous," institutionalization, keeping in mind Western institutionalization.

If you consider it for a moment, ASEAN's diversity is amazing. The level of economic development also varies greatly among countries. Even with respect to historical experience, all countries, with the exception of Thailand, were colonized by different colonial powers. Indonesia was a Dutch colony. Malaysia, Singapore, and Myanmar were English colonies. Gaining membership in the 1990s, Vietnam, Laos, and Cambodia were French colonies. While some countries adopted a democratic system, others adopted a socialist system. Some countries maintained a monarchy, while others up to recently were military administrations. There is also a large variation in population size, language, and culture. It is due to the aspiration for development in the midst of such diversity that, perhaps, the "reverse" institutionalization was created. Based on this, there is a possibility of expansion and development toward an East Asian system. In this section, we shall consider East Asian regional integration and institutionalization, focusing on ASEAN.

Considering institutionalization of the East Asian region from the perspective of the ASEAN's economic cooperation and development, we could provisionally identify four different periods. The first period is centered on political factors, beginning from the establishment of ASEAN in 1967 up to the end of the Vietnam War in 1975. The second period is from 1975/1976 up to 1997, when economic cooperation was added to ASEAN's objectives. This period can be divided into two sub-periods. The first part is up to 1987 wherein development is pursued through import substitution policy, and the second part is from 1988 to 1997 wherein development is pursued mainly through the acceptance of foreign direct investment. The third period is from the outbreak of Asian currency crisis of July 1997 to the global financial crisis of 2009 during which East Asia regional cooperation was gaining momentum. The fourth period is from the global financial crisis of 2009 up to the present, searching for an East Asian economic integration and regional security that goes beyond the framework of the third period in response to the awareness of the critical nature of China's emergence. At the same time, it is a period where US President Obama is attempting a return to Asia and the start of the strengthening of Japan's collective security system with America under the Shinzo Abe administration. In particular, the TPP broad agreement reached in October 2015 would bring to this region the possibility of a split in the framework of regional cooperation. However, former President Obama's legacy was denied by his successor, President Donald Trump, who had won presidential election in November 2016 and in January 2017 issued an order to withdraw from the TPP. On the other hand, in

November of the same year, the remaining 11 menber countries of the TPP reached a broad agreement. The TPP 11 agreement (the Comprehensive and Progressive Agreement for Trans-Pacific Partnership) was signed in March 2018, and was expected to come into effect in 2018.

Anyway, let us first take a look at the first and second periods. Going back to the creation of ASEAN in 1967, ASEAN's biggest concern was regional peace and stability and national security amidst the unstable international environment. ASEAN was inaugurated as a system for political security cooperation (Yamakage 1991: 114–15; ditto 1997: 17). At that time, Southeast Asia was a region of conflict giving rise to mutual distrust. Indonesia and the Philippines had a "confrontational" policy to the forming of Malaysia. There was a feud between Malaysia and Singapore that led to separation and independence. There was also the communist threat. The history of this region is one where a strong foreign country would force the adoption of a "system." The region was led around by the nose from the tribute system of China from BC up to the second half of the nineteenth century, to the succeeding colonial system of Europe, and to the "Co-Prosperity Area" and "New Order" of Japan's Greater East Asia War (Chawla et al. 1974). Owing to this, the establishment of ASEAN holds a historical significance in the sense of creating by itself an intra-regional framework, even though it was established to cope with the issues that it confronted at that time.

The second period of East Asia's institutionalization starts from the holding of the ASEAN economic ministerial meeting in November 1975 and the first ASEAN summit meeting in February 1976. The summit meeting's objective was coping with the international environment after the end of the Vietnam War, and the economic cooperation discussed in the economic ministerial meeting of the previous year was first added to the ASEAN's objectives. The leaders signed the Declaration of ASEAN Concord, adopted the Treaty of Amity and Cooperation (TAC) in Southeast Asia, and discussed important issues such as territorial integrity, nonintervention in internal affairs, and the peaceful resolution of conflicts. This provided a basic philosophy to ASEAN, which did not have a basic treaty (Yamakage 2001: 117–18). At the same time, ASEAN Industrialization Project (AIP) and other economic cooperation were ironed out. This project aimed at the industrialization, as a region, of products such as urea, phosphate fertilizer, potassium, petroleum chemicals, iron and steel, soda ash, newspaper paper, and rubber products (Joint Press Statement 1976). However, this project failed, with the exception of the urea projects of Indonesia and Malaysia. Member countries were unable to adjust interests, as each one pursued import substitution industrialization.

The later part of the second period of institutionalization starts with the third ASEAN summit meeting in December 1987, where intra-regional industrialization policy, for the acceptance of direct investments by foreign firms, was initiated. In the economic ministerial meeting of 1988, the ASEAN Brand-to-Brand Complementation (BBC) plan was set up, and a 50% tariff concession was granted for intra-regional procurement for brands of foreign automotive companies. BBC became the ASEAN Industrial Cooperation (AICO) in 1996, whereby zero to 5% special tariffs were granted to certified firms not in the automotive industry. In the fourth ASEAN summit meeting held on December 1992, there was agreement to create the ASEAN Free Trade Area (AFTA), which started in January 1993 and aims to be completed in 2018. Later, AFTA's completion was advanced by 15 years to 2003. In the sixth ASEAN summit meeting held amidst the Asian currency crisis on December 1998, the completion, as a "bold measure," was advanced by one more year to 2002 (ASEAN Secretariat 1998). The economic integration of ASEAN was proceeding in earnest.

Since the second half of the 1980s, big changes in the international environment were behind ASEAN's pushing for foreign capital introduction policy and economic integration (Shimizu 1998). It was necessary for ASEAN to cope with the new situation such as (a) the yen appreciation after the 1985 Plaza Accord, (b) the spread of economic integration and Free Trade Agreements in the USA and Europe, and (c) the emergence of China. There was a growing awareness that the acceleration of the economic integration was needed in order to receive foreign investments from outside the ASEAN region (Hirakawa 2008:101–102). During this period, ASEAN began to adopt an aggressive expansionist policy even with regard to diplomatic affairs. In the 25th ministerial meeting of July 1992, Vietnam and Laos were admitted as TAC members and were immediately given observer status in ASEAN. Vietnam was granted membership in 1995, Laos and Myanmar in 1997, and Cambodia in 1999.

But, what was the reason for this orientation of ASEAN to expand membership even transcending ideologies? After the end of the Cold War in Southeast Asia, the issue became the emergence of China with the reduced influence of the USA and the collapse of the Soviet Union. In actuality, "the power projection of China toward the South, that is, its heading toward the Southeast Asian waters was a huge threat" (Yamakage 2001:3). Owing to this, ASEAN adopted the "South China Sea (ASEAN) Declaration" in the ASEAN Foreign Ministerial meeting of 1992; established the ASEAN Regional Forum (ARF), as a system for security dialogues involving China (Yamakage 2001:3); and, at the same time, deemed it necessary, through regional expansion, to strengthen its voice in international affairs and to ensure a plea for the economic activities of ASEAN companies. This is what made ASEAN head for expansion. For the four new member nations, membership into ASEAN became useful to build stability for their national development. Especially for Vietnam, its accession to ASEAN was expected as measures to cope with the issue of territorial right in the South China Sea with China.

3.4.2 *Asian Currency Crisis and East Asian Regional Cooperation*

The third period of East Asia's institutionalization starts on the occasion of the 1997 Asian currency crisis. The dramatic recession, which occurred in the rapidly growing East Asia, made ASEAN people aware of the limits in ASEAN alone confronting the instability accompanying globalization. In this period, the acceleration of ASEAN integration, which proceeded from the second period, and the wider ASEAN+3 regional cooperation frameworks, having ASEAN as a core, were pursued.

First, let's take a look at the acceleration of the ASEAN economic integration. The second ASEAN unofficial summit held in December 1997 in the very middle of the Asian currency crisis, the "ASEAN Vision 2020", was adopted for building the ASEAN community by 2020. The community initiative was concretized by the "2nd ASEAN Joint Declaration" (Bali Accord) adopted in the 9th ASEAN Summit of October 2003. The ASEAN community was created through the three communities of (a) the ASEAN Security Community (ASC), (b) ASEAN Economic Community (AEC), and (c) ASEAN Social and Cultural Community (ASCC). The 12th ASEAN summit meeting held in January 2007 advanced the completion of the ASEAN community by 5 years to 2015. The 13th ASEAN summit meeting held on the 40th anniversary of ASEAN in November 2007 enacted the ASEAN Charter, giving the highest standard to ASEAN that till then lacked any legal basis as an international institution.

The ASEAN Charter declared in article one: "to maintain and enhance peace, security and stability," "to live in peace with the world at large in a just democratic and harmonious environment," and "to create a single market and production base which is stable, prosperous, highly competitive and economically integrated with effective facilitation for trade and investment in which there is free flow of goods, services and investment." Besides, it stipulates that ASEAN summit meeting shall be held twice a year (ASEAN Secretariat 2008).

The Asian currency crisis of 1997 became an opportunity for ASEAN to expand the institutionalization that it was then promoting. In retrospect, the East Asia Economic Group (EAEG) proposed by then Malaysian Prime Minister Mahathir at the end of 1990 was frustrated due to the resistance of the USA and Australia. Moreover, the Asia Monetary Fund (AMF) initiative proposed by Japan did not materialize due to the resistance of the USA and the IMF. However, on the 30th anniversary of the creation of ASEAN in 1997, the leaders of Japan, China, and South Korea were invited, and quite naturally the response to the crisis became a matter for discussion. This is because they recognized the necessity of regional cooperation amidst the callous attitude of the USA and international institutions, which criticize East Asia as the crony capitalism.

The leaders of ASEAN+3 that met again on December 1998 agreed to regular holding of such meetings. The third ASEAN+3 of November 1999 issued for the first time in the region's history the "Joint Declaration for Regional Cooperation in East Asia" and proclaimed the "strengthening of the self-help and assistance mechanisms in East Asia." The fifth ASEAN+3 Summit of November 2001 approved the "Towards an East Asian Community" report of the East Asia Vision Group (EAVG), which was established in the meeting of 1998. The sixth ASEAN+3 Summit of November 2002, in accordance with the final report of the East Asia Study Group (EASG), which was established based on leaders' agreement at the fourth ASEAN Summit of November 2000 in Singapore, agreed to (a) the future establishment of an East Asian Summit and (b) the creation of an East Asian free trade area. The 8th

ASEAN+3 Summit of November 2004 decided on holding the East Asia Summit (EAS) in 2005. On December 2005, the 9th ASEAN+3 Summit was held, followed by the first EAS. The 11th ASEAN+3 Summit held in November 2007 issued the "2nd Joint Declaration related to the East Asian Cooperation."

A big feature in the progress of this East Asian cooperation is ASEAN's "centrality." The ASEAN+3 and EAS Summits were formed on the invitation of ASEAN. The meetings were chaired by the ASEAN host country. The EAS in December 2005 issued the Kuala Lumpur Declaration, which confirms various principles, such as (a) ASEAN playing an "important role" together with the EAS as "driver" in the future goal of forming an East Asian community, with ASEAN+3 becoming a "major means", and (b) EAS striving for the strengthening of global standards and universal values through an open, inclusive, and transparent framework.

With regard to economic integration, research started in 1998 on a Japan-Korea FTA, as proposed by Korea, and in January 2001, on a proposal by Singapore, negotiations started for a Japan-Singapore Economic Partnership Agreement (JSEPA). However, Japan's early economic integration schemes invited an FTA competition with China. In November 2000, China proposed the holding of a summit with ASEAN and in the Summit of November 2002 entered into a China-ASEAN economic cooperation framework. However, since then, ASEAN has come to take the initiative in entering into East Asia's FTA. In 2010, ASEAN practically concluded the ASEAN+1 FTA. At the start of that year, AFTA, ASEAN-China FTA, and ASEAN-Korea FTA entered the stage of tariff elimination, and the ASEAN-India FTA and ASEAN-Australia-New Zealand FTA were inaugurated. The Japan-ASEAN FTA was inaugurated as an EPA (Ishikawa 2011:10–12).

Amidst all these, Japan, under then Prime Minister Junichiro Koizumi, and very conscious especially of China, proposes the East Asia Community Initiative. Owing to this, Koizumi's Community Proposal included the addition of Australia and New Zealand to ASEAN+3 in order to reduce the influence of China.

While the moves in multilateral economic integration were promoted by private research of the East Asia Free Trade Area Initiative (EAFTA, ASEAN+3 Prospective Members) proposed by China in April 2005, Japan proposed the private research of the Comprehensive Economic Partnership of East Asia (CEPEA) in June 2007. Consequently, ASEAN set up task groups in September 2010 for both the EAFTA and CEPEA and has initiated discussions. In August 2011, Japan and China jointly proposed to ASEAN the setting up task groups for both ASEAN+3 and ASEAN+6. In November of the same year, the host country Indonesia proposed the Regional Comprehensive Economic Partnership (RCEP), which this time emphasized the centrality of ASEAN. In November 2012, the rites for starting up the RCEP negotiations were carried out in the ASEAN-related Summit (Gaimusho 2012).

Ultimately, institutionalization of economic cooperation and integration in East Asia started from ASEAN and advanced through the initiative of ASEAN under the struggle for leadership between Japan and China. Moreover, it seems to be headed toward the construction of an Asian community which consolidates the political and economic factors. This is systematically shown in Fig. 3.9.

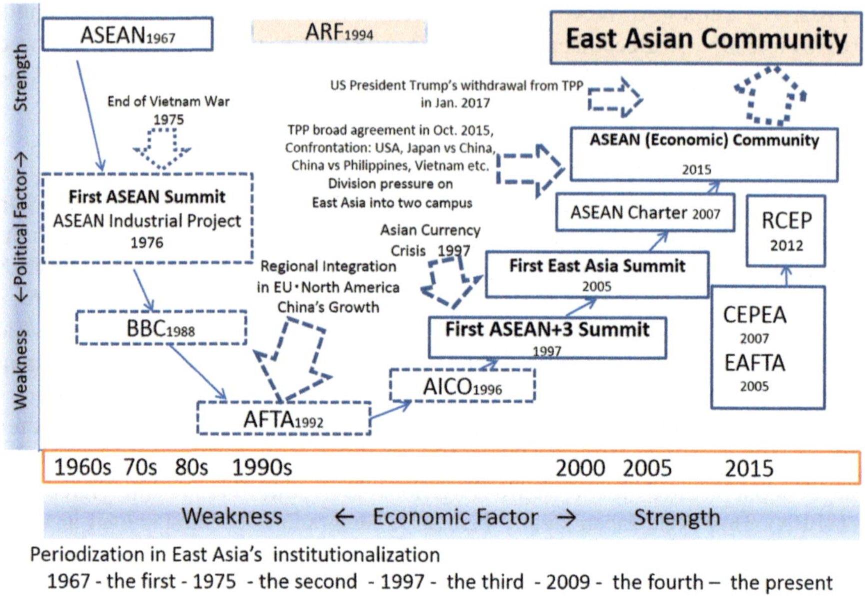

Fig. 3.9 ASEAN and "reverse" institutionalization of East Asia. (Source: Author's creation) Note: BBC, AFTA, and AICO stand for Brand-to-Brand Complementation, ASEAN Free Trade Area, and ASEAN Industrial Cooperation respectively. EAFTA (East Asia Free Trade Agreement) has been led by China and Korea, CEPEA (Comprehensive Economic Partnership of East Asia) has been led by Japan, and RCEP (Regional Comprehensive Economic Partnership) has been led by ASEAN

Despite having its weaknesses often pointed out, ASEAN has existed for half a century and has developed through a process of "reverse" institutionalization. After the Asian currency crisis, it played an important role, beyond the ASEAN framework, in the stability and development of the East Asian region. However, as can be seen in the next section, this framework is currently confronted with a major issue. This is in the fourth period of institutionalization of East Asia, wherein there is exposure to pressures to disperse. Behind this is the structural shift in the world and Asian economies accompanying the growth of East Asia.

3.5 Structural Transformation and New Issues

3.5.1 The Rising Chinese Issue and the TPP

The fourth period of the institutionalization of East Asia, which started some time after the global financial crisis of 2009, was a new stage in institutionalization as well as regional integration. There was a change in the character of the East Asian

Summit (EAS). In the determination process of the 16 member countries of the first EAS (ASEAN 10, Japan, China, South Korea, Australia, New Zealand, and India), there was a leadership struggle between Japan and China. In the ASEAN+3 Foreign Ministerial Meeting of April and May of 2005, the conditions for membership were fixed, and the participation of Australia, New Zealand (hereafter NZ), and India was decided in the July meeting (http://www.mofa.go.jp/mofaj/area/eas/eas.html). China emphasized ASEAN+3, while Japan, in order to reduce the influence of China, "proposed a way for the US to participate in some form during the adjustment phase" (Shimamura 2006: 46). However, this proposal was not accepted, and Japan advocated ASEAN+6, which included Australia, New Zealand, and India (*The Asahi Shimbun* 2005.12.4; *The Mainichi Shimbun* 2005.12.4). It should be noted that Russian President Vladimir Putin, who was invited by the host country Malaysia to this meeting, indicated at the start of the meeting his hope in formally participating from the next meeting, but this was not accepted.

However, at the fifth EAS of October 2010, the USA and Russia were allowed to participate. Moreover, there were informal foreign ministerial discussions by EAS member countries held in Hanoi in July 2010. In conflict with China regarding territorial rights to the Spratly Islands in the South China Sea, Vietnam, as hosting country of the meeting, wished for the participation of the USA. As such, the US State Department Secretary and the Russian Foreign Minister were invited as representatives of the US and Russian Presidents. Japan also welcomed the participation of both countries. Since the sixth EAS held in November of the next year, both countries became formal members. The territorial rights problem between China and ASEAN, in particular the Philippines and Vietnam, was worsening. For a gathering of small countries that is ASEAN, the conflict with and threat of a rising China paved the way for the participation of extra-regional big countries.

Later, it was found out that China has been forcibly forming land filling of coral areas, and constructing ports and military bases, prompting the expression of the following critical view of the ASEAN Foreign Ministerial Meeting and Summit of April 2015. "We share the serious concerns expressed by some Leaders on the land reclamation being undertaken in the South China Sea, which has eroded trust and confidence and may undermine peace, security and stability in the South China Sea" (ASEAN Chairman's Statement 2015). At the time, the Obama-led US government also strongly criticized China's "deviation from the international standard." In July 2016, the International tribunal for the Law of the Sea (ITLOS) concluded "that there was no legal basis for China to claim historic right to resources within the sea areas within the 'nine-dash line'" and also that "China has violated Philippine sovereign rights in the South China Sea" (Santos 2016). There is also a territorial dispute between Japan and China in the East China Sea.

In June 2016, in the Philippines, Rodrigo Duterte who wanted to enhance ties between his country and China became the new president as Benigno Aquino's successor, and in January of the next year, Trump was inaugurated as the president in the USA. They seem to refrain from criticizing China's hard-line stance in the South China Sea. President Trump appears to have much more concern about North Korea's nuclear test and firing of missiles than territorial dispute with China in the

South China Sea. However, such problems between ASEAN countries and China have remained substantially unresolved. It serves to deepen conflicts among countries in the East Asian region.

ASEAN cannot always be one against China. In July 2012, the 45th ASEAN Foreign Ministerial Meeting and related meetings held in Phnom Penh was unable to reach a consensus about the South China Sea problem, leading to the host country Cambodia not issuing an ASEAN common declaration. A week later, the "Six Principles of ASEAN Regarding the South China Sea" was announced, but this type of incident was the first in the 25-year history of the ASEAN Foreign Ministerial Meetings. At the 50th ASEAN Foreign Ministerial Meeting held in Manila in August 2017, ASEAN and China agreed on a negotiating framework for a Code of Conduct in the South China Sea. It is without doubt that ASEAN will continue to be challenged in its coping with a stronger China.

The situation is the same with regard to economic integration. As mentioned before, amidst the rivalry between Japan and China, ASEAN took the initiative in setting up the RCEP negotiations. However, in 2009, there was a move to challenge this attempt at economic integration. In 2015, a broad agreement was reached on the Trans-Pacific Partnership (TPP) proposed by the USA.

The TPP was based on the FTA (P4) inaugurated in 2006 among Brunei, Chile, New Zealand, and Singapore. However, in 2008, then US President Bush indicated an interest in participating. Australia, Peru, and Vietnam later on joined in, forming the eight-country TPP negotiations. President Obama, who was sworn into office in January 2009, was at first not receptive to the TPP but in time had a change of policy. In November of the same year in Tokyo, he indicated participating in the TPP negotiations during his visit to Japan. In the following month, he reported this decision to the US congress. The reason for participating is increasing US exports and employment through TPP. Malaysia joined the negotiations in 2010, and Canada and Mexico in November 2012, for a total of 11 negotiating countries. In March 2013, Prime Minister Shinzo Abe, throwing away his election promise, revealed formal participation in the negotiations. Japan formally became a member in July of the same year.

What was the TPP? Former US President Obama considered it was "a regional agreement that will have the high standards worthy of a 21st century trade agreement" (*The Wall Street Journal*, Nov.14, 2009; *The Japan Times*, Nov.15, 2009). It was plainly an integration initiative, with a high level of freedom, and covering a wide area. But, what was the reason for America's promoting it?

From Table 3.3, we can confirm that, at least until the time when Japan participated in negotiations, within the TPP participating countries, the economic strength of the USA was disproportionately large. In short, it was almost impossible for the USA to obtain the trade liberalization effect with just the initial negotiating countries. It must be said that the USA also had other objectives. The USA perhaps had mainly two objectives. Firstly that would be the participation of Japan. With the addition of Japan, the USA could expand its exports and businesses. Secondly, that would be the determination of Asia-Pacific's trading rules that would be beneficial for the USA. This was the China policy. The conditions for TPP membership are the

Table 3.3 The GDP composition of TPP agreement signed countries

	GDP in 2010	Share/TPP 9 Nov. 2009- Sep. 2012	Share/TPP 11 Oct. 2012- June 2013	Share/TPP 12 July 2013- Jan. 2017	Share/TPP11 Feb.2017- present
	Billion $	%			
Brunei	12.37	0.07	0.06	0.05	0.12
Chile	203.3	1.21	1.02	0.82	1.96
New Zealand	140.51	0.83	0.7	0.56	1.35
Singapore	222.7	1.32	1.11	0.89	2.15
P4	578.88	3.44	2.89	2.32	5.58
Australia	1,237.36	7.35	6.18	4.97	11.92
Malyasia	237.96	1.41	1.19	0.96	2.29
Peru	153.8	0.91	0.77	0.62	1.48
Vietnam	103.57	0.62	0.52	0.42	1.00
U.S.	14,526.55	86.27	72.53	58.32	
Canada	1,577.04		7.87	6.33	15.19
Mexico	1,034.31		5.16	4.15	9.96
Japan	5,458.80			21.92	52.58
TPP12 Total	24,767.76	100.00	100.00	100.00	
TPP11 Total(after 2917)	10,381.72				100.00
ref. China+HK/TPP12 or TPP1 after 2017	6,327.18			25.55	60.95

Source: Created from IMF, World economic outlook database, September 2011
Note: New Zealand estimated. November of 2009 is the month when President Obama announced the US intention to participate in the TPP negotiations. October of 2012 and July of 2013 were months when Canada and Mexico and Japan entered into negotiations, respectively. On October 5, 2015, a broad agreement of the TPP was reached among 12 countries. January of 2017 is the month when US President Trump signed order to withdraw from the TPP of 12 nations. Then, remaining 11 countries reached agreement on the new free trade deal, TPP 11, in November 2017

same as those of WTO. Once the TPP rules have been successfully determined, countries wanting to participate after the conclusion of negotiations would need the approval of all the member countries. The applying country may have to make large concessions. In retrospect, China was forced to actually negotiate for 15 years before becoming a WTO member in December 2001. Japan has also experienced this at the time to participate in its negotiation. This was a powerful pressure on China, which had a high trade dependence on the USA (Hirakawa 2012). Nonmember countries must have more or less the same concern.

In short, TPP is a strategy for the return of the USA to the East Asian economic zone where sits China that is now at the economic center of the largest economic zone of the world. It is an attempt of the USA to prevent East Asia from determining its own rules (Hirakawa 2014). With the TPP agreement, Obama blatantly announced this objective in his statement made at the White House "we can't let countries like China write the rules of the global economy. We should write those rules, opening new markets to the US products while setting high standards for protecting workers and preserving our environment" (Office of the Press Secretary, the White House 2015). This gives rise to the possibility of East Asia being divided into two camps through economic integration.

Actually, why did Singapore, which was a P4 member, and other ASEAN member countries, namely, Vietnam and Malaysia, participated in and signed the

TPP agreement? Why were other countries such as Thailand, the Philippines, and South Korea leaning toward participation just after the TPP had reached a broad agreement in 2015? One of the major conditions for this is the change in the development mechanics inside and outside of the region, which was brought about by the structural changes in East Asia due to the rise of China. The one-sided economic dependence on China is a dangerous choice for every country in East Asia in terms of national security. Participation in the TPP became a move toward a political economic balance.

This situation has not changed since the time when President Trump ordered to withdraw the USA from the TPP. In East Asia, the new TPP 11 agreement is expected to come into effect in 2018, and RCEP continues to be negotiated toward an agreement in the same year. Even though they are not going to be realized, strengthened regional cooperation and institutionalization are needed in East Asia much more than before.

3.5.2 Global Structural Transformation and the Asia Infrastructure Investment Bank

In March and April 2015, China shook the world with its advocacy to establish the Asian Infrastructure Investment Bank (AIIB). The AIIB was announced in 2013 by Chinese Chairman Xi Jinping, and in 2014 a Memorandum of Understanding (MOU) regarding the AIIB framework was signed in Beijing by a total of 21 countries from the ASEAN and the Middle East. In March 2015, with the deadline for participating in the establishment soon coming up, the major advanced nations, starting with the UK's announcement of participation, decided to participate, with the exclusion of Japan, Canada, and the USA. A total of 57 countries announced their participation, and at the end of the same year, it was officially inaugurated by 57 countries. Consequently, the early funding target of 50 billion dollars doubled to 100 billion dollars. The basis for establishment was the Asian Development Bank's expectation of an infrastructure demand of 8 trillion dollars by 2020 in Asia. It is said that the AIIB was established given that this demand could not be met by the existing international financial institutions.

In April 2017, 13 new countries, including Canada, were approved to join by the AIIB, and the number of member countries reached the number of 70, which is bigger than the Asian Development Bank's number of 67. According to the AIIB President (Jin Liqun's address at the second annual meeting held at Jeju, Korea, in June of the same year), the AIIB approved 3 more countries to join and the number of member states "is expected to reach 85 to 90 this year." There are 16 of the bank's financing initiatives, totaling 2.5 billion dollars (The Nikkei Asian Review, June 17, 2017). Many initiatives that the AIIB approved are related to One Belt, One Road (OBOR), including loans in favor of hydropower station investments in Pakistan in July 2016 and a project to strengthen a power transmission and distribution system in the State of Andhra Pradesh, India, in 2017 (AIIB Home page accessed Sept. 8, 2017). In June 2017, Moody's Investors Service assigned Triple-A Credit Rating to the AIIB (https://www.aiib.org/en/news-events/news/2017/20170629_001.html).

Incidentally, Japan's easily following wishes of the USA with regard to joining the AIIB was generally regarded as falling behind the times. A rivalry and disgust for a rising China would also have led to the decision not to participate. Right after the announcement of the Chinese government that 57 countries indicated their wishes to become founding members of AIIB, the quick vote conducted by the Nikkei Co. showed that 71.0% of Japanese respondents were against participation (*The Nihon Keizai Shimbun*, April 15, 2015). Newspapers reported that Prime Minister Abe was containing AIIB by stating in a Japanese TV program on April 20, "companies that borrow money from a loan shark may have survived momentarily but shall lose its future" (The Nihon Keizai Shimbun Electronic Version, Apr. 21, 2015). Taking the perspective of the UK, the Financial Times says that the decision for having China establish the AIIB was due to international financial institutions such as the IMF not giving China voting rights proportionate to its national strength (*The Financial Times*, Mar. 26, 2015). Transformation of the global economy is causing a large swell in its wake.

3.6 Concluding Remarks: The Era of PoBMEs and Institutionalization of East Asia

In this chapter, we confirmed a dramatic transformation accompanying the development of East Asian economy and have seen the changing of the shift mechanism from a NIEs model of development through exports to a PoBMEs model of development interested in potential markets. In this transformation, BRICs, especially China, is in an advantageous position. On the other hand, ASEAN played a large role with regard to the institutionalization of East Asia, which is characterized by a "reverse" institutionalization that is different from the experience of America and Europe. Since the Asian currency crisis, ASEAN promoted the development of the meeting diplomacy such as ASEAN+3 and the East Asia Summit and economic integration having the future goal of an East Asian community. However, the resulting institutional framework is at present confronted with big issues from both inside and outside the region. One is the rise in pressures to breakdown in the cooperation within ASEAN as well as East Asia with respect to policies regarding China.

With regard to territorial disputes in the South China Sea between China and the Philippines, and between China and Vietnam, China fundamentally continues to apply hard-line measures in the South China Sea. With regard to the collision incident between a Chinese fishing boat and a Japanese Coast Guard's patrol boat near the Senkaku Islands in 2010, and Senkaku Islands territorial disputes triggered by Governor of Tokyo Shintaro Ishihara in 2012, China's stance is the same. The former Japanese diplomat Hitoshi Tanaka indicates as follows: "The hard-line measure in the territorial dispute of the East China Sea in 2010, the one-sided measures regarding the Chinese vessel collision incident near Senkaku Islands, among others, are notable for their extremely aggressive foreign policy posture. When former Prime Minister Junichiro Koizumi visited the Yasukuni Shrine in 2001, China called this "Cold Politics Warm Economics" and adopted political measures such as the cancellation of the bilateral summit, but no economic measures were adopted. In contrast, regarding the Chinese vessel collision in 2010, China took one-sided and hard-line countervailing measures, which did not differentiate between politics and economics, such as the de facto stoppage of rare earth exports and the arrests of Japanese. With the nationalization (by Japanese Government) of the Senkaku Islands, China took the policy of showing the strength of China's "nationalism" (Tanaka 2012). Both sides have their excuses with respect to their assertions on territorial rights. Actually, Chinese foreign policy posture is clearly changing.

As East Asia's economic development structure enters the PoBMEs stage and China grows larger, there undeniably is an aspect that arises from within the change in relationships with other member countries. The issue of the Takeshima landing of then South Korean President Lee Myung-bak in August 2012 could be understood within the same structure regarding Japan. The economic development of East Asia and the relative decline of Japan's position have caused the eruption of the territorial rights problem, which in the past has been vaguely considered. In a growth trajectory and growing in confidence, a country gives rise to a big nationalistic movement, more so if suppressed emotions were hidden. In China, a mechanism is at work for intensifying such a movement amidst the growth and expansion of the gap between the rich and the poor. In response, Japan's Abe administration has aroused nationalism and a remarkably hard-lined posture in policy toward China. In September 2015, amidst voices of a constitutional violation by an overwhelming majority in Japan, the Abe administration steamrolled in Parliament the security bill that granted collective security. Abe administration aggressively promoted the TPP, and after Trump's withdrawal from the deal in January 2017, he wants to conclude the PPT 11. This can be judged as a phenomenon that arose from within transformation of the global economy and the international order. The picture is one where the rising China will be pressed to restructure, and Japan, which stands in the old order, will be busy with supporting this. It looks like the following questions are being asked: will it split into two camps? Or, will there be cooperation that leads to the creation of regional stability and affluence? How shall East Asia handle these problems? The meeting diplomacy, in the East Asian region's institutionalization nurtured for half a century with ASEAN as pivot, is an extremely important development and peace framework. China and Japan have a responsibility for the future of the East Asian region. It is an extremely heavy one.

References

ADB (2011) Asia 2050: realizing the Asian century. Asian Development Bank, Manila

ASEAN Chairman's Statement (2015) Chairman's statement of the 26th ASEAN summit, April 27

ASEAN Secretariat (1998) Statement on bold measures. 6th ASEAN Summit

ASEAN Secretariat (2008) The ASEAN charter. Association of Southeast Asian Nations. Jakarta

Chawla S, Gurtov M, Marsot AG (eds) (1974) Southeast Asia under the new balance of power. Praeger Publishers Inc, New York

Gaimusho (2012) PPT material: Higashi ajia chiiki hokatuteki renkei kyotei Kosho (negotiation for the Regional Comprehensive Economic Partnership (RCEP). Division of Economic Partnership, Ministry of Foreign Affairs, Japan (in Japanese)

Gill I, Kharas H (2007) An east Asian renaissance: ideas for economic growth. World Bank, Washington, DC

Hirakawa H (1999) East Asia's industrialization and the currency and financial crises within the world economy. J Intl Econ Stud 13:1–24

Hirakawa H (2008) Higashiajia no chiikitogo niokeru ASEAN no yakuwari (roles of ASEAN in East Asia's regional integration). Kokusai Ajia Kyodotai Janaru (J Intl Asian Commun Assoc). Tokyo 1:94–111 (in Japanese)

Hirakawa H (2011) Higashi ajia no keizaitogo to kozotenkan – NIES kara PoBMEs heno kozotenka to sekaikeizai (East Asia's economic integration and its structural shift: structural shift from NIEs to PoBMEs and the world economy. In Ito M, Motoyama Y (eds) Sekai to nihon no seijikeizai no konmei (Chaos in the world's and Japan's politics and economy) Ochanomizu Shobo, Tokyo, pp 104–119 (in Japanese)

Hirakawa H (2012) The TPP and Japan's response. In: Foreign trade university international conference: trans-Pacific partnership agreement: prospects and implications. Information and Communications Publishing House. Hanoi, pp 28–66

Hirakawa H (2013) East Asia's integration and structural shift. In: Yagi K, Yokokawa N, Hasegawa S, Dymski GA (eds) Crises of global economies and the future of capitalism. Routledge, London/New York, pp 272–287

Hirakawa H (2014) Kozo tenkan no sekaikeizai to higashiajia chiiki no seidoka (The world economy in structural shift and East Asia's institutionalization), In: Uemura H, Uni H et al. (eds) Tenkanki no ajia shihonshugi (Asian capitalism in transition). Fujiwara Shoten, Tokyo, pp 25–57 (in Japanese)

Hirakawa H (2017) Global ICT-based services offshoring and Asia. In: Hirakawa H et al (eds) Innovative ICT industrial architecture in East Asia: offshoring of Japanese firms and challenges faced by East Asian firms. Springer, Tokyo

Hirakawa H, Aung TT (2011) Globalization and emerging economies: Asia's structural shift from the NIEs to potentially bigger market economies (PoBMEs). Evol Instit Econ Rev 8(1):39–63

IMF (2012, 2014) World economic outlook. International Monetary Fund, Washington, DC, October

IMF (2016, 2018) World economic outlook. International Monetary Fund, Washington, DC, April

Ishikawa K (2011) Shindankai ni susumu ajia taiheiyo no chiikitogo (Asia and Pacific regional integration advancing to a new stage). Japan Association for Asian Studies. Ajia kenkyu (Asian Stud) 57(3):1–24 (in Japanese)

ITI (2008) International trade matrix by goods. Tokyo, Kokusai Bokeki Toshi Kenkyusho (Institute of International Trade and Investment)

Joint Press Statement (1976) The 2nd ASEAN economic ministerial meeting, 8–9 March. ASEAN Secretariat, Kuala Lumpur

Kokusai Boeki Toshi Kenkyusho (2008) ITI international trade matrix by goods 2008 version. Institute of International Trade and Investment, Tokyo (in Japanese)

Kokusai Kyoryoku Ginko (various issues) Wagakuni seizogyo kigyo no kaigai jigyo tenkai ni kansuru chosa houkoku (Survey report of overseas business development of Japan's manufacturing firms). Japan Bank for International Cooperation, Tokyo (in Japanese)

Maquito FC, Hirakawa H (2010) Kyoyugata seicho to shiteno higasi ajia no keizaitogo (East Asia's economic integration as shared growth). In Higashi ajia no sangyo syuseki (East Asia's industrial agglomeration). Gakujutsu Shuppankai, Tokyo, pp 539–558 (in Japanese)
Ministry, Economy, Trade, and Industry (2005, 2007, 2009, 2011, 2013, 2014) Tsusho hakusho (White paper on international economy and trade). Keizai Sangyo Sho (in Japanese)
National Intelligence Council (2008) Global trends 2025: a transformed world. The National Intelligence Council, New York
National Intelligence Council (2012) Global trends 2030: alternative worlds. USA: The National Intelligence Council. wwww.dni.gov/nic/globaltrends
Nihon Bokeki Shinko Kiko (2010) ASEAN wo chusin to shita boeki matorikkusu (Trade matrix centering on ASEAN). JETRO, Tokyo (in Japanese)
O'Neill J (2001) Building better global economic BRICs. Goldman Sachs Glob Econ Pap 66:3–12
O'Neill J, Wilson D, Purushothaman P, Stupnytska A (2005) How solid are the BRICs. Goldman Sachs Glob Econ Pap 134:3–21
Office of the Press Secretary, the White House (2015) Statement by the president on the trans-Pacific partnership. The USA, October 5
Santos M (2016, July 12) Key points of arbitral tribunal's verdict on PH-China dispute. INQUIRER.net (Philippines news for Filipinos)
Sato K (2003) ASEAN rejiimu (ASEAN regime). Keiso Shobo, Tokyo (in Japanese)
Shimamura T (2006) Higashi ajia shunokaigi (EAS) no sosetsu to kongo no kadai (Building of the East Asia summit (EAS) and forthcoming tasks). Reference (National Diet Library, Japan) 664:39–47 (in Japanese)
Shimizu K (1998) ASEAN ikinaI keizaikyoryoku no seijikeizaigaku (Political economy of ASEAN regional economic cooperation). Mineruva Shobo, Koto (in Japanese)
Suzuki S (2004) East Asian cooperation through conference diplomacy: institutional aspects of the ASEAN plus three (APT) frameworks. IDE APEC study center working paper series. 03/04-No.7, March
Tanaka H (2012) Chugoku to do mukiauka (Jo) Takokukan de juusoteki wakugumi wo (how to face China (part 1) building multi-layered framework). The Nihon Keizai Shimbun (newspaper). September 26 (in Japanese)
Wilson D, Purushothaman R (2003) Dreaming with BRICs: the path to 2050. Goldman Sachs Glob Econ Pap 99:1–22
Wilson D, Stupnytska A (2007) The N-11: more than an acronym. Goldman Sachs Glob Econ Pap 153:2–21
World Bank (2005) World development indicators 2005. World Bank, Washington, DC
Yamakage S (1991) *ASEAN: Shinboru kara shisutemu he* (from symbol to system). Tokyo Daigaku Shuppankai, Tokyo (in Japanese)
Yamakage S (1997) ASEAN pawaa: Ajia taiheiyo no chukaku he (ASEAN power: towards a Core of the Asia Pacific). Tokyo Daigaku Shuppankai, Tokyo (in Japanese)
Yamakage S (2001) ASEAN no kihon rinen no doyo (ASEAN's Turmoil of basic principles). In: Yamakage S (ed) Tenkanki no ASEAN – Aratana kadai heno chosen (ASEAN in transition: challenge to new tasks). Kokusai Mondai Kenkyusho (Japan Institute of International Affairs), Tokyo (in Japanese)
Yun C (2009) Tonan ajia keizai togo no genjo to kadai (current status and issues of East Asia's economic integration). Toa Keizai Kenkyu (East Asian Stud) Yamaguchi: Yamaguchi University 67(2):81–103 (in Japanese)

Chapter 4
Comparative Analysis of Regional Trade Imbalance in East Asia and the Eurozone

Hiroyuki Uni

4.1 Introduction

The purpose of this chapter is to analyze the structure and the causes of intra-regional trade imbalances in East Asia and the eurozone since 1995. The current account imbalance expanded globally in the 2000s. This global current account imbalance is one of the important factors of the global financial crisis in 2008 and the Euro crisis from 2010. In this chapter, I want to clarify the mechanism behind this expanding trade imbalance by analyzing mainly the international input-output tables created by the World Input-Output Database (WIOD) project.[1] The main cause of expanding trade imbalance in East Asia is the export-led growth regime in China, Korea, and Taiwan. Today, however, some of the conditions that supported export-led growth are collapsing. Transformation to domestic demand-led growth has become a policy agenda in these countries to some degree, although there are some issues for this transformation. The main cause of expanding trade imbalance in the eurozone is the present system of monetary integration without fiscal integration. Therefore, development toward fiscal integration is needed despite strong objection in some member countries.

The structure of this chapter is as follows. In Sect. 4.2, in order to focus on the typical structural problems in East Asia, I examine in detail the trade structure between two groups, one consisting of China, Korea, and Taiwan and the other consisting of Japan and the United States. In the past, the electrical machinery industry and transport machinery industry in China, Korea, and Taiwan used imported capital goods and parts made in Japan and the United States for production

[1] See Timmer et al. (2015) and http://www.wiod.org/

H. Uni (✉)
Kyoto University, Kyoto, Japan
e-mail: uni@econ.kyoto-u.ac.jp

R. Boyer et al. (eds.), *Evolving Diversity and Interdependence of Capitalisms*, Evolutionary Economics and Social Complexity Science 11,
https://doi.org/10.1007/978-4-431-55001-3_4

and exported the final goods to Japan, the United States, and European countries. Such "triangular trade" led to a trade deficit in intermediate machinery products in these three countries against Japan and the United States. However, in recent years, these three countries have accomplished trade surpluses in intermediate machinery products. In other words, traditional "triangular trade" is coming to an end. This change in the trade structure is behind the recent expanding trade surplus in China, Korea, and Taiwan.

In Sect. 4.3, in order to focus on the typical structural problems in the eurozone, I examine in detail the trade structure between two groups, one consisting of Spain, Portugal, and Greece and the other consisting of Germany and France. In the former three countries, competitiveness declined in the field of textile and leather products which traditionally were competitive, and the trade surplus in these products shrank. Moreover, they failed to construct export competitiveness in the field of machinery products, and the trade deficit in these products expanded.

Section 4.4 explains the theoretical framework for analyzing the causes of this structural change. Based on the input-output tables, I precisely measured labor productivity of export goods and non-tradable goods (the method is described in detail in the Appendix of this chapter). Focusing on changes in labor productivity of export goods, hourly wages, and the exchange rate, I show the three conditions that supported export-led growth, namely, "export-biased productivity growth" (Hicks 1953), the suppression of wages, and the undervalued exchange rate. In addition, I show the advantages and disadvantages with export-led growth.

Section 4.5 presents the results of a measurement of labor productivity of East Asian countries. In China, Korea, and Taiwan, export-biased productivity growth is remarkable, and wage growth rate is less than the growth rate of labor productivity of export goods. Although these two rates are almost equal in the United States, Korean and Taiwanese currencies depreciated against the US dollar. This became possible through unilateral management of the float system that many Asian countries adopted after the Asian currency crisis in 1997. China significantly devalued its currency in 1993–1994. In addition, suppressed wages are also a sequela of the Asian currency crisis. Under such circumstances, mainly in regard to machinery products, a virtuous cycle, such as decreases in export goods' prices → increases in export volume → productivity growth of export goods → decreases in export goods' prices, was realized. A fundamental cause of the expanding trade imbalance is the success of the export-led growth in China, Korea, and Taiwan.

Section 4.6 presents the results of a measurement of labor productivity of the eurozone countries. In Spain, Portugal, Greece, and other countries, the wage growth rate exceeded the growth rate of labor productivity of export goods, and in Germany it was the opposite. Under monetary integration, however, it was impossible to adjust for these differences through changes in exchange rates. Unequal changes in unit labor costs under monetary integration are fundamental causes for the expanding trade gap in the eurozone.

In Sect. 4.7, based on the above analysis, I examine some limitations in the East Asian export-led growth regime and consider the issues for transformation to domestic demand-led growth. The first limitation of export-led growth is the cumulative expansion of trading partners' deficit accompanied with decreases in output volume and employment in their manufacturing industry. The Trump government is trying to convert the trade policy of the United States to a protectionist one in order to maintain employment in the manufacturing industry. This means that East Asian export-led growth has reached its limit. Second, in Asian countries including China, Korea, and Taiwan, in recent years, the number of labor disputes and the growth rate of wages continues to increase. This means that a condition that supports export-led growth is breaking down. Reflecting these situations, in China, Korea, and Taiwan, the transformation to domestic demand-led growth has already become a policy agenda. For that, these countries need to solve some issues. I explain these issues, drawing from the lessons learned from failed economic policies in Japan.

In Sect. 4.8, I examine alternative solutions for trade imbalance in the eurozone. The austerity policies implemented in the Southern European countries after the Euro crisis aim not only to restrain imports but also to increase exports through productivity growth and wage suppression like East Asian countries in the past. However, as far as looking at the results of the Southern European countries after the Euro crisis, export growth slowed down compared to before the crisis, although they are successful in restraining the import of final goods. In order to reduce the trade imbalance without relying on restraining imports via austerity policies, it is necessary to realize fiscal integration of the eurozone countries and fiscal transfers from the trade surplus countries to the deficit countries.

4.2 Structure of Trade Imbalance in East Asia

Figure 4.1 shows the current account balance in percentage of GDP in East Asian countries and the United States. While the increasing trend of the current account surplus is seen in China, Korea, and Taiwan, the deficit expanded significantly in the United States until 2006.

Current account is the sum of the four types of foreign economic transactions: balance on goods, balance on services, balance on primary income, and balance on cash transfers. As amounts of exports and imports of goods are greatly larger than amounts of other types of transactions, the trend of the trade balance determines most of the trend of the current account. Hereafter, I analyze the changes in the structure of the trade balance of East Asian countries using the international input-output tables created by the World Input-Output Database (WIOD) project. One of the merits of using the international input-output table is that we can see the trade structure separately for intermediate goods and final goods, in addition to the trade balance by partner country and by product. That is, we can see in what products significant change has occurred, whether it has occurred in intermediate goods or in final goods, and against what country trade deficit or surplus is expanding significantly.

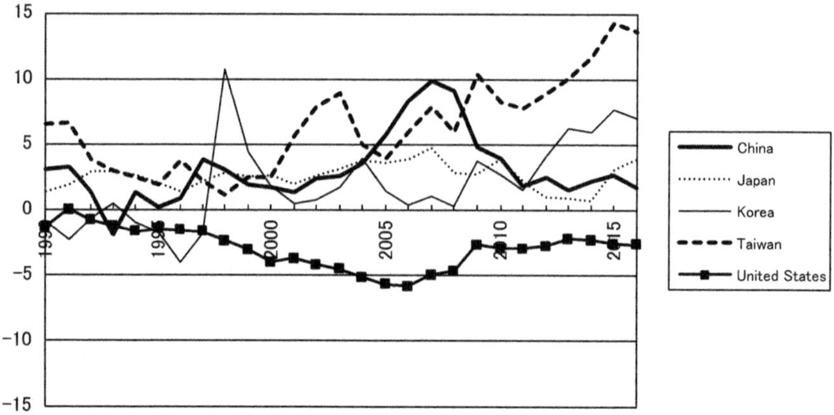

Fig. 4.1 Current account balance in East Asian countries, Percent of GDP (Unit: %)
Sources: Made by the author from IMF, World Economic Outlook Database, April 2017. Taiwanese data: Central Bank of the Republic of China and The Directorate General of Budget, Accounting and Statistics (DGBAS)

Next, let us take a look at changes in the trade balance between the following two groups: the first one consists of China, Korea, and Taiwan, and the second one consists of Japan and the United States. The former group recorded a surplus of 27.7 billion US dollars against the latter group in 1995. It increased to 179.2 billion US dollars in 2010. That is, the trade imbalance between these two groups expanded by 6.5 times in 15 years. This trade imbalance can be divided into that of intermediate goods trade and that of final goods trade. In the intermediate goods trade, the former group recorded a deficit of 18.4 billion US dollars against the latter group, and, in the final goods trade, the former group recorded a surplus of 46.1 billion US dollars in 1995. They changed to a deficit of 6.6 billion US dollars and a surplus of 195.7 billion US dollars, respectively, in 2010. Therefore, increases in trade surplus have occurred in the final goods trade. Figure 4.2 shows the trend of exports and imports between these two groups. Although imports of final goods grew slowly, exports of final goods and exports and imports of intermediate goods increased rapidly. As will be described later, export-led growth with an undervalued exchange rate and suppression of wage increases has side effects such as increases in import prices and stagnation of purchasing power of workers, which leads to the slow growth in imports of final goods.

Figure 4.3 shows the trade balance between these two groups by products.[2] The group that consists of China, Korea, and Taiwan recorded large surplus in textile and leather products against the group that consists of Japan and the United States in 1995. Although, the surplus in textile and leather products increased in 2010, the largest surplus was achieved in electrical products. In other words, China, Korea,

[2]Although Fig. 4.3 shows only products of the primary industry and the secondary industry, only these products cover 80–90% of the trade balance.

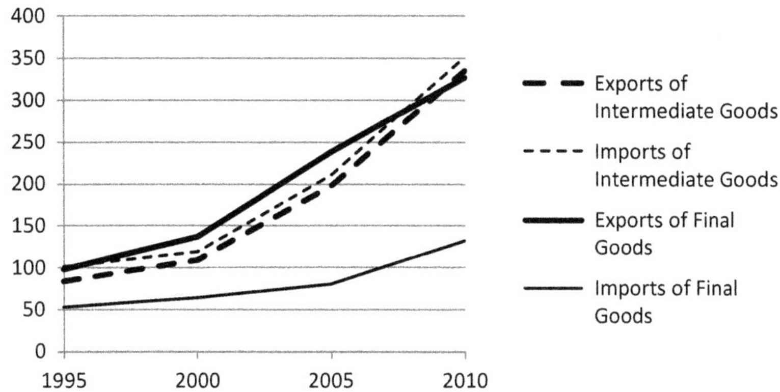

Fig. 4.2 Trade between China+Korea+Taiwan and Japan+US (Unit: billion dollars)
Sources: Calculated by the author from the World Input-Output Database

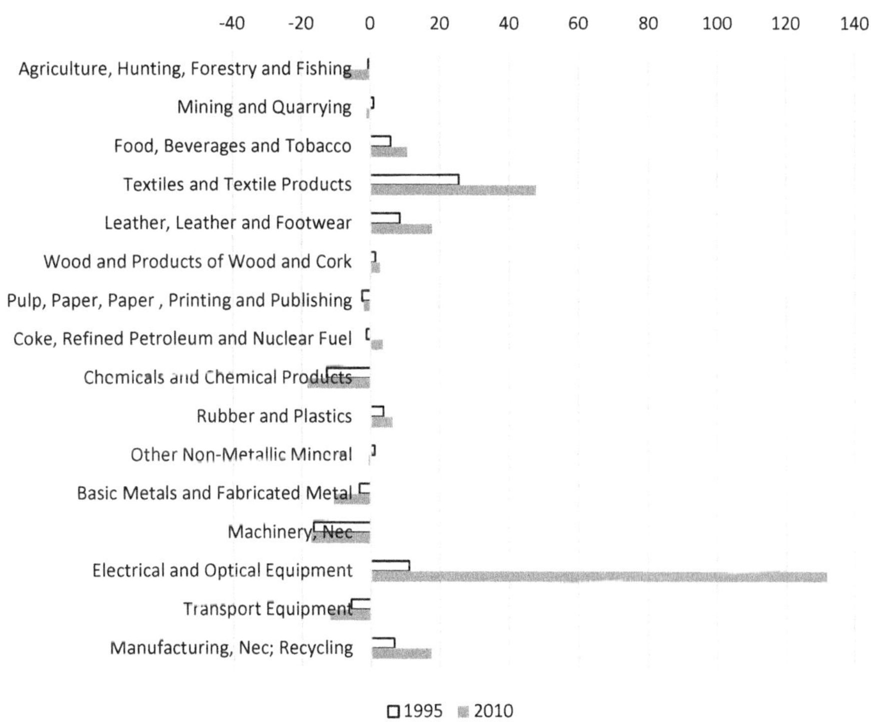

Fig. 4.3 Trade balance between China+Korea+Taiwan and Japan+US (Unit: billion dollars)
Sources: Calculated by the author from the World Input-Output Database. Products of tertiary industry are omitted

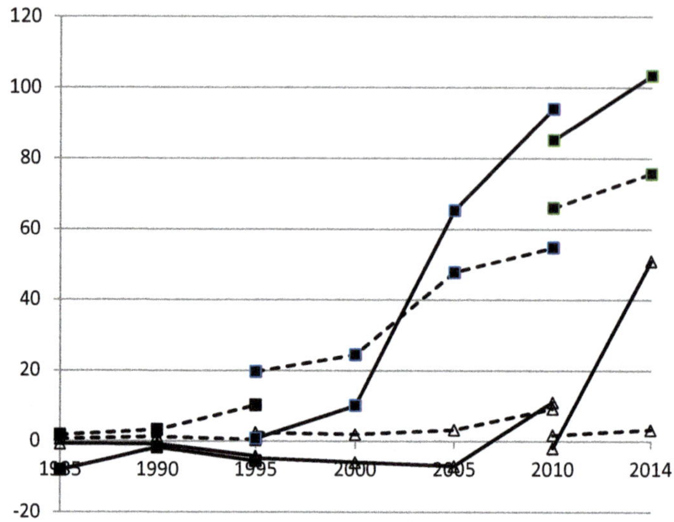

Fig. 4.4 China's trade balance against Japan and US (Unit: billion dollars)
Notes: Solid lines, machinery products; dotted lines, textile and leather products; triangular markers, intermediate goods; square markers, final goods
Sources: Calculated by the author from the Asian International Input-Output Table (1985–1995); the World Input-Output Database, Release 2013 data (1995–2010), Release 2016 data (2010–2014)

and Taiwan succeeded in the conversion of major export goods, by increasing their international competitiveness in the electrical machinery industry.

Next, in order to clarify the process of this conversion of major export goods, let us take a look at changes in the trade balance of textile and leather products[3] and machinery products[4] in China, Korea, and Taiwan, respectively. Figures 4.4, 4.5, and 4.6 show the trade balance of China, Korea, and Taiwan, respectively, against Japan and the United States. In these figures, I used the 56 sectors tables in 2014 (Release 2016 data of WIOD), in addition to the 35 sectors tables from 1995 to 2010 (Release 2013 data of WIOD).[5] Moreover, I added data from 1985–1995 derived from *Asian International Input-Output Table* (Institute of Developing Economies, 24 sectors tables).

First, let us look at the trade balance of textile and leather products that are indicated by dotted lines. Although there are not any remarkable trend changes regarding intermediate goods, indicated by dotted lines with triangular markers, there are decreasing trends in the surplus of Korea and Taiwan and an increasing

[3]"Textile and leather products" are the sum of "Textiles and Textile Products" and "Leather, Leather and Footwear" in the industry classification in WIOD, Release 2013.

[4]"Machinery products" are the sum of "Machinery, Nec," "Electrical and Optical Equipment," and "Transport Equipment" in the industry classification in WIOD, Release 2013.

[5]Because of difference in the number of sectors, etc. between Release 2013 data and Release 2016 data, numerical values in 2010 differ slightly.

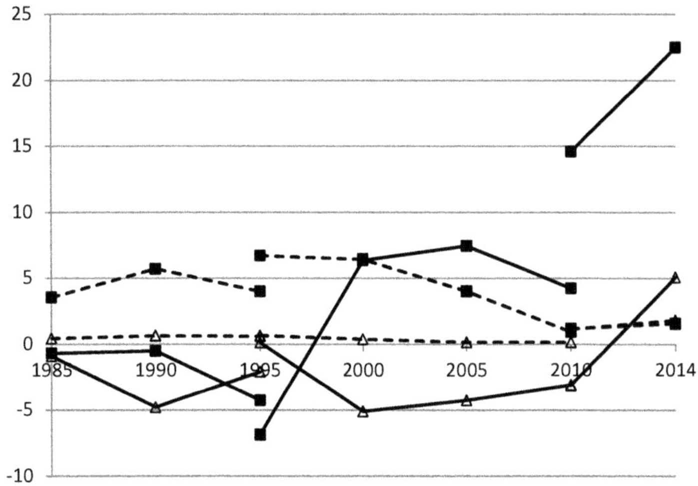

Fig. 4.5 Korea's trade balance against Japan and US (Unit: billion dollars)
Notes and Sources: See Fig. 4.4

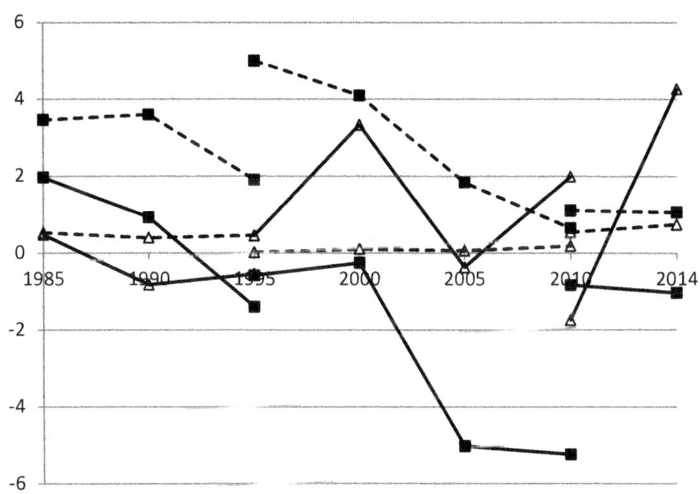

Fig. 4.6 Taiwan's trade balance against Japan and US (Unit: billion dollars)
Notes and Sources: See Fig. 4.4

trend in the surplus of China regarding final textile and leather products indicated by the dotted lines with square markers. The cause of such changes is the following well-known fact. Regarding the final textile and leather products, mainly clothing, Korea's and Taiwan's shares in the international market were reduced by an increase in China's share. However, in recent years, due to rising wages in China, the production bases of textile and leather products have moved to low-wage countries, such as Bangladesh and Vietnam. Therefore, the trade surplus of final textile and leather products in China is likely to decrease in the future. On the other hand, its downward trends in Korea and Taiwan are likely to continue in the future. Therefore, these countries need to create an alternative major export good, the hopeful candidate of which is machinery products.

Next, let us look at the trade balance of machinery products indicated in solid lines. Significant changes occurred in all three countries both in intermediate goods and in final goods. Although the trade balance of intermediate machinery products was in deficit in most years until 2010 in the three countries, it changed to surplus in 2014. A cause of this turnaround in intermediate machinery products is the following fact. In the past, the electrical machinery industry and transport machinery industry in China, Korea, and Taiwan produced using imported capital goods and parts made in Japan and the United States and exported the final goods to Japan, the United States, and European countries. Such "triangular trade" led to trade deficit in intermediate machinery products in these three countries against Japan and the United States. However, in recent years, the percentage of local procurement of parts is rising as a result of technology transfer from advanced countries and technological progress in local parts manufacturers. Through such changes, these three countries have accomplished trade surpluses in intermediate machinery products. In addition, regarding final machinery products indicated by solid lines with square markers, the trade surplus has increased dramatically since 2000 in China and Korea. After all, China and Korea succeeded in developing the intermediate and final machinery products as a new major export good; also Taiwan succeeded in developing the intermediate machinery products as a new major export good.

4.3 Structure of Trade Imbalance in the Eurozone

Figure 4.7 shows the current account balance in percentage of GDP in the eurozone countries. While the current account *surplus* in Germany increased cumulatively, in Spain, Portugal, and Greece, the current account *deficit* increased cumulatively until 2008. In other words, even in the eight countries shown in this figure, the imbalance expanded year by year until 2008, between surplus countries such as Germany and the Netherlands and the other six deficit countries.

Next, I look at the trade structure between two groups, one consisting of five countries called GIIPS (Greece, Ireland, Italy, Portugal, Spain) and the other consisting of other eurozone countries. Even in 1995, the GIIPS group had a trade deficit of 23.1 billion US dollars against the other eurozone countries. This deficit increased to 73 billion US dollars in 2010 (86.9 billion dollars in 2005 before the global financial crisis). The trade deficit in the GIIPS group against other eurozone countries increased about three times over the 15 years from 1995 to 2010, and the regional trade gap greatly expanded. I divide this trade deficit into that of intermediate goods trade and that of final goods trade. Figure 4.8 shows the trends of exports and imports in the GIIPS group against the other eurozone countries. In intermediate

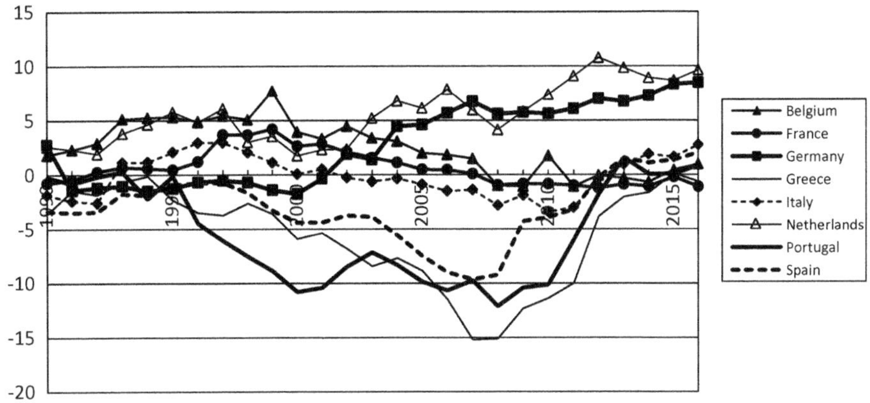

Fig. 4.7 Current account balance in eurozone countries, Percent of GDP (Unit: %)
Sources: Made by the author from IMF, World Economic Outlook Database, April 2017

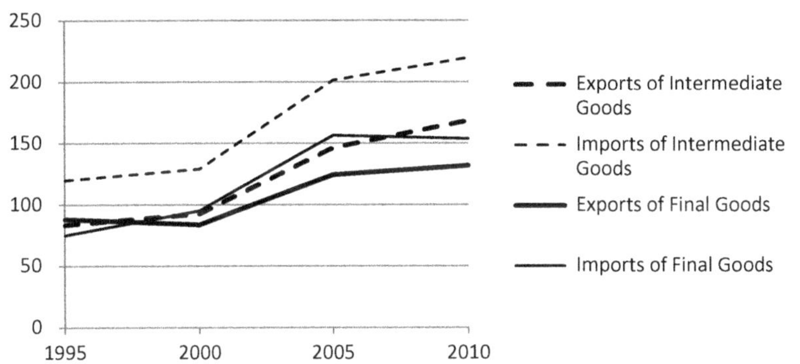

Fig. 4.8 Trade between GIIPS and other eurozone countries (Unit: billion dollars)
Sources: Calculated by the author from the World Input-Output Database

goods trade, the GIIPS group recorded a deficit of 36.2 billion US dollars against the other eurozone countries, and in final goods it recorded a surplus of 13.1 billion US dollars. In 2010, however, it fell to a deficit of 51.3 billion US dollars in intermediate goods trade and a deficit of 21.8 billion US dollars in final goods trade. As such, a significant part of the GIIPS group's trade deficit arises from intermediate goods trade.

According to Fig. 4.8, the reason why the trade deficit of the final good contracted slightly from 2005 to 2010 is due to a decrease in imports of final goods, not due to an increase in exports of final goods. The shrinking imports of final good are an effect of so-called austerity policies. In other words, the declining export competitiveness of GIIPS countries continued in both intermediate goods and final goods.

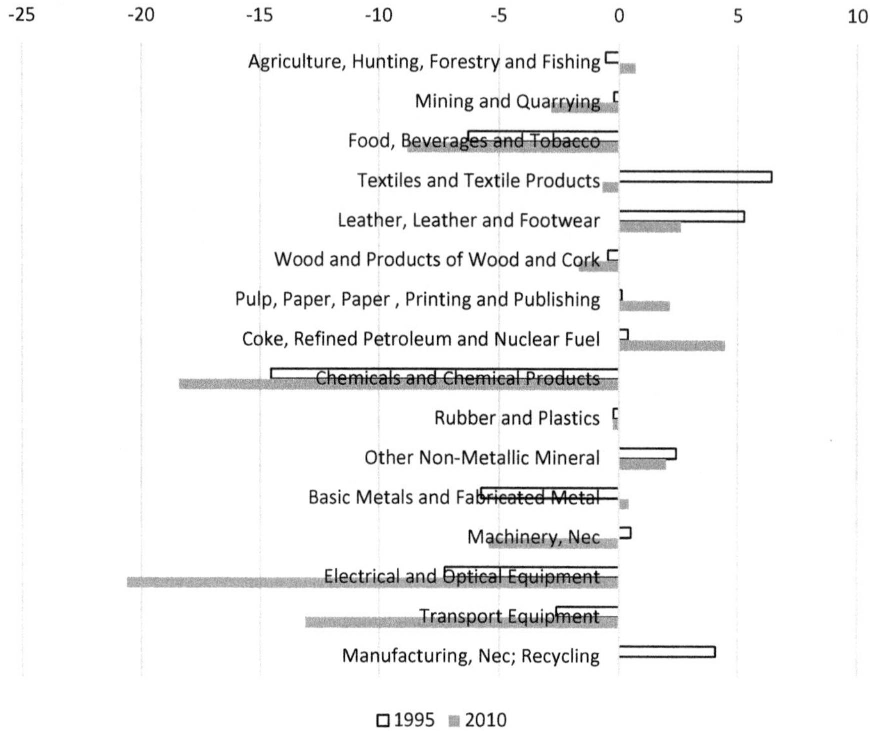

Fig. 4.9 Trade balance between GIIPS and other eurozone countries (Unit: billion dollars)
Sources: Calculated by the author from the World Input-Output Database. Products of tertiary industry are omitted

Figure 4.9 shows the trade balance between these two groups by products. Although the GIIPS group recorded large trade surpluses in textile and leather products against the other eurozone countries in 1995, these surpluses shrank in 2010. The GIIPS group recorded a trade deficit in machinery products in 1995, and this deficit increased greatly in 2010. Therefore, the GIIPS group lost traditional competitiveness in the field of textile and leather products, and they failed to construct export competitiveness in the field of machinery products.

Next, let us examine the trends in trade imbalance in these two fields in each country. I will analyze the trade balance of Spain, Portugal, and Greece against Germany and France. The former three countries, in total, had a deficit of 10.8 billion US dollars against the latter two countries in 1995, and this deficit increased to 23.1 billion US dollars in 2010 (the deficit in 2005 was $ 44.9 billion). Therefore, about half of the trade deficit in the GIIPS group against the other eurozone countries group arose between the former three countries and the latter two countries.

Figures 4.10, 4.11, and 4.12 show the trade balance of Spain, Portugal, and Greece, respectively, against Germany and France. First, let us look at the trade balance of textiles and leather products that are indicated by dotted lines. Although there are not any remarkable trend changes regarding intermediate goods, indicated

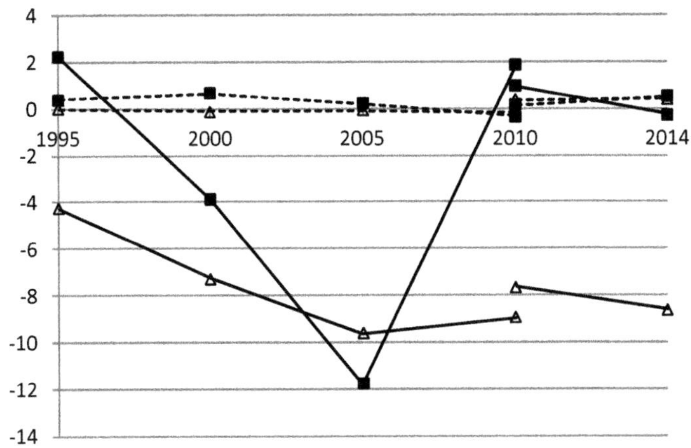

Fig. 4.10 Spain's trade balance against Germany and France (Unit: billion dollars)
Notes: Straight lines, machinery products; dotted lines, textile and leather products; triangle markers, intermediate goods; square markers, final goods
Sources: Calculated by the author from the World Input-Output Database, Release 2013 data (1995–2010), Release 2016 data (2010–2014)

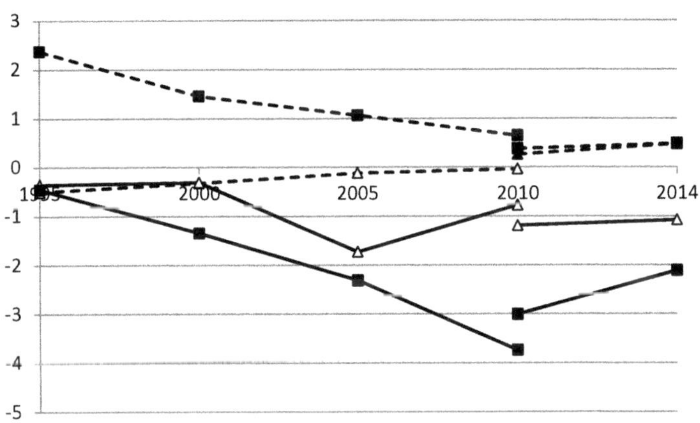

Fig. 4.11 Portugal's trade balance against Germany and France (Unit: billion dollars)
Notes and Sources: See Fig. 4.10

by dotted lines with triangular markers, there are decreasing trends in the surplus of Portugal and Greece regarding final textile and leather products indicated by the dotted lines with square markers. This is the result of the increased market share of Chinese products in the international market with respect to the final goods in textiles and leather products, mainly clothing, as seen above. There is also a high possibility that this decreasing trend of the surplus of Portugal and Greece will continue in the future. In these countries, it is necessary to create new major export goods instead of textiles and leather products. Machinery products are potential candidates.

Next, let us look at the trade balance of machinery products indicated by solid lines. Significant trend changes are seen in all countries, both for intermediate goods

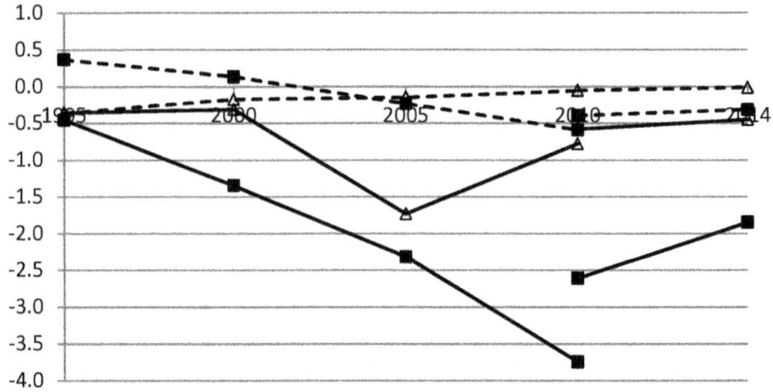

Fig. 4.12 Greece's trade balance against Germany and France (Unit: billion dollars)
Notes and Sources: See Fig. 4.10

and for final goods. The direction of these changes is greatly different from the East Asian countries shown in Figs. 4.10, 4.11, and 4.12. First, the trade balance of intermediate goods of machinery products indicated by solid lines with triangular markers shows an expanding deficit for Spain, Portugal, and Greece from 1995 to 2005. After 2005, although the expansion of this trade deficit has ceased, the considerably large deficits remain. Also in the trade of final goods of machinery products indicated by solid lines with square markers, these three countries increased the trade deficit until 2005. After the Euro crisis, this trade deficit has decreased because consumption and investment were suppressed and imports of final goods of machinery products were decreased through austerity policies.[6] In this way, since the decline in trade deficits in final goods of machinery products in these three countries is not due to the increase in exports, it can be said that these three countries failed to make machinery products the new major export goods instead of the traditional major export products. This is the main cause of the structural trade deficit in these three countries. This is quite contrary to the East Asian countries which succeeded in converting the trade structure by making intermediate goods and final goods of machinery goods new major export goods.

4.4 Method for Analyzing Causes for Trade Imbalance

This section explains the theoretical framework for analyzing the causes of these structural changes in the East Asian countries. A major cause determining the trade balance is the international competitiveness of export goods. While competitiveness

[6]In Spain, the trade of final goods of machinery products has nearly balanced since 2010. This is because imports of final goods of transportation machinery from Germany and France abruptly declined to less than half due to import restraints from austerity policies, not due to an increase in exports.

in forms other than price, such as in quality and brand, is also important in some products, I focus on the price competitiveness.

Export goods priced on an international currency basis (p) can be expressed as follows:

$$p = (1 + \mu)\left(ew/\lambda_f + m\right)$$

Here, μ is profit markup rate including capital costs, e is exchange rate (dollar rate against national currency), w is hourly wages, λ_f is labor productivity of export goods, and m is imported resource costs on an international currency basis per one unit of product. As will be explained in Appendix, I precisely measured labor productivity of export goods and non-tradable goods based on the input-output tables,[7] and this labor productivity is the reciprocal of the quantity of labor directly and indirectly required to obtain one physical unit of the product. Therefore, ew/λ_f represents the vertically integrated unit labor costs on an international currency basis including domestically produced resource costs.

When α is a ratio of the imported resource costs in the total costs

$$\alpha = m/\left(ew/\lambda_f + m\right)$$

$$\widehat{p} = \left(\widehat{1+\mu}\right) + (1 - \alpha)\left(\widehat{e} + \widehat{w} - \widehat{\lambda}_f\right) + \alpha\widehat{m}$$

We pay attention to the vertically integrated unit labor cost of export goods on an international currency basis ($u = ew/\lambda_f$), which is the product of the exchange rate, the hourly wages, and the reciprocal of labor productivity of export goods for the following reasons. First, the weight of the vertically integrated unit labor cost in the price of an export good is the largest.[8] Second, my analysis is a long-term one. In general, the imported resource cost and the capital cost do not have significant long-term trends. Productivity and wages, both of which are components of the unit labor cost, have significant long-term trends. Therefore, the vertically integrated unit labor cost is suitable as the object of our long-term analysis. As such, the long-term trend of export prices is greatly influenced by long-term trend of the unit labor cost. The growth rate of unit labor cost is decomposed to three components: the appreciation rate of the national currency, the wage growth rate, and the growth rate of labor productivity of export goods:

[7]In most previous studies (Canzoneri et al. 1999; Égart 2002; Kovács 2004; Kawai et al. 2003), the manufacturing and service sectors are, respectively, considered as the tradable and non-tradable goods sectors. It is evident that this dichotomy is not satisfactory.

[8]The ratio of the imported resource costs in the total costs (α) in the East Asian countries is about 0.1 to 0.4.

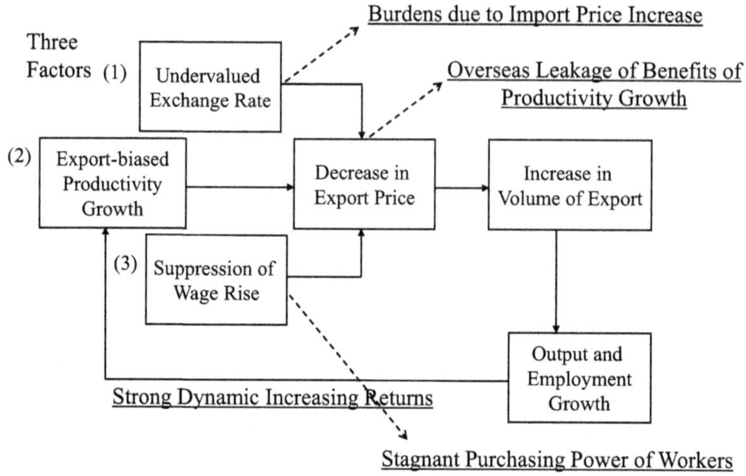

Fig. 4.13 A model of export-led growth
Source: Made by the author

$$\widehat{u} = \widehat{e} + \widehat{w} - \widehat{\lambda_f}$$

By focusing on changes in labor productivity of export goods, hourly wages, and the exchange rate, I can show three factors that contribute to decreases in export prices. The three factors are "export-biased productivity growth" (Hicks 1953), suppression of wages, and undervalued exchange rates.

In the case of export-led growth, cumulative causation works as follows (see Fig. 4.13). Under export-biased productivity growth, discretionary and depreciatory control of the exchange rate or repression of wage rise leads to decreases in export prices. When the export prices decline, output and employment in export goods sectors increase. Consequently, it brings about productivity increase in these sectors through strong dynamic increasing returns. In this case, the purchasing power of other countries' consumers rises when they purchase these goods. In other words, a significant part of the benefit of productivity growth leaks abroad, and it is distributed to consumers in other countries. Advantages of export-led growth are output and employment growth and the rapid technological change through strong dynamic increasing returns in export goods sectors. Disadvantages of export-led growth are the overseas leakage of the benefit of the productivity growth and the stagnant purchasing power of domestic workers. Moreover, a decisive limitation in export-led growth is accumulative trade deficits in trading partner countries.

The role of cumulative causation in domestic demand-led growth is clear (see Fig. 4.14). Wage and profit increase, which is distributed as a benefit of productivity growth, makes growing consumer demand and investment demand possible. This growing domestic demand brings about an increase in output, which gives rise to productivity growth in turn through dynamic increasing returns. However, since a significant part of consumption is service consumption, this effect is smaller than in

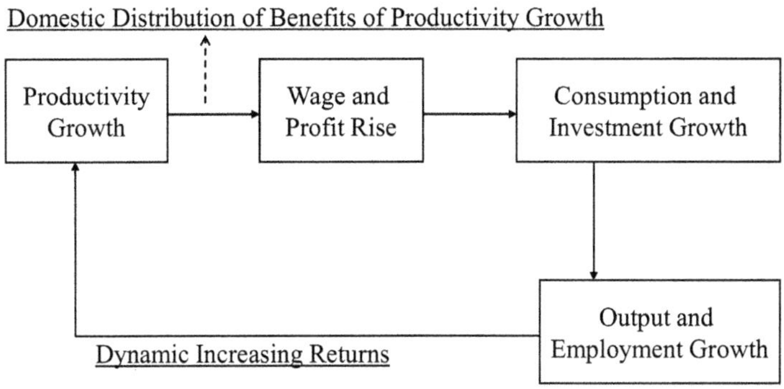

Fig. 4.14 A simple model of domestic demand-led growth
Source: Made by the author

the case of export-led growth. The route from productivity growth to demand growth is mediated by income distribution. In general, the range of income distribution is limited within national economies. Therefore, under domestic demand-led growth, cumulative causation plays its role domestically.

4.5 Export-Led Growth in East Asian Countries

According to the input-output tables in 2005, export shares in the domestic production of machinery manufacturing industries (13, 14, and 15 in the industry code) are 33% in China, 44% in Korea, and 74% in Taiwan. Annual real growth rates of exports from 2000 to 2008 in these three countries are 15.2%, 9.5%, and 6.8%, respectively, which are 1.5 times, 2.2 times, and 1.8 times larger than real GDP growth rates (10.1%, 4.3%, and 3.7%, respectively). These facts show that economic growth was driven by the high growth in exports.

Figure 4.15 shows the growth rate of labor productivity of export goods, the wage growth rate, and the appreciation rate of the national currency in East Asian countries and the United States. Labor productivity was measured using the method explained in the Appendix. Each growth rate is represented by an average annual rate over 13 years from 1995 to 2008.

The abovementioned three factors that contribute to decreases in export prices in these countries are as follows. Although the growth rate of labor productivity of non-tradable goods is not shown in this figure, "export-biased productivity growth" is remarkable in China, Korea, and Taiwan. Disparities of productivity growth between export goods and non-tradable goods are 3.4%, 6.0%, and 4.4%, respectively. The high productivity growth of export goods evidently contributed to the export-led growth. The first reason for this is serious efforts by these countries to introduce foreign capital and technology and to implement an export promotion policy. As a result of these endeavors, the export-oriented factories that were

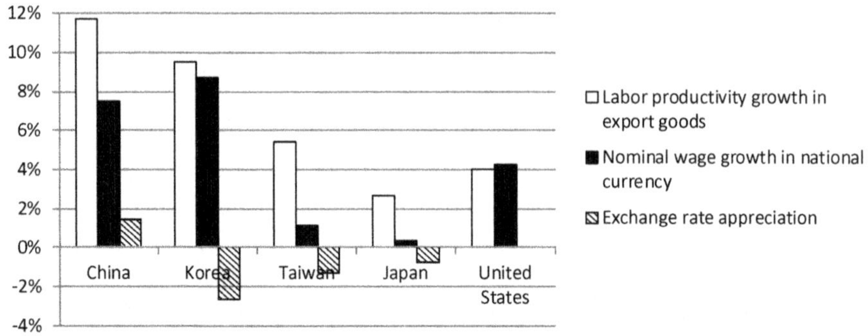

Fig. 4.15 Growth in productivity and wages (1995–2008, annual average growth rates)
Source: Calculated by the author by the method noted in the Appendix, using the World Input-Output Database, Release 2013 data

equipped with this new technology succeeded in achieving high labor productivity growth through large-scale production. The second reason is strong dynamic increasing returns, which mean that high output growth brings about high productivity growth.

Second, the suppression of wage rise is obvious in Taiwan and China. The wage growth rates were greatly lower than the growth rate of labor productivity. For example, in Taiwan, the annual wage growth rate of 1.2% was significantly lower than the annual labor productivity growth rate of 5.4%. In addition, Taiwan devalued their currency at 1.3% annual rate, so the unit labor cost decreased at a rate of 5.6% annually.

Third, depreciation of the exchange rate occurred in Taiwan and Korea in this period from 1995 to 2008. For example, in Korea, the annual wage growth of 8.7% is almost equal to the 9.5% annual labor productivity growth of export goods. Therefore, if there were no changes in exchange rate, the unit labor cost would not have changed greatly. In fact, however, as the exchange rate depreciated by 2.7% annually, the unit labor cost decreased by 3.5% annually. Although China's RMB appreciated in this period by 1.4% annual rate, China devalued the RMB by 33% from 1993 to 1994 as shown in Fig. 4.16. Taking this substantial devaluation into account, China also discretionally devalued the exchange rate in order to increase exports.

The annual growth rates of unit labor costs can be calculated from the data in Fig. 4.15, based on

$$\widehat{u} = \widehat{e} + \widehat{w} - \widehat{\lambda}_f$$

As a result, the annual growth rates of unit labor costs are −2.8% in China, −3.5% in Korea, and −5.6% in Taiwan. These decreases in unit labor cost surely caused decreases in export prices. For example, we can recall the fierce declines in price of LCD TVs and personal computers made in these countries.

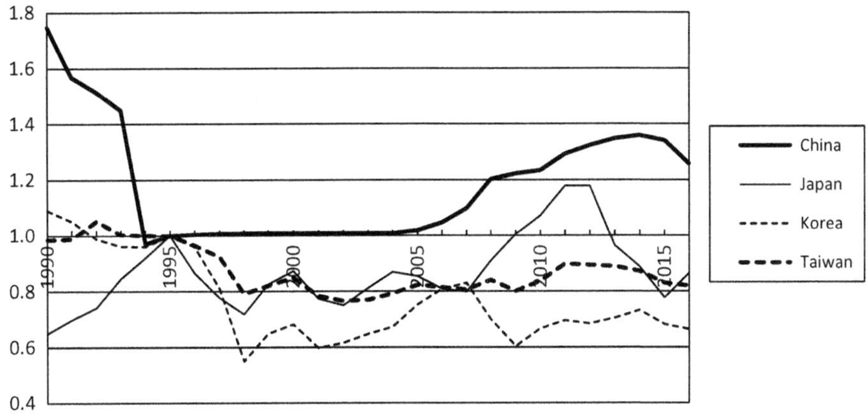

Fig. 4.16 Exchange rates in East Asian countries from 1990 to 2016 (US dollar/National currencies, 1995 = 1)
Sources: IMF, *International Financial Statistics*. Taiwan: The Directorate General of Budget, Accounting and Statistics (DGBAS). The base year (1995) is selected because trade imbalances in 1995 were the minimum in the Fig. 4.1.

Next, I explain that the suppression of wage rise and undervalued currencies are sequelae of the Asian currency crisis in 1997 (for more information, see Uni (2012)). From 1990 to 1995, the productivity of export goods and wages grew at the same rate in the United States, China, Korea, and Taiwan. In this period, as most Asian currencies were pegged to the US dollar, their exchange rates were almost constant against the US dollar, as shown in Fig. 4.16. A prerequisite for the "dollar peg system" is that wages and the productivity of export goods grow at the same rate. However, the Chinese government devalued the RMB by 33%, from 5.76 yuan per dollar in 1993 to 8.62 yuan per dollar in 1994, as shown in Fig. 4.16. Consequently, the exchange rate in Asian countries appreciated greatly against the RMB. Another prerequisite for the "dollar peg system" in small countries is that the large competitors in exports, such as China, maintain this system. This system was destroyed by the devaluation of the RMB. Proportional growth in wages and the productivity of export goods in most Asian countries meant that their relative unit labor costs compared with China did not change. In this situation, if their exchange rates against the RMB appreciated, their export competitiveness declined. Most Asian countries compete with China. Since the mid-1990s, China's exports have tended to grow rapidly, and other Asian countries' exports have tended to grow slowly. The correction of this imbalanced growth of exports started in 1997 as a speculative attack on overvalued currencies; it was accomplished by a sharp erosion of the currency value. This rapid and violent adjustment of exchange rates had a destructive effect on real economies: outflow of short-term capital, sharp fall of asset prices, banking crises, decline in production, increase in unemployment, etc.

Although export-biased productivity growth continued in China, Korea, Taiwan, and Malaysia after the crisis, in Indonesia and the Philippines, labor productivity decreased due to the economic crisis, which was accompanied by the currency crisis in 1997. In these countries, except Indonesia, the nominal wage rise slowed down compared with the previous period. This slowdown could be explained by the rise in unemployment. Lower wage growth than the productivity growth shown in Fig. 4.15 is a sequela of the Asian currency crisis in 1997.

In countries other than China, the exchange rates depreciated sharply in the currency crisis in 1997. Furthermore, in these countries, except China and Malaysia,[9] the exchange rate regime changed from the dollar peg system to the managed floating system.[10] In a managed floating system, the monetary authority influences the exchange rate dynamics through active market intervention without specifying an exchange rate target.

The slowdown of wage increases and the depreciation of currencies in many Asian countries after the currency crisis of 1997 brought about decreases in their export prices on a US dollar basis and enabled them to recover export competitiveness with China. Then, as shown in Fig. 4.16, Korean and Taiwanese currencies have not returned to the values they were at before the Asian currency crisis, and the Chinese RMB has not returned to its original value before its devaluation in 1993–1994. On the other hand, in the United States, as shown in Fig. 4.15, the nominal wage growth substantially equaled to labor productivity growth and the unit labor cost of export goods did not decrease. These facts indicate that price competitiveness of East Asian export goods has increased against the United States. Thus, in the 2000s, as shown in Fig. 4.1, the US trade deficit, especially that against East Asian countries, increased greatly.

As described above, the unique historical situation in which wage rise was suppressed and the currencies were devalued as sequelae of the Asian currency crisis of 1997 contributed to a virtuous cycle of export-led growth: export price reductions → export volume growth → export-biased productivity growth → export price reductions. As a result, China, Korea, and Taiwan succeeded in the conversion of major export goods from textile and leather products to the machinery products. Moreover, although these countries recorded a deficit in the trade of intermediate machinery products initially, it became a surplus in 2014.

---

[9]Malaysia also devalued the ringgit, maintaining the dollar peg system.

[10]The IMF definition of "managed floating with no predetermined path for the exchange rate" is as follows: "The monetary authority attempts to influence the exchange rate without having a specific exchange rate path or target. Indicators for managing the rate are broadly judgmental (e.g., balance of payments position, international reserves, parallel market developments), and adjustments may not be automatic. Intervention may be direct or indirect." The IMF definition of "independently floating" is as follows: "The exchange rate is market-determined, with any official foreign exchange market intervention aimed at moderating the rate of change and preventing undue fluctuations in the exchange rate, rather than at establishing a level for it."

According to the IMF classification in 1999, the exchange rate regimes in Korea, Indonesia, Thailand, and the Philippines were "independently floating," similar to Japan's case. However, as the monetary authorities in these countries frequently and discretionally intervened in the market, their exchange rate regimes were similar in practice to managed floating (Corden 2002).

4.6 Unequal Change in Unit Labor Cost in the Eurozone Countries

One of the necessary conditions for preventing the expansion of the current account imbalance within the eurozone is the stabilization of relative prices of export goods in member countries. Since the major component of export goods prices is a vertically integrated unit labor cost on an international currency basis, it is necessary to equalize the rates of change of this cost in all member countries for stabilizing the relative prices of export goods in member countries. As explained in Sect. 4.4, the growth rate of unit labor cost on an international currency basis is decomposed to three components: the appreciation rate of the national currency, the wage growth rate, and the growth rate of labor productivity of export goods:

$$\widehat{u} = \widehat{e} + \widehat{w} - \widehat{\lambda}_f$$

This equation shows that if there is a difference between wage growth rate ($\widehat{w}$) and productivity growth rate of export goods ($\widehat{\lambda}_f$) in one country, this country's unit labor cost on a national currency basis would change and that this change can be offset on an international currency basis by change in exchange rate ($\widehat{e}$). For example, if the wage growth rate exceeds the productivity growth rate of export goods, the unit labor cost in a national currency basis would rise. Then, if the exchange rate remains unchanged, exports of this country would decrease due to the rise in the export price on an international currency basis. However, if the national currency is devalued as much as offsetting this rise in unit labor cost, it is possible to avoid an increase in export price on an international currency basis. Thus, the exchange rate plays a role as an adjustment variable to mitigate the negative impact of excessive wage increases on exports. As shown in Fig. 4.17, in fact, such adjustments have been frequent in Spain, Portugal, Greece, etc. before the creation of the Maastricht Treaty in 1992.

After monetary integration, in the trade between member countries, the above adjustment became impossible. In other words, in order to stabilize the relative price of export goods in member countries, it is required to equalize wage growth rate ($\widehat{w}$) to productivity growth rate of export goods ($\widehat{\lambda}_f$) directly in each country.

In the case where labor productivity increases at a uniform rate in export goods and non-tradable goods, the price of export goods and that of non-tradable goods become constant by equalizing the wage growth rate to this uniform rate of labor productivity growth. Therefore, in this case, the relative price of export goods in member countries will also be stabilized by achieving the first Maastricht convergence criterion that the inflation rate should be no more than 1.5% above the rate for the three member countries with the lowest inflation over the previous year.

However, the reality is that most member countries after the adoption of the euro in 1999 did not have a uniform productivity growth in export goods and non-tradable goods but instead had "export-biased productivity growth" (Hicks 1953). Figure 4.18

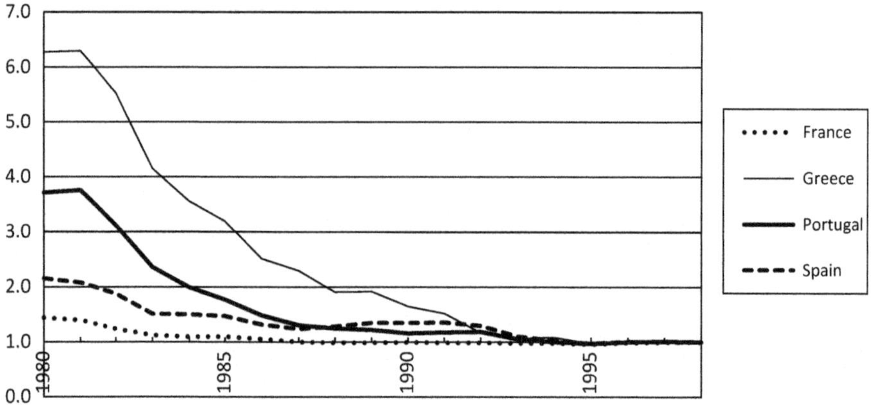

Fig. 4.17 Exchange rates in European countries from 1980 to 1998 (Deutschemark / National currencies, 1998=1)
Sources: IMF, *International Financial Statistics.*

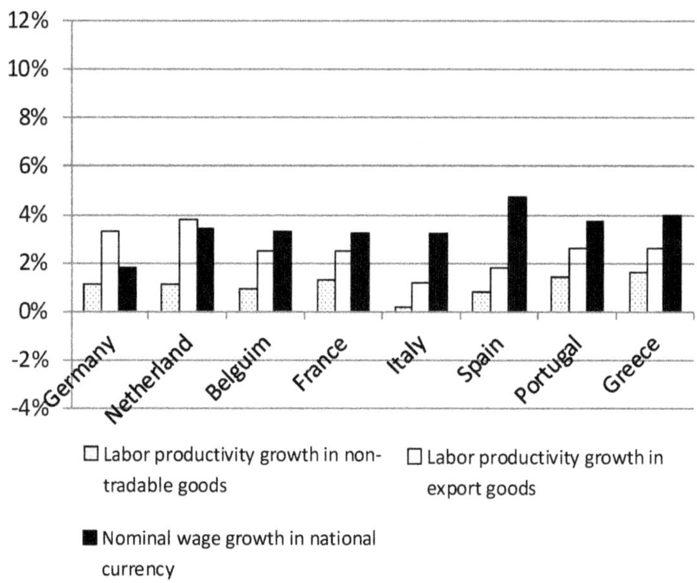

Fig. 4.18 Growth in productivity and wages (2000–2008, annual average growth rates)
Source: The author calculated from the World Input-Output Database, Release 2016 data, using the method noted in the Appendix
Note: Although 37% (in 2000) and – 49% (in 2008) of the total export of Greece are "water transport," this sector's share in the total labor input is only 1.0% (in 2000) and – 0.7% (in 2008). A reason seems to be that foreign sailors are not counted in the number of employees. As there exists this inconsistency in the "water transport" sector, I omitted this sector in the calculation of labor productivity of expert goods in Greece

shows the result of this measurement using the World Input-Output Database. These rates of change are the average annual rate in eight eurozone countries from 2000 to 2008. In all of these countries, the growth rate of labor productivity of export goods exceeds that of non-tradable goods. The differences between the two are 1.0% to 2.7%. However, these differences are smaller than the differences of 4% to 6% in China, Korea, and Taiwan. The biggest problem in the eurozone countries is that the member countries split into the following two groups. On the one hand, in Germany and the Netherlands, the wage growth rate was lower than the labor productivity growth rate of export goods, and their unit labor cost declined. On the other hand, in Belgium, France, Italy, Portugal, Spain, and Greece, the wage growth rate exceeded the labor productivity growth rate of export goods, and their unit labor cost rose. As mentioned earlier, since it is impossible to adjust the exchange rate under the monetary union, the change in unit labor cost directly affects the change in export price. The difference between the wage growth rate and the labor productivity growth rate of export goods results in an increase in the current account surplus in Germany and the Netherlands and an increase in the current account deficit in other countries as shown in Fig. 4.7.

The background of the chain of Europe's debt crisis and the Euro crisis that began with the downgrade of government bonds such as in Greece, Portugal, and Spain at the end of 2009 was the current account deficit and the fiscal deficit caused by the reasons described above. In Greece, Portugal, Spain, etc., austerity policies for suppression of wages and fiscal spending were implemented as measures to deal with the crisis. If these excessive wage increases which exceed the growth rate of labor productivity of exports are moderated in these Southern European countries, the rise in export prices will stop, and the current account deficit will slow down. In fact, as shown in Fig. 4.7, the current account deficit of these countries has shrunk since 2010. Also, in Germany, raising the wage growth rate which is lower than the growth rate of labor productivity of export goods would be effective for reducing the current account imbalance (Flassbeck and Lapavitsas 2015). Figure 4.19 shows the average annual growth rates of productivity and wages in the eight eurozone countries from 2008 to 2014. Compared with the growth rates from 2000 to 2008 shown in Fig. 4.18, the wage growth slowed down greatly in Southern European countries, and the German wage growth increased from 2000 to 2008. However, productivity growth slowed down not only in the Southern European countries but also in the Northern European countries. A reason for this is that the shrinking current account deficit in the Southern European countries was brought about not by expanding exports but by shrinking imports. This caused the slowdown of exports in the Northern European countries. In order to convert the trade balance into surplus in the Southern European countries, without relying on the shrinking imports by the austerity policies, it is important to create new major export goods instead of the traditional major export goods that lost international competitiveness in the competition with China, etc. Is it possible to convert the trade structure in these Southern Europe countries only by adjusting the wage growth rate? We discuss this problem in Sect. 4.8.

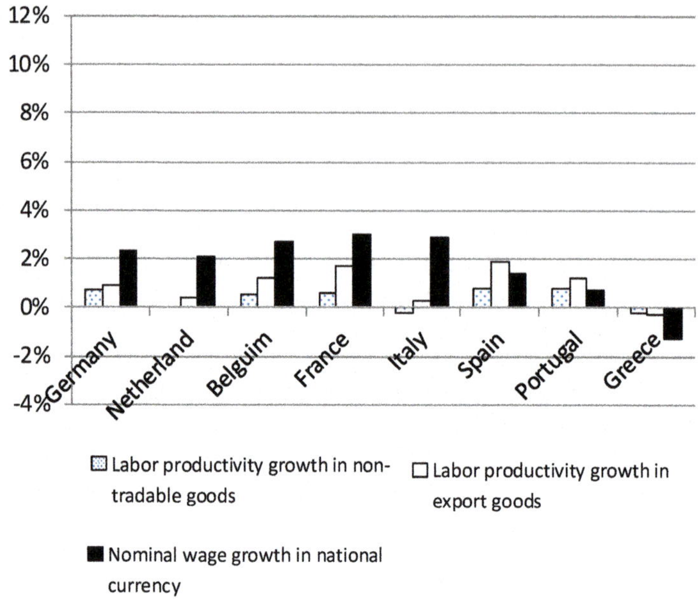

Fig. 4.19 Growth in productivity and wages (2008–2014, annual average growth rates)
Source and Note: See Fig. 4.18

4.7 Toward Transformation of Export–Led Growth in East Asian Countries

Today, export-led growth has become difficult in East Asian countries, so transformation of the growth regime is required. First, the cumulative increase in the trade surplus in East Asian countries resulted in a cumulative expansion of the trade deficit in the United States, a major trading partner. It's accompanied with the reduction of output and employment in the US manufacturing industry. The Trump government is trying to convert the trade policy of the United States to a protectionist one in order to maintain employment in the manufacturing industry. This means that East Asian export-led growth has reached its limit. Second, in Asian countries including China, Korea, and Taiwan, in recent years, the number of labor disputes and the growth rate of wages continue to increase. This means that a condition that supports export-led growth is breaking down.

Figure 4.20 shows the average annual growth rates of labor productivity in export goods and nominal wages from 2008 to 2014. Although the wage growth was slower than the productivity growth in the East Asian countries from 2000 to 2008 as shown in Fig. 4.15, the wage growth became faster than the productivity growth in China and Korea from 2008 to 2014. Although the productivity growth from 2008 to 2014 became slower than that from 2000 to 2008, the productivity growth in the East

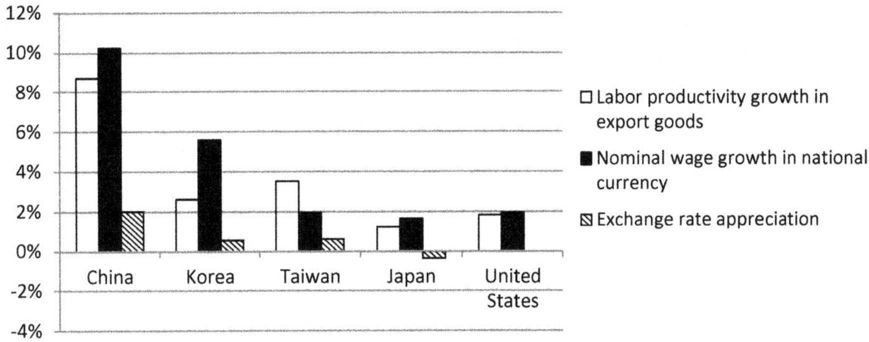

Fig. 4.20 Growth in productivity and wages (2008–2014, annual average growth rates)
Source: Calculated by the author by the method noted in the Appendix, using the World Input-Output Database, Release 2016 data

Asian countries continued to be higher than that in the European countries shown in Fig. 4.19.

For example, an owner-manager of a Japanese clothing manufacturer with a factory in China and Bangladesh said "the miracle that happened in the past in China has not reappeared in the present Asia and companies expanding into Asia cannot make great profit" because there are big differences in workers, materials, and/or money when comparing the present situation with the situation around 1990 (Kojima 2013). He stressed a change in workers between then and now as "abundant low-wage workers with no rights in 1990" and "labor shortage, a storm of strikes and workers claiming their rights at present." In many Asian countries, wage labor relations are transforming. The real wages continuously increase in China (urban area) and Korea from around 2000.[11] The global financial crisis in 2008 did not bring about as large a suppression of wage increases as did the Asian currency crisis in 1997. Although the nominal wages in Japan and Taiwan stagnated in Fig. 4.20, Taiwanese real wages tended to increase in the 2010s. The number of the labor disputes has increased rapidly in China and Taiwan.[12] The number of labor disputes in 2015 was about 7.6 times in China and about 5.5 times in Taiwan compared to 1998. The situation of "labor shortage, a storm of strikes and workers claiming their rights at present" indicates that export-led growth is transforming from the inside of East Asian countries.

In addition, Hirakawa (2013) mentioned that rather than the existence of an abundant low-cost labor force, the potential existence of a market has become a critical factor in a firm's decision to enter a developing country. Such capital in

[11]Calculated by the author from nominal wages and CPIs in IMF, *International Financial Statistics*, *China Statistical Yearbook*, and *The Directorate General of Budget, Accounting and Statistics (DGBAS)*.

[12]Sources: *China Statistical Yearbook* (number of cases accepted by arbitration committees) and *The Directorate General of Budget, Accounting and Statistics (DGBAS)*.

developed countries would expect the establishment of a virtuous cycle of domestic demand-led growth, such as "Fordism," in the developing countries. However, a transformation from export-led growth to domestic demand-led growth requires the resolution of some issues regarding (1) exchange rate regime, (2) wage growth, and (3) productivity growth. Hereafter, I discuss these issues referring to lessons from the failure of economic policies of the Abe administration since 2012 ("Abenomics") in Japan.

4.7.1 Exchange Rate Regime

In order to eliminate unilateral discretionary currency devaluation, a cooperative system of governments should be institutionalized. Even if proportional wage growth with productivity growth is realized, it may be possible to continue export-led growth through an undervalued exchange rate. If one of the countries adopts such policy, this could induce competition for currency devaluation, and the collective benefits of entire international community may be destroyed. In order to solve such a "dilemma of collective action," it is necessary to institutionalize multilateral coordination regarding the setting of the target rates, even if member countries continue to maintain a managed floating system (Uni 2007).

However, as the construction of this kind of international cooperation is a difficult agenda, exchange rate fluctuations will likely continue. Therefore, price setting behavior of export companies facing exchange rate fluctuations is important for a transformation from export-led growth to domestic demand-led growth. Regarding this point, the recent changes in price setting behavior of Japanese export companies are informative. In the period of depreciation of the yen, traditional Japanese companies did not change export prices on a yen basis. Therefore, depreciation of the yen resulted in a decrease in export prices on an international currency basis, which led to an increase in the volume of exports. However, in the recent period of depreciation of the yen, many Japanese companies raised export prices on a yen basis. For example, the yen depreciated by 14% from 106 yen per dollar in 2014 to 121 yen per dollar in 2015 as a result of the quantitative and qualitative easing the Bank of Japan started in 2013. Then, automobile companies raised their export prices on a yen basis by 6.8%. As a result, a decrease in export prices on a US dollar basis became small (i.e., rates of exchange rate pass-through declined), and the export volume of Japanese automobiles increased only by 0.9%. In other words, in recent years, Japanese companies seek an increase in their profit margin rather an increase in the volume of exports. This is the first step for getting out of export-led growth. Problems in Japanese companies exist in the distribution of increased gains, of which most are reserved in companies and not distributed to workers as wage increases.

4.7.2 Wage Growth

While slower wage growth than productivity growth is a necessary condition for export-led growth, proportional wage growth with productivity growth is necessary for the domestic demand-led growth. However, as export-biased productivity growth is prominent in East Asian countries, the following problem occurs in wage setting. Proportional wage growth with productivity growth of export goods is desirable for the stability of export prices but will result in the socially uniform growth rate of wages exceeding the productivity growth of non-tradable goods. In this case, companies producing non-tradable goods may try to pass this increase in costs on to the prices of products. However, if these companies are subject to intense price competition each other, they may oppose such a wage increase.

The Japanese government continued to urge a wage increase to employers' associations from 2014, which is called "government-laid spring offensive." However, wages have not increase. In Japan, annual wage rises are determined in negotiations between individual companies and enterprise unions. The "spring offensive system" is a mechanism for diffusion of high wage increases in high-performance companies to other companies. However, the wage bargaining power of labor unions weakened because the labor union density declined due to non-regularization of employment. In order to create agreements on proportional wage growth with productivity growth, it is necessary to organize non-regular workers and reinforce wage bargaining power of labor unions.

4.7.3 Productivity Growth

As mentioned above, in the case of export-biased productivity growth, low labor productivity growth in sectors producing non-tradable goods tends to prevent wage growth and a shift to domestic demand-led growth. Therefore, it is particularly important to increase labor productivity in the non-tradable goods sector. As the population is declining in Japan, and will likely continue to decline in the long term, labor productivity growth is necessary for alleviating the constraints on labor supply. The Abe administration started to examine "work style reforms" from September 2016. Key issues are the correction of the long working hours of full-time workers, improvement of non-regular workers' situation, etc. However, gaps in opinions between the government, employers' associations, trade unions, and women' associations are quite large.

Employers' associations think that an increase in labor productivity is important for enhancing competitiveness and ensuring profits, mainly through the relaxation of Japan-specific stringent labor regulations. Their immediate targets are the relaxation of dismissal regulations for firing low productivity workers and realizing white-collar exemption that would allow firms to exempt well-paid professional workers from working hours regulations.

On the other hand, labor unions' target is stricter restriction on excess working hours. They aim for institutional reforms that strengthen the involvement of trade unions in the determination of the upper limit of working hours in individual companies. In principle, labor unions favor shrinking disparities between regular and non-regular workers. However, they opposed balancing the reduction of working conditions of regular workers because the majority of union members are regular workers. They also opposed the white-collar exemption and the introduction of foreign workers.

When Prime Minister Abe met the president of the Japanese Trade Union Confederation (RENGO) in July 2017, they agreed to the following compromise. The management side concedes stricter restriction on excess working hours, and the labor side concedes white-collar exemption. However, immediately after this meeting, various objections appeared in the Japanese Trade Union Confederation, and consequently this compromise was withdrawn. This example indicates that raising labor productivity is a difficult agenda with conflicts of various interests, and deliberative discussion is necessary for creating social compromise.

4.8 Toward Monetary Integration with Political Integration

When we pay attention to the current account in the eurozone countries after the mid-1990s, deficits increased cumulatively in Greece, Spain, and Portugal until 2008, while the surplus of Germany increased cumulatively. In the usual case, the current account deficit is offset by the capital account surplus. In fact, in the early stage, the current account deficit was financed by the continuous private capital inflow into the Southern European countries from the late 1990s. This private capital inflow included direct investments to the manufacturing industry, and it contributed to the industrial development in the Southern European countries. However, the private capital started to outflow in 2008 with the global financial crisis, and this private capital outflow from the Southern European countries increased after the Euro crisis in 2011. It is a change in TARGET balances in the ECB that financed the current account deficits in the Southern European countries instead of the lost private capital.[13] In TARGET2, which is the payment system of the eurozone, TARGET balances are formed between the ECB and each country's central bank, and these sovereign debts increase automatically in the countries where private capital was lost. As an example, in TARGET balances, the total balance of the following five countries, namely, Italy, Spain, Portugal, Greece, and Ireland (so-called GIIPS), increased rapidly from −110.8 billion euro in the end of 2008 to −813.5 billion euro

[13]The public financial support by the "Troika" (EU, IMF, and ECB) also played a role in financing these countries' current account deficits. But, quantitatively, the change in TARGET balances is much larger.

in the end of 2012.[14] The total private capital inflow to these five countries from 2003 to 2008 was 900 billion euro, but most of it had moved out of these countries by 2012. In contrast, in German TARGET balances, credit piled up from 115.3 billion euro in the end of 2008 to 655.7 billion euro in the end of 2012. Even in the end of 2016, the TARGET balance of the five countries mentioned above was −829.6 billion euro, and Germany had 754.3 billion euro credits. Most of the imbalances in TARGET balances have not disappeared.

This cumulative imbalance in TARGET balances is a result of a structural defect in the system design called "monetary integration without political integration." We may well understand this defect by imagining monetary integration with political integration. On the inside of the politically integrated community, the principle of equal pay for equal work and common working conditions would become general standard. The integrated government would subsidize regions or industries where these general standards cannot be realized because of low productivity due to technological or structural reasons. In other words, through an integrated taxation-fiscal system, a part of income is transferred from technologically or structurally strong regions or industries to weak ones. Through this income transfer, even if there are differences in productivity between regions or industries, equal competitiveness to some extent will be maintained with equality in wage and working conditions.

However, with the monetary integration without political integration realized in Europe, movements to equalize wages directly lead to the expansion of gaps in competitiveness and current account imbalances between countries. This is because there is no correction mechanism through a taxation-fiscal system and the former correction mechanism through exchange rate adjustment does not work. For example, after monetary integration, in Germany, the wage growth rate was kept lower than the productivity increase rate; on the other hand, in the Southern European countries, the wage growth rate was higher than the productivity increase rate. However, such cross-border equalization of wages is natural after the liberalization of cross-border movement of the labor force.

These actual unsustainable cumulative current account imbalances give impetus for Europe to fundamentally reform the system design of "monetary integration without political integration." After the Euro crisis, several institutional reforms were implemented, such as the establishment of the European Stability Mechanism (ESM) and the establishment of the Bank Union consisting of the Single Supervisory Mechanism, the Single Resolution Mechanism, and Deposit Guarantee Scheme, but they are partial reforms far from full-scale political integration or taxation-fiscal system integration. In addition, the European Commission began to watch budget deficits, wage increases, and productivity increases in order to prevent macroeconomic imbalance and to correct it. Moreover, the European Commission can enforce corrective actions to deviating countries. However, these new institutions have little effects for upgrading industry and enhancing productivity in the stagnating Southern

[14]TARGET balances, *Statistical Data Warehouse*, European Central Bank, (http://sdw.ecb.europa.eu/reports.do?node=1000004859)

European countries, because fiscal expansion policy is prohibited. As a result, gaps in wages and working conditions between the eurozone countries will not shrink and are more likely to spread. In other words, the eurozone is likely to be polarized real economically, even though it was unified monetarily.

Appendix

The productivity growth of export goods and non-tradable goods was estimated in the following manner from the input-output tables (Uni 1995).

X is a column vector in which each entry shows the total amount of output of each commodity.

Y is a column vector in which each entry shows the total final demand for each commodity. It is the sum of the domestic final demand (denoted by D) and exports (denoted by F).

A is the input coefficient matrix in which entries in each column show the amount of domestic commodity used by the industry to obtain one unit of output.[15]

a is a row vector in which each entry shows the amount of labor directly required to obtain one unit of output in each industry.[16]

L is a scalar to denote the total labor input.

The following two equations show the quantity system in a country:

$$(I - A)X = Y$$

$$aX = L$$

We obtain the following from these equations:

$$a(I - A)^{-1}Y = L$$

We denote $a(I - A)^{-1} = v$,

where v is a row vector in which each entry shows the amount of labor directly and indirectly required to produce one physical unit of each commodity, that is, "the vertically integrated labor input coefficient" (Pasinetti 1973) and "labor value" in classical economics:

[15] In the World Input-Output Database, I used National Input-Output Tables Analytical in current prices (with 35 sectors; unit, the US dollar). As they are noncompetitive import type tables, the input coefficient matrix of domestic products is obtained directly. However, for China, data of "Sale, maintenance and repair of motor vehicles and motorcycles; retail sale of fuel" sector is missing.

[16] Regarding labor input by sector, I used "Total hours worked by persons engaged" in the socioeconomic accounts included in the World Input-Output Database.

$$vY = v(D + F) = L$$

Column vector D is the product of the total domestic final demand (denoted as ΣD) and the share of each commodity in this total (denoted as column vector d). Therefore

$$D = d\Sigma D$$

Similarly

$$F = f\Sigma F$$

We obtain the following equation:

$$v(d\Sigma D + f\Sigma F) = vd\Sigma D + vf\Sigma F = L$$

where vd and vf are scalars. These represent the quantity of labor directly and indirectly required to obtain one nominal unit of domestic final demand and export, respectively. Labor productivity is the reciprocal of the quantity of labor directly and indirectly required to obtain one physical unit of the product. As the unit of the World Input-Output Database is the US dollar at current prices, I converted them to the US dollar at constant prices by multiplying vd by the domestic demand[17] deflators (π_d) and vf by the export deflators (π_f) derived from the national accounts.[18] These are "the vertically integrated labor input coefficients." The labor productivity of non-tradable goods (λ_d) and export goods (λ_f) are as follows:

$$\lambda_d = 1/vd\pi_d$$
$$\lambda_f = 1/vf\pi_f$$

References

Canzoneri MB, Cumby RE, Diva B (1999) Relative labor productivity and the real exchange rate in the long run: evidence for a panel of OECD countries. J Int Econ 47:245–266

Corden WM (2002) Too sensational: on the choice of exchange rate regimes. MIT Press, Cambridge, MA

[17]For example, in the United Nations' *National Accounts*, domestic demand is the sum of "Final consumption expenditure" and "Gross capital formation."

[18]Except for Taiwan, deflators are derived from the table of GDP by type of expenditure at current prices (US dollars) and that at constant prices (US dollars) in the United Nations, *National Accounts Main Aggregates Database* (http://unstats.un.org/), and for Taiwan, from Republic of China, *National Statistics* (http://eng.stat.gov.tw/).

Égart B (2002) Estimating the impact of the Balassa-Samuelson effect on inflation and the real exchange rate during the transition. Econ Syst 26:1–16

Flassbeck H, Lapavitsas C (2015) Against the troika: crisis and austerity in the Eurozone. Verso, London

Hicks J (1953) An inaugural lecture. Oxford Econ Pap 5(2):117–135 (Republished in Hicks J (1983) Classics and moderns. Basil Blackwell, Oxford)

Hirakawa H (2013) East Asia's integration and structural shift: the shift from newly industrializing economies to potentially bigger market economies under the global economy. In: Yagi K et al (eds) Crises of global economy and the future of capitalism. Routledge, New York

Kawai M, Kasuya M, Hirakata N (2003) Analysis of the relative price of nontradable goods in the G7 countries, Bank of Japan working paper series, No.03-E-5

Kojima M (2013) The miracle in China do not reappear in Asia. In: Ohmori T et al (ed) Gekidousuru Asia wo iku. Institute for Northeast Asian Studies, Obirin University (in Japanese)

Kovács MA (2004) Disentangling the Balassa-Samuelson effect in CEC5 countries in the prospect of EMU enlargement. In: Szapáry G, von Hagen J (eds) Monetary strategies for joining the Euro. Edward Elgar, Cheltenham

Pasinetti LL (1973) The notion of vertical integration in economic analysis. Metoroeconomica 25:1–29

Timmer MP, Dietzenbacher E, Los B, Stehrer R, de Vries GJ (2015) An illustrated user guide to the world input–output database: the case of global automotive production. Rev Int Econ 23:575–605

Uni H (1995) Export-led growth in Japan. Bull Japan Soc Polit Econ 32:90–105 (in Japanese)

Uni H (2007) Export-biased productivity increase and exchange rate regime in East Asia. Kyoto Econ Rev 76(1):117–138

Uni H (2012) Comparative analysis of conditions for monetary integration: Europe and Asia. In: Boyer R, Uemura H, Isogai A (eds) Diversity and transformations of Asian capitalisms. Routledge, New York

Chapter 5
The Evolving Diversity and Interdependence of Growth Regimes and De-industrialization in European Countries and Japan

Hiroyasu Uemura and Shinji Tahara

5.1 Introduction

The transformations of growth regimes have proceeded with industrial structural changes in the increasing economic interdependence of European and East Asian countries. Most of the European economies have experienced de-industrialization as a long-term industrial structural change since the 1970s. De-industrialization is usually defined as a relative decline in output and employment in the manufacturing industry. This phenomenon has been observed universally, not only in European economies but in other advanced economies as well. In Japan, in particular, de-industrialization has accelerated rapidly since the 1990s amid institutional changes in the domestic economy and structural changes in international economic relations with other Asian countries in the process of Asian economic integration. In Europe, de-industrialization has exhibited different patterns with the evolving diversity and interdependence of European capitalisms in the process of European integration.

We analyze the transformation and interdependence of growth regimes and industrial structural changes to understand the structural characteristics of de-industrialization in Germany, France, Italy, the UK, and Japan. We attempt to extend the theoretical framework of the "growth regime" in the *régulation* theory, taking account of long-term industrial structural changes and the evolution of

H. Uemura (✉)
Yokohama National University, Yokohama, Japan
e-mail: huemura@ynu.ac.jp

S. Tahara
Chiba University of Commerce, Ichikawa, Japan
e-mail: stahara@cuc.ac.jp

R. Boyer et al. (eds.), *Evolving Diversity and Interdependence of Capitalisms*,
Evolutionary Economics and Social Complexity Science 11,
https://doi.org/10.1007/978-4-431-55001-3_5

international economic interdependence through analyses using the World Input-Output Database (WIOD).

Our analysis is conducted under four themes. First, we analyze the patterns of international economic interdependence occurring during regional integration in Europe and East Asia. Second, we analyze growth regimes and de-industrialization in Germany, France, Italy, the UK, and Japan, focusing on changes in domestic economic structures and international economic relations from the viewpoint of the *régulation* theory (Petit 1986, 2005; Boyer 1988, 2015). Third, we analyze the structural linkages between the manufacturing industry and the service industry to understand the characteristics of de-industrialization in each economy. We thus extend the method of studying de-industrialization based on input-output analysis that was developed by Franke and Kalmbach (2005) to analyze the German economy. In particular, we use World Input-Output Database (WIOD) in our structural analysis of de-industrialization. Fourth, we consider the socioeconomic implications of de-industrialization and the increase in various service activities within several varieties of capitalism in the process of regional integration.

5.2 Theoretical Framework of Growth Regime and De-industrialization

5.2.1 Growth Regime and De-industrialization in the Open Economy

De-industrialization can be analyzed in the framework of the "growth regime" with industrial structural change. The interaction of demand formation and production activities plays a key role to determine the dynamics of economic growth, and the interaction between real and financial factors influences the stability of the economy. Furthermore, industrial structural changes occur in tandem with the increasing economic interdependence of growth regimes in the open economy.

From this theoretical perspective, we explain the dynamics of growth regimes and de-industrialization from the perspective of the *régulation* theory (Petit 1986, 2005; Boyer 1988, 2015). First, the cumulative interaction of productivity growth and output growth determines the dynamics of a growth regime in the national economy. This dynamic effect operates most strongly in the manufacturing industry (Kaldor 1978). The theoretical framework of cumulative growth and de-industrialization in the open economy framework is depicted in Fig.5.1.

The basic logic of demand formation in a growth regime is as follows. Productivity growth creates national incomes, which are distributed into wages and profits. Furthermore, an increase in profits has a positive effect on the expected profit rate and investment, and an increase in investment realizes more profits. Therefore, cumulative interactions occur between the profit rate and the accumulation rate. Furthermore, increased investment leads to an increase in intermediate inputs from

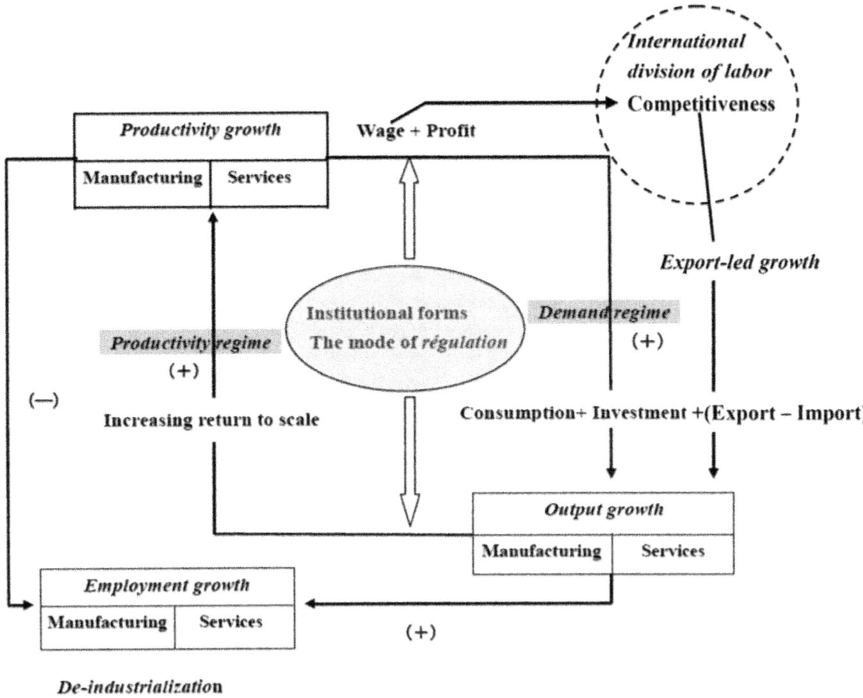

Fig. 5.1 Growth regime and de-industrialization in the open economy
Source: This figure is the modified version of the figure in Uemura and Tahara (2014) by taking account of export/import and the international division of labor.

either the manufacturing or service sector. At the same time, an increase in wages leads to more consumption demand (Rowthorn 1982; Taylor 1991). The markets for consumer durable goods and consumer services expand accordingly.

Next, there is an effect from consumption to investment, consisting of both short-term and long-term effects. In the former, changes in demand influence investment through the adjustment of capacity utilization in the manufacturing industry. In the latter, a continuous expansion of consumption influences the expected return of investment, leading to an increase in investment. In the actual process of investment decision, these effects are integrated into investment decision. The growth rates are not uniform across the industries as profitability differentials exist at the industrial level. In this context, two patterns of demand formation are observed, depending on the patterns of coordination in the financial system, the wage-labor nexus, and international economic relations. If investment is highly sensitive to profits, the causal chain of "profit-led (or investment-led) growth" (i.e., profits-investment-economic growth) is realized. On the contrary, if investment is sufficiently sensitive to demand expansion in the market, the casual chain of "wage-led (or consumption-led) growth" (wage-consumption-investment-economic growth) is realized (Marglin and Schor 1990).

Furthermore, in the open economy framework, export/import plays a very important role in economic growth with the evolving international division of labor amid the interdependence of growth regimes in the process of regional integration. This creates the dynamic causal chain (productivity-unit labor costs-export) also plays a crucial role in the growth of the manufacturing industry, which is the basic logic of "export-led growth" in the open economy.

In summary, all of the linkages from productivity growth to demand formation are called the "demand regime" in the *régulation* theory (Boyer 1988, 2015).[1] The demand regime can be expressed as

$$\Delta y = f(\Delta\lambda) \tag{5.1}$$

where y is a final demand vector and λ is a labor productivity vector. Demand vector y is divided into three components: domestic final demand vector y^{dfd}, export vector y^{ex}, and import vector y^{im}. The final demand vector is further divided into consumption vector y^{con}, investment vector y^{inv}, and government spending vector y^{gov}.

$$\begin{aligned} \Delta y &= \Delta y^{dfd} + \Delta y^{ex} - \Delta y^{im} \\ &= \Delta y^{con} + \Delta y^{inv} + \Delta y^{gov} + \Delta y^{ex} - \Delta y^{im} \end{aligned} \tag{5.2}$$

Each of the components can be regarded as a function of productivity growth. Furthermore, final demand induces intermediate demand, which can be studied by the input-output analysis. In our framework of input-output analysis, input coefficient matrix A is divided into the matrix of domestic input ratios H and technological coefficient matrix A^* by following the framework by Franke and Kalmbach (2005), as follows:

$$A = H \circ A^* \tag{5.3}$$

In mathematical terms, the input coefficient matrix is the Hadamard product of the matrix of the domestic shares of intermediate inputs and the matrix of technological coefficients.

$$a_{ij} = h_{ij} \cdot a^*_{ij} \quad i, j = 1, 2 \ldots n \tag{5.4}$$

This can distinguish between domestic intermediate inputs and foreign intermediate inputs into the production process. By using the Leontief inverse matrix, $B = (I - A)^{-1}$, and Eq. (5.3), the increase in the output vector can be calculated

[1]The growth pattern differs from country to country, depending on the specific institutional arrangements involved. In the Japanese case, "profit-led growth" played a leading role in the high economic growth in the 1960s, and "export-led growth" became dominant after the 1980s (Uemura 2000, 2012; Uemura et al. 2016).

from the final demand vector, technological coefficient matrix, and domestic intermediate inputs, as follows:

$$\begin{aligned}\Delta x = & B_0\Delta y + (B_1 - B_0)\Delta y \\ & + B_0(H_0 \circ \Delta A^*)x_0 + [B_1(H_1 \circ \Delta A^*) - B_0(H_0 \circ \Delta A^*)]\ x_0 \\ & + B_0(\Delta H \circ A_0^*)x_0 + (B_1 - B_0)(\Delta H \circ A_0^*)x_0\end{aligned} \tag{5.5}$$

where x is the output vector, the suffixes are period 0 and period 1, and Δx shows the increase in output from period 0 to period 1, and the suffixes are the period 0 and the period 1. The first item shows the change in output caused by a change in final demand. The third item shows the change in output caused by a change in the technological coefficient. The fifth item shows the change in output caused by a change in domestic intermediate inputs. The second, fourth, and sixth items are the output changes caused by the residual. Therefore, the output can be divided into eight factors: consumption, investment, government spending, export, import, technological change, domestic intermediate inputs, and the residual.

$$\begin{aligned}\Delta x = & B_0(\Delta y^{con} + \Delta y^{inv} + \Delta y^{gov}) + B_0\Delta f^{ex} - B_0\Delta f^{im} + B_0(H_0 \circ \Delta A^*)x_0 \\ & + B_0(\Delta H \circ A_0^*)x_0 + RES\end{aligned} \tag{5.6}$$

where RES is the residual. Furthermore, dividing each item by output x at period 0, we obtain the contribution of each components to output growth. The advantage of this framework is the fact that this makes us to consider the transformation of growth regime on the basis of the analysis of changes in these components.

Next, the linkage from demand growth to productivity growth is another major causal chain in the growth regime. An increase in investment leads to an increase in productivity through the replacement of capital equipment. This effect is more remarkable in the manufacturing industry than in the service industry with the dynamics of introducing new capital equipments and scrapping old capital equipments. Furthermore, an increase in demand leads to productivity growth through increasing return to scale especially in the manufacturing industry. This effect is often called the "Kaldor-Verdoorn Law" (Kaldor 1978; Boyer and Petit 1991). In addition, innovation contributes to productivity growth, depending on the social system of innovation in each national and regional economy (Amable et al. 1997). In summary, these linkages from demand growth to productivity growth are called "the productivity regime" in the framework of the *régulation* theory (Boyer 1988).

$$\Delta\lambda = f(\Delta x) \tag{5.7}$$

As for the linkages between the manufacturing and the service industries, which are reflected by the input coefficient matrix A, the following theoretical points are usually noted in the study of de-industrialization (Petit 1986). First, cumulative causation between output growth and productivity growth operates strongly in the manufacturing industry. Second, the manufacturing industry has its own "subsystem dynamics" (Landesmann and Scazzieri 1996) and causes changes in the linkage between the manufacturing industry and the business-related service industry with the externalization of business activities, which are reflected by the technological coefficient matrix A^*. Third, the spillover effect of intermediate demand for both domestic and international production linkages of the manufacturing and service industries contributes to output growth and productivity growth in those industries.

The dynamism of output growth and productivity growth determines employment growth in the national economy, which provides a basic framework of structural change and de-industrialization in terms of employment (Pasinetti 1981).

$$\widehat{N} = \widehat{x} - \widehat{\lambda} \tag{5.8}$$

where $\widehat{N}$ is the vector of employment growth rates ($\widehat{N}_i = \Delta N_i / N_i$), $\widehat{x}$ is the vector of output growth rates ($\widehat{x}_i = \Delta x_i / x_i$), and $\widehat{\lambda}$ is the vector of productivity growth rates ($\widehat{\lambda}_i = \Delta \lambda_i / \lambda_i$).

Therefore, in a matured national economy in which the share of agricultural employment has become very small, de-industrialization occurs in terms of the relative share of employment when the growth rate of real output minus the growth rate of productivity in the service industry is greater than that in the manufacturing industry. This dynamic pattern was first formalized by W. Baumol and was applied to the process of de-industrialization in R. Rowthorn's de-industrialization model (Baumol 1967; Rowthorn and Wells 1987). De-industrialization increases service employment with a skill bifurcation, depending on the institutional characteristics of the labor market, and this shift of employment influences the transformation of the social welfare system (Emmengger et al. 2012).

Furthermore, international trade and foreign direct investment have important effects on de-industrialization in many countries in the process of regional integration. Trade specialization between manufactured goods and services, which is influenced by the international division of labor and production linkages, determines the dynamism of industrial structural change in national economies, influenced by the exchange rate system. For example, the export goods manufacturing industry could be a starting point of "cumulative causation," producing tradable products with increasing returns to scale. On the contrary, if the national economy depends heavily on the export of natural resources, this may exacerbate long-term economic stagnation. The pattern of trade specialization in regional integration causes either a "virtuous circle" or a "vicious circle" with the conflicts of interest among various industrial sectors. Foreign direct investment can have both the positive effect of promoting the international division of labor in the region and the negative effect of accelerating de-industrialization in the national economy.

5.2.2 Four Types of De-industrialization in the Open Economy

The conditions for de-industrialization in terms of employment are usually explained by focusing on the difference between the growth rate of real output and that of labor productivity (Baumol 1967; Rowthorn and Wells 1987). In this study, we focus on the interdependent industrial structures between the manufacturing and service sectors in the open economy framework and define four types of de-industrialization.

The first type is "positive de-industrialization," in which the growth differentials of labor productivity between the manufacturing sector and the service sector bring about a shift in employment from the manufacturing sector to the service sector. Labor productivity is influenced by the international division of labor. The second type is "negative de-industrialization," which is caused by decreasing demand and stagnant output in the manufacturing sector in the open economy. These two types were formalized originally by Rowthorn and Wells (1987). The third type is "de-industrialization through manufacturing-service linkages," which is brought about by an increase in intermediate inputs from the business-related service industry to the manufacturing industry, inducing an increase in employment in the business-related service industry. This was formalized by Petit (1986). This type of de-industrialization also happens with the international division of labor in the interdependence of growth regimes. The fourth type is "de-industrialization by the shift of final demand to the service sector," which includes the long-term changes in final demand structures driven by the transformation in the international division of labor and economic interdependence. These four types of de-industrialization are summarized in Table 5.1.

Table 5.1 Four types of de-industrialization in the open economy

	Output		Labor productivity		Employment	
	Manufacturing	Service	Manufacturing	Service	Manufacturing	Service
Positive de-industrialization	Increase or constant	–	Considerably increase	–	Constant or decrease	Increase
Negative de-industrialization	Decrease	–	–	–	Decrease	Increase
De-industrialization through manufacturing-service linkages	Increase	Increase	–	–	–	Increase
De-industrialization by the shift of final demand to the service sector	–	Increase	–	–	Decrease	Increase

Note: (–) shows that the direction cannot be determined

5.3 Patterns of Regional Interdependence in Europe and East Asia

Different growth regimes are interdependent on each other through the trade of final and intermediate goods/services in regional integration. In particular, the international division of labor and economic interdependence are evolving in the processes of regional integration in Europe and East Asian, where the patterns of regional integration have influenced growth regimes and de-industrialization. We analyze the evolving pattern of regional integration in Europe and East Asia by investigating the trade of both final goods/services and intermediate goods/services, using World Input-Output Database (WIOD).[2] We analyze changes in trade patterns between 1995 and 2014, as shown in Table 5.2. The patterns and changes in international economic interdependence can be clearly identified for both the EU and East Asia.

In Europe, the pattern of interdependence of capitalisms is relatively stable among EU member countries over the 20 years. In both 1995 and 2014, Germany was a key player in the trade of final and intermediate goods in the single European market. In particular, Germany created stronger ties in final goods trade with other EU member countries after the Euro was introduced as a single currency in the process of European integration. This caused more trade imbalance between Germany and southern European countries.

In East Asia, interdependence through the intermediate goods trade has been intensified among major Asian economies over the same 20-year period. Furthermore, the pattern of the international division of labor has also changed very drastically due to the rapid growth of the Chinese economy. In 1995, Japan was a key player in the supply of intermediate goods to other Asian countries, especially China. By 2014, however, China was supplying not only final goods but also intermediate goods to other Asian countries and was importing final goods from other countries. Therefore, China with the rapidly growing market has become the center of Asian economic integration. This may influence industrial structural changes and de-industrialization in the Japanese economy.

Furthermore, looking at the interdependence among the EU, East Asia, and the USA, East Asian economies have established their own international division of labor and have become relatively independent of the EU member countries over the 20-year period. Even in this transformation of relatively independent regional interdependence, however, both intermediate and final goods trade have been stronger between Germany and China as the market has expanded rapidly in China. This may impose competitive pressure on the German economy and, in turn, may influence the economies of other EU member countries such as France, Italy, and Spain.

[2]As for the study of the patterns of regional integration by using WIOD, Baldwin and Lopez-Gonzalez (2013) is an important foundation.

Table 5.2 Interdependence in trade in Europe and East Asia

Input Coefficient Matrix in WIOD, 1995

Supply/Demand	Japan	South Korea	China	Taiwan	Indonesia	India	US	UK	France	Germany	Italy	Other EU countries	LOW
Japan	0.446	0.018	0.010	0.033	0.018	0.004	0.004	0.004	0.002	0.002	0.001	0.002	0.013
South Korea	0.002	0.445	0.006	0.007	0.008	0.001	0.001	0.001	0.001	0.001	0.001	0.001	0.003
China	0.001	0.005	0.559	0.004	0.004	0.002	0.001	0.001	0.000	0.001	0.001	0.001	0.002
Taiwan	0.001	0.002	0.006	0.391	0.003	0.000	0.001	0.001	0.000	0.001	0.000	0.001	0.002
Indonesia	0.001	0.002	0.002	0.003	0.389	0.001	0.000	0.001	0.000	0.000	0.001	0.000	0.001
India	0.000	0.000	0.000	0.001	0.001	0.446	0.000	0.001	0.000	0.000	0.001	0.000	0.001
US	0.004	0.017	0.005	0.025	0.007	0.003	0.413	0.010	0.008	0.005	0.005	0.009	0.030
UK	0.000	0.002	0.002	0.003	0.003	0.002	0.002	0.394	0.005	0.005	0.004	0.009	0.005
France	0.000	0.001	0.001	0.002	0.003	0.001	0.002	0.007	0.401	0.006	0.009	0.010	0.005
Germany	0.001	0.004	0.002	0.008	0.007	0.004	0.002	0.013	0.012	0.377	0.012	0.023	0.008
Italy	0.000	0.001	0.001	0.002	0.001	0.001	0.001	0.004	0.006	0.005	0.419	0.006	0.004
Other EU countries	0.001	0.005	0.003	0.012	0.008	0.006	0.003	0.023	0.019	0.025	0.017	0.406	0.010
LOW	0.010	0.032	0.015	0.039	0.019	0.020	0.017	0.016	0.013	0.014	0.019	0.023	0.387
Total imput	0.468	0.536	0.611	0.531	0.472	0.490	0.447	0.474	0.467	0.443	0.490	0.492	0.469
Value added	0.532	0.464	0.389	0.469	0.528	0.510	0.553	0.526	0.533	0.557	0.510	0.508	0.531

Note: Cells with a value ≧0.005 are shadowed.
Source: WIOD2016

Input Coefficient Matrix in WIOD, 2014

Supply/Demand	Japan	South Korea	China	Taiwan	Indonesia	India	US	UK	France	Germany	Italy	Other EU countries	LOW
Japan	0.411	0.014	0.003	0.029	0.008	0.002	0.002	0.001	0.001	0.002	0.001	0.001	0.004
South Korea	0.004	0.468	0.004	0.016	0.006	0.002	0.001	0.001	0.000	0.001	0.001	0.001	0.004
China	0.008	0.022	0.629	0.027	0.013	0.006	0.004	0.004	0.004	0.006	0.004	0.007	0.015
Taiwan	0.002	0.003	0.003	0.374	0.002	0.001	0.001	0.001	0.000	0.001	0.000	0.001	0.002
Indonesia	0.002	0.003	0.001	0.006	0.398	0.002	0.000	0.000	0.000	0.000	0.000	0.001	0.002
India	0.000	0.001	0.000	0.002	0.002	0.395	0.001	0.001	0.001	0.001	0.001	0.001	0.003
US	0.005	0.009	0.002	0.010	0.003	0.003	0.393	0.008	0.008	0.007	0.003	0.014	0.017
UK	0.001	0.002	0.000	0.001	0.000	0.002	0.002	0.385	0.007	0.005	0.003	0.009	0.004
France	0.001	0.001	0.001	0.001	0.001	0.001	0.001	0.007	0.373	0.008	0.007	0.010	0.003
Germany	0.001	0.004	0.002	0.005	0.001	0.002	0.002	0.011	0.016	0.371	0.013	0.027	0.006
Italy	0.000	0.001	0.000	0.001	0.001	0.001	0.001	0.003	0.008	0.006	0.425	0.006	0.002
Other EU countries	0.002	0.004	0.001	0.005	0.002	0.002	0.003	0.023	0.028	0.055	0.024	0.393	0.015
LOW	0.045	0.066	0.027	0.088	0.050	0.053	0.027	0.025	0.025	0.025	0.027	0.045	0.457
Total imput	0.482	0.599	0.672	0.563	0.487	0.471	0.438	0.469	0.472	0.488	0.510	0.514	0.535
Value added	0.518	0.401	0.328	0.437	0.513	0.529	0.562	0.531	0.528	0.512	0.490	0.486	0.465

Note: Cells with a value ≧0.005 are shadowed.
Source: WIOD2016

Trade Matrix of Final Goods and Services in WIOD, 1995

Supply/Demand	Japan	South Korea	China	Taiwan	Indonesia	India	US	UK	France	Germany	Italy	Other EU countries	LOW	Total
Japan	96.4%	0.2%	0.2%	0.2%	0.0%	0.0%	1.1%	0.1%	0.1%	0.2%	0.0%	0.2%	1.2%	100.0%
South Korea	1.7%	89.6%	0.4%	0.2%	0.2%	0.1%	2.5%	0.3%	0.2%	0.5%	0.1%	0.6%	3.5%	100.0%
China	2.4%	0.2%	87.9%	0.1%	0.1%	0.1%	3.9%	0.6%	0.3%	0.0%	0.2%	0.8%	2.5%	100.0%
Taiwan	3.5%	0.2%	1.4%	80.5%	0.2%	0.1%	6.4%	0.5%	0.3%	1.1%	0.2%	1.0%	4.6%	100.0%
Indonesia	1.6%	0.1%	0.1%	0.1%	93.5%	0.0%	2.0%	0.3%	0.2%	0.5%	0.3%	0.4%	0.9%	100.0%
India	0.4%	0.0%	0.0%	0.0%	0.0%	95.4%	1.2%	0.4%	0.2%	0.6%	0.3%	0.5%	1.0%	100.0%
US	0.4%	0.1%	0.1%	0.1%	0.0%	0.0%	96.7%	0.1%	0.1%	0.2%	0.1%	0.2%	1.9%	100.0%
UK	0.5%	0.1%	0.2%	0.1%	0.1%	0.1%	1.5%	89.1%	1.0%	1.3%	0.6%	2.8%	2.7%	100.0%
France	0.4%	0.1%	0.2%	0.1%	0.0%	0.0%	0.7%	0.8%	90.3%	1.6%	0.8%	2.2%	2.8%	100.0%
Germany	0.4%	0.1%	0.2%	0.1%	0.1%	0.1%	0.9%	0.8%	0.9%	89.6%	0.8%	3.1%	2.8%	100.0%
Italy	0.5%	0.2%	0.2%	0.1%	0.0%	0.1%	1.2%	0.7%	1.4%	2.0%	88.1%	2.4%	3.1%	100.0%
Other EU countries	0.4%	0.2%	0.1%	0.1%	0.1%	0.1%	0.9%	1.3%	1.5%	3.1%	0.9%	88.4%	2.9%	100.0%
LOW	0.6%	0.1%	0.1%	0.1%	0.1%	0.0%	2.0%	0.3%	0.3%	0.6%	0.2%	0.6%	94.2%	100.0%
Total	17.6%	1.7%	2.4%	0.9%	0.8%	1.3%	25.8%	3.7%	4.9%	7.9%	3.6%	8.9%	20.4%	100.0%

Note: Cells with a value ≧1.0% are shadowed.
Source: WIOD2016

Trade Matrix of Final Goods and Services in WIOD, 2014

Supply/Demand	Japan	South Korea	China	Taiwan	Indonesia	India	US	UK	France	Germany	Italy	Other EU countries	LOW	Total
Japan	92.9%	0.2%	1.0%	0.2%	0.1%	0.0%	1.3%	0.1%	0.1%	0.2%	0.0%	0.2%	3.8%	100.0%
South Korea	1.0%	80.9%	3.8%	0.3%	0.2%	0.2%	2.5%	0.3%	0.1%	0.3%	0.1%	1.0%	9.4%	100.0%
China	1.0%	0.3%	88.5%	0.1%	0.1%	0.2%	2.1%	0.3%	0.2%	0.4%	0.1%	0.7%	6.0%	100.0%
Taiwan	1.0%	0.2%	5.4%	82.5%	0.1%	0.2%	2.0%	0.4%	0.1%	0.5%	0.1%	0.6%	6.8%	100.0%
Indonesia	0.6%	0.2%	0.4%	0.1%	93.7%	0.1%	1.4%	0.1%	0.1%	0.2%	0.1%	0.3%	2.7%	100.0%
India	0.1%	0.0%	0.3%	0.0%	0.0%	92.9%	0.7%	0.3%	0.1%	0.1%	0.1%	0.3%	5.0%	100.0%
US	0.1%	0.1%	0.3%	0.0%	0.0%	0.0%	96.2%	0.2%	0.1%	0.2%	0.0%	0.3%	2.5%	100.0%
UK	0.1%	0.1%	0.5%	0.0%	0.0%	0.0%	1.2%	90.3%	0.5%	0.7%	0.3%	1.8%	4.5%	100.0%
France	0.2%	0.2%	0.5%	0.1%	0.0%	0.1%	0.7%	0.9%	88.2%	1.6%	0.7%	2.4%	4.3%	100.0%
Germany	0.4%	0.3%	1.9%	0.1%	0.1%	0.2%	2.0%	1.4%	1.5%	79.4%	0.9%	5.4%	6.5%	100.0%
Italy	0.2%	0.2%	0.6%	0.0%	0.0%	0.1%	1.2%	0.8%	1.1%	1.5%	86.9%	2.5%	4.8%	100.0%
Other EU countries	0.2%	0.1%	0.5%	0.1%	0.0%	0.1%	1.0%	1.5%	1.4%	3.0%	0.9%	84.5%	6.9%	100.0%
LOW	0.4%	0.2%	0.7%	0.1%	0.1%	0.1%	2.3%	0.3%	0.3%	0.5%	0.2%	0.9%	94.0%	100.0%
Total	6.0%	1.6%	13.0%	0.6%	1.2%	2.8%	23.7%	3.7%	3.5%	4.3%	2.6%	7.9%	29.0%	100.0%

Note: Cells with a value ≧1.0% are shadowed.
Source: WIOD2016

5.4 Evolving Diversity of Growth Regimes and De-industrialization in EU and Japan

5.4.1 Varieties of Capitalism and Growth Pattern

De-industrialization has proceeded along with the transformation of growth regime in most advanced countries since the 1970s. After the 1990s, it accelerated in some countries owing to financial globalization and the deepening international division of labor. De-industrialization has shown different features in different varieties of capitalism, depending on the institutional arrangements and international economic relations (Hall and Soskice 2001; Amable 2003; Harada 2007).

According to a study on the EU by Robert Boyer (see Chap. 2 in this book), four types of growth regime in European capitalisms can be identified: “finance-led accumulation capitalism” (UK), “export- and innovation-led capitalism” (Germany, Sweden), “consumption-led capitalism” (France, Italy, Greece), and “hybrid regime, price taker, and export and consumption-led capitalism” (Spain). Furthermore, Harada and Tohyama (2012) also classified five types of Asian capitalism: “innovation-led capitalism” (Japan, Korea, Taiwan), “city capitalism” (Singapore, Hong Kong), “trade-led industrializing capitalism” (Thailand, Malaysia), “insular semi-agrarian capitalism” (Indonesia, the Philippines), and “continental mixed capitalism” (China).

These different types of capitalism have different institutional arrangements and institutional complementarity in the production systems, wage-labor nexus, the financial system sector, and social protection. Taking account of the typology, our comparative analysis of de-industrialization focuses on advanced countries with different types of advanced capitalism, as follows: Germany (export and innovation-led capitalism) and France (consumption-led capitalism), Italy (consumption-led capitalism), the UK (finance-led accumulation capitalism), and Japan (export and innovation-led capitalism). We investigate how different varieties of capitalism with different institutional arrangements and international economic relations show different patterns of de-industrialization.

We review the dynamic patterns of growth regimes in these advances economies. Figures 5.2 and 5.3 show the real growth rates and unemployment rates in Germany,

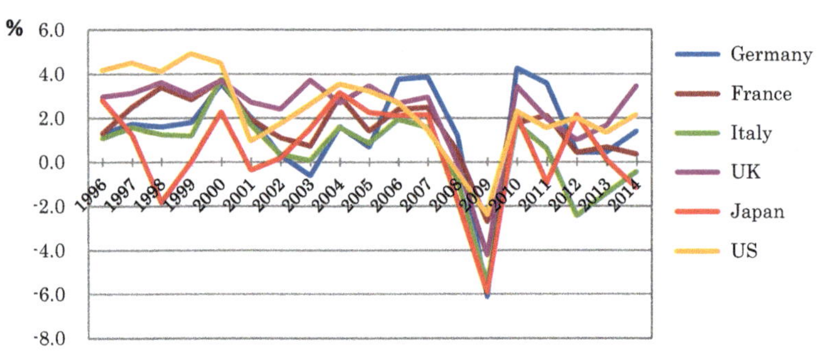

Fig. 5.2 Growth rates of real GDP. (Source: WIOD 2016 and WIOD 2013)

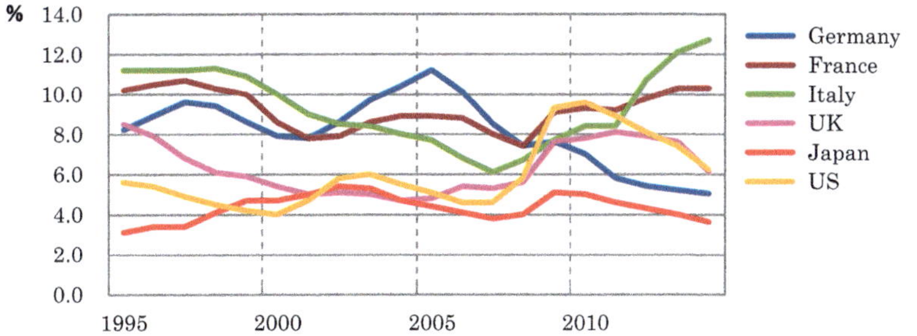

Fig. 5.3 Unemployment rate. (Source: Eurostat)

Table 5.3 Industrial classification for the analysis of de-industrialization

1	Agriculture	Agriculture, forestry, fisheries, livestock and sericulture farming
2	Export core manufacturing	Transportation equipment, general machinery, electronic and electrical equipment, etc. (export/output ratio is more than 20% in each country)
3	Other manufacturing	Other manufacturing industries than the export core
4	Other industries	Construction, electricity and gas, water supply, mining
5	Financial services	Financial and insurance services
6	Business-related services	Rental of office equipment's and goods, advertisement, information services and internet-based services, wholesale, research and development, telegraph and telephone, mail, transportation
7	Consumer services	Retail, insurance, real estate, broadcasting, entertainment, eating and drinking places, accommodation
8	Public services	Public administration, education, medical, hygiene

France, Italy, the UK, Japan, and the USA. De-industrialization has occurred in all of these advanced countries.

To investigate the pattern of de-industrialization, we use the detailed classification of industrial sectors, shown in Table 5.3, in which "the export core manufacturing" industry is defined as that with more than 20% of exports per unit of output in each country.

Following the industrial classification outlined in Table 5.3, the employment shares of "export core manufacturing," "financial services," "business-related services," "consumer services," and "public services" are seen for Germany, France, Italy, the UK, Japan, and the US in Table 5.4.

The ratio of "export core manufacturing" is very high in Germany, which is a core EU exporter. By contrast, the ratio of "financial services" is relatively high in the UK and the US, which are typical "market-based capitalism" or "finance-led capitalism" countries, where financialization has proceeded very rapidly. In this regard, the growth pattern in each country is reflected in its type of capitalism and pattern of de-industrialization. The ratio of "business-related services" has been high in the UK and France and has been increasing in Germany and Japan. According to Franke and

Table 5.4 Employment share of industries, 2009

		Germany	France	Italy	UK	Japan	US
1	Agliculture	2.1	3.0	3.9	1.7	4.9	1.4
2	Export core manufacturing	13.7	5.2	9.5	5.8	4.9	2.8
3	Other manufacturing	2.7	5.4	7.7	3.4	9.7	5.4
4	Other industries	6.6	8.3	9.7	7.7	9.7	6.4
5	Financial services	3.0	3.2	2.6	5.3	2.4	4.1
6	Business-related services	24.6	25.2	21.8	25.0	22.4	21.0
7	Consumer services	18.5	15.4	21.9	19.5	18.2	21.7
8	Public services	28.8	34.2	22.9	31.7	27.8	37.2

Source: WIOD 2013

Kalmbach (2004) and Uemura and Tahara (2014, 2017), "export core manufacturing" and "business-related services" have very strong linkages in Germany and Japan.[3] Both countries are the "coordinated market economy (CME)" (Hall and Soskice 2001), or examples of "export- and innovation-led capitalism." When analyzed more closely, however, they have different institutional arrangements and are different types of capitalism, even though they show rather similar patterns of de-industrialization. Furthermore, the ratio of "public services" is relatively high in the USA and France and has been increasing very rapidly in Japan. The "public services" play the role of employment absorber in the process of de-industrialization (Iversen and Cusack 2000). A "negative de-industrialization" is often compensated for by the expansion of "public services," which causes the political problem of increasing public debt.

5.4.2 *Comparative Analysis of Growth Regimes and De-industrialization*

Before conducting a comparative analysis of de-industrialization across national economies, we review our framework of analysis which integrates quantitative analyses of growth regime and de-industrialization. From Eqs. (5.6) and (5.8), we obtain the structural relations which are used in our analysis.

[3]De-industrialization has also occurred with "business-related services" in South Korea (export- and innovation-led capitalism). For the Korean pattern of de-industrialization, see Ok (2016). This study examines the determining factor of de-industrialization in Korea, focusing on the increase in service intermediate outsourcing for the purpose of cost-saving, which has a negative productivity effect on the Korean economy. Therefore, a comparative analysis of de-industrialization among the German, Japanese, and Korean patterns is an interesting research topic. As for the Japanese pattern, see Tahara (2009, 2010), Tahara and Uemura (2014), Uemura and Tahara (2014).

Table 5.5 Variables and symbols

Variable	Symbol
Growth rate of real output	*RX*
Contribution of domestic final demand	*DFD*
Contribution of export	*Ex*
Contribution of import	*Im*
Contribution of technological coefficient	*Tech*
Contribution of domestic input	*DIn*
Residual	*Re*
Growth rate of employment	*Em*
Growth rate of labor productivity	*LP*

(the growth rate of real output) = *(the contribution of domestic final demand)* + *(the contribution of export)* − *(the contribution of import)* + *(the contribution of technological coefficient)* + *(the contribution of domestic input)* + *(residual)*

(the growth rate of employment) = *(the growth rate of real output)* − *(the growth rate of labor productivity)*

In the tables that show the results of our analysis, we use the following symbols for these components as shown in Table 5.5.

Based on these equations, a comparative analysis of de-industrialization is conducted for the UK, Germany, France, Italy, and Japan. The period of analysis is from 1995 to 2014, conditioned by the data limitations of the WIOD.[4] During this period, the Euro was established as a single currency for most EU countries in 1999, resulting in a large trade imbalance between Germany ("export- and innovation-led capitalism") and Italy ("consumption-led capitalism"), amplifying the heterogeneity of the Eurozone economies. The subprime crisis hit all the European economics in 2008, followed by the Euro crisis in 2011. The Euro crisis exacerbated the sovereign debt crises in southern European economies, causing governance problems for European integration (Boyer 2013). The subprime crisis also affected the Japanese economy, which was also damaged by the Great East Japan Earthquake in 2011 (see Fig. 5.2). Amid these events, Japanese firms have been shifting their productive activities to other East Asian countries.

In what follows, the results of the analysis of growth regimes and the pattern of de-industrialization are explained for Germany, France, Italy, the UK and Japan in reference to their specific institutional arrangements to respond to economic fluctuations and crises.

[4]The WIOD data are calculated in dollars, so we convert them into data in real terms. The conversion procedures are explained in the Appendix at the end of this paper.

5.4.2.1 Germany (Export and Innovation–Led Capitalism)

Germany has large firms and an institutionally coordinated system of employment and skill formation in a strong manufacturing sector with high competitiveness and exports final and intermediate goods to other EU member countries and to the rest of the world. The dynamic pattern is a core in Germany's growth regime (Table 5.6).

1995–2000 (European Integration Proceeded) Led by a large increase in export demand, "the export core manufacturing" industry realized high rates of output growth and productivity growth, thus exhibiting overall cumulative growth. As a result, employment decreased only slightly and very weak "positive de-industrialization" occurred. Furthermore, growth in "the business-related services" occurred mainly through the technological coefficient effect, leading to increased employment. Therefore, the German economy exhibited "de-industrialization through manufacturing-service linkages," which corresponds to the analysis of Franke and Kalmbach (2005).

2000–2005 (After the Euro Was Introduced) After the Euro was introduced as a single currency in 1999, export demand increased continuously though this was counterbalanced by imports of final and intermediate goods in Germany. Therefore, "the export core manufacturing" industry showed high growth rates, and "positive de-industrialization" occurred in the German economy. Moreover, growth in "consumer services" was weak due to the low level of consumption, and "public services" absorbed employment, putting pressure on the German welfare state.

2005–2010 (Hit by the Subprime Crisis) The "export core manufacturing" industry, hit by the subprime crisis, showed negative growth, which is exceptional in the German economy. At the same time, output fell in "the other manufacturing" industry, mainly due to a decrease in consumption. Therefore, "negative de-industrialization" occurred in Germany in this period. Even in this situation, however, "business-related services" retained a sufficient employment-absorption capacity by absorbing workers released from the manufacturing sector. This reduced unemployment even during the economic recession (see Fig. 5.2 and Fig. 5.3).

2010–2014 (During the Euro Crisis) The Euro crisis happened during this period. Even during the crisis, the German economy performed very well and showed positive growth in all sectors except agriculture. Both labor productivity and employment increased in "the export core manufacturing," "other manufacturing," and "other industries," so de-industrialization ceased during this period. The main factor in the increased output in those sectors was export, especially export to other EU member countries. On the contrary, in "financial services," output growth declined, and this caused a decrease in employment in the sector during the Euro crisis. Even in this situation, "business-related services" still absorbed employment.

Table 5.6 Growth regime and de-industrialization in Germany: annual growth rate of components (%)

Germany			RX	DFD	Ex	Im	Tech	DIn	Re	Em	LP		RX	DFD	Ex	Im	Tech	DIn	Re	Em	LP
1995–2000	1	Agliculture	1.8	2.3	3.0	−3.4	1.5	−1.5	−0.2	−2.8	4.6	2000–2005	−0.2	−1.3	2.2	−1.4	0.5	−0.2	0.0	−2.5	2.3
	2	Export core	4.4	2.1	6.3	−5.0	3.0	−1.7	−0.2	−0.8	5.2		1.7	−0.8	4.2	−1.4	0.6	−0.8	−0.1	−1.6	3.2
	3	Other Manu.	0.5	1.4	2.6	−2.6	0.7	−1.3	−0.2	−0.5	1.1		0.9	−0.9	2.3	−0.5	0.1	0.0	−0.1	−1.5	2.3
	4	Other in.	−1.0	−0.2	1.2	−2.1	2.2	−1.1	−0.9	−3.3	2.4		−2.0	−2.7	1.2	−1.2	2.0	−0.8	−0.5	−4.2	2.2
	5	Financial S.	6.3	5.9	2.8	−2.3	0.7	−0.8	0.0	0.3	5.9		−0.1	−0.2	0.8	−0.4	0.0	−0.2	−0.1	−0.4	0.3
	6	Business S.	4.3	1.2	2.7	−2.7	3.7	−1.0	0.3	3.2	1.1		2.5	−0.2	2.7	−0.9	1.3	−0.3	0.0	1.1	1.4
	7	Consumer S.	1.9	1.8	1.0	−1.2	0.9	−0.5	0.0	2.3	−0.4		0.6	0.1	0.6	−0.2	0.1	−0.1	0.0	0.1	0.4
	8	Public S.	2.1	1.7	0.2	−0.3	0.6	−0.1	0.0	1.3	0.8		1.1	0.7	0.1	0.0	0.2	0.1	0.0	0.6	0.5
2005–2010	1	Agliculture	−1.0	−1.9	2.2	−2.5	3.9	−2.5	−0.3	−0.2	−0.8	2010–2014	−4.1	−1.9	1.6	0.6	−3.5	−0.6	−0.3	−0.4	−3.7
	2	Export core	1.1	0.5	3.4	−2.2	2.2	−2.4	−0.3	−0.3	1.4		2.3	0.5	3.8	−1.8	1.0	−1.1	−0.2	1.8	0.5
	3	Other Manu.	−0.2	−0.4	1.7	−1.7	1.3	−1.1	0.0	−0.3	0.1		1.2	0.8	2.3	−1.4	0.3	−0.7	−0.1	0.6	0.6
	4	Other in.	2.9	0.1	0.4	−0.6	2.9	−0.2	0.3	0.3	2.6		0.5	1.2	1.5	0.1	−2.0	−0.2	−0.2	1.0	−0.5
	5	Financial S.	2.1	1.3	1.9	−1.0	0.6	−0.6	−0.1	−0.7	2.9		1.8	1.7	1.1	−0.8	0.3	−0.4	−0.1	−0.3	2.0
	6	Business S.	2.6	2.2	2.0	−2.4	2.3	−1.6	0.0	2.0	0.6		1.3	1.1	2.2	−1.8	1.2	−1.2	−0.2	1.7	−0.3
	7	Consumer S.	1.1	0.5	0.5	−0.4	0.8	−0.3	0.0	0.6	0.4		0.1	0.0	0.8	−0.5	0.2	−0.3	0.0	0.7	−0.6
	8	Public S.	2.4	1.9	0.1	−0.1	0.4	0.0	0.1	1.3	1.2		1.3	1.2	0.2	−0.2	0.3	−0.2	−0.1	0.7	0.5

Source: WIOD 2016 and WIOD 2013

RX Real output, *DFD* Domestic final demand, *Ex* Export, *Im* Import, *Tech* Technology, *DIn* Domestic input, *Re* Residual, *Em* Employment, *LP* Labor productivity

5.4.2.2 France (Consumption–Led Capitalism)

France has various kinds of manufacturing industries and a relatively competitive agricultural sector. It also has strong institutional regulations governing wages and unemployment assistance in the labor market. Consumption and public spending often support demand formation in France's growth regime (Table 5.7).

1995–2000 (European Integration Proceeded) In France, export demand was very strong in "the export core manufacturing" industry, and "the other manufacturing" industry generated high rates of output and productivity growth and thus cumulative growth. As a result, employment decreased only slightly, and very weak "positive de-industrialization" occurred. Furthermore, the growth of "the business-related services" occurred mainly by an increase in final demand as well as technological coefficient effects, which led to an increase in employment. In other words, "de-industrialization through manufacturing-service linkages" was weaker in France than in Germany. Furthermore, "public services" supported by sufficient consumption demand absorbed employees in the French welfare state.

2000–2005 (After the Euro Was Introduced) Even after the establishment of the Euro in 1999, export demand remained high, although it was counterbalanced by large volumes of imports of final and intermediate goods. Therefore, "the export core manufacturing" industry showed high growth rates, and "positive de-industrialization" occurred. All the service industries, "financial services," "business-related services," "consumer services," and "public services" were supported by sufficient consumption and continued to absorb employment in France.

2005–2010 (Hit by the Subprime Crisis) The effect of the subprime crisis was relatively mild in France, and "the export core manufacturing" industry and "the other manufacturing" industry maintained positive growth rates. Therefore, in those industries, "positive de-industrialization" continued with a slightly increased unemployment rate (see Fig. 5.3). At the same time, "agriculture" maintained competitiveness due to an increase in domestic consumption demand and export demand, showing relatively high growth rates of output and labor productivity. This pattern in the agriculture industry is a typical feature in France.

2010–2014 (During the Euro Crisis) Employment decreased in "export core manufacturing," "other manufacturing," and "other industries" due to a sharp decrease in domestic final and intermediate demand in the Euro crisis. In this situation, "negative de-industrialization" proceeded in "other manufacturing" and "other industries." Employment that was released by the manufacturing sector was partly absorbed by both private and public service sectors.

Table 5.7 Growth regime and de-industrialization in France: annual growth rate of components (%)

France			RX	DFD	Ex	Im	Tech	DIn	Re	Em	LP		RX	DFD	Ex	Im	Tech	DIn	Re	Em	LP
1995–2000	1	Agliculture	2.9	3.0	2.6	−2.3	0.2	−0.1	−0.5	−1.8	4.7	2000–2005	−0.6	0.6	0.5	−1.0	0.1	−0.7	−0.1	−1.4	0.8
	2	Export core	8.7	5.8	9.0	−8.0	3.9	−1.8	−0.2	−0.7	9.5		0.4	1.4	2.3	−2.9	3.6	−3.4	−0.7	−2.6	2.9
	3	Other Manu.	7.1	4.7	3.7	−3.7	2.8	−0.2	0.0	0.1	7.1		0.0	1.1	0.9	−1.6	1.0	−1.4	−0.2	−0.9	0.9
	4	Other in.	−3.3	0.4	1.4	−2.6	0.0	−1.5	−1.1	−0.2	−3.1		2.7	2.1	0.4	−1.1	2.5	−1.0	−0.1	2.0	0.7
	5	Financial S.	3.7	1.6	1.3	−1.0	1.3	0.4	0.1	−0.2	3.9		3.4	2.5	0.4	−0.7	1.6	−0.5	0.0	1.4	2.1
	6	Business S.	4.6	4.3	3.0	−2.8	1.2	−0.7	−0.4	3.8	0.7		3.1	2.2	0.6	−1.0	2.0	−0.8	0.0	1.3	1.7
	7	Consumer S.	3.4	3.3	1.0	−1.0	0.4	−0.2	−0.1	1.5	1.9		1.9	1.7	0.2	−0.2	0.5	−0.2	0.0	0.7	1.2
	8	Public S.	1.9	2.1	0.2	−0.4	0.1	−0.1	−0.1	1.5	0.4		1.3	1.4	0.0	−0.1	0.0	−0.1	0.0	0.6	0.7
2005–2010	1	Agliculture	−0.2	−1.2	0.7	−0.1	1.1	−0.6	−0.1	−2.7	2.5	2010–2014	1.3	0.5	0.9	−1.1	1.8	−0.7	−0.1	−0.1	1.4
	2	Export core	−1.8	−1.7	−0.7	−0.6	1.0	0.3	−0.2	−3.6	1.8		0.8	0.4	3.0	−2.8	4.7	−3.6	−0.8	−1.0	1.8
	3	Other Manu.	−1.2	−1.0	−0.2	−0.3	0.5	−0.1	−0.1	−1.9	0.7		−0.7	−0.1	1.1	−1.5	1.3	−1.3	−0.2	−1.0	0.3
	4	Other in.	0.9	−0.3	−0.1	0.2	0.6	0.7	−0.1	2.0	−1.1		−0.9	−0.5	0.5	0.1	−0.6	−0.2	−0.1	−0.7	−0.2
	5	Financial S.	3.5	−0.1	1.1	−0.6	3.1	−0.2	0.2	0.5	3.0		1.1	0.7	0.6	−0.7	1.2	−0.5	−0.1	0.6	0.5
	6	Business S.	1.1	0.8	1.2	−1.4	1.4	−0.8	−0.1	0.6	0.6		1.7	0.7	1.9	−1.6	2.1	−1.2	−0.1	0.9	0.8
	7	Consumer S.	1.4	2.5	−0.2	−0.3	−0.4	−0.2	0.0	1.3	0.1		0.7	0.9	0.3	−0.4	0.3	−0.3	0.0	0.5	0.1
	8	Public S.	1.3	1.4	0.0	−0.1	0.0	0.0	0.0	0.7	0.6		1.3	1.2	0.1	−0.1	0.3	−0.1	0.0	0.6	0.8

Source: WIOD 2016 and WIOD 2013

RX Real output, *DFD* Domestic final demand, *Ex* Export, *Im* Import, *Tech* Technology, *DIn* Domestic input, *Re* Residual, *Em* Employment, *LP* Labor productivity

5.4.2.3 Italy (Consumption–Led Capitalism)

Italy has a large number of heterogeneous small- and medium-sized firms in the manufacturing and consumer service industries, which are supported by domestic consumption demand. The labor market is relatively inflexible, with many workers having diversified skills, and the manufacturing and service industries with low productivity play an important role in absorbing employment. These characterize Italy's growth regime (Table 5.8).

1995–2000 (European Integration Proceeded) Output growth continued in "the export core manufacturing" industry, "the other manufacturing" industry, and "the other industries," but productivity growth was not as high in these industries. Therefore, de-industrialization was mitigated by a sufficient output growth in the Italian economy. A remarkable feature of the Italian economy is low productivity growth in the manufacturing industry. While "financial services" and "business-related services" were expanding, productivity growth remained very low, especially in "business-related services."

2000–2005 (After the Euro Was Introduced) After the Euro was established as a single currency in 1999, "the export core manufacturing" industry lost its international competitiveness and exhibited negative growth rates. The main cause of this sharp decline was stagnant export demand and sharply increased imports. In this period, the transformation of the growth regime occurred alongside an increasing trade deficit in Italy. Under this condition, productivity growth was low in "the export core manufacturing" industry, and thus, a mildly "negative de-industrialization" proceeded in the Italian economy.[5]

2005–2010 (Hit by the Subprime Crisis) "The export core manufacturing" and "the other manufacturing" industries showed negative growth rates in output and labor productivity, and thus, a strongly "negative de-industrialization" occurred in the Italian economy. In this situation, workers were absorbed by "consumer services" and other private services, which are traditionally an employment sponge. Generally, the private service industries play an important role in absorbing employment in the Italian economy, even while causing a very sharp increase in the unemployment rate (see Fig. 5.3).

2010–2014 (During the Euro Crisis) The Euro crisis hit the Italian economy very strongly, and Italy's output growth rates became negative due to a sharp decrease in domestic final demand. Furthermore, the growth rates of productivity were negative in "other manufacturing" and "other industries." Employment declined sharply in "export core manufacturing," "other manufacturing," and "other industries,"

[5]After the Euro was established, the trade imbalance expanded between Germany and southern European counties expanded rapidly. In this situation, the Euro system made de-industrialization accelerate, causing severe unemployment problems, in the southern European economies (see Boyer 2013). De-industrialization has been influenced strongly by the currency system in Europe.

Table 5.8 Growth regime and de-industrialization in Italy: annual growth rate of components (%)

Italy			RX	DFD	Ex	Im	Tech	DIn	Re	Em	LP		RX	DFD	Ex	Im	Tech	DIn	Re	Em	LP
1995–2000	1	Agliculture	1.3	3.6	1.3	−1.7	−0.9	−0.6	−0.3	−3.5	4.8	2000–2005	−0.5	−0.2	0.6	−0.4	−0.7	0.2	−0.1	−1.3	0.8
	2	Export core	3.2	3.3	2.6	−3.6	1.4	−0.6	0.0	−0.5	3.7		0.1	0.5	0.8	−1.0	0.4	−0.6	0.0	−0.8	0.9
	3	Other Manu.	2.7	2.8	1.7	−2.1	0.9	−0.4	−0.1	0.2	2.5		1.3	0.8	1.0	−0.6	0.3	−0.1	0.0	0.4	0.9
	4	Other in.	2.1	2.0	0.7	−2.1	2.9	−1.0	−0.4	0.4	1.7		2.3	1.9	0.3	−0.8	1.5	−0.5	0.0	3.6	−1.3
	5	Financial S.	4.9	0.8	0.7	−0.7	3.0	0.3	0.7	−0.4	5.3		1.3	0.8	0.2	−0.2	0.5	0.0	0.0	0.7	0.6
	6	Business S.	4.9	2.9	1.1	−1.8	2.9	−0.4	0.3	5.0	−0.1		1.6	1.1	0.5	−0.7	0.9	−0.2	0.0	2.2	−0.6
	7	Consumer S.	2.4	2.3	0.6	−0.8	0.5	−0.2	0.0	0.5	1.9		1.1	0.8	0.2	−0.2	0.3	0.0	0.0	1.9	−0.9
	8	Public S.	1.6	1.2	0.1	−0.1	0.4	0.0	0.0	0.8	0.8		1.2	1.2	0.0	0.0	−0.1	0.1	0.0	0.5	0.7
2005–2010	1	Agliculture	−0.2	−4.2	0.7	−1.2	5.2	−0.3	−0.3	−0.8	0.6	2010–2014	−0.6	−3.8	0.9	0.0	3.2	−0.7	−0.2	−1.4	0.8
	2	Export core	−1.1	−3.0	0.7	−1.0	3.9	−1.1	−0.5	−2.1	1.1		−1.0	−4.1	2.9	0.8	1.4	−1.9	−0.2	−1.3	0.2
	3	Other Manu.	−1.8	−3.2	0.5	−0.7	2.2	−0.5	−0.2	−1.3	−0.6		−2.3	−3.5	1.6	0.3	0.6	−1.2	0.0	−1.5	−0.8
	4	Other in.	−1.7	−2.9	−0.1	−0.4	1.6	0.3	−0.2	0.4	−2.1		−5.2	−5.0	0.7	1.5	−1.6	−1.1	0.4	−4.1	−1.1
	5	Financial S.	2.2	−2.1	−0.2	−0.2	4.9	0.1	−0.2	0.6	1.7		−0.7	−2.8	0.6	0.7	1.3	−0.3	−0.1	−1.0	0.3
	6	Business S.	−0.6	−0.1	−0.3	−0.4	0.7	−0.4	−0.1	0.8	−1.4		−2.2	−2.7	1.1	0.4	−0.1	−0.8	0.0	0.5	−2.7
	7	Consumer S.	0.3	1.2	0.1	−0.1	−0.9	−0.2	0.1	1.3	−1.1		−0.9	−1.2	0.3	0.1	0.1	−0.2	0.0	0.7	−1.6
	8	Public S.	0.2	−0.3	0.0	0.0	0.4	0.0	0.0	−0.1	0.3		−0.7	−1.0	0.1	0.0	0.4	0.0	0.0	−0.3	−0.4

Source: WIOD 2016 and WIOD 2013

RX Real output, *DFD* Domestic final demand, *Ex* Export, *Im* Import, *Tech* Technology, *DIn* Domestic input, *Re* Residual, *Em* Employment, *LP* Labor productivity

showing a pattern of "negative de-industrialization," and the unemployment rate increased very sharply (see Fig. 5.3). The service sectors, especially "financial services" and "business-related services," are very stagnant during the Euro crisis.

5.4.2.4 The UK (Finance-Led Capitalism)

De-industrialization started in the UK early in the 1950s and has been accelerating ever since the structural crisis of the 1970s (Rowthorn and Wells 1987). Furthermore, "financial services" and "business-related services" have expanded rapidly in tandem with the financial liberalization and deregulation which were brought about by neoliberalist policies after the 1980s. Therefore, the UK's growth regime is characterized "finance-led" (Table 5.9).

1995–2000 (The UK Was Relatively Independent of European Integration) While "the export core manufacturing" industry, "the other manufacturing" industry, and "the other industries" grew firmly owing to the increase in consumption demand and export demand, productivity growth was higher than output growth. Therefore, "positive de-industrialization" occurred in the UK during this period. Moreover, output and employment grew in "financial services," "business-related services," and "consumer services." However, productivity growth was so high in "financial services" and "business-related services" that employment growth in these sectors was rather modest in the British economy.

2000–2005 (The UK Was Outside the EUROZONE) This period includes a time of recession in the British economy, and output and employment fell considerably in "the export core manufacturing" due to a decline in export demand. Therefore, "negative de-industrialization" occurred in "the export core manufacturing" and "the other manufacturing." In this period, "financial services" did not grow sufficiently, so employment was absorbed sufficiently by only "public services."

2005–2010 (Hit by the Subprime Crisis) The subprime crisis hit the British economy in 2008, and "financial services" and "business-related services" showed low growth rates owing to a sharp fall in final demand and export demand. Furthermore, productivity growth was negative in many industries, so the British economy exhibited very strong "negative de-industrialization" in this period. This shows that the British economy is relatively vulnerable to a financial crisis.

2010–2014 (During the Euro Crisis) As the UK is situated outside the Eurozone, the British economy was not heavily affected by the Euro crisis. A decline was seen only in "other industries" and "financial services." During this period, de-industrialization continued. In particular, "positive de-industrialization" proceeded in "export core manufacturing" and "other manufacturing" industries. "Business-related services" were very active, showing high growth rates of output and employment during this period.

Table 5.9 Growth regime and de-industrialization in the UK: annual growth rate of components (%)

UK			RX	DFD	Ex	Im	Tech	DIn	Re	Em	LP		RX	DFD	Ex	Im	Tech	DIn	Re	Em	LP
1995–2000	1	Agliculture	−1.3	6.4	0.6	−2.1	−5.0	−1.0	−0.1	−3.0	1.7	2000–2005	2.4	4.6	0.6	−3.9	2.2	−1.0	−0.2	−0.3	2.6
	2	Export core	2.5	4.6	4.1	−6.0	2.7	−2.4	−0.5	−1.4	3.9		0.9	2.7	2.2	−4.1	3.4	−2.6	−0.7	−5.3	6.2
	3	Other Manu.	0.7	3.8	0.7	−1.6	−1.6	−0.3	−0.4	−1.0	1.7		−0.5	2.2	0.9	−2.5	0.3	−1.2	−0.2	−3.6	3.0
	4	Other in.	2.3	2.5	0.8	−1.2	0.5	−0.3	0.0	0.3	2.1		1.5	2.3	−0.1	−1.3	1.6	−0.9	−0.1	2.0	−0.5
	5	Financial S.	7.6	5.4	2.9	−1.4	1.3	−0.5	−0.1	0.5	7.1		−1.1	0.7	0.9	−0.8	−1.2	−0.6	−0.1	0.0	−1.0
	6	Business S.	8.9	4.9	1.9	−1.8	3.3	−0.3	0.9	2.6	6.3		3.1	2.2	1.4	−1.5	1.8	−0.8	0.0	1.5	1.5
	7	Consumer S.	4.3	4.2	0.5	−0.7	0.6	−0.2	0.0	2.2	2.1		3.4	3.3	0.5	−0.4	0.3	−0.2	0.0	1.6	1.8
	8	Public S.	2.7	2.0	0.2	−0.1	0.5	0.0	0.1	1.3	1.4		3.5	3.3	0.1	−0.1	0.2	0.0	0.0	2.6	0.9
2005–2010	1	Agliculture	−1.6	−4.4	0.5	0.1	2.0	0.2	0.0	2.1	−3.7	2010–2014	7.4	4.7	−0.1	−1.3	2.6	1.1	0.3	2.0	5.4
	2	Export core	−1.5	−1.4	−0.9	−2.5	3.8	0.2	−0.6	−3.8	2.3		2.0	3.7	−1.1	−1.6	−0.9	1.9	−0.1	−0.2	2.2
	3	Other Manu.	0.4	−2.2	0.4	−1.9	3.7	0.3	0.2	−2.5	2.9		1.8	2.0	−0.7	0.3	−0.8	1.2	−0.2	−0.3	2.1
	4	Other in.	1.0	−0.9	−0.1	−0.6	2.4	0.0	0.1	−0.4	1.3		−1.2	1.0	−0.5	0.5	−2.8	0.8	−0.2	0.4	−1.6
	5	Financial S.	2.2	0.6	−0.1	0.1	1.0	0.4	0.2	−0.6	2.8		0.2	0.5	1.2	−0.2	−1.2	0.1	−0.2	−0.1	0.3
	6	Business S.	1.1	−0.3	2.1	−1.0	0.6	−0.3	0.0	0.9	0.3		4.4	1.7	1.5	−0.6	1.3	0.4	0.0	2.6	1.8
	7	Consumer S.	2.7	3.8	0.4	−0.4	−0.9	−0.3	0.1	−0.1	2.9		2.1	1.6	0.2	0.0	0.0	0.2	0.0	1.7	0.4
	8	Public S.	1.7	1.4	0.2	−0.1	0.1	0.0	0.0	1.7	0.0		1.1	1.0	0.1	0.0	0.0	0.0	0.0	0.4	0.7

Source: WIOD 2016 and WIOD 2013

RX Real output, *DFD* Domestic final demand, *Ex* Export, *Im* Import, *Tech* Technology, *DIn* Domestic input, *Re* Residual, *Em* Employment, *LP* Labor productivity

5.4.2.5 Japan (Export and Innovation–Led Capitalism)

Large firms in "the export core manufacturing" industry have played a crucial role in Japan, supported by their subcontracting networks (Boyer and Yamada 2000). These firms realize an "export and innovation-led" growth regime. The externalization of business activities and workers from the manufacturing sector to the service sector has been remarkable in tandem with increasing non-regular workers since the recession in the 1990s, and this has exacerbated inequality in Japanese society (Table 5.10).

1995–2000 (Structural Crisis After the Collapse of the Bubble) Even during the long-lasting recession of the 1990s, output increased in "the export core manufacturing" industry, which had sufficient export demand in sharp contrast to the negative growth of output in "the other manufacturing" and "the other industries." Accordingly, "positive de-industrialization" proceeded in "the export core manufacturing" industry, while "negative de-industrialization" occurred in "the other manufacturing" and "the other industries." Furthermore, "business-related services" and "public services" grew steadily in terms of output and employment. Especially, the growth in "public services" was supported by government spending. The strong linkages between "the export core manufacturing" sector and the "business-related service" sector showed patterns similar to those in the German economy (see Uemura and Tahara 2014, 2017).

2000–2005 (Unbalanced Recovery) This period includes a recovery process from the long-lasting recession, when "the export core manufacturing" industry exhibited very high output growth and productivity growth, leading to "positive de-industrialization." The growth of labor productivity was enhanced by the externalization of business activities and workers to "business-related services." Furthermore, both output and employment increased in "financial services," "business-related services," and "public services." Thus, a new growth pattern emerged in the first half of the 2000s, but this did not lead to a new and stable growth regime. In this situation, new rules and mechanisms of coordinating Japanese firms' overseas activities and domestic structural changes were not established.

2005–2010 (Hit by the Subprime Crisis) When the subprime crisis hit the Japanese economy in 2008, growth in "the export core manufacturing" industry became stagnant, and "the other manufacturing" and "the other industries" showed negative growth rates due to a sharp decline in investment demand. Accordingly, the Japanese economy exhibited overall "negative de-industrialization." In this situation, "financial services" and "business-related services" also showed negative growth rates, and their labor productivity fell sharply. As a result, employment was sustained via intrinsic institutional mechanisms in the Japanese labor market, even though many non-regular workers were fired. In this situation, "public services" absorbed employees, thus keeping the unemployment rate relatively low (as seen in Fig. 5.3), but this caused severe problems for public finance.

Table 5.10 Growth regime and de-industrialization in Japan: annual growth rate of components (%)

Japan			RX	DFD	Ex	Im	Tech	DIn	Re	Em	LP		RX	DFD	Ex	Im	Tech	DIn	Re	Em	LP
1995–2000	1	Agliculture	−0.3	−0.2	−0.3	0.2	−0.1	0.1	0.0	−4.2	3.9	2000–2005	−1.6	−0.9	1.1	−1.4	1.1	−1.1	−0.4	−2.9	1.3
	2	Export core	3.1	0.7	−1.8	0.9	1.6	1.5	0.2	−1.0	4.2		4.4	1.6	3.8	−1.7	1.4	−0.6	−0.1	−1.4	5.9
	3	Other Manu.	−1.4	−1.6	0.2	0.0	0.9	−0.7	−0.1	−2.6	1.2		−0.5	−0.3	1.7	−1.6	1.3	−1.0	−0.6	−3.2	2.7
	4	Other in.	−1.4	1.0	−1.7	−0.1	−0.6	−0.9	0.9	−1.6	0.2		−1.8	−1.8	0.5	−2.5	5.9	−1.9	−2.0	−2.6	0.8
	5	Financial S.	0.3	0.1	0.1	−0.1	0.1	0.0	0.0	−1.9	2.2		2.2	1.6	0.9	−0.7	1.3	−0.4	−0.4	−1.8	4.0
	6	Business S.	2.6	3.7	0.6	−0.4	−0.9	−0.3	−0.1	0.3	2.3		1.9	0.9	1.1	−0.7	1.5	−0.5	−0.4	0.8	1.0
	7	Consumer S.	0.4	0.4	0.0	0.0	0.0	0.0	0.0	0.2	0.2		0.4	0.7	0.4	−0.3	0.0	−0.2	−0.2	−0.4	0.8
	8	Public S.	2.1	−0.4	2.4	−2.1	2.1	−0.1	0.2	1.5	0.5		2.4	2.4	0.0	0.0	0.1	0.0	0.0	2.7	−0.3
2005–2010	1	Agliculture	0.7	−1.5	0.1	0.3	2.3	−0.1	−0.4	−1.8	2.5	2010–2014	−0.8	0.2	1.1	−3.5	4.1	−2.5	−0.3	−1.1	0.3
	2	Export core	−0.3	−0.3	0.0	−0.4	0.6	−0.2	−0.1	−0.3	0.0		0.2	0.6	4.0	−3.9	1.6	−2.0	−0.2	−2.0	2.2
	3	Other Manu.	−2.5	−2.0	0.2	0.7	−1.3	0.0	0.0	−2.4	−0.1		−1.4	0.4	1.6	−3.2	2.1	−2.1	−0.2	0.0	−1.4
	4	Other in.	−3.5	−3.6	0.0	2.1	−3.4	1.6	−0.3	−2.3	−1.2		0.7	1.5	0.5	−2.2	4.4	−2.4	−1.0	−2.6	3.3
	5	Financial S.	−3.8	−1.5	0.0	0.1	−2.3	−0.1	0.0	1.1	−4.9		−0.2	−0.2	0.4	−0.9	1.3	−0.7	−0.1	−3.1	3.0
	6	Business S.	−2.2	−2.1	0.3	0.2	−0.4	0.0	−0.1	0.5	−2.6		0.5	0.7	0.4	−1.2	1.6	−0.9	−0.2	−0.3	0.8
	7	Consumer S.	0.3	−0.2	0.0	0.2	0.2	0.1	−0.1	−0.3	0.6		0.1	0.3	0.2	−0.4	0.4	−0.3	−0.1	−1.0	1.2
	8	Public S.	1.4	1.2	0.0	0.0	0.1	0.0	0.0	1.1	0.3		0.4	0.5	0.0	−0.1	0.0	0.0	0.0	0.5	−0.2

Source: WIOD 2016 and WIOD 2013

RX Real output, *DFD* Domestic final demand, *Ex* Export, *Im* Import, *Tech* Technology, *DIn* Domestic input, *Re* Residual, *Em* Employment, *LP* Labor productivity

2010–2014 (Recovery from the Earthquake) After the Great East Japan Earthquake in 2011, the Japanese government followed expansionary monetary and fiscal policies, supporting an increase in domestic final demand. The "export core manufacturing" and "business-related services" recovered under this condition. However, domestic inputs decreased in all the manufacturing industries, reflecting a shift in the production of intermediate goods to other Asian countries. Even in this situation, "export core manufacturing" and "other industries" showed "positive de-industrialization." Therefore, sufficient employment growth did not occur in the manufacturing sector.

5.4.3 *Diversified Growth Regimes at the Tipping Point of European Integration and Japan's De-industrialization in China-Driven Asia Integration*

The institutional varieties of capitalism in the four European countries (Germany, France, Italy, and the UK) and the structural characteristics of their integration into the EU as a polity-led process determine the evolving diversity and interdependence of growth regimes and the patterns of de-industrialization, as seen in "Europe" in Fig. 5.4.

Germany exhibited a very dynamic growth regime with high productivity growth in its export core manufacturing sector and can thus be termed "export and innovation-led growth regime." Therefore, "positive de-industrialization" has occurred in Germany's manufacturing sector. After the Euro was introduced as a single currency in 1999, Germany enhanced its international competitiveness and realized a huge trade surplus with other EU member countries. Even during the Euro crisis, Germany maintained a superior trade performance and was even exposed to international competition with Asian economies. The strength of manufacturing-service linkages determines the pattern of output-employment dynamics in both industrial sectors and the nature of the conflicts and compromises between its domestic political groups.

France maintained export levels even after the establishment of the Euro. However, this was counterbalanced by large amounts of imports of final and intermediate goods. The manufacturing sector showed positive growth rates, and "positive de-industrialization" proceeded. France's service industries, especially consumer services and public services, have all been supported by sufficient consumption and have continued to absorb employment. Therefore, France can be termed "consumption-led growth regime." During the Euro crisis, employment decreased in the manufacturing sector due to a decrease in domestic final demand. In this situation, "negative de-industrialization" occured in France's "other manufacturing industry" and "other industries." In this situation, the employment released by the manufacturing sector was partly absorbed by the service sector, such as public services.

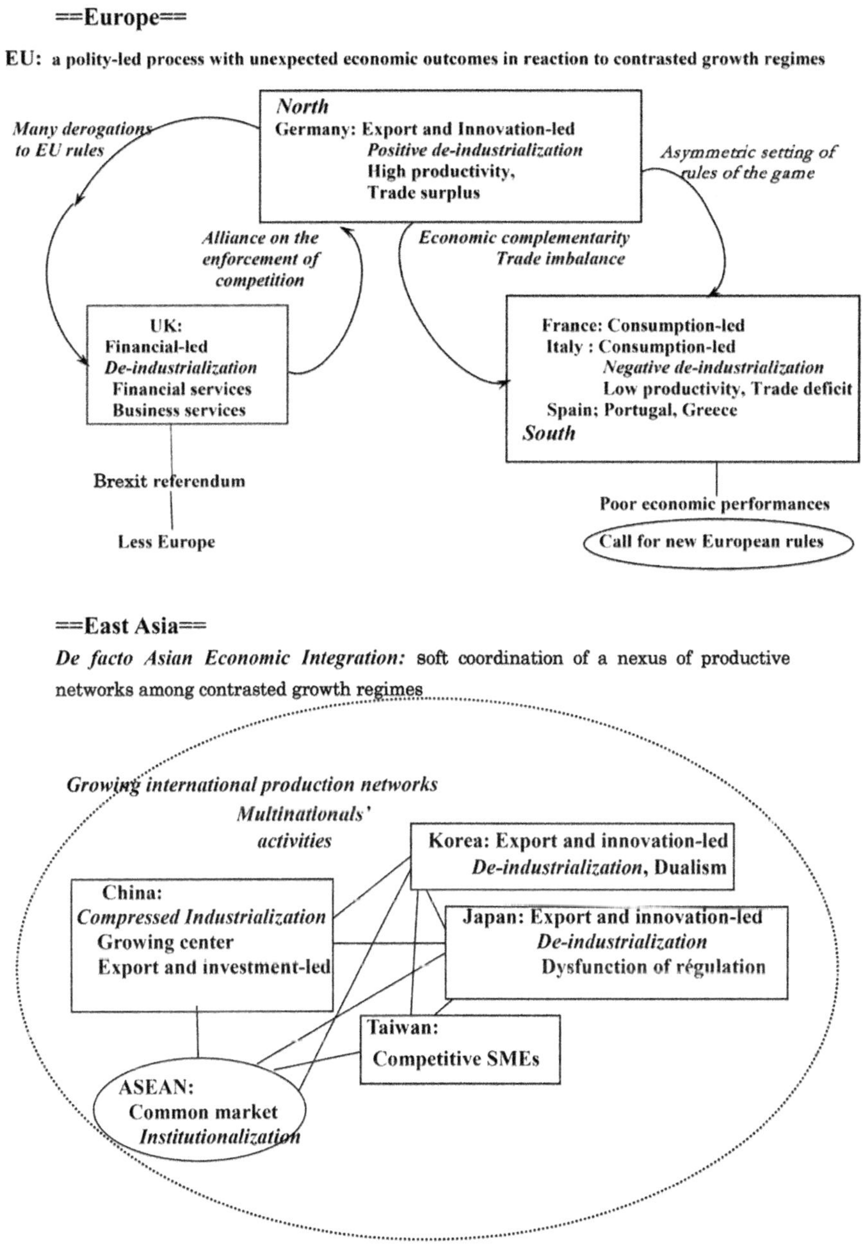

Fig. 5.4 Evolving diversity and interdependence of growth regimes in EU and Asia

Remarkably, Italy's manufacturing sector has exhibited low growth rates and low productivity. After Italy joined the Eurozone in 1999, the "export core manufacturing" industry lost its international competitiveness and often exhibited negative growth rates. The main factors in this decline were stagnant exports and sharply increased imports. The transformation of the growth regime proceeded alongside an increasing trade deficit in Italy. Under these conditions, productivity growth was low in the manufacturing industry, so "negative de-industrialization" occurred in the Italian economy. Italy has "consumption-led growth regime," but during the Euro crisis, the growth rates became negative due to the sharp decrease in domestic final demand, especially in investment and consumption. Furthermore, productivity growth rates were often negative in some manufacturing industries and employment declined sharply, causing a sharp increase in the unemployment rate.

The UK has been relatively independent of the continental European economies. It maintained its position outside the Eurozone and did not join the Schengen zone, too. De-industrialization has accelerated in the British economy since the structural crisis of the 1970s. Financial and business-related services expanded rapidly due to financial liberalization and deregulation which were brought about by neoliberalist policies after the 1980s. The UK has "finance-led growth regime," but the British economy was not affected so strongly by the Euro crisis. A decline was seen only in financial services and some manufacturing industries. De-industrialization has been always proceeded, and, in particular, either "positive de-industrialization" or "negative de-industrialization" has occurred in the manufacturing industries under various economic conditions. Business-related services have been active, showing relatively high growth rates of output and employment. The UK's semidetached relationship with the EU has benefited the British economy, but this will be eroded after Brexit.

During European integration with the Euro as a polity-led process (Wiener and Diez 2009), the four countries under study have formed diversified growth regimes and different patterns of de-industrialization. There have been economic complementarity and trade imbalance between Germany and southern European countries (Boyer 2013). Furthermore, Brexit may be bringing about more diversified paths of growth regime in these countries.

In Japan, the growth regime has been determined by domestic institutional structures and international economic relations in the process of de facto regional economic integration, as seen in "East Asia" in Fig. 5.4. De-industrialization has accelerated rapidly since the structural crisis in the 1990s (Uemura and Tahara 2014). Even in this situation, a productivity growth differential has been maintained between the export core manufacturing industry with cumulative growth and the other industries during the long-lasting recession. Employment decreased with the mechanism of "positive de-industrialization" in the export core manufacturing industry and decreased even more remarkably with the mechanism of "negative de-industrialization" in the other manufacturing industries.

On the contrary, employment increased in the business-related service industry via the mechanism of "de-industrialization by manufacturing-service linkages." Business process outsourcing accelerated, producing more service employment. In this process, the employment discharged from the manufacturing industry was absorbed into the service industry. Since the 1990s, employment has continuously increased, even amid with a decrease in labor productivity in the service sector. Most of the service industries absorbed employment, acting as an "employment sponge," and showed positive growth rates of employment even during the global financial crisis.

The absorption of employment by the service industry can often lead to a decrease in per capita incomes along with decreasing labor productivity. In fact, workers who were fired by manufacturing firms were often reemployed as non-regular workers by smaller firms in the business-related service industry. In this situation, a polarization emerged between the manufacturing industry with high productivity and the consumer service industry with low productivity, weakening the coordinating mechanism for wages and employment. This phenomenon was seen in the export core manufacturing industry in the 2000s, which had not seen even in the export-led growth in the 1980s. After the Japanese economy was hit by the subprime crisis in 2008 and earthquake in 2011, the export core manufacturing industry was damaged, and thus Japanese multinational corporations shifted productive activities to other Asian economies, exacerbating the polarization of the Japanese economy and society and the dysfunction of *régulation* (Boyer et al. 2012; Lechevalier 2014). Growing international production networks as well as competition with China's growing economy and other Asian economies in the process of de facto Asian economic integration puts very strong pressure on the Japanese economy to initiate a shift in the domestic industrial structures (Uemura et al. 2014; Yokokawa et al. 2016).

Overall, the results of our international comparative analysis point to three important implications concerning research on growth regimes and de-industrialization in advanced economies. First, it is important to identify what types of de-industrialization have proceeded in certain industries, specifically whether the patterns are "positive" or "negative" in the output-productivity-employment dynamics. This depends on the varieties of the growth regimes, which are determined by domestic institutional arrangements as well as final and intermediate goods trade in the process of regional economic integration. Second, the strength of manufacturing-service linkages determines the pattern of output-employment dynamics in the manufacturing and service sectors as well as the nature of the conflict between domestic political groups. Very strong linkages are observed in Germany and Japan, where large manufacturing firms dominate in the manufacturing sector and have several interests in common with firms in the business-related service industry. Furthermore, these linkages are influenced by the international division of labor in the process of regional integration. Third, we should carefully investigate which service sectors absorb workers who have been released from the manufacturing sector. As mentioned in the analyses above, service sectors absorb workers in Germany, France, Italy, the UK and Japan. In general, "public services" and "consumer services" absorbed workers in the process of de-industrialization, but this has been influenced by the recent transformation of the welfare state, which causes more dualistic and fragmented structures in these countries (Emmenegger et al. 2012; Magara 2017; Martine and Thelen 2007; Palier and Thelen 2012; Thelen 2014).

5.5 Conclusion

In this study, the theoretical framework of growth regimes and de-industrialization was explained from the viewpoint of the *régulation* theory, and a comparative analysis of the dynamics of growth regime and de-industrialization was conducted for Germany, France, Italy, the UK and Japan. The structural characteristics of regional integration in the EU and East Asia as well as growth regimes and de-industrialization can be summarized as follows.

First, national growth regimes are heterogeneous in EU and East Asia and are evolving continuously, influenced by the process of regional integration. De-industrialization in terms of employment is seen universally in all advanced economies, but each economy shows different features, depending on its pattern of capital accumulation, institutional arrangements, and international economic relations. In particular, employment dynamics at the industrial level occurs within the framework of "the growth regime," which is determined by the dynamic interactions between "the demand regime" and "the productivity regime" in the open economy, as suggested by the *régulation* theory.

Second, four types of de-industrialization can be theoretically formalized: "positive de-industrialization," which occurs via productivity growth differentials between the manufacturing and service sectors; "negative de-industrialization" which is caused by stagnant output in the manufacturing sector; "de-industrialization through manufacturing-service linkages," in which services increase as intermediate inputs to the manufacturing sector; and "de-industrialization caused by the shift in final demand to services," which is often influenced by international economic relations and national patterns of demand formation. The different logic of de-industrialization is often dominant on different varieties of capitalism as well as space and time involved.

Third, in the historical process of regional integration in Europe and East Asia, the interdependence among growth regimes has evolved in several patterns. In Europe, the pattern of interdependence of growth regimes is relatively stable, and Germany has been a key player in the final and intermediate goods trade. In particular, Germany created stronger ties of final goods trade with other EU member countries, after the Euro was introduced, leading to the Euro crisis during the process of European integration. In East Asia, interdependence has deepened through intermediate goods trade between major Asian economies over the past 20 years. The pattern of the international division of labor has changed drastically as the Chinese economy has rapidly grown. In 1995, Japan was a key player in the supply of intermediate goods to other Asian countries. In 2014, however, China was supplying not only final goods but also intermediate goods to other Asian countries. This shift in the international division of labor may influence industrial structural changes and de-industrialization in the Japanese economy.

Fourth, different patterns of de-industrialization are identified in different countries. In Germany, "the export core manufacturing" industry has grown with a high growth rate of labor productivity, which has caused "positive de-industrialization" with strong linkages between "export core manufacturing" and "business-related services" in the process of European integration. In France, the manufacturing industry has shown steady growth, usually leading to "positive de-industrialization," supported by domestic consumption. In Italy, especially after the introduction of the Euro as a single currency, "the export core manufacturing" and "the other manufacturing" industries have showed negative growth rates along with rapidly increasing imports. The growth of labor productivity has also been very low, so this caused only slightly "negative de-industrialization" in Italy. In the UK, "financial services" and "business-related services" have grown with high productivity in the boom period, while "the export core manufacturing" industry often showed negative growth, exhibiting "negative de-industrialization." The Japanese pattern is somewhat similar to the German one with strong linkages between "export core manufacturing" and "business-related services." Furthermore, the externalization of business activities and workers from the manufacturing industry to the "business-related services" industry has been remarkable in the Japanese economy, faced with fierce competition and growing interdependence with the Chinese economy in the process of Asian economic integration.

Growth regimes are evolving along with growing national interdependence in the process of regional integration in the EU and East Asia. In this context, de-industrialization is a universal and inevitable phenomenon in all advanced economies, but its patterns and structural characteristics differ from country to country, depending on economic structures, institutional coordinating mechanisms, growth regimes, and international economic relations. Faced with the fierce international competition, the serious socioeconomic effects of de-industrialization may include dualization and inequality in an economy and society, but these effects can be mitigated, conditional on the creation of institutional rules and social policies in the each national economy.

Appendix: Method of Converting WIOD Data to Real-Term Data

World Input-Output Database (WIOD) used in the analysis comprises nominal data in dollars. The only real-term data available are World Input-Output Tables (WIOTs) in previous year prices (PYP). The PYP data is not suitable for the purpose of the input-output analysis in this chapter. To conduct our time-series analysis of industrial structural change, we convert the WIOD data to real-term data by utilizing the exchange rate of each country and an output deflator for each industrial sector. The exchange rate data are taken from the WIOD (2013, 2016), and the deflators for outputs and intermediate inputs in each industry are provided by Socio-Economic Accounts (SEA) and the WIOD. The SEA deflators are compiled for the values in each column, causing discrepancies in the values in each row. Therefore, we use the "double inflation method" to adjust for this gap in values.

References

Amable B (2003) The diversity of modern capitalism. Oxford University Press, Oxford

Amable R, Barré R, Boyer R (1997) Les systèmes d'innovation à l'èere de la globalisation. OST/Economica, Paris

Baldwin R, Lopez-Gonzalez J (2013) Supply chain trade: a portrait of global patterns and several testable hypotheses, NBER working paper 18957

Baumol WA (1967) Macroeconomics of unbalanced growth: the anatomy of urban crisis. Am Econ Rev 57(3)

Boyer R (1988) Formalising growth regimes. In: Dosi G et al (eds) Technical change and industrial transformation. Pinter Publishers, London

Boyer R (2013) The Euro crisis: history and policies of European integration, Fujiwara-shoten, Tokyo

Boyer R (2015) Économie politique des capitalismes : Théorie de la régulation et des crises. La Découverte, Paris

Boyer R, Petit P (1991) Kaldor's growth theories: past, present and prospects for the future. In: Nell E, Semmler W (eds) Nicolas Kaldor and Mainstream Economics: Confrontation or Convergence? Macmillan, London

Boyer R, Yamada T (eds) (2000) Japanese capitalism in crisis: a regulationist interpretation. Routledge, London

Boyer R, Uemura H, Isogai A (eds) (2012) Diversity and transformations of Asian capitalisms. Routledge, London

Emmenegger P, Häusermann S, Palier B, Seeleib-Kaiser M (eds) (2012) The age of dualization: the changing face of inequality in deindustrializing societies. Oxford University Press, Oxford

Franke R, Kalmbach P (2005) Structural change in the manufacturing sector and its input on business related services: an input-output study for Germany. Struct Chang Econ Dyn 16:467–468

Hall P, Soskice D (eds) (2001) Varieties of capitalism: the institutional foundations of comparative advantage. Oxford University Press, Oxford

Harada Y (2007) Varieties of industrial structural change: an attempt of typology based on a multivariate analysis. In: Yamada T, Uni H, Nabashima N (eds) A new aspect of cotemporary capitalism. Showado, Kyoto

Harada Y, Tohyama H (2012) Asian capitalisms: institutional configurations and firm heterogeneity. In: Boyer R, Uemura H, Isogai A (eds) Diversity and transformations of Asian capitalisms. Routledge, London

Iversen T, Cusack TR (2000) The cause of welfare state expansion: de-industrialization or globalization. World Polit 52(3):313–349

Kaldor N (1978) Further essays on economic theory. Gerald Duckworth, London

Landesmann MA, Scazzieri R (eds) (1996) Production and economic dynamics. Cambridge University Press, Cambridge

Lechevalier S (ed) (2014) The great transformation of Japanese capitalism. Routledge, New York

Magara H (2017) Policy change under new democratic capitalism. Routledge, London

Marglin S, Schor J (eds) (1990) The golden age of capitalism: re-interpreting the Postwar experience. Clarendon, Oxford

Martine CJ, Thelen K (2007) The state and coordinated capitalism: contributions of the public sector to social solidarity in postindustrial society. World Polit 60(1):1–36

Ok W (2016) The Korean exception: service outsourcing by manufacturing firms and the role of institution. Evol Inst Econ Rev 13(1):165

Palier B, Thelen K (2012) Dualization and institutional complementarities: industrial relations, labor market, and welfare state changes in France and Germany. In: Emmenegger, Häusermann, Palier, Seeleib-Kaiser (2012)

Pasinetti LL (1981) Structural change and economic growth: a theoretical essay on the dynamics of the wealth of nations. Cambridge University Press, Cambridge
Petit P (1986) Slow growth and the service Economy. Frances Pinter, London
Petit P (2005) Croissance et richesse des nations. La Découverte, Paris
Rowthorn R (1982) Demand, real wages and economic growth. Studi Econ 18
Rowthorn R, Wells J (1987) Deindustrialization and foreign trade. Cambridge University Press, Cambridge
Tahara S (2009) Mutual linkages between the manufacturing industry and the service industry: an input-output analysis of the Japanese economy 1980–2000. Yokohama J Soc Sci 14(3)
Tahara S (2010) Structural changes in the manufacturing industry and their impact on sectoral output and employment. Yokohama J Soc Sci 15(3)
Tahara S, Uemura H (2014) Growth regime and de-industrialization in Japan. In: Uemura H, Uni H, Isogai H, Yamada T (eds) (2014)
Taylor L (1991) Income distribution, inflation, and growth: lectures on Structuralist macroeconomic theory. MIT Press, Cambridge
Thelen K (2014) Varieties of liberalization and the new politics of social solidarity. Cambridge University Press, Cambridge
Uemura H (2000) Growth, distribution, and structural change in the post-war Japanese economy. In Boyer and Yamada (eds) (2000)
Uemura H (2012) Institutional changes and the transformation of the growth regime in the Japanese economy: facing the impact of the world economic crisis and Asian integration. In: Boyer R, Uemura H, Isogai A (eds) (2012)
Uemura H, Tahara S (2014) The transformation of growth regime and de-industrialization in Japan. Revue de la régulation:15
Uemura H, Tahara S (2017) The political-economic implications of de-industrialization with varieties of capitalism: an EU-Japan comparative analysis. In Magara H (2017)
Uemura H, Uni H, Isogai A, Yamada T (eds) (2014) Asian capitalism in transition. Fujiwara-shoten, Tokyo
Uemura H, Yamada T, Harada Y (2016) Regulation approach to Japanese and Asian capitalism: understanding varieties of capitalism and structural dynamics. In Yokokawa, Yagi, Uemura and Westra (eds) (2016)
Wiener A, Diez T (eds) (2009) European integration theory, 2nd edn. New York, Oxford University Press
Yokokawa N, Yagi K, Uemura H, Westra R (2016) The rejuvenation of political economy. Routledge, New York

Chapter 6
East Asian Monetary Regimes and Comparison with the European Case: A Stock-Flow Consistent Approach

Jacques Mazier, Myoung-keun On, and Sebastian Valdecantos

6.1 Introduction

The Asian crisis of 1997 has shown the limits of a simple dollar peg policy and of a market-driven regional integration without formal institutions. During the 2000s a lot of efforts have been devoted to improve monetary and financial cooperation at the regional level, especially with the Chiang Mai and the Asian Bond Market initiatives. But results have been limited, mainly due to political issues associated to the competition between China and Japan. The financial crisis of 2008 has given new interest to the question of monetary cooperation at the regional level.

The Chinese increasing role in the world economy has raised new issues. The nature of the yuan has been progressively changing at the international level. In 2005 the exchange rate system of China officially shifted to a managed floating regime, which consisted of a flexible exchange rate within some predetermined limits given by a basket of currencies mainly composed of the dollar, euro, yen, and won. After 2005 the yuan has gradually appreciated against the dollar, except for a period between July 2008 and June 2010 when the Chinese central bank pegged the yuan against the dollar, in the context of the global financial crisis. The limits the yuan's daily movements against the dollar due to the narrow trading band and the control of international capital movements made the Chinese exchange rate system closer to a fixed regime rather than to a floating system. Despite the appreciation of the yuan against the dollar, the yuan remained undervalued until the beginning of the 2010s

J. Mazier (✉) · M.-k. On
University Paris 13, CEPN-CNRS, Paris, France
e-mail: mazier@univ-paris13.fr

S. Valdecantos
Universidad Nacional de Mar del Plata, Mar del Plata, Argentina

R. Boyer et al. (eds.), *Evolving Diversity and Interdependence of Capitalisms*, Evolutionary Economics and Social Complexity Science 11,
https://doi.org/10.1007/978-4-431-55001-3_6

(Aflouk et al. 2010). Since 2010 the peg of the yuan to the dollar has been transformed into a more flexible regime using a basket of currencies as reference with an intraday fluctuation band, which has been enlarged in 2012. The huge foreign reserves of the Chinese central bank allowed it to keep the yuan parity under control with a target of real moderate appreciation in the medium term. However, since 2014 China has faced financial crunch with large capital outflows ($700 billion until the end of 2015) and a limited depreciation against the dollar which has only partly compensated a real effective revaluation of nearly 20% since 2012. Chinese authorities have now to define a new exchange rate policy with three possibilities: a progressive devaluation which would have the default of encouraging more capital outflows, a large devaluation to boost the exports which would be a major shock at world level and would not help the Chinese economy to upgrade its international specialization and adopt a new growth regime more devoted to domestic demand, a strengthening of capital controls to stabilize the yuan's value which would be in conflict with the past effort to raise the yuan's international status. The internationalization of the yuan and its convertibility has been a long-term project. They suppose huge institutional transformations. Internationalizing a currency means authorizing nonresidents to hold domestic and foreign assets denominated in national currency and allowing their conversion in foreign currencies without restriction. China has a long way to go in this regard.

Since the burst of the financial crisis in 2008, the development of monetary and financial cooperation in East Asia has gained interest. First, some measures aimed at giving more formal structures to the Chang Mai initiatives have been taken. Second, the project of an Asian Monetary Fund to face short-term adjustment problems has been relaunched. However, the great heterogeneity of East Asia, both in terms of level of development and of countries' size, pleads for keeping an adjustable exchange rate system in the future monetary regime, at least for a long transition period (Jeong et al. 2012). To go beyond the present system based on managed floating with various forms according to the different countries, two main forms of monetary cooperation have been proposed, one based on a common currencies basket (Williamson 1998) and the other based on the Asian Currency Unit (ACU).

The ACU project is the more ambitious. Since the end of the 2000s, in the context of financial crisis, it has gained interest (Shimizutani 2009). It is a long-term project. The first step would be centered on the re-building of the institutions created with the Chiang Mai initiative and on the reinforcement of financial supervision. The second step, to be taken after 2020, would be the settlement of the ACU composed of the yen, yuan, won, and other East Asian currencies and its promotion for public and private uses. These years would be used to achieve the financial liberalization and reinforce the financial regulation before the transition to an exchange rate regime based on the ACU in the 2030s. Even at this long term, the perspective of a single currency seems problematic at the level of an area which will always be characterized by huge heterogeneity. On the contrary, the use of the ACU in an East Asian monetary regime where the national currencies would be preserved and would be in a system of fixed, but adjustable, exchange rates against the ACU, would be a more realistic project. The nature of the ACU remains open. It could be, as it is now planned, a currency basket. It could also be a new international currency floating against the dollar and the euro.

Concretely, a possible alternative to the ACU in the long term could be the yuan, once it has become fully convertible and the Chinese banking and financial system have been restructured and consolidated. Another possibility could be that of the "block yuan," where the yuan would be used as an anchor for the other East Asian currencies, while the yen would be in a position rather similar to the one of the pound sterling against the euro. The point in debate is what should be the level of rigidity or flexibility of this regime. Whereas a rigid one would mean that this block yuan would be close to a yuan zone with fixed exchange rates (which would not be suitable for the heterogeneity of the zone), a more flexible one would give more room of manoeuver to face asymmetric economic performances.

The problem raised by these flexible monetary regimes, whether with an anchor on the yuan or an ACU, is the risk of instability associated to capital flights and recurrent exchange rate adjustments. Hence, some form of capital controls would have to be maintained to provide the system with more stability. This question of capital controls is more debated than it was as the financial crisis of 2008 has shown the limits of a full liberalization and the need of tighter regulation.

A comparison with the European case is enlightening. The economic and monetary integration has followed a completely different path in Europe. The march toward monetary union has resulted of a strong political will from the Werner report in 1970 to the Maastricht Treaty in 1992. However, the road has not been without accident. In the early 1970s, the European snake proved to be very unstable and has been abandoned. The European Monetary System (EMS), launched in 1979, was based on fixed, but adjustable exchange rates, with respect to the European Currency Unit (ECU), a European currencies' basket. The EMS has also suffered from many speculative attacks but became progressively more rigid after 1987 until the main crisis of 1992–1993. Large exchange rate adjustments and a new design of the EMS, with enlarged fluctuation margins, were decided. Simultaneously the project of monetary union continued in order to achieve more stability. After a painful convergence process, the euro was adopted in 1999. This was regarded as a major political success. Contrary to what was initially expected by most of the observers, no new speculative attack happened between 1993 and 1999. Two factors explained this successful transition. First, the monetary authorities underlined the credibility and the strength of the political willingness to march toward the single currency. They praised the efficiency and the flexibility of the modes of intervention of the central banks. Second, thanks to the exchange rate adjustments of 1992 and 1993 and to the costs for Germany of the German reunification, exchange rate misalignments had disappeared between European countries, contrary to what was prevailing during the 1980s when most of the time the deutschmark was undervalued, while the French franc and the Italian lira were overvalued (Couharde and Mazier 2001). But this monetary union has been realized without any other institutional change in order to face the huge heterogeneity which existed, and still exists, between the members of the euro area and, more precisely, between the German block and the Southern European countries, France included. During the 2000s intra-European misalignments have reappeared due divergent evolutions between the two groups of countries. Without federal budget and with very limited intra-European labor force mobility, there is almost no adjustment mechanism to compensate asymmetric shocks or evolutions. Real devaluations through wage and employment cuts have a high social cost and a limited efficiency, especially in countries with a reduced degree of openness like Greece or Portugal. The consequences of this institutional framework have been the blocking of European growth during the 1990s with the transition period following the Maastricht Treaty and after the financial crisis when deflationist policies have been imposed to the Southern countries.

The contrast is clear with East Asia where the intra-regional integration is also high at the level of ASEAN+3. After the Asian crisis of 1997, more pragmatic exchange rate regimes have been adopted, and exchange rate misalignments have been more limited during the 2000s than in the European case, with some exception like the undervaluation of the yuan during a rather long period.

To investigate the impact of various exchange rate regimes on East Asian economies, we construct a four-country stock-flow consistent (SFC) model which consists of four areas (China, East Asian countries, the USA, and the rest of the world). The simulations analyze the adjustment mechanisms following demand or supply shocks. Various forms of exchange rate regimes are considered for East Asia (yuan/dollar, East Asia/dollar, and East Asia/yuan fixed or floating or managed). We show the characteristics of the adjustment mechanism and the interactions among regions under each alternative setting. A second set of models is based on a more detailed decomposition of East Asia with a split between Japan and the rest of East Asia, while the USA is gathered with the rest of the world for more simplicity. It allows for the study of more elaborated flexible exchange rate regimes (fixed but adjustable beyond a certain threshold) and based on alternative forms of the ACU (ACU as a currency basket, global ACU as an international currency, ACU bancor or even ACU as a single currency).

The same type of four-country SFC model can be applied to the eurozone with a split between North Europe (the German block), South Europe, the USA, and the rest of the world. It is possible to describe the history of the European monetary integration and its failure from the European Monetary System (EMS) to the current eurozone. In the same framework, two types of alternative monetary regimes can be proposed, the first one is a multispeed eurozone going from a multi-eurozone to an eurozone without Germany and the second, more ambitious, based on an euro-bancor model and a European Clearing Union (Mazier and Valdecantos 2014, 2015).

The chapter is organized as follows: Sect. 6.2 presents the alternative exchange rate regimes for East Asia and the associated closures of the four-country SFC model, first for the basic and intermediate regimes and second for the ACU regimes. The results of simulations are given in each case. Lessons are drawn from a comparison with the European experience in Section 6.3, using the same type of approach. The last section concludes.

6.2 East Asian Exchange Rate Regimes and SFC Model

The theoretical background will be summarized before presenting the alternative monetary regimes for East Asia and the associated closures of the four-country SFC model, first for the basic and intermediate regimes and second for the ACU regimes.

6.2.1 *Theoretical Background*

The stock-flow consistent approach, which a growing literature has been using in recent years, has several virtues. Especially, it can track the trajectory of flows and stocks and model the financial sector explicitly as well as the production sector. The general methodology of SFC models is well explained in the founder book of Godley and Lavoie (2007b). SFC models comprise a set of behavioral equations which describe the transactions and decisions of institutional agents (households, firms, government, banks, central bank, rest of the world) within the accounting framework in flows and stocks framed in complete balance sheets.

The contributions of Godley and Lavoie (2007a) and Lavoie and Zhao (2010) are seminal to analyze international monetary regimes with the SFC approach. They construct a three-country model based on the portfolio balance models which incorporate the imperfect asset substitutability and valuation effects caused by the changes of exchange rates. In contrast to Blanchard et al. (2005), they endogenize GDP and the supply of securities, and thereby the interaction between the real and financial variables can be considered more explicitly. They examine the impact of the diversification of the foreign reserves of China through some simulation experiments.

Mazier and Tiou-Tagba (2012) generalized the previous work by introducing the managed floating exchange rate system with the target variable such as foreign reserves or a current account surplus and by analyzing the cases with flexible prices instead of constant prices. These three-country models are extended to four-country models. Mazier and Valdecantos (2014) describe the institutional setting of the Eurosystem in detail in order to reproduce some of the events that happened during the crisis of the eurozone. Mazier and Valdecantos (2014) analyze the implications regarding the intra-zone imbalances in euro area. They divide the euro area into two parts, North and South, and compare various alternative exchange rate regimes (monetary union, EMS, multiple euros, euro-bancor) which can be thought as a way out of the current crisis.

Godley and Lavoie (2007b) present two main closures for an open economy model: one for the case where the exchange rate is flexible and the other one for the case of fixed exchange rates. In the first case, the bond market of one of the countries (say, the UK) is cleared through exchange rate movements, which may be upward or downward depending on the gap between supply and demand. The purchases and sales of domestic bonds by the central bank ensure that its balance sheet identity holds at every point of time. The other country's (say, the USA) bond market is balanced through purchases and sales by the monetary authority. So we are left with the explanation of how the balance sheet identity of the monetary authority of the USA is satisfied. As it happens in every SFC model, there is an equation that does not need to be written, since it can be derived from the remaining equations of the model. In this closure, this is the case of the balance sheet identity of the central bank of the USA.

In the second case, i.e., when the exchange rate is fixed, this variable can no longer ensure that the bond market of the UK is in equilibrium. Thus, it is the central bank that must intervene to make supply equal demand. Moreover, since the exchange rate is fixed, the monetary authority must intervene in the foreign exchange market in order to ensure equilibrium between supply and demand at the targeted exchange rate. These interventions bring about changes in the stock of foreign reserves held by the monetary authority. As regards the bond market of the other county, it is cleared through interventions of the central bank. Once the equations for the aforementioned processes have been written, we are left with the equation that guarantees that the balance sheet identity of the central bank of the USA is being held. As it happened in the flexible exchange rate closure, this is the redundant equation of the model.

6.2.2 Exchange Rate Regimes in East Asia and SFC Model: The Basic Alternatives

The world economy is divided in four areas: the USA, China, East Asia, and the rest of the world. Areas have their own currencies, dollar $, yuan ¥, East Asian ₩, and rest of the world #. The whole structure of the SFC model is close to the one used by the previous authors and will not be described in detail. All the equations are presented in Mazier et al. 2014. The institutional agents (households, firms, government, banks, central bank) and their financial assets and liabilities are described in the annex with the balance sheet of the four countries. Households receive wages and interests, pay taxes, and consume and hold cash and bank deposits. Firms accumulate capital, pay taxes and interests, and finance their investments with undistributed profits and credit. Government expenditures are financed by taxes, after payments of interests, and by issuing public bonds to cover their deficit. These public bonds are the main international financial assets. Commercial banks receive households' deposits, hold reserves at the central bank, supply credit to the firms without restriction, hold domestic or foreign bonds with a portfolio behavior, and can be refinanced by the central bank. Banks' profits are redistributed to households as dividends. The central bank provides cash to households, receives reserves from the commercial banks and refinances them, and holds domestic bonds and foreign reserves. Bonds issued by the US government work as the unique foreign reserve. Profits of the central bank coming from interest payments are paid as taxes to the government. Interest rates are supposed constant. International trade is described through bilateral imports with demand effects and price effects linked to bilateral exchange rates. The flow of funds and the accumulation of capital, financial assets and liabilities, and wealth are described in a SFC manner, including the reevaluation effects due to exchange rates variations.

The emphasis of this study is put on alternative exchange rate regimes within Asia. The dollar and the rest of the world currency are supposed to be freely floating. Regarding East Asia and China, four basic regimes can be considered:

- The regime XX, where the yuan and the East Asian currency are both pegged to the dollar in a fixed regime. This reflects broadly the middle of the 1990s when the yuan was anchored to the dollar after a long period of devaluation and adjustment, while East Asian currencies were also pegged to the dollar. This was seen as an informal form of cooperation between them.
- The regime XL, where the yuan is pegged to the dollar while the East Asian currency and the dollar are floating. This situation corresponds roughly to what prevailed during the end of the 1990s and the beginning of the 2000s.
- The regime LL, which is a rather hypothetical regime where the yuan and the East Asian currencies are both supposed to be freely floating. This could be thought as a situation where the yuan has achieved its long transition period toward internationalization and is floating against the dollar. As in the regime XL, the East Asian currency floats. This regime would correspond to a world economy dominated by the finance and the market.
- The regime LX is another long-term scenario where the yuan is also floating after a complete liberalization. But the East Asian currency would now be pegged to the yuan. In other words China and East Asia are supposed to have formed a yuan zone in a long-term perspective.

Beyond these corner regimes, intermediate monetary regimes can be considered reflecting more managed floating exchange rate policies. Without analyzing all the possible combinations, four cases will be distinguished:

- The regime XA, where the yuan is still pegged to the dollar but the East Asian currency is now in a managed regime against the dollar, instead of being purely floating like in the regime XL. This regime would still correspond to the regime of the end of the 1990s and the beginning of the 2000s.
- The regime AL, where the Chinese monetary authorities follow a managed regime against the dollar with a target for their foreign reserves or their current account surplus while East Asia lets its currency float against the dollar. This regime is closer to the current monetary regime.
- The regime AX is another version of the yuan area where the yuan follows a managed exchange regime against the dollar and the East Asian currency is in the fixed regime with the yuan. The Chinese financial liberalization is supposed to be less advanced, and the Chinese authorities keep the yuan more under control.

Table 6.1 The alternative exchange rate regimes in East Asia

E_4 or E_5 EA/ US or EA/CH	E_2 between US and CH		
	Fixed system (X)	Managed system (A)	Floating system (L)
Fixed system (X)	Regime XX Fixed E_2, fixed E_4	Regime AX Managed E_2, fixed E_5	Regime LX Floating E_2, fixed E_5
Managed system (A)	Regime XA Fixed E_2, managed E_4		Regime LA Floating E_2, managed E_5
Floating system (L)	Regime XL Fixed E_2, floating E_4	Regime AL Managed E_2, floating E_4	Regime LL Floating E_2, floating E_4

- The regime LA is a last version of the yuan area or, more precisely, of a yuan block where the yuan is still freely floating after a period of liberalization. It is now used as a reference by the East Asian currencies engaged in a managed floating regime or in a fixed, but adjustable, exchange rate regime.

Table 6.1 summarizes the different exchange rate regimes. Since there are four areas, six bilateral exchange rates should be determined for fulfilling transactions: 1 $\$ = E_1\#$ (between US and RW), $1\$ = E_2¥$ (between US and CH), $1\ \# = E_3¥$ (between RW and CH), $1\$ = E_4₩$ (between US and EA), $1₩ = E_5¥$ (between EA and CH), and $1\ \# = E_6₩$ (between RW and EA). Table 6.1 of the exchange rate systems has two axes. The horizontal axis stands for the exchange rate regime between the USA and China. Moving from left to right means more liberalization for the yuan regime. The vertical axis represents the relation between East Asia and the USA or China. Moving down means an evolution from a fixed regime for the East Asian currency toward a floating regime.

6.2.2.1 Alternative Closures of the Four Basic Exchange Rate Regimes

In SFC models the exchange rate determination is based on the adjustment between supply and demand of bonds on the different markets. It can be shown also that this is equivalent to a more traditional determination where exchange rates result from the sum of the flows in and out linked to trade, income, and capital movements.

The Dollar-Pegged Regime XX (Yuan/Dollar and East Asia/Dollar Fixed)

The starting point is the regime XX, where the exchange rates between both the yuan E_2 and the East Asian currency E_4 against the dollar are fixed. This regime can be interpreted as the one prevailing in the middle of the 1990s, when the yuan was anchored to the dollar but also most of the East Asian currencies. This anchorage of the East Asian currencies on the dollar was regarded as a de facto form of regional cooperation for countries already economically integrated. As a consequence, the exchange rate of the East Asian currency against the yuan is also fixed ($E_5 = E_2/E_4$). The dollar and the rest of the world currency (E_1) are floating.

To keep fixed their exchange rates against the dollar (E_2 and E_4), the Chinese and East Asian central banks adjust their foreign reserves and purchase or sell bonds issued by the US government. The Chinese and East Asian bond markets are cleared by the demand of the domestic bonds by the central banks. Since the exchange rate between USA and the rest of the world (E_1) is floating, the US bonds held by the central bank of rest of the world, which represent their foreign currency reserves, remain constant, while the equilibrium of the rest of the world central bank balance sheet determines the level of the domestic bonds it holds.

The Regime XL (Yuan/Dollar Fixed, East Asia/Dollar Floating)

We now turn to the regime XL where the East Asia currency floats against the dollar, while the yuan remains fixed against the dollar, as it was in the end of the 1990s and beginning of the 2000s. The modeling of this new regime is simple. Since the exchange rate between the East Asian currency and the dollar (E_4) is floating, it is defined in the same way as the case of E_1. Foreign reserves held by the East Asian central bank are constant, while its balance sheet equilibrium determines the domestic bonds it holds. E_4 is determined equating the demand of East Asian bonds by US banks and the supply of these bonds to US banks given by the equilibrium of their market.

The Floating Regime LL (Yuan/Dollar and East Asia/Dollar Floating)

The transition from a fixed regime to a floating regime reflects the tendency toward financial liberalization. It corresponds to a regime which could be implemented only at the end of a long period of transition. By modifying the basic model, we can model the exchange rate of the yuan against the dollar E_2 determined under the floating regime. The foreign reserves of the Chinese central bank are now constant, while its balance sheet equilibrium determines the domestic bonds it holds. E_2 is determined by equating the demand of Chinese bonds by US banks and the supply of these bonds to US banks given by the equilibrium of their market.

The Yuan Area Regime LX (Yuan/Dollar Floating and East Asia/Yuan Fixed)

On the one side, the exchange rate regime between the USA and China is liberalized, and the yuan is floating against the dollar. On the other side, the regional cooperation between Asian countries is sufficiently developed in order to form a yuan area with fixed exchange rates. The modeling of the floating yuan has already been presented and requires no changes. The modeling of the yuan area with fixed exchange rate E_5 between East Asia and yuan implies variable foreign reserves for the East Asian

Table 6.2 Alternative closures of basic exchange rate regimes

	Variable determined in bond market			Variable determined by CB		
	B^{RW}	B^{CH}	B^{EA}	CB^{RW}	CB^{CH}	CB^{EA}
Regime XL Fixed E_2, floating E_5	E_1	$Bcb^{d}{}^{CH}_{CH}$	E_4	$\Delta Bcb^{d}{}^{RW}_{RW}$	$\Delta Bcb^{d}{}^{US}_{CH}$	$\Delta Bcb^{d}{}^{EA}_{EA}$
Regime XX Fixed E_2, fixed E_4	E_1	$Bcb^{d}{}^{CH}_{CH}$	$Bcb^{d}{}^{EA}_{EA}$	$\Delta Bcb^{d}{}^{RW}_{RW}$	$\Delta Bcb^{d}{}^{US}_{CH}$	$\Delta Bcb^{d}{}^{US}_{EA}$
Regime LL Floating E_2, floating E_4	E_1	E_2	E_4	$\Delta Bcb^{d}{}^{RW}_{RW}$	$\Delta Bcb^{d}{}^{CH}_{CH}$	$\Delta Bcb^{d}{}^{EA}_{EA}$
Regime LX Floating E_2, fixed E_5	E_1	E_2	$Bcb^{d}{}^{EA}_{EA}$	$\Delta Bcb^{d}{}^{RW}_{RW}$	$\Delta Bcb^{d}{}^{CH}_{CH}$	$\Delta Bcb^{d}{}^{US}_{EA}$

central bank. The exchange rate E_4 between East Asia and dollar is no more constant but derived from the exchange rate E_2 between yuan and the dollar ($E_4 = E_2/E_5$).

Table 6.2 shows the alternative closures for each exchange rate regime. The first three columns refer to variables that ensure the equilibrium with respect to each country's bond market. The last three columns indicate the variables which ensure the equilibrium of each central bank's balance sheet. We can recall, first, that the US bond market is always equilibrated by the domestic bonds held by the US central bank $B_{cb}{}^{d}{}_{US}{}^{US}$ and, second, that the equilibrium of the US central bank balance sheet is not written as it is the missing equation of the model.

6.2.2.2 The Closure of the Intermediate Regimes

Regime XA (Yuan/Dollar Fixed; East Asia/Dollar Managed)

In the regime XA, the yuan is still pegged to the dollar, but the East Asian currency is now in a managed regime against the dollar, instead of being purely floating like in the regime XL. It is another illustration of the regime of the end of the 1990s and beginning of the 2000s. This regime can be constructed by modifying the exchange regime that determine E_4 from the basic model XX. We can use two kinds of targeting. The former is based on the foreign reserves held by the East Asian central bank and uses the ratio of US bonds held by central bank to GDP $\left(Bcb^{d}{}^{US}_{EA}/Y^{EA}\right)$ as a target; the latter uses simply the ratio of the current account to GDP (CA^{EA}/Y^{EA}). The last equations are the same as in the regime XX with variable foreign reserves of East Asia.

$$E_4 = E_{4-1} + \gamma_1 \cdot \left(Bcb^{d}{}^{US}_{EA}/Y^{EA} - \left(Bcb^{d}{}^{US}_{EA}/Y^{EA}\right)^{e}\right)$$

$$E_4 = E_{4-1} + \gamma_2 \cdot \left(CA^{EA}/Y^{EA} - \left(CA^{EA}/Y^{EA}\right)^{e}\right)$$

Regime AL (Yuan/Dollar Managed, East Asia/Dollar Floating)

In the regime AL, the Chinese monetary authorities follow a managed regime against the dollar with a target for their foreign reserves or their current account surplus while East Asia is floating against the dollar. This regime is closer to the current monetary regime. The system of equations is equivalent to the basic model XL with variable Chinese foreign reserves, except for the equation giving the yuan/dollar exchange rate E_2 which is replaced by one of the following equations.

$$E_2 = E_{2-1} + \gamma_1 \cdot \left(Bcb^{d}{}^{\text{US}}_{\text{CH}} / Y^{\text{CH}} - \left(Bcb^{d}{}^{\text{US}}_{\text{CH}} / Y^{\text{CH}} \right)^{e} \right)$$

$$E_2 = E_{2-1} + \gamma_2 \cdot \left(CA^{\text{CH}} / Y^{\text{CH}} - \left(CA^{\text{CH}} / Y^{\text{CH}} \right)^{e} \right)$$

The Yuan Area Regime AX (Yuan/Dollar Managed, East Asia/Yuan Fixed)

The regime AX is another version of the yuan area where the yuan follows a managed exchange regime against the dollar and the East Asian currency is in the fixed regime with the yuan. The Chinese financial liberalization is supposed to be less advanced and the Chinese authorities keep the yuan more under control. Equations are the same as in the fixed regime XX, except for the yuan/dollar exchange rate E_2 which is under control like in the regime AL while the Chinese foreign reserves are variable. However, the East Asian currency is no more anchored on the dollar, but on the yuan (E_5 is constant instead of E_4).

The Yuan Block Regime LA (Yuan/Dollar floating, East Asia/Yuan Managed)

The regime LA describes the situation where the East Asian monetary authorities are engaged in a managed floating regime with the yuan, while the yuan is floating against the dollar. This regime can be labeled a yuan block as the yuan plays a role of anchor but in a more flexible way than in a yuan area with fixed East Asia/yuan exchange rate. The equations are the same as in the regime LX, except for the exchange rate E_5 (EA/yuan) which is adjusted by the intervention of East Asian monetary authorities to meet the target on the foreign reserves or the current account. East Asian foreign reserves are variable but under control.

$$E_5 = E_{5-1} + \gamma_1 \cdot \left(Bcb^{d}{}^{\text{US}}_{\text{EA}} / Y^{\text{EA}} - \left(Bcb^{d}{}^{\text{US}}_{\text{EA}} / \text{Y}^{\text{EA}} \right)^{e} \right)$$

$$E_5 = E_{5-1} + \gamma_2 \cdot \left(CA^{\text{EA}} / Y^{\text{EA}} - \left(CA^{\text{EA}} / Y^{\text{EA}} \right)^{e} \right)$$

6.2.2.3 Simulations of the Basic and Intermediate Regimes

We focus on an asymmetric supply shock inside the whole East Asia area which is the main challenge for East Asian monetary regimes and consider a gain of competitiveness of China against East Asia (the income elasticity in equation giving the Chinese imports from East Asia is reduced from 0.6 to 0.5). Figure 6.1 gives the main results for China and East Asia (in relative difference from the baseline).

The Basic Regimes

We start with the regime XX (dollar pegged) which corresponds roughly to the middle of the 1990s with a de facto cooperation between East Asian countries by the anchorage on the dollar and also with the interventions of the Chinese monetary authority to limit the fluctuations of the yuan and anchor the yuan on the dollar. It is a kind of dollar standard with only the rest of the world floating against the dollar. The gain of Chinese competitiveness against East Asia induces a boom of Chinese GDP and trade surplus at the expense of East Asia, which suffers from symmetric losses. With fixed exchange rates, there is no mechanism of adjustment. Imbalances between China and East Asia remain without adjustment.

The regime XL (yuan/dollar fixed, East Asia/dollar floating) corresponds to the end of the 1990s and beginning of the 2000s when Chinese monetary authority limited the fluctuation of exchange rates within a certain range while the East Asian currencies were more floating against the dollar. The gains of competitiveness of China against East Asia induce a boom in China with increasing current surplus to the detriment of East Asia. But the floating exchange rate of East Asia absorbs the shock with a devaluation against the dollar which reduces the current deficit and the slowdown in East Asia to the detriment of the USA.

The main characteristic of the floating regime LL is the existence of adjustment mechanisms alleviating the persistent imbalances through flexible exchange rates. In case of an improvement of Chinese competitiveness against East Asia, the current account surplus or deficits which occur in the early periods after the competitiveness shock are reduced gradually, as the exchange rates are adjusted. Chinese current account surplus makes the yuan appreciate against the dollar, while the currency of EA depreciates.

The regime LX (yuan/dollar floating, East Asia/yuan fixed) is representative of a yuan area with the East Asian currency anchored on the yuan which floats freely after a long period of liberalization. Although this regime is rather unlikely, it is worth studying it. In case of gains of Chinese competitiveness against East Asia, this is another illustration of the negative effect of fixed exchange rates when asymmetric shock occurs. Thanks to the gains of Chinese competitiveness, the yuan appreciates against the dollar, followed by the East Asian currency which is pegged to the yuan. The East Asian slowdown and current deficit are amplified without mechanism of rebalancing. The USA appears as the main winner of this evolution.

The Intermediate Regimes

In the managed exchange rate equation, we introduce only the results using the ratio of US bond held by central bank to GDP. Even though results are a little bit different depending on the selected target variable, it will be sufficient to show the feature of adjustment mechanisms. The shock corresponds as previously to a loss of East Asian competitiveness against China (see Fig. 6.1).

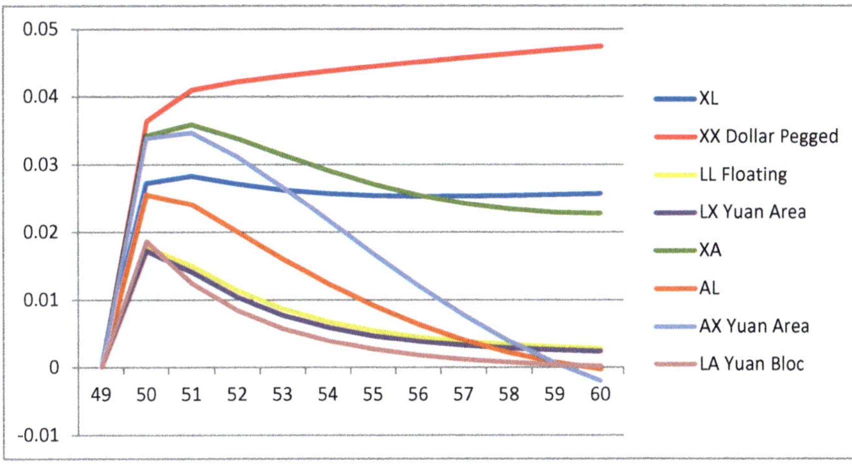

GDP of East Asia

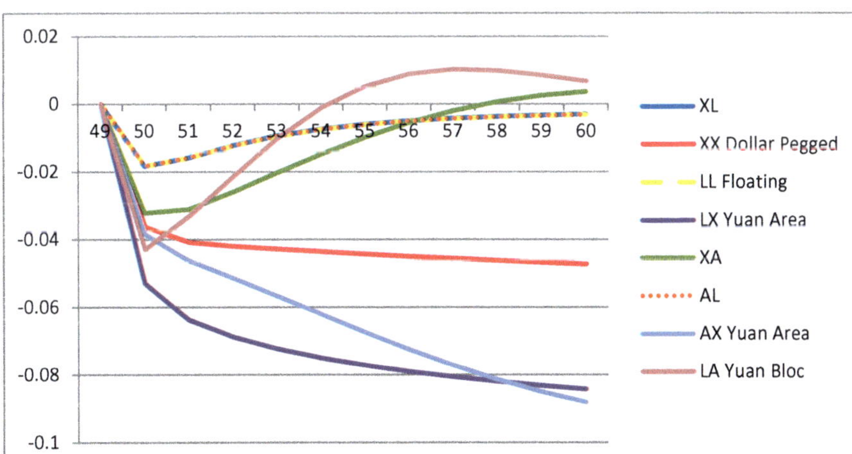

E_2 (1$= E_2 yuan)

Fig. 6.1 Improvement of the competitiveness of China toward EA (in relative difference from the baseline)

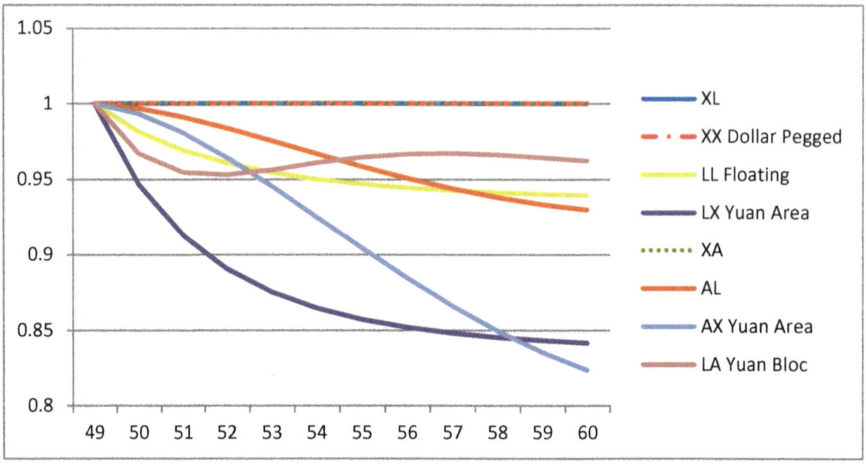

E_4 (1\$= E_4 ₩)

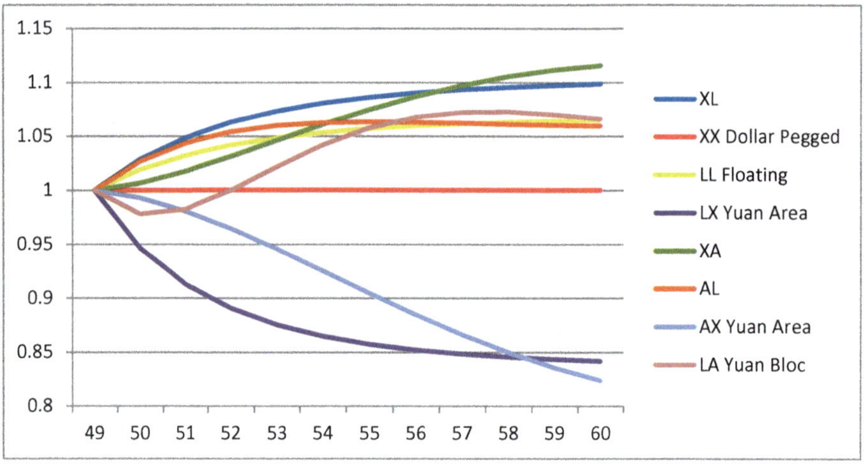

Fig. 6.1 (continued)

In the regime XA (yuan/dollar fixed, EA/dollar managed), the results are very similar to the regime XL where the yuan/dollar was fixed and the EA/dollar floating. The only significant difference is that the movements of exchange rates are slower to meet the target value. Both regimes XL and XA are representative of the end of the 1990s and beginning of the 2000s.

In the regime AL (yuan/dollar managed, EA/dollar floating), the features are rather similar to the floating regime LL. The velocity of adjustment in the early periods is slower than in the case of pure floating system. Consequently the simulation shows that the scale of the fluctuation in current account is enlarged. China is able to better preserve its gains in terms of growth and current surplus, thanks to a reduced appreciation of the yuan. The regime AL corresponds broadly to the 2010s.

The regime AX (yuan/dollar managed, EA/yuan fixed) is another version of the yuan zone where, instead of having a pure floating yuan as in the regime LX, the yuan follows a managed regime, while the EA currency remains anchored rigidly to the yuan. Without surprise, the results resemble to those of the regime LX. However, once again, Chinese results in terms of growth and trade are better preserved due to the more limited appreciation of the yuan at short term. The evolution is also less unfavorable to East Asia at short-medium term, thanks to the more limited appreciation of the yuan (and of the EA currency) and the better situation of China. But the rigid anchorage on the yuan remains highly painful.

The regime LA (yuan/dollar floating, East Asia/yuan managed) is another version of a yuan block which is a more flexible regime. The exchange rate of EA currency/ yuan is managed and no more rigid, as in the yuan zone. The results for China are close to those of the floating regime LL or to the yuan zone LX but with a more reduced yuan appreciation, as Chinese surpluses increase less due to the EA currency depreciation. Thanks to this EA depreciation, a recovery and an improvement of the current account are observed in East Asia. On the whole this is the more favorable regime for East Asia facing a shock of competitiveness from China.

6.2.2.4 Lessons from the Simulations

This first set of simulations has given a rough description of East Asian monetary regimes as they have been observed in the past or could evolve in the future. It is of course a highly simplified representation, but it describes the interdependency between real and financial spheres in stocks and flows in a consistent way at the world level. Beyond the Chinese gain of competitiveness against East Asia, other shocks have been observed since the end of the 1990s and can be simulated: a demand shock due to stronger Chinese rate of accumulation, another supply shock reflecting gains of Chinese competitiveness against the USA, and a revaluation of the yuan in the case of fixed exchange rate between the yuan and the dollar (see Mazier et al. 2014, for the main results).

The regime XX (dollar pegged) represents roughly what was prevailing during the middle of the 1990s. It reflects a weak form of de facto coordination between East Asian countries by anchoring on the dollar to avoid divergent evolutions. Strong Chinese growth diffuses toward East Asia and the USA with current accounts in surplus, while the rest of the world appreciates moderately and does not benefit the boom. Improving Chinese competitiveness against the USA leads to a boom in China at the expense of the USA with large current imbalances and no diffusion effect to East Asia, as the gains on China and the losses on the USA compensate with weak exchange rate adjustment mechanisms. Gains of Chinese competitiveness against East Asia give similar results at the detriment of East Asia. The Asian crisis of 1997–1998 can be interpreted in this context with an East Asian speculative boom and declining competitiveness leading to large current deficits with no adjustment mechanisms.

The regimes XL and XA (fixed yuan/dollar and floating or managed East Asia/ dollar) corresponds to the main lines of the end of the 1990s and beginning of the

2000s. Chinese boom induces US recovery, which is also sustained by a dollar depreciation, with small impact on East Asia and rest of the world who suffer from exchange appreciation. Improving Chinese competitiveness against the USA also leads to Chinese boom at the detriment of the USA who faces large current deficit. Here again there is no diffusion to East Asia and rest of the world and very limited exchange rate adjustments. On the opposite, Chinese gains of competitiveness against East Asia can be better balanced, thanks to East Asian depreciation against the dollar. A yuan revaluation against the dollar is also a partial solution, as it rebalances the disequilibrium between China and the USA but without effect on East Asia and the rest of the world, as their currencies appreciate against the dollar. In case of managed exchange rate for East Asia (instead of pure floating), the evolution of East Asia is more favorable. As it is known, this yuan revaluation has remained modest before the burst of the financial crisis in 2007–2008, which has contributed to the reduction of the world imbalances mainly through cuts in imports. However, thanks to more flexible exchange rate policy in East Asia, intra-East Asian imbalances have been reduced.

The regime AL (yuan/dollar managed, East Asia/dollar floating) presents some similarities with the present situation of the 2010s. The results obtained are also rather close to the regime LL of pure floating. The main difference is that, with floating exchange rates, the velocity of adjustment is higher which reduces the scale of current account variations and of the GDP growth. Increasing Chinese investment boosts Chinese growth and deteriorates its current account which depreciates the yuan. This depreciation stimulates more Chinese growth and reduces its current deficit. On the opposite, the other areas are less stimulated and their current surplus decreased. Similarly, gains of competitiveness of China against the USA induce opposite evolutions of GDP and current account in the two countries with a return to the initial position, thanks to the yuan appreciation. Last, improving Chinese competitiveness against East Asia is also balanced by East Asian depreciation.

These simulations illustrate once again that floating exchange rates are a powerful tool to reduce international imbalances. But the large instability is the intrinsic drawback of this exchange rate system. The economic policy instruments to preserve the stability should be implemented with some form of capital controls. Even though the adjustments are realized more gradually and the scale of the fluctuation is larger compared to the case of the pure floating system, the managed exchange rate system could be a feasible political alternative as an intermediate stage. Compared with the present situation, two points must be underlined. First, the yuan is not floating, and the managed exchange rate of the yuan is under control of the Chinese central bank. Second, East Asian currencies are not also freely floating. However, since the end of the 2000s, the East Asian current surpluses have been reduced significantly.

The regimes LX and AX (yuan/dollar floating or managed, East Asia/yuan fixed) is a different type of regime which can be called yuan area with the East Asia currency anchored to the yuan which is floating or managed against the dollar. It is a long-term scenario which could be achieved after a difficult process of economic and politic integration in East Asia. Although rather unlikely, it is worth being examined.

Following a stimulation of Chinese investment, China and East Asia benefit of the yuan depreciation which improves both the current account and the GDP growth. On the opposite the USA suffers large losses due the dollar appreciation. In this demand shock, East Asia benefits of Chinese recovery. But in case of Chinese gains of competitiveness against the USA, the induced growth leads to an appreciation of the yuan and of the East Asia currency which penalizes its growth and deteriorates its current account. Conversely the USA benefits of the dollar depreciation. The same results are observed in case of China increasing competitiveness against East Asia.

Asymmetric shocks in a fixed exchange rates regime induce divergent evolutions which are difficult to manage in the absence of exchange rate adjustments. This is a well-known result, often forgotten however. Even if a yuan area is a long-term perspective, it does not play in its favor, more especially as this yuan area is characterized by strong structural heterogeneities between participant countries.

Last, the regime LA (yuan/dollar floating, East Asia/yuan managed) is also a long-term scenario but with a more managed exchange rate regime for East Asia. It can be called a yuan block, where the exchange rate of EA currency/yuan is managed and no more rigid, as in the yuan zone. In case of Chinese gains of competitiveness against East Asia, the results for China are close to those of the floating regime LL or to the yuan zone LX but with a more reduced yuan appreciation, as Chinese surpluses increase less due to the EA currency depreciation. Thanks to this EA depreciation, a recovery and an improvement of the current account are observed in East Asia. On the whole this is the more favorable regime for East Asia facing a shock of competitiveness from China.

6.2.3 *Exchange Rate Regimes in East Asia: The ACU Regimes*

A second set of models allows for the study of more elaborated intermediate monetary regimes (with fixed but adjustable exchange rates beyond a certain threshold) and is based on alternative forms of Asian Currency Unit (ACU): traditional ACU as a currency basket, ACU bancor, global ACU as an international currency, or even ACU as a single currency. They are based on a more detailed decomposition of East Asia with a split between Japan and the rest of East Asia, while the USA is gathered with the rest of the world for more simplicity. Consequently, in the SFC model the world economy is divided into four areas: China, Japan, the rest of East Asia, and the rest of the world. The whole structure of the SFC model remains the same.

6.2.3.1 The Traditional ACU Regime

The traditional ACU is a currency basket composed of the yuan, the yen, and the East Asian currency ($1UC^{RW} = E_{10}$ ACU) which is used only as a unit of account.

The ACU/rest of the world exchange rate (E_{10}) is built as a weighted average of the yen (E_1), the yuan (E_2), and the EA currency (E_4) compared to the rest of the world currency.

$$\frac{1}{E_{10}} = \frac{Y^{JP}}{Y^{JP}+Y^{CH}+Y^{EA}} \cdot \frac{1}{E_1} + \frac{Y^{CH}}{Y^{JP}+Y^{CH}+Y^{EA}} \cdot \frac{1}{E_2} + \frac{Y^{EA}}{Y^{JP}+Y^{CH}+Y^{EA}} \cdot \frac{1}{E_4}$$

The yen, the yuan, and the EA currency are floating against the rest of the world currency and are pegged to the ACU (1 ACU= E_7 yen =E_8 yuan= E_9 UC^{EA}). For the sake of simplicity, it is supposed there is no fluctuation margin, but these exchange rates are adjustable when the current account in % of GDP is permanently under a certain threshold. The yuan/rest of the world exchange rate (E_2) is determined in a floating regime, and the yuan is acting as anchor of the whole system. The EA currency/yuan and the yen/yuan exchange rates are fixed but adjustable within the ACU regime. Consequently, the EA currency/rest of the world (E_4) and the yen/rest of the world (E_1) exchange rates can be simply deduced from the yuan exchange rate (E_2). Under this hybrid regime, the EA and Japanese central banks accumulate foreign reserves under the form of bonds issued by the rest of the world government (${Bcb^s}^{RW}_{JP}$ and ${Bcb^s}^{RW}_{EA}$).

$$E_{7_t} = E_{7_{t-1}} \cdot (1+\varphi), \text{if } \frac{{CA^{JP}}_{t-i}}{{Y^{JP}}_{t-i}} < -0.001, \forall i = 1,2,3,4,5$$

(same equations for E_8 and E_9)

$$E_1 = E_2.E_7/E_8 \text{ and } E_4 = E_2.E_9/E_8$$

$${Bcb^s}^{RW}_{JP} = {Bcb^d}^{RW}_{JP}/E_1$$

$$\Delta {Bcb^d}^{RW}_{JP} = \Delta RSV^{JP} + \Delta {H^d}^{JP} - \Delta A^{JP} - \Delta {Bcb^d}^{JP}_{JP}$$

$${Bcb^d}^{JP}_{JP} = B^{sJP} - {Bb^d}^{JP}_{JP} - {Bb^s}^{JP}_{RW} - {Bb^s}^{JP}_{CH} - {Bb^s}^{JP}_{EA}$$

(same equations for East Asia)

The ACU regime can also be organized without Japan or China which would prefer to preserve their autonomy.

6.2.3.2 The ACU Regime Without Japan

In this regime Japan remains outside the ACU regime and floats against the rest of the world. This regime is very similar to the previous one. The yuan is still the anchor of the ACU regime (E_2). The only difference is the determination of the yen/rest of the world exchange rate (E_1) which is now floating.

$$\frac{1}{E_{10}} = \frac{Y^{\mathrm{CH}}}{Y^{\mathrm{CH}} + Y^{\mathrm{EA}}} \cdot \frac{1}{E_2} + \frac{Y^{\mathrm{EA}}}{Y^{\mathrm{CH}} + Y^{\mathrm{EA}}} \cdot \frac{1}{E_4}$$

$$\mathrm{E}_{8_t} = \mathrm{E}_{8_{t-1}} \cdot (1+\varphi), \text{if } \frac{CA^{\mathrm{CH}}{}_{t-i}}{Y^{\mathrm{CH}}{}_{t-i}} < -0.001, \forall i = 1,2,3,4,5$$

(same equations for E_9)

$$\mathrm{E}_4 = \mathrm{E}_2.\ \mathrm{E}_9/\mathrm{E}_8$$

$$Bcb^{d}{}^{\mathrm{RW}}_{\mathrm{JP}} = \text{constant}$$

$$Bcb^{s}{}^{\mathrm{RW}}_{\mathrm{JP}} = Bcb^{d}{}^{\mathrm{RW}}_{\mathrm{JP}}/E_1$$

$$\Delta Bcb^{d}{}^{\mathrm{JP}}_{\mathrm{JP}} = \Delta RSV^{\mathrm{JP}} + \Delta H^{d\mathrm{JP}} - \Delta A^{\mathrm{JP}} - \Delta Bcb^{d}{}^{\mathrm{RW}}_{\mathrm{JP}}$$

$$E_1 = \left(B^{s\mathrm{JP}} - Bb^{d}{}^{\mathrm{JP}}_{\mathrm{JP}} - Bb^{s}{}^{\mathrm{JP}}_{\mathrm{CH}} - Bb^{s}{}^{\mathrm{JP}}_{\mathrm{EA}} - Bcb^{s}{}^{\mathrm{JP}}_{\mathrm{JP}}\right)/Bb^{d}{}^{\mathrm{JP}}_{\mathrm{RW}}$$

6.2.3.3 The ACU Regime Without China

In this alternative ACU regime, China remains outside the system to preserve its autonomy, and the yuan floats alone against the rest of the world (E_2). This regime is similar to the previous ones. The yen becomes the new anchor of the ACU regime (E_1).

$$\frac{1}{E_{10}} = \frac{Y^{\mathrm{JP}}}{Y^{\mathrm{JP}} + Y^{\mathrm{EA}}} \cdot \frac{1}{E_1} + \frac{Y^{\mathrm{EA}}}{Y^{\mathrm{JP}} + Y^{\mathrm{EA}}} \cdot \frac{1}{E_4}$$

$$\mathrm{E}_{7_t} = \mathrm{E}_{7_{t-1}} \cdot (1+\varphi), \text{if } \frac{CA^{\mathrm{JP}}{}_{t-i}}{Y^{\mathrm{JP}}{}_{t-i}} < -0.001, \forall i = 1,2,3,4,5$$

(same equations for E_9)

$$\mathrm{E}_4 = \mathrm{E}_1.\ \mathrm{E}_9/\mathrm{E}_7$$

6.2.3.4 The ACU Bancor

A more ambitious regime would borrow some of the ideas proposed by Keynes (1941) in his report on an international monetary reform. An Asian bancor would be introduced and would in practice be very similar to the traditional ACU, a basket currency of the national currencies. More important, an Asian Clearing Union (CU) would be created, and the participant countries would accumulate bancor balances (AB) at this Clearing Union according to their external performances, both in terms of current account and capital movements. A surplus country would register an increase in its bancor account at the CU whereas a country in deficit would register a decrease in its stocks of bancors. The East Asian currencies would be pegged to the Asian bancor with a system of fixed, but adjustable, exchange rates. The adjustment criterion of each East Asian currency vis-à-vis the Asian bancor would depend on the intra-regional external performance of the associate country ($CA^{\mathrm{JP}}_{\mathrm{CH}} + CA^{\mathrm{JP}}_{EA}$, for instance). But the East Asian currencies would float against the currency of the rest of the world, with one of them acting as an anchor for the whole system (the yuan for instance). Its exchange rate against the rest of the world (E_2) would be determined by the supply and demand of its domestic bond markets, while its central bank would keep constant its foreign reserves ($Bcb^{s\,\mathrm{RW}}_{\mathrm{CH}}$). As the other East Asian currencies are pegged to the Asian bancor and engaged in a fixed exchange rate system, their exchange rates against the rest of the world can be simply deduced, while their central banks accumulate foreign reserves ($Bcb^{s\,\mathrm{RW}}_{\mathrm{JP}}$ and $Bcb^{s\,\mathrm{RW}}_{\mathrm{EA}}$).

$$1 \text{ Asian bancor} = \mathrm{E}_7\text{yen} = \mathrm{E}_8\text{yuan} = \mathrm{E}_9\mathrm{UC}^{\mathrm{EA}}$$

$$\frac{1}{E_{10}} = \frac{Y^{\mathrm{JP}}}{Y^{\mathrm{JP}} + Y^{\mathrm{CH}} + Y^{\mathrm{EA}}} \cdot \frac{1}{E_1} + \frac{Y^{\mathrm{CH}}}{Y^{\mathrm{JP}} + Y^{\mathrm{CH}} + Y^{\mathrm{EA}}} \cdot \frac{1}{E_2} + \frac{Y^{\mathrm{EA}}}{Y^{\mathrm{JP}} + Y^{\mathrm{CH}} + Y^{\mathrm{EA}}} \cdot \frac{1}{E_4}$$

$$E_{7t} = E_{7t-1} \cdot (1 + \varphi), \text{ if } \left(CA^{\mathrm{JP}}_{\mathrm{CH}} + CA^{\mathrm{JP}}_{EA}\right)/Y^{jp} < 0.001 \text{ (same equation for E8 and E9)}$$

$$E_2 = \left(B^{s\mathrm{CH}} - Bb^{d\,\mathrm{CH}}_{\mathrm{CH}} - Bb^{s\,\mathrm{CH}}_{\mathrm{JP}} - Bb^{s\,\mathrm{CH}}_{\mathrm{EA}} - Bcb^{s\,\mathrm{CH}}_{\mathrm{CH}}\right)/Bb^{d\,\mathrm{CH}}_{\mathrm{RW}}$$

$$Bcb^{s\,\mathrm{RW}}_{\mathrm{CH}} = \text{constant}$$

$$\Delta Bcb^{d\,\mathrm{RW}}_{\mathrm{CH}} = Bcb^{s\,\mathrm{RW}}_{\mathrm{CH}-1} \Delta E_2$$

$$\mathrm{E}_1 = \mathrm{E}_2 .\ \mathrm{E}_7/\mathrm{E}_8 \text{ and } \mathrm{E}_4 = \mathrm{E}_2 .\ \mathrm{E}_9/\mathrm{E}_8$$

The transactions undertaken within the Clearing Union can now be presented. This is the institution where all the payments are cleared. Every East Asian country would have an account at the Clearing Union. This account would be an asset for each national central bank and a liability for the Clearing Union. However, bancor balances (AB) would not only be composed of international trade and portfolio investment within East Asia. They would also include specific flows characterizing Keynes' proposals.

First, in order to make the adjustment process more symmetric within East Asia, the rule would make both debtor and creditor countries share the burden of the debts. Thus, all countries would pay interests on their bancor balances, positive as well as negative (e.g., $r^{JP}_{-1} \cdot \left|AB^{JP}_{-1}\right|$). This rule would encourage countries to make their account at the Clearing Union be as close to zero as possible. A second flow incorporated in the bancor balances would be the one related to the distribution of the funds collected by the Clearing Union and resulting from the interest payments on the bancor balances (the profit of the Clearing Union PAB). This intra-Asian adjustment (IAA) would be distributed to member countries according to their external performance. Last, the balance sheet identity of the East Asian central banks holds through the purchases or sales of foreign reserves.

$$\Delta AB^{JP} = \Delta CL^{JP} + r_{-1}^{JP} \cdot \left|AB_{-1}^{JP}\right| + IAA^{JP} \cdot E_7$$

$$\Delta CL^{\mathrm{JP}} = \mathrm{CA}_{\mathrm{CH}}^{\mathrm{JP}} + \mathrm{CA}_{\mathrm{EA}}^{\mathrm{JP}} + \mathrm{KA}_{\mathrm{CH}}^{\mathrm{JP}} + \mathrm{KA}_{\mathrm{EA}}^{\mathrm{JP}}$$

$$PAB = r_{-1}^{JP} \cdot \left|AB_{-1}^{JP}\right|/E_7 + r_{-1}^{CH} \cdot \left|AB_{-1}^{CH}\right|/E_8 + r_{-1}^{EA} \cdot \left|AB_{-1}^{EA}\right|/E_9$$

$$\Delta Bcb^{d}{}_{\mathrm{JP}}^{\mathrm{RW}} = \Delta RSV^{\mathrm{JP}} + \Delta H^{d\mathrm{JP}} - \Delta A^{\mathrm{JP}} - \Delta Bcb^{d}{}_{\mathrm{JP}}^{\mathrm{JP}} - \Delta AB^{\mathrm{JP}}$$

Finally, another feature suggested by Keynes could be introduced. In Keynes' proposals surplus countries are encouraged to use their positive bancor balances to increase imports, since otherwise they would be wasting their balances. The government is the only agent that could internalize the loss that the central bank would incur if bancor balances were gradually reduced through interest payments. Consequently, it is assumed that the government of surplus countries augments its public expenditures to purchase imported products from other member countries. This adjustment process is non-recessionary as only surplus countries would be pushed to pursue more expansive policies.

$$\begin{cases} \psi^{i}{}_{t} = \mu \cdot \log\left(1 + r \cdot AB^{i}{}_{t-1}\right), & \text{if } AB^{i}{}_{t-1} > 0 \\ \psi^{i}{}_{t} = 0, & \text{elsewhere.} \end{cases}, \quad \text{for } i = \mathrm{JP}, \mathrm{CH}, \mathrm{EA}$$

$$G^{i}{}_{t} = G^{i}{}_{0} \cdot \left(1 + gr^{i}\right)^{t} + \psi^{i}{}_{t}, \text{for } i = \mathrm{JP}, \mathrm{CH}, \mathrm{EA}$$

6.2.3.5 The Global ACU as a New International Currency

In a more ambitious perspective, the ACU would not be a simple basket currency but a true international currency, the global ACU (AG), acting as an international store of value. East Asian governments would issue bonds in national currencies (yen, yuan, EA) which would be purchased only by national agents (domestic banks in the model). The gap between the financial needs of the government ($B^{s\mathrm{JP}}$ for instance) and the demand for bonds denominated in domestic currency ($Bb^{s}{}_{\mathrm{JP}}^{\mathrm{JP}}$) would be filled by issuance of bonds denominated in global ACU ($B^{s\mathrm{JP},\ \mathrm{AG}}$) and purchased by foreign creditors to get external financing ($Bb^{s\mathrm{JP,AG}}_{\mathrm{CH}} + Bb^{s\mathrm{JP,AG}}_{\mathrm{EA}} + Bb^{s\mathrm{JP,AG}}_{\mathrm{RW}} + Bb^{s\mathrm{JP,AG}}_{\mathrm{ACB}}$). This global ACU would float at the world level and its exchange rate against the rest of the world currency ($1\text{UC}^{\text{RW}} = \text{E}_{10}$ AG) would be determined as usual by the interaction between supply and demand of global ACU-denominated bonds.

$$B^{s\text{JP,AG}} = \frac{B^{s\text{JP}} - Bcb^{s\,\text{JP}}_{\text{JP}} - Bb^{s\,\text{JP}}_{\text{JP}}}{E_7}$$

$$E_{10} = \frac{\begin{array}{c} B^{s\text{JP,AG}} + B^{s\text{CH,AG}} + B^{s\text{EA,AG}} - Bb^{s\text{JP,AG}}_{\text{CH}} - Bb^{s\text{JP,AG}}_{\text{EA}} - Bb^{s\text{CH,AG}}_{\text{JP}} \\ -Bb^{s\text{CH,AG}}_{\text{EA}} - Bb^{s\text{EA,AG}}_{\text{JP}} - Bb^{s\text{EA,AG}}_{\text{CH}} - Bb^{s\text{JP,AG}}_{\text{ACB}} - Bb^{s\text{CH,AG}}_{\text{ACB}} - Bb^{s\text{EA,AG}}_{\text{ACB}} \end{array}}{Bb^{d\,\text{JP,AG}}_{\text{RW}} + Bb^{d\,\text{CH,AG}}_{\text{RW}} + Bb^{d\,\text{EA,AG}}_{\text{RW}}}$$

In order to give flexibility to this exchange rate regime, the exchange rates of the national currencies (yen, yuan, EA) against the global ACU (1 AG = E_7 yen $=\text{E}_8$ yuan = E_9 UC^{EA}) are fixed but can be adjusted according to the external performance vis-à-vis their trading partners. A rule similar to the one used in the traditional ACU regime can be retained. Once the intra-East Asian exchange rates are defined, it is possible to derive the exchange rates of the national currencies vis-à-vis the rest of the world ($\text{E}_1=\text{E}_{10}.\text{E}_7$; $\text{E}_2=\text{E}_{10}.\text{E}_8$ and $\text{E}_4= \text{E}_{10}.\text{E}_9$).

The same type of Clearing Union as in the bancor regime is adopted. Each national central bank has a balance at the Clearing Union equal to its current account and portfolio balance with the other countries participants (CL^{JP}). As the global ACU is floating and as the national central banks accumulate these balances at the Clearing Union in global ACU, they have no need of foreign reserves which are supposed to be constant, with the possibility of valorization effects. Last, the balance sheet identity of the East Asian central banks holds through the purchases or sales of domestic bonds.

$$\Delta CL^{\text{JP}} = \text{CA}^{\text{JP}}_{\text{CH}} + \text{CA}^{\text{JP}}_{\text{EA}} + \text{KA}^{\text{JP}}_{\text{CH}} + \text{KA}^{\text{JP}}_{\text{EA}}$$

$$\Delta Bcb^{d\,\text{JP}}_{\text{JP}} = \Delta RSV^{\text{JP}} + \Delta H^{d\text{JP}} - \Delta A^{\text{JP}} - \Delta Bcb^{d\,\text{RW}}_{\text{JP}} - \Delta CL^{\text{JP}}$$

$$Bcb^{s\,\text{RW}}_{\text{JP}} = \text{cst}$$

$$\Delta Bcb^{d\,\text{RW}}_{\text{JP}} = Bcb^{s\,\text{RW}}_{\text{JP}-1}.\Delta E_1$$

6.2.3.6 The ACU as a Single Currency

This monetary regime is rather unlikely as it supposes a strong political will to accept the settlement of a monetary union between all the East Asian countries which remain highly heterogeneous. Unlike the traditional ACU, which is a basket currency, the new ACU is a true currency in which real and financial transactions are denominated. There are no more national currencies and all national bonds are denominated in ACU. The ACU floats against the rest of the world and the

Table 6.3 Alternative closures of ACU exchange rate regimes

	Variable determined in bond market			Variable determined by CB		
	B^{CH}	B^{EA}	B^{JP}	CB^{CH}	CB^{EA}	CB^{JP}
ACU regime Floating E_2, fixed but adjustable E_3 E_5	E_2	$Bcb^{d\,EA}_{EA}$	$Bcb^{d\,JP}_{JP}$	$\Delta Bcb^{d\,CH}_{CH}$	$\Delta Bcb^{d\,RW}_{EA}$	$\Delta Bcb^{d\,RW}_{JP}$
ACU regime without JP floating E_1 E_2, fixed but adjustable E_5	E_2	$Bcb^{d\,EA}_{EA}$	E_1	$\Delta Bcb^{d\,CH}_{CH}$	$\Delta Bcb^{d\,RW}_{EA}$	$\Delta Bcb^{d\,JP}_{JP}$
ACU regime without yuan floating E_1 E_2, fixed but adjustable E_6	E_2	$Bcb^{d\,EA}_{EA}$	E_1	$\Delta Bcb^{d\,CH}_{CH}$	$\Delta Bcb^{d\,RW}_{EA}$	$\Delta Bcb^{d\,JP}_{JP}$
Bancor ACU	E_2	$Bcb^{d\,EA}_{EA}$	$Bcb^{d\,JP}_{JP}$	$\Delta Bcb^{d\,CH}_{CH}$	$\Delta Bcb^{d\,RW}_{EA}$	$\Delta Bcb^{d\,RW}_{JP}$
Global ACU	$B^{sCH,\,AG}$	$B^{sEA,\,AG}$	$B^{sJP,\,AG}$	$\Delta Bcb^{d\,CH}_{CH}$	$\Delta Bcb^{d\,EA}_{EA}$	$\Delta Bcb^{d\,JP}_{JP}$
ACU single currency	$E_2=E_4=E_1$	$E_2=E_4=E_1$	$E_2=E_4=E_1$	$\Delta Bcb^{d\,CH}_{CH}$	$\Delta Bcb^{d\,EA}_{EA}$	$\Delta Bcb^{d\,JP}_{JP}$

traditional flexible exchange rate closures prevail. The ACU/rest of the world exchange rate clears the ACU-denominated bond market and the national central banks purchase/sell domestic bonds to balance their balance sheet. There is no foreign reserves accumulation by the East Asian countries (they are kept constant) with only valuation effects when the reserves are expressed in ACU.

Table 6.3 shows the alternative closures for the different ACU exchange rate regimes. As previously, the first three columns refer to variables that ensure the equilibrium with respect to each country's bond market. The last three columns indicate the variables which ensure the equilibrium of each central bank's balance sheet. We can recall first that the rest of the world bond market is always equilibrated by the domestic bonds held by the rest of the world central bank and second that the equilibrium of the rest of the world central bank balance sheet is not written as it is the missing equation of the model.

6.2.3.7 Simulations of the ACU Regimes

As previously, we focus on the same type of asymmetric supply shocks inside the whole East Asia area. We consider first a loss of competitiveness of East Asia against Japan (the income elasticity in equation giving the Japanese imports from East Asia is reduced from 0.6 to 0.5) and second a loss of competitiveness of East Asia and Japan against China. Figures 6.2 and 6.3 give the main results for China and East Asia (in relative difference from the baseline) for the traditional ACU regimes. Figures 6.4 and 6.5 examine the case of the bancor ACU regime and of the global ACU regime. The regime XL (yuan pegged to the dollar, East Asia and Japan floating) and the single currency regime are used as reference regimes.

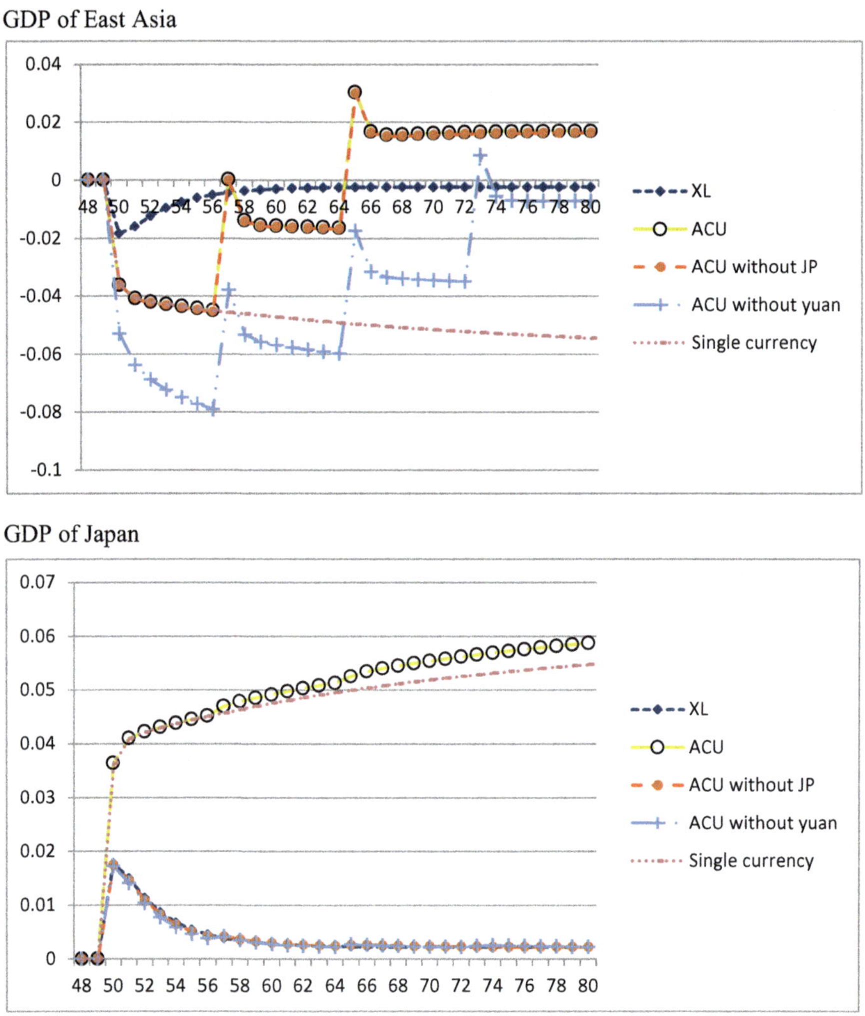

Fig. 6.2 Loss of competitiveness of East Asia against Japan for ACU regimes (in relative difference from the baseline)

A loss of competitiveness of East Asia against Japan induces a negative shock with a slowdown and current deficit. With fixed exchange rate regimes like the regime XX (all the East Asian currencies pegged on the rest of the world) or the single currency, there is no adjustment mechanism. The slowdown and the current deficit remain on the long term. On the contrary more flexible regimes like the ACU regimes with or without the yen allow a progressive adjustment by successive steps with a recovery and a reduction of the current deficit, thanks to a depreciation of EA

Exchange rate E_1 (1\$= E_1 yen)

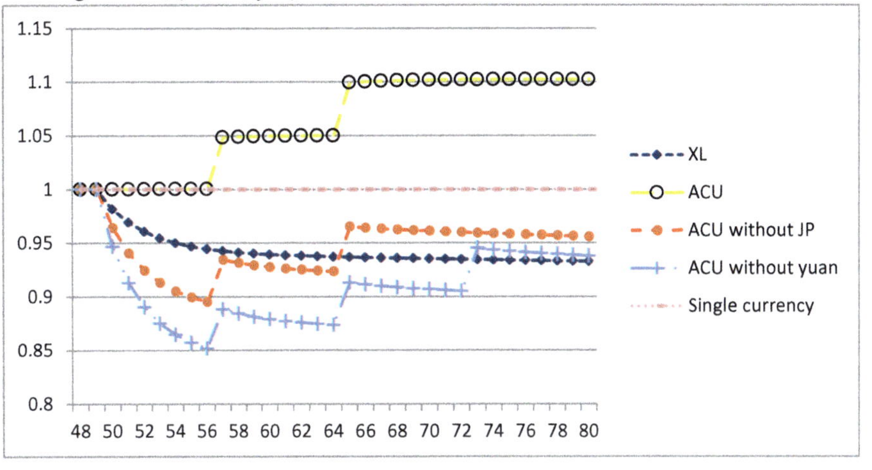

Exchange rate E_2 (1\$ = E_2 yuan)

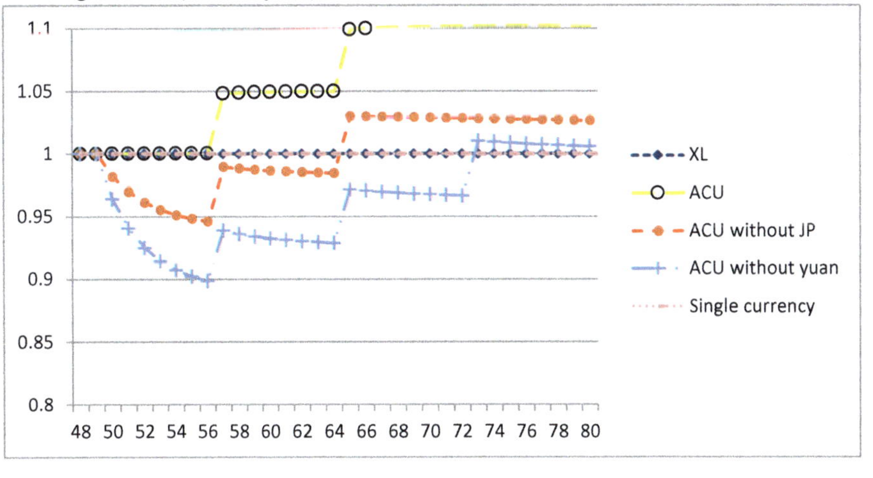

Fig. 6.2 (continued)

Exchange rate E_4 (1\$ = E_4 EA)

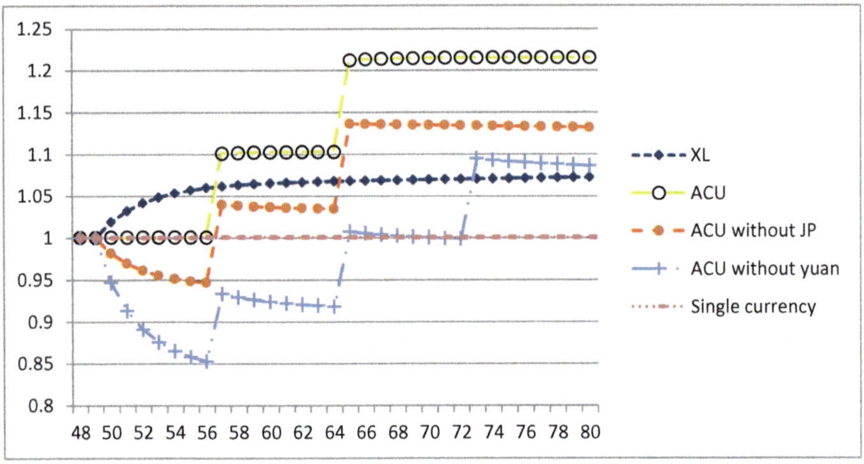

Fig. 6.2 (continued)

currency. More surprisingly an ACU without the yuan gives negative results with a more dramatic GDP decline and current deficit. This can be easily understood, since, in this regime, the Japanese currency is the new anchor of the ACU regime and appreciates strongly due to the gains of competitiveness. EA currency follows this appreciation which increases the initial negative shock. An adjustment is observed only in the long term. Also surprisingly, in the ACU regime, in spite of the gain of competitiveness of the Japanese economy, the yen depreciates against the dollar, which leaves a large advantage to Japan in terms of growth. This is due to the fact that the yuan is the anchor in this regime and slightly depreciates, inducing also the yen depreciation. These mechanisms reflect the fact that the ACU regime gives some flexibility in the adjustment but is not well adapted to face asymmetric shocks between the country participants. The same type of conclusions can be drawn from the loss of competitiveness of East Asia and Japan against China (Fig. 6.3). Partial adjustment can be obtained with the ACU regimes in contrast with more fixed ones. But it is mainly when the yuan is outside the ACU that adjustment can be obtained, thanks to a devaluation of the EA currency and of the yen.

We now turn to Asian bancor regimes with the same type of shocks. In case of a loss of competitiveness of East Asia against Japan a bancor regime without exchange rate adjustment (due to restrictive criterion) allows almost no correction and the initial decline of East Asian GDP remains at the advantage of Japan. When exchange

GDP of EA

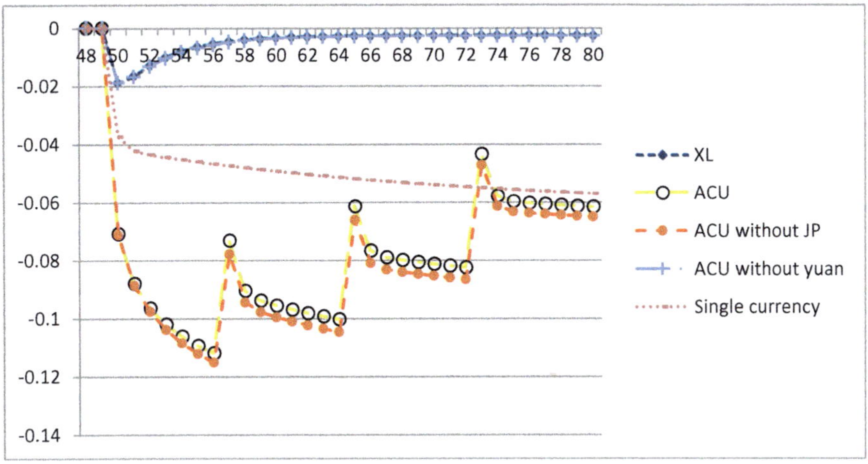

Exchange rate E_4 (1\$ = E_4 EA)

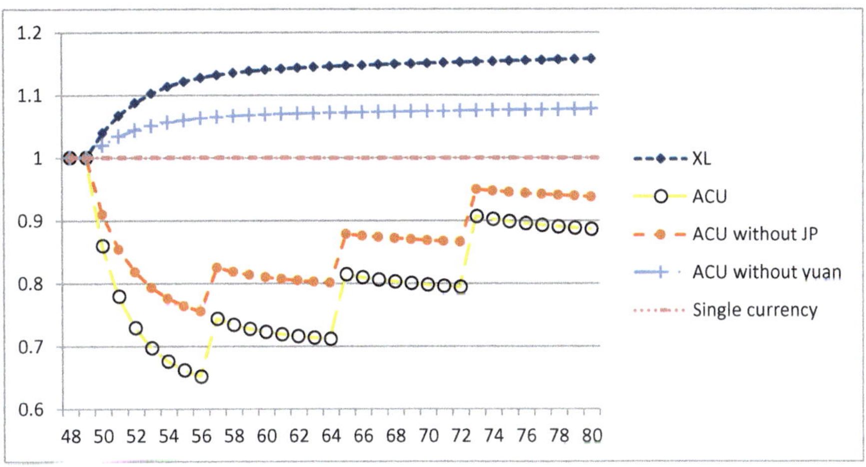

Fig. 6.3 Loss of competitiveness of East Asia and Japan against China for ACU regimes (in relative difference from the baseline)

rate adjustments are introduced, a devaluation of the EA currency by successive steps allows a progressive rebalancing. Last, a bancor regime where the surplus country is supposed to increase its public expenditures and imports more from the rest of East Asia gives the best performance, especially when it is combined with exchange rate adjustments. But this hypothesis of rebalancing policy by the surplus country is rather exigent and would need important improvement of coordination at the level of East Asia (Fig. 6.4). The same observations can be made in the case of a loss of competitiveness of East Asia and Japan against China (Fig. 6.5).

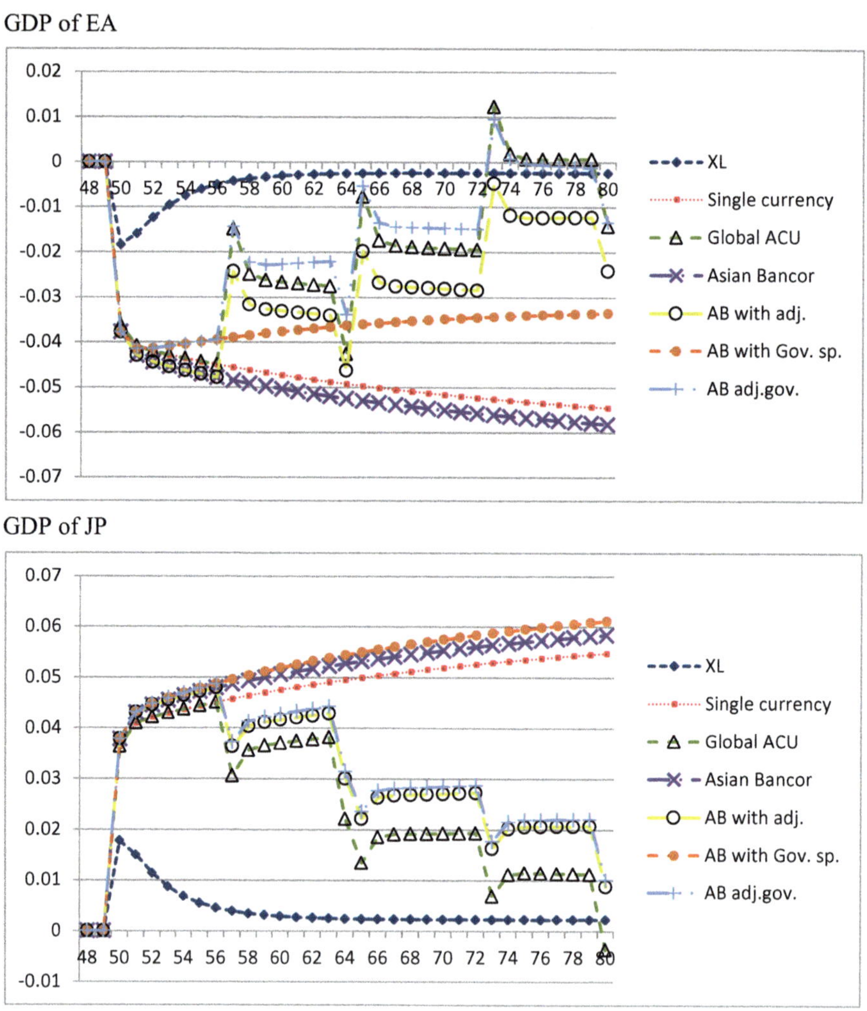

Fig. 6.4 Loss of competitiveness of East Asia against Japan for bancor and global ACU regimes (in relative difference from the baseline)

Exchange rates
E1 (1 RW = E1 Yen)

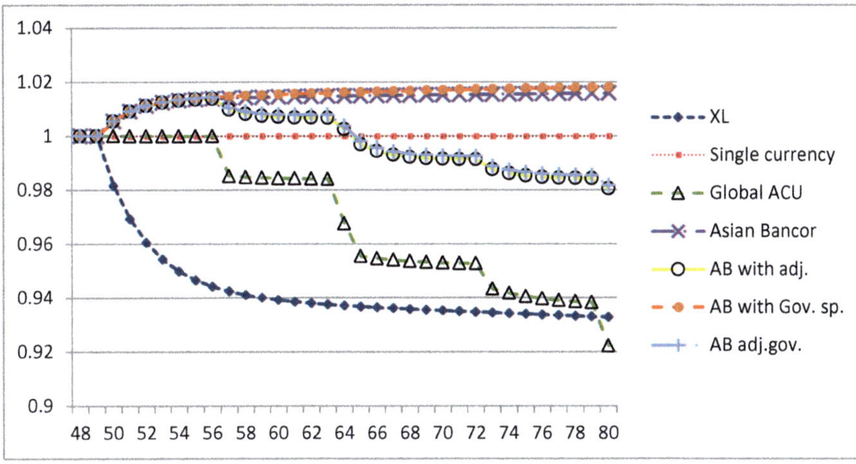

E4 (1 RW = E4 EA)

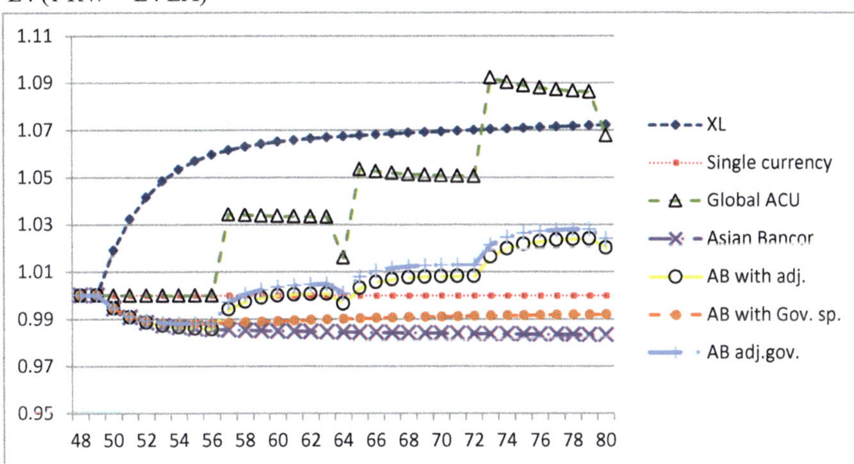

Fig. 6.4 (continued)

In the global ACU regime, the rebalancing are larger than those observed with the Asian bancor and the traditional ACU regimes (Figs. 6.4 and 6.5). In case of a loss of competitiveness of East Asia against Japan, the global ACU is floating and remains stable. The intra-East Asian exchange rate adjustments (devaluation of the EA currency and revaluation of the yen) are more limited than with the ACU, but more efficient. In the ACU regime, the devaluation of the EA currency is indeed partly offset by a devaluation of the ACU and of the yen.

Finally, the case of the ACU as a single currency is worth to be examined although it seems very unlikely due to the lack of political will in such a direction (Figs. 6.4 and 6.5). Without surprise the single currency regime appears as the less adapted to face asymmetric shocks. There is no mechanism to compensate the initial loss of competitiveness, and the GDP of the country negatively shocked remains durably depressed.

GDP of EA

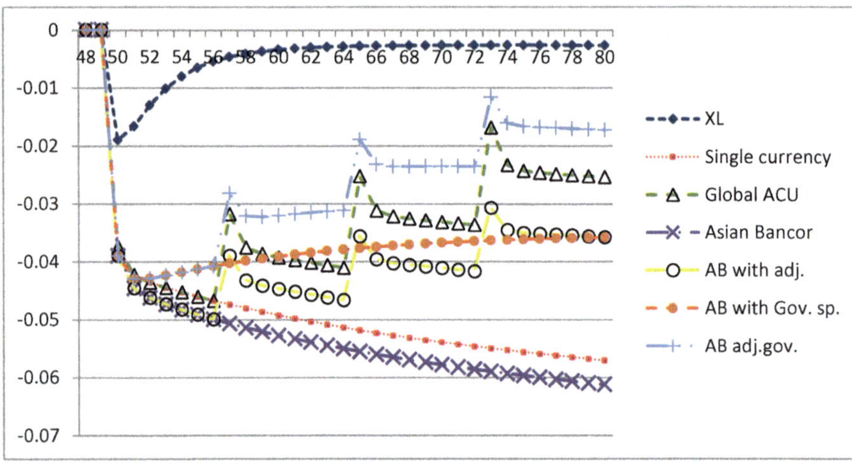

Exchange rates

E2 (1 RW = E2 Yuan)

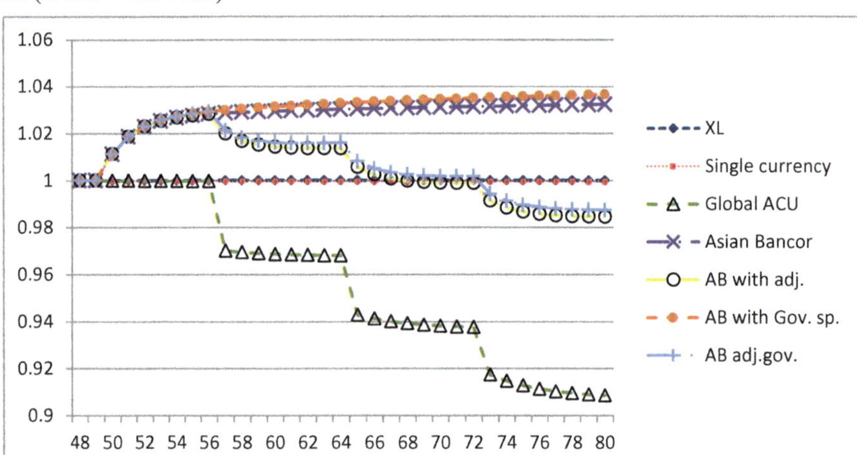

E4 (1 RW = E4 EA)

Fig. 6.5 Loss of competitiveness of East Asia and Japan against China for bancor and global ACU regimes (in relative difference from the baseline)

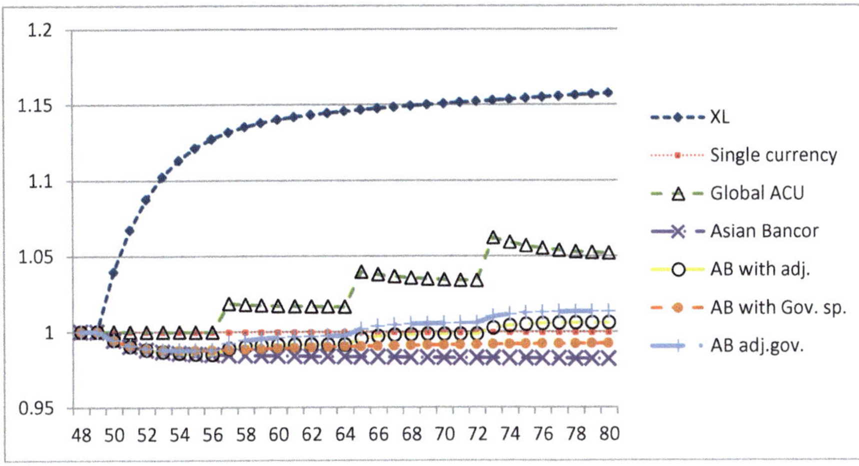

Fig. 6.5 (continued)

The current exchange rate regime in East Asia is characterized by a progressive liberalization of the yuan and pragmatic managed floating regimes for the other currencies. With the increasing economic and financial regional integration, monetary and financial cooperation has been debated a lot since the 2000s without clear improvement. The previous simulations have illustrated alternative exchange rate regimes which could be implemented to go beyond this current regime (yuan block, ACU regime, global ACU regime, bancor ACU, yuan area). An assessment of the European experience will be highlighting as the European monetary regime has been deeply transformed since the first steps of monetary cooperation in the 1970s.

6.3 Comparison with the European Monetary Integration

The eurozone crisis has been analyzed in Chapter 5, and alternative European scenarios have been already presented. The history of the European monetary integration and its failure from the European Monetary System (EMS) to the current eurozone can be described using a four-country SFC model of the eurozone (North Europe, South Europe, the USA, and rest of the world) similar to the one used to analyze the East Asian regimes. Beyond the EMS and the current monetary union, two types of monetary regimes can be proposed, the first one is a multispeed eurozone going from a multi-eurozone to a eurozone without Germany and the second based on an euro-bancor model and a European Clearing Union (Mazier and Valdecantos 2014, 2015).

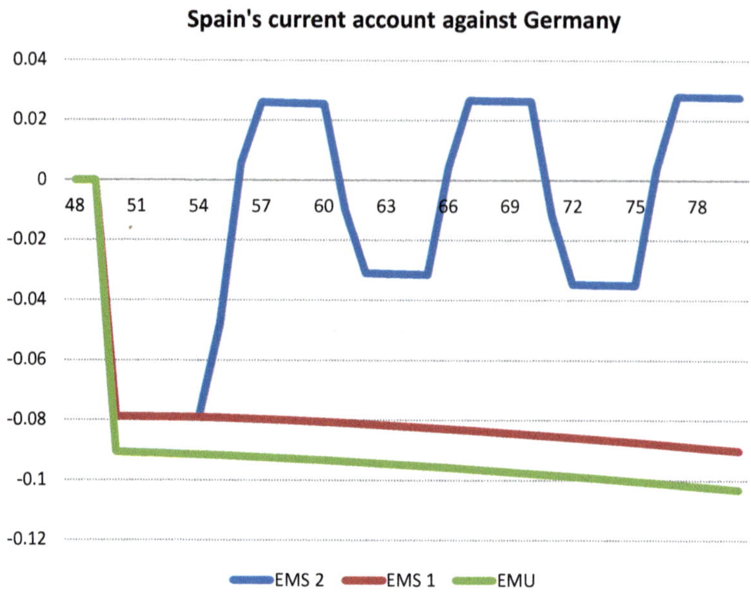

Fig. 6.6 Southern European current account against Northern European country (Spain/Germany) facing a competitiveness shock (due to overvaluation). (Source: Mazier and Valdecantos 2015)

6.3.1 From the EMS to the Eurozone

In the EMS the national currencies were pegged to the ECU which was a basket currency that only served as a unit of account. The currencies were allowed to fluctuate slightly around the ECU but the fluctuation bands were insufficient to correct the imbalances that could arise as a result of structural or temporary divergences between countries. That is why currency realignments were frequent in this regime, at least during the first period. When the EMS became more rigid, imbalances increased inducing larger adjustments like in 1992–1993. These evolutions have been reproduced using the four-country SFC model. It shows that an intra-European exchange rate misalignment produces a loss of competitiveness and a negative shock on Southern country which can be corrected, thanks to monetary adjustments. The simulations give two versions of the EMS according to the thresholds chosen for the devaluation rule (Fig. 6.6). In the EMS1 the threshold is higher allowing larger current deficit, while in the EMS2 the threshold is lower and the size of the current deficit allowed smaller. The EMS1 regime is more stable but is less efficient to reduce the imbalances and is not sustainable in the long term, as it has been illustrated by the burst of the rigid EMS in 1992–1993. The EMS2 is less stable with recurrent devaluations but the initial negative shock is better corrected. More stability can be obtained, thanks to higher threshold or to criterion of adjustment using the stock of foreign reserves or the reintroduction of some kind of capital controls. But this problem of stability remains with more or less of acuity.

This has been a major argument in favor of the single currency. In 1999 the ECU has been replaced by the euro and there are no more national currencies. The euro is a true currency in which real and financial transactions are denominated and which floats against the dollar. The national European central banks have TARGET2 balances at the ECB, as an asset, which are the sum of all intra-European transactions (current operations and portfolio investment) in a given period. But this monetary union has no mechanism to face the structural heterogeneity which exists between the Southern European countries and the German block. With divergent evolutions between the two groups of countries intra-European misalignments have reappeared. There is almost no adjustment mechanism, and imbalances between Southern and Northern countries remain, as it is illustrated by a shock of a loss of competitiveness in the South using the SFC model (Fig. 6.6). In the absence of a federal budget, the main adjustments have been obtained through wage and employment cuts with a high social cost and a reduced efficiency. Furthermore, contrary to what was expected by the advocates of the single currency, the euro has not led to financial stability. National currencies could not be attacked as they were no more existing, but the financial markets have clearly discriminated between foreign debts in Southern or German euros. Southern European countries have faced a huge increase of their public bonds interest rates, and this has been the beginning of the euro crisis. This can be also described using a SFC model of the monetary union (Duwicquet and Mazier 2010).

6.3.2 From a Multispeed Eurozone to a Euro-Bancor Regime

In such a context, the reintroduction of an adjustment of nominal exchange rates within the eurozone could imply a positive competitiveness shock that could help troubled countries to deal with the crisis. This appears as a necessary, but not sufficient, condition, and it would have to be accompanied by other policies, especially on the supply side. The first type of monetary regime which can be proposed is a multispeed eurozone going from a multi-eurozone to a eurozone without Germany and the second based on a euro-bancor model.

6.3.2.1 A Multispeed Eurozone

First, a multi-eurozone can be considered where national euros are reintroduced at the national or regional level, while a global euro is preserved to support the role of the current euro in financial markets as an international store of value. The global euro will be floating against the dollar and determined as the result of the interaction between supply and demand of euro-denominated bonds. Issuances of European bonds for foreign creditors are only denominated in global euro and can be bought by domestic banks whereas private agents (firms and households) purchase only bonds denominated in national euro. National euros against global euro exchange rates are fixed but adjustable according to different types of criterion reflecting the intra-European performance of the country against the rest of the zone (intra-European current account or stocks of foreign reserves). National central banks accumulate foreign reserves under the form of dollar-denominated bonds issued by the USA.

Second, another solution is a system in which Germany leaves the eurozone and lets its currency float, while the remaining European countries keep the euro, which would either be pegged to the German currency with a fixed, but adjustable, exchange rate or float freely against the dollar. If the euro is pegged to the mark, the ECB adjusts its foreign reserves in consequence. If the euro is floating against the dollar and the mark, the ECB keeps its reserves constant. The weak point of this regime is that the intra-European exchange rates fluctuate, but this adjustment concerns only the relations between Germany and the rest of the eurozone which is preserved. The strong point of this regime is precisely that the main source of the intra-European imbalances, the unequal relations with the German bloc, disappears.

6.3.2.2 A Euro-Bancor Regime

Last, a euro-bancor model can be considered. This proposal borrows from the experience of the EMS, from Keynes' proposals on bancor and International Clearing Union (ICU), and from the current existence of the ECB and the SEPA. First, it borrows from the EMS the existence of a nonmaterial unit of account to which national currencies are pegged and which is now called euro-bancor (a basket currency of national European currencies). Second, in Keynes' proposal countries accumulated bancor balances according to their external performance (increasing bancor account at the ICU for countries with trade surpluses, decreasing stock of bancors for countries running trade deficits). The idea of accumulating balances of a simple unit of account currency as a result of international transactions is the same that we observe in the current TARGET2 system at the ECB. It implies that most of the institutions that are required to implement a regime of this nature (a Clearing Union, an international unit of account and a system that registers the transactions within the region) already exist (the ECB could play the role of the ICU, and the SEPA is the system that registers all the transactions) or have existed and could be restored (the ECU that would play the role of the bancor).

European currencies are pegged to the Euro-bancor (thereby fixed with respect to each other), but they float against the dollar, with one of them having a role of anchor. This system is close to the EMS but more symmetric as it will be shown. The adjustment criterion of European currencies vis-à-vis the Euro-bancor depends on the intra-regional external performance of each country. The national European central banks are engaged in a fixed exchange rate arrangement, although adjustable. They accumulate foreign reserves, which close their balance sheet, except the one which is acting as anchor and keeps its foreign reserves constant. The Clearing Union is the institution where all the payments are cleared. Every country has an account at the Clearing Union. This account is an asset for each national central bank and a liability for the Clearing Union, just as it happens in the current TARGET2 system.

Some other Keynes' proposals can be introduced. First, in order to make the external adjustment process more symmetric than it is today, all countries would pay interests on their bancor balances, shall them be positive or negative. This would be another major change compared with the eurozone where the external adjustment process is asymmetric because only debtor countries are forced to introduce the structural policies aimed at correcting the imbalances. This new rule should encourage countries to make their accounts at the Clearing Union be as close to zero as possible. Second, the funds collected by the Clearing Union, which result from the interest payments on Euro-bancor balances, could be redistributed in favor of countries in deficit to help them in strengthening their supply side by more investment.

6.3.2.3 Simulations

Simulations have been made using the four-country SFC mode with the eurozone split between the South and the German block. A first set of simulations present a comparative analysis of different exchange rate regimes (from the current system of the eurozone to multiple euros) after a negative competitiveness shock in South Europe due to the overvaluation of the euro for South Europe (Fig. 6.7). Results show that after some delay, a depreciation of the South currency against the dollar induces an improvement of the trade balance and of the GDP (at the detriment of Germany). However, as the ancient EMS, a multiple euro framework might produce recurrent exchange rate adjustments (unless criterions adjustment would be based on stock of foreign reserves or would allow small but persistent current deficits). Results would be better in case of Germany leaving the eurozone (South euro pegged to North euro or both euros floating in Fig. 6.7)

Another set of simulations represent the same shock (a loss of competitiveness in the South due to an overvaluation) for different euro-bancor regimes, always compared with the euro regime (EMU, Economic and Monetary Union). In the euro regime, the overvaluation has a negative impact on the South current account and growth. The euro-bancor regime improves the South European countries, thanks to payment of interests by the surplus country and transfer to the deficit countries (Fig. 6.8). Euro-bancor 1 is the basic one with a large devaluation threshold which avoids exchange rate adjustments and has a more limited impact. Euro-bancor 2 with a smaller threshold gives more favorable effects, thanks to the devaluation which is combined with the payment of interests and its transfer. As previously, if the adjustment criterion is too strict (almost no deficit is allowed in Euro-bancor 3), the model could be more instable with one exchange rate adjustment following another. Euro-bancor 4 includes, in addition to the Euro-bancor 1 regime with a large devaluation threshold, a supply shock effect for the South country with increasing imports of capital goods, more investment and later an import substitution effect.

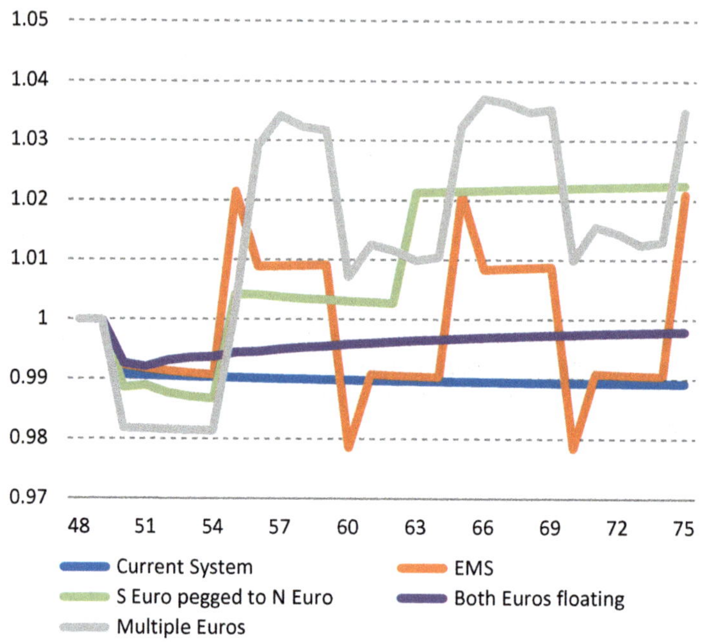

Fig. 6.7 Effects of a loss of competitiveness of the South due to an overvaluation on the South GDP

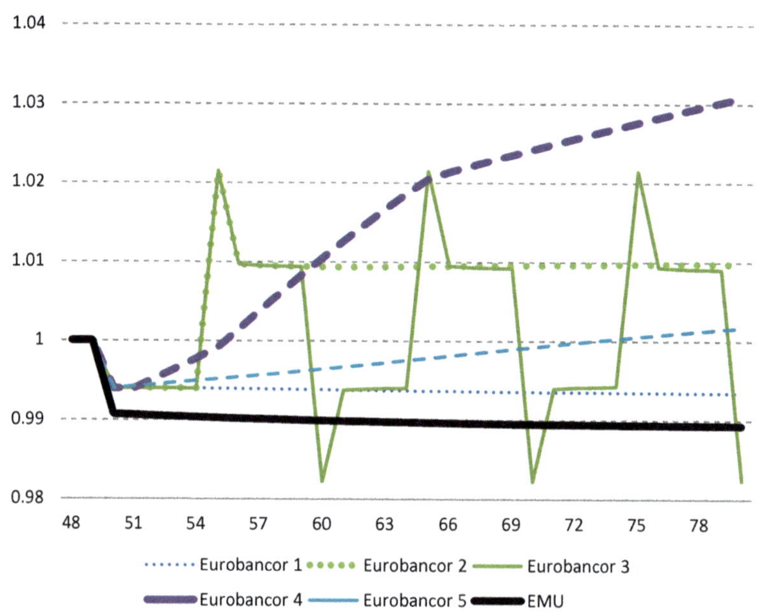

Fig. 6.8 Effects of a loss of competitiveness of the South due to an overvaluation on the South GDP. (Source: Mazier and Valdecantos 2014)

Euro-bancor 5 introduces a higher propensity to import for the surplus country with more public expenditures. They illustrate, beyond the question of exchange rate adjustments, the effectiveness of other institutional arrangements implying supply side policies for deficit countries or more expansionist policies for surplus countries.

6.3.3 Three Lessons

Three lessons for East Asia can be drawn from this brief analysis of the European experience of monetary integration.

First, the EMS was a mechanism trying to manage fixed but adjustable exchange rates which was adapted to answer to asymmetric shocks and to the heterogeneity of the European Union but could lead to recurrent devaluations with the possibility of speculative attacks, as it has been the case in the 1980s and early 1990s. It is a risk that could exist in the ACU regime if too large exchange rate misalignments appear or if some forms of capital control are not preserved.

Second, a premature settlement of a monetary union between heterogeneous countries without the necessary institutional changes leads to unsustainable imbalances and permanent blocking, as the euro crisis clearly shows since 2009. This seems a strong argument against the implementation of too rigid monetary regimes at the scale of the whole East Asia. However, some deeper forms of monetary cooperation could be considered within a more limited and more homogeneous group of countries.

Third, the reintroduction of the possibility of exchange rate adjustments in South European countries could give significant room of manoeuver. Its main advantage would be to be focused on manufacturing sector and more generally on tradable goods which are the key driver of intra-European imbalances. By itself it is not sufficient and must be completed by other measures, on the supply side to consolidate the initial positive shock and on income distribution to avoid an inflationist drift. Two regimes are more attractive, a eurozone without Germany as it gives an answer to one of the main source of intra-European imbalances but implies a split which can have a political cost and Euro-bancor regime which reintroduces exchange rate adjustments while keeping many of the institutional achievements of the last 20 years in the monetary field. In the European case, the transition toward this kind of exchange rate regime is a difficult task due to the debt burden and the risk of capital flights. It is very different in East Asia as the starting point is already a pragmatic regime. The target is to build a more institutionalized framework.

6.4 Conclusion

With the new issues raised by the financial crisis of 2008 and the increasing role of China at the world level, the aim of this paper was to assess the pragmatic exchange rate regimes adopted in East Asia since the 2000s and to evaluate alternative monetary regimes such as the ACU regime or the yuan block. A clear opposition has appeared with the European case where more rigid monetary regimes have been implemented since the end of the 1970s, from the EMS to the launching of the euro. An estimation of the exchange rate misalignments since the 1990s has shown that these misalignments were more limited in East Asia during the current period than in the 1990s, in contrast with what has been observed between the European countries. To investigate these exchange rate regimes, a four-country SFC model of East Asia has been proposed. It is of course a highly simplified representation, but it describes the interdependency between real and financial spheres in stocks and flows in a consistent way at the world level, which is not always done in other approaches. In this SFC approach there is no opposition between a determination of the exchange rates by the capital flows and by the current account. Both are taken into account simultaneously. Two versions of the SFC model have been used.

The first one, based on a simple structure China, East Asia, the USA, and rest of the world, has given a rough description of the East Asian monetary regimes as they have been observed in the past. The dollar-pegged regime during the middle of the 1990s has shown its limits with the lack of adjustment mechanisms and the persistent international imbalances. The hybrid regime of the end of the 1990s and the beginning of the 2000s has introduced more flexibility to absorb the asymmetries and reduce exchange rate misalignments, thanks to the managed or floating East Asian exchange rates against the dollar, but the yuan pegged on the dollar was a source of disequilibrium. The more flexible regime of the 2010s, where the yuan/dollar parity is managed and the East Asia/dollar parity more floating, has been able to limit the consequences of major international imbalances. Its main drawback is its potential instability and the necessity to implement some forms of capital control to make it more resilient. Pure floating remains a rather theoretical regime. Last two regimes corresponding to rather long-term scenarios have been examined. The yuan zone where East Asia currency is anchored to the yuan which is floating or managed against the dollar is rather unlikely as it could be achieved only after a long process of political and economic integration in East Asia. The difficulty to manage the shocks in an area characterized by strong structural heterogeneity between participant countries remains a major problem which has been clearly observed in the euro area during the 2000s and the 2010s. A yuan block where the East Asia/yuan parity is managed (and not fixed) is also a long-term scenario, but it allows a better absorption of asymmetric shocks. It seems a more promising perspective in the case where the yuan would strengthen its position at the world and regional level.

The second set of SFC models with a split between China, Japan, and East Asia has been used to analyze more formalized exchange rate regimes. In general, the ACU regimes, thanks to the possibility of exchange rate adjustments, allow a progressive reduction of imbalances and appeared well adapted to heterogeneous area like East Asia. However, they are very sensitive to the currency acting as anchor and to the countries participating or not to the ACU basket. On the whole they present the same advantages and limits than the EMS in the European case. The Asian bancor regimes, based on a Clearing Union, are more exigent in terms of institutions and bancor balances play a key role. But the amplitude of the adjustments is more limited than in the traditional ACU regimes. The bancor regime becomes more efficient when it is supposed that surplus countries are engaged in public expenditures policy to increase their demand and reduce their surplus. Although desirable, such an engagement would be difficult to obtain.

Last, the global ACU allows larger rebalancing effects than the bancor or ACU regimes. It is more balanced than the ACU regime as the global ACU is floating vis-à-vis the rest of the world. It could appear as an attractive compromise, but it is rather exigent as it implies the launching of a new international currency (the global ACU) and the limitation of the role of the national East Asian currencies. The East Asia context is on that point very different from the European experience where the euro is equivalent to the global ACU and exists already. In the eurozone case, the challenge is to reintroduce the possibility of exchange rate adjustments.

The case of the ACU as a single currency, although very unlikely, illustrates the negative effects of the lack of any exchange rate adjustment to face asymmetric evolutions in a heterogeneous area. It confirms the results already observed with the so-called yuan area. On this respect East Asia seems in the exact opposite situation compared with the euro area. The single currency has been launched since 1999 without the institutional changes which would have been necessary but were almost impossible to implement due to political reasons (mainly the very limited solidarity between European countries and the refuse to go toward fiscal federalism). Its failure has been particularly clear since the burst of the euro crisis. It confirms how unwise it would be for East Asian countries to go toward this kind of monetary regime.

References

Aflouk N, Jeong S-E, Mazier J, Saadaoui J (2010) Exchange rate misalignments and world imbalances, a FEER approach for emerging countries. Intl Econ 124:31–74

Blanchard O, Giavazzi F, Fa F (2005) International investors, the U.S. current account, and the dollar. Brookings Pap Econ Activit 1:1–49

Couharde C, Mazier J (2001) The equilibrium exchange rates of European currencies and the transition to the Euro, Applied economics, vol 33. Routledge, London, pp. 1795–1801

Duwicquet V, Mazier J (2010) Financial integration and macroeconomic adjustments in a monetary union. J Post Keynesian Econ 33(2):333–370

Godley W, Lavoie M (2007a) A simple model of three economies with two currencies: the eurozone and the USA. Camb J Econ 31(1):1–23

Godley W, Lavoie M (2007b) Monetary economics: an integrated approach to credit, money, income, production and wealth, 2nd edn. Palgrave Macmillan, New York

Jeong S-E, Mazier J, Saglio S (2012) Given the heterogeneity of Asian countries, is a monetary integrationor coordination possible? In: Boyer R, Uemura H, Isogai A (eds) Diversity and transformation of Asian capitalisms. Routledge, London

Keynes JM (1941) Proposals for and International Clearing Union. 15 December 1941, Collect Writings 25:74

Lavoie M, Zhao J (2010) A study of the diversification of China's foreign reserves within a three country stock-flow consistent framework. Metroeconomica 62(3):434–458

Mazier J, Tiou-Tagba Aliti G (2012) World imbalances and macroeconomic adjustments: A three-country stock-flow consistent model with fixed or flexible prices. Metroeconomica 63 (2):358–388

Mazier J, Valdecantos S (2014) A detailed representation of the eurosystem and the current crisis in the eurozone: a stock-flow consistent approach', CEPN, working paper, no. 2014-02

Mazier J, Valdecantos S (2015) A multi-speed Europe: Is it viable? : A stock-flow consistent approach. Euro J Econ Econ Policies Intervent 12(1):93–112

Mazier J, On M, Valdecantos S (2014) East Asian monetary regimes: a SFC approach, CEPN, working paper 2014-11

Shimizutani S (2009) Asian common currency as a driving force of economic integration in East Asia: a prospect. Asia Pac Rev 16(2):26–41

Williamson J (1998) The case for a common basket peg for East Asian currencies. In Collignon S, Pisani-Ferry J, Park YC (eds) Exchange rate policies in emerging Asian countries, Routledge, London

Part II
Origins and Ways Out of the EU Crisis

Chapter 7
Can We Explain German and French Trajectories in the 2000s by Their Institutional Setting During Fordism?

Nicolas Canry

7.1 Introduction

A common explanation to German economic success for 10 years has been its ability to reform its labour institutions: from 1990, the percentage of firms abiding by the traditional sectoral contracting wage-setting system decreased significantly, allowing new firms to pay lower wages. This increasing heterogeneity of firms would explain, to some extent, the rising wage inequality observed in Germany for 25 years (Dustmann et al. 2009; Card et al. 2013). The Hartz laws (2003–2005) were also supposed to strengthen labour market flexibility by reducing reservation wage and implementing active labour market policy, by creating mini-jobs, etc. (Eichhorst and Marx 2009. The adoption of working time accounts also allowed to adjust employment volume by working hours rather than hiring and firing (Burda and Hunt 2011; Blot et al. 2015). This widespread set of reforms implemented by Germany would explain how Germany managed to cross the *subprime* crises without lasting fall of employment. This success also contrasts with "sclerotic" French economy, unable, according to many economists, to evolve so as to take globalization constraints into account and to reform its institutions (Hairault 2015) or to promote trust and cooperation (Aghion et al. 2010).

In previous works (see Canry 2005 for a synthesis), I showed that German economy had experienced a Goodwin cycle (Goodwin 1967) between 1950 and 1990. In the 1980s, German followed the Helmut Schmidt "theorem" and succeeded in restoring profits, investment, competitiveness and eventually employment (unemployment rate is below 5% in Federal Republic of Germany just before the reunification). Approximately at the same period, France launched competitive

N. Canry (✉)
Université Paris 1 Panthéon-Sorbonne, Centre d'Economie de la Sorbonne, Paris, France
e-mail: nicolas.canry@univ-paris1.fr

R. Boyer et al. (eds.), *Evolving Diversity and Interdependence of Capitalisms*,
Evolutionary Economics and Social Complexity Science 11,
https://doi.org/10.1007/978-4-431-55001-3_7

disinflation, but profit recovery did not translate into sufficient capital accumulation, in spite of commercial balance recovery during the 1990s: France remained trapped in a high profitability/low employment equilibrium at this period.

Following Soskice and Iversen (Soskice and Iversen 2005), we can assert that German growth regime rested for a long time on strong institutional complementarity between a non-accommodative central bank (the Bundesbank) and a wage bargaining led at a macroeconomic level (Calmfors and Driffill 1988) by trade unions (especially IG Metall), sufficiently "concentrated" to take central bank reaction into account. We can imagine that this original wage labour nexus has been destabilized by the entry of Germany in the Eurozone, which weakened the narrow relationship between central bank, employer associations and trade unions: domestic unions could have considered that their "responsible" action would be far less likely to have a sensible effect on wages at the European level. Central bank would now react to Eurozone's inflation, which would depend on strategies of all European unions. This fear may have increased the willingness of employer associations to leave branch agreements and decentralize wage setting process (Dustmann et al. 2014). Germany would then have switched from a coordinated to a more liberal market economy (Hall and Soskice 2001).

The objective of this paper is not to minimize the importance of institutional change in Germany. Nevertheless, I show in this paper that beyond reforms and institutional transformations implemented by Germany for two decades, the economic success that this country has been currently experiencing rests fundamentally on the same devices and macroeconomic closure as before (since WWII). To support my analysis, I compare France and Germany growth regimes since 2000. In fact, I assert that France and Germany have been facing common characteristics and pretty close macroeconomic constraints, i.e. a significant excess of private saving on domestic private investment, especially investment by firms.

7.2 Analytical Framework

I adopt a very simple Keynesian perspective, in which excess of saving has depressive effect on production level and activity. In the simple Keynesian model (closed economy, no state), the higher the saving rate of the households (or the national saving rate), the weaker the level of activity.

Since 2000, continental Europe – more specifically northern continental Europe – suffers from saving glut (as worldwide economy, Bernanke 2005). Nevertheless, continental Europe (contrary to worldwide economy) is not a closed economy; thus equilibrium on the financial market between global net borrowing and lending rests on the following equation:

$$S = I + (G - T) + (X - M)$$

In that perspective the issue of excess saving in some area can be solved by:

- Increasing (private) investment.
- Increasing public deficit, by raising government spending and/or reducing fiscal policy. State may be more likely to adopt this "solution" if it expects a reverse situation, (i.E. an excess of private demand over the supply of goods) in the future. In that sense, dig public deficit could be considered as an intertemporal equilibrium solution.
- Increasing commercial balance of trade (net exports). This last strategy can be considered as the "supply" strategy to overcome macroeconomic demand constraints: For an open economy, competitiveness reflects the ability to sell production abroad, regardless of domestic income distribution. In a worldwide economy, competitiveness and positive commercial balance may be the most efficient way to ensure that supply creates its own demand. On the contrary, the lack of competitiveness can exacerbate the gap between domestic supply and demand of goods, as a growing part of national incomes flies away through imports. That is the main reason why some wage-led economies in the closed framework of Fordism have become profit-led with deepening globalization (Bowles and Boyer 1995).

7.3 French and German Economic Situations for 20 Years

Figure 7.1 displays that France and Germany have been facing a pretty similar "constraint" – i.e. a significant private saving glut – from 1995 to, at least, 2008 (note that we usually present data since 1950 for France and only since 1991 for Germany, as German national accounts have available data only from this date).

The two countries have nevertheless adopted very different ways to escape from (or "solve") this constraint and fill the gap between S and I. The way that each country took last decade is closely related to the "*mode de régulation*" that had been adopted after WWII, during the Fordist era:

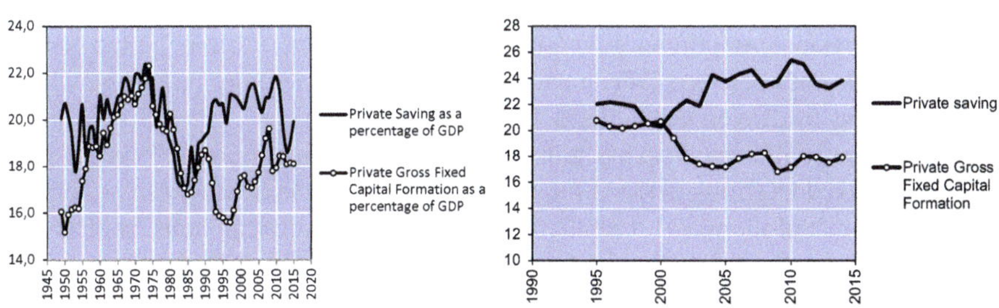

Fig. 7.1 Private saving and investment as a percentage of GDP, France 1949–2014 (left) and Germany 1995–2014 (right). Database: National Accounts, INSEE (France) and Eurostat (Germany)

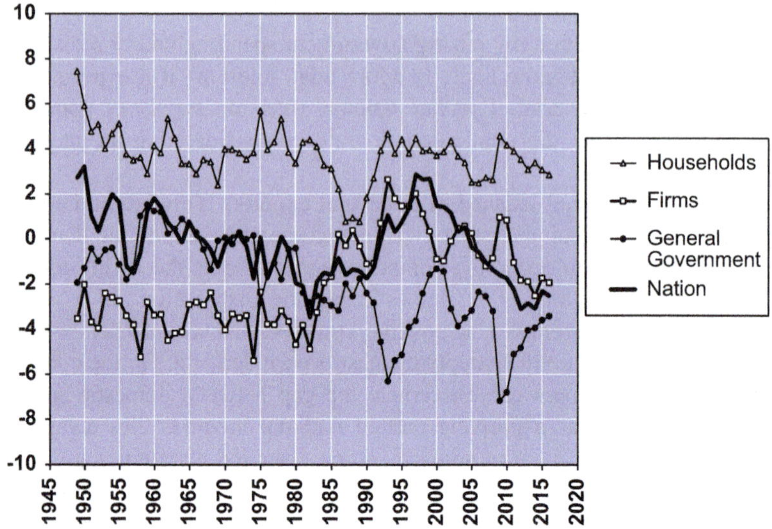

Fig. 7.2 Net borrowing/lending of sectors as a percentage of GDP, France, 1949–2014. Database: National Accounts, INSEE

- Figure 7.1 clearly displays the tenuous relation between private saving and investment in France up to the middle of the 1980s. Then, saving rate increases as investment drops. French saving excess has translated into higher government deficit (as shown on Fig. 7.2). The gap between private investment and saving narrows from 2000 to 2007 as investment takes off. Unfortunately, the bulk of this private investment comes from real estate by households (as it is displayed by Fig. 7.3 describing the evolutions of French households investment), which eventually fed bubble rather than "productive" capital accumulation and, eventually, productivity of firms. Moreover, the increase of real estate prices has exacerbated investment increase (at current prices). If we focus on saving, the main fact concerning France is that the national (private) rate is quite stable in the long run, if we except the deterioration over the periods 1980–1985 (period of deep wage austerity) and 2010–2015. In that perspective, French trajectory for 20 years seems to be very similar by many aspects (real estate bubble, growing trade imbalance, important government intervention, etc.) to the United States' (the similarities between French and American growth regimes had already been underlined by Boyer and Julliard 1992), even though the United States didn't suffer from a domestic saving glut (but rather from an "imported" saving glut, consecutive to a strong demand for safe assets – American treasury bills – coming from the rest of the world (Caballero et al. 2016), as American household saving rate was very weak for 15 years (around 2% in 2008, just before the triggering of *subprime* crisis).
- On the contrary, Germany has bypassed the Keynesian constraint or the Say's law – I.E. German produced far more industrial goods than the quantity its own domestic demand could absorb – By managing to export massively its domestic production (it is also noticeable that Germany didn't experience any real estate

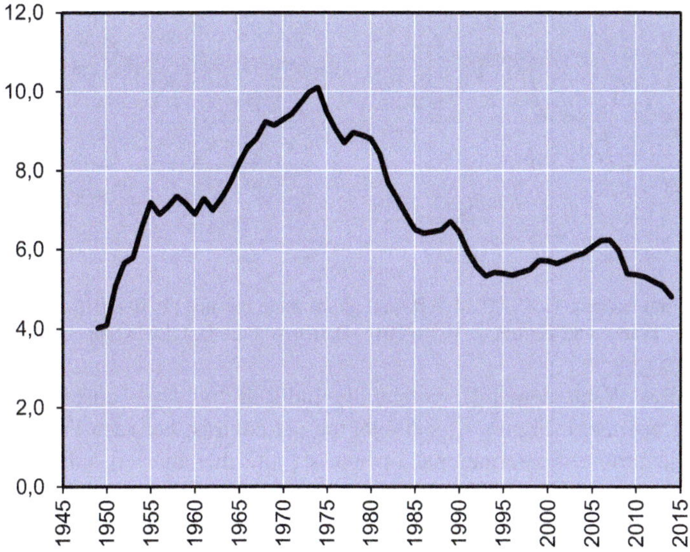

Fig. 7.3 Real gross fixed capital formation by households (excluding unincorporated enterprises) as a percentage of real GDP, France, 1949–2014. Database: INSEE, National Accounts

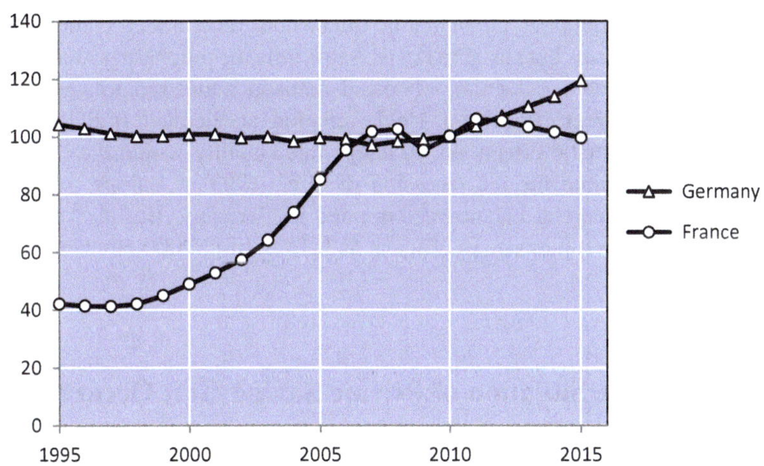

Fig. 7.4 Nominal house price indices, 2010 = 100, France and Germany, 1995–2015. Database: OECD, OECD.Stat

bubble, at least before the *subprime* crisis; see Fig. 7.4). In that sense, Germany macroeconomic regulation during the 2000s does not differ so much from that which was led during the 1980s (as West Germany became the first worldwide exporter) or even in the 1950s: German industrial and geographical specializations allow this country to counterbalance weak domestic consumption (more

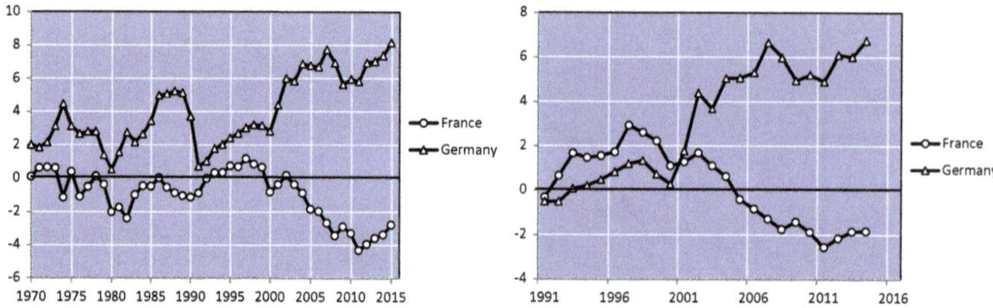

Fig. 7.5 Trade balance (1991–2014, left) and goods trade balance (1970–2015, right) as percentage of GDP, France and Germany, 1970–2015. Database: OECD, OECD.Stat

generally: Weak demand), potentially induced by wage austerity, by wider trading openness. Figure 7.5 exhibits the net contrast between France and Germany in terms of international openness (note that the left side of the figure focuses on goods trade balance, for which OECD data are available from 1970): Goods trade balance as percentage of GDP reaches 5% for Germany in 1987. Actually, the strong demand shock consecutive to reunification and the decision to fix the exchange rate between Ostmark and Deutschmark to unity have temporarily concealed, during the 1990s, this long-lasting German "export strategy". This decision of parity between the two currencies by H. Kohl (which had probably a very political and symbolic dimension) deteriorated competitiveness of east German firms but sustained in the same time the purchase power of eastern households, which spectacularly boosted demand addressed to west German companies. Between 1990 and 1995, inflation accelerated (the Bundesbank reaction had dramatic effects on exchange rate stability within the "Eurozone" and was responsible for the recession of 1992–1993 in Europe; see Fitoussi 1995), and commercial balance deteriorated in Germany. But the "export-led" strategy reappeared globally as efficient as before, from 2000 onwards.

7.4 Why Did a Situation of Private Saving Glut Occur?

Some leading European countries have been facing a saving glut for many decades. By this, I mean that private saving largely exceeds the needs or desires of investment by private domestic agents, as it is emphasized on Fig. 7.1 in the French and German cases.

Data show that saving glut in France primarily results from a relative investment shortage arising from the end of Fordism during the 1970s (private saving seems to have remained pretty stable over time, so that we should rather speak either of a relative saving glut or an investment shortage). We can bring two main explanations to this investment slowdown: on the one hand, the volume of investment in real estate (at constant prices) by households reached a peak at the beginning of the 1970s

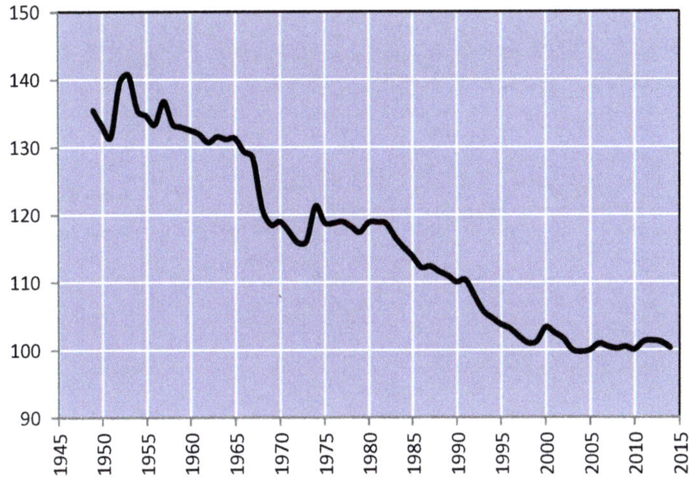

Fig. 7.6 Relative price of gross fixed capital formation (by corporations and unincorporated enterprises) to GDP. Relative price = 100 in 2010. France, 1949–2014. Database: INSEE, National Accounts

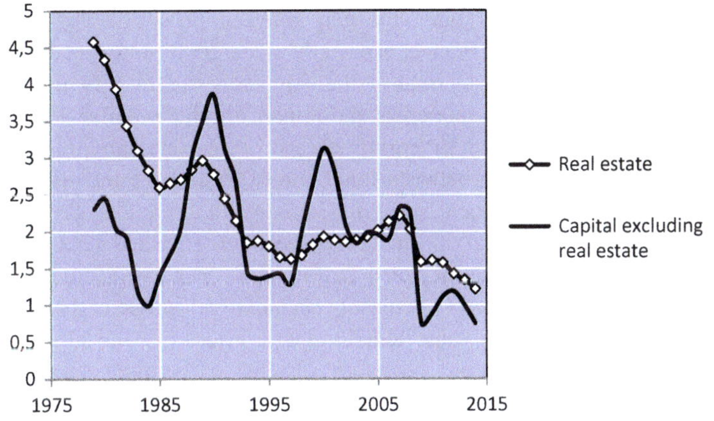

Fig. 7.7 Rate of net capital accumulation (%), France, 1979–2014. Database: INSEE, National Accounts

then decreased for 20 years before stabilizing after 1995. On the other hand, the relative price of GFCF to GDP has sharply fallen between 1950 and 2000 in France (around – 35%; see Fig. 7.6) as in the bulk of developed countries.

According to Summers (2015), this price effect might explain a large part of the saving glut which appeared all around the world since 2000: the accumulation of capital in volume did not significantly decline (if we exclude real estate) over this period (see Fig. 7.7 in the case of France), but capital accumulation at current prices did, as capital price has been falling (nonetheless such an assumption requires an

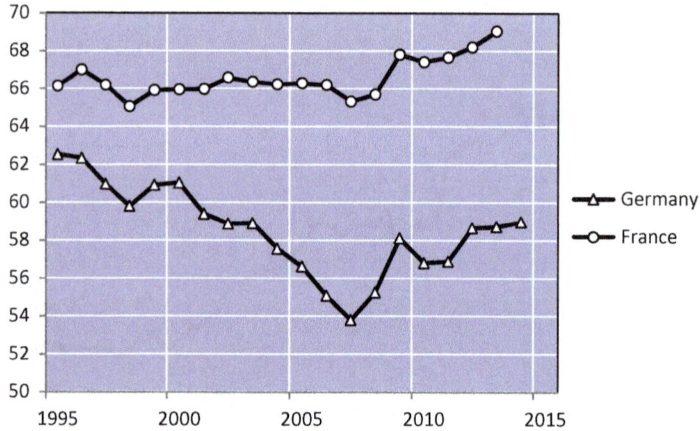

Fig. 7.8 Wage share in value added at factor prices (%) in nonfinancial corporations, France and Germany, 1995–2014. Database: Eurostat

elasticity of substitution inferior to one between labour and capital in the production function).

If we now focus on Germany, the gap between private saving and private investment is greater than in France, especially since 2000 (unfortunately, data are not available before 1995 for Germany): the gap reaches up to 7 points of GDP for the years preceding the *subprime* crisis and remains high thereafter. For Germany, this is the consequence of two diverging effects: on the one hand, the increase of national (private) saving rate between 2000 and 2005 and, on the other hand, the concomitant drop of investment rate. In Germany, households' saving rate has remained pretty stable since 2000, fluctuating between 15% and 17% (a bit higher than in France). However, as depicted in Fig. 7.8, primary income distribution fluctuated a lot over this period (whereas it remained very stable at the same period in France): the wage share in value added at factor prices (i.e. the sum of compensations of employees and gross operating surplus) of nonfinancial corporations dropped of 7.2 points of percentage between 2000 and 2007 (and even 8.5 points since 1995). As saving rate (gross saving related to gross value added) by firms is bigger than households' one, such a change in income distribution mechanically increased national saving rate.

The sharp wage share decline in the 2000s could result from institutional change (previously mentioned) that occurred on the labour market in Germany, but it can also be consecutive to the high level of unemployment faced by the country during the 1990s (the unemployment rate reached 9.7% in 1998). This high unemployment level might have weakened the bargaining power of trade unions, as in the beginning of the 1980s. Actually, Fig. 7.9 confirms that unemployment rate has remained a strong determinant of real wages in Germany (unlike France where the relationship between unemployment and real wage growth is insignificant). Furthermore, Fig. 7.10 shows that unit labour costs, which had increased significantly just after

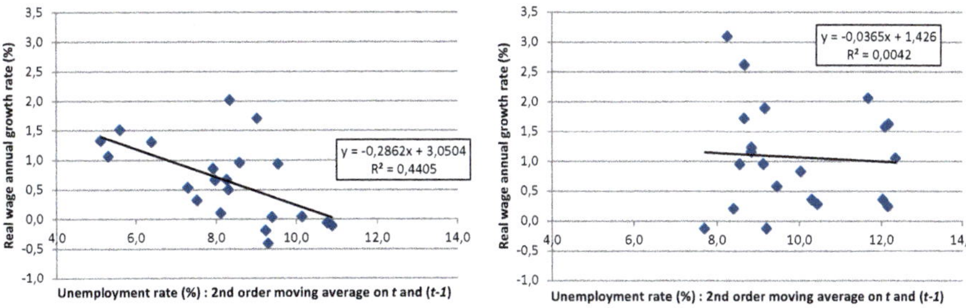

Fig. 7.9 Annual real wage growth and unemployment rate, Germany (left) and France (right), 1994–2014. Database: OECD. Statistics on employment and the labour market

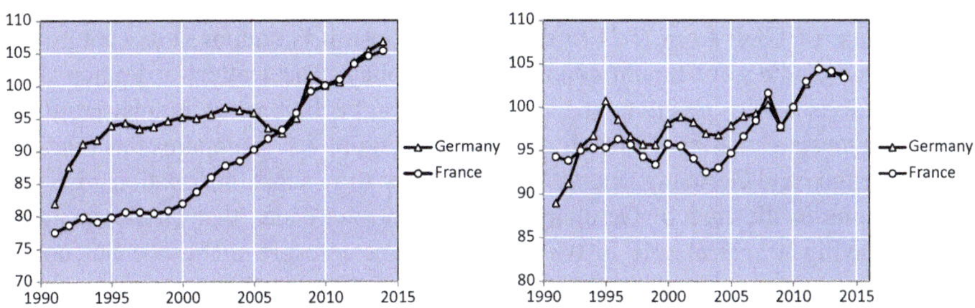

Fig. 7.10 Unit labour costs based on worked hours (left) and export price deflator (right), France and Germany, 1995–2014. Database: Eurostat

reunification, remained quite stable between 1995 and 2007 in Germany: even though it is often underlined that specialization on high-quality goods make German exports weakly sensitive to prices, wage austerity most probably allowed Germany to keep very stable export prices (at least before the *subprime* crises), without squeezing markups, which strengthened its competitiveness (Kollmann et al. 2014).

The dramatic change in income distribution that resulted from austerity during the 2000s had very likely a strong negative incidence on domestic demand (Carlin and Soskice 2009), as France painfully experienced it after competitive disinflation in the 1980s, but the "extraverted" growth regime that Germany set up in the 1950s actually allows this country to avoid such a "domestic demand trap": exports absorb the gap between production and domestic consumption. Moreover, the wage austerity was more likely to be sustainable as households didn't face any real estate bubble. Nevertheless, such a *mode de régulation* requires "consumers of last resort" overseas. . . .

7.5 The Very Contrasting Role of the State in France and Germany

This article fundamentally rests on (and supports) the idea developed by Bofinger (2016). According to Bofinger, the "German macroeconomic paradigm" since WWII is the legacy of Walter Eucken's thought which departs strongly from Keynesian analysis and gave birth to ordoliberalism. According to Eucken, macroeconomic policy must rely on price stability, prices flexibility and balanced fiscal budget. This analysis rejects any strong economic role to government, especially concerning cyclical regulation and countercyclical policy.

Figures 7.11 and 7.12 plot the scatter linking public deficit at date *t* and the average annual growth rate of real GDP 2 years before (i.e. the annual average growth rate of GDP from *(t-2)* to *t*). This relationship is supposed to capture the importance of the government countercyclical policy. The scatter for France since 1960 exhibits a very positive, stable and significant relationship, emphasizing the very "Keynesian" nature of French government. Figure 7.12 compares this relationship in France and Germany since 1991 and clearly shows that this relationship is far less tenuous in the case of Germany. This supports our idea that public spending keeps playing a central role in the macroeconomic closure in France but not in Germany, where government does not seem to play historically a central role to fill the gap between private investment and saving, unlike France.

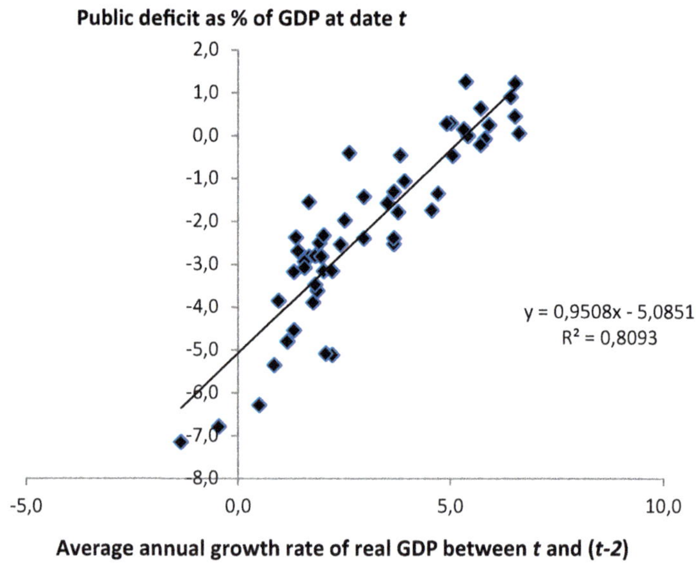

Fig. 7.11 Moving average annual growth rate of real GDP (%) between dates $(t - 2)$ and t and public deficit (%) at date t, France, 1960–2014. Database: National Accounts, INSEE

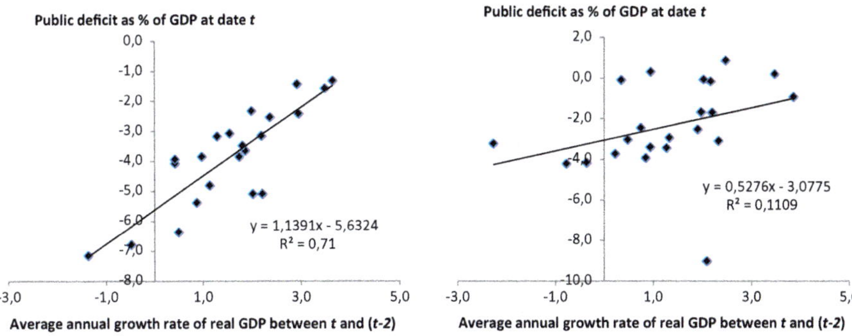

Fig. 7.12 Moving average annual growth rate of real GDP (%) between dates ($t-2$) and t and public deficit (%) at date t, France (left) and Germany (right), 1991–2014. Database: National Accounts, INSEE (France) and Eurostat (Germany)

7.6 Consequences for European Integration

Germany is very representative of the economic situation in Northern Europe. Indeed, it turns out that Eurozone has been divided for 15 years between "North" – the bulk of Scandinavian countries, the Netherlands and Germany, all exhibiting significant trade surpluses – and "South," Spain, Portugal, Greece and, to a less extent, Italy and France (these countries exhibit trade deficits, and they can be considered as consumers of last resort). Actually this kind of "European imbalances" could be sustainable from a theoretical standpoint: Northern Europe can be considered as a very mature economy, richly doted in capital, whereas Southern Europe keeps on catching up, especially by accumulating capital. In this frame, saving from northern households is lent to firms in the South, where (marginal) capital productivity is higher. South countries finance their capital accumulation and development by borrowing abroad. Higher productivity induced by additional capital should eventually reduce competitive gap between North and South. . . . These two different "growth regimes" could therefore coexist in the European frame, thanks to their complementarity in terms of saving.

In practice, unfortunately, saving glut from Northern European countries fuelled real estate bubbles, rather than productivity, in southern countries, where inflation has eventually been higher (compared to Northern Europe). In that sense, Europe suffers from a bad allocation of capital (too little has been dedicated to productivity growth and innovation), which has destabilized the complementarity between North and South. Finally, as European Union is not an optimal monetary zone yet, inflation differentials and the impossibility for southern countries to devaluate their currency have exacerbated the competitive gap between North and South. Europe is then confronted to the difficulty, underlined by R. Boyer (Boyer 2018) in this present book, to make coexist different *modes de régulation* in the absence of exchange rate flexibility.

Moreover, focusing on international competitiveness to deal with the issue of domestic demand failure consists for Northern Europe in exporting its own constraints on other European "partners". Such a strategy clearly appears nowadays as non-cooperative from a European standpoint (especially since crises in Greece, Ireland and Spain have broken out). What was considered as competitive institutional device in the frame of nation-states might be viewed as a brake to European integration from now on. In that perspective, a "cooperative" strategy for Germany could be to further support its domestic demand and to accept, for example, to increase its own wages, which would release competitiveness constraints currently faced by Southern Europe (available data for the last years suggest that such a dynamics might be beginning). We think this cooperative solution, joined with the building of a strong fiscal harmonization, might be the only way to continue successfully the European integration process.

7.7 Conclusion

In this article, I try to characterize the mean by which two countries, France and Germany, manage the potentially destabilizing (for economic activity) gap between private investment and saving. I show that in spite of the very sensitive institutional changes that the two countries set up since 2000 (in particular Germany on its labour market), the two countries maintained, broadly speaking, specificities of the *mode de régulation* they had built few decades ago, during Fordism: in Germany, weak public intervention, wage bargaining focusing on unemployment and export-led growth to compensate the possible deficit of domestic demand and in France, stronger importance given to government spending to stabilize activity.

References

Aghion P, Algan Y, Cahuc P, Shleifer A (2010) Regulation and distrust. Q J Econ 125 (3):1015–1049

Bernanke B (2005) The global saving glut and the U.S. current account deficit. The Federal Reserve Board, remarks by Governor Ben S. Bernanke at the Sandridge Lecture, Virginia Association of Economists, Richmond, Virginia

Blot C, Chagny O, Le Bayon S (2015) Faut-il suivre le modèle allemand ? La documentation française, Paris

Bofinger P (2016) German macroeconomics: the long shadow of Walter Eucken. VoxEU, 9th of June

Bowles S, Boyer R (1995) Wages, aggregate demand, and employment in an open economy: an empirical investigation. In: Epstein GA, Gintis HM (eds) Macroeconomic policy after the conservative era. Cambridge University Press, Cambridge

Boyer R (2018) Two Dialectics between Polity and Economy: European and Asian Integration Processes Compared, contribution in the present book

Boyer R, Juillard M (1992) The new endogenous growth theory versus a productivity regime approach: one century of American economic history revisited. Couverture Orange n° 9210, CEPREMAP
Burda M, Hunt J (2011) What explains the German labor market miracle in the great recession? Brook Pap Econ Act 42(1):273–335
Caballero RJ, Farhi E, Gourinchas P-O (2016) Safe asset scarcity and aggregate demand. Am Econ Rev 106(5):513–518
Calmfors L, Driffill J (1988) Bargaining structure, corporatism and macroeconomic performance. Econ Policy 3(6):13–61
Canry N (2005) Régime *wage-led*, régime *profit-led* et cycles: un modèle. Écon Appl 58(1):143–163
Card D, Heining J, Kline P (2013) Workplace heterogeneity and the rise of West German wage inequality. Q J Econ 128(3):967–1015
Carlin W, Soskice D (2009) German economic performance: disentangling the role of supply-side reforms, macroeconomic policy and coordinated economy institutions. Soc Econ Rev 7:67–99
Dustmann C, Ludsteck J, Schönberg U (2009) Revisiting the German wage structure. Q J Econ 124 (2):843–881
Dustmann C, Fitzenberger B, Schönberg U, Spitz-Oener A (2014) From sick man of Europe to economic superstar: Germany's resurgent economy. J Econ Perspect 28(1):167–188
Eichhorst W, Marx P (2009) Reforming German Labor Market Institutions: a dual path to flexibility. IZA discussion paper n° 4100
Fitoussi J-P (1995) Le débat interdit. Arléa, Paris
Goodwin RM (1967) A growth cycle. In: Feinstein CH (ed) Capitalism and economic growth. Cambridge University Press, Cambridge
Hairault J-O (2015) Ce modèle social que le monde ne nous envie plus. Albin Michel, Paris
Hall P, Soskice D (2001) Varieties of capitalism: the institutional foundations of comparative advantage. Oxford University Press, Oxford
Kollmann R, Ratto M, Roeger W, In't Veld J, Vogel L (2014) What drives the German current account? And how does it affect other EU member states? Economic Papers n° 516. European Commission
Soskice D, Iversen T (2005) The nonneutrality of monetary policy with large price or wage setters. Q J Econ 115(1):265–284
Summers LH (2015) Demand side secular stagnation. Am Econ Rev 105(5):60–65

Chapter 8
EU Multi-layered Migration Governance and the Externalization of French Migration Management: Analysis of Political Dynamics Driving the Construction of Complex Migration Regime

Mitsuru Uemura

8.1 Introduction

In the 2010s, extreme right-wing parties gained more popularity in member countries of the EU than academic scholars expected. The issue of migration, pertinent in each member country, led to the rise of the extreme right-wing parties. In particular, at the beginning of 2015, a split of opinion occurred between and within EU member countries regarding the acceptance of a large number of refugees into to the EU. In this situation, asylum seekers are considered a threat to national security, and the extreme right-wing parties that promoted an anti-immigrant mentality gained popularity among the people. In this regard, it is clear that the immigration control is related to not only an increasing welfare burden but also national security, which is a major problem in a political sphere for national sovereignty.

However, in EU member countries, immigration control is not governed entirely by each sovereign state, but rather, in the EU area, "multi-layered governance" is formed at different levels: common migration policies at the EU level and cooperation between the EU member countries and third countries outside the EU area. Namely, the EU member countries, the EU with the common immigration control

This chapter is a fully revised version of the original article, Mitsuru Uemura "The Externalization of French Migration Control Policies and EU Multi-layered Migration Governance," *International Relations*, Vol. 190, 2018, with the permission of The Japan Association of International Relations.

M. Uemura (✉)
University of Tokyo, Tokyo, Japan
e-mail: mitsuru-uemura@g.ecc.u-tokyo.ac.jp

R. Boyer et al. (eds.), *Evolving Diversity and Interdependence of Capitalisms*, Evolutionary Economics and Social Complexity Science 11,
https://doi.org/10.1007/978-4-431-55001-3_8

	Polity	Policies	Politics
External Policy Area	・Multi-layered migration govenance (External dimension)	・Bilateral agreement ・EU Mobility Partnership ・EU Readmission Agreement	・EU-third countries ・France- third countries ・Intervention by International organizations
EU	・Strengthening European Commission's competence ・Qualified majority voting ・Extension of ECJ's jurisdiction	・EU common migration policies ・EU common asylum policies ・Transposition of EU directives to domestic laws	・Coordination of interests between European Commission and member states ・More coordination in EU Summit
Member state (France)	・Strengthening the government's competence ・Changes in the structures of domestic opportunity	・National migration policies ・National asylum policies	・Conflicts of interests among domestic actors ・Preferences of the ruling party

Fig. 8.1 EU Multi-layered migration governance: polity, policies, and politics

system, and third countries play important roles as relevant actors to the immigration control, and as a result of negotiation among these actors, institutions are formed to control immigration. These negotiations are conducted in multilevel arenas. Figure 8.1 summarizes the negotiations and institutions which are formed as the result thereof. This analytical framework includes the internal dimension (relation between the EU and member states) and external dimension (relation between the EU and third countries) of EU common immigration policies and includes the perspectives of "polity," "policies," and "politics" to which researchers of "Europeanization" recently often refer.[1]

While the dimension of polity is not so addressed in detail in this article, we need to analyze the complex and multi-layered dimensions of migration issues comprehensively.

Immigration control consists of two policy areas, namely, the formation of immigration standards for legal immigrants and the official treatment of illegal immigrants. Regarding the policy on legal immigration, that is, deciding who is

[1]For a similar theoretical framework, see Aglietta and Leron (2017). Some researchers have used a framework of "polity, policies, and politics" to analyze the dynamics in some policy fields. However, in the migration policy field, the framework has not yet been used in the analysis. For the multi-levels of *régulation*, or governance, in the EU, see Boyer (2015). For more information on "Europeanization," see Guiraudon (2010); Bretherton and Mannin (eds.) (2013).

permitted to enter a country legally with a visa, the gradual formation of common policies is observed at the EU level.[2]

Regarding policy on illegal immigration, strict official treatment is sanctioned to deal with illegal immigrants. In order to make the official treatment of illegal immigrants effective with the need to send immigrants back to their countries of origin, cooperation with third countries is a very important factor. In the illegal immigration policies at the EU level, external migration policies such as the EU Readmission Agreement and the Mobility Partnership have been formulated with increasing complexity in the competence of migration management of EU member states.[3]

Therefore, in this article, the nature of the multi-layered governance of external migration management is investigated by focusing on France as a core EU member state. Furthermore, the meaning of political dynamics is clarified in terms of the intention France and third countries by participating in the construction of institutions. By doing so, we aim to contribute to the academic field of global politics of the international movement of people.

Stating the conclusions in advance, in the multi-layered migration governance of the EU external policies, which consists of the EU, EU member states, and third countries, there is a conflicting configuration between the EU and third countries. While the EU tries to establish effective migration policies based on the harmonization of policies among member states and active cooperation by third countries, both parties seek to maximize their own interests. Therefore, the EU Readmission Agreement and the Mobility Partnership between the EU and third countries were initially ineffective because of the lack of bargaining power of the EU as a negotiation actor, the pursuit of some member states to keep strong ties with ex-colonial countries, and the lack of cooperativeness of third countries. To overcome this ineffectiveness, it is important how the EU manipulates the interests of the other actor, and it can be pointed out that the EU's function has been strengthened since the late 2000s.

This article is organized as follows. In Sect. 8.2, the existing researches on the EU common policies on migration management are summarized, and the research agendas are clarified. In Sect. 8.3, a brief history of the externalization of illegal immigrant management is provided, and the transformation of illegal immigrant management in France and driving factors of bilateral agreements with third countries are clarified. Furthermore, the EU Readmission Agreements, the Mobility Partnership, and the EU Return Directive are referred to, and the nature of the methods employed by the EU and member states for the return of illegal immigrants is explained. In addition to these explanations, we visualize the factors driving the

[2]In the 2000s, under the initiatives of the European Commission, the EU Family Reunification Directive (2003/86/EC) and the EU Blue Card Directive (2009/50/EC) were proposed, and the transposition of directives into domestic laws has been developed in the EU member states.

[3]"External migration policy" in this article refers to an "external policy for migration." In particular, we pay attention to the security issue aspect of migration policies, which has become increasingly important in repatriating illegal immigrants and border control.

evolution of these institutions. Then, "the dual character" of the EU and member states is described. In Sect. 8.4, a case study is presented based on an investigation of the bilateral agreements between France and third countries such as Senegal, Cape Verde, and Tunisia. Furthermore, the EU-third country international agreements and the intentions of the French government are considered by examining official documents from the French government in public consultations about the EU Return Directive. In doing so, the possibility and viability of "the dual character of immigrant management" and intentions of each actor in the construction of institutions are identified. In the conclusion, the clarified points and their implications in this article are summarized.

8.2 The Research Agendas

8.2.1 Survey of Existing Researches

The development of EU common migration policies is characterized by conflicting relationships between EU institutions such as the European Commission, which promotes communization, and the member states, who continue to pursue their autonomy. Much existing research discusses these political dynamics and institutional development.

The epoch-making research in the area of the EU common migration policies including immigrant management was the "vertical venue-shopping" which was proposed by V. Guiraudon. She contended that both neo-functionalism and liberal inter-governmentalism, which had been the mainstreams in the European integration theory, cannot adequately explain the EU migration policies. She argued that the government of each member state committed the EU with a roundabout strategy that it makes use of the EU as a venue for the decision-making process of migration policies, making it as a form of "vertical venue-shopping." For example, she explained that the reason why "the Schengen Area" was created is a result of the fact that the Ministry of Internal Affairs and the Ministry of Justice pursued their autonomy in pursuing migration and refugee policies and that they chose "the Schengen Area" at the level of Europe which is situated above each member state.[4] Furthermore, the Ministry of Internal Affairs of each member state shifted the venue of consultation to the EU to escape from the restrictions placed on them by the norm of human right which are strongly shared by the Ministry of Labor, the Ministry of Foreign Affairs, and the Court of Justice, and they tried to create immigration-restricting policies. As it is different from the liberal inter-governmentalism that focuses on the preferences of the government of each member state as a whole in the political decision-making, Guiraudon clearly explained clearly

[4]The epoch-making research on EU common migration policies is Guiraudon (2000).

the relevant actors to the development of EU migration policies and their political dynamics, paying attention to conflicts among the governmental organizations in each member state.

S. Lavenex extended Guiraudon's framework of "vertical venue-shopping," characterizing it as an "Escape to Europe" (Lavenex 2006). Furthermore, she explained that the Ministries of Internal Affairs of member states shifted their policies to "Escape to Foreign Policy," strengthening their autonomy when faced with the constraint of human rights norms at the EU level which were enacted after the Amsterdam Treaty.[5] She also explained that the migration and refugee policies converged to foreign policies that pursued cooperation with immigrant-sending countries, shifting their venue to the outside of the EU. The "Escape to Foreign Policy" refers to international agreements between the EU member states and third countries. Since Lavenex's pioneering work, much research focusing on the foreign aspect of EU common migration policies has investigated the nature of common institutions between the EU and third countries.

What we should be careful about is the fact that most research regards the EU as a virtually a single actor in international migration management.[6] However, the EU cannot be a single actor as we see disagreement among the member states on how to respond to the refugee crisis. In fact, the EU signs international agreements with third counties on migration, and at the same time, the member states also reach bilateral agreements with the third countries. In this regard, the perspective of multi-layered governance is indispensable in the research on EU external migration policies that seeks to understand the relationships between the EU and member states. For example, R. Kunz, S. Lavenex, and M. Panizzon noted the fact that international migration governance is multi-layered at the bilateral, the regional, and the multi-lateral levels.[7] Regarding this state of affairs in the research, it is very rare, but significantly suggestive, to empirically study what intentions sovereign states, the EU as a regional community, and the third countries have in constructing international institutions.[8] The argument of Guiraudon and Lavenex can be summarized from the viewpoint of "polity, policies, and politics," as shown in Fig. 8.2.

[5] As for the implication of "Escape to Europe" and "Escape to Foreign Policy," see Lavenex (2006).

[6] See Jurje and Lavenex (2014).

[7] See Kunz, Lavenex and Panizzon (eds.) (2012). "Multi-layered migration governance" refers to the multi-layered negotiations and agreements on migration in the EU external migration policies (Panizzon 2012). In this sense, the research coverage is different from that of the general framework of the EU multilevel governance which has been discussed by P. Schumitter and G. Marks.

[8] As major Japanese literature on the EU and France, we refer to Yasue (2012) and Miyajima (2009).

	Polity	Policies	Politics	
External Policy Area	•Multi-layered migration governance (External dimension)	• Bilateral agreement • EU Mobility Partnership • EU Readmission Agreement	•EU-third countries •France-third countries •Intervention by International organizations	**Lavenex "Esecape to Foreign Policy"**
EU	•Strengthening European Commission's competence •Qualified majority voting •Extension of ECJ's jurisdiction	• EU common migration policies • EU common asylum policies • Transposition of EU directives to domestic laws	•Coordination of interests between European Commission and member states •More coordination in EU Summit	
Member state(France)	•Strengthening the government's competence •Changes in the structures of domestic opportunity	• National migration policies • National asylum policies	• Conflicts of interests among domestic actors • Preferences of the ruling party	**Guiraudon "Vertical Venue-Shopping"**

Fig. 8.2 Arguments by Guiraudon and Lavenex

8.2.2 Analytical Framework and Research Method

In order to clarify the multi-layered governance structure and actors' preferences in the EU external migration policies, the case studies are approached by taking into account the following points. Namely, we consider general institutional relations in the EU policies and French bilateral agreements with third countries in the area of migration policies and analyze actors' preferences in the multi-layered governance, that is, France, the EU, and the third countries, by examining documents issued by the French government and official EU documents. Then, the viability of the institutions is clarified by analyzing their contents and consistency between actors' intentions and their outcomes identified by deducing the implications thereof. In addition to this static analysis of institutional content, we investigate politics at the EU level and in France to determine the reason why these institutions are formed in this way. In so doing, we make explicit our understanding based on the empirical study of the multi-layered governance which is produced by the EU, the member states, and third countries.

The objects of our analysis are the bilateral agreements on immigrant management between France and third countries, who also have agreements with the EU. As third countries that satisfy this condition, Senegal and Tunisia, which are ex-colonies of France, and Cape Verde were selected, and the international agreements between these three countries and France and the EU are analyzed.

8.3 Historical Overview of the Externalization of Migration Management

8.3.1 French Policies for Illegal Immigrants and Bilateral Agreements

8.3.1.1 Transformation of French Policies for Illegal Immigrants

In France, illegal immigrant management originated in "*Ordonnance*" which became effective in November 2, 1945. This has long been a fundamental law on the entrance and stay of foreigners.[9] However, it is after the discontinuation of the acceptance of foreign workers in 1974 that the illegal immigrant problem was actualized. After this, immigrants who were born in ex-colonial countries in North Africa entered France with a tourist visa and stayed without an "Application de carte séjourt" to get a job in France. They became illegal immigrants. Furthermore, this restriction to the way of legal migration status gave some employers incentives to use illegal immigrants to compensate the lack of labor force, which increased the number of illegal immigrants.[10] How did the French government deal with these illegal immigrants?

The attitude and policies of the French government for illegal immigrants explicitly reflect the preferences of the ruling party.[11] Namely, restrictive or liberal policies traditionally depended on the Right or Left government. For example, in the Jospin government of *Le Parti Socialiste* established in 1997, the extension of the legalization of illegal immigrants was realized, so the existence of illegal immigrant did not become an urgent political agenda. In contrast, in the 2000s, with the rise of *Front National* (FN), an extreme right-wing party, more restrictive immigration management was implemented, irrespective of the Right or the Left.

In the formation of immigration policies when the bilateral agreements-the objectives of analysis in this article-were signed, Nicolas Sarközy played a leading role in promoting restrictive immigration policies in the *Union pour un Mouvement Populaire* (UMP). The immigration law (Sarközy Law II) enacted in 2006 includes restrictive measures for illegal immigrants. For example, when "Application de carte séjourt" is not rejected, a "deportation obligation" is possibly imposed at the same time.[12]

---

[9]This *Ordonnance* became a code of law, enacted as the "Code de l'entrée du séjour des étrangers et du droits d'asile (CEDEA)" by the Ordonnance on November 24, 2004.

[10]OCDE (2017), Le recrutement des travailleurs immigrés: France 2017, Éditions OCDE, Paris. https://doi.org/10.1787/9789264276741-fr p.292

[11]In the *cohabitation* period in which the parties of the president and the parity of the majority in the parliament were different, it was the party of majority to organize the cabinet that took charge of migration policies.

[12]Loi n° 2006-911 du 24 juillet 2006 relative à l'immigration et à l'intégration.

8.3.1.2 Bilateral Agreement Between France and Third Countries and "Immigration Choisie"

Bilateral agreements existed between France and the third countries, but after 2006, however, the agreements came to follow the principle of "immigration choisie," which was pursued under Nicolas Sarközy's initiative as a policy measure to enhance the effectiveness of illegal immigrant management. Furthermore, these bilateral agreements are constructed on the premise of a strong association between the control of migration and development.[13] In 2006, the agreement was developed by Brice Hortefeux of the Ministry of Migration which was newly established. From 2006 to 2014, France signed 13 agreements.[14] The contents of these agreements differ for each different third country, but they all follow the principle embodied in the law revisions in 2006 and 2007. The common characteristics of the agreements are as follows. First, the disordered entrance of immigrants was regarded as a security issue, so the cooperation of the police office in border control and the cooperative measures for forged documents and the readmission of immigrants without reasonable documents (*sans-papier*) from third countries are written in the law. Second, the issuing of a Circulation visa ensures the acceptance of labor immigrants, the promotion of the return of skilled workers to their home countries, and cooperation to contribute to the development of immigrant-sending countries.[15] Third, the aim of solidarity between France and the third countries is explicitly stated.

Among these three characteristics, the first is the most important, namely, the problem of the securitization of immigration. The intention of making the readmission from third counties a clause stemmed from the concern regarding the legalization of illegal immigrants which was implemented by the Spanish government. This fear of the mass legalization of illegal immigrants is declared in the first draft of European Pact on Immigration and Asylum, which was proposed by the French government.[16] Furthermore, the issuing of a Circulation visa was conditional on immigrant-sending countries' cooperation in controlling illegal immigrants when readmitting them.

In this regard, the agreements between France and the third countries were pursued to maximize French benefits in managing illegal immigrants, making issue linkages between access to the labor market and measures for illegal immigrants rather than strengthening solidarity characterized by reciprocal relations. The

[13]Website of the French Interior Ministry https://www.immigration.interieur.gouv.fr/Europe-et-International/Les-accords-bilateraux/Presentation-generale-des-accords-bilateraux

[14]Ibid.

[15]As for "circulation immigrants" who are promoted to move by "Circulation visa," see Tsuchiya (2009), pp.11–24, in which it is explained that the EU takes advantage of the resolution of labor shortage and that the immigrant-sending countries take advantage of money transfer and knowledge transmission.

[16]Le gouvernement français (2008) "European pact on immigration and asylum version I Draft of 25.01.08" cmr.jur.ru.nl/cmr/docs/pacte.europeen.sarkozy.pdf

	Polity	Policies	Politics
External Policy Area	* * *	French Bilateral Agreements with third countries.	France vs Third countries (transit or sending countries)
EU	* * *	European pact on immigration and asylum	France vs Spain, Germany European Commission was influenced.
France (Member state)	* * *	2003 Sarközy law(I) 2006 Sarközy law(II) 2007 Hortefeux law	Sarközy Initiative (I)immigration choice (II)Prevention of mass legalization (III) co-development with sending countries

Fig. 8.3 Political dynamics originated from French politics and impacted other dimensions and levels (2003–2009)

agreements were signed between Francophone countries such as Bénin, Burkina Faso, and Senegal as well as with newly emerging countries such as Russia.

Under the initiative of French President Sarközy, who was also the president of the Council of the EU in the second half of 2008, measures to control illegal immigrants were proposed in the European Pact on Immigration and Asylum 2008.[17] In particular, it is interesting that Sarközy strongly intended to establish external migration policies, emphasizing the fact that the legalization of a large number of illegal immigrants increases the number of illegal stays and that cooperation with the immigrant-sending countries is important for migration control. Sarközy's intention was "uploaded" to the EU level and to a certain extent influenced the strategies of the European Commission (Fig. 8.3).

[17]Council of the European Union (2008b).

8.3.2 EU Readmission Agreement, Mobility Partnership, and EU Return Directive

8.3.2.1 Development of the External Dimension of Border Control Policies

Here, the EU Readmission Agreement, the Mobility Partnership, and the EU Return Directive as typical tools to manage illegal immigrants with the cooperation of the third countries are investigated.[18]

In the 1999 Tampere program, the EU first acknowledged the possibility of cooperation with third countries in migration management. The Tampere program proposed a "comprehensive approach" to migration, and several principles were proposed therein.[19] These included that immigration should be coordinated in a balanced manner from the viewpoint of human rights and the economy, and immigrants from third countries should as far as possible be afforded the same rights and duties as European citizens. Furthermore, the aim of establishing migration management strategies that included more cooperation from immigrant-sending countries was proposed. At the same time, it was decided to establish the High-Level Working Group on Asylum and Migration (HLWG) as an EU institution that deals with the external aspect of migration policies.[20] In 2005, the European Council drafted the "Global Approach to Migration" proposing an action plan for African and Mediterranean countries. This provided a concrete picture of the strategies of foreign affairs for aiming migration control. In the Hague Programme of 2005 and the Stockholm Programme of 2010, the foreign aspect of migration policies was strengthened. Furthermore, *The Global Approach to Migration and Mobility* (GAMM) was proposed as an EU Commission Communication in 2011. This Communication was published based on the results of the inquiry on relevant actors in June 2011. *Le Secrétariat Général des affaires européennes* (SGAE) responded to the inquiry process. In this way, after the late 1990s, cooperation with third countries was pursued as a method of EU-level migration management.

8.3.2.2 EU Readmission Agreement

At first, the EU Readmission Agreement can be briefly explained as follows. The agreement decided that immigrant-sending countries shall have the responsibility for the readmission of immigrants whose entry and stay in the EU member countries are

[18]Besides the three policies mentioned in this section, "the European Return Fund" was established in 2007, and organizations at the EU level provide financial support to send illegal immigrants back to their home countries.

[19]European Council (1999) 'Presidency Conclusions' Tampere European Council, 15-16 October.

[20]For the detailed information on the members and activities of the High-Level Working Group on Asylum and Migration (HLWG), see Okabe (2014).

not permitted or whose update of stay admission is rejected. This agreement is recognized as an important part of the external migration policies of the European Commission. In the Amsterdam Treaty of 1999, the competence to sign the EU Readmission Agreement with the third countries was implicitly given to the EU as a common competence. Furthermore, in the revision of the Lisbon Treaty in 2009, the competence was explicitly provided to the EU, in the Treaty on the Functioning of the European Union 79 (3).[21] In 2004, at first, the Admission Agreement was signed with Hong Kong and, since then, has been signed with ten countries outside of the EU area including Russia and Turkey. The contents of the agreement depend on the conditions of each country.[22]

In the EU Communication, in which the European Commission reports on the assessment of the practice of the EU Readmission Agreement until 2011 and showed the points for further improvement, the following problems were pointed out.[23] First, the arrangement for data on readmission such as Eurostat is insufficient. Second, the practice of the EU Readmission Agreements is not uniform among the EU member countries. The European Commission explains that most member countries utilize the EU Readmission Agreement to repatriate illegal immigrants with a third country nationality staying in a member country, but the other member countries utilize bilateral agreements that have existed before the EU Readmission Agreements came into effect. In this regard, the European Commission pointed out that the inconsistent practice of the EU Readmission Agreement by the member countries impaired their credibility and recommended that all member states apply the EU Readmission Agreement to repatriate the illegal immigrants. Third, the European Commission pointed out the problem that some EU Readmission Agreements had not yet started, or had not been accomplished with the negotiation, and suggested that there are a lack of incentives for third countries to advance the negotiations and a lack of flexibility related to technical problems in third countries.[24] In fact, the reciprocity between the EU and third countries is not high enough with the more costs of third countries, because they do not have sufficient administrative abilities to readmit illegal immigrants. In the EU Communication, the European Commission identified the following ways to promote the third countries' cooperation. Namely, they are the promotion of issuing visa, financial support and the global approach to migration control, and the quota system for legal immigrants' access to the labor market.[25] The lack of flexibility of the member states is mainly due to concern over time constraints for sending back illegal immigrants.

[21] European Commission (2011), p.2.

[22] According to websites of European Commission (Migrations and Home Affairs DG) https://ec.europa.eu/home-affairs/what-we-do/policies/irregular-migration-return-policy/return-readmission_en, EU has signed 17 agreements.

[23] European Commission (2011).

[24] Ibid., p. 6.

[25] Ibid., p. 8.

In this regard, while more the EU Readmission Agreements are gradually being signed with third countries, in some cases, the member states sometimes repatriate illegal immigrants based on existing bilateral agreements. Moreover, the EU does not necessarily have sufficient resources to provide incentives to third countries to sign an agreement under negotiation. Therefore, while the EU has the competence, as decided in the Lisbon Treaty, it does not have absolute authority in its bargaining power and effectiveness.

8.3.2.3 Mobility Partnership

The Mobility Partnership is composed of soft laws that embody the joint declaration between the EU and third countries and do not have legally binding power. Negotiations are advanced between third countries and the Council of Europe and the European Commission, which represents the member states. The Mobility Partnership lists common measures for migration problems such as the integration of immigrants, human trafficking, border control, and forged documents, and each member state can choose the issues on which it cooperates with a third country. As such, the Mobility Partnership aims to provide a uniform framework for cooperation on migration, ensuring consistency among member states.

In 2008, the Mobility Partnership was first signed with Moldova and Cape Verde and, until now, has been signed with Eastern European countries such as Moldova and Georgia and those on the southern coast of the Mediterranean including Morocco and Tunisia. In particular, since the 2000s, an increasing number of third countries have signed the agreements.[26] The official aim of the Mobility Partnership is to promote reciprocity among EU member states, immigrant-sending countries, and migrant workers born in third countries. This contrasts the EU's external migration policies, which prioritize the security issues and border control. The Mobility Partnership tries to establish a transnational framework for migrant workers including the "Circulation visa" scheme[27] and is recognized as an important policy that integrates the problem of migrant workers into the EU's external migration policies. In the "Stockholm Programme" of 2009, the Mobility Partnership was referred to as a long-term and comprehensive framework for cooperation on migration control.[28]

Existing research on the implementation of the Mobility Partnership argues that it is a "dangerous partnership," because the contents thereof are too abstract. In particular, the issue of the "Circulation visa" sometimes compromises the consistency of EU policies on migrant workers among the EU member states and reduces

[26]By December 2016, the Mobility Partnership had been signed with Moldova, Cape Verde, Georgia, Almena, Azerbaijan, Tunisia, Jordan, and Belarus.

[27]See Carrera et al. (2012), p.97.

[28]Council, The Stockholm programme (17024/09). Brussels: Council of the European Union (2009)

the protection of human rights for migrant workers who came from the third countries.[29] On the other hand, the Mobility Partnership plays the role of setting in motion negotiations between institutions with legally binding power such as the Readmission Agreement.

8.3.2.4 EU Return Directive

The EU Readmission Agreement and Mobility Partnership attempt to ensure consistency in terms of policies among EU member states from an external point of viewpoint. In contrast, the EU Return Directive is an attempt to promote consistency in the application of policy among EU member states by transposing the contents of the directive into a domestic law within a certain time limit.[30]The EU Return Directive was adopted in 2008 and came into effect in 2010. The contents of the directive decided the establishment of the human rights protection and the minimum criteria for the procedures in the return system of the EU member states, maximum detention period of illegal immigrants, and improvement of detention conditions, setting the time limit for voluntary leave, establishment of monitoring for repatriating illegal immigrants, and the maximum period in which to refuse entry and the conditions thereof.

The assessment of the effectiveness of the EU Return Directive was delineated into different periods in the official documents of the European Commission. According to a document published by the DG Home Affairs of the European Commission in 2013, the directive ascertained the conditions for sending back illegal immigrants, even though this is a minimum requirement. Under these conditions, the directive contributed to the establishing the provision of immigrants' return when it has not been established and promoted the human rights protection of illegal immigrants by formulating a uniform standard for the maximum detention period.[31] However, a document dated March 2017 explained that the EU Return Directive still remained a lot of discretion in the transposition of the directive into a domestic law and that the inconsistent transposition among the member states had a negative impact on the effectiveness of the EU return policy.[32] In any case, the EU Return Directive aimed to promote consistency in the policies of EU member states.

In this regard, when we consider measures to solve the problem of illegal immigration and return policies at the EU level, we need to understand the complexity of the issue that is composed of the EU Readmission Agreement with legal

[29]Carrera et al. (2012), pp.97–115

[30]These attempts and harmonization of laws are the primary subjects of research on "Europeanization" research. See Faist and Ette (2007).

[31]European Commission (2013), pp.9–17.

[32]European Commission (2017b), p.1. In the area of the EU common migration policies including the measures against illegal immigrants, the EU directives are likely to imply optional clauses as they attempt to communalize the core elements of the sovereignty of the EU member states.

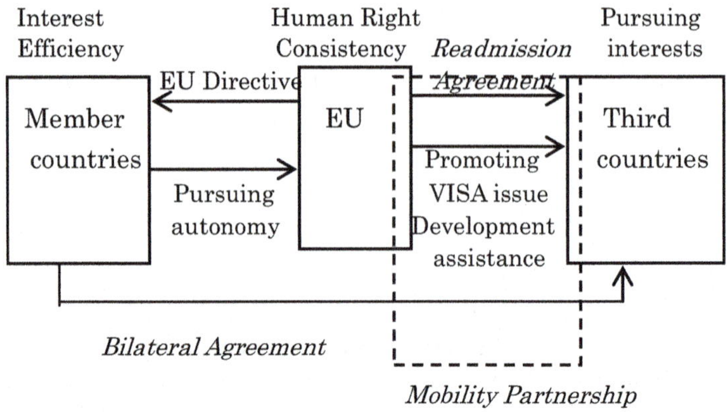

Fig. 8.4 Tripartite EU multi-layered migration governance

	Polity	Policies	Politics
External Policy Area	• Multi-layered migration governance (External dimension)	• EU Mobility Partnership • EU Readmission Agreement	• EU-third countries ***Externalisation***
EU	• Strengthening European Commission's competence. Ex. Article 79(3) of TFEU by Lisbon Treaty	• Transposition of EU directives to domestic laws Ex.Directive2008/115/EC	Active European Commission propositions. 2005 GAM 2010 GAMM
France (Member state)	* * *	• French immigration policies. Loi n°2011-672 du 16 juin 2011 Décret no 2011-820 du 8 juillet 2011	***Europeanization***

Fig. 8.5 Political dynamics originated from the EU level

binding power, Mobility Partnership as a soft law, and the EU Return Directive legislated for EU member states. The tripartite multi-layered governance in the EU is summarized in Fig. 8.4, and the political dynamics that has been originated from the EU level is shown in Fig. 8.5.

8.4 Intention of France as an EU Member State and the Demarcation of the EU Readmission Agreement and Mobility Partnership: A Case Study of Bilateral Agreements/EU Readmission Agreements and the French Government's Response in the Inquiry Process in 2011

In this section, the migration management enforced by the bilateral agreements between France and third countries and the EU Readmission Agreement and the Mobility Partnership in the EU-level framework are analyzed, and the differences in their characteristics and the intention of each actor are considered. The third countries focused on in this analysis are Senegal, Carpe Verde, and Tunisia. Senegal signed the bilateral agreement with France in 1980 but did not sign the Mobility Partnership. Cape Verde signed the EU Readmission Agreement and the Mobility Partnership with the EU and also has a bilateral agreement with France. Tunisia signed the Mobility Partnership with the EU as well as signed a bilateral agreement with France. These three countries belong to the "Zone de Solidarité Prioritaire" and have strong ties with France.[33] Furthermore, in the inquiry process of *The Global Approach to Migration and Mobility* (GAMM) in 2011, the position and intention of the French government was investigated by examining official documents published by the relevant ministries.

8.4.1 Analysis of France's Bilateral Agreement and the EU External Migration Policies

8.4.1.1 Senegal

Senegal is an ex-colonial country of France, and even now, half of the Senegalese who are moving to Europe are actually immigrants entering France.

There is a long history of bilateral agreements between Senegal and France. In particular, the agreement on the co-management of the flow of immigrants signed on September 23, 2006, inherited many legacies of the bilateral agreements instituted after the 1980s. Most important, the agreement on migration that was signed between France and Senegal provided an opportunity for professional training to immigrant workers who intended to return to Senegal by themselves.[34] Furthermore,

[33]See La Cimade (2009).

[34]Loi n° 81–1139 du 24 décembre 1981 autorisant l'approbation d'un accord entre le Gouvernement de la République française et le Gouvernement de la République du Sénégal sur la formation en vue du retour et de l'insertion dans l'économie sénégalaise des travailleurs ayant émigré temporairement en France Accord signé à Dakar le 1er décembre 1980.

in the 1990s, opportunities for student exchange were implemented between France and Senegal. The 2006 agreement included the following aspects: first, the establishment of a general monitoring system for migration management; second, the circulation of people and the issue of Circulation visa; third, the agreement on the acceptance of students and workers as well as provisions for family reunification; fourth, border monitoring for illegal immigrants and their return management by both countries; and fifth, the establishment of common patrols in border control in the coastal area. Regarding the return of illegal immigrants to their home countries, either France or Senegal is obligated to accept illegal immigrants of their nationality who are staying in the other country, while respecting human dignity and basic human rights. The agreement also dictated that France shall make arrangements for effective measures to promote the voluntary return of illegal residents who have a duty or leave France and that the Senegalese benefit from exceptional acceptance into their home countries with a "temporary residence card."

As such, the bilateral agreement between France and Senegal stipulates the cooperation of border control and exceptional acceptance of illegal residents and contributes to French migration management. Moreover, the promotion of legal immigration through the Circulation visa is a measure to provide a benefit to Senegal, too. In this sense, the bilateral agreement is reciprocal for both actors.

In the EU-Senegal relationships, negotiations pertaining to the Mobility Partnership between the EU and Senegal were initiated in 2008 but stopped indefinitely just 1 year later. The reason for the breakdown of the negotiation was explained by M. Chou and M. Givert, based on their interviews with negotiators on both the EU side and the Senegalese side, as follows. The Mobility Partnership was recognized as a political risk because of the increasing costs of border control rather than benefits for Senegal, and the negotiation failed because of Senegal's rational decision.[35]

However, despite that negotiations on the Mobility Partnership failed, the EU sought a way to continue cooperation with Senegal as a major immigrant-sending country to EU member states.[36] Official documents of the European Commission in 2016 explained that the negotiations on the policy coordination of returning illegal immigrants had advanced and that the employment creation project for young Senegalese was adopted through "the EU trust fund."[37] In particular, significant economic assistance has been provided to solve the causes underlying the problem of illegal immigration, and in Senegal, 600 companies are provided with financial support by the EU, creating 24,000 new jobs.[38] Namely, according to the official documents of the European Commission, the EU began to economically assist

[35]See Chou and Gibert (2012), pp.409–427.

[36]See European Commission (2017a). According to this document, 1,0300 irregular migrants arrived in Italy in 2016.

[37]European Commission Communication from the Commission to the European Parliament, The European Council and the Council "Second Progress Report: First Deliverables on the Partnership Framework with third countries under the European Agenda on Migration (2016).

[38]Ibid, p.6.

Senegal after the breakdown of negotiations regarding the Mobility Partnership. Thus, the EU strategy became similar to the bilateral agreement between France and Senegal to elicit Senegal's cooperation in managing migration.

8.4.1.2 Cape Verde

Cape Verde signed the bilateral agreement with France in 2008,[39] the Mobility Partnership in 2008, and the Readmission Agreement in 2014 with the EU. Cape Verde is an ex-colonial country of Portugal.

The preface of the bilateral agreement refers to the Cotonou Agreement, Europe-Africa Conference, and the Mobility Partnership at the EU level. The contents of the prescription are as follows: first, the promotion of the short-term mobility of people with a "Circulation visa"; second, the issue of "Competence and Human Resource visa" for students and young skilled workers; third, the acceptance of their own nationals who have become illegal immigrants; and fourth, the provision of financial assistance for Cape Verde, indicating an issue linkage with the anti-illegal immigrant measures, promotion of legal immigrants, and development assistance.

In contrast, the contents of the Mobility Partnership on migration management included the following six points in the negotiation process:[40] first, the establishment of a monitoring system on immigrant inflow; second, the management and promotion of the employment and integration of legal immigrants; third, the issue of a "Temporary Visitor visa"; fourth, the linkage between migration and development; fifth, asylum seekers and immigrants; and sixth, measures regarding illegal immigrants.

These actions aimed to strengthen the existing cooperation between Cape Verde and EU member states. At the same time, Cape Verde and France began promoting the employment of legal immigrants and strengthened the existing bilateral agreement, reconfirming the joint development program, measures against drug and human trafficking, investigation of forged documents, and the strengthening of border control. Besides France, Cape Verde also signed a partnership with Portugal, the former colonial power, and Spain, with whom it is geographically close. As an agreement that is concerned with all EU member countries, the Mobility Partnership stipulated the promotion of student exchange, cooperation with FRONTEX (the European Border and Coast Guard Agency) regarding the return of immigrants, and cooperation with Europol (the European Police Office) to establish an information exchange system for police cooperation and crime.[41]

---

[39] Accord entre le Gouvernement de la République Française et le Gouvernement de la République du Cap-Vert relatif à la gestion concertée des flux migratoires et au développement solidaire (ensemble trois annexes).

[40] Council of the European Union (2008a).

[41] In 2016, FRONTEX was reorganized and renamed as the European Border and Coast Guard Agency (EBCG).

According to these stipulations, there is no mutually exclusive relation between the Mobility Partnership and bilateral agreement. Rather, the Mobility Partnership promotes cooperation in the policy area in which the bilateral agreement does not make up a concrete prescription.

Next, Cape Verde drafted the EU Readmission Agreement as follows. The EU Readmission Agreement that was signed by the EU and Cape Verde in 2013 prescribes a bilateral obligation on the acceptance of the nationals from Cape Verde and EU member states as well as third country's nationals.[42] Furthermore, in this agreement, the time limit for the readmission procedure, the transportation of repatriates, and a joint readmission committee were decided. As the visa promotion agreement was signed in 2012, in the EU Readmission Agreements, the benefits of promoting visas for legal immigrants and costs of readmitting illegal immigrants were connected. Therefore, the contents of the EU Readmission Agreement are more concrete than those of the bilateral agreement.

8.4.1.3 Tunisia

Tunisia signed a bilateral agreement with France in 2008.[43] Tunisia is an ex-colonial country with strong historical ties with France. The 2008 bilateral agreement inherited the content of former agreements, namely, the 1998 agreement on residence and work and 2003 agreement on the exchange of young skilled workers. The 2008 agreement comprises two types of protocols and bylaws. One is concerned with the joint management of migration and the other with development assistance. Regarding the joint management of migration, the agreement stipulates the activation of the movement of people between the two countries via the issuance of a visa such as the "Competence and Human Resource visa" and the "Circulation visa," the bilateral duty on the readmission of illegal residents, and cooperation in technical tasks pertaining to controlling illegal immigrants. With regard to development assistance, the agreement specifies the socioeconomic integration and employment creation for Tunisians residing in France and financial support for other projects. According to these prescriptions, it is clearly identified that France actively practices development assistance together with the joint management of migration. In other words, through the agreement, while Tunisia bears the costs of migration management, France provides the benefits of economic development to Tunisia.

The agreements between the EU and Tunisia are explained as follows. Tunisia signed the Mobility Partnership with France in 2014.[44] The counties that participated

[42]Council Decision of October 7, 2013, on the Conclusion of the Agreement between the European Union and the Republic of Cape Verde on the Readmission of Persons Residing without Authorization; OJ L282 of 24/10/2013, p. 13.

[43]Accord Cadre relatif à la gestion concertée des migrations et au développement solidaire entre le Gouvernement de la République Française et le Gouvernement de la République Tunisienne.

[44]European Commission (2014) "Déclaration conjointe pour le partenariat de mobilité entre la Tunisie, l'Union Européenne et ses Etas membres participants."

Table 8.1 External migration policies with Senegal, Cape Verde, and Tunisia

	Bilateral agreement with France	EU readmission agreement	Mobility partnership
Senegal	It has started since the 1980s. Signed in 2006	In negotiation since 2016	Negotiation started since 2008, but it has stopped indefinitely just one year later
Cape Verde	Signed in 2008	Signed in 2014	Signed in 2008
Tunisia	It has started since the 1980s. Signed in 2008	In negotiation since 2016	Signed in 2014

in the Mobility Partnership are ten EU member states including France. The contents of the Mobility Partnership with Tunisia are as follows: the promotion of the movement of people by simplifying the issuing of visas; the EU's assistance to the Tunisian government to establish a protection system for refugees and asylums seekers, providing employment, education, and the opportunities of training to Tunisian with qualifications in the EU; the social integration of legal Tunisians in the EU; the setting up of the negotiation on the Readmission Agreement for illegal immigrants; and the establishment of cooperation regarding human trafficking and border control. Moreover, the Mobility Partnership aims to link migration and development. For example, according to the European Commission fact sheet published by European Commission, the EU and Tunisia launched negotiations on visa facilitation and readmission agreements in October 2016.[45]

Comparing the bilateral agreement with France and the Mobility Partnership, we can point out that both agreements have a framework under which Tunisia receives development assistance in exchange for bearing the costs of migration management. The relations between the countries are considered compatible, because some projects resulting from the EU Mobility Partnership are implemented through French expertise.[46]

External migration policies, namely, bilateral agreement, the EU Readmission Agreement, and the Mobility Partnership, with Senegal, Cape Verde, and Tunisia, are summarized in Table 8.1.

8.4.2 *Analysis of French Government Documents Responding to the Inquiry Process in 2011*

In the inquiry process of 2011 which was mentioned above, relevant ministries, specialists, and individuals responded to the European Commission's questions on the Global Approach to Migration. The questions proposed by the European

[45]European Commission (2017c), p.3.

[46]See Lemma Project (Projet Lemma) which was launched in July 2016.

Commission were concerned with the role of EU external relations, priority order for a dialogue process among regions,[47] and priority order in the Global Approach.

The preferences of the French government, which were determined based on its responses, focused on the following three points.[48] First, promoting the return of illegal immigrants and border control was prioritized over the protection of immigrants' human rights. Second, the development of third countries as immigrant-sending countries was considered very important, so the issue of a "Circulation visa" and the flexibility of the various kinds of funds which were established at the EU level must be promoted. Third, the French government favored the development of policies at the EU level, but showed a cautious stance for concrete measures that may reduce France's autonomy. For example, the French government set the maximum number of Mobility Partnerships signed in a year, and opposed the attempt to jointly coordinate and manage the resources of EU member countries with third countries.

Therefore, while France favored the establishment of the Mobility Partnership, it wanted this to remain at the level of a joint partnership that does not infringe on the country's sovereignty. Furthermore, the priority of human rights protection for immigrants was relatively low.

8.5 Conclusion

In this section, the results of the empirical analysis are summarized, and the situation of multi-layered migration governance and intention of France as an EU member state are considered. In so doing, implications for the global politics of the international movement of people are highlighted.

As a summary of the empirical analysis, the following three results are pointed out. First, there are many overlapping areas between bilateral agreements and EU-level agreements with third countries. This structure is identified by a comparative analysis of the contents of bilateral agreements and the EU-level institutions. Furthermore, bilateral agreements and EU-level agreements are not mutually exclusive but complementary in that the EU institutions are complementary to the bilateral agreements and apply them under the conditions of the EU's limited bargaining power. In particular, there is the EU's intention to integrate the existing bilateral agreements into the EU Mobility Partnership as a framework for soft law and as an extension thereof to create an EU Readmission Agreement that can be legally enforced. Furthermore, the Tunisian case revealed the Lemma project, which was implemented through French expertise. This case substantiated the compatibility

[47]As for the dialogue processes on migration which are set by the EU, for example, there are the "Asia-Europe meeting on migration (ASEM)" and "EU-Africa Partnership on Migration, Mobility and Employment."

[48]Secrétariat général des affaires européennes (2011) Consultation relative à l Approche globale sur les migrations, Questionnaire.

between the French bilateral agreements and EU external migration policies. In fact, after the 2010s, the number of Mobility Partnerships has increased, and further negotiations are ongoing. Second, third countries such as Senegal and Tunisia integrated the issue of a "Circulation visa" and development assistance, which benefit them, into their bilateral agreements with France. Specifically, it was suggestive that negotiations for the Mobility Partnership between Senegal and the EU failed in 2009, because of third countries' preference not to bear the burden of migration management costs.

Regarding France's intention as an EU member state, the country signed bilateral agreements on immigration with third countries after the 1980s and, initiated by Sarközy, signed an agreement to increase the effectiveness of the return policy after the mid-2000s. Based on our analysis of the contents of the agreement and response documents for the 2011 inquiry process, it can be noted that France made their policies to deal with illegal immigrants more effective by enhancing third countries' ability for migration control and also provided incentives for third countries' cooperation by creating a linkage between development assistance and the problem of migration. Participating in all Mobility Partnerships, France considers EU-level initiatives important in gaining the cooperation of third countries. However, France shows cautious attitudes in cases where the Mobility Partnerships diminish her autonomy.

Next, the multi-layered migration governance structure is summarized from the viewpoint of polity, policies, and politics in European integration. As suggested at the beginning of this chapter, in the multi-layered governance, the actors are the EU, EU member states, and third countries. There is a conflicting configuration in the areas of policies and politics between the EU, which pursues enacting effective migration policies based on policy harmonization among member states and active cooperation with third countries, and the EU member states and third countries, which want to maximize their benefits. However, established institutions are not mutually exclusive but complementary when bilateral agreements are extended to the EU-level agreements in the areas of polity and politics. In particular, though member states have a consistent attitude to pursue their autonomy, the EU has tried to exercise its power of negotiation by establishing the development fund and creating an all-encompassing negotiation package. In fact, the gradual development was seen in these areas after the 2010s. Moreover, the resilience of the EU is evident in the external aspect of migration policies. The European Commission and other EU institutions continue to establish solidarity among member states by promoting the implementation of the EU Readmission Agreement, enhancing the effectiveness of the Mobility Partnership, and transposing the EU Return Directives into domestic laws. Possibly, this EU resilience will receive political backlash, because EU policies and regimes directly influence the lives of citizens whose opportunities to participate in the decision-making process are limited. This is the very nature of the EU decision-making process. Namely, even though the EU and political leaders of member states can find the appropriate areas free from other constrained effects, the policies they constructed would be fixed by the strong will of citizens, as seen in the example of Brexit. Therefore, we must be cautious about the political discussion among EU member states. Furthermore, we should acknowledge that the stability of constructed governance is still not valid.

Finally, the contribution of the analysis of multi-layered migration governance to global politics on the international movement of people is explained as follows. As noted in this article, in the multi-layered governance, there are multiple potential venues for negotiation and politics; thus, actors with their own interests may engage in "forum shopping." Therefore, in order to increase the effectiveness of multi-layered migration governance, we should identify the interests of each actor and, rather than imposing norms on actors unilaterally, establish complementary institutions more compatible with these interests of each actor from the long-term perspective.

References

Aglietta M, Leron N (2017) La double démocratie: Une Europe politique pour la croissance. Édition du Seuil, Paris

Boyer R (2015) Économie politique des capitalismes: Théorie de la régulation et des crises, La Découverte, Paris

Bretherton C, Mannin LM (eds) (2013) The Europeanization of European politics. Palgrave Macmillan, Basingstoke

Carrera S, Hernadez R, Sagrera I (2012) Mobility partnerships: 'insecurity partnerships' for policy coherence and migrant workers' human rights in the EU. In: Kunz R, Lavenex S, Panizzon M (eds) (2012), pp 97–115

Chou M-H, Gibert M (2012) The EU-Senegal mobility partnership: from launch to suspension and negotiation failure. J Contemp Eur Res 8(4):409–427

Council of the European Union (2003) Council directive on the right to family reunification. Brussels, 2003/86/EC (28 February 2003)

Council of the European Union (2008a) Joint declaration on a mobility partnership between the European Union and the Republic of Cape Verde. Brussels (21 May 2008)

Council of the European Union (2008b) European pact on immigration and asylum. Brussels, 24 September 2008

Council of the European Union (2009) Council directive on the conditions of entry and residence of third-country nationals for the purpose of highly qualified employment. 2009/50/EC (25 May 2009)

European Commission (2011) Communication from the Commission to the European Parliament and the Council evaluation of EU readmission agreement. Brussels, 23.2.2011 COM(2011) 76 final

European Commission (2014) Déclaration conjointe pour le partenariat de mobilié entre la Tunisie, l'Union Européenne et ses États members participants

European Commission (2016) Communication from the Commission to the European Parliament, The European Council and the Council "Second progress report: first deliverables on the partnership framework" with third countries under the European Agenda on migration, Brussels

European Commission (2017a) Fourth progress report on the partnership framework with third countries under the European agenda on migration

European Commission (2017b) Fact sheet questions and answers: making return and readmission procedures more efficient. Brussels, March 2017

European Commission (2017c) Fact sheet: relations between the EU and Tunisia

European Commission – DG Home Affairs (2013) Evaluation on the application of the Return Directive (2008/115/EC), 22 October 2013
Faist T, Ette A (2007) The Europeanization of national politics and politics of immigration between autonomy and the European Union. Palgrave Macmillan, Basingstoke
Guiraudon V (2000) European integration and migration policy: vertical policy-making as venue shopping. J Common Mark Stud 38(2):251–271
Guiraudon V (2010) Les effets de l'européanisation des politiques d'immigration et d'asile. Politique européenne no° 31: 7–32
Jurje F, Lavenex S (2014) Trade agreements as venues for 'market power Europe? ' The case of immigration policy. J Common Mark Stud 52(2):320–336
Kunz R, Lavenex S, Panizzon M (eds) (2012) Multilayered migration governance. The promise of partnership. Routledge, London
La Cimade (2009) Document d'analyse les accords relatifs à la gestion concertée des flux migratoires et au codéveloppment Version Actualisé. (20 Octobre 2009)
Lavenex S (2006) Shifting up and out: the foreign policy of European immigration control. West Eur Policies 29(2):329–350
Le gouvernement français (2008) European pact on immigration and asylum version I Draft of 25.01.08. cmr.jur.ru.nl/cmr/docs/pacte.europeen.sarkozy.pdf
Loi n° 1981–1139 du 24 décembre 1981 autorisant l'approbation d'un accord entre le Gouvernement de la République française et le Gouvernement de la République du Sénégal sur la formation en vue du retour et de l'insertion dans l'économie sénégalaise des travailleurs ayant émigré temporairement en France Accord signé à Dakar le 1er décembre 1980
Loi n° 2006–911 du 24 juillet 2006 relative à l'immigration et à l'intégration
Miyajima T (2009) Social integration and exclusion of immigrants: the French equality questioned. The University of Tokyo Press, Tokyo
Okabe M (2014) The study of the EU migration control as foreign policies: the reconstruction of borders and the diffusion of norms. Doctoral thesis, The University of Tokyo
Panizzon M (2012) Franco-African pacts on migration: bilateralism revisited in multilayered migration governance. In Kunz, Lavenex, Panizzon (eds) (2012)
Secrétariat général des affaires européennes (2011) Consultation relative à l Approche globale sur les migrations, Questionnaire
Tsuchiya T (2009) The development of EU common migration policies: the prosperity of "immigrants" and "ours". J Takasaki City Univ Econ 52(3):11–24
Yasue N (2012) The EU and France: the swaying tricolor in the European integration. Horitsu Bunka-sha, Kyoto

Chapter 9
Transforming the Role of Public Policies for Innovation: The Role of Institutional Foundations in Finland as a Nordic State

Norio Tokumaru

9.1 Introduction

One of the trends in "growth strategies" in advanced countries since the beginning of the twenty-first century has been to emphasize innovations in areas where services and infrastructures are provided largely by the public sector. The Japanese "new growth strategy," established in 2010, is a typical example, in which both "green innovation" and "life innovation" were at the core of the strategy. In line with this trend, Boyer (2004) argued that economic growth in advanced economies will be generated by human-related services[1] rather than the production of durable goods, as in the postwar period. His argument was based on the consumption expenditure record in the United States, which showed the salient increase in expenditure on interpersonal services, in contrast with the almost unchanged expenditure on durable consumer goods. If his argument is correct, then the main locus of innovation in advanced countries will be human-related services. Because a large part of human-related services are provided by the public sector, innovation policies may require novel approaches, partly because diverse sociopolitical factors such as regulations,

This research is supported by JSPS Grant-in-Aid for Scientific Research (C) No. 25380225. This paper has been presented at several annual conferences, including the Society for the Advancement of Socio-Economics (SASE) 2014 and the Japan Association for Evolutionary Economics (JAFEE) 2015. I highly appreciate Ville Valovirta (VTT) for providing information on the survey conducted at VTT. I am also grateful for the detailed information and discussion by all the interviewees.

[1]Boyer (2004) termed this emerging growth model the "anthropogenetic model," in which interpersonal service provision activities, such as healthcare and education, are the main sources of economic growth.

N. Tokumaru (✉)
Nagoya Institute of Technology, Nagoya, Japan
e-mail: tokumaru.norio@nitech.ac.jp

R. Boyer et al. (eds.), *Evolving Diversity and Interdependence of Capitalisms*, Evolutionary Economics and Social Complexity Science 11,
https://doi.org/10.1007/978-4-431-55001-3_9

institutions, political processes, and even cultural norms affect innovations in human-related services. As we will see in this paper, the European Union, and particularly Northern European countries, has been quite active in implementing novel approaches to innovation policies.

At the same time, latecomer countries have upgraded their capacity for innovation (Tokumaru 2013), which suggests that it will become increasingly difficult for advanced countries to differentiate themselves from latecomer countries simply by enhancing their technical and organizational capacity (cf. Brown et al. 2011). Moreover, governments in advanced countries and in latecomer countries have implemented conventional, "supply-side" innovation policies, such as education policies, intellectual property rights policies, and entrepreneurship policies, to enhance the supply of technical personnel and knowledge. This also suggests that the governments of advanced countries will need to develop novel approaches to innovation policies other than supply-side policy measures in order to differentiate themselves from latecomer countries.

A novel policy approach to innovation policy emerging in Europe, namely, the *demand- and user-driven (DUI) innovation policy*, deserves special attention in this context and will be examined in detail in this paper. It remains an open question as to whether the DUI policy requires a deep transformation of the role of the public sector, as well as whether it is merely a shift of attention from the supply side to the demand side.

Based on a detailed case study of the implementation of a DUI policy in Finland, this study examines how the role of the public sector has been transformed in implementing innovation policies. This paper is organized as follows. Section 9.2 briefly examines the concept of a DUI policy in the context of innovation studies. Then, Sects. 9.3 and 9.4, based on policy documents, show how innovation policies have transformed since 2000 in the EU and Finland, respectively. Section 9.5 examines the DUI policy implementation in Finland, including the roles *actually* played by public and semi-public actors. Section 9.6 argues that the novel role of the public and semi-public sectors in a DUI policy can be understood as the governance of the evolutionary process of innovation, where the public and semi-public sectors should be deeply involved in the innovation process. This is contrary to the conventional role of the public sector to provide useful complementary resources such as institutional frameworks, funding, and education while standing *outside* the innovation process. From institutionalist perspectives, the Nordic welfare and corporatist institutions, including the active third-sector organizations, might play a key role in implementing DUI policies. Lastly, this is followed by a discussion on possible implications for East Asian countries.

9.2 Demand- and User-Driven Innovation (DUI) Policy as a Novel Approach to Innovation Policy

In this section, we briefly review the concept of a demand- and user-driven innovation (DUI) policy in the context of innovation policy[2] research. "Market failure" has been the traditional criterion to justify innovation policies, of which the public funding of basic research is a typical example (Nelson 1959; Arrow 1962). Moreover, innovation studies have recognized that innovation is the result of the interaction among agents, and, as a result, the concept of an "innovation system" has become widely used (Freeman 1987; Lundvall 1992; Nelson 1993). Therefore, the criteria for innovation policies have been extended so that policy measures to correct market failures and "systemic failures" are also justified (Chaminade and Edquist 2010). In fact, Chaminade and Edquist (2010) point out that (1) ensuring interaction among organizations, (2) avoiding negative lock-in, and (3) catalyzing the structural change in industries in order to promote product innovation are examples of policy targets used to correct the systemic failures of innovation systems. In summary, policymakers try to intervene in the interactions among agents rather than the behavior of individual agents in this new, systemic failure perspective of innovation policy.

The DUI policy is understood to be a typical policy measure used to solve systemic failure problems. OECD (2011) defined the DUI policy as a "set of public measures to increase demand for innovations, to improve conditions for the uptake of innovations, or to improve the articulation of demand in order to spur innovations and allow their diffusion." According to Edler (2010), the DUI policy is "public action to induce innovation and/or speed up the diffusion of innovation through increasing the demand for innovation, defining new functional requirements for products and services and/or improving user involvement in innovation production (user-driven innovation)." Both of these definitions understand the DUI policy as a measure used to promote innovations by stimulating the demand for innovations rather than increasing the resources put into innovative activities.[3]

Edler (2010) notes that (1) the public procurement of innovation (PPI) and (2) the promotion of private demand are concrete policy measures for a DUI policy. Here, the promotion of private demand comprises (a) subsidizing the private demand for innovation, (b) enhancing the attitude to accept innovations, and (c) regulatory changes to promote innovations. Among these policy measures, this paper focuses on PPI, which has been pursued actively in Europe since the 2000s.

---

[2]In this paper, an innovation policy is defined as various policy measures that aim to enhance the innovative performance of economic entities such as firms, regions, and nations. Thus, as Lundvall and Borrás (2005) point out, an innovation policy is a broader concept than that of a science and technology policy. Moreover, other policy areas, such as labor market policies, can serve as innovation policies.

[3]On important roles of demand and user for innovation, see a detailed study by Von Hippel (1988).

9.3 The Transformation of Innovation Policies in the EU

Because the innovation policies in Finland have evolved closely with EU innovation policies, in this section, we briefly examine the transformation of EU innovation policies since the 2000s.

9.3.1 Emphasis on the DUI Policy

While the innovation policy in the EU emphasized conventional, supply-side policy measures, such as funding for science- and technology-related activities in the first half of the 2000s, the European Commission has since begun to emphasize demand-side policy measures, as shown in the following policy documents.

9.3.1.1 *Creating an Innovative Europe* (2006)

This report, known as the *Aho Report*, fundamentally defined the novel direction of the EU innovation policy and was written by a group of specialists led by Esko Aho (the former prime minister of Finland), who were appointed at the Hampton Court summit meeting. The report points out three challenges for the EU innovation system: (1) the globalization of research and development (R&D) activities, which might decrease R&D activities in the EU; (2) weakened incentives to invest in R&D in Europe as a result of the delayed market integration and the fragmentation of small national economies; and (3) a lack of demand-side measures to promote innovations.

In order to respond to these challenges, they proposed the following three policy recommendations: (a) creating an integrated European market for innovative products and services, (b) increasing the level of R&D investment as high as 3% of GDP, and (c) enhancing the mobility of human resources and capital. Of these, they placed the strongest emphasis on (a). In particular, they proposed concrete measures such as the strategic use of innovation-friendly regulations and public procurements, as well as large-scale public investment in key areas, such as "e-health," in order to promote the demand for innovative products and services.

9.3.1.2 *Putting Knowledge into Practice: A Broad–Based Innovation Strategy for the EU* (2006)

This document represented the renewal of EU innovation policy, following the recommendation by the *Aho Report*. The strategy proposed here is "broad-based" in the sense that it includes the promotion of R&D but also the implementation of innovation-friendly and broad social conditions. This was a significant departure from previous policy documents, including *More Research and Innovation* (2005), shifting from encouraging *supply-side* R&D activities to encouraging *demand-side* innovations.

Sharing the idea proposed by the *Aho Report* that innovative markets and demand are important, this document proposed the following six measures to promote innovation: (1) education, (2) mobilizing the potential of a single EU market, (3) the strategic use of regulation and standardization, (4) more collaboration among stakeholders, (5) increasing investment in research and innovation, and (6) improving public procurement. The goal of the strategic use of regulation and standardization is to enhance the competitiveness of EU companies by playing a leading role in implementing regulations and set standards. Improving public procurement aims to promote innovations by strategically using *pre-commercial* public procurement, where the public sector procures products and services that have not yet been commercialized.[4]

The particular emphasis was on the creation of a *lead market* in the EU, where leading-edge products and services are created and sold. In concrete terms, this document claimed lead markets should be created in limited areas, such as environment and healthcare,[5] based on the above six measures in order to develop leading-edge products and services to be exported to areas outside the EU.

9.3.1.3 *Europe 2020 Flagship Initiative: Innovation Union* (2010)

This document described innovation policies for the new growth strategy of the EU, *Europe 2020*, which assumed that innovations were necessary to recover from the current economic crisis. While it largely followed the above, broad-based concept of an innovation policy, four novel points were emphasized: (1) creating a single EU market as a large market for innovation, (2) promoting open innovations, (3) promoting social innovations, and (4) creating the European Innovation Partnership (EIP). Of these, creating the EIP aimed to increase the speed of innovation by concentrating development resources in a limited number of areas.

Based on the brief examination of the three documents, Europe appears to have decided to enhance its competitiveness by mobilizing an innovation-friendly single market and creating leading edge products and services to be exported. This implies that the focus of innovation policies has gradually shifted from supply-side to demand-side measures.

---

[4]The basic idea here is that public procurement might be able to influence companies to develop products and services in certain directions by focusing its demand.

[5]According to *Communication on the Lead Market Initiatives* (Commission of the European Communities 2007), the European Commission decided on several lead market areas, including e-health, sustainable construction, protective textiles, bio-based products, and recycling and renewable energies. For more on the concept of a leading market, see Beise (2004).

9.3.2 Regulatory Reforms for the Public Procurement of Innovation Policy

As described in Sect. 9.2, one of the main policy measures for the DUI policy is the *public procurement of innovation* (PPI). The PPI aims to procure innovative products and services that do not exist, rather than buying existing products and services, as in conventional public procurement. Sharing 19% of the GDP in the EU, the European Commission expects public procurement to stimulate innovations effectively (European Commission 2014, *Public Procurement as a Driver of Innovation in SMEs and Public Services*).

However, the European Commission pointed out that one of the biggest obstacles for the PPI is the tendency of public procurers to avoid taking risks, largely owing to the EU legislation on public procurement, in which competitive bidding is the norm. In fact, because the PPI often requires intensive dialog between public procurers and private companies, public procurers tend to avoid trying the PPI because they are afraid of violating EU legislation (Procurement of Innovation Platform 2014, *Guidance for Public Authorities on Public Procurement of Innovation*).

It was in this context that the European Commission issued a new directive, the *Public Procurement Directives 2014/24/EU*, which allowed for "competitive dialog" enabling public procurers and private companies to have intensive discussions *before* the tender. According to this new directive, competitive dialog is allowed in that the public sector tries to procure large-scale, complex products and services, the requirements of which cannot be specified before the tender, which is expected to ease the PPI. While the public procurer exclusively specifies the requirements in the case of conventional competitive bidding, in competitive dialog, the public procurer proposes brief requirements, and the detail is gradually specified during discussions between the public procurer and the private companies.[6]

9.4 The Transformation of Innovation Policy in Finland[7]

In this section, we shift our attention to the case of Finland and examine how the Finnish innovation policy has transformed since the 2000s. In the 1990s, Finland adopted the idea of "national systems of innovation" as the basis of policymaking. Here, the capacity to connect different sectors was seen as a strength of Finland (Lemola 2004; Edquist et al. 2009). It has been often claimed that innovation policies since the 1990s have been effective for the rapid development of the ICT industry (Hämäläinen and Heikala 2007).

[6]Based on the concepts of Hirschman (1970), it can be said that this legislation justifies public procurers using the *voice* and the *exit* option.

[7]This section is partly supplemented by interviews at the Ministry of Employment and the Economy on March 14, 2011, and March 8, 2013.

However, since the 2000s, some authors have criticized the previous approaches to innovation policies, stating that they place too much emphasis on "science and technology push" measures with heavily "top-down" initiatives (Kotiranta et al. 2009; Sabel and Saxenian 2009; Miettinen 2012), where bottom-up, regional initiatives are often ignored (Jauhiainen 2008). It was against this background that the innovation policy in Finland gradually transformed.

9.4.1 Finnish Economy Under the Big Structural Change

Finland has been a good location for knowledge-intensive work such as engineering. Average monthly earnings of professionals in Finland in 2014 amount to 4212 euro, less than Denmark (5017) and Germany (4615) and slightly higher than Sweden (4091), which implies the salary of engineer is relatively modest compared with other competing European countries (Eurostat 2017). In terms of the resources devoted to research and development (R&D) activities, Finland has been one of the advanced countries that put highest portion of resources into R&D. Even after the decline due to the economic downturn, the ratio of R&D to GDP in Finland in 2014 is 2.90%, ranked 9th in OECD countries following Denmark (2.96%) and Germany (2.93%). The same figure was highest, 3.75%, in 2009, ranked second in OECD countries following Israel (4.14%). Finland has also 15.3 researchers in 1000 employees in 2014, the highest number among OECD countries, followed by Denmark (14.8) and Sweden (14.1) (*OECD Main Science and Technology Indicators 2017*). Finnish workplaces tend to have organizational practices that support innovative activities. According to the *European Work Conditions Survey 2015*, 50% of Finnish respondents answered that teams at work have at least some autonomy, following only Denmark (55%), Sweden (53%), and Norway (53%). In the same survey, when the respondents were asked whether or not they had opportunities to learn at work, 89% of Finnish respondents answered "yes," quite similar with Sweden (90%), Norway (89%), and Denmark (89%), while the EU average was 71%.

In sum, Finland has some foundations attractive for knowledge-intensive industries such as ICT. In fact, the percentage of value added of ICT sector in the total value added in Finland amounts to 5.6% in 2013, ranked 8th in OECD countries, following countries including Korea (10.7%), Japan (7.2%), Sweden (6.8%), and the United States (5.9%) (*OECD Digital Economy Outlook 2015*). Relatedly, the share of value added of industry sector in the total value added in Finland is still as high as 20.3% in 2014, the same as in Japan and higher than the EU average (18.9%) (*OECD Factbook 2016*).

However, it is also the fact that despite the continuing strength in ICT and manufacturing, Finnish economy is under the significant structural change, largely due to the decline of the handset business of Nokia. In fact, the share of value added of industry sector in the total value added dropped from 28.8% in 2002 to 20.3% in 2014, second largest decline, 8.5 point, among OECD countries following only

Table 9.1 Share of ICT goods export in total export (%)

	2000	2005	2010	2015
Korea	34.5	30.0	21.4	21.7
Finland	23.6	20.3	6.4	2.5
Japan	22.7	16.9	10.7	8.5
United States	20.1	14.3	10.6	9.4
Sweden	17.7	11.2	9.7	6.9

Source: *World Development Indicators 2017* (World Bank)

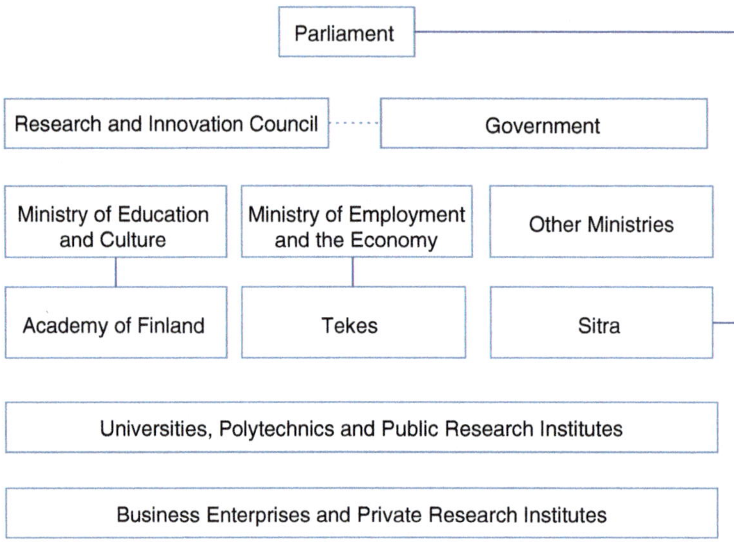

Fig. 9.1 Organizations for innovation policies in Finland. (Source: www.research.fi)

Ireland (decline in 9.8 point) (*OECD Factbook 2016*). The share of export in GDP also dropped from 45.1% in 2008 to 35.2% in 2016, second largest drop, 9.8 point, following Norway (drop in 11.7 point), among OECD countries (*World Development Indicators 2017*). At the same time, Table 9.1 shows the share of ICT goods export in the total export has declined steadily and most rapidly than any other countries. All these show that the Finnish age of ICT-dominated, export-led development completely ended in the end of the 2000s. It is also in this context that the new approach to innovation policies, different from the ones that supported the rise of ICT industries in the 1990s, is needed.

9.4.2 The Innovation System in Finland

Figure 9.1 shows the organizations related to the science, technology, and innovation (STI) policies in Finland. The Ministry of Education and Culture and the Ministry of Employment and the Economy are the two ministries deeply involved

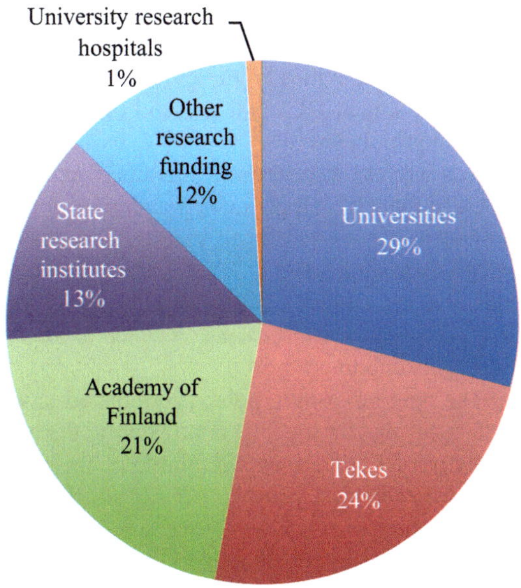

Fig. 9.2 Sources of public funding for research and development (2015). (Source: Tilastokeskus)

in STI policies. In particular, the Academy of Finland (AF) and Tekes, being affiliated to those ministries, play important roles in implementing STI policies. While AF provides competitive funds for basic research, Tekes provides subsidies and loans to applied research and development, of which one-third is for universities and the remaining two-thirds go to private companies. Figure 9.2 shows the sources of public funding for research and development (R&D).

9.4.3 Emphasis on the DUI Policy

Along with the transformation of innovation policies in the EU, as described in Sect. 9.3, Finland has also started to emphasize "demand-side" measures in innovation policies.

9.4.3.1 *Proposal for Finland's National Innovation Strategy* (Ministry of Employment and the Economy 2008)

This document was a proposal for the renewal of innovation policies, prepared by a joint committee of employers, employees, and the government and led by Esko Aho, the former prime minister who also led the group that wrote the document *Creating an Innovative Europe* for the EU innovation policy. Following the idea behind the new innovation policies in the EU, this document proposed the concept of a "broad-based innovation policy,"[8] under which the following four "action plans" were taken up: (1) to influence global innovation networks and to create an environment that can attract R&D activities from abroad, (2) to develop clusters as international hubs, (3) to implement DUI policies, and (4) to coordinate the various measures of the innovation policies.

It is easy to discern from this document that the Finnish government aims to leverage the EU's single market and innovation policies in order to overcome their limited resources and small market. For instance, the plan recommends that the government implement DUI policies in areas similar to the EU's "lead markets." The plan also recommends influencing the European Commission[9] when it decides on research and innovation areas on which to focus, so that Finland can effectively use the EU's support.

The new innovation policy, formulated based on this document, specified concrete measures for the DUI policy for the first time. According to a document by the Ministry of Employment and the Economy, *Demand and User-driven Innovation Policy: Framework (Part I) and Action Plan (Part II)* (2010), there are four pillars around which concrete policy measures are formulated: (1) knowledge and capability development, (2) regulatory reform, (3) renewal of the infrastructure, and (4) incentivizing demand- and user-driven innovations. Examples include promoting public-private partnerships by means of the pilot "Living Lab" projects, promoting innovations using public procurement, and encouraging innovative entrepreneurship by opening data owned by the government in such areas as weather and traffic.

9.4.3.2 *Mini Country Report: Finland* (European TrendChart Innovation Policies, 2011)

In this country report, the European TrendChart innovation policies, an EU organization, critically evaluated the Finnish innovation policy with the aim of benchmarking the innovation policies of the member states. According to this report, the limit of the Finnish innovation policy lay in its strong emphasis on supply-side measures, which has been gradually overcome by introducing DUI policies. One of the difficulties faced by Finnish innovation policymakers was that they had to

[8] It is possible to point out the vagueness of this concept, as noted by Edquist et al. (2009), when the Ministry of Education and Culture and the Ministry of Employment and the Economy in Finland asked them to critically assess the innovation policies. However, at the same time, they appreciated that the "broad-based" concept encompassed both technological and *non-technological* innovations and emphasized demand- and user-driven innovations.

[9] In fact, during the interviews with the author, policymakers repeatedly emphasized that the Finnish government tried to influence the policymaking processes in the European Commission. To quote from the interviews with Tekes and Sitra, "Finland has tried to make the European Commission adopt the demand-driven innovation policy as an important policy agenda" (Tekes: March 1, 2011), and "It is an important role (of Sitra) to lobby the European Commission to adopt the demand-driven policy" (Sitra: March 8, 2011).

develop concrete policy measures by themselves, because Finland was one of the forerunners of DUI policies.

On the one hand, the report points out that Finnish innovation policymakers had to collaborate and coordinate with the EU innovation policies in order to overcome the small size of the domestic market. On the other hand, the smallness of the market could serve as an efficient, flexible pilot..[10]

Based on the above examination, it is possible to argue that the Finnish innovation policy has expanded its original, supply-side measures, such as the promotion of R&D investment and industrial clustering, by emphasizing DUI policy measures, which is in line with the transformation of the EU's innovation policy. It is also possible to discern the strategy of the Finnish government to influence the evolution of the EU's innovation policy with the aim of diffusing domestic innovations. In this sense, the evolution of the Finnish innovation policies should be understood in the context of the EU.

9.5 Case Study on PPI in Finland

This section analyzes the policy implementation process in order to understand whether and how the role of the public and semi-public sectors changed after adopting the DUI policy. We examine the case of PPI, which represents the DUI policy, to better understand the nature and the potential of the DUI policy.

9.5.1 Public and Semi-public Organizations Involved in PPI

Before the detailed case study, we describe how the public and semi-public organizations are involved in the PPI, based on interviews with managers at some of the key organizations directly involved in PPI projects. Interviews were conducted mainly in March 2011, and lasted for 90–120 minutes. These were followed up every year until November 2015. While Tekes is a government agency in charge of funding to public procurers for selected PPI projects, Forum Virium and Culminatum were both semi-public, nonprofit companies, partly owned by the municipalities, including the city of Helsinki.

[10]For instance, the point of view expressed by an interviewee at Sitra strongly suggests that the Finnish government tried to leverage the domestic market as a test bed for experimentations of innovative ideas: "As Finland is the pioneer of the demand- and user-driven innovation policies, we want to demonstrate here and then scale up in the EU market. Then, the EU will pay attention to the experiences here if we can experiment and learn from failures more quickly than other countries" (Interview March 8, 2011).

9.5.1.1 Tekes (Finnish Funding Agency for Innovation)

Funding selected projects is the main task of Tekes, which has begun to focus on DUI projects as well. In this context, Tekes has funded mainly municipalities and private companies that have participated in PPI projects. Tekes funded about 70 PPI projects from 2008 to 2013 and organized the new program, the "smart procurement program," from 2013 to 2016, with a budget of 30 million euro. Under this new program, Tekes funded 48 projects by September 2015. As in other projects, only part of the project costs are covered by Tekes funding.

For instance, in several projects of the public procurement of energy-efficient, "zero-energy buildings" for public kindergartens in the metropolitan area, funded by Tekes, the goal of municipalities was to develop energy-efficient buildings using only mature, existing technologies. On the other hand, the ultimate goal of Tekes was to develop the market of "zero-energy buildings" by establishing the concept and design of such buildings in these PPI projects, which was why Tekes decided to fund these municipalities. In addition to the municipalities that owned the kindergartens, Tekes, engineering and construction consultants, and researchers participated in these PPI projects. Here, Tekes led the discussions by providing concrete technical advice when the owners tried to specify the buildings in detail. According to the claim by the interviewee, Tekes could engage in the discussion processes largely because of its rich knowledge on the innovation processes, because about half of the people at Tekes had worked for private companies. While these PPI projects succeeded and the municipalities as public procurers were satisfied, one of the challenges was to diffuse the energy-efficient buildings by developing a new market.

9.5.1.2 Forum Virium

Forum Virium is owned by the city of Helsinki, as well as several private companies. Its mission is to develop new digital, public services and to network relevant private companies and other organizations for these development activities. Forum Virium adopted the user-centric approach to development, in principle, in which the users of the services are involved in development activities.

The city of Helsinki has eagerly adopted the public-private partnership for the purpose of efficient service provision because, while a large part of the public services are provided by the public sector, it would soon become difficult to continue this model of service provision because of the rapid aging of the population. It was in this context that the city decided to organize and own this nonprofit company. After Forum Virium submitted proposals to the city, the city decided whether and how much funding to provide to all or some of the proposals. Then, it organized participants in the development projects, private companies, and users and carried out the projects.

For example, the "Healthy Borough" project, organized by the health center of the city of Helsinki, aimed to use digital technologies to enhance the health of the citizens. Here, participants included several major ICT companies and NPOs, including Forum Virium. Forum Virium was in charge of organizing the participant companies and developing digital services, for example, the "electronic health card" and the "health stand." Using an electronic health card containing their personal health information, people can receive relevant advice from a preventive medicine perspective at the local, lightweight health stations, called health stands.

9.5.1.3 Culminatum

Culminatum was a nonprofit company established in 1995 to implement a regional cluster policy of the central government, namely, the "center of excellence" program[11] (OSKE: kansallinen osaamiskeskusohjelma), owned by the metropolitan cities of Helsinki, Vantaa, and Espoo, as well as by private companies, science parks, and universities. The goal of Culminatum was to network academy, industry, and government in southern Finland by managing the projects and organizing partners.

Supporting public procurement by these municipalities was one of their major businesses. As mentioned above, while the European Commission and Finland both started to emphasize *pre-commercial* public procurement, the municipalities lacked suitable rules and practices to do the same thing. For instance, while the city of Helsinki enacted the new legislation for public procurement in 2011, it was not possible to ask for the opinions of end users or to discuss issues with suppliers because the basic idea of the new legislation was to ensure competition among the suppliers.

The main task of Culminatum was to help municipalities procure more innovative products or services by organizing relevant companies and research institutions and managing the projects. Despite these shortcomings in the rules of the municipalities, the style of public procurement changed gradually from one based on price competition, in which the municipalities specified the products or services, to one based on competition in terms of the concepts of the products or services, which should be user-oriented. It was in this context that the municipalities needed nonprofit companies such as Culminatum, which had wide networks with various practitioners and organizations with broad competences, because the cities were not used to implementing user-oriented procurement processes and were not aware of the possibilities of innovation.

[11]Because the OSKE program finished in 2013, Culminatum closed in June 2013.

9.5.2 A Case of Public Procurement of Energy-Efficient Public Housing in the City of Naantali[12]

In order to understand how the introduction of the DUI policy changed the role of the public sector in implementing innovation policies, this subsection examines the process of public procurement of energy-efficient public housing[13] in the city of Naantali as a typical case of a PPI project in Finland.

The actual procurer in this case was Vaso (Varsinais-Suomen Asumisoikeus Oy: Right of Occupancy Housing in Southwest Finland), a public corporation owned by the local municipalities in Southwest Finland, which own the *social housing* for middle- and low-income people who buy only the right of occupancy (ROO). In this context, a government organization under the Ministry of Environment, ARA (Asuminen Rahoitus- ja Kehittämiskeskus: Housing Finance and Development Center of Finland),[14] provides loans and subsidies to residents and to social housing corporations such as Vaso. The goal of ARA is to ensure the supply of high-quality, low-cost dwellings for citizens as an integral part of the welfare policy. The main missions are as follows: (1) to provide loans and subsidies for providers of the social housing for middle- and low-income people, (2) to provide loans for those who buy the ROO of the social housing, and (3) to participate in development projects of social housing. It was in the third mission that ARA started to provide subsidies for the initial planning phase in the development projects in 2008. Their goal was to encourage innovative plans to reduce the costs of construction and maintenance. In order to engage in the development process, ARA started to hire architects.

This project started when Vaso consulted ARA on how to procure the new dwellings and to obtain funding from ARA. ARA required social housing corporations like Vaso to meet the tough conditions of low costs and high quality in order to obtain funding. However, it was difficult for Vaso to control these costs owing to the conventional "turnkey" procurement, where the construction companies only realized the specifications defined by Vaso. It was in this context that ARA proposed that Vaso apply for funding from Tekes under the scheme of the "smart procurement program," which funded the planning phase of selected PPI projects. In fact, Tekes funded only the planning phase in order to impact the funded PPI projects in the most effective way with a small amount of money. This was based on the idea that the

[12]This subsection is based mainly on the following interviews, each of which was for 90–120 minutes long: Tekes (March 5, 2013; May 27, 2013; and November 26, 2014), ARA (May 31, 2013, and November 25, 2014), Vaso (March 4, 2013), RAKLI (May 31, 2013, and November 27, 2014), and Hartela (June 4, 2013).

[13]The energy-efficient houses are called "passive houses," which are highly isolated from the outside air and able to sustain a comfortable temperature and humidity while greatly reducing energy consumption. According to the new legislation of the Finnish government, all new houses built after 2016 should be passive houses.

[14]With regard to the ARA and its engagement in the Naantali project, see also ARA (2013), *Asumisen Uudistaminen 2009–2012: Loppuraportti*. ARA, Tengbom Eriksson Arkkitehdit Oy, and Gaia Consulting Oy.

planning phase is where the most important decisions are made. In addition, Tekes ensured that only limited resources were allocated to the planning phase, which was another reason why the target of Tekes' funding was the planning phase.

One of the salient features of the application process for Tekes' funding was that Vaso and Tekes had already held intensive discussions *before* Vaso actually applied, which enabled Vaso to improve their application documents significantly. In fact, it was 4 months before Vaso actually applied when Vaso contacted Tekes and Tekes assigned four designated staff to Vaso to help prepare the application documents. Finally, Vaso decided to follow Tekes' ambitious advice to challenge to procure the low-cost, technically advanced passive houses by using innovative procurement methods, including the intensive dialog among stakeholders. According to Tekes, at the beginning of this 4-month dialog, the technical target set by Vaso was not at all challenging, because Vaso had planned turnkey, cost-based procurement. At last, Vaso could complete the ambitious application documents well enough to be selected. Note that the essential role of Tekes in this context was to "raise the bar" for the applicants by holding intensive dialog sessions while ensuring the technical feasibility of the project.

Vaso actually applied for Tekes' funding in October 2009, and Tekes decided to provide funding to Vaso in December 2009, following the competition where just half the applicants could obtain funding. As was usually the case in funding by Tekes, it funded only half the budget for the planning phase. At the same time, ARA decided to fund Vaso for the planning phase.

Tekes also introduced qualified, external engineers, architects, technical consultants, and other specialists to Vaso, who could help Vaso achieve the ambitious target, although Vaso had employed some in-house architects and engineers. It is notable that these specialists were specified in the application document submitted to Tekes, because they were introduced before the application.

To summarize, the essential roles of Tekes was to encourage applicants to take risks but also to mobilize and combine resources to enable applicants to realize the ambitious plan. Note that all of these important roles of Tekes were almost complete *before* the competition among applicants, which means Tekes provided funding and *real services* to enhance applicants' capability to innovate.

The participants in the planning phase were as follows: Vaso, an architect Kimmo Lylykangas, an energy consultant company Olof Granlund, a project consultant company Pöyry, ARA, the city of Naantali, and several construction companies, including Hartela, which eventually won the competition. While ARA took part in the planning activities to provide technical advice to reduce the energy consumption and the cost, Tekes did not engage in the planning, only following the progress. RAKLI (The Finnish Association of Building Owners and Construction Clients), an association that represented the real estate industry, played an important role in this planning phase by managing the discussions among the above participants and other stakeholders. In the series of discussions, RAKLI implemented its own method, called a "procurement clinic,"[15] where all stakeholders, including the *potential* constructors, gathered and intensively discussed relevant issues for several months before the tender. RAKLI developed this "clinic" as a method of procuring cheaper but higher-quality dwellings, which was a common interest for the members of that association, by promoting intensive dialog between procurers and suppliers.

RAKLI gathered the relevant stakeholders to the "clinic," which continued between February and November, 2010, and managed the dialog and negotiations there. It is notable that despite being long before the bid process, 11 rival constructors had also participated in the "clinic" meetings since June 2010. The purpose behind RAKLI inviting them was to examine whether it was possible to actually build the dwellings as cheaply as the architect planned. Because the constructors tried to avoid disclosing relevant information in front of competitors at the meetings, Vaso held meetings with each constructor individually to make them disclose enough information. This enabled Vaso to gather many proposals in order to change the original design. In fact, after having this kind of intensive dialog, Vaso could change the original design and the method of implementation to reduce the cost. An interviewee at Vaso claimed that he could learn how to implement the innovative public procurement while adhering to the EU legislation during these "clinic" meetings.

Eventually, 11 constructors bid for the construction contract in November 2010, which failed because the cost was 25% higher than planned. In fact, the constructors realized the *real* cost was much higher than they expected for the first time when they estimated the detail. The initial plan was modified in early 2011 when the original, one-storied buildings were, for example, changed to two-storied buildings. The renewed competitive bidding process was in March 2011, and Hartela won the contract. The detailed design and construction phases started in May and November 2011, respectively. Vaso applied for ARA funding again for construction costs, which they would eventually obtain, based on the ARA's decision.

9.5.3 The Impact of the PPI on Participating Private Companies

Lastly, we try to assess the impact of the PPI policy on the firms involved. Before the tender, Hartela, the construction company that won the contract in the aforementioned project, originally decided to participate in the "clinic" meetings because it expected to acquire many new competences, because the passive house project at Naantali was quite demanding in terms of technology and cost. In fact, Hartela did not at all expect the project to yield a profit but planned to leverage the competences obtained during the passive house project to other energy-efficient housing projects.

[15]For details on the "procurement clinic" method, see RAKLI and Vaso (2011), *Vaso/Soininen-hankintaklinikka: Tulosraportti 17.11.2011*. See also a case study of ex staff of RAKLI, by Kuronen and Vaara (2012).

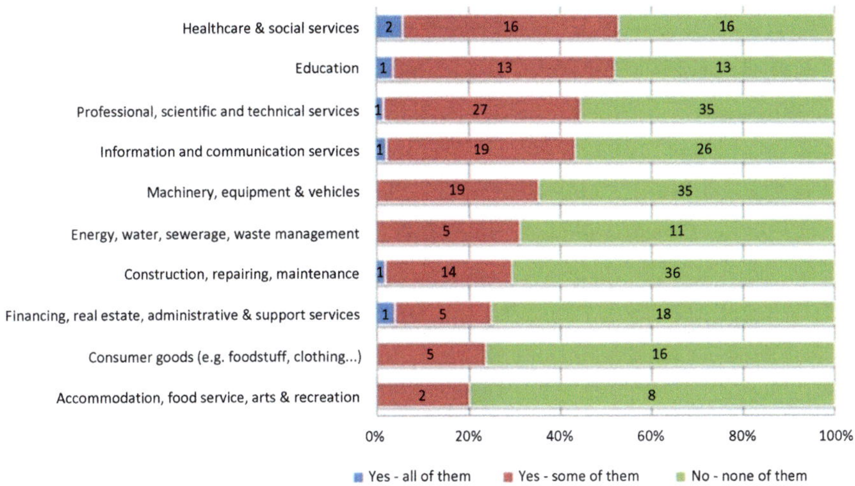

Fig. 9.3 The impact of public procurement on innovations by firms. (Source: Ville Valovirta (VTT)

An interviewee claimed: "Toyota has engaged in the F1 car development projects in order to utilize the knowledge obtained during the F1 projects to the ordinary car development projects. We understood what the F1 projects meant for Toyota was just what the passive house project meant for us because generally passive house is quite demanding compared with the ordinal energy-efficient building."

In fact, Hartela could obtain novel technical competences, including how to calculate energy use and how to reduce energy consumption, while using wood as the basic material, which has been transferred to and utilized in more common, energy-efficient construction projects. The company expected it would be 5 or 10 years before the high-standard, low-cost passive houses, similar to those in this project, would diffuse, which means the impact of PPI might continue for a long time, at least in some cases, including this one.

Next, we examine the impact of the public procurement in general on the capacity of private companies to innovate, based on the result of a questionnaire survey conducted by VTT (Technical Research Centre of Finland). Figure 9.3 shows how much innovation firms generated in the course of public procurement projects. In sectors such as "healthcare and social services" and "education," where the public actors provide a large share of services, over 50% of the respondents indicated that at least some of the innovations were generated in public procurement projects.

Figure 9.4 exhibits how and to what extent each of the public procurement practices affects innovations by firms. Here, "early interaction with procuring organization" was the practice that encouraged innovation most, followed by

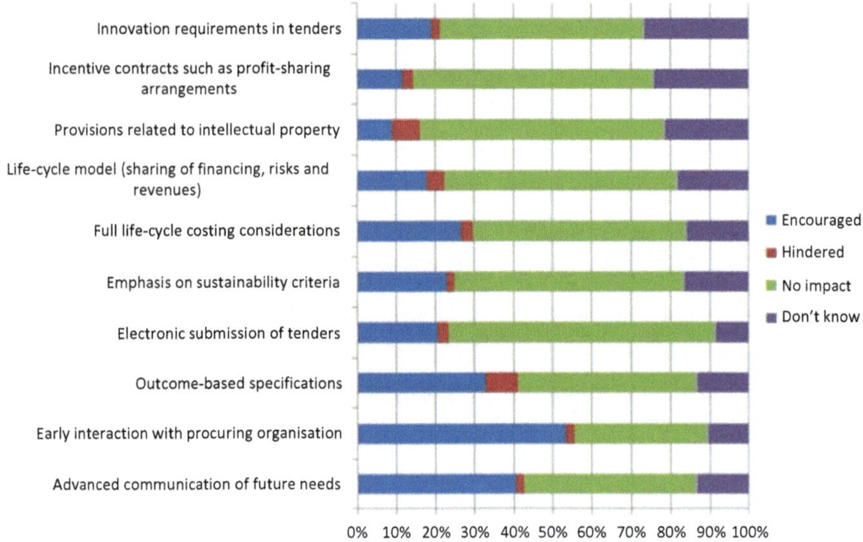

Fig. 9.4 The impact of public procurement practices on innovations by firms. (Source: Ville Valovirta (VTT)

"advanced communication of future needs" and "outcome-based specifications."[16] Based on the observation that at least these three practices are generally emphasized when the PPI policy is implemented, Fig. 9.4 implies that the PPI policy has significant impacts on firms wanting to innovate.

9.6 Discussion: A Novel Approach to Innovation Policies and its Implications

9.6.1 Emerging Policy Approach: Governing the Evolutionary Process of Innovation

From the cases above, it is possible to discern that, rather than playing passive roles as merely buyers of given innovative products, the public and semi-public organizations actively managed the innovation process. For instance, they provided key knowledge and introduced relevant firms, individuals, research institutions, and

[16]In the context of outcome-based specifications, procurers present only the outcomes of the products or services that they are going to procure, and firms have to respond by finding concrete ways to meet all the outcomes, which means large rooms are left for firms to innovate. In contrast, in the cases of conventional public procurement, procurers specify the products and services in detail, leaving little room for firms to innovate.

government institutions to public procurers. In other words, rather than providing incentives and monitoring from outside the innovation process, the public and semi-public organizations are actively engaged in the innovation process.

Based on this consideration, it could be argued that a salient, novel feature of the PPI policy is that the public and semi-public organizations that were involved in the policy implementation process had to engage in a highly uncertain process of innovation to govern the process. This feature can be contrasted clearly with the conventional approaches to innovation policies, in which public organizations design systems that provide *optimal* resources and incentives, such as R&D subsidies and patent systems, without being involved in the innovation process. Any innovations emerge from trial and error processes that consist of, on the one hand, creating options and, on the other hand, selecting from among these options. Thus, innovation processes under the PPI policy can also be understood as *evolutionary* processes[17] (Nelson and Winter 1982). Therefore, it is possible to see that the public and semi-public organizations tried to govern the evolutionary process of innovation in the PPI policy. In this sense, the PPI policy is a novel approach to innovation policies, where public organizations, including the policymakers, actually try to govern the evolutionary process of innovation. This can be understood as an important case of an "experimental innovation policy," proposed by authors such as Charles Sabel (Dutz et al. 2014).

In the case of the public procurement of energy-efficient public housing, the governance of the evolutionary process of innovation consists of three factors. First, it tried to broadly direct the evolutionary process. For instance, while Tekes tried to raise the bar during the planning phase, ARA, as the social housing organization representing the idea of the welfare state, enforced the idea of "low-cost, high-quality energy-efficient housing," which means that both organizations determined the broad direction of innovations pursued. However, it should be emphasized that the technical and economic details are almost totally left for further dialog and experimentation. Second, it tries to get relevant people and organizations together who have the necessary competence to plan and implement the innovative public procurement project. In fact, Tekes helped the public procurer, Vaso, develop ambitious plans by introducing relevant architects and engineering firms. Third, it managed the dialog among the stakeholders, which was actually the role of RAKLI.

With regard to the official policy documentation on the DUI policy, which includes a PPI policy, the transformation of the innovation policy has been understood merely as a shift of emphasis from "technology push" to "demand pull." However, if we consider how the PPI policy is actually implemented, the shift of emphasis is highly likely to engender a deep transformation in the nature of the policy. It is in this context that public organizations in charge of the PPI policy have to understand both technological possibilities and markets for innovation in order to govern the evolutionary process of innovation. In this sense, the role of public and

[17] In this paper, evolution is understood as a generic principle that accounts for changes using the combination of mutation, retention, and selection. See Nelson and Winter (1982) and Hodgson and Knudsen (2010) for a detailed discussion on applying the Darwinian concept of evolution to social sciences.

semi-public organizations in the PPI policy suggest some of the emerging novel roles public organizations can play to encourage innovation. This deserves particular attention, because the role of the public sector in innovation has often been downplayed in the influence of the neoliberal ideas (Mazzucato 2014).

9.6.2 The Influence of Institutional Conditions and Implications for East Asia

In terms of institutional foundations, there are two salient features in the cases examined in Sect. 9.5. First is the idea of a welfare state directing innovation. Second, several public organizations (e.g., Tekes) or semi-public organizations (e.g., Forum Virium, Culminatum, RAKLI) are intermediated with local municipalities as public procurers and private companies. These two features enabled the public procurement to promote innovations with public values by avoiding the too narrow focus on cost reduction, as has been often observed in the cases of "new public management" (Osborne 2010; Bevir 2012). In this sense, it is possible to understand that the evolutionary innovation process under the PPI policy is governed not by a single public organization but by the network of several related organizations with different interests and legal statuses. Furthermore, the mode of governance is similar to what Bevir (2012) called "network governance." This suggests that the existence of the thick "third-sector" organizations,[18] representing the collective or public interests, constitutes a significant precondition for the PPI policy, which enables the intermediation among different organizations and institutions.

While the European Union adopted the DUI and PPI policy to be implemented widely in the member countries, it could be argued that the Nordic countries have favorable conditions to implement these policies. This is because they are still strong welfare states,[19] but they also have thick, active third-sector organizations,[20]

[18]Here I adopt the definition by Pestoff (1998), who defines the third sector as the sector that intermediates other sectors, namely, market (private firms), state (public institutions), and community (households and families). It includes both private and public organizations, for-profit and nonprofit organizations, and formal and informal organizations.

[19]According to the OECD Social Expenditure Statistics, the average of the Nordic countries was ranked as the highest (26.9%) in terms of public social expenditure as a percentage of GDP in 2012. The averages of the OECD member countries and the European countries, excluding the Nordic countries, were 21.4% and 23.4%, respectively. These figures do not include the public expenditure for education, one of the most significant elements of welfare states.

[20]Salamon et al. (2004) summarized the result of their project, Johns Hopkins Comparative Nonprofit Sector Project, and compiled the Johns Hopkins Global Civil Society Index (JHU/GCSI) to enable international comparisons of third-sector organizations. According to this index, Nordic countries are ranked top, followed by the Anglo-Saxon countries, in terms of capacity, sustainability, and the impact of civil society organizations. However, authors such as Evers and Laville (2004) pointed out that the third-sector activities are underestimated in JHU/GCSI because it excludes several organizations, including cooperatives active in Europe. For the definition, history, and current situation of civil society organizations in Finland, see Harju (2006) and Seppo (2013).

connected by the corporatist traditions of building consensus at the societal level. Several authors have argued that Nordic corporatist welfare states have transformed themselves to ones that enable innovations (Kristensen and Lilja 2011; Miettinen 2012; Ornston 2012). Their main argument is quite similar to the "flexicurity" thesis in that the measures of social protection and skill formation provided by the welfare state enable firms to pursue innovations. However, it could be difficult to sustain the "welfare state—social protection and skill formation—innovation" nexus because, as I argued in Sect. 9.1, advanced countries will sooner or later face difficulties in differentiating between supply-side measures, as a result of the increasing competition from the latecomer countries. This paper proposes another potentially important mechanism by which the welfare state institutions enable innovations.

According to Amable (2003), Japan and Korea belong to "Asian capitalism," one of the five types of capitalism, as identified in his empirical analysis where he examined five institutional areas, including "product market competition," "wage-labor nexus," "financial sector," "social protection," and "education." Based on his analysis, a salient feature of the Asian capitalism, in comparison with "social democratic economies" of Nordic countries, is the low level of expenditure on social protection and education,[21] which reflects the dominant "companyist *règulation*,"[22] characterized by a strong and weak coordination capacity of a firm and the societal level, respectively, as far as Japanese capitalism is concerned. At the same time, the third sector is less active in "Asian industrialized countries," including Japan and Korea (Salamon et al. 2004). Considering the case of the PPI policy, these facts imply that there are relatively weak institutional mechanisms that connect social problems to innovative efforts in Japan, when compared with the Nordic countries. Solving social problems is becoming increasingly important as a source of economic growth and innovation (Boyer 2004), which means the roles of the public sector and the third sector are important.

[21]The public social expenditure as a percentage of GDP in 2012 in Japan (23.1%) was higher than the average of OECD member countries (21.4%). However, a larger part of the expenditure in Japan was for the elderly than in the OECD, including pensions and health services. This reflects the fact that social protection for the working age population has been provided mainly by employers as long-term employment and seniority wages. In addition, the public expenditure on all levels of education as a percentage of GDP in 2011 was 3.6% in Japan, significantly lower than the average of 5.3% in the OECD, 6.2% in Sweden, and 6.3% in Finland (OECD 2014).

[22]According to Yamada and Hirano (2012), one of the two pillars of the companyist *règulation* is "labor-management compromise," which ensures employment security in exchange for accepting unlimited duties. It should be emphasized that the secured employment served as a de facto social protection measure, replacing the public expenditure for social protection.

9.7 Concluding Remarks

This paper showed that a novel approach to innovation policies, namely, a demand- and user-driven innovation (DUI) policy, including a public procurement of innovation (PPI) policy, has been emerging in the EU and Finland since the late 2000s. This means public and semi-public organizations try to govern the evolutionary process of innovation during the implementation of a PPI policy. Thus, this paper contributes to innovation study literature by showing how "evolutionary innovation policy," proposed by Nelson and Winter (1982) and Metcalfe (1997) and outlined by Nill and Kemp (2009) and Dodgson et al. (2011), is implemented. In addition, we describe the kind of social and organizational capabilities required for public and semi-public organizations.

Further research is needed to examine the following issues. Firstly, the impact of PPI and DUI policies on private firms should be analyzed empirically. Secondly, and more importantly, from the perspective of an institutional political economy, we should examine how different institutional configurations influence the implementation and performance of PPI and DUI policies by comparing similar projects of public procurement of innovation in other countries. This is an important research agenda, not only because the role of the public and semi-public sector is expected to become more important but also because countries have different capacities to mobilize public and semi-public organizations to implement PPI and DUI policies.

References

Amable B (2003) The diversity of modern capitalism. Oxford University Press, Oxford

Arrow KJ (1962) Economic welfare and the allocation of resources for invention. In: Nelson RR (ed) The rate and direction of inventive activity: economic and social factors. Princeton University Press, Princeton

Beise M (2004) Lead markets: country-specific drivers of the global diffusion of innovations. Res Policy 33(6–7):997–1018

Bevir M (2012) Governance: a very short introduction. Oxford University Press, Oxford

Boyer R (2004) The future of economic growth: as new becomes old. Edward Elgar, Cheltenham

Brown P, Lauder H, Ashton D (2011) The global auction: the broken promises of education, jobs, and incomes. Oxford University Press, Oxford

Chaminade C, Edquist C (2010) Rationales for public policy intervention in the innovation process: a Systems of Innovation Approach. In Smits RE, Kuhlmann S, Shapira P (eds) The theory and practice of innovation policy. Edward Elgar, Cheltenham

Dodgson M, Hughes A, Foster J, Metcalfe S (2011) Systems thinking, market failure, and the development of innovation policy: the case of Australia. Res Policy 40(9):1145–1156

Dutz MA, Kuznetsov Y, Lasagabaster E, Pilat D (eds) (2014) Making innovation policy work: learning from experimentation. OECD, IBRD, World Bank, Paris

Edler J (2010) Demand-based innovation policy. In Smits RE, Kuhlmann S, Shapira P (eds) The theory and practice of innovation policy. Edward Elgar, Cheltenham

Edquist C, Luukkonen T, Sotarauta M (2009) Broad-based innovation policy. In: Evaluation of the Finnish national innovation system: full report. Helsinki, Taloustieto Oy

Evers A, Laville J-L (eds) (2004) The third sector in Europe. Edward Elgar, Cheltenham

Freeman C (1987) Technology policy and economic performance: lessons from Japan. Pinter Publishers, London/New York
Hämäläinen TJ, Heiskala R (eds) (2007) Social innovations, institutional change and economic performance: making sense of structural adjustment processes in industrial sectors, regions, and societies. Edward Elgar, Cheltenham
Harju A (2006) Finnish civil society. Helsinki, Kansanvalistusseura
Hirschman AO (1970) Exit, voice, and loyalty: responses to decline in firms, organizations, and states. Harvard University Press, Cambridge, MA
Hodgson GM, Knudsen T (2010) Darwin's conjecture: the search for general principles of social and economic evolution. The University of Chicago Press, Chicago
Jauhiainen JS (2008) Regional and innovation policies in Finland: towards convergence and/or mismatch? Reg Stud 42(7):1031–1045
Kotiranta, A, Nikulainen T, Tahvanainen AJ, Deschryvere M, Pajarinen M (2009). Evaluating national innovation systems: key insights from the Finnish INNOEVAL survey. Discussion papers no. 1196, ETLA (The Research Institute of the Finnish Economy)
Kristensen PH, Lilja K (eds) (2011) Nordic capitalisms and globalization: new forms of economic organization and welfare institutions. Oxford University Press, Oxford
Kuronen M, Vaara P (2012) "purchasing clinics" in public procurement and urban development. Paper presented at the 19th annual European real estate society conference, Edinburgh, Scotland
Lemola T (2004) Finnish science and technology policy. In: Schienstock G (ed) Embracing the knowledge economy: the dynamic transformation of the Finnish innovation system. Edward Elgar, Cheltenham
Lundvall B-Å (ed) (1992) National Systems of innovation: towards a theory of innovation and interactive learning. Pinter, London
Lundvall B-Å, Borrás S (2005) Science, technology, and innovation policy. In Fagerberg J, Mowery D, Nelson RR (eds) The Oxford handbook of innovation. Oxford University Press, Oxford
Mazzucato M (2014) The entrepreneurial state: debunking public vs. private sector myths. Anthem Press, London
Metcalfe S (1997) Technology systems and technology policy in an evolutionary framework. In Archibugi D, Michie J (eds) Technology, globalisation and economic performance. Cambridge University Press, Cambridge
Miettinen R (2012) Innovation, human capabilities, and democracy: towards an enabling welfare state. Oxford University Press, Oxford
Nelson RR (1959) The simple economics of basic scientific research. J Polit Econ 67(3):297–306
Nelson RR (ed) (1993) National innovation systems: a comparative analysis. Oxford University Press, Oxford
Nelson RR, Winter SG (1982) An evolutionary theory of economic change. The Belknap Press of Harvard University Press, Cambridge
Nill J, Kemp R (2009) Evolutionary approaches for sustainable innovation policies: from niche to paradigm? Res Policy 38(4):668–680
OECD (2011) Demand-side innovation policies. OECD, Paris
OECD (2014) Education at a glance 2014. OECD, Paris
Ornston D (2012) When small states make big leaps: institutional innovation and high-tech competition in Western Europe. Cornell University Press, Ithaca
Osborne SP (ed) (2010) The new public governance? Emerging perspectives on the theory and practice of public governance. Routledge, London
Pestoff VA (1998) Beyond the market and state: social enterprises and civil democracy in a welfare society. Ashgate Publishing, Farnham
Sabel C, Saxenian A (2009) A fugitive success: Finland's economic future. Helsinki, Sitra
Salamon LM, Sokolowski SW, Associates (2004) Global civil society: dimensions of the nonprofit sector volume two. Kumarian Press, Bloomfield

Seppo M (2013) Finnish civil society now: its operating environment, state and status. KEPA's working papers no. 39

Tokumaru N (2013) Varieties of clustering and capability development in the Indian IT industry. In: Hirakawa H, Lal K, Shinkai N, Tokumaru N (eds) Servitization, IT-ization, and innovation models: two-stage industrial cluster theory. Routledge, Abingdon

Von Hippel E (1988) The sources of innovation. Oxford University Press, Oxford

Yamada T, Hirano Y (2012) How has the Japanese mode of *Règulation* changed?: the whereabouts of companyism. In: Boyer R, Uemura H, Isogai A (eds) Diversity and transformations of Asian capitalisms. Routledge, Abingdon

Chapter 10
Brexit: Lessons for the Viability of the European Union and Other Regional Integration

Robert Boyer

10.1 Introduction

Since the Eurozone crisis of the early 2010s, the future of European integration has been highly debated among experts and has become a hot topic during member state elections. Many North American economists believe that sticking to a dysfunctional Euro is bound to fail and that it would trigger the risk of the disintegration of 60 years of patient transnational institution building (Stiglitz 2016). The rise of anti-European movements and parties is a threat to European stability since they defend a complete repatriation of national sovereignty. For other economists, mainly European, the perils can only be overcome by a step forward in the direction of a more coherent distribution of economic policy responsibilities among Brussels and national capitals that would embed democratic principles (Aglietta and Leron 2017; Piketty et al. 2017). The May 2017 French presidential election surprisingly won over the issue of pursuing new avenues of European integration and not a nationalistic withdrawal.

Understanding the complex process that led to the Brexit vote is quite interesting; is it an accident originating from a miscalculation by the British Prime Minister, and/or does it reveal the deep transformation of social stratification and individual attitudes toward the loss of sovereignty? This chapter proposes some steps in that direction. For standard economic theoreticians, Brexit is seemingly a paradox; a converging bulk of research suggests that the British economy has largely benefited from adhesion to the Single Market, but a majority has rejected belonging to the European Union (EU). The growing gap between the winners and the losers of internationalization is a preliminary explanation. A second one stresses that the irruption of a new political offer by the UK Independence Party (UKIP) pushes a divided Conservative Party to organize a referendum that singles out the European

R. Boyer (✉)
Institut des Amériques, Vanves, France
e-mail: r.boyer2@orange.fr

R. Boyer et al. (eds.), *Evolving Diversity and Interdependence of Capitalisms*, Evolutionary Economics and Social Complexity Science 11,
https://doi.org/10.1007/978-4-431-55001-3_10

issue: the deeply rooted anti-European feelings of the least privileged part of the population, usually silenced by Westminster representative democracy, thus find an expression. Therefore, the surprise brought by the outcome of the June 23, 2016, referendum points out the irrelevance of many conventional analyses: successive polls and financial markets were not efficient forecasting tools; the governmental elite's perceptions were different from grassroots attitudes; and the votes could not be derived from the dispassionate assessment of economic cost/benefit associated with Leave or Remain, since emotions, passions, and affects (Lordon 2016) played a definitive role in the choice offered to the British population (Sect. 10.2).

The apparent contradiction between the overall macroeconomic benefits derived from the European integration and its rebuttal by a small majority of the citizens reveals that there is no such entity as a representative agent when in a society highly polarized according to education level, age, and the rural/urban divide. The vote reveals a Great Social Divide between those who can prosper in a highly mobile internationalized environment and those whose fate strictly depends on belonging to a given territory. This division is the outcome of nearly three-decade-long transformation of British society, largely neglected by the political establishment and pollsters that continue to rely upon dated representations of the country (Sect. 10.3).

These shifts in social identities have knockdown effects upon political orientations and demands addressed to governments, such as control over immigration; however, this issue transcends the traditional opposition between the Conservative and Unionist (Conservative) and Labour Parties. This gives a clear opportunity for a political entrepreneur to build a new party. UKIP exclusively focused on opposition to the EU's ideal of free mobility, which includes immigrants and refugees. Many other European countries have also experienced an equivalent crisis of their party system that puts at the forefront the issue of national sovereignty. It is seen as a shield against the destructive impact of globalization, relayed by the directives of the EU (Sect. 10.4).

The Brexit vote is a total social fact according to Marcel Mauss (1925). It can only be understood as the outcome of the interactions between three different processes: a changing geographical distribution of jobs, the transformed attitudes within and across classes and socioeconomic groups, and innovation in the political arena expressed as a vigorously anti-European agenda. The integration of various subdisciplines is necessary to understand regional integration and disintegration. Is this nexus of causalities specific to the UK, or does it feature a more general configuration of the new relationships between transnational economic forces and the reconfiguration of political dividing lines? In fact, the rise of anti-European movements is quite general, and similar processes have been observed in the USA (Sect. 10.5).

This analytical framework helps understand why the UK-EU negotiations that began in March 2017 have been so slow and inconclusive. The British government has reluctantly recognized that the economic dividends promised by Brexit should be transformed into slower growth, but this finding has not shifted the Brexiter/Remainers divide. The government must navigate contradictory demands in society, polity, and economy, and it dramatically underestimates the intricacies between the UK and EU value chains and regulations (Levell 2018). It takes time to develop a strategy that would overcome a purely rhetorical approach and consider the realities of interdependencies and partial irreversibility involved. The fact that the regions and citizens most negatively affected by the abandonment of the EU have, in fact, voted for Brexit points out a false attribution of the social divide to Europe, whereas I argue it is the long-term consequence of the neoliberal strategies launched by Margaret Thatcher; remunerations have been individualized, and redistribution by public policies has been reduced (Sect. 10.6).

This dilemma is quite common to many member states of the EU. What should be the new balance between responses to citizens' demands and the pressures brought by international actors? But it is not the only issue to be addressed. How to overcome the dysfunctionality of the Eurozone and prevent the repetition of the 2010 major crisis? What are the responses to the rise of nationalist feelings of citizens who face unprecedented flows of immigrants and political refugees? Can the European leaders overcome these sources of disintegration and thus prevent an effective Brexit to trigger a destructive domino effect, away from the pooling of national sovereignty that had been steadily developing since the Treaty of Rome (1957) (Sect. 10.7)? Conversely is there a chance for the UK to build a more inward-looking growth model that would reduce the Great Social Divide revealed by the Brexit vote, or does it mean a complete reorientation of the integration of the UK into the world economy under the motto of a "Global UK"?

Many other scenarios are possible, and this plurality is the source of major uncertainties about the future relations between the UK and the EU. Whereas a soft Brexit is aimed at and preferred by both partners, is not a hard Brexit the possible outcome of the inability to rationally redesign the layering of multiple interdependencies that have been piling up since 1974 when the UK joined European integration (Sect. 10.8)? In conclusion Brexit is not an exceptional event, since it is an anticipation of the problems and processes that most other EU countries must face and overcome. As a preliminary case study of these problems, we can ask: What competences should be efficiently pooled at the continental level, and what other ones should be repatriated at the nation-state level? How can the democratic principles at home and in Brussels be strengthened? Will migrations destroy public opinion's acceptance of free mobility and put at risk the solidarity that is required for a definite push in the direction of a federal Europe?

10.2 A Surprise in Search of Explanations and Theorizing

The UK economy was booming and unemployment was rather low, the UKIP was perceived as an outsider in the political arena, and the surveys conveyed the prognosis of an easy success of the referendum. Then how to explain the vote in favor of Brexit?

Table 10.1 Macroeconomic performance: UK versus EU and Eurozone (2015)

Index	Entity UK	EU	Eurozone
GDP per capita (USD)	43.963	34.168	31.275
Growth rate (2015)	2.2%	1.9%	1.6%
Unemployment	5.4%	9.5%	11.0%
Inflation	0.0	0.0	0.0
Current account/GDP	−4.3%	+2.0%	+3.7%

Source: Extracted from European Commission (2016), *Economic Forecast*, Winter 2016, February

10.2.1 The Brexit Paradox: Economic Success But Rejection of the EU

Typically, the models formalizing electoral choices state that the more likely a government is to win an election, the more satisfactory the economic situation of the voters. Under this respect, the macroeconomic situation of the UK was fairly good when citizens had to decide between Remain and Brexit; the economy was growing faster than continental Europe, unemployment had dramatically decreased much more rapidly than in other countries, and the income per capita was higher than average. Macroeconomists generally attributed this good position to the degree of freedom enjoyed by the British government who had decided in the past not to join the Euro (Table 10.1).

This stable economic health was precisely the origin of large inflows of foreign workers, especially from Eastern Europe who were attracted by a very fluid and active labor market. Consequently, the adhesion to the Single European Market has meant a renewed economic dynamism, but simultaneously, the free mobility principle across member states has promoted an unprecedented migration in the direction of the most successful countries. In their evaluation of the costs and benefits of the EU, citizens were divided. Some had the skills, competences, and inclusion in social networks to benefit from the extra dynamism associated with European integration, while others perceived themselves as victim of the unfair competition exerted by migrant workers. Such a feeling was diffused but had no explicit political voice in the Conservative and Labour Parties. UKIP—founded in 1993—is first a democratic libertarian party, but, via a succession of crises, the party finds a way for winning votes in anti-Europeanism (Maddock 2017). In 2015, UKIP received four million votes at the general election but gained only one member of parliament. By contrast, when a referendum was called solely upon the issue of EU adhesion, the ideological impact of UKIP became evident. Quite dialectically, a successful integration of the UK into the EU Single Market is converted into the rejection of one of its pillar: free mobility of citizens (Fig. 10.1).

Brexit is also a defeat for rational choice theory as taught by standard economic theory. Given the de facto large interdependency between the UK and continental Europe, international trade theory suggests that in the short to medium time frame, most British people would lose in economic terms, even when they were not among

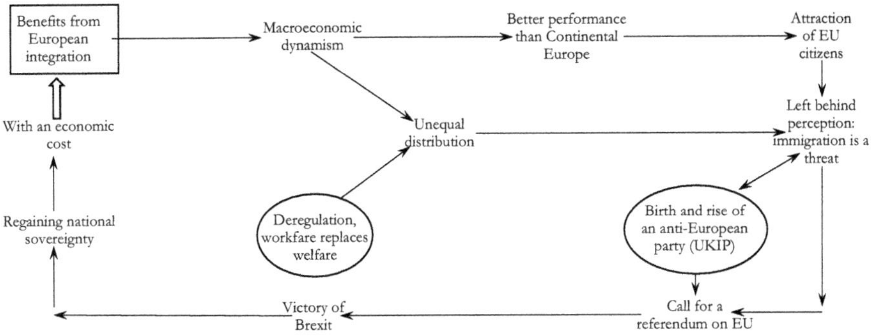

Fig. 10.1 The Brexit paradox: national sovereignty more important than economic benefits from the EU

the winners of Europeanization and globalization. But contemporary *social psychology* and *experimental economics* stress that rational action has a limited scope; quite different mechanisms are involved in every day decision-making (Kahneman and Tversky 1984). Experimental game theory suggests that the rationality principle must be taught and learned through experience. In many other circumstances, emotions and passions prevail (Frank 1988; Petit 2015), and the framing of the future by expectations, fictions, and imaginaries has become crucial in the epoch of finance-led regimes (Beckert 2016; Boyer 2016), and it has replaced the conception of an economic world moved by objective and invariant laws. This reframing is especially so for the political debates around Brexit; issues of dignity, pride, and sense of belonging do matter much more than a cold calculus of economic costs and benefits. The more these issues matter, the more difficult it is to explicitly quantify the link between macro-political decisions and personal trajectories.

The Brexit vote is de facto destroying two decades of British efforts to get the best of both worlds, i.e., access to the large European Single Market without adhesion to Schengen border control or the Euro. Last-minute negotiations by David Cameron had extended this list of exemptions, for instance, allowing transitory barriers to intra-EU mobility and increased control of national parliaments over European decisions. More fundamentally, the British government had become a central player in the EU by stopping any progress toward political integration and frequently allying with Germany in the defense of competition against the pressures by the governments of Southern European countries to build more solidarity in Europe. Retrospectively, I argue that this Brexit referendum will appear as an incredible strategic mistake of the UK, at odds with a century of quite clever European diplomacy.

10.2.2 The Impact of the New Political Offer of UKIP Upon the Party System and Brexit

Clearly, a referendum belongs to the *political sphere* and not directly to the economic one. This is a fundamental objection to standard economic approach according to which polity is simply a projection of the economy without any diffraction or modification. Again, general economic-sociological theory warns us that the various spheres that compose a given society do not deploy the same principles and they tend to become more autonomous through time (Luhmann 1997). These spheres exchange information, and all of them require economic resources, but they develop their own logic and try to be immunized from the perturbations of the rest of the society. This is quite enlightening regarding Prime Minister David Cameron's decision to organize a referendum on the belonging of the UK to the EU as a clever device to discipline a fraction of dissident members of parliament within the Conservative Party. It was a reply to the UK Independence Party (UKIP) that decided to exclusively promote the withdrawal of the UK from the EU. Its increasing popularity was perceived as a threat to the domination of the Conservative Party. The call for a referendum changed the normal political game; traditionally both pro- and anti-EU sentiments coexisted within both the Labour and Conservative Parties, and this opposition was supposed to be secondary. In 2016, the citizens could express themselves independently from the intermediation of parties over the future of the UK in the EU.

Few observers really considered the fact that this political bet could be lost, implying an effective Brexit. The British political elite could have learned from the 2005 Dutch and French referenda on the project of the EU constitution that delivered an unambiguous *no* from citizens, whereas the majority of parties had promoted adoption. What was supposed to be a *Machiavellian game* turned sour: the government had to assume the economic, financial, and social consequences of the referendum. In addition, comparative political analysis suggests that such referenda are a very dangerous tool. Fundamentally, voters not only reply to the question at stake; they also express their adhesion or rejection of the current policy of the government. Furthermore, the phrasing of the question may twist the outcome of the referendum in one direction or another. It was thus especially risky to decide on such an important issue by a referendum as it was relatively disconnected from the Westminster style of debate and the intensive deliberation typical of a political system that gives primacy to the parliament (Binzer and Hobolt 2009; *Société de Législation compare* 2011).

Social surveys suggested that the issue at stake was not at all how to share the benefits from European integration but whether immigration could be curbed down. The narrative of UKIP was becoming the dominant one, and the traditional parties were unable to impose their own. A significant fraction of the population anticipated that the British economy would be worse off in the event of Brexit; however, citizens were not hoping for greater influence of the UK in the world, nor for a reduction of unemployment. The Brexit vote was politically motivated without an explicit intent to promote more economic benefits, but in order to defend citizens from the competition exerted by migrant workers. Few people (24%) expected a better economic outcome, but a majority anticipated lower immigration (57%); only 17% were skeptical about an increase in Britain's influence in the world (NatCen Social Research 2015, p. 6).

10.2.3 The Misery of Foresight: The Overconfidence of the Elites

It was therefore to be expected that the referendum would be highly contested. By contrast, the methodology of political polls is built upon the hypothesis of a continuum of voters distributed along a single variable such as income (Jackson 2016). The outcome of the referendum was then supposed to depend upon the choice of a median voter. Furthermore, in the past the Prime Minister had called for early elections in response to favorable polls but lost their bet and thus their power. This error was repeated with the 2016 referendum and the 2017 general elections (Allen 2018). Finally, in all these votes, the politicians have been neglecting the impact of the political campaign upon the outcome of the vote that can change the distribution of votes. In the context of the British referendum, Brexiters were praising the return to a full national sovereignty, a quite positive image indeed, whereas the Remainers were stressing the catastrophic economic consequences of leaving the EU without a clear motto, explicating a positive role of European integration. Finally, the analysts had been confusing a series of snapshots with the dynamic process of public opinion evolution. The polling since September 2015 had described a highly erratic sequence difficult to interpret even though the rolling average seemed to detect a majority for a Remain vote.

The confidence of the British Prime Minister about the results of the referendum was also sustained by a series of econometric studies:

- On one hand, sophisticated techniques had been developed to compute counterfactuals, whereby the UK should not have adhered to regional integration: the gains were impressive and significant even if declining through time (Nauro et al. 2014). Furthermore, the gains from regional integration were positive for all countries with the exception of Greece (Nauro et al. 2015).
- On the other hand, in the period preceding the referendum, a consensus had emerged concerning the consequences of Brexit at the macroeconomic level: lower productivity, growth, and standard of living (HM Treasury 2016a; Gudgin et al. 2016; House of Commons 2018). Other econometric exercises pointed out similar results for growth and standard of living (Dhingra et al. 2016a). Another exercise measured the negative impact of Brexit upon foreign direct investment (FDI) (Dhingra et al. 2016b), and still another one convincingly showed that immigration was not detrimental to British citizen wage and standard of living (Dhingra et al. 2016c).

Therefore, at the aggregate level, adhesion to the EU had been beneficial, and a way out of the EU would be costly. This optimistic assessment totally neglected popular sentiments about the legitimacy of European integration. Citizens cannot be considered to decide their vote according to a pure and exclusive economic calculus of its impact upon expected gains and costs respective of Remain or Leave: they form a more general appreciation about the European integration per se independently from its direct consequence upon their personal wellbeing. In fact, the British people express many effects of the role of Brussels in their personal life. Among all national public opinion, the British are the most adverse concerning the benefits of economic and monetary integration: in early 2016, only 17% of the population had a positive appraisal, the lowest percentage among the EU, less than in Denmark (29%) and Sweden (25%) that refused to join the Euro. No comparison with adhesion was observed in France (70%) or Germany (73%) (European Community 2016a, b). Similarly, much of public opinion within the EU is overwhelmingly favorable to internal labor mobility, but nearly a third of citizens express their opposition in the UK—the country with the lowest recognition of the legitimacy of free mobility (European Community 2016a, b). All these data were available, but they did not capture the attention of the leaders of the Conservative Party.

This gap between Westminster and Main Street explains the disarray of Theresa May. In April 2016, she stated, "On balance, and given the tests I set earlier in my speech, I believe the case to remain a member of the European Union is strong." A week after the vote she launched her leadership campaign with the words, "Brexit means Brexit" (*Financial Times* 2017). Since then, she has been recurrently oscillating between two opposite positions: "a hard Brexit is better than a bad agreement" (May 2017) when addressing domestic public opinion but a more conciliatory approach when speaking to EU politicians or Brussels negotiators.

10.3 The Brutal Perception of a Wide Social Divide

What is the origin of this political turmoil? Exclusive political factors do not explain it since it is the spillover effects originating from the economy and society transformed by the acceleration of the internationalization that explains the vote for Brexit.

10.3.1 An Unprecedented Social and Geographical Polarization

An unnoticed shift in social stratification was brutally revealed by the unprecedented decision to organize a referendum on European integration issues, typically a topic addressed within parliament: the adding up of a series of silent transformations ends

Table 10.2 Two sources of social divide

A. A generational divide

Age	Remain	leave
18–24	71%	29%
25–49	54%	46%
50–64	40%	60%
65–	36%	64%

Source: Extracted from You Gov (2016) June 23–24 https://yougov.uk/new/2016/06/27/howBritainvoted

B. The educational divide

		Remain	Leave
Education	Lower	30%	70%
	A level	50%	50%
	Intermediate	48%	52%
	Degree	68%	32%

Source: Extracted from you Gov (2016) June 23–24 https://yougov.uk/new/2016/06/27/howBritainvoted

up having a powerful impact (Jullien 2009). Traditionally, political scientists analyze regional economic integration as a matter of legitimacy and not only of economic efficiency. When sovereignty is shared on multiple levels between national governments and supranational authorities, the issue of national identity is dramatically underestimated (Bartel 2002).

All the surveys about the distribution of votes between Brexit and Remain point out a specific pattern of voters' distribution (Ashcroft 2016; BBC 2016; You Gov 2016). The younger citizens under 25 years were primarily in favor of Remain, whereas the older ones largely joined the Brexiter camp (Table 10.2A). A similar inversion is observed concerning the level of education: the people with higher education preferred to stay within the EU, but low-skilled citizens voted for Brexit (Table 10.2B).

The location also matters: small towns voted Brexit, but larger more cosmopolitan cities preferred Remain (BBC 2016). Scotland had a majority in favor of Remain, and this exacerbated the confrontations with London about the demand for independence or at least more autonomy. Finally, the voters that declared to be proud to be British were logically the supporters of Brexit. Seemingly, two conflicting visions of the future of the UK emerged from the referendum, even though idiosyncratic configurations defined a multiplicity of socioeconomic groups' attitudes with respect to EU: left behind citizens, right or centrists traditionalists, disengaged pessimists, cosmopolitan critics, and optimistic centrists (Clarke et al. 2017). The result of the referendum came as a dramatic surprise for both camps: the Brexiters won against the own prognosis of UKIP, and Remainers discovered that they belong to the minority. The political elite were lost and still experience many difficulties in coping with this radiography of British society.

10.3.2 A Slow But Powerful Transformation of the British Society

Macroeconomists and policy makers have long been quite myopic in the perception and recognition of the explosion of inequalities in the UK and the USA. This might explain the surprising success of Thomas Piketty' book *Capital in the Twenty-First Century* (2014) that made accessible to the public an interesting long-run analysis of nature and source of economic inequalities. During a long period, growth has been assumed to be the solution to job access and a general increase in standard of living. The economic profession was victim of an erroneous hypothesis about the existence of representative agents. The damage was not so severe during post-World War II Golden Age, when powerful collective agreements, a progressive income tax, and easy access to public services such as education and healthcare had stabilized wage inequality at very low levels. With the crisis of this growth regime, inequalities have exploded from 1979 to 1990 as measured by Gini coefficient that grew from 0.24 to 0.34 during the period and then stabilized during 2010 (Equality Trust 2013).

With the surge of subcontracting, delocalization of jobs abroad, the deregulation of labor markets, and the dynamism of financial innovations, a growing heterogeneity of income progression has been observed across and within sectors, among individuals according to their diploma, and an impressive gap now opposes the rich and superrich to the rest of population. The sources of this emerging dualism are well-known, and the UK is a good example of this new pattern:

- On one hand, markets that used to be regional or national became global, and they entitle the emergence of new oligopolies or monopolies that capture increasing return to scale. Within the productive systems, this brings a structural source of inequality.
- On the other hand, the domination of stock markets against bank intermediation allows a huge concentration of wealth according to a patrimonial form of capitalism (Piketty 2014).

The concentration of wealth is still more important than the concentration of income because the diffusion of shareholder value has increased the required rate of return on equity, in a context of slow growth. Consequently, mechanically, the income derived from capital skyrockets, whereas the income of wage earners progresses at most along modest productivity increases. The top 0.1% income exploded from 500.000 £ in 1993 to more than 1.400.000 £ in 2009, whereas the income of the top 1% is nearly stagnant during the same period (Equality Trust 2013).

This inequality is also observed at the geographical level: certain regions and large cities specialize according to research, innovation, finance, and business services, whereas small towns and isolated regions experience a painful des-industrialization, a possible deterioration of public services, and a loss of opportunity for getting access to promising new jobs. The North East of the UK exhibits the lowest wealth per capita (150.000 £) with the highest level in the South

East (340.000 £) and South West (305.000 $) but not necessarily in London (245.000 £) (Equality Trust 2013).

10.4 A Crisis of Political Representations and Intermediation

This polarization of income and wealth is so spectacular that the representation of various groups by the old party system is challenged. The traditional Westminster democracy used to channel strategic decisions, but the call for a referendum destabilizes this political intermediation process. The outcome is a poor collective decision, whereby promised economic gains are converted into less growth and job creation.

10.4.1 A Shift in Political Attitudes of the Working Class

Brexit brutally reveals the growing divergence between political, financial, and economic elites and the perceptions of citizens at the grassroots level. With the delocalization of manufacturing employment including the shrinking of blue-collar workers and the specialization of the UK in financial intermediation at the world level along with the delivery of sophisticated business services, the geographical polarization of income and wealth has increased; therefore, the political map of the UK has significantly changed during the last two decades. The extreme polarization of votes manifests the structural transformations of society. Young people and the highly educated are a fraction of the population who live in large cities, especially in London, and they have voted in favor of Remain. By contrast, older people with low education, welfare dependents, and modest employees living in Northern England in small cities favored Brexit (Ashcroft 2016).

> The dividing line is up to the everyday perception; Some of those core Remainers reported waking up the day after the Brexit vote feeling, at least briefly, that they were living in a foreign country. If that was, indeed, the case they were merely experiencing, in political reverse, what a majority of people apparently feel every day. (Goodhart 2017, p. 2)

This polarization manifests the general perception by the middle and working class that social mobility has been significantly reduced during the last two decades. It is important because the belief that the majority of the population now belonged to the middle class played an essential role in pacifying social conflict and the design of a rather consensual political program, only moderately affected by the succession of the right and left parties, the Conservative and Labour Parties in the UK (Table 10.3A).

The social categories in favor of Brexit were largely dependent on the supply of public goods such as education, health, and an intense redistribution via the tax

Table 10.3 From the social divide to political orientation

A. A growing perception of barriers to mobility between classes 2005 and 2015		
Class identity	Mobility is not very difficult (% of responses)	
	2005	2015
Middle class	40	30
Working class	32	24

Source: NatCen Social Research (2015), British social attitudes, social class, p.5

B. A move toward authoritarian and anti-immigrants' feelings 2015		
	Authoritarian	Anti-immigrants
Occupational class	(%)	(%)
Middle class	45	48
Working class	60	65

Source: NatCen Social Research (2015), British social attitudes, social class, p.13

system. With the triumph of the liberalization program, a universal welfare state has shifted toward a "workfare," with major inequality now being related to access to a job, however reduced its remuneration. Despite the persistence of a collective and redistributive institution such as the national healthcare system, welfare dependent and low-skilled workers have endured the cost of this transition from a system based upon equality of outcomes toward an equal opportunity model. The rest of the world did not directly impose all these evolutions, but result from domestic political choices, sometime in the name of national competitiveness.

The Brexit vote reveals a second confusion; the general process of *internationalization* of the British economy is presented as mainly a consequence of *Europeanization*. The successive governments have been very clever in negotiating and obtaining many opt-out clauses: social charter, no adhesion to the Euro, reduced participation to the European budget, and rejection of the Schengen Treaty regarding internal mobility. Thus, the institutional constraints from belonging to Europe have been reduced to those that are compatible with domestic objectives. Nevertheless, the popular press has been attributing many, if not all, the domestic problems to Brussels' regulations and directives. This alliance between the media and nationalistic politicians (e.g., via UKIP) builds a discourse that blames the EU for transformations that have been caused by the internationalization of the British economy and its excessive reliance upon its financial sector.

This erroneous diagnosis was further confirmed in public opinion when an unprecedented flow of refugees entered the EU; the danger was coming from abroad and especially from the European Commission that tried to organize a coordinated sharing of refugees among member states, according to rather technocratic criteria. De facto, this runs against the feeling from blue-collar workers and the self-employed who declared themselves preoccupied with immigration, whereas upper classes did not express the same fear. Similarly, the less privileged tended to favor authoritarian parties, at odds with the rest of society. The social surveys about Britain were pointing out this divergence, largely unnoticed and neglected by policy makers (Table 10.3B. supra).

The referendum on the EU is an opportunity for the expression of such polarization at the personal and geographic levels (Ashcroft 2016). The danger associated with migration, both real and imaginary, probably played a major role in explaining the Brexit vote. Finally, the fact that a member of parliament in favor of Remain was murdered makes clear the deep social division among British society and the impact of deep sentiments about identity and sovereignty. The voice of academic researchers who proposed an analytical approach to the overall benefits of past migration could not be heard by public opinion (Dhingra et al. 2016c). The political arena was far away from Habermas' ideal of an *agora* where all stakeholders express their point of view and defend their interests to finally acquire a common decision via deliberation. In a sense, the Brexit vote is a good example of the consequences of such a weakness of contemporary democracy. This ideal deliberation about the best method of integration into a supranational order is possible, as evidenced by the extensive and intensive consultation of all sociopolitical groups in order to determine whether Sweden was interested in joining the Euro (Calmfors 1997).

10.4.2 The Crisis of Parties and Representative Democracy

The Swedish society organized itself to decide whether the country adheres to the Euro by collecting the diversity of attitudes and expectations of various socioeconomic groups operating in different sectors. The government had to take the final decision in light of a very detailed and somehow contradictory appraisal of the possible consequences of the Euro. Such a process was not at all contemplated in the UK. Two channels have been mixed: the referendum where every vote counts and parliament that enacts public opinion via the electoral code. Traditionally, the debate opposes Conservatives to Labour via the transitory mediation of a liberal democratic party or, more recently, the UKIP and the Greens. The dilemma is that European integration has both defenders and critics within each of the two major parties. Only UKIP and the Greens displayed quasi-unanimity (Table 10.4).

An equivalent diversity prevails when members of the two main parties are interviewed about the precise content of Brexit. Only the payment to the EU for

Table 10.4 The Leave/Remain divide crosses party affiliation

VOTE 2016		Vote 2016	
		Leave	**Remain**
	Conservative	61%	39%
	Labour	35%	65%
	Scottish National Party	36%	64%
	Liberal Democrats	32%	68%
	UKIP	95%	15%
	Green	80%	20%

Source: Extracted from You Gov (2016) June 23–24 https://yougov.uk/new/2016/06/27/howBritainvoted

Table 10.5 The distribution of political options within parliament

Acceptance by/of	Conservatives	Labour	
EU freedom of movement	26%	72%	Agreement: no
ECJ after march 2019	37%	90%	Agreement: no
Payment into EU central budget	53%	81%	Possible agreement: maybe
Payment for specific services/ arrangements	96%	91%	Agreement: yes

Source: Phillip Cowley and Alan Wager (2018)

specific services and the participation to European independent agencies have a clear majority in accepted Conservative and Labour MPs. By contrast, Labour is in favor of freedom of movements, which is at odds with the preference of the Conservatives. A similar opposition emerges concerning the role of the European Court of Justice after Brexit; the Labour Party is largely in favor, but less than a third of the Conservative MPs share this opinion. A possible agreement could be observed concerning the payment into the EU central budget, but the Minister in charge of negotiating Brexit has resisted this payment, only recognized by the Prime Minister on May 2018 (May 2018). As a matter of fact, parliament experiences difficulties obtaining a majority in favor of one form or another of Brexit. This is evidence of the emerging crisis of the British party system and Westminster representative democracy (Table 10.5).

10.4.3 Is a Citizens' Assembly Better than a Parliament Deadlock?

Calling a referendum was supposed to be a clever device for overcoming a possible deadlock in the conduction of negotiations with the EU. Nevertheless, this political tool reduced choice to "yes" or "no," and for instance, it did not address what Brexit would be exactly. Furthermore, citizens may have decided their vote by responding to a separate issue: do they agree or not with the current policy of the government, independently from the issue of EU? In line with a philosophical approach (Habermas 2013), a representative group of citizens can be put at work; they receive detailed information, they discuss among themselves, and this deliberative process possibly changes the initial perception of the issue at stake. Furthermore, the choice is not between "yes" and "no" but among more precise options such as staying in the Single Market, searching for a comprehensive trade deal, or, on the contrary, a limited one, accepting the absence of any deal between the UK and the EU (Table 10.6).

The outcome is that a majority prefers a negotiated deal to the absence of deal, but this is not necessary the opinion of the Prime Minister who declared that no deal was better than a bad deal. A similar gap between the options of the government and the

Table 10.6 The preference of citizens' assembly

TRADE DEAL WITH EU	SINGLE MARKET	COMPREHENSIVE TRADE DEAL	LIMITED TRADE DEAL	NO TRADE DEAL	
Trade deal with the EU	14 %	14 %	19 %	3 %	
	Negotiated deal				
MIGRATION BETWEEN THE UK AND THE EU	FREE MOVEMENT	FREE MOVEMENT WITH CONTROL	EU FAVORED FREE MOVEMENT	EU NOT FAVORED TOTAL IMMIGRATION AS NOW	EU NOT FAVORED, IMMIGRATION DOWN
	9 %	26 %	5 %	4 %	7 %
		Targeted immigration			

Source: Elaborated from Alan Renwick (2018)

assembly of citizens relates to the issue of immigration: a significant fraction is in favor of targeted immigration instead of a dramatic reduction of inflow of EU citizens. This partial experiment, recognized as such by its initiators, is further evidence for a creeping crisis of the political intermediation delivered by the Westminster style democracy (Renwick 2018; Renwick et al. 2017).

10.5 Brexit: A Total Social Fact Calls for an Original Approach

Clearly, a purely economic approach to Brexit is bound to fail because a holistic approach requires consideration of the role of both rationality and emotions. Narratives, social transformations, and changing political attitudes are to be considered within an integrated social science approach.

10.5.1 How Society, Polity, and Economy Jointly Interact

In the absence of a coordinating mechanism, *a sequential process* takes place when successive decisions in one domain, for instance, in the economy, transfer impulses to another one. This process begins at the level of social stratification and moves finally to the political sphere. All the actors involved only perceive after the fact how their successive strategies result in an unintended configuration. For example, the winners of the referendum refused to form a government, and thus Theresa May, a politician from the Remain camp, decided to assume the responsibility to negotiate

Brexit, against her own convictions. She hides her perplexity beneath a wonderful tautology, “Brexit is Brexit.”

Therefore, the sequencing of transformation and decisions matters. The British economy is slowly transforming in the context of its internationalization as a world financial intermediation center and the partial transfer of national sovereignty to the European level. The logic of the European Commission is to build supranational rules and regulations—in the American definition—to monitor competition in the Single Market. Some of these European interventions are far from popular since a seemingly bureaucratic approach breaches the principle of economic freedom and subsidiarity. Consequently, a fraction of the population may think that any difficulty experienced by the UK originates from Brussels, presented by some popular media sources as a variant of a Soviet-type approach. The more so, if a new party can capitalize all the discontents into a unique objective of leaving the EU. David Cameron had cleverly used this threat and was successful in obtaining the exemption from a significant number of European rules that were unpopular in the UK. As they say, kill two birds with one stone: he negotiated political gains for the Conservative Party in its fight against UKIP, and as a side effect, a higher probability of a Remain victory and recognition of the Prime Minister’s determination and competence. Brutally, on June 2016, the whole set of expectations from pollsters, financiers, and party leaders collapsed against the spectacular rise of conflicting political visions of the future of the UK (Tilford 2016; Gilles 2017). Since then, all actors have desperately tried to work out new strategies, and as of writing, no new dominant paradigm has emerged (Fig. 10.2).

On the academic side, mono-disciplinary and mono-causal approaches fail to deliver a convincing analysis and interpretation of the origins, the meaning, and the likely consequences of the British referendum on Brexit. This fact emphasizes the merits of an alternative approach that interconnects all the factors in a given society that can be set into motion. Brexit can be qualified as a total social fact, as indicated by Marcel Mauss. His definition remains useful for understanding highly complex societies, “The facts we have studied are. . .total social facts. . .they set in motion in some cases all of society and its institutions. . .and in other cases only a large number of institutions” (Mauss 1925:5).

10.5.2 A Rather Common Configuration in the EU

In retrospect, such a transformation was not so difficult to diagnose. First, this polarization of public opinion between pro- and anti-Europe movements is not specific to the UK. It is present in Central and Eastern Europe—Hungary, Poland, and the Czech Republic—but also in the core founding nations of the EU, including France and the Netherlands. During the process leading to the Euro, surveys had shown a clear opposition between, on one hand, the likely winners (large firms, professionals, young people with academic degrees) who thought that they would gain and on the other hand probable losers (small firms, low-skilled workers, welfare

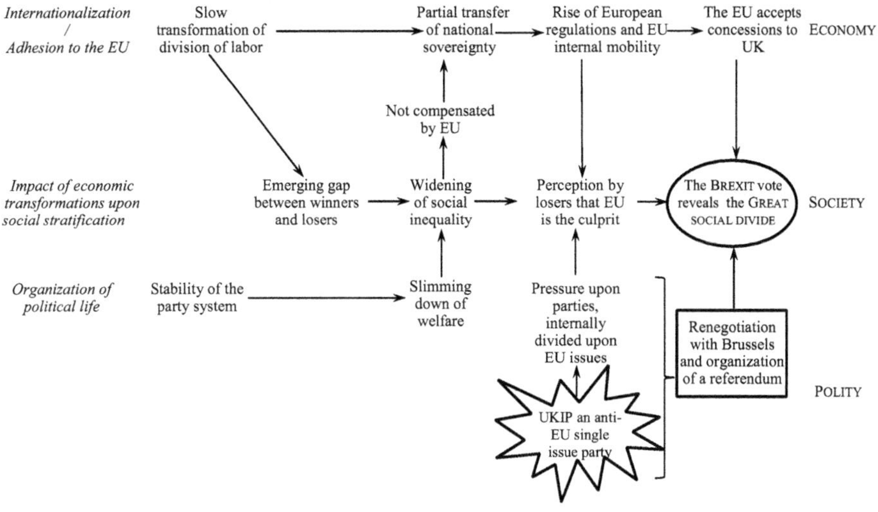

Fig. 10.2 A synoptic presentation of the argument of the chapter

dependent, retirees) who declared to be pessimistic about the evolution of their personal position after the Euro (Boyer 2000). In 2005, the Dutch and the French had rejected by referendum the project instituting the Euro, but parliament finally adopted a slightly modified European Treaty. The Brexit vote was simply updating this polarization of European societies; for the Remain group, multiculturalism and acceptation of immigration were assumed to be good for society, but detrimental for Brexiters (Ashcroft 2016).

During the 2000s, the high degree of international liquidity and easy access to credit for individuals and States had been hiding the deflationary bias of the Lisbon Treaty, but after the Lehman Brothers collapse and its subsequent conversion into a wider Euro crisis, this structural property of the European policy mix manifested itself and sharpened the division between the losers and winners, in the context of widening inequalities. Yet, here is the British paradox: the country is deeply integrated into the world economy, but the slimming down of welfare and industrial employment have not allowed for a sharing of the benefits of globalization (*The Economists* 2016a). Such a pattern is, to some extent, also observed in continental Europe. The impact of globalization is still more violent on other continents; the restructuring of capital has implied the exclusion of various social groups (Sassen 2014). In Europe, this process is converted into the vote for nationalistic and xenophobic parties. Around the mid-2010s, in France, the Front National captured 25.4% of the votes, and in Hungary, the scores for the extreme right are also high—14.7%. In other countries, the extreme right also garnered significant percentages: the Netherlands (13.4%), Finland (12.9%), Greece (9.4%), and Italy (6.2%). Most impressive is the resurgence of an extreme right party in Germany, blocking the soft functioning of a governmental coalition (McCarthy 2014).

The American presidential election confirmed and extended the lesson from the British referendum. The winner has built his success with a simple but powerful motto, "Make America Great Again." Whereas social scientists, including economists (Stiglitz 2016), pointed out the explosion of inequalities and their negative impact upon economic growth and social order, most of the evils of American society are attributed to unfair competition and an excessive internationalization of American firms. Therefore, the very framing of the election is redefined by this narrative. In the past, a central issue was the balance between workers and firms, but it has shifted toward the opposition between the elite in Washington and the people on Main Street. Simultaneously, the elite are assumed to be internationalist, betraying the American population's interest and well-being. This process has been converting blue-collar workers, who traditionally voted for Democrats, into vocal supporters of Republicans (Frank 2005). Very daring promises exploit the credibility of the fraction of the population that has experienced a stagnation of real income, and who fear a decline in the standard of living of their children stemming from de-industrialization and urban crises. Anger and pessimism find expression in the violence of the Republican candidate's discourse. "Alternative facts" are the direct consequences of this primacy of narratives over analyses, "Arguments based on reason and facts alone make little headway when confronted with powerful metaphors, deep stories, and moral intuitions, which in turn may be powerfully supported by habit, stories, and ritual" (Nelson 2017: 2).

Nevertheless, the USA and the EU do not follow the same trajectory; the first is a fully fledged federal state, and the second exhibits an incoherent mode of governance. The EU is facing the most severe crisis since its foundation because it has been perceived as promoting a form of free market economy without building at the federal level a safety net that would guaranty efficient and fair adjustments to the vacillation of the world economy. This core orientation dates back from the very beginning of the European integration. The project was indeed rather technocratic; lucid and informed experts should promote rules of the economic game that should prevent the repetition of the European wars. The economic complementarities thus created would imply spillovers to the rest of society concerning technical norms, social welfare, and finally economic policy coordination. This was the hope clearly expressed by Jean Monnet (1988), and it has inspired many of the advances in European integration. Nevertheless, if it was relatively easy to remove trade barriers linked to tariffs, the strengthening in competition has made more and more difficult the extension of welfare at the domestic level, and the diversity of national configurations has blocked the constitution of a coherent European welfare. Thus, the weakest groups have perceived the EU as an obstacle to the defense of their well-being, and new parties have been exploiting these social demands not fulfilled by the implicit alliance between Christian and Social democrats in the management of European institutions.

Brexit points out the extreme social polarization in England and the fragility of the UK to the issue of Scotland independence, but it might also have dramatic consequences for continental Europe. In the past, recurring crises have been used as drivers for a deepening of economic integration, and they have strengthened the idea of "an ever-closer European integration," the motto of the EU. Integration is no longer the case with the Euro; some countries have joined, Greece for instance, while others have declined, including Denmark and the UK. Similarly, the members of the Schengen agreement represent another grouping. This "Europe à la carte" (flexible Europe) seemed to have won but Brexit means that one country may decide to quit this club and some other governments might use this precedent to negotiate as many opting-out clauses as nationalist movements demand or they may even exit from the European Single Market.

10.6 The Difficult Process of Brexit Negotiations

Immediately after the June 23, 2016, referendum, the campaign of the Brexiters had spread a very optimistic vision: more funding for the NHS by the redeployment of the UK contribution to EU budget, expression of full sovereignty and strict control of immigration, stimulation of innovations by the removal of "silly" European regulations, and the ability to negotiate free trade agreements with the most dynamic regions of the world. These promises were stated with the expectation that the withdrawal of the UK would trigger a domino effect and a quick exit from the EU, following the British initiative. In the last quarter of 2018, must this discourse be reassessed? At least four obstacles have emerged since Article 50 was declared on March 2017.

10.6.1 The Enduring Polarization of Public Opinion

Unfortunately, most of these promises did not fit with the legal obligations of the European treaties. The European regulations had to be adopted at least transitorily because their British equivalent could not be developed from scratch; the negotiations with new free trade agreement (FTA) partners could only begin after Brexit, and they could not compensate the loss of market share within the Single Market. Finally, the EU member states have manifested a surprising unanimity in defending the past achievements of the European integration. Logically, all these disappointments should have induced some Brexiters to regret their vote; however, polls suggest that nearly the same proportion of Brexiters continue to think they were right and that the Remainers made a wrong decision (Hobol et al. 2018).

Two contrasting visions of the world do coexist in the UK. For the Remainers, a clear majority considers that the British economy is likely to be worse off out of the EU, and they are not totally convinced that the control of immigration will be more efficient. At odds with this vision, the Brexiters put a higher valuation on the limitation of immigration, and they are less concerned by economic prosperity (Fig. 10.3).

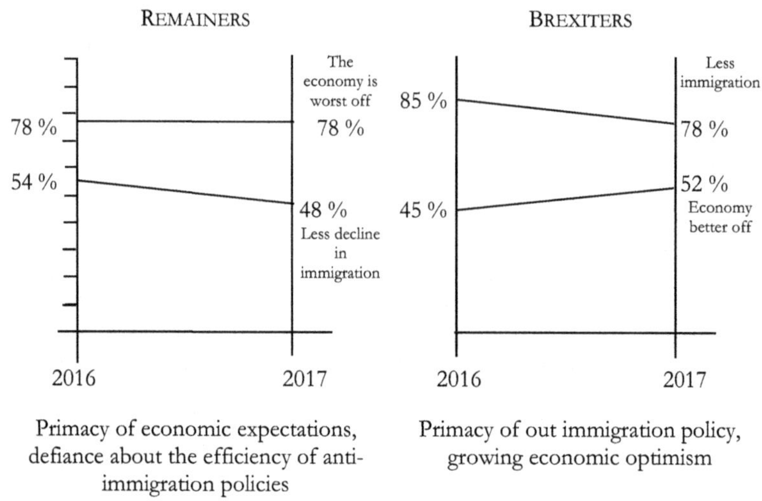

Fig. 10.3 One year after Brexit: two contrasted and unchanging visions. Source: Elaborated from Goodwin (2018)

This opposition has not been reduced at all by the evidence of government difficulties in defining what Brexit precisely means. In place of a rational median voter that would evaluate objectively the impact on his personal situation and evolution of the British economy as a whole, the process of socialization has produced two distinctive entities.

- As previously mentioned, the Remainers enjoy a good education, they are younger than the rest of the population, they usually live in large cities, and they have a positive perception of internationalization and Europeanization. For them, the vote of the referendum is a surprise since they now must realize that they belong to a minority (Goodhart 2017). They are aware of the significant costs of Brexit, even soft ones, and they are convinced that minor adjustments of the present policies could be sufficient to curb down significantly migratory flows. This reduction could have been the reason for the compromise negotiated by Prime Minister Cameron, limiting access of newly entering EU workers to welfare benefits to 4 years out of a period of 7 years (Korski 2016). In fact, the outcome of the referendum has been to dampen the appetite of many Central Europe workers to stay in or come to the UK. Thus the social position largely determines the probability of the vote and the anticipation of the consequences of Brexit. In a sense, the expectations of the Remainers are framed by their habitus, the concept framed by Pierre Bourdieu (2017) (Fig. 10.4).
- Low-skilled citizens, especially when they are aging and live in small towns, do not have the same perception of the issues at stake. They are comforted in their vision that Brexit will bring more growth and employment opportunities evidenced by the fact that the UK economy is still booming 18 months after the referendum; the campaign of the Remainers anticipating depression and

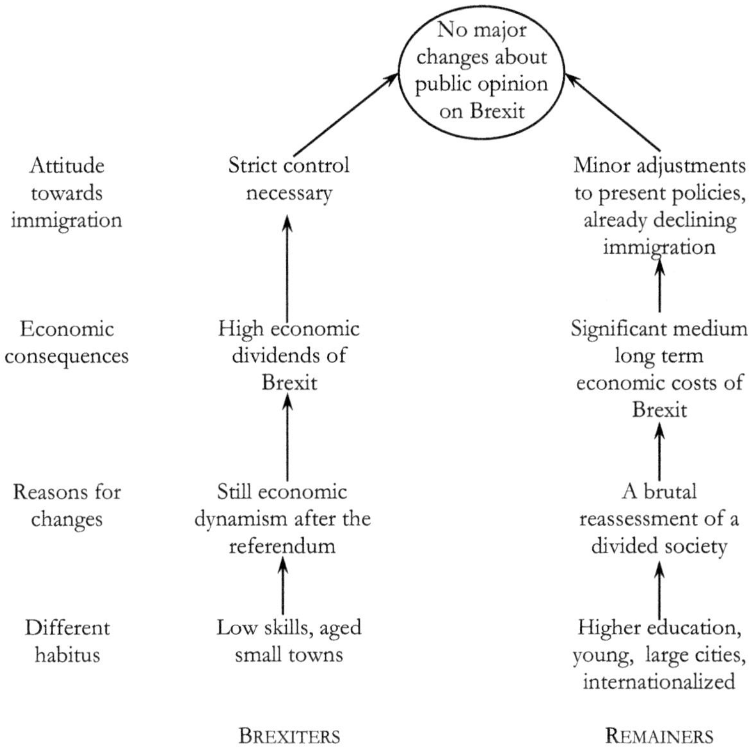

Fig. 10.4 Why the social divide revealed by Brexit persists until early 2018

chaos was erroneous. Consequently, the economic cost of Brexit is not a relevant issue for them since the priority is to reaffirm British sovereignty on regulations, trade, and economic policy. The control of immigration continues to be a priority in the fulfillment of Brexit. A different social, political, and individual history sets into motion a specific realm of expectations.

Thus, one observes a remarkable stability in the Brexiter/Remainer divide (Green 2016; Elliott and Kanagasooriam 2017; Evans 2018). There is no reason for a convergence toward a consensual anticipation of the future of the UK. This suggests the importance of the economic sociology proposed by Pierre Bourdieu (2017). Consequently, it is especially difficult for a government to negotiate a way out of the EU in the context of a socially and politically divided country.

10.6.2 *The EU as a Scapegoat: The Forgotten Role of Neoliberal Reforms of Welfare*

The referendum on Brexit has shifted the political agenda in the direction of the opposition between domestically and internationally oriented social groups. The more conventional opposition between liberalism and interventionism, i.e., between right- and left-wing parties, has been concealed. Therefore, the European integration has been attributed with a major role in the widening of social and economic inequalities. Nordic social democratic regimes have succeeded in limiting inequality despite the adhesion to globalization; the contrast is very clear compared with the UK and the USA (Piketty 2014). Such a gap is mainly explained by the resilience of a progressive tax system and an extended universal welfare, accessible to any citizens whatever his current employment (Boyer 2014).

In fact, the international literature tries to disentangle two sources of inequality: the new productive paradigm that destabilizes past labor division and the internationalization process that opposes two categories of wage earners. In the case of the UK, the culprit is supposed to be internationalization, and this might be the consequence of the referendum. The issue of skill formation is somehow neglected within official statements of the parties and government (*The Conservatives* 2017). There is a still more important absence; the slimming down of welfare and tax reforms has been unable to counteract the vicious circle that produced the losers of globalization. A significant fraction of the population has been marginalized or pauperized by the replacement of welfare by a workfare. Social marginalization goes along with difficult access to the political arena, and consequently welfare issues are not central to public policy decisions.

There is thus a paradox: the concealing of distributive and redistributive issues puts at the forefront of the political debates first anti-globalization movements and second a diffused fear about the long-term consequences of robot diffusion and artificial intelligence (Fig. 10.5). This partial view does not help overcome the structural problem of the UK, i.e., the search for a positive sum game both at home and internationally.

10.6.3 *A Dramatic Underestimation of the Complexity of the Processes Involved by Brexit*

An initial blocking of the negotiations relates to the fact that the economic dividends of Brexit have been converted into a minimization of the costs of abandoning the Single Market and custom union. There is no doubt that the UK will be worse off. First, retrospective analyses have estimated the large benefits of joining the EU (Nauro et al. 2014). Second, whatever the final configuration of Brexit, nearly all quantitative estimates conclude in a reduction of growth, employment, and productivity (OECD 2016; Dhingra et al. 2016a; Gudgin et al. 2016; HM Treasury 2016b);

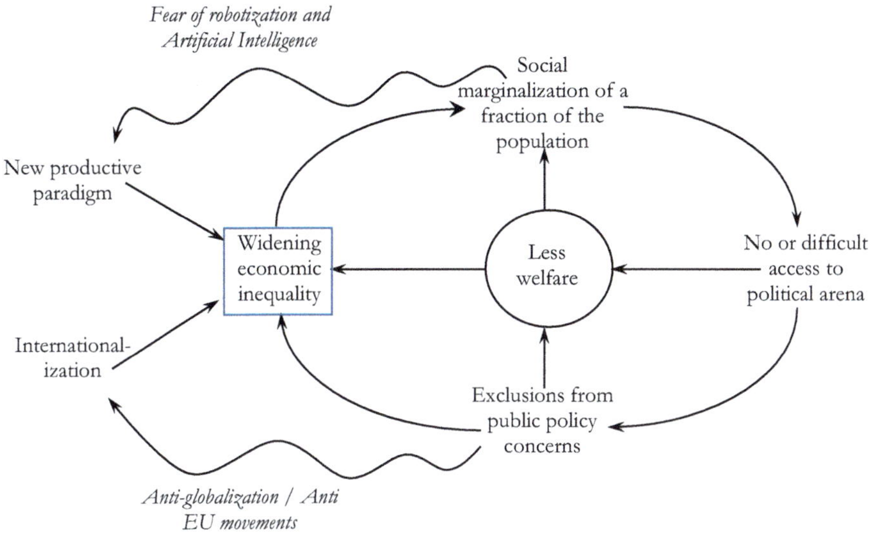

Fig. 10.5 Anti-EU movements: the forgotten origin of inequalities and less redistribution by welfare and public spending

the harder the Brexit, the higher the costs to be shared by the various social groups. All sectors, regions, and socioeconomic groups will have to bear a fraction of these costs (Gasiorek et al. 2018; Nardelli 2018). By contrast, the negotiations of new free trade agreements will take time and bring only a modest contribution to UK growth compared with a continuing of EU links.

Nevertheless, Brexiters have dramatically downplayed the sunk costs and irreversibility associated with belonging to the EU over four decades. Designing new regulations concerning product norms and quality and implementing the UK border controls will generate extra costs that were previously shared at the European level. Brexiters can argue that this recovered sovereignty will remove cumbersome constraints imposed by Brussels and that renewed innovations will compensate the loss of market share on continental Europe; however, note that the costs are large and certain, whereas the expected returns are relatively modest and quite uncertain (Table 10.7).

The clear benefits for the UK relate to the control of immigration; ideologically and politically, this sustains the popularity of the government and the acceptance of Brexit, but from an economic point of view, many British sectors are operating successfully based on the inflow of foreign workers, whatever their skill, which is high in the national health services in the city of London and in universities and low in most services (retailing, restauration, cleaning,services to the person, and so on) and agriculture (Dhingra et al. 2016c). A brutal decline in immigration may soothe the antagonisms against foreigners, but simultaneously, the losses in value added will make redistribution via public spending and welfare still more difficult. In any

Table 10.7 Why most forms of Brexit are so difficult: highly probable costs and few and hypothetical advantages

	The present obstacles	The potential benefits
Economic	1. Economic direct costs for all sectors and all regions; the larger are the costs, the harder is Brexit	1. Search for new trade flows by extended FTA outside the EU
	2. Cost of implementing new border controls	2. Economic autonomy from EU regulations
Social	3. Time required for reorienting value chains	3. More dynamism of innovation by deregulation
	4. Tension over NHS, university, services, agriculture	4. Chosen immigration
	5. Less resources for redistribution via public spending and welfare	5. Defense of Britishness
Political	6. A dysfunctional party system	6. Less conflicts between nationals and migrants
International	7. Need to negotiate all former EU FTA	7. Primacy of people's choices over economic logic
	8. The weight of geography: Distant partners	8. Global Britain superior to European Britain

case, the impact of immigration on wage is not as large as imagined by Brexiters (Nickell and Saleheen 2015). The growing dysfunctional nature of the British contemporary party system explains the impossible task of the Prime Minister, permanently oscillating between contradictory objectives and forms of Brexit (*Financial Time* 2017).

It is not easy to replace dense links with European neighbors with sparse ones with distant and powerful partners such as the USA or China; is it realist to anticipate that British diplomacy will get more favorable FTA than the EU? Similarly, the attractiveness of the UK might originate from light-touch regulations in terms of labor and finance, but it was so because the UK belonged to the EU. The inflow of foreign direct investment will necessarily be lower after Brexit (Dhingra et al. 2016b), and this will have a negative impact upon productivity and employment. An ironic observer pointed out: "One does not cut in one night ties woven for thirty years (…) This process involves taking out the English egg from the European omelet" (Pascal Lamy, former Director General of WTO 2018). More seriously, the Brexiters postulated an easy reversibility toward more independence, whereas the diffusion of world value chains and geographical specialization imply significant irreversibility and persisting interdependency.

10.6.4 Are Free Trade Agreements Better Forms of Internationalization?

The British government has announced the negotiation of a multiplicity of FTAs around the world. By definition, they respect national sovereignty, and they allow direct control over immigration, i.e., the crucial objective of the Brexiters. Are these treaties the solution to the economic and social divides, a major factor in the split revealed by the referendum? Not necessarily, since the vicious circle associated with EU liberalization and competitive policy is likely to persist. When the division of labor is organized according to the competitiveness of territories, the coherence of the domestic productive system is at risk; the dynamism of domestic demand is now satisfied by the world supply, and this erodes the very possibility of the mass production/mass consumption virtuous circle. In this new configuration, and in the context of the decentralization and individualization of income formation, solidarity among wage earners is difficult to obtain. In addition, wage austerity policies replace the synchronization of wage increase by collective agreements: the mechanism of productivity distribution operates via the reduction of the relative price of consumption goods.

On one hand, unions have more and more difficulties in defining and defending the collective rights of workers. On the other hand, many investigations suggest that underprivileged workers vote less frequently than other citizens and no traditional party fully defends the interests of the underprivileged. Consequently, this unbalance in the representation of population diversity dramatically reduces the demand for welfare and new social rights (Fig. 10.6).

As time elapsed, this discontent of the left behind sparked the emergence of populist parties, and they exerted a growing influence on national political debates (Wyplosz 2016). The British referendum is the first example of an agenda set by the capitalization of xenophobic feelings. The election of Donald Trump against the traditional ideology of the Republican Party is a second example: the rejection of free trade and restrictive immigration policy are two similarities with the British case though Europeanization does not always play a role. The September 2017 German general election showed the declining audience of the Christian Democratic Union (CDU) and the Social Democratic Party (SPD) and the affirmation of the *Alternative für Deutschland* (AfD) that shifted from anti-Euro and anti-EU to anti-migrant. The blocking of government formation for 5 months is evidence of the general crisis faced by parties and electoral democracy. Finally, the March 2018 Italian election has the same consequences; the erosion of the long-established traditional parties and the recomposition of the political offer around anti-immigrant and anti-globalization programs. Clearly, free trade is at risk both as a response to public opinion and as the offensive of the USA against multinational negotiations in charge of organizing free trade.

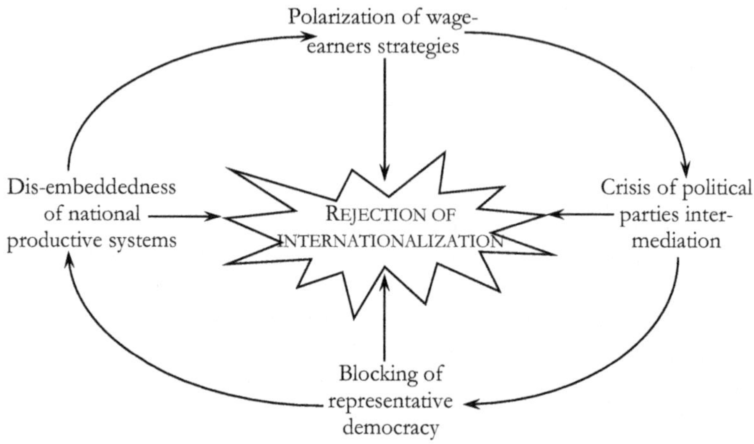

Examples:	Brexit referendum in the UK	2016
	Trump's Presidency in the US	2017
	General elections in Germany	2017
	General elections in Italy	2018

Fig. 10.6 Why internationalization face many difficulties after three-decade-long liberalization

10.6.5 A Painful Adaptation of British Government Strategy

Ideologies display simplified representations of the world at the very moment when the interdependencies operating internationally feature unprecedented complexity. It took 6 months for the British government to launch the process codified by Article 50 of the European Treaties. Therefore, when negotiations between the British and EU representatives began, the bargaining stance of the UK was in line with the rhetoric of the Brexiters, with the hope to calm the anxiety of the Remainers with the proposal of complete access to the Single Market as usual. On the European side, the consensual objectives were to preserve the Single Market and the custom union, according to which the four free mobility—goods, services, capital, and labor—could not be separated at will, contrary to demands of British negotiators. In terms of game theory, the equilibrium set was empty. Furthermore, the government tried variants between a hard and soft Brexit in order to tentatively build a consensus within the Conservative Party. The return to reality was especially slow since the EU negotiators only developed a nearly consistent proposal in early March 2018 May's Mansion House Discourse (Fig. 10.7).

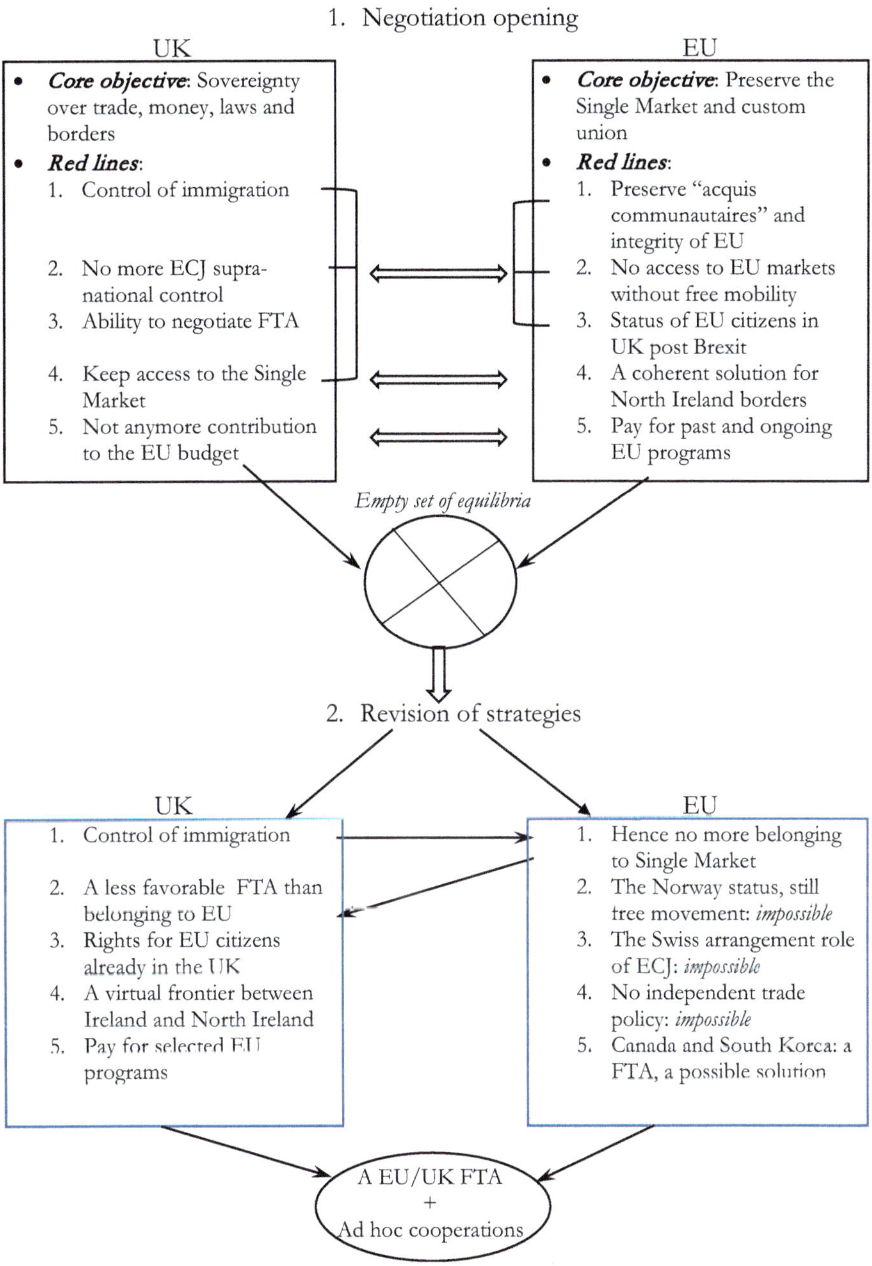

Fig. 10.7 The UK-EU relations after Brexit. A simple game theory approach

The British government then recognized the difficult tradeoff between the national control of immigration and a reduced access to the Single Market to the European Economic Area (EEA) (Whiteman 2016). This position also excludes a Norwegian-style agreement, and the belonging to a FTA as a favorable alternative to belonging to the EU is therefore out of reach; the rights of the EU citizens already in the UK are the counterpart of the symmetric rights granted to British citizens in the EU. The British agree to pay for past EU programs and new ones in proportion to remaining within some European agencies. One source of frontal disagreement remains the continuity between Ireland and North Ireland (Gouez 2017). British negotiators propose an unspecified virtual British frontier, whereas to the European negotiators, it is a legal matter, since a territory cannot be simultaneously in and out of the EU. This incoherence of the British position—torn between the necessity of preserving the peace process between the two Irelands and the definite will to quit the EU—might prove to be a potential source of hard Brexit, by lack of an admissible compromise.

10.6.6 The Perils of an Unintended Hard Brexit

The European and British negotiators are fully conscious that an aggressive and rigid strategy would be detrimental for both partners. Nevertheless, the probability of a hard Brexit is significant because many hurdles must be crossed (Fig. 10.8).

A good compromise should simultaneously satisfy three conditions: no dramatic economic costs, social transformations reducing the gap between the winners and the losers of internationalization, political recognition and legitimacy. The task is quite challenging indeed because it assumes a reversal of decades long structural transformations.

This alignment must take place in the UK, and it is far from currently evident: how to overcome the issue of the two Irelands? Will Scotland accept a compromise that essentially fits the English preoccupation? Can a slower growth induce a more intensive redistribution among individuals and localities? What should be the

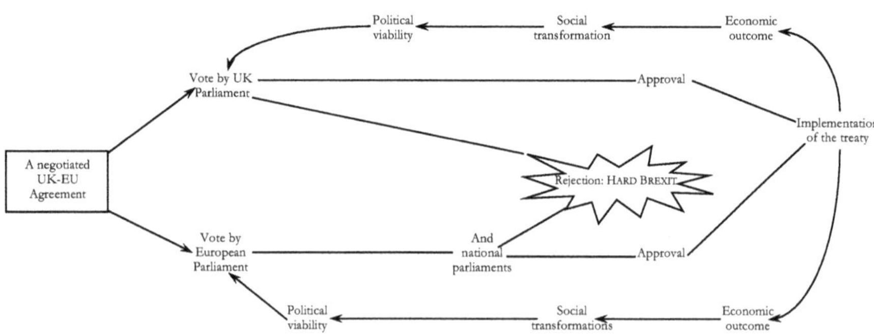

Fig. 10.8 The future of any negotiated agreement: social and political long-run viability

reconfiguration of parties that would be entitled to consider not only the opposition between internationalists and locals but also the traditional distinction between right and left in terms of the choice between trust in market and necessary state intervention?

Any new trade treaty between the UK and the EU requires the majority at the European Parliament. In the past, the explicit or implicit alliance of Christian democrats and social democrats warranted a relatively easy compromise. Given the rise of Euro-skeptic or anti-EU parties, the 2019 elections to the European Parliament might destroy this past equilibrium, as a significant fraction of the members belonging to populist movements possibly become allied to block any progression toward a more integrated Europe.

Following an initiative proposed by the Netherlands concerning the admission of new EU members, many national parliaments will ask for a full deliberation about the relevance of any new treaty. Given the current governments with Euro-skeptic parties—Poland, Hungary, Austria, the Czech Republic, and possibly Italy—the rebuttal of any proposal by the European Council is a probability.

10.7 The Critical State of the EU: A Destructive Crisis

The Brexiters imagined that their bold decisions would mean the next collapse of the EU through domino effects from one Euro-skeptic public opinion to another. This bet has not been successful in early 2018; nevertheless, European integration faces totally new challenges that cannot be overcome by a new wave of technocratic innovations, such as the banking union. The past cannot be extrapolated, and simple projections of past trends must be replaced by imaginative scenarios.

10.7.1 The Three Structural Crises of Old Europe

The process of Europeanization triggered a vast theoretical literature. The dominant approach was typically a neo-functionalist approach. Each advance in the integration of markets would call for the next step, i.e., an institutionalization of the rules of the game (Fligstein and Sweet 2002; Fligstein 2008). The stabilization of exchange rates necessary for the viability of the Single Market called for monetary integration, and this anticipated a political move toward a pooling of national sovereignty into the embryo of a federalist European State that was required for the sustainability of the Euro. The process was quite uneven since it proceeded from one crisis to another, but each of them finally turned out to be productive. For the first time, the 2010s may open the possibility of a destructive crisis (Schmitter and Lefkofridi (2015), wherein defection overcomes solidarity, and the Brexit vote could mean a tipping point in the history of Europe.

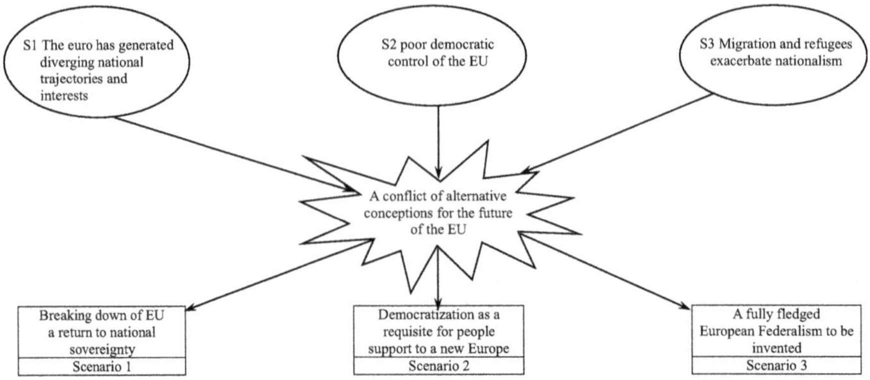

Fig. 10.9 Three sources in the EU contemporary crisis and possible scenario

Since intergovernmental bargaining has replaced the construction of European commons, many emerging EU structural problems have been neglected since the launching of the Euro. All of them violently and simultaneously develop in the early 2010s when the 2008 American crisis reaches Europe. At least three series of contradictions and unbalances have been piling up without adequate and sequential institutional and political reforms (Fig. 10.9).

Since the very launching of the Euro, any analytical investigation could easily prove that the European Treaties were implying a *dysfunctional economic policy* between member states and the ECB and between monetary and budgetary policies (Boyer 2000). Only the redeployment of financial portfolios across Europe has transitorily removed this incoherence (Boyer 2013), but 2016 is the year of reckoning.

The primacy of capital over labor, the hierarchical domination of competition over solidarity and of *technocratic "expertise"* over *democratic deliberation* all these factors have become evident with the Greek crisis. There is no doubt that past governments had extended public deficits and hidden them by special financial instruments; the responsibility of Greece was clearly involved. This was not a reason for denying the expression of citizens' will and replacing the government by the troika European Central Bank, European Commission, and IMF; no autonomous decision was left to the Greek government (Boyer 2015a). Thus, the rights of creditors are defended by European international organizations, and a technocratic approach is replacing democracy (Streeck 2014). This is a clear contradiction with the objectives and motto of the EU, i.e., the promotion of democracy and "unity within diversity."

With the inflow of *political refugees and economic migrants* from the Middle East and Africa, the public opinion of Central and Eastern European countries challenges the legitimacy of European institutions. In 2015, Brussels tried to impose quota for the integration of the refugees, but it was a failure; only a few wanted to migrate to France, while the clear majority preferred Germany. Hungary, Poland, and the Czech Republic bluntly refused to welcome more migrants, despite their limited number. This point revealed a third European divide between Eastern and Western Europe, compounding the conflict between Northern European creditors and Southern debtor, and the traditional opposition between finance-led and export-led capitalisms, i.e., continental Europe versus the UK (Boyer 2015b).

10.7.2 Conflicting Strategies and Reforms

European policy makers now have to address these three challenges they have been unable to overcome when they first emerged. The crisis is far more complex than all the previous ones, and the probability of a breaking down of 60 years of patient European integration exists (Schmitter 2012) and grows along with the lack of determination of national governments preoccupied by the defense of their own interests, at the detriment of the common European public goods and commons. This moment reveals the structural limits of a neo-functionalist approach to economic integration; rather, technocratic processes have been unfolding without clear political mobilization (Hooghe and Marks 2008). On each of the three core issues, completely different solutions can be given, and it is quite challenging to imagine an ambitious reform that would solve all of them.

- Diverging national trajectories
  The *diverging national trajectories* can be given two opposite solutions. If the principle of a no-transfer union is defended by northern member states, especially Germany, the centrifugal forces will prevail and provoke, whether they like it or not, the *exit of the weakest* European economies. The recurring dilemma raised by the successive structural reforms imposed on the Greek government has yet to be overcome. Similarly, the rise of nationalism in Eastern European member states, such as Poland or Hungary, may result in an exit from the EU. The unity of Europe could only be maintained by the implementation of *a solidarity principle*, associated with permanent transfers to ailing economics. Unfortunately, the federalists have been on the defensive because public opinion is attracted by nationalist and xenophobic programs and a few clumsy defenses by the EU have exacerbated the rejection of a supranational solution to most pressing contemporary problems.
- The lack of democratic accountability
  The lack of *democratic accountability* of many decisions by the EU has become a major source of discontent and criticism. The Brexiters have presented themselves as the defenders of national democracy against a distant and inefficient bureaucracy. The current trend of public opinion is about the *repatriation of many competences* delegated to Brussels or jointly exerted; it is especially so for social policy, welfare, labor laws, and some other norms. *The exit from the EU* can be a brutal reassessment of the democratic principle as superior to any international treaty, at odds with the transatlantic negotiation of extended free trade agreements. Since 2017, the Trump presidency has denounced transatlantic

and transpacific FTAs, and it has consolidated anti-European movements. Similarly, few European politicians are eager to follow the path of a new phase in the construction of a genuine federalism built upon a complex set of checks and balances by democratic deliberation at any level of all EU interventions (Pisani-Ferry et al. 2016; Aglietta and Leron 2017; Piketty et al. 2017). Was the defeat of extreme right parties in Austria, the Netherlands, and France during the 2017 elections the early signal of a reversal of citizens' opinion in favor of a *greater intra-European solidarity* and the permissive condition for a tighter European Integration? In early 2018, German and Italian elections contradicted this renewed Euro-optimism.

- The free mobility of European citizens and the flow of refugees
  The choice is still harder concerning the issues of internal *free mobility* of European citizens and the response to the flow of candidates to *political refugees' status*. A significant fraction of public opinion considers that these are the exclusive concerns of each national sovereign state. But since internal mobility of labor is part of the free exchange principle of goods, services and capital, any permanent and significant control of national borders works against European integration, even if from a legal point of view, the Schengen agreement is distinct from the treaties instituting the EU. An alternative solution would be to transfer the control of *external borders* to a common entity in counterpart of the removal of *internal mobility* control. Nevertheless, this is a quite difficult step in a period of recurring inflows of refugees and migrants escaping Middle East and Africa turmoil when violent terrorist attacks propagate the feeling that immigration, refugees, and terrorism are a common threat to national identity. A technocratic approach of migration cannot replace the commonly held sentiments that build a new supranational identity.

The Brexit vote is not an anecdotal event in the long process of regional integration; it might imply a *watershed* between supranational identity formation and regression to an exclusive definition of identity at the level of existing or future nation states. They could emerge from the collapse of the international cooperation at the apex of three decades of globalization. This was the missing component of many analyses of economic integration (Bartel 2002).

10.8 The Uncertain Future of UK–EU Relations

Any recovery of the British economy supposes the emergence of a sociopolitical coalition to drive a coherent growth regime and to acquire some legitimacy for citizens (Gramsci 1978; Poulantzas 1968). This general hypothesis has been updated and converted into an analytical framework (Amable 2003). It has proven to be quite useful to understand the Italian crisis (Palombarini 2001) but also the transformations of French polity during the last two decades (Amable 2017; Amable and Palombarini 2017). The Brexit vote reveals the inadequacy of existing parties to represent the variety of social and economic interests: the Conservatives, Labour, Liberal Democrats, and the Greens are all divided over the Brexit/Remain issue. Only UKIP voters are unanimous, but they do not represent the majority. The party has been unable to form a Brexit alliance, and its leader Nigel Farage has refused to be part of a future coalition in charge of negotiating the divorce of the UK from the EU. His successor is said to be waiting for the disappointment associated with a bad deal with the EU to manifest before launching a new ascending role for UKIP (Maddock 2017: 12).

The party system is in trouble and any reconfiguration will take time. Traditionally the political spectrum opposes a liberal right to an interventionist left, but the polls about Brexit's reasons do explicate the fact that the opposition between inward-looking individuals and internationalists has probably become more important (Ashcroft 2016). Sociopolitical analyses confirm a deeply rooted divergence between the *Somewhere* voters who absolutely need a domestic anchor and the *Anywhere* voters who thrive by crossing national boundaries (Goodhart 2017). The UK is only one extreme configuration, but in Greece, for reasons already mentioned, and France—the economy the most destabilized by the internationalization and financial globalization—a majority thinks that the EU has had unfavorable outcomes (*The Economist* 2016b).

10.8.1 The Time of Radical Uncertainty

If one accepts the previous diagnosis, no determinist prevision is possible; everything is up to the strategic interactions between key British and European actors. The interdependencies and issues at stake are so numerous that they challenge the conventional methods of standard economic theory (formal modelling, rational expectations, market equilibrium) in order to find an optimum Brexit strategy and sequencing.

- Let us suppose first that the will of the Brexiters will be considered by the new government that gathers politicians belonging to two camps. Either the way out is unilateral at the initiative of the UK, and then the short- to medium-term costs might be very large after the breaking down of access to the Single Market. Conversely, both partners might try to negotiate a win-win agreement that would limit simultaneously the economic and political costs of Brexit for the UK and the EU. No doubt, many other intermediate scenarios can be invented (Barker 2016).
- In any case, given the uncertainty about the scenario that will prevail, firms will wait and see before massively investing again. Some may prefer to delocalize, whereas the political instability will reduce the confidence in the future of the City as a world financial center. We must go back to the long-neglected analysis opposing risk to uncertainty (Knight 1921) as rejuvenated by Keynes and his contemporary followers (Lavoie 2014). This uncertainty has impacted

investment for various sectors (Tetlow et al. 2016). It will be the more so the longer the period before the start of the negotiations and their conclusions.

- The fact that the new Prime Minister had (mildly) supported Remain and that none of the leaders of Brexit tried to form a government suggests a rather different scenario. On one hand, with the progressive recognition of the adverse consequence of Brexit erosion of the purchasing power of wages, less FDI, and productivity increases, a fraction of the voters in favor of Brexit might realize that they had an erroneous assessment of the consequences of their vote upon their economic situation. On the other hand, the ruling elite formed by politicians, financiers, professionals, and media may grasp the opportunity for organizing another poll to get a new parliament that would reconsider such a drastic decision or even organize a new referendum around a slightly different issue.
- Alternatively, long and inconclusive negotiations may convince politicians that EU member states will not accept the UK as belonging to the European market without accepting internal citizens' mobility (Barker 2016). Symmetrically, the European negotiators would be happy with this abandonment of Brexit that would have been a very bad signal for the future of European integration.

These two-tier radical uncertainties—among the variants of Brexit and between Brexit and Remain—will have a negative impact that may be partially compensated by the devaluation of the currency. Initially, although relatively mild in terms of macroeconomic figures, the costs of Brexit could progressively diffuse into the British economy if the representations of the financial community become pessimistic and a recession could tilt public opinion (Artus 2016). Keep in mind the misjudgment by financiers about the consequences of the Lehman Brothers' collapse: seemingly small losses finally accumulated into spillovers triggering the unfolding of the worst crisis since 1929. This is a third source of uncertainty.

10.8.2 Some Possible Futures for the UK's International Relations

This political uncertainty makes quite problematic the setting of an economic strategy in line with the expression of Brexit. The past political alliance was closely associated to a typical finance led in the UK along a variant of the US model; the consequences have been de-industrialization, regional imbalances between declining industrial Northern regions, and booming Southern England under the aegis of financial domination. Finally, inequalities are widening both among wage earners and between working class and upper class. A reply to the Brexiters' demands could be quite diverse (Table 10.8).

- They can be interpreted as the request of *a more inward-looking growth* regime that would restrict opening to world trade, control immigration, and accept a decline of the City in world financial intermediation. This first scenario would

Table 10.8 After BREXIT: some alternative strategies for the UK

	Consequences			
Strategy	Content	Merits	Weaknesses	Likelihood
An isolationist *UK*	WTO regime with EU	An effective reply to Brexiters' demands	Slower productivity, growth and lower living standards	A dull scenario
	An active redistribution policy toward the left behind of globalization	A possible reduction of the great social divide	End of the illusion of a stronger UK	Difficult reduction of over indebtedness
	An industrial policy	A cure of trade deficit	A destruction of past institutional competitive advantages (City, low tax, single market)	A rupture with a secular strategy of opening to the world
Global UK, away from the EU	Multiplicity of FTA with distant partners (China, India, Common Wealth, etc.)	Acceptance of the benefits from international division of labor	Benign neglect for the importance of distance in international trade	Does not address the issue of globalization pushed inequalities
	No special relation with EU	Full control of migration	Long periods (one or two decades) of painful adjustment	Less bargaining power outside the EU
	No change in social policy	Renascent British empire	Decline of the City	A part of wishful thinking
A free zone at the borders of the EU	A hard and aggressive Brexit	A clear choice	UK size prevents the imitation of Singapore or Hong Kong	A probable new rebellion of Brexiters
	A fiscal competition	Britain first: a key political argument	Exacerbation of wage earners' inequality	Poor political sustainability
	Competitive exchange rate	Ruling by dividing the EU	Retaliation by the EU	Ex post worse situation than before Brexit

mean an active innovation and industrial policy to reduce the trade deficit no longer financed by a massive net inflow of FDI and portfolio investment. To gain political legitimacy, an intensive redistribution via taxation and welfare should be welcome. The initial statement by the new Prime Minister after June 23, 2017, pointed to that direction, and the Conservative manifesto reiterates this promise:

> The work of the government under her leadership will be driven not for the benefit of a privileged few but by the interests of ordinary, working families: people who have a job but do not always have job security; people who own their own home but worry about paying the mortgage; people who can just about manage but worry about the cost of living and getting their children into a good school. (The Conservatives 2017, p. 8).

A transitory reduction of productivity and standards of living is to be expected since in the interim period, the UK destroys the many advantages derived from the integration into the Single Market. Those who voted Remain may protest, and some may emigrate toward the next European financial center.

- *A global Britain free from the EU rules* is a second possibility contemplated by the same manifesto.

> The United Kingdom is a global nation. Our history is a global history; our future must be global too. We believe Britain should play an active, leading role in the world. Not because it is our right or inheritance, but because our leadership in the world is the surest way to defend and advance the interests of the British people, and to extend around the world those values that we believe to be right. (ibid., p. 37).

A multiplicity of Free Trade Agreements is supposed to compensate for Brexit, and this recognizes that internationalization is a stimulus to productivity and innovation. Thus, it helps to sustain a better life of the people provided they do not continue to widen income and wealth inequalities. Past historical experience suggests that it is a general feature of these treaties when a strong social democratic tradition is not warranting a fair share of the dividends of internationalization. This scenario assumes that the geopolitical power of the UK will be stronger outside the EU. Such a statement requires discussion, and it raises a paradox: why to look faraway places when until now the more active trade has taken place in Europe?

- Could England become a *tax haven at the margins of the EU?* While explicating her negotiating strategy, the Prime Minister has mentioned several times that:

> Negotiations will undoubtedly be tough, and there will be give and take on both sides, but we continue to believe that no deal is better than a bad deal for the UK. (The Conservatives. 2017:36).

A typically noncooperative game could then imply a currency war to regain the competitiveness lost by higher tariffs of exports to the EU or the City could be transformed into a fully fledged fiscal haven. Can the UK really become a large Singapore or Honk Hong? Will the Brexiters approve this quite extreme strategy that threatens to exacerbate present inequalities? Has the lesson of the interwar rise of economic nationalism been forgotten? Let us hope that this is only a potential threat in order to extract the maximum concessions from the EU.

- None of these strategies successfully reconciles the search for dynamic efficiency with a renewed solidarity pact among all British citizens. Why? It is simply because Brexit was sold to public opinion with the argument that national sovereignty would open a bright economic future: no more any contribution to the EU budget, immense new markets because Brussels regulations were the source of poor British dynamism. In theory, there would be easier financing of welfare once the foreigners were back home and British workers would enjoy better wages once the Polish plumbers and the Italian doctors were replaced by

British citizens. Consequently, more credit could easily be reimbursed by the extra incomes thus generated. All these statements were good for winning the Brexit vote, but as time elapses, they will become obstacles to a more prosperous and fair society. Recognizing this error could open a last and more promising strategy: *back to economic realism.* Europe is bound to evolve toward a multiplicity of adhesion forms within which the UK could easily find its niche. Thus, it would not lose the benefits of four decades of close interactions with the Old Continent.

10.8.3 Narratives and Political Discourses Matter

This analysis stresses the importance of narratives that are necessary to sustain an existing or an emerging growth regime. The politicians in favor of Remain were unable to work out an attractive future, compared with the nirvana promised by the Brexiters. Are there convincing discourses able to correct the misrepresentations that have been so efficient in attracting the votes of the losers of globalization? A prospective about the future of London stresses how difficult this exercise is (Leadbeater 2016). A complete isolation from the world economy would transform London into a modern Petra. This trajectory would be more imposed from outside than chosen by British citizens. According to a second possibility, London could become a national, as opposed to global capital, and this assumes the victory of nationalistic, if not xenophobe discourses. A third scenario would transform London into the equivalent of Hong Kong or Shenzhen, i.e., a special European economic zone. This would mean the deconstruction of the national state with recurring conflicts with the hinterland: a quite difficult transition indeed.

These overlapping strategies could probably be pursued simultaneously, and this "muddling through" would make political discourses quite problematic. Can learning by experimenting and pragmatism define a new political discourse? In such a configuration, Hayek's conceptions would prevail far away from the constructivism associated with previous regimes: Fordism, innovation-led growth, or a regime dominated by finance. This implies a chaotic and long transformation toward a still unknown socioeconomic regime. Understanding how social transformations, economic restructuring, and political discourses interact could define a promising agenda for contemporary research allying socio-economists with a *régulation* approach.

10.9 Conclusion

Understanding the origins and the processes that led to the Brexit vote may enlighten the future of the EU and the risks associated with the pursuit of globalization observed since the 1980s.

1. European integration has proceeded via the succession of severe political crises that have always been overcome by *new advances* in common rules and institutions with the Euro being the achievement of this 60 years old process. The severity of the Euro crisis, not yet totally overcome, and the British referendum both call for a dramatic reappraisal: Greece was nearly excluded from the Eurozone, and in March 2017 the negotiations about the withdrawal of the UK from the EU began. For the first time the basic project of an ever closer economic and political integration is at risk: one member state prefers to get rid of the opportunities and constraints associated with a supranational negotiated order. If its negotiators are successful, it might spark a domino effect against the resilience of the EU. This European crisis could move from *constructive* to become *destructive.*
2. For conventional economic theories, the Brexit vote is *a paradox*: the UK has largely benefited from its adhesion to European integration in 1973, but a fraction of British citizens is ready to accept a significant reduction of their standards of living in exchange for Brexit. Therefore, the abstraction of a representative *homo economicus* is misleading in the assessment of the viability of the EU: the *defense of national sovereignty* is part of a conception of equal dignity for all citizens whatever their economic status or success, and they are right to ask for a voice in the design of an autonomous economic policy. Economic rationality cannot govern political choice, the more so, the more dominant *the passions and the affects* that transcend Cartesian logic.
3. The Brexit vote is the most spectacular event among the rise of anti-European movements all over Europe. It probably means *a turning point* in the long history of the European integration. Previously, the process of supranational rules building delivered economic results that were deemed as positive by the various public opinions: faster growth, less trade frictions among member states, and reduction of currency crises. This *indirect and ex post legitimation* was sufficient to counterbalance the critiques that denounced the democratic gap between the national and European arenas. Since the Euro crisis, the austerity policies led to the dramatic "adjustment" program imposed on Greece and the poor macroeconomic performance of the Old Continent compared to the USA and Asia. The very delegation of so many competences to the European level is more and more challenged: *Brussels' interventions are inefficient and undemocratic* without national parliament control. The Brexit vote captures these sources of protest and becomes the reference for nationalist programs in the rest of Europe.
4. The Brexit raises *another paradox*: why has the belonging of the UK to the EU not been challenged earlier in response to a widely diffuse and strong disbelief about the very objective of the Europeanists, i.e., to progressively forge a new supranational identity? *A series of silent transformations*, long unnoticed by policy makers, can progressively alter the society and the economy; thus, *an event* may brutally reveal to the actors that they now live in a new socioeconomic regime. They discover this rupture via a crisis that is a surprise even for the best informed "experts." It is so for the 2008 world financial and economic crisis and for the 2016 US presidential election. So, Brexit makes apparent *two*

structural changes: first, the intense transformation of jobs under the impact of a finance-led regime favored by a deep internationalization and, second, a polarization of society in terms of expectations and attitudes concerning immigration. The switch that alters the system is the *entry of a new party* that calls for leaving the EU. The tactical call for a referendum turns into a disaster for the elite, massively in favor of Remain. Nevertheless, the very same elite must manage the consequences of the vote since the Brexiters refuse the responsibility for forming a new government.

5. This hypothesis appears to be rather powerful not only for the UK but for many other member states of the EU. On one side, *economic liberalization* of product, labor, and financial markets has been promoted by the European Commission, and it has transformed economic specialization and the hierarchy of jobs. On the other side, at the individual level, the *social polarization* has increased along with the level of education, age, and locality. Similarly, spatial and geographical inequalities have grown, and this makes problematic the national identity. The mapping of the votes confirms the quite different demands addressed to governments, respectively, by the optimist winners and the disappointed losers, as shown, for example, by the 2017 French presidential elections. Nevertheless, the threat over the belonging to the EU is the more severe, the more convincing the political program of *nationalist/populist and anti-immigration parties*. They are present in Denmark, France, Austria, Hungary, the Netherlands, Finland, and finally Italy since the 2018 elections. The Euro crisis had opposed the healthy Northern Europe to a hailing South (Italy, Portugal, Greece, and Spain). The refugee and immigration crisis of the 2015–2016 is exacerbating another divide between Central and Eastern Europe on the issue of internal mobility within the Single Market.
6. The present crisis of the European integration displays an *unprecedented complexity*. Most of the previous ones were focused on quite difficult but single issues such as the future of common agricultural policy, the transformation of the European Monetary System, the adoption of the Euro as the single currency, the rescue of the banks after the Lehman Brothers crisis, and more recently the crisis of sovereign debt of the weakest economies. When these crises occurred, recurrently some experts have anticipated a possible collapse of the EU, since they observed the acute conflicts of interests and conceptions about regional integration. The perils are still more preoccupying at the end of the 2010s because national governments must find *an overall solution to three nagging threats*.

   First, the dysfunctionality of the Eurozone has generated *divergent evolutions* for productivity, standards of living, and economic specialization. This would call for more solidarity, but the resurgence of nationalism is blocking this avenue.

   Second, the transfer of many policies at the EU level has been perceived as a shift from local democratic deliberation to a *technocratic imposition by Brussels of a free market strategy*, far away from the protection that the left behind requires.

   Third, the EU principle states that individual mobility is the necessary complement to the free trade of goods, services, and capital. This hurts the popular belief—generally not confirmed by the literature—that *migrations* are the source of unemployment for domestic workers and welfare and public budget deficits.

Adding up the solutions for each evil (dysfunctional federalism, poor democratization of EU institutions, perceived threat of immigration) takes time and does not delineate any coherent and viable solution. A radical political innovation is needed to give a chance to the revival of a *community spirit*, currently blocked by the legacy of an intergovernmental approach to regional integration.

7. An equivalent uncertainty prevails concerning *the existence of a successful post-Brexit socioeconomic regime* by which the British citizens would be definitely better off than remaining in the EU. Can the long negotiation of new free trade treaties with distant countries replace the access to the large and nearby Single Market? Will FDI and international finance continue to flow to the UK without an easy access to continental European economies and the ECB? Is it realist to consider that the UK can become a tax haven or emulate Singapore as a leading innovation center? Could not the implicit ideology of the Brexit voters imply an inefficient inward-looking model, unable to sustain the reduction of inequalities that would reunite the UK? Can the breaking down of the UK be prevented if the final agreement with the EU is not agreed upon by Scotland? Or if no solution is found to the Irish border dilemma: Ireland still in the EU. Northern Ireland out but no real frontier between them? If on the contrary a hard Brexit takes place, will not the Brexiters reassess their position and admit their possible dramatic error and their contribution to the—unintended—second secular decline of the UK?

Bettering our understanding of Brexit is an important task for both the nationalist and Europeanist agenda: what will be the direction of the bifurcation? It is also a social laboratory experiment about the future of globalization, regional integrations, and the possible revival of economic nationalism.

References

Aglietta M, Leron N (2017) La Double Démocratie. Une Europe politique pour la croissance. Seuil, Paris

Allen K (2018) Are the UK's political polls wrong again? Financial Times. February 28th

Amable B (2003) The diversity of modern capitalism. Oxford University Press, Oxford

Amable B (2017) Structural crisis and institutional change in modern capitalism; French capitalism in transition. Oxford University Press, Oxford

Amable B, Palombarini S (2017) L'illusion du bloc bourgeois. Raisons d'agir, Paris

Artus P (2016). Brexit: le choc économique est de petite taille, mais les effets peuvent venir de l'incertitude, de l'aversion pour le risque, des effets de richesse.... Flash Economie. n° 734. 7 juillet. Natixis, Paris

Ashcroft L (2016) How the United Kingdom voted on Thursday...and why. Friday 24th June. http://lordashcroftpolls.com/2016/06/how-the-united-kingdom-voted-and-why

Barker A (2016) Four scenarios: how Brexit process could unfold. Nasty, neutral or friendly... or it might not happen at all. Financial Times. July 20th. http://www.ft.com/cms/s/0/5ec21720-49c1-11e6-8d68-72e9211e86ab.html#axzz4G4w8DlpE

Bartel L (2002) Economic inequality and political representation. Department of Politics and Woodrow Wilson School of Public and International Affairs. Princeton University, Princeton, November

BBC (2016) The 23 June 2016 referendum vote. www.bbc.com/news/UK-politics-36616028

Beckert J (2016) Imagined futures. Fictional expectations and capitalist dynamics. Oxford University press, Oxford

Binzer Hobolt S (2009) Europe in question: referendums on European integration. Published to Oxford Scholarship online, Oxford, May. http://www.oxfordscholarship.com/view/10.1093/acprof:oso/9780199549948.001.0001/acprof-9780199549948

Bourdieu P (2017) Anthropologie économique - Cours au Collège de France 1992–1993. Raisons d'Agir. Seuil, Paris

Boyer R (2000) The unanticipated fallout of European monetary union: the political and institutional deficits of the euro. In: Crouch C (ed) After the euro. Oxford University Press, Oxford, pp 24–88

Boyer R (2013) Origins and ways out of the Euro crisis. Rev Polit Econ 25(1):1–38

Boyer R (2014) Mundos de la desigualdad (los): un analisis a partir de la teoria de la regulation y una respuesta a Thomas Piketty. Buenos Aires, Editorial Octubre

Boyer R (2015a) L'accord entre Athènes et ses créanciers est inefficace et dangereux. *Le Monde.* 4 septembre, p 6

Boyer R (2015b) Economie politique des capitalismes. La Découverte, Paris

Boyer R (2016) From economics as fiction to fiction-led capitalism. In: Coste J-H, Dussol V (eds) *Representations of capitalism in American fiction.* Routledge, London To be published

Calmfors L (1997) EMU: a Swedish perspective. Kluwer: Academic Publisher, Boston

Clarke D, Goodwin M, Whiteley P (2017) Brexit why Britain voted to leave the European Union. University of Essex Publication

Cowley P, Wager A (2018) Brexit and public opinion. The UK in a Changing Europe, pp 29–31. http://ukandeu.ac.uk/wp-content/uploads/2018/01/Public-Opinion.pdf

Dhingra S, Ottaviano G, Sampson T, Van Reenen J (2016a) The consequences of Brexit for UK trade and living standards. http://cep.lse.ac.uk/pubs/download/brexit02.pdf

Dhingra S Ottaviano G, Sampson T, Van Reenen J (2016b) The impact of Brexit on foreign investment in the UK. LSE. http://cep.lse.ac.uk/pubs/download/brexit08_book.pdf#page=40

Dhingra S, Ottaviano G, Van Reenen J (2016c) Brexit and the impact immigration on the UK. LSE. http://ceplseacuk/pubs/download/brexit05pdf. October 2017

Elliott M, Kanagasooriam J (2017) Public opinion in the post-Brexit era: economic attitudes in modern Britain. https://www.li.com/activities/publications/public-opinion-in-the-post-brexit-era-economic-attitudes-in-modern-britain

Equality Trust (2013) How has inequality changed. https://www.equalitytrust.org.uk/how-has-inequality-changed

European Community (2016a) Eurobarometer. July

European Community (2016b) Economic forecast. Winter, February

Evans G (2018) Voting in the 2017 general election: a Brexit election? In The UK in a Changing Europe .Brexit and public opinion, pp 15–17. http://ukandeu.ac.uk/wp-content/uploads/2018/01/Public-Opinion.pdf

Financial Times (2017) Theresa May's 9 U-turns, May 22. https://www.ft.com/content/e021c208-3ede-11e7-9d56-25f963e998b2

Fligstein N (2008) Euroclash, the EU, European identity, and the future of Europe. Oxford University Press, Oxford

Fligstein N, Sweet AS (2002) Constructing polities and markets: an institutionalist account of European integration. Am J Sociol 107(5):1206–1243

Frank RH (1988) Passions within reason. The strategic role of emotions. Norton, New York

Frank T (2005) What's the matter with Kansas? How conservatives won the heart of America. Holt, Paperback

Gasiorek M, Serwicka I, Smith R (2018) Which manufacturing sectors are most vulnerable to Brexit?. UK trade policy observatory. Briefing paper 16 February
Gilles C (2017) Three visions of UK economy take shape on verge of Brexit talks. 12 March. https://www.ft.com/.../a73023ce-034f-11e7-aa5b-6bb07f5c8e12
Goodhart D (2017) The road to somewhere: the populist revolt and the future of politics. Hurst and Co, London
Goodwin M (2018) The perceived costs and benefits of Brexit. In The UK in a changing Europe. Brexit and public opinion. pp 24–26. http://ukandeu.ac.uk/wp-content/uploads/2018/01/Public-Opinion.pdf
Gouez A (2017) Le Brexit et l'imbroglio frontalier irlandais. Policy paper n°210. Institut Jacques Delors, novembre
Gramsci A (1978) Cahiers de prison. Gallimard, Paris
Green RA (2016) Brexit poll: six months on. Brits stand by EU referendum decision CNN, December 19
Gudgin G, Coutts K, Gibson N (2016) The macro-economic impact of Brexit: using the CBR macro-economic model of the UK economy (UKMOD). WP 483. Center for Business Research. University of Cambridge, December
Habermas J (2013) Demokratie oder Kapitalismous?. Blätter für deutsche und internationale Politik 5:59–70
HM Treasury 2016a. HM Treasury analysis: the immediate economic impact of leaving the EU. May. https://www.gov.uk/government/publications/hm-treasury-analysis-the-immediate-economic-impact-of-leaving-the-eu
HM Treasury 2016b. HM Treasury analysis: the long-term economic impact of EU membership and the alternatives. www.gov.uk/government/publication
Hobol SB, Leeper T, Tilley J 2018) Emerging Brexit identities. In The UK in a Changing Europe Brexit and public opinion, pp 18–20 http://ukandeu.ac.uk/wp-content/uploads/2018/01/Public-Opinion.pdf
Hooghe L, Marks G (2008) A post functionalist theory of European integration: From permissive consensus to constraining dissensus. Br J Polit Sci 39:1–23
House of Commons (2018) EU exit analysis cross Whitehall briefing. Exiting the European Union Committee, January. https://www.parliament.uk/documents/commons-committees/Exiting-the-European-Union/17-19/Cross-Whitehall-briefing/EU-Exit-Analysis-Cross-Whitehall-Brief ing.pdf
Jackson N (2016) Comment les sondages sur le Brexit ont raté la victoire du « Leave ». Huffipost. 24 juin. http://www.huffingtonpost.fr/2016/06/24/sondages-brexit-rate-leave_n_10654474.html
Jullien F (2009) Les transformations silencieuses. Grasset / Fasquelle, Paris
Kahneman D, Tversky A (1984) Choices, values, and frames. Am Psychol 39:341–350
Knight F (1921) Risk. uncertainty and profit. Hart. Schaffner & Marx/Mifflin Co, Boston/ Houghton
Korski D (2016) Why we lost the Brexit vote. Behind the scenes of the flawed campaign to keep the UK in the EU. Politico 20 October. Why we lost the Brexit vote. https://www.politico.eu/article/why-we-lost-the-brexit-vote-former-uk-prime-minister-david-cameron/
Lavoie M (2014) Post-Keynesian economics: new foundations. Edward Elgar Publishing Ltd, Cheltenham
Leadbeater C (2016) London's future: a brief guide. Five scenarios for the city post-Brexit, from 'renationalised' British capital to European enclave. Financial Times, July 23th–24th, p 1, "Life & Arts"
Levell P (2018) Firms' supply chains form an important part of UK-EU trade: what does this mean for future trade policy? Institute for Fiscal Studies, 8 January
Lordon F (2016) Les affects de la politique. Seuil, Paris
Luhmann N (1997) Theory of society. Stanford University Press, Stanford

Maddock R (2017) The rise and fall of UKIP. Financial Time Weekend Magazine, May 27/28, pp 12–17
Mauss M (1925) Essai sur le don. Forme et raison de l'échange dans les sociétés archaïques. Reprint Quadrige /Presses Universitaires de France, 2007
May T (2017) Theresa may confirms: Britain is heading for Brexit Max. The Economist, January 17. https://www.economist.com/blogs/bagehot/2017/01/countdown-2019
May T (2018) The May's mansion house discourse. 2 March. http://brexitcentral.com/full-text-theresa-mays-mansion-house-speech/http://brexitcentral.com/full-text-theresa-mays-mansion-house-speech/
McCarthy N (2014) Far-right leads Eurosceptic earthquake, May 26. https://www.statista.com/chart/2293/far-right-leads-eurosceptic-earthquake/
Monnet J (1988) Mémoires. Fayard, Paris
Nardelli A (2018) Brexit analysis says the UK will be worse off in every scenario. January 29. BuzzFeed News Europe. https://www.buzzfeed.com/albertonardelli/the-governments-own-brexit-analysis-says-the-uk-will
NatCen Social Research (2015) British social attitudes. Social class. p 13
NatCen Social Research (2016) Brexit: what will it mean for Britain? Findings from British Social attitudes 2015
Nauro C, Coricelli F, Moretti L. (2014) Economic growth and political integration; estimating the benefits from membership in the European Union using the synthetic counterfactuals methods. DP n° 8162. IZA. Bonn, Germany
Nauro C, Coricelli F, Moretti L (2015) Norwegian rhapsody? The political economic benefits of regional integration. DP n° 9098. IZA, Bonn
Nelson J (2017) Nature abhors a vacuum: sex, emotion, loyalty and the rise of illiberal economics. Real-World Econ Rev Issue n° 79:35–42. http://www.paecon.net/PAEReview/issue79/Nelson79.pdf
Nickell S, Saleheen J (2015) The impact of immigration on occupational wages: evidence from Britain. Bank of England. Staff Working Paper N° 574, 18 December
OECD (2016) The economic consequences of Brexit: a taxing decision. OECD economic, policy paper, April No. 16
Palombarini S (2001) La Rupture du compromis social italien. Éditions du CNRS, Paris
Petit E (2015) Economie des émotions. La Découverte, Paris
Piketty T (2014) Capital in the 21st century. Harvard University Press, London
Piketty T, Hennette S, Sacriste G, Vauchez A (2017) Pour un traité de démocratisation de l'Europe. Seuil, Paris
Pisani-Ferry J.et al (2016). Europe after Brexit: a proposal for a continental partnership, 29 August
Poulantzas N (1968) Pouvoir politique et classes sociales de l'état capitaliste. Maspero, Paris
Renwick A (2018) The citizens' assembly on Brexit. In: The UK in a changing Europe, Brexit and public opinion, pp 32–35. http://ukandeu.ac.uk/wp-content/uploads/2018/01/Public-Opinion.pdf
Renwick AS, Jennings W, Mckee R, Russell M, Smith G (2017) A considered public voice on Brexit: the report of the citizens' assembly on Brexit. The Constitution Unit. UCL, London http://citizensassembly.co.uk/wp-content/uploads/2017/12/Citizens-Assembly-on-Brexit-Report.pdf
Sassen S (2014) Expulsions: brutality and complexity in the global economy. Belknap Press/ Harvard University Press, Harvard
Schmitter PC (2012) European disintegration? A way forward. J Democracy 4:39–48
Schmitter Philippe and Zoe Lefkofridi (2015) Neo-functionalism as a theory of disintegration 'European Disintegration – a blind spot of integration theory? 22nd CES conference, Paris
Société de Législation Comparée (2011) Théorie et pratiques du référendum. Actes de la journée d'étude du 4 novembre. Collection Colloques. Vol. 17. Université Panthéon Assas Paris II. Centre d'études constitutionnelles et politique – Institut Cujas

Stiglitz J (2016) The Euro: and its threat to the future of Europe. Allen Lane
Streeck W (2014) Buying Time: the delayed crisis of democratic capitalism. Verso, London/New York
Tetlow G, Cadman E, Giles C (2016) Brexit barometer: slowdown fears vie with investment optimism. Financial Times, July 29th. http://www.ft.com/cms/s/0/d3e8002a-53e2-11e6-9664-e0bdc13c3bef.html#axzz4G4w8DlpE
The Conservatives (2017) The conservative and unionist party. Manifesto 2017. Forward together. Our plan for a stronger Britain and prosperous future
The Economist (2016a) An aggravating absence. Britain's decision to leave the European Union will cause soul searching across the continent – and beyond. July 2nd–8th, pp 19–22
The Economist (2016b) Drawbridges up: the new divide in rich countries is not between left and right but between open and closed, July 20th–August 5th, pp 14–16
The UK in a Changing Europe (2018) Brexit and public opinion. http://ukandeu.ac.uk/wp-content/uploads/2018/01/Public-Opinion.pdf
Tilford S 2016) Brexit Britain: the poor man of Western Europe? September. http://cer.eu/publications/archive/policy-brief/2016/brexit-britain-poor-man-western-europe
Whitman R (2016) The EEA: a safe harbour in the Brexit storm, 27 June. https://www.chathamhouse.org/expert/comment/eea-safe-harbour-brexit-storm
Wyplosz C (2016) La révolte mondiale des sans-grade. http://www.slate.fr/story/118281/revolte-mondiale-sans-grade#
You Gov (2016) How Britain voted, June 23–24. https://yougov.uk/new/2016/06/27/howBritainvoted

Chapter 11
Ways Out of the Eurozone Crisis: Some Alternative European Scenarios

Jacques Mazier, Pascal Petit, and Dominique Plihon

11.1 Introduction: An Overview of the Impasse Facing the EU

One has to take a mid-long-term view of the challenges that the EU had to face to assess how to get out of its actual impasse. The 1970s stands as a major turning phase where two challenges emerged. The first one is directly linked with the collapse of the gold exchange standard and the necessity to restructure the international relations accordingly. The neoliberal option, giving full priority to market mechanisms, largely boosted by the US and the UK governments, became the dominant motto within the EU and strongly impacted its integration process. The second challenge came from the rising acknowledgment of the limits to growth, e.g., the fact that current processes of production and consumption were not sustainable as some resources were nonrenewable and some activities were deteriorating the environment. A report to the US president [1]and the report of the Club of Rome (1972)[2] were both very clear on the emergency to respond to these challenges. Still this second challenge had a limited impact on the EU integration process, beyond a leading role in the Kyoto Protocol. By and large these warnings were rather minimalized and partly considered as controversial until the last decade. In the 2000s, the deterioration of the environment started to raise the credit of these warnings, stressing increasingly the negative impact of human activities on the climate and the environment. This relative inertia to meet this second challenge was also tied to the idea that the neoliberalization of markets could have coped with it setting up a new

[1]The Charney Report to Jimmy Carter (1979) was both pretty clear and pressing for action.
[2]*Limits to Growth* by Meadows et al. (1972).

J. Mazier (✉) · P. Petit · D. Plihon
University Paris 13 Sorbonne Paris Cité, Paris, France
e-mail: mazier@univ-paris13.fr; pascal.petit@ens.fr

R. Boyer et al. (eds.), *Evolving Diversity and Interdependence of Capitalisms*, Evolutionary Economics and Social Complexity Science 11,
https://doi.org/10.1007/978-4-431-55001-3_11

governance of the world economy which would have faced the environmental challenge. It rapidly turned out in the 2000s that such would not be the case. The first reason for such inaction is that market liberalization benefitted in the first place to the financial sector, inducing a mobility of capital and a pressure in favor of short-term financial results for the shareholders. This short termism clearly hampered taking into account the long-term investments required by the environmental challenge.

Meanwhile the neoliberal turn followed by the EU had detrimental effects on the integration process. It has pushed to the construction of a poorly designed eurozone, unable to cope with the disequilibria induced by the international financial crises, favored by the global diffusion of the neoliberal turn.

This chapter will in its second section explore the incoherence of the euro regime and how it prevents the EU to get out of the crisis, brought by the worldwide neoliberal economic turn and the ensuing global financial crises. The third section considers how some sharing of the debt burden, induced by the crisis, could help to overcome the inequalities brought by a too rigid eurozone regime. The fourth section investigates whether a more flexible euro regime could have avoided the divergences that increased in the EU after the global financial crisis, which even split the old typology of the varieties of the EU capitalisms, leading to single-out Germany. Section 11.5 finally checks how, facing at last the second major challenge, e.g., the environmental one could open the way to investment policies toward sustainable EU development goals, reversing the diverging trends provoked by a lasting systematic reliance on straightforward market mechanisms.

This liberalization of finance has been one of the major factors of these divergences, with mobile industries tempted to localize worldwide their production processes, according to wage levels and other competitive advantages. Specific EU investment schemes such as the structural funds were not large enough to overcome the competition from low wage (or low-energy price) countries. This process of internationalization/delocalization was also fueled by internationalized trading houses (like Wallmart and the like) and audit firms as well as other specific business services. The same process of liberalization of finance, allowing capital mobility, boosted speculative runs on various currencies. Exchange rate crises soon appeared in the 1990s as the most pressing danger. The 1997 financial crisis showed how unsteady was this liberal globalization of finance. One has to recall that the eurozone was created, clearly prematurely, under such pressure of speculative runs.[3] Needless to say, the collapse of the Soviet block at the turn of the 1990s pushed further the trend of product market liberalization and especially its financial dimension. This globalized finance was not any better in supporting investments in innovative industries. Financial support for dot.com enterprises led the way to speculative runs ending in the dot.com crisis of 2001. The shortsightedness of the finance industry, being so bluntly demonstrated in the domain of innovative investments, turned in the

[3]Whereby most European currencies had to align with the deutsche mark, by then the strongest European currency, against the dollar.

2000s toward more traditional fields, e.g., lending to government and administrative bodies or households but with new instruments, diluting the risks or passing it over to official bodies warranting the loans. These "innovations" of the finance industry altogether fueled various speculative runs, in particular in housing. Construction thus fueled economic growth in countries like the USA, the UK, Spain, or Ireland (the country models for the OECD at the turn of the century). No wonder that it led rapidly to a financial crisis, initiated by the US subprime crisis in 2007. The same exhilarating financial activity (to quote Nobel Prize winner Schiller) had fueled debt increases of public bodies, from cities and local administrations to national governments. Chiefly this widespread rise in indebtment weakened the capacity of these public bodies to react to the detrimental effects of the financial crisis. The social costs of an increased unemployment induced by the economic recession that followed the global financial crisis and the costs of bailing out enterprises (most of them financial) bankrupted by this very financial crisis raised public expenditures to unprecedented levels, which had to be faced by further indebtment. EU countries, especially from the south of Europe, were differently affected and unequally able to borrow at reasonable rates. It fueled speculative runs against the weakest EU countries, betting that they will be forced out of the eurozone.

In less than 3 years, the global financial crisis had led to a crisis of the euro. Since then the EU and especially the eurozone have been marred in a lasting economic stagnation which is largely due to the austerity policy imposed on all members suppressing all room for manoeuver to get out of the crisis. This has been widely reckoned, even by orthodox economists.[4] Major institutions such as the IMF are also reconsidering the relevance of such policy. The ECB has itself slightly moved away from this strict austerity policy, announcing in mid-2012 it will help countries under speculative attacks, all of which led to a pause in the euro crisis. Still recovery is too slow, and austerity policies are still too binding and uniquely aimed at down pressing wages to get out of stagnation, giving credit to a threat of deflation. Meanwhile in this process of stagnation, inequalities among EU countries have increased, especially in terms of competitiveness, e.g., in their abilities to find their place in the international economy in which they are by now largely integrated. All this leads to forecast a widening of the gap between EU members if the same policy is maintained (see Table 11.1).

[4]Last but not the least was the Nobel Prize winner Christopher Sims at an international conference held in Lindau in Germany in August 2014.

Table 11.1 Per capita GDP relative to the European average without new policies

	Estimate	Projections	
	2013	2020	2030
Nordic countries	138	153	173
Germany	123	133	147
Other Western Europe (NL, BE, LU, AT, CH)	136	135	135
UK	118	109	88
France	113	102	87
Italy	94	94	87
Spain	94	89	87
Other Southern Europe (GR, PO, IE)	84	82	80
Poland	66	67	82
Other Eastern Europe	51	53	60

Source: CAM scenario N2, January 2014 (Eatwell et al. 2014)

11.2 The Trap of the Single Currency

11.2.1 A Dividing Tool from Its Start

The euro resulted from a political compromise between France and Germany which paid little attention to economic realities. France wanted to avoid simply being integrated into an expanded mark zone. Germany agreed to the elimination of the mark in return for the acceptance of its reunification but imposed its own rules. The initial compromise of 1992 presupposed a limited eurozone because it was thought that the restrictive Maastricht criteria for inflation and public finances would prevent the two main southern countries – Italy and Spain – from participating. But the adjustment efforts made by these countries in the first half of the 1990s so as not to be left outside allowed them to qualify although the criteria were far from being strictly satisfied, especially as regards the level of public debt in Italy.

In fact, inflation and real interest rate differentials were not eliminated among northern and southern countries in the eurozone for nearly a decade. At the beginning of the 2000s, the debt securities of Greece, Spain, or Portugal appeared to be equivalent to German debt securities. This led to an investment boom, stimulated by low real interest rates, with capital flowing in from Northern Europe, including massive speculation in Spanish and Irish real estate. Growth was slower in Germany, held back by higher real interest rates and wage adjustments under the Schröder reforms of the early 2000s. This apparent convergence disguised important imbalances. There was a wide divergence in unit wage costs with, in relative terms, big increases in Spain, Ireland, Greece, and Italy and falls in Austria, Finland, and, above all, Germany. Current account imbalances widened enormously, with deficits in the South in contrast to surpluses in the North. But these current account disequilibria were regarded as a secondary matter in the monetary union where the overall current account was close to balance. Rather, the key issue for governance in the eurozone was seen as government deficits and debts. Here things seemed to be going well:

European countries had reduced their public sector deficits; Germany returned to balance in 2007, while Spain, Portugal, and Ireland were regarded as models of budgetary rigor in complete conformity to the Maastricht norms.

On the eve of the global financial crisis of 2008, the wide disequilibria due to heterogeneity appeared to be hidden. They were characterized by an undervalued euro for countries in the German bloc and an overvalued euro for the countries of Southern Europe (including France), while for the eurozone as a whole, the euro was close to its equilibrium value (Duwicquet et al. 2013). These misalignments of real exchange rates among the countries of the eurozone were the source of important transfers at the expense of the export sector of countries with an overvalued exchange rate and to the advantage of export sectors of countries where there was an undervaluation. Taking into account the size and the degree of openness of the different economies, it can be estimated that, for a misalignment of 10% in the real exchange rate, the implicit transfers are of the order of +4% to +5% of GDP for Germany and − 3% to −4% for France, Italy, and Spain.

These misalignments of exchange rates reflected the structural heterogeneity between Northern and Southern Europe, with France in several respects in an intermediate position. The north of Europe is more specialized in manufactures, while the south of Europe is increasingly specialized in non-tradeable goods. The size of industrial firms is clearly smaller in Greece, Portugal, Spain, and Italy than in the rest of Europe. In general, small firms have lower productivity. Innovation efforts are significantly weaker in the South than in the North, and the active population is clearly less qualified.

11.2.2 The Incoherence of the Eurozone Regime

The financial crisis of 2008 revealed these disequilibria. Our contention is that a monetary union between heterogeneous countries with no other adjustment mechanisms than wage deflation can only lead to divergent evolutions and rising intra-European disequilibrium with a polarization of economic activity on the most competitive block. To face the eurozone crisis, European governments have generalized austerity policies in order to achieve internal devaluations and reduce the public deficits. New European institutions and rules were designed to achieve this financial objective (European Stability Mechanism, Outright Monetary Transactions, Banking Union, Quantitative Easing, Capital Markets Union). But the monetary and financial federalism monitored by the ECB (European Central Bank), combined with the rules of the Fiscal Treaty, cannot solve the eurozone crisis.

The nonconventional monetary policy of quantitative easing (QE) of the ECB, put in place in 2012, had more limited effects than thought. QE is not allowed to absorb more than one third of the debt of any issuer of bonds, and bond purchases have to be in proportion to the economic weight of the country concerned. This rule limits the assistance which can be given to countries in difficulty and makes it difficult over time to keep the promise of *whatever it takes.*[5] The limits on purchases of German bonds are close to being reached – it is the largest economy but with a declining amount of debt – while it would be easy to buy more Italian bonds but that would exceed the Italian quota. Moderation of the rules would be necessary (raise the fraction of debt that can be bought to 50%, for example, and permit bond purchases above the economic weight of the country concerned), but this would be difficult to negotiate. The provision of emergency liquidity assistance (ELA) to banks which are solvent but under pressure raises a further problem: the decision is taken by the central bank of the country concerned and not, as would be logical, by the EU-level authority responsible for banking supervision. Here again we see the incomplete nature of the federal project and the different levels of confidence in different countries.

ECB policy poses a further problem. The ECB has helped to put out the fire or, at least, to stop it spreading. QE has only been effective to a limited extent. By adding to liquidity, the ECB policy was meant to reinforce the low interest rates and to encourage the banks to increase their loans or to buy financial assets. It has had only a limited impact on real growth and inflation. Most of the liquidity created by the ECB has gone toward financial markets, both in the eurozone, pushing up the price of assets, and outside, with a corresponding outflow of capital and a decline in the euro exchange rate. The very low interest rates did not have a strong impact on productive investment because of the low level of demand and a climate of uncertainty which favors the holding of financial assets. The two main channels through which QE has affected the economy are the boom on financial markets which can give rise to wealth effects on expenditure but also lead to dangerous asset price bubbles and the depreciation of the euro which can advantage sectors producing tradable goods and services. All in all, the unconventional monetary policy implemented by the ECB had limited effects on the real economy.

Given the weak state of the economy, equity prices seem very high with the possible development of a financial bubble. The risk of a bubble on bond markets is even more worrying. European banks and central banks have bought enormous quantities of bonds. If bond prices should fall because of a political crisis, because of financial problems in one country, or because interest rates rise in the rest of the world, there could be significant losses on bond holdings which, in the last resort, would impact on the central bank. The central bank would have to recognize the losses in its accounts, and this would require it to be recapitalized. In itself this can be a difficult operation. It would be all more difficult in the eurozone because, unlike the Fed in the USA, the central bank is not backed by a single state but by 17 states. Recapitalization of the European system of central banks would be financed by all member states in proportion to their share in its capital, while it might be only one country, or a limited number of them, which was involved in the losses on bonds. This could make the operation even more complex.

[5]To echo the statement in July 2012 of Mario Draghi, director of the ECB, to show his commitment to defend the euro.

Finally, even though current account imbalances have been reduced, overall payment imbalances are still widening. The ECB plays the role of a clearing house and records in its TARGET2 (Trans-European Automated Real-time Gross settlement Express Transfer) system the deficits of the South and the surpluses of the North, that is, for each country, the sum of its current account and net inflows of capital. Until 2008 the current account deficits of the South were matched by capital inflows so that the TARGET2 system as a whole was close to balance. Since 2009 this has no longer been the case. The deficits and surpluses now being registered in TARGET2 reflect net outflows of capital from South to North which cannot be sustained indefinitely because they arise from a loss of confidence by investors in the countries concerned. These deficits rose even further in 2016 and reached very high sums for Italy and Spain because of the size of the two countries. In the American case, where *Fedwire* is the equivalent of TARGET2, supervisory mechanisms exist at the level of the regional central banks. Balances are brought back close to equilibrium every year through incentives for local banks to help finance intra-regional imbalances and, above all, by asset transfers among the regional central banks. Such mechanisms do not exist at the level of the eurozone, and, in present circumstances, it is hard to envisage them, given the incomplete character of European integration.

11.2.3 In Spite of Everything, a Sustainable Regime?

In a context of continuing tension, some modifications can be seen since 2015. Wages have risen more in Germany under pressure from IG Metall, and infrastructure investment (becoming in any case increasingly necessary) has been relaunched. Although these changes are much less than Germany could achieve, they head in the right direction. At EU level the Juncker investment plan, launched in 2015, contains some very impressive numbers, but one should not be mistaken. In theory 315 billion euros of additional investment are expected by the end of 2018, that is, 0.8% of EU GDP and an increase in investment of 4% per year. In practice the Juncker plan is to be managed by the EIB (European Investment Bank) where a special fund has been set up but endowed with only 21 billion euros (of which 16 are being raised from an existing line of credit). The EIB can lend up to 60 billion by borrowing. The rest must come from the participation in the plan of other public or private investors. Overall, although the size of the plan has been increased to 500 billion and its period of operation extended to 2020, the value added by the plan is very small. These difficulties remind us of the problems faced by European-level plans to relaunch investment since the 1980s.

Macroeconomic conditions in several countries have improved somewhat since 2015, sustained by the depreciation of the euro, the fall in petroleum prices, and a slight relaxation of the severe budgetary constraints imposed by the European Commission. One should not build false hopes on this slightly sunnier interval – and this for two reasons. Firstly, although a real recovery is taking place in the eurozone in 2017 and 2018, unemployment remains very high in the south of the zone, and income inequalities are still wide. All this leads to persistent social tensions. Secondly, destabilizing factors remain, with high levels of both public and private debt, fragile banks, and the threat of higher interest rates to come. There continue to be serious misalignments of real exchange rates among the countries of the zone, mainly at the advantage of Germany. For countries where the real exchange rate does not adjust, this means a slow asphyxiation as illustrated by the French and Italian cases. The sustainability of the eurozone growth regime in the absence of thoroughgoing reforms remains a completely open question.

Persistence with a growth regime which performs so badly may seem surprising. It is to be explained by the interests of two groups – on the one hand, the countries of Northern Europe and on the other the European elite. The first, grouped around Germany, benefit from an undervalued currency and do reasonably well, even if they are affected by the weakness of the southern countries. The small, very open economies can also adapt more easily. The second, the "European elite," consisting of the dominant strata in industry and finance and the European technocracy, uses the crisis to deepen and extend neoliberal policies: increased flexibility on the labor market; reduction in social expenditures leading households to resort increasingly to private insurance; tighter budgetary frameworks to reduce the role of the state and relaunch the process of privatization; refusal to increase taxes on financial revenues; high incomes or big wealth holdings, which have all seen considerable tax reductions; and failure to impose adequate constraints on the financial sector. These express also the relative indifference to developments in the internal market of the big European corporations which are more global than European.

The present contribution wants to stress nevertheless that there are ways, quite feasible, e.g., without running risks of dramatic economic collapses, to get out of this impasse, while the pursuit of austerity policies runs the risks of provoking major social and economic crisis.

We hereafter consider three alternative ways out.

One will investigate to which extent a more open approach on public debts, based on both a wider solidarity between EU members and a wider range of publicly controlled financial instruments, could do the job (Sect. 11.3).

The other way out will appreciate how the straight jacket of a unique euro could be overcome in allowing strictly monitored adjustments of "national" currencies (Sect. 11.4).

The third option will stress the opportunity to quit austerity policies for investment schemes, fully legitimized and pragmatic in helping both to face the environmental challenge and to reduce the competitive gap between member countries (Sect. 11.5).

To support these assessments and stress the feasibility of their policy recommendations, we shall draw on the work of calibration done in a European project AUGUR (www.augurproject.eu). The project used a world model (CAM) of blocs[6] with detailed coverage of trade and the balance of payments with separate subsystems for primary products, energy, manufactures, services, income transfers, and capital movements that make it possible to investigate the influence of world markets and financial flows on each bloc and the transmission of policy adjustments across blocs (see Cripps 2014). The impact of exchange rate movements on each component of the current account is represented explicitly, and the model is closed by assumptions about adjustment of domestic spending and inflation in each block. Long-term accumulation of government debt, bank lending and deposits, exchange reserves, and other external assets and liabilities are tracked in money terms and as a ratio to GDP. Projected outcomes include employment, productivity, per capita income, and government spending on goods and services (Eatwell et al. 2014; Mazier et al. 2013).

11.3 Sharing the Sovereign Debt Burden

The majority of EU member states are now highly indebted in the sense that the ratio of government debt to GDP exceeds the 60% ceiling laid down by the Stability and Growth Pact, and budget deficits are far in excess of the 0.5–1.0% objective for the structural deficit prescribed by the Stability Pact. As budget cuts are perpetuating stagnation, it is very difficult for governments to bring deficits down to the prescribed level, and debt-to-GDP ratios may remain high or even increase for a long time to come. Table 11.2 shows the projected outcome under the assumption that

Table 11.2 Government debt and deficits without new policies

	Government debt as % of GDP			Government surplus or deficit as % of GDP		
	2013	2020	2030	2013	2020	2030
Europe	87	90	74	−4.5	−0.8	−1.7
Nordic countries	45	49	60	1.6	1.7	0.7
Germany	78	63	60	−1.0	0.5	−1.0
Other Western Europe (NL, BE, LU, AT, CH)	74	83	73	−4.1	−1.8	−2.6
UK	93	92	83	−6.1	−1.1	−2.1
France	92	108	98	−5.0	−2.0	−2.7
Italy	133	127	93	−6.3	−1.6	−2.8
Spain	93	124	87	−9.6	−1.9	−1.8
Other Southern Europe (GR, PO, IE)	155	181	121	−9.6	−1.8	−1.6
Poland	65	60	45	−5.1	−0.9	−2.7
Other Eastern Europe	52	54	43	−3.4	−0.2	−1.6

Source: CAM scenario N2, January 2014 (Eatwell et al. 2014)

[6]The model distinguishes five subregions of Europe (North, South, East, West, and the UK), four large countries (USA, Japan, China, India), and ten other country groups in the rest of the world.

current policies and institutions are maintained unchanged. Debt ratios in most countries remain at around their present level or increase in the period up to 2020 and decline gradually thereafter. Budget deficits fall in the next few years in response to cuts and stabilize or increase slowly in the 2020s. The gap is widening between Nordic countries, with government surplus, and other countries of the Union which continue to experience government deficits.

The prospects are that the new fiscal policy rules will no more be enforced than those in force before 2008. The major reason for this outcome is that austerity policies are counterproductive and lead to slower growth and hence to a mechanical increase in the debt-to-GDP ratio. A major concern is ongoing financial risks. Highly indebted member states will remain under pressure and largely unprotected in the event of a new crisis. No government will want to ask for assistance from the ESM (European Stability Mechanism) given the strict conditions and de facto loss of sovereignty that this implies, as experienced by the Greek government. There is a risk of financial instability, as southern countries of the eurozone, including France, may be under speculative attacks, since they will not be able to reduce the burden of their sovereign debt.

To summarize, the above projections (Table 11.2) suggest that the perpetuation of current policies aiming at reducing deficits and debts of governments is not sustainable for three reasons. First, it will have a depressing impact on the eurozone with high social costs. Second, heterogeneity and imbalances will increase among countries in the eurozone. Third, there is a high risk of new crises on government bond markets in the future. This risk will be amplified by the coming upward trend in interest rates due to the decision of large central banks to exit progressively from low interest rate policies in the near future.

A way out of such a difficult situation is a more open approach of the management of government debt, based on a wider solidarity among country members of the eurozone. In fact, three types of policies could be implemented to achieve a process of mutualization of government debts in the euro area: (1) the restructuration of government debts, (2) intervention of the ECB on the government bond market, and (3) issuance of Eurobonds.

(1) *Restructuring government debts*. Several southern countries of the eurozone have accumulated unsustainable public debts because their high level of debt reduces economic growth and prevents the use of fiscal policy, the only macroeconomic instrument left in a monetary union. The implication is that public debts must be restructured in these countries, at least in the smallest ones like Greece and Portugal which face major difficulties and for which the cost of debt restructuring is not too high. The problem is more delicate for larger countries like Spain, or even France and Italy, where the size of the public debt is more important. Several proposals have been put forward. One plan involves the creation of an agency that would acquire at face value 50% of existing public debts for the relevant countries and swap them into zero-interest perpetuities.[7]

[7]Mutual Agreement for Public Debt Restructuring in the Eurozone, Madre Plan, CEPR, May 2014.

This means that the corresponding debts are wiped out. To that effect, the agency borrows on the financial markets the amount needed to acquire the debts. The agency best suited for this task is the ECB, because, as all major central banks, it has a good credibility, can sustain some losses, and is the only institution which can mobilize large resources on the markets.

(2) *Intervention of the ECB on government bond markets*. The ECB plays its role of lender of last resort in a very restrictive way with respect to governments. In September 2012, the ECB announced a new Outright Monetary Transactions (OMT) program which consists of buying short-term and medium-term government bonds. This OMT program – contrary to the FED and the BoE – takes only place on the secondary market, and the ECB does not have any official target for interest rates on government bonds. Furthermore, it is conditional to the acceptance of adjustment programs imposed by the Troika in accordance with the ESM. This is one of the causes of the depth of the sovereign debt crisis in the euro area. Therefore, a change in the ECB doctrine is necessary. The ECB has to become an active player on the government bond market, including the primary market, as it has been the case in the USA, the UK, and Japan. The ECB is holding around 10% of government debt of the eurozone countries, which is much lower than the 40% percentage for the Bank of Japan. Such a policy would have two positive effects. First, it would put a downward pressure on government bond rates and reduce the cost of debt. Second, it would reduce the probability of crisis on the bond market in the future, thanks to the interventions of the ECB as a LLR.

Since the beginning of 2015, the ECB has launched a quantitative easing (QE) policy buying each month 60 billion euros of securities, mainly public bonds, which will increase its balance sheet up to 10% of eurozone GDP in September 2016. It is welcomed but arrives too late in many senses. Furthermore this QE suffers from some limits. It concerns only the secondary market and is implemented mainly through national central banks, which reduces the potential effect of mutualization in case of losses. Its impact will be rather limited to support growth or inflation. By itself QE does not induce more credit distribution. Its main effects are twofold. Financial institutions which sell securities to the ECB can buy domestic securities (which increase their prices and sustain the financial markets) or foreign securities (which induces capital outflows and a euro depreciation). As the wealth effects are more limited in the eurozone than in the Anglo-Saxon countries, the main impact of the QE is the euro depreciation. In spite of its positive effect on growth, it raises some questions. The German euro is now hugely undervalued, and the German current surplus has reach 8.6% of GDP in 2015 (8.3% in 2016 and 7.8% in 2017) which reinforces global imbalances and can contribute to a revival of currencies war.

(3) *The common issue of Eurobonds* is a third promising way to deal with the question of public debt in the EU. Each country's debt would be guaranteed by all the others. The rationale is that the overall level of European debt is not so high, when compared to the USA and Japan; but it is distributed in an uneven way. The biggest benefits from such a policy of debt mutualization would accrue

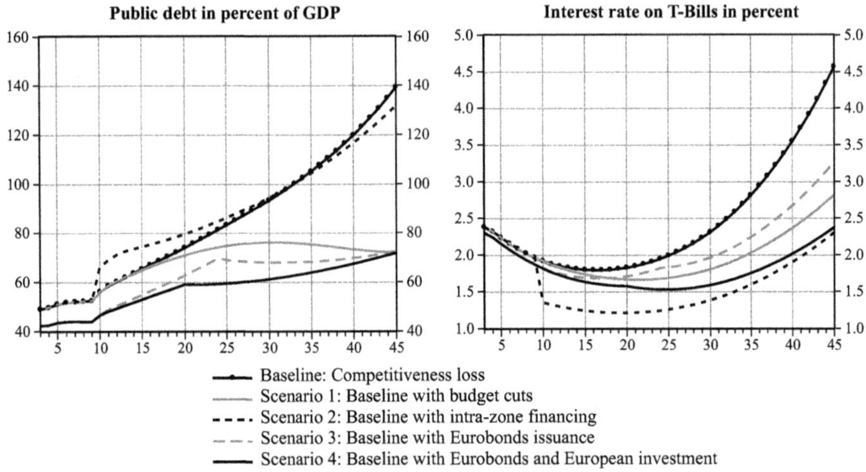

Fig. 11.1 Evolution of the public debt (in % du GDP) and of interest rate (in %) in Southern Europe. (Source: Duwicquet et al. 2014)

to Southern European countries and help them to limit their debt burden. Different schemes have been proposed. One is to have Eurobonds issued jointly up to the value of 60% of each eurozone member state's GDP. But it leaves the remaining debt above the 60% threshold more exposed to the market pressure with a risk of higher rates of interest. A more progressive solution is to issue guaranteed debt above the 60% threshold, because the cost of that share of the public debt is more expensive since markets consider it more risky. Eurobonds can also be a useful instrument to finance common policies at the European level (see Sect. 11.5).

Simulations have been made using a two-country stock-flow consistent model of the eurozone where the southern country suffers from the overvaluation of its currency and of a loss of competitiveness (Duwicquet et al. 2013, 2014). Issuing Eurobonds above the 60% threshold helps to slow down the increase of the rate of interest in the south and partly to preserve the growth (scenario 3 in Figs. 11.1 and 11.2). When Eurobonds are used to finance European investment projects in new technologies, infrastructures, and energetic transition, the positive impact is larger (scenario 4).

However the difficulties raised by issuing Eurobonds must not be underestimated for at least two sets of reasons. First it implies the creation of a European Debt Agency in charge of this issue. It means a strict control of the national public expenditures by this new European agency in order to guarantee the quality of the debt. It represents another form of mutation toward more federalism that few European countries are ready to accept. Second, Eurobonds and mutualization induce a larger charge for Northern European countries in the medium run at the advantage of southern countries, at least through the interest charges. Even if ex post,

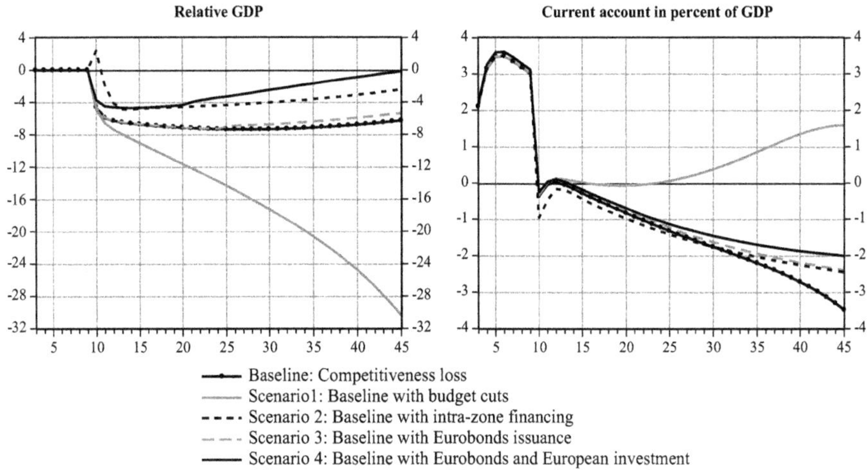

Fig. 11.2 Relative GDP (in %) and current account (in absolute variation in % of GDP) in Southern Europe. (Source: Duwicquet et al. 2014)

there is a global gain for all participants, thanks to a more sustained growth, the Eurobond project faces rather strong resistance from northern countries, as it has been illustrated in 2012–2013. Beyond these obstacles, two basic problems would remain unresolved, macroeconomic stabilization and the heterogeneity and unequal competitiveness of member states or, in other words, the persistence of misaligned real exchange rates.

11.4 Toward a Multiple Euro Regime

The main structural problem of the eurozone lies in its large heterogeneity which makes it impossible for southern countries to compete against the German bloc at the same exchange rate parity.

11.4.1 Structural Heterogeneity Between European Countries

Strong structural heterogeneity can be observed at almost all levels between the German bloc and the southern countries. The northern countries are more specialized in manufacturing activities, the size and the level of productivity of the firms are higher, the effort of research and development is more important, and the labor force

Table 11.3 Misalignments in real effective terms (in %)

	EU	FRA	GER	ITA	SPA	FIN	IRL	PRT	GRC
1994	−3.4	2.4	−7.4	6.9	1.4	−5.8	−0.7	0.9	15.1
1995	1.2	−0.7	−7.5	8.2	9.6	5.1	−1.7	3.8	−0.1
1996	4.2	3.2	−4.8	6.7	−0.1	8.3	−0.8	−10.4	−11.3
1997	3.5	12.9	−1.6	5.4	1.1	20.1	−1.5	−18.5	−8.2
1998	0.6	14.0	−4.3	2.1	0.5	22.9	−2.6	−16.8	−1.7
1999	2.0	19.2	−7.3	−1.5	−5.0	21.6	−0.3	−21.4	−7.2
2000	0.1	8.7	−8.1	−3.8	−7.6	24.9	−0.6	−29.3	−16.8
2001	6.9	6.8	−2.9	−3.1	−7.9	25.3	−4.0	−36.1	−17.4
2002	6.6	2.5	3.8	−6.3	−4.8	25.6	−4.8	−30.1	−19.0
2003	2.2	−2.9	1.3	−8.5	−3.2	15.2	−3.6	−26.1	−9.1
2004	7.2	−0.1	5.6	−5.4	−15.4	19.6	−3.8	−40.1	5.0
2005	1.9	−4.6	5.3	−4.1	−20.3	7.8	−4.8	−46.1	−7.6
2006	1.6	−4.8	9.1	−3.8	−24.6	9.7	−2.0	−47.9	−6.3
2007	−0.2	−6.0	13.1	−0.7	−26.4	15.5	−0.9	−34.5	−5.2
2008	0.9	−13.3	13.0	−4.5	−33.3	11.7	−4.7	−46.3	−3.7
2009	6.6	−8.3	13.9	−2.9	−10.2	0.2	−0.7	−34.4	−8.5
2010	4.9	−6.9	16.8	−4.2	−14.6	2.5	−0.9	−28.1	−21.1
2011	8.6	−10.1	16.8	−5.8	−22.9	−5.9	−2.5	−19.6	−53.1
2012	16.3	−12.6	19.3	−2.5	−14.1	−8.9	−7.9	−12.2	−30.9
2013	18.0	−5.0	18.7	1.5	−3.6	−7.2	1.4	6.8	−20.3
2014	20.1	−10.1	19.4	3.8	−2.7	−7.4	5.9	4.4	−15.4
2015	26.1	−8.2	18.7	2.4	6.1	−6.7	12.8	8.6	1.9

Source: Duwicquet et al. (2014)
Note: A positive (negative) number indicates an undervaluation (overvaluation) expressed in percent of the observed value

is more qualified. This heterogeneity can be illustrated by estimation of exchange rate misalignments, using a FEER (Fundamental Equilibrium Exchange Rate) approach. The FEER is defined as the exchange rate prevailing when the economy simultaneously reaches the external equilibrium and the internal equilibrium for all the trading partners. This measure was derived from a standard world trade model in which all the variables are endogenous, except the external equilibrium (sustainable current account) and the internal equilibrium (full utilization of the productive potential). The external equilibrium is estimated with panel regression techniques. The internal equilibrium is reached when the output gap is closed (see Jeong et al. (2010) for further details). Since the early 2000s, we have assisted to a sharp increase of the heterogeneity of misalignments in the eurozone (Table 11.3) with a split within the eurozone between some countries increasingly undervalued (like Germany, Austria, the Netherlands, and Finland) and others increasingly overvalued (like Greece, Portugal, Spain, and France). On average between 2005 and 2010, Germany, Austria, the Netherlands, and Finland have been undervalued by 13%, while Greece, Portugal, Spain, and France have been overvalued by 23%.

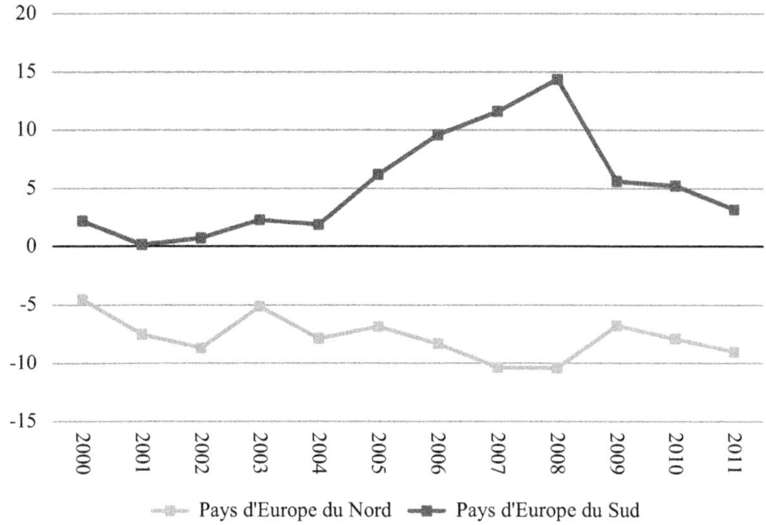

Fig. 11.3 Increase or reduction of costs induced by exchange rate misalignments (in % of GDP). (Source: Duwicquet et al., 2013)

These exchange rate misalignments are at the source of implicit and large transfers between the north and the south of Europe. Thanks to the undervaluation of their currencies, the countries of the German bloc have benefited of a reduction of their costs of around 10% of GDP at the end of the 2000s, while on the opposite, the southern countries supported, with their overvalued currencies, an increase of their costs close to 15% of the GDP (Fig. 11.3).

However, since the beginning of the eurozone crisis in 2010, a reduction of misalignments is observed for most of the Southern European countries. Irish, Spanish, Italian, and even Portuguese euros seem no more overvalued in 2012. But Greek and French euros remain overvalued around 15% and German euro undervalued around 20%. These movements have been mainly driven by large real effective devaluations in Ireland, Spain, Portugal, and Greece, as shown in Fig. 11.4 with the evolutions of the relative unit labor cost (ULC), i.e., real effective exchange rates based on ULC. These politics of internal devaluation are very painful and have led to a deep recession in Greece, as in other Southern European countries, with a reduction of current deficits mainly due to the shrink of imports, but with limited improvement of public finance.

Adjusting the real exchange rate through the so-called internal devaluations implies unacceptable social costs. Hence, the reintroduction of an adjustment of nominal exchange rates within the eurozone could imply a positive competitiveness shock that could help troubled countries to deal with the crisis and, in the medium run, stay or come back in the eurozone in a sustainable way. This, of course, would have to be accompanied by other policies, especially on the supply side. Two types of monetary regimes can be proposed; the first one is a multispeed eurozone going

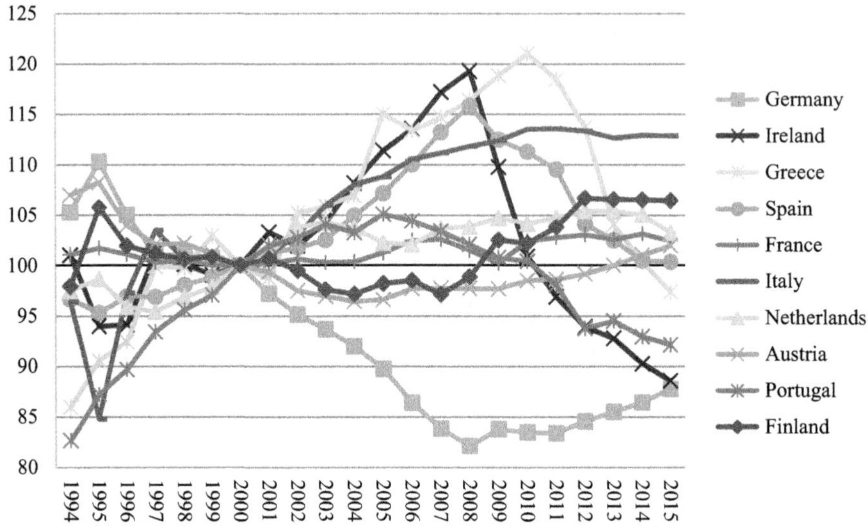

Fig. 11.4 REERs based on unit labor cost (relative ULC). (Source: Duwicquet et al. 2014)

from a multi-eurozone to a eurozone without Germany and the second, more ambitious, is based on an euro-bancor model and a European Clearing Union (Mazier and Valdecantos 2014, 2015).

11.4.2 A Multispeed Eurozone

11.4.2.1 A Multi-Eurozone

First, a multi-eurozone can be considered where national euros are reintroduced at the national or regional level, while a global euro is preserved to support the role of the current euro in financial markets as an international store of value. The global euro will be floating against the dollar and determined as the result of the interaction between supply and demand of euro-denominated bonds. Issuances of European bonds for foreign creditors are only denominated in global euro and can be bought by domestic banks, whereas private agents (firms and households) purchase only bonds denominated in national euros. National euros against global euro exchange rates are fixed but adjustable according to different types of criteria, reflecting the intra-European performance of the country against the rest of the zone (intra-European current account or stocks of foreign reserves). National central banks accumulate foreign reserves under the form of dollar-denominated bonds issued by the USA.

11.4.2.2 A Return to the European Monetary System

Second, a simple return to the European Monetary System (EMS) of the 1980s and 1990s can be taken up. As in the previous case, there will be a split up of the eurozone into national euros, but, instead of keeping a global euro used as an international currency, there will be a European Currency Unit (ECU) playing the role of a simple unit of account. The ECU will be a basket currency composed of the national euros according to the weight of each country. The ECU will be the reference to which national euros are pegged following the same mechanism as in the previous case (fixed but adjustable exchange rates of national euros against ECU according to different criterion of external performance). National central banks continue to accumulate foreign reserves in the same way as before. But national euros will now be floating against the dollar. In practice the German euro is floating, while the other national euros are anchored on it through the peg on the ECU.

11.4.2.3 A Eurozone Without Germany

Third, another solution is a system in which Germany leaves the eurozone and lets its currency float, while the remaining European countries keep the euro, which would either be pegged to the German currency with a fixed, but adjustable, exchange rate or float freely against the dollar. If the euro is pegged to the mark, the ECB adjusts its foreign reserves in consequence. If the euro is floating against the dollar and the mark, the ECB keeps its reserves constant. The weak point of this regime is that the intra-European exchange rates fluctuate, but this adjustment concerns only the relations between Germany and the rest of the eurozone which are preserved. The strong point of this regime is precisely that the main source of the intra-European imbalances, the unequal relations with the German bloc, disappears.

11.4.2.4 Simulations

Simulations have been made using a four-country SFC model of the world economy with the eurozone split in two countries, Spain for the south and Germany for the German block. A first set of simulations present a comparative analysis of different exchange rate regimes (from the current system of the eurozone to multiple euros) after a negative competitiveness shock in Southern Europe due to the overvaluation of the euro for Southern Europe. Results show that after some delay a depreciation of the Spanish currency against the dollar induces an improvement of the trade balance and of the GDP (at the detriment of Germany). However a multiple euro framework or a return to the EMS might produce recurrent exchange rate adjustments (unless criterion adjustment would be based on stock of foreign reserves or would allow small but persistent current deficits). Results would be better in case of Germany leaving the eurozone (Figs. 11.5 and 11.6).

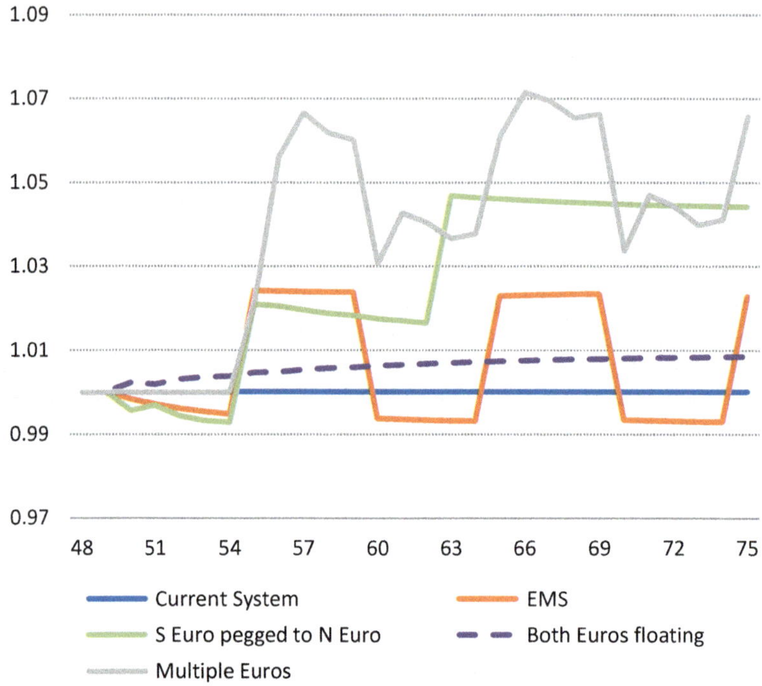

Fig. 11.5 Effects of a loss of competitiveness of the South due to an overvaluation on the parity of the Spanish euro against the dollar

11.4.3 A Euro–Bancor Regime

Last, a euro-bancor model can be considered. This proposal is more ambitious as it borrows from the experience of the EMS, from Keynes' proposals on bancor and International Clearing Union (ICU), and from the current existence of the ECB and the SEPA. First, it borrows from the EMS the existence of a nonmaterial unit of account to which national currencies are pegged and which is now called euro-bancor (a basket currency of national European currencies). Second, in Keynes' proposal, countries accumulated bancor balances according to their external performance (increasing bancor account at the ICU for countries with trade surpluses decreasing stock of bancors for countries running trade deficits). The idea of accumulating balances of a simple unit of account currency as a result of international transactions is the same that we observe in the current TARGET2 system at the ECB. It implies that most of the institutions that are required to implement a regime of this nature (a clearing union, an international unit of account, and a system that registers the transactions within the region) already exist (the ECB could play the role of the ICU, and the SEPA is the system that registers all the transactions) or have existed and could easily be restored (the ECU, which would play the role of the bancor).

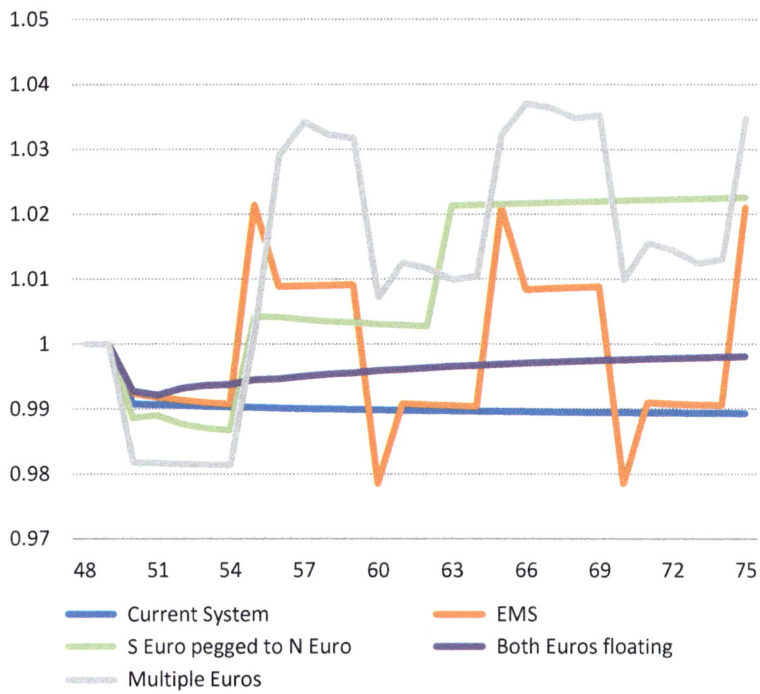

Fig. 11.6 Effects of a loss of competitiveness of the South due to an overvaluation on the Spanish GDP

European currencies are pegged to the euro-bancor (thereby fixed with respect to each other), but they float against the dollar. This feature of the system is also borrowed from the EMS. The adjustment criterion of European currencies vis-à-vis the euro-bancor depends on the intra-regional external performance of each country, unlike the case of the EMS where the overall performance was considered. As regards the balance sheet of national European central banks, the German and the other central banks are in an asymmetric position. The German central bank does not need to accumulate foreign reserves as its currency is floating against the dollar. The situation is different for the other European central banks which have to hoard reserves in order to make the necessary interventions to allow their currencies to keep the peg against the German currency. The role of the clearing union (the ECB in practice) can be developed more in detail. The clearing union is the institution where all the payments are cleared. Thus, every country would have an account at the clearing union. This account would be an asset for each national central bank and a liability for the clearing union, just as it happens in the current TARGET2 system.

However, some other Keynes' proposals can be introduced. First, in order to make the external adjustment process more symmetric than it is today, this system

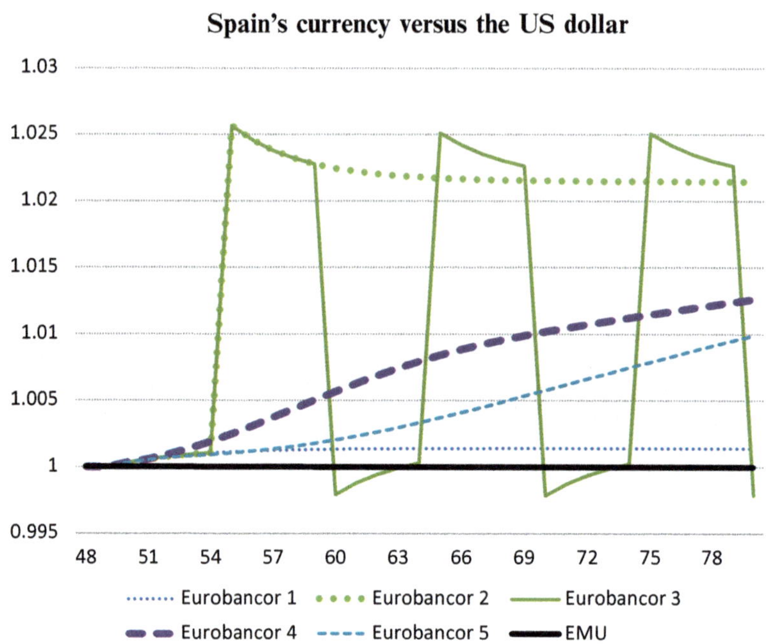

Fig. 11.7 Spain's currency versus the US dollar

would make both debtor and creditor countries share the burden of the debts.[8] All countries would pay interests on their bancor balances, shall them be positive or negative. This rule should encourage countries to make their accounts at the clearing union be as close to zero as possible. Second, the funds collected by the clearing union, which result from the interest payments on euro-bancor balances, could be redistributed in favor of countries in deficit to help them in strengthening their supply side by more investment.

11.4.3.1 Simulations

Simulations have been made using a four-country SFC model of the world economy of the same type as before with the eurozone split in two countries, Spain for the south and Germany for the German block (Figs. 11.7 and 11.8). They represent the same shock (a loss of competitiveness in the south due to an overvaluation) for different euro-bancor regimes, always compared with the current system (EMU, Economic and Monetary Union). In the euro regime (EMU), the overvaluation has a

[8]As it has been widely pointed out, in the current setting of both the international monetary system and the euro area, the external adjustment process is asymmetric because only debtor countries are forced to introduce the structural policies aimed at correcting the imbalances.

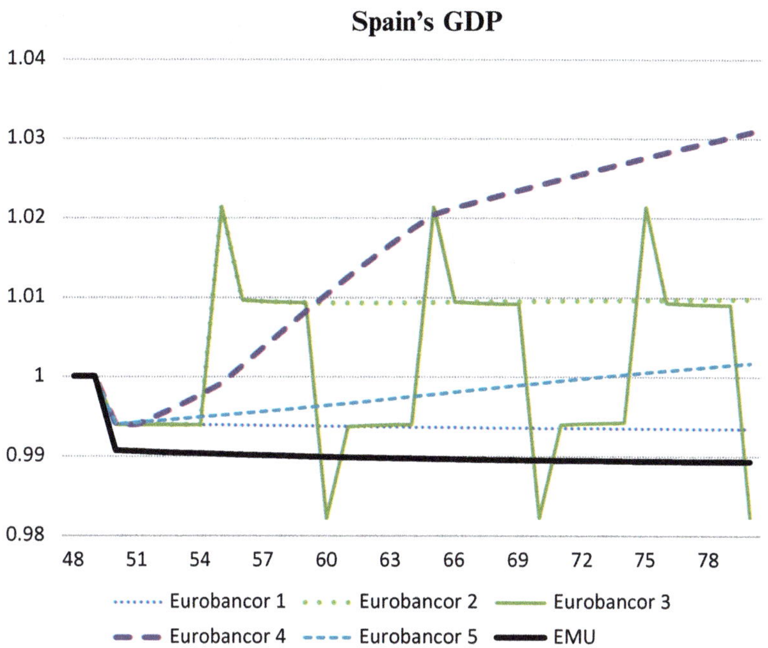

Fig. 11.8 Spain's GDP

negative impact on the Spanish current account and growth. The euro-bancor regime improves the Southern European countries thanks to payment of interests by the surplus country and transfer to the deficit countries. Euro-bancor 1 is the basic one with a large devaluation threshold which avoids exchange rate adjustments and has a more limited impact. Euro-bancor 2 with a smaller threshold gives more favorable effects thanks to the devaluation which is combined with the payment of interests and its transfer. As previously, if the adjustment criterion is too strict (almost no deficit is allowed in euro-bancor 3), the model could be more instable with one exchange rate adjustment following another. Euro-bancor 4 includes a supply shock effect for the southern country with increasing imports of capital goods, more investment, and later an import substitution effect. Euro-bancor 5 introduces a higher propensity to import for the surplus country with more public expenditures.

11.4.4 Conclusion

On the whole, beyond the different monetary regimes which can be adopted, the reintroduction of the possibility of exchange rate adjustments for Southern European countries gives significant room of manoeuver. Its main advantage is to be focused on manufacturing sector and more generally on tradable goods which are the key driver of intra-European imbalances. By itself it is not sufficient and must be completed by other measures, on the supply side to consolidate the initial positive shock and on income distribution to avoid an inflationist drift. Two regimes are more attractive, a eurozone without Germany as it gives an answer to one of the main sources of intra-European imbalance but a split which can have a political cost and a euro-bancor regime which reintroduces exchange rate adjustments while keeping many of the institutional achievements of the last 20 years in the monetary field.

But the transition to a new exchange rate regime faces two major difficulties. First, the external debt in euros will have to be renegotiated in order to avoid a too large increase of the debt burden in case of depreciation of the new national currency. Since a large part of this debt is intra-European, it will be possible to find a compromise, even if it raises some tensions between European countries. As we have seen, debt restructuring seems inevitable anyway at least for the weakest countries. Second, the risk of financial crisis with capital flights is important as soon as the possibility of a split of the euro will reappear. The introduction of technical measures of capital controls is possible, but their efficiency is limited. The conclusion is that it will be difficult to avoid a financial crisis. The crisis can be short if the new monetary regime is correctly designed with more realistic national exchange rates avoiding misalignments and with more favorable perspective of growth than the current impasse.

11.5 A Recovery Plan Based on a Pro-environment Investment Scheme

There is a third way out of the present impasse of the EU which could easily be combined with the two sets of policies presented in the above sections. The one we want to investigate rapidly hereafter can straightforwardly be seen as a specific case of the policies of project bonds introduced in Sect. 11.3. The specificity of this way out is to bank on the rising pressure of the environmental challenge, which gives to the related investment schemes a full legitimacy across the board of countries and also hints at workable designs of investment. Let us recall beforehand how this shift took place. For over three decades, political discourses have alternatively stressed two challenges: first, the necessity of a successful integration in a world economy, continuously transformed by a worldwide process of liberalization of international transactions forcing a generalized retreat of the economic power of the states, and, second, the need of a shift toward more sustainable development paths following the warnings on the environment threat given by scientists in the 1970s.[9] The first challenge has been voiced strongly in the 1980s and 1990s by the governments and the international institutions. The second challenge has for a long time remained purely rhetorical. Integration in the world economy has been the overdominant

[9]Of which the emblematic Meadows et al.' s report on the limits to growth.

motto in its most crude form, searching for cost competitiveness in pressing down wages and pushing forward non-price competitiveness, supporting hi-tech multinational firms and the rent of innovations drawn from their R&D activities. All this process has mainly led over three decades to increase income inequality and unemployment. Meanwhile the threat of speculative runs on currencies in a world of global liberalized finance pushed a majority of EU countries to adopt a single currency despite its detrimental impact on the convergence among EU member states which remains a key issue for the success of a regional integration process. In the year 2000, the deterioration of the environment became more obvious, leading the UN to take action and international agreements to develop, such as the Kyoto agreement (protocol), to reduce CO2 emissions. While the voice of. Climate skepticism was strongly declining,[10] the reports of the IPCC (International Panel on Climate Change) gained increasing attention. The financial crisis of 2007 and the ensuing public debt crisis of the early 2010s led to a reinforcement of austerity policies especially in the EU. But these policies rapidly turned out to be such a dead end that even some conservative politicians and orthodox institutions called for alternative policies.

The problem then is how to define these alternative policies. It is difficult to rally EU members to help financing or allow public indebtment to support unconditionally household consumption, which would increase chiefly imports, without boosting the competitiveness of the country. Agreement among member states to support investment schemes would be easier to reach, but it remains highly conditional, raising issues traditionally opposed to industrial policies: How should investments be selected if not through the market? Which body is going to check that the objective of the investment will be efficiently reach? The investment scheme has to be effective and the operation accountable (no transfers to firms or households without controlling that they are effectively used for what they are purposed). The investment under view has to be legitimate, meaning that it should concur objectively to boost the competitiveness of firms without harming households. All this implies some kind of control all along and loss of sovereignty which is difficult for member states to accept. The experience of the EU "structural funds" thus showed the pros and cons of such schemes. It finally ended by stricter requirements on the objects and conditions of realization of the subsidized investments. At the time being, investment schemes around environmental issues seem best positioned to meet such stricter standards. Still they have to be easily tractable, to be fairly allocated and simply controlled. Focusing on one environmental variable such as CO2 emissions is in that sense a strong advantage, even if discarding other environment variables can be counterproductive (be it neglect of biodiversity, increasing threats of nuclear accidents or changing the role of agriculture). Aglietta and Hourcade (2012) give an example of a simple decarbonization scheme which is meeting the above requirements. The criterium to support an investment is then the

[10] http://www.ft.com/intl/cms/s/0/46a65844-05f4-11e4-8b94-00144feab7de.html#axzz3CuHNaaUq

reduction of CO2 emissions it allows. A premium is fixed at EU level which is equivalent to a carbon price but is not determined on any market but fixed by the authorities who are managing the investment fund. Recent past has shown that market mechanisms work very poorly to support long-term investment as required to preserve environment in an economic world still strongly dominated by a liberalized and internationalized finance, therefore caring most exclusively for short- or medium-term projects. Moreover the investments in question concern all sectors of an economy, from energy, transport, housing, and agriculture to basic manufacturing industries. Supports to these industries therefore impact in terms of jobs and incomes throughout all activities, notwithstanding their direct impact on the well-being of all the users of the productions under view. One of the simplest design for such investment scheme would be to create a European Ecological Fund (EEF) which would receive contributions from member states of a small percentage points of their GDP. A more sophisticated scheme (if EU members are more daring) would be to use Eurobonds to finance it. The EEF would monitor the distribution of these subventions, taking into account (a) the CO2 emissions saved, (b) the sectors of activity (to distribute between housing, energy producing, transport, and other activities), and (c) the level of development of the country of the investor (to allow some redistributive effect). The overall level of the contributions of member states to this fund and the target of CO2 reduction would finally correspond to some average carbon price with the big difference that this price would in effect be differentiated to take into account the differences in development levels and to involve all activities, while a single market of CO2 reduction would not allow such redistributive effects. Such scheme would open an evolutionary process by which member states would progressively increase their respective efforts to meet constantly higher targets of reduction in CO2 emissions, in an effort constantly fueled by the catching up and widespread impacts of the scheme.

Indeed a key issue is then to know if the initiative launched by the EEF would reach rapidly enough an order of magnitude sufficient to lead to a cumulative process of pro-environment investments. The simulations done in the AUGUR project (see Cripps et al. 2014) provide a calibration which supports the idea that it is possible for such scheme to gain some momentum. An increase of public spending of around 1% across the board of all activities clearly changes the 2030 horizon. The simulation aims at reducing unemployment within a 5%–8% range and to reduce the productivity gap between member states. The contributions vary among them to meet the redistributive objective, but overall the new efforts are of an order of magnitude similar to the present contributions to the EU budget. It is not negligible but should be compared to the national plans of economic recovery launched in various member states. For instance, in France when the contribution to the 2013 EU budget was of some 22 billion euros, the pact of responsibility of 2014 would cost twice as much (some 41 billion euros[11]). It thus requires sizeable but feasible efforts by member

[11]See http://www.vie-publique.fr/actualite/dossier/rub1786/pacte-responsabilite-solidarite-allegements-charges-contre-embauches.html

states. The main factor for such cumulative dynamics to take place is that such a pro-environment scheme would have a full legitimacy (increasing with the observation of the environment problems around the world) and a transparent tractable design, where the effectiveness of the investments and their distributive impacts among activities and countries could be monitored in transparent ways, forging a learning process, whereby trust would continuously increase. No alternative investment scheme can make the same claims.

Is Europe really ready for such an effort? The answer remains uncertain as the EU is giving positive and negative signs on such outcome. Let us list three positive signs before assessing their shortcomings. In the first place, the Juncker plan (2014) to boost investments in member states clearly showed a rising concern over the low level of investment that has prevailed in Europe for some decades and has worsened in the aftermath of the 2008 global financial crisis. The Juncker plan suggested to create a specific European investment fund of some 16 billion euros to subsidize private and public investment projects. This leverage effect was supposed to rally some 320 billion euros of investment. Clearly a consistent selection of projects with a fund of such magnitude could help both to reverse the divergence trend among EU member states and to support a good deal of environment-friendly projects. If the selection criteria are adequate, such plan could effectively put the EU on a sustainable trajectory in economic, social, and environmental terms. A second positive sign has been the series of action that came to compose the 2020 climate and energy package which in the early 2010s achieve to set three key targets: (a) a 20% cut in greenhouse gas emissions (from 1990 levels), (b) 20% of EU energy from renewables, and (c) 20% improvement in energy efficiency. Table 11.4 details the three main schemes involved to reach these objectives.

A third positive sign can be seen in various propositions put forward at the COP21 Paris conference by diverse EU institutions. The European Commission proposed to reduce global emissions by at least 60% below 2010 level by 2050. This proposition was followed by a statement of the Committee of the Regions, suggesting a global target of zero emission by 2050 and a 50% reduction in EU emissions by 2030. The EU parliament asking for a more ambitious climate policy urged also for a phasing out of carbon emissions by 2050, adding a demand for a 5-year commitment period for the Paris Agreement and a scaling up of the aid to developing countries.

The negative signs that make the issue uncertain are of two kinds. On one side the series of directives and official assessments of central EU institutions does not imply that the measures will be enforced. Thus the delays of member states to fully apply, for instance, the EU directive on energy passed on in 2012 (by 2015 it had still to be fully integrated in national laws by 19 EU countries out of 28) are worrying for the success of the 2020 climate and energy action plan.

On the other side, a major reflation plan such as the Juncker investment plan is only feebly linked with the EU proclaimed priority for a strong climate policy that would maintain the EU as a major global actor in the domain. There is only a vague consensus to allow a quota of 20% of the scheme to environment-friendly projects. Moreover the Juncker investment scheme is broadly based on market incentives, all

Table 11.4 EU 2020 climate and energy package

Emission trading system (ETS) A key tool to cut greenhouse gas emissions from large-scale facilities in the power and industry sectors, as well as in the aviation sector. The ETS covers around 45% of the EU's greenhouse gas emissions. In 2020, the target is for the emissions from these sectors to be 21% lower than in 2005
National emission reduction targets This covers the sectors not in ETS (some 55% of total EU emissions), i.e., housing, agriculture, waste, and transport (excluding aviation). EU countries have taken binding annual targets until 2020 for cutting emissions in these sectors (compared with 2005) under the "Effort sharing decision." The targets differ according to national wealth, from a 20% cut for the richest countries to a maximum of 20% increase for the least wealthy
Renewable energy – national targets EU member states have taken binding national targets to raise the share of renewable in their energy consumption, under the renewable energy directive. The targets vary according to the starting points, from 10% in Malta to 49% in Sweden. As a whole the EU will thus be able to reach a target of 20% of renewable energy for 2020 (from 9.8% in 2010) and a share of 10% of renewables in transport
Innovation and financing The EU supports the development of low carbon technologies, for example, through the: NER 300 program for renewable energy technologies and carbon capture and storage Horizon 2020 funding for research and innovation
Energy efficiency measures for increasing energy efficiency are set out in the: – Energy efficiency plan Energy efficiency directive

Source: http://ec.europa.eu/clima/policies/strategies/2020/index_en.htm

of which leaves space to large rebound effects, whereby decrease of energy prices could lead to increases in energy consumption, an issue which is not given enough attention. Not to mention the fact that the reform of the financial system which is important for the success of any investment scheme with specific targets and transparency requirements is progressing slowly. Such lack of consistency is largely based on lasting divergences among member states which have to be overcome in order to launch a virtuous cumulative process of investment in a comprehensive and "redistributive" environment policy.

11.6 Tentative Conclusions on the Ways Out of the EU Crisis

The previous sections have clearly stressed that ways out of the crisis do exist that would not change the situation overnight but would set the EU on a sustainable development path of recovery. It has also been stressed that divergence trends and shortcomings of the institutional fabric of the EU make it difficult to opt for the major institutional changes that are required.

A first example has been given by the role of the European Central Bank (ECB), first severely constrained in its power to deal with the debt crisis of the aftermath of the 2008 financial crisis. Progresses have been made, letting initiatives of the ECB to cope with the legal constraints of its statute and allowing some easing of its ability to manage the euro crisis of 2012. Its power to intervene directly to boost the EU economy remains though rather limited if compared with the US Fed. However, the ECB should play a major role in the financing of the transition, for instance, by implementing new forms of nonconventional policies, such as "green QE" policies.

A second example of the shortcomings of the EU construction mainly concerns the functioning of the Euro, a central piece in the EU dynamics of integration. It has been clearly showed that the creation of the euro, even if defensive or because it was a defensive move, has left open the issue of ensuring the convergence of member states, though it is a crucial issue for the sustainability of a currency union. If divergence trends occur, some institutional mechanisms should be available to set the union back on a sustainable track. Clearly such mechanism does not exist with the order of magnitude required by the extent of the divergence. The existing tools of redistribution among member states were clearly short of being able to reverse the diverging trends that developed in the 2000s and increased after the 2008 financial crisis. Flexible exchange rate mechanisms could have helped as shown in Sect. 11.4 providing that a multiple euro system would have received sufficient political support to facilitate a delicate transition and incorporate some mechanisms of solidarity; it is all the more striking of the straight jacket effect of the euro union that such alternatives have not been debated.

A third example of ways out could have been given in taking advantage of the momentum of the climate policies as shown at the Paris COP21 conference to launch well-targeted investment schemes that would have reversed the diverging trends and set the EU on a transition path toward an economically, socially, and environmentally sustainable development path. It is certainly a deep structural turn not so easy to reach. There are clear pros and cons in the many policy initiatives taken by the EU institutions, but the level of uncertainty remains worrying.

By all means the EU is clearly at a crossroads. Its crisis is obvious as shown in the rise of political parties in favor of (more or less) exiting the EU. Its interest to keep some voice in the governance of a globalized world is also clear. The ways out of this crisis, in economic terms as we listed them in the above sections, are not so much controversial in their logic. But as they required important institutional changes, the political possibilities of their implementations are disputed. We do believe though that the drawbacks of the neoliberal economic ideology that drove the process of globalization for the past four decades have clearly appeared and that conversely the importance of the environmental challenge is by now widely acknowledged and gives some room for internationally concerted policies on "sustainable development goals," a forum where the EU can be an important player, and all the more so if major historical actors of the construction of the EU, such as Germany and France, can jointly push in that direction. Any recovery of the global economy, out of the global financial crisis, even if only technical and short termed as the one that emerged in 2017, can help such accord, while at the heart of the crisis, the interests of these two countries diverge. There is a window of opportunity for such rally to occur in the EU around some kind of large convention on environment issues. The balance sheet of the commitments taken at the COP21 on December 2015 in Paris, due to be done in 2022, will be telling in that respect. Either the EU has effectively appeared as a global promoter of the construction of a sustainable world order which can be the basis of a sound reconstruction of the EU or the EU integration project may be bound to become "passé."

References

Aglietta M, Hourcade JC (2012) Can indebted Europe afford climate policy? Can it bail out its debt without climate policy? Intereconomics 47(3)

Cripps F (2014) Macro model scenarios and implication for European Policy Chapter 2. In Eatwell J, Petit P, Mc Kinley T (eds) (2014)

Cripps F et al (2014) Charting ways out of Europe 's Impasse – a policy memorandum. Policy notes and reports. May WIIW. www.wiiw.ac.at

Duwicquet V, Mazier J, Saadaoui J (2013) Désajustements de change, fédéralisme budgétaire et redistribution. Revue de l'OFCE 127:57–93

Duwicquet V, Mazier J, Saadaoui J (2014) « Interest rates, eurobondss and intra-european exchange rates misalignments: the challenge for sustainable adjustments in the euro zone », CEPN Working Paper n° 2014-11

Eatwell J, Petit P, Mc Kinley T (2014) Challenges for Europe in the world, 2030. Sage, London

Jeong S-E, Mazier J, Saadaoui J (2010) Exchange rate misalignments at world and European levels: a FEER approach. Économie Internationale 121(3):25–58

Mazier J, Valdecantos S (2014) Gathering the pieces of three decades of monetary coordination to build a way out of the European crisis. Working paper CEPN n° 2014–2010

Mazier J, Valdecantos S (2015) A multispeed Europe: is it viable? Intervent Eur J Econ Econ Policy 12(1):93–112

Mazier J, Petit P, Plihon D (eds) (2013) L'économie mondiale en 2030: ruptures et continuités, Economica, Paris

Meadows DH, Meadows DL, Randers J, Behrens W (1972) The limits to growth: a report for the club of Rome's project on the predicament of mankind. Universe Books, New York

Part III
China and Japan in Asian Diversity of Capitalisms

Chapter 12
Institutional Diversity, Industrial and Innovative Specialization in Asian Capitalism

Hironori Tohyama and Yuji Harada

12.1 Introduction

Since the 1990s, numerous studies have focused on comparative institutional analyses dealing with advanced capitalist countries (e.g., Hall and Soskice 2001; Amable 2003). Nevertheless, the diversity of Asian capitalisms was left to be investigated in the field of comparative studies of capitalism.

However, as the Asian economy has emerged as the center of the global economy, attention on the Asian regions has led to an increasing number of studies on institutional diversity in Asian capitalism (e.g., Witt and Redding 2013; Walter and Zhang 2012; Zhang and Whitley 2013). Harada and Tohyama (2012) conducted multiple factor analysis (MFA) and cluster analysis and identified five types of Asian capitalism, by focusing on six institutional domains such as financial market, production market, labor market, international trade, education, and social security.[1]

As Amable (2003) and Hall and Soskice (2001) pointed out, the institutional structure of an economy is closely connected with the specialization of economic activities in the relevant economy. Institutions define incentives to invest in specific assets, which are sources of comparative advantage in some economic activities.

This theoretical hypothesis in varieties of capitalism (VoC) asserts that different institutional characteristics are associated with different capabilities of innovation, leading to different patterns of industrial specialization (Hall and Soskice 2001;

[1]Tohyama and Harada (2014) have identified six types of Asian capitalism including India.

H. Tohyama (✉)
Shizuoka University, Shizuoka, Japan
e-mail: tohyama.hironori@shizuoka.ac.jp

Y. Harada
Setsunan University, Neyagawa, Japan
e-mail: yuji.harada@econ.setsunan.ac.jp

R. Boyer et al. (eds.), *Evolving Diversity and Interdependence of Capitalisms*, Evolutionary Economics and Social Complexity Science 11,
https://doi.org/10.1007/978-4-431-55001-3_12

Amable 2003). Thus, we can find some coherent relationships among institutional diversity at the macro level, innovative capabilities of firms, and patterns of industrial specialization. The purpose of this chapter is to investigate whether and how such a relationship is established in Asian capitalism. In other words, we will examine whether the coherence among macro institutional diversity, innovative capabilities, and industrial specialization exists.

We organize the chapter as follows. In the next section, we confirm the diversity of institutional configuration in Asian capitalism by applying the method and data sources used in Harada and Tohyama (2012) to an extended period of time. In Sect. 12.3, we identify that the patterns of industrial specialization in Asian capitalism are connected with the institutional diversity in the region. In Sect. 12.4, we investigate how the institutional diversity of Asian capitalisms is associated with cross-national patterns of specialization regarding innovative activities and in industries. Finally, in Sect. 12.5, we derive some implications from our findings and conclude the chapter.

12.2 Institutional Diversity of Asian Capitalisms

12.2.1 Five Types of Asian Capitalism

Harada and Tohyama (2012) applied MFA to the data related to different institutional domains from 2004 to 2007 in order to analyze the diversity of institutional configuration in Asian capitalism. First, they placed the social systems consisting of a bundle of institutions in common dimensions to facilitate comparison. Second, they positioned different institutional domains in common dimensions and compared the domains' distribution between Asian and advanced economies.

Considering the socioeconomic context of each economy and the preceding research outcomes in addition to the statistical analyses, Harada and Tohyama (2012) identified the following five types of Asian capitalism, which were distinctively differentiated from advanced capitalisms.

12.2.1.1 Insular Semi-agrarian Capitalism: Indonesia and the Philippines

This group is characterized by a lower degree of liberalization of various markets. Both Indonesia and the Philippines had experienced severe crises in terms of their political and economic regimes. Whereas Indonesia experienced the Asian financial crisis in 1997, the Philippines faced the external debt crisis in the early 1980s. Both countries were subsequently subject to structural adjustment policies imposed by the International Monetary Fund (IMF). Such experiences might have stymied progress there, in terms of market liberalization, industrialization, and the introduction of FDI—unlike in Malaysia and Thailand, which are usually recognized as ASEAN countries with relatively similar kinds of economies.

12.2.1.2 Trade–Led Industrializing Capitalism: Malaysia and Thailand

This type of Asian capitalism has characteristics similar to those of *insular semi-agrarian capitalism*, with respect to the degree of liberalization of markets. Moreover, it is characterized by relatively higher public expenditure for education, a higher dependence on external trade, and less rigidity vis-à-vis employment and hours worked. Compared to Indonesia and the Philippines, Malaysia and Thailand have not been severely affected by economic crises. It can be said that these countries feature *trade-led industrializing capitalism*, because liberalization and industrialization have steadily advanced there, and these countries are integrated into the world-trade network via a global supply chain.

12.2.1.3 City Capitalism: Hong Kong and Singapore

The following characteristics are shared among the countries in this group: a significant degree of liberalization of different markets, higher trade dependence, lower domestic social protection, and high profitability of the banking system. These countries can be termed as having *city capitalism*, a type analogous with the category specified in Berthelier et al. (2003).

12.2.1.4 Innovation–Led Capitalism: Japan, South Korea, and Taiwan

Higher economic development and barriers to entry in the product market are observed as common characteristics in these countries. It might be difficult to categorize these countries as a single group, since each country has its own distinct features with regard to other variables. In particular, it is observed that Japan is not highly integrated. Nevertheless, these three countries comprise a cluster from a statistical viewpoint, not only because of their relative distance from other clusters but also because they have experienced historical success in export-oriented industrialization, based on a number of innovations in the electrical goods industry. As such, the countries can be considered to have *innovation-led capitalism*. It should also be noted that this categorization aligns with the results of Berthelier et al. (2003).

12.2.1.5 Continental Mixed Capitalism: China

Based on the result of the previous analysis, China has many similar institutional characteristics with Malaysia and Thailand. It implies that a typical characteristic of China is that its institutional configuration is heavily capitalist. Such characteristics can be defined as a "selective embrace of capitalism" (Chowdhury and Islam 2007, p. 15). On the other hand, the political and economic regime of China also has very specific features such as socialist market economy. Furthermore, as will be detailed below, the analysis based on firm-level data also suggests that China is distinctive in how it pays attention to the relationship between institutions and innovation activities within firms. As Harada and Tohyama (2012) indicated, the share of domestic market-oriented firms in China is much larger than that found in other economies. Therefore, we consider China to have *continental mixed capitalism* (see also Boyer 2012).

12.2.2 The Diversity of Asian Capitalisms During 2004–2011

Based on the above typology of Asian capitalism, we confirm that the institutional diversity can be observed even in the extended period from 2004 to 2011.

12.2.2.1 Methodology and Data

In line with Harada and Tohyama (2012), we apply MFA to our data, instrumenting for institutions. As mentioned above, we recognize each economic system as a bundle of institutions from multiple domains.

Technically, an institution is instrumented by a range of variables. Accordingly, the institutional configuration is represented by multiple sets of variables because each configuration of institutions consists of one or more domains of institutions. As a result, these variables contain data in which a set of observations is described by several sets of variables.

MFA is useful to analyze these data, that is, a set of observations described by several groups of variables. We compare the social systems, which require us to make those groups of variables comparable. To do so, MFA performs a principal component analysis (PCA) on each group of variables, where each group is normalized by dividing all its elements by its first singular value. This weight is practically the first eigenvalue of a PCA on the group. Next, all the normalized data are aggregated into one table, which is analyzed through a PCA. This gives a set of factor scores for the observations and loadings for the variables. The influence of the groups of variables in the global analysis is balanced, and the structure of each group is retained. In this sense, MFA can be referred to as a weighted PCA or the method of rescaling the principal components (Pagès 2014).

Then, we apply cluster analysis to the dimensions from the MFA. Doing so is instrumental to distinguish the institutional architecture among Asian economies.

We examine the following 11 Asian economies: China (CHN), Hong Kong (HKG), Indonesia (IDN), India (IND), Japan (JPN), South Korea (KOR), Malaysia (MYS), the Philippines (PHL), Singapore (SGP), Thailand (THA), and Taiwan (TWN). In addition, we include 20 advanced economies: Australia, Austria, Belgium, Canada, Denmark, Finland, France, Germany, Greece, Ireland, Italy, the Netherlands, New Zealand, Norway, Portugal, Spain, Sweden, Switzerland, the

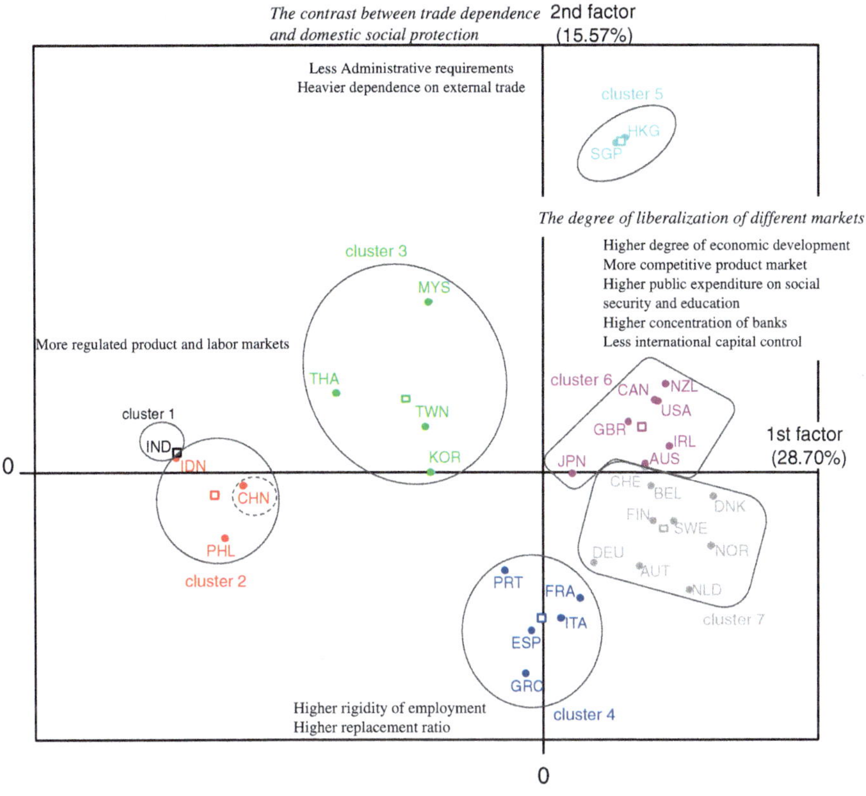

Fig. 12.1 Institutional diversity of advanced and Asian capitalism: 2004–2011

United Kingdom, and the United States. Each economy is described by the same six institutional domains, where each domain is instrumented by a range of variables. Accordingly, we have 31 economies with 53 variables maintaining consistency of variables with our previous analysis as far as possible. As a result, our data table is a matrix of 31 rows and 53 columns. All the variables are averaged over 2004–2011 as long as the data for each variable is available in order to maintain the coherence between the analyses of institutional configuration and industrial specialization conducted below. However, the data are not available for all years and economies.

12.2.2.2 Findings

Figure 12.1 illustrates the results derived from MFA of the aforementioned Asian and advanced economies. Overall, 44.27% of the variance among the economies can be explained by the first two factors. As indicated on the horizontal axis of Fig. 12.1, the first factor has a contribution rate of 28.70%. It correlates positively with the degree of economic development,[2] less regulation on product market, higher public expenditure on social security and education, higher concentration of banks, and less international capital control, and negatively with more regulations on product and labor markets, to be more precise, redundancy cost in labor market and barrier to entry and exit in product market. The vertical axis, representing the second factor (contribution rate of 15.57%), is determined by the burden of governmental administrative requirements, by ratio of external trade on its positive side, and by rigidity of employment and replacement rate on its negative side. The variables that primarily determine these factors almost correspond to those that resulted from our previous analysis (Harada and Tohyama 2012) in spite of the turnover of a couple of variables. Therefore, we can summarize them as *the degree of liberalization of different markets* and *the contrast between trade dependence and domestic social protection*, respectively, as shown. It could imply that the factors determining the diversity of institutional configuration are to some extent stable over the course of time.

Conducting cluster analysis based on the result of MFA, we realize that several groups in Asian and advanced capitalism are similar to those identified by the previous analysis. This implies that most of the targeted economies in the figure are situated at almost the same position as in the mid-2000s. However, the cluster analysis divides individual economies into groups according to the relative distance between economies, so that the number and composition of clusters can be changed depending on the change in distances among economies. We find that some clusters of Asian economies are recomposed differently. For instance, some countries of *innovation-led capitalism*, South Korea and Taiwan, comprise another group with countries of *trade-led industrializing capitalism*, Malaysia and Thailand. While China and countries of *insular semi-agrarian capitalism*, Indonesia and the Philippines, make up one group together, one can recognize two types of Asian capitalism shown in the previous section at the inferior level in the hierarchical tree of clusters. Therefore, Asian economies are distinctively differentiated from advanced ones, although Japan has an exceptional position among Asian economies because it is included in the group of Anglo-Saxon countries, which was called *advanced liberal capitalism* in Harada and Tohyama (2012).

The same holds for the analysis solely targeting Asian economies. We find similarities in terms of the factors determining the institutional diversity and the relative positions of economies with those identified in the analysis in the mid-2000s (see Fig. 12.2). The first factor determining 36.70% of the total variance among economies, that is, the horizontal axis in the figure, can be called *liberalization of different markets and progress of financialization and globalization*, similar to that

[2]It should be noted that it is difficult to clearly distinguish whether the dissimilarity among Asian economies results from the diversity of those institutional configurations or merely from the difference of the stage of economic development which each economy has reached because the degree and the process of economic development of Asian economies considerably diverge. The result of our analysis implies that institutional characteristics as well as economic development of each economy undeniably determine the diversity of Asian capitalisms to some extent.

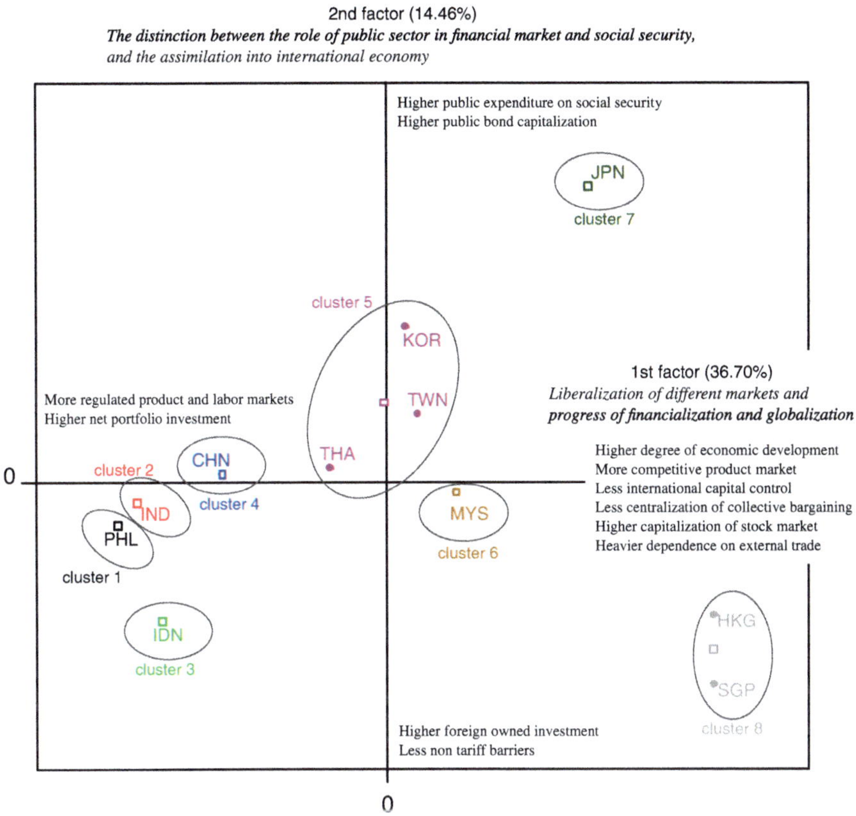

Fig. 12.2 Institutional diversity of Asian capitalism: 2004–2011

in Harada and Tohyama (2012). Concerning the second factor which contributes 14.46% to the explanation of the variance, we define it as *the distinction between the role of public sector in financial market and social security, and the assimilation into international economy* although determining variables of the principal factors are slightly different than those in our previous analysis.

However, by cluster analysis, Asian economies are fragmented into small groups different from those in the previous analysis. Regarding the five types of Asian capitalism mentioned above, we find that although *city capitalism* is maintained, Japan is isolated from *innovation-led capitalism*, and South Korea and Taiwan comprise another group with a country of *trade-led industrializing capitalism*, Thailand. Another country of the group, Malaysia, comes into being an independent cluster. As for *insular semi-agrarian capitalism* and *continental mixed capitalism*, each country belonging to these groups, Indonesia, the Philippines, and China, comprises its own cluster. Furthermore, India stays as an independent group that Tohyama and Harada (2016) revealed with the data from 2007 to 2011, although the country was not treated in Harada and Tohyama (2012). This cluster was named as *IT-led dirigiste capitalism.*

While the results of the above analyses do not produce an unequivocal representation of five types of Asian capitalism, it should be noted again that the determining factors of the diversity of Asian capitalisms resulted from both analyses with advanced economies and within Asian economies are quite similar to those in our previous analyses and that the relative position of most economies from this analysis is analogous to that in the previous analysis even in the extended period of time. Although the result of cluster analysis appears to be different from the previous one, what should be noticed is that cluster analysis heavily depends on distance connectivity between individuals/groups. Furthermore, although institutional changes in some economies such as Japan seem to be rather substantial leading to a new configuration of the relevant economy, we should also note that an economy would be deeply embedded in a specific socioeconomic context in a region from the long historical perspective. Therefore, considering socioeconomic context of each economy in addition to the result of these statistical analyses, it would be reasonable that we could still retain the hypothesis of five types of Asian capitalism clearly distinguished from advanced capitalism in terms of institutional configuration at this stage. As far as the statistical analysis would rely on the current set of variables, this typology of Asian capitalisms could not be sustained in the future because some economies such as Japan seem to be in the middle of institutional changes. Nevertheless, it is worthy to investigate theoretical foundations of the typology (Boyer 2015, pp.236–7). In order to facilitate such an investigation along with these results, we examine the diversity of industrial structure and specialization in Asian capitalism in the next section.

12.3 The Diversity of Industrial Structure and Specialization in Asian Capitalism

Next, we investigate how the institutional configuration of a particular economy determines economic activities in that economy. Considering firms are the ones that actually undertake economic activities in the economy, it is necessary to examine the influence of institutional configuration on firm behavior and the resulting industrial structure and specialization. For this purpose, comparative institutional advantage (CIA) presented by Hall and Soskice (2001) can be used. According to them, "the basic idea is that the institutional structure of a particular political economy provides firms with advantages for engaging in specific types of activities there" (Hall and Soskice 2001; p. 37). It implies that the institutional environment of an economy constrains the patterns of firm behavior and, consequently, builds a particular type of industrial specialization in that economy.

However, this argument is faced with the following problem: It is originally employed just for the analysis of advanced countries. As shown above, the institutional configurations of Asian economies are distinctly different from those of advanced countries. If the logic of CIA is applied to the Asian economies, one might suppose that the types of industrial specialization of Asian economies would be dissimilar from those of advanced countries as well. One of the reasons for this dissimilarity could be explained by the existence of different types of specialization.[3] Thus, we define three types of specialization in order to deeply investigate the diversity of industrial specialization in Asian capitalism. First, we specify a specialization index with regard to external trade as shown in many statistics provided by international organizations such as the World Bank. This is defined as the ratio of trade balance (export minus import) in an industry to that in the whole economy. We adopt the calculation in Amable (2003), although there are several methods of calculation to represent such a specialization. The actual form of definition is as follows:

$$L_{i,j} = \frac{X_{i,j} - M_{i,j}}{Y_j} \frac{X_{i,j} + M_{i,j}}{X_j + M_j} \cdot \frac{X_j - M_j}{Y_j}$$

where L, X, M, and Y stand for the specialization index, export, import, and value added, respectively. Moreover, subscripts i and j represent industry and economy, respectively.

Second, we take the shares of output and employment of an industry in the entire economy, as an index of industrial specialization or industrial structure. In the analysis of industrial specialization in Asian capitalism, it is noteworthy that there are economies with different degrees of economic development in the region. It is often believed that economic development could considerably affect the evolution of industrial structure. Petty-Clark's law supports such an induction. It explains that the weight, such as share of employment or value added, of industries shifts away from primary (agriculture) and secondary (manufacturing) sectors to the tertiary (services) sector through the process of economic development (e.g., Clark 1957). Furthermore, the specialization in the manufacturing sector is designated as ratios of output and employment in an industry to those in manufacturing as a whole. This measure can capture the evolution within the manufacturing sector, which describes the catching-up process of some Asian economies in the overlapping dynamics of import, production, and export in industries, as shown in the flying geese model proposed by Akamatsu (1961, 1962).[4]

Third, we account for the effect of the global value chain (GVC), which is considered to be significantly developed in the Asian region, depending on the division of roles in the region. It is pointed out that the production process of a

[3]Another reason can be attributed to the lack of data concerning innovation that Hall and Sosikice (2001) utilized in Asian economies.

[4]For a detailed survey, see Kasahara (2004) and Kojima (2000). According to them, the flying geese model per se has evolved along with the development of Asian economies, such as the deepening relationship among them through foreign direct investment.

product is fragmented into different economies. Thus, it is important to specify the role of an industry in an economy in the international network of production. That can be measured by the ratio of value added in the export of an industry. Furthermore, this indicator is calculated for final and intermediate products because the production process in the Asian region is complex, and the role of an industry in each economy is different. The fragmentation of production process results from the activities of transnational companies (TNCs), such as FDI, licensing, and subcontracting, which might enhance the growth of a particular industry. The activities of TNCs and the construction of international network of production would enable closer connection among economies, so that the development of an institution and/or an industry in an economy would improve that of institution and evolution of another economy (cf. Aoki 2010). Therefore, the varieties of industrial structure and specialization among Asian economies may be partly understood by differences in their institutional configurations.

12.3.1 Methodology and Data

Similar to the analysis in the previous section, we conduct MFA and cluster analysis in order to investigate the diversity of Asian capitalisms with regard to industrial specialization. Concerning data, we define four types of variables: specializations in output, employment, external trade, and composition of value added. The first two types consider both the ratio in the whole economy and that in manufacturing. The last two types are concerned with final product and intermediate product, respectively.

We obtained data on the national shares of output and employment targeting 12 industries from the Asian Development Bank (ADB) and 23 industries in manufacturing from the United Nations Industrial Development Organization (UNIDO). As for specialization in external trade and in composition of value added, we manipulate the data from the OECD Trade in Value Added (TiVA) database.

We examine 11 Asian economies as specified in the previous section. Each economy is described by four types of specialization, where each type is instrumented by a range of variables (24 industries in manufacturing, 12 industries (sectors) in an economy for output and employment shares, 23 industries for the specialization in external trade and in value added).[5] Accordingly, we have 11 economies with 164 variables. However, it depends on variables in which economy and for which period data are available. Thus, all the variables are averaged over 2005–2011 as long as the data are available in order to avoid missing data for the analysis.

[5]See data appendix for details.

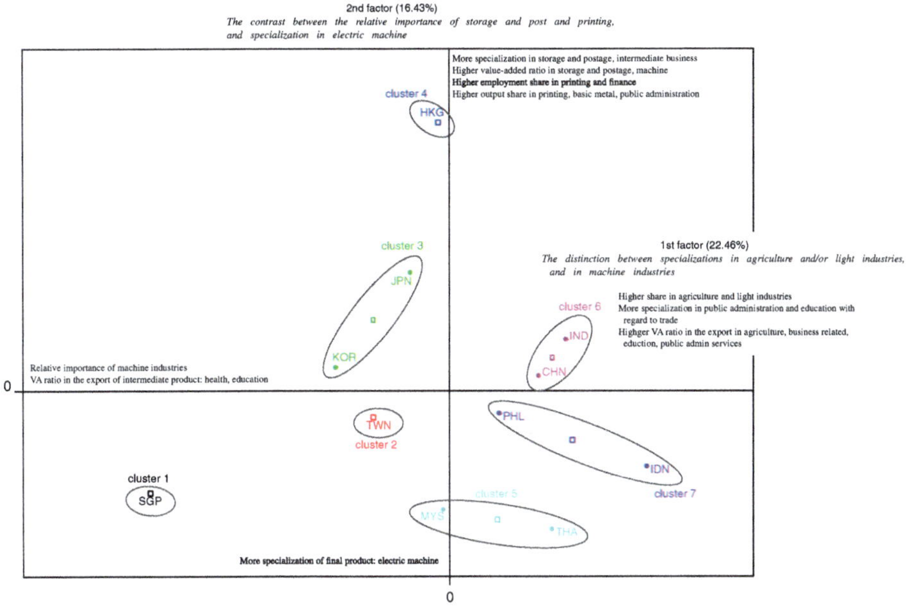

Fig. 12.3 The diversity of Asian capitalism in terms of industrial specialization: 2005–2011

12.3.2 Findings

12.3.2.1 Results of MFA

The number of factors that explain more than 10% of variance of objects (economies) is four. Figure 12.3 shows the factorial plane composed of the first two factors. The first factor explains 22.46% of the total variance. The factor is represented as the horizontal axis of Fig. 12.3. It is positively correlated with the "relative importance in agriculture and light industries with regard to output and employment," "specialization in public administration and education with regard to trade," and "high value-added ratio in export in agriculture and business-related service." On the negative side, the factor is dependent on variables associated with "relative importance of machine industries" and "high value-added ratio in the export of intermediate product in health and education industries." The axis can be interpreted as *the distinction between specializations in agriculture and/or light industries and in machine industries*.

Regarding the second factor, it determines 16.43% of the variance. The variables which affect the factor on the positive side are "specialization in storage and postage and intermediate business," "high value-added ratio in the export of storage and postage and machine," "high employment share in printing and finance," and "high output share in printing, basic metal, and public administration." The negative side of the factor is determined by "specialization in electrical equipment as final product." It is recognized that the vertical axis in Fig. 12.3 represents *the contrast between the relative importance of storage and post and printing on the one hand and specialization in electric machine on the other.* The former in particular distinguishes the peculiarities of Hong Kong from those of other economies as pointed out below; the latter emphasizes the features of *innovation-led capitalism.*

The other two factors also explain the variance of economies to some extent, while they are not pictured in the figure. The third factor, which just contributes to 13.55% of the variance, is positively correlated with "high employment share in manufacturing" and "high value-added ratio in the export of intermediate product in textile, retail, and wholesale industries" and negatively with "high value-added ratio in the export of final product in chemical industry" and "specialization of final product in finance."

The fourth factor explaining 11.03% of the variance has a sizeable effect. It categorizes economies in the order of "relative importance of construction with regard to output share and value-added ratio" and "specialization in health and wood."

12.3.2.2 Results of Cluster Analysis

Cluster analysis is executed based on the result of MFA. Figure 12.3 reveals seven clusters.

The first cluster comprises just Singapore and the second does Hong Kong. These countries together comprise *city capitalism*, which is identified in the analysis of institutional diversity. Singapore has high employment and output shares of office, radio, and medical machines. It specializes in chemical, electrical equipment, and financial intermediation in terms of final and intermediate products. Its value-added ratio in export of intermediate product in construction is high. In contrast, concerning Hong Kong, the specificity of the cluster is displayed in such indicators as high employment and output shares of printing, machine, transport, and finance, specialization in storage and post, and financial intermediation.

The third cluster is composed of Japan and Korea, which partly corresponds to a type of institutional configuration, *innovation-led capitalism.* This cluster is characterized by high employment and output shares of machine industries and specialization of final product in machine industries. Although *innovation-led capitalism* in the analysis of institutional diversity also includes Taiwan, the countries comprising the cluster in terms of institutional configuration are considered not to be tied closely to each other with regard to institutional characteristics. Such a feature is distinctively confirmed in terms of industrial specialization.[6]

The fourth cluster solely comprises Taiwan, which is very close to the countries of the third cluster in the hierarchical clustering tree. It is characterized by

[6]Nevertheless, these three countries are at similar level of the third factor.

specialization of final product in machine industries, especially in electric equipment, resulting in the fact that Taiwan is situated below the third cluster in Fig. 12.3.

The fifth one includes two very large-scale and idiosyncratic countries, China and India. These two countries feature high shares of basic metal in terms of employment and output. They also show high value-added ratio in the export of final product in agriculture, business service, retail, and education.

The sixth cluster is composed of Malaysia and Thailand, corresponding to *trade-led industrializing capitalism* in relation to the diversity of institutional configuration. They have common characteristics as follows: High employment share in food, rubber, and radio machine industries; high share of output in food and radio machine industries; specialization of final product in electric machine and retail industries. It is also confirmed that they have a low degree of specialization of intermediate product in intermediate business service.

The seventh cluster consists of Indonesia and the Philippines, which is called *insular semi-agrarian capitalism* in the analysis of institutional diversity. This cluster is characterized by large shares of output and employment in light industries such as food, wearing apparel, and specialization of final product in agriculture and textiles.

12.3.3 Implications

We confirm the similarity and difference between the diversity of industrial specialization and that of institutional configuration in Asian capitalism. As shown above, we can verify the similarity between the two sorts of diversity. To be more precise, we can figure out the correspondence in the case of *insular semi-agrarian capitalism* and *trade-led industrializing capitalism*. Regarding *innovation-led capitalism*, though this group is divided into two clusters of industrial specialization, these clusters are relatively close to each other. In other words, while all countries of *innovation-led capitalism* specialize in machine industries in the broad sense, Taiwan especially has high specialization in electric machine.

We also find discrepancies between institutional configuration and industrial specialization. On the one hand, the industrial specialization patterns of economies diverge, while the relevant economies belong to the same group together in terms of institutional configuration. This is the case of Hong Kong and Singapore. Although these two economies are considered to belong to the same type of institutional configuration, *city capitalism*, the industrial specialization pattern of Hong Kong is clearly distinguished from that of Singapore by characteristics such as relative importance of printing and specialization in storage and post. It might imply that the industrial development would depend not only on the institutional environment of an economy but also on the specific history of industries such as printing industry in Hong Kong. On the other hand, the industrial specialization pattern of an economy is similar to that of another economy, despite the fact that the relevant economies have different institutional characteristics and are included in contrasting groups with regard to institutional configuration. China and India share similar characteristics regarding industrial specialization such as high employment shares in chemical, mineral product, and basic metal in manufacturing, and in agriculture and mining in the whole economy, and high output share in basic metal in manufacturing, but belong to different groups of institutional configuration. This may be partly due to the fact that both countries are in the process of industrialization.

Therefore, we substantially confirm the coherence between institutional configuration and industrial specialization with some discrepancies that should be explained by further research. It can be said that the analysis in this section to some degree supports the CIA hypothesis even in Asian capitalism. However, to be more exact, the CIA proposed by Hall and Soskice (2001) dealt with the specialization in innovative activities of firms. The next section explores this issue.

12.4 Cross–National Patterns of Specialization in Innovative Activities

We focus our attention on the question of how the institutional configuration specific to each economy determines the economic activities within that economy. Hall and Soskice (2001) imply that the institutional environment of an economy constrains the patterns of firm behavior and, consequently, constitutes a particular type of industrial specialization. However, little is known about how firms behave in institutional environments, and so the question of interaction between institutional environments and firm behavior is still open for discussion.

In this section, we undertake a systematic analysis of the interaction between these factors by focusing on the innovative activities of Asian firms because innovations are becoming the main drivers of their growth nowadays as well as absorptive capabilities for them. More specifically, we are concerned with the problem of whether the five types of institutional frameworks provide companies with better capacities to absorb or advance in certain types of technologies, resulting in cross-national patterns of specialization in innovative activities. In other words, we focus on how the varieties of Asian capitalism are relevant to cross-national patterns of specialization in innovation.

In the following subsection, we first observe the trends in the US patents granted to inventors in Asian economies from 1980 to 2004 and then conduct a sector-level analysis, which gives a clear picture of cross-national patterns of specialization in patenting activities.

Table 12.1 Total number of patents granted for each period

	1980–1984	1985–1989	1990–1994	1995–1999	2000–2004
China	4	76	128	168	581
Hong Kong	94	153	149	412	847
Indonesia			4	6	17
India	12	18	46	181	836
Japan	41,374	76,273	104,540	128,166	169,926
Korea	26	222	2507	10,923	17,984
Malaysia	2	3	14	14	74
The Philippines	1	2	2		3
Singapore	12	26	53	303	1201
Thailand		1	5	29	19
Taiwan	30	207	1250	5854	18,277

Note: Figures denote the total number of US patents granted to each country in a particular period

12.4.1 A Brief Overview of Patenting Activities Across Economies

In investigating national patterns of specialization in innovative activities, we use patent data from a single patent granting country, i.e., the USA, to standardize the unit of innovation. These data facilitate cross-country comparisons (Hall et al. 2001). Table 12.1 summarizes the trends in US patents granted to inventors in Asian economies from 1980 to 2004.

As Table 12.1 indicates, the overall patenting activity of Asian economies had been quite low during the 1980s except for Japan; however, since the 1990s, it has increased substantially in Korea and Taiwan, followed by Hong Kong and Singapore. The growth in patenting activity has been much more dramatic for Taiwan and Korea than for Hong Kong and Singapore, suggesting that the former in particular have experienced a massive increase in innovative activities since the 1990s.

The overall patenting activity in China and India began to increase in the 2000s. Accordingly, the number of patents in these countries is almost close to that in Hong Kong and Singapore. The result concerning China seems to be consistent with that in Tohyama and Harada (2016), indicating that the scientific level and innovative capabilities are relatively high (see also Table 12.2). The number of patents in Indonesia and the Philippines, and to a lesser extent in Malaysia, is the lowest among our sample economies. This result implies that innovative activities in those economies would stagnate.

The overall trends in innovative activities in Asian economies seem to be consistent with the results of the above institutional analysis, meaning that the institutional diversity of Asian capitalisms provides firms with better capacities to advance in certain types of technologies. It possibly could lead to cross-national patterns of specialization in innovative activities.

Table 12.2 Typology of capitalism and innovation in Asian economies

Cluster	Diversity of Asian capitalism	Relevant variables to cluster (v.test)	RTA industries
(Cluster 1) Indonesia The Philippines	***Insular semi-agrarian capitalism*** This group is characterized by a lower degree of liberalization of various markets	**Product market** Closing business time (days) Starting business time (days) Closing business recovery rate (cents on the dollar) **Financial market** Net interest margin **Labor market** Centralized collective bargaining Minimum wage	NA
(Cluster 2) Malaysia Thailand	***Trade-led industrializing capitalism*** This group has characteristics similar to those of Group 1, in terms of the degree of liberalization of markets. Moreover, it has relatively higher public expenditure for education, a higher dependence on external trade, and less rigidity vis-à-vis employment and hours worked.	**Education** Public expenditure on education as % of total government expenditure	**Malaysia:** Mechanical (materials processing and handling; metal working; miscellaneous), others (agriculture, husbandry, food; amusement devices; apparel and textile; furniture, house fixture; heating; pipes and joints; receptacles; miscellaneous) **Thailand:** NA
(Cluster 3) Hong Kong, Singapore	***City capitalism*** The following characteristics are shared among the countries in this group: a significant degree of liberalization of different markets, higher trade dependence, lower domestic social protection, and high profitability of the banking system	**International trade** Ratio of import to GDP; Ratio of export to GDP; Non-tariff trade barriers Foreign ownership/ investment restrictions; Net portfolio investment (% of GDP) Mean tariff rate; Capital controls **Financial market** Stock market capitalization/GDP; Bank concentration **Product market** Price controls; Administrative requirements; Starting business procedures (number) **Labor market** Rigidity of employment index; Difficulty of redundancy index;	**Hong Kong:** Electrical and electronics (electrical devices; electrical lighting; power systems; miscellaneous), others (agriculture, husbandry, food; amusement devices; apparel and textile; furniture, house fixture; heating; receptacles; miscellaneous) **Singapore:** Electrical and electronics (electrical devices; measuring and testing; semiconductor devices)

(continued)

Table 12.2 (continued)

Cluster	Diversity of Asian capitalism	Relevant variables to cluster (v.test)	RTA industries
		Redundancy costs **Economic development** GDP per capita	
(Cluster 4) Japan, Korea, Taiwan	***Innovation-led capitalism*** Higher economic development and barriers to entry into product markets are observed as common characteristics in these countries	**Education** Adult literacy rate (% of population aged 15 years and above) **Financial market** Public bond market capitalization / GDP; Private bond market capitalization / GDP **Social security** Public expenditure on health (% of GDP); Public social protection and health expenditure as percentage of GDP **International trade** Standard deviation of tariff rates	**Korea:** Computers and communications (computer peripherals; information storage), electrical and electronics (electrical lighting; semiconductor devices; miscellaneous) **Japan:** Computers and communications (computer hardware and software; computer peripherals; information storage), electrical and electronics (electrical devices; electrical lighting; nuclear and X-rays; power systems; semiconductor devices; miscellaneous), mechanical (metal working; motors, engines and parts) **Taiwan:** Electrical and electronics (electrical devices; power systems; semiconductor devices)
(Cluster 5) China	***Continental mixed capitalism*** China shares many institutional characteristics with Malaysia and Thailand, as shown in the analysis with advanced economies. This would imply that its institutional configuration is heavily capitalist. However, it is distinct from these two countries in the analysis among Asian economies	**Financial market** Interest rate controls/negative real interest rates Ownership of banks **Social security** Private expenditure on health (% of GDP) **Product market** Starting business, Min. capital (% of income per capita)	**China:** Chemical (organic composition; resins, miscellaneous-chemicals), drugs and medical (drugs; biotechnology; miscellaneous), others (agriculture, husbandry, food; amusement devices; earth working and wells; furniture, house fixture; heating; receptacles; miscellaneous)

Note
For grouping of Asian economies in Column 1, see also Harada and Tohyama (2012)
Relevant variables to clusters in Column 3 are ones with a v.value of 2 and higher
Column 4 indicates industries with more than one RTA, based on industry category (subcategory)

12.4.2 Cross-National Patterns of Innovative Specialization

In order to identify cross-national patterns of specialization in patenting activities, we utilize the relative technological advantage (RTA) index, which measures the relative distribution of a country's inventive activity in each industry (Mahmood and Singh 2003). Formally, the RTA index for country i in sector j is defined as the ratio of country i's share of total patents in sector j to the share of total world patents in that sector, i.e.,

$$RTA_{ij} \equiv \frac{n_{ij}/\sum_i n_{ij}}{\sum_j n_{ij}/\sum_i \sum_j n_{ij}}$$

where n_{ij} is the number of patents of country i in sector j. By definition, this index equals 1 if the country holds the same share of worldwide patents in a given technology as in the aggregate and is below (above) 1 if there is a relative weakness (strength) (see also Hall and Soskice (2001)).

Column 3 in Table 12.2 presents the list of industries with an RTA above 1.[7] According to the table, Malaysia, *trade-led industrializing capitalism*, shows comparative advantages in "mechanical" and "other" industries, which includes subcategories such as "agriculture, husbandry, food"; "amusement devices"; "apparel and textile"; "earth working and wells"; "furniture, house fixture"; "heating"; "pipes and joints"; "receptacles"; and "miscellaneous others."

Economies referred to as a *city capitalism* show comparative advantages in the "electrical and electronics" industry, which is similar to an *innovation-led capitalism*. Hong Kong also advances in the "other" industry.

As for cluster 4, these economies share certain similarities in that they all show a comparative advantage in the so-called high-technology industry. For example, Korea and Japan have comparative advantages in "computers and communications" and "electrical and electronics." In addition, Japan advances in the "mechanical" industry, which includes subcategories such as "motor, engines, and parts" and "transportation." Innovative activities in Taiwan are outstanding in the "electrical and electronics" industry, especially in "semiconductor devices."

The last cluster, i.e., China, shows comparative advantages in such industries as "chemical," "drugs and medical," and "others."

In the following, we visualize the results of Table 12.2 in Figs. 12.4, 12.5, and 12.6, which makes it easier to understand the relationship between institutional characteristics and cross-national patterns of specialization in innovative activities. In these figures, we map sample economies on the space described by the first two dimensions derived from the analysis of institutional diversity within Asian economies, and at the same time, we indicate the characteristics of each dimension and the

[7]If we consider a very limited number of samples in Indonesia, the Philippines, and Thailand, information on RTA of these economies would be irrelevant, and hence they are not indicated in Table 12.2.

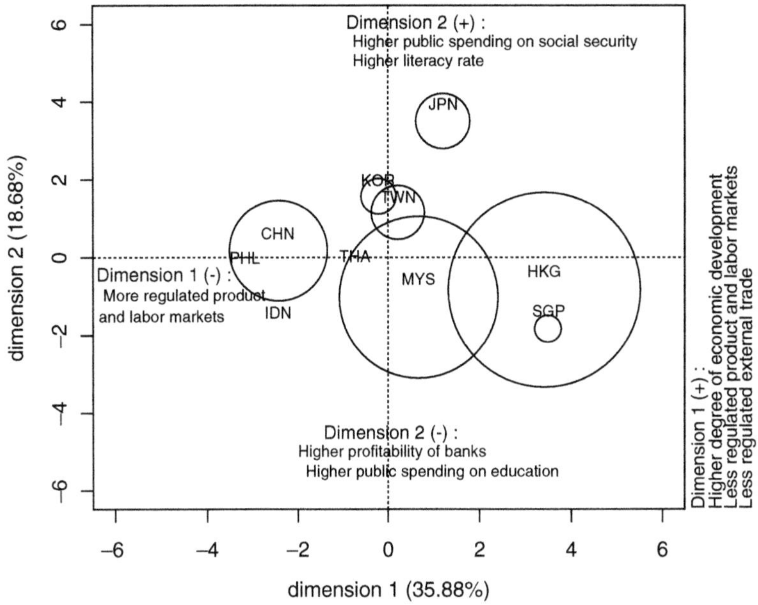

Fig. 12.4 RTA in others (Note: The size of circle represents the RTA index)

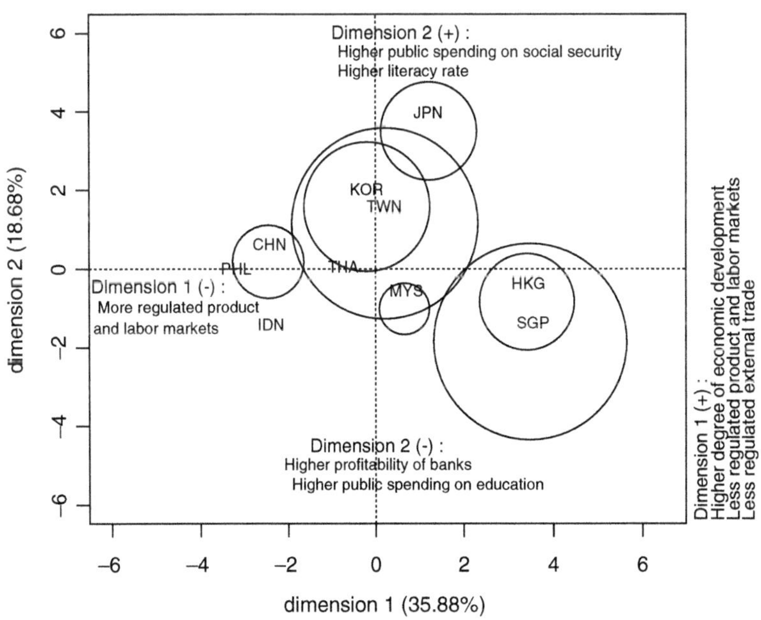

Fig. 12.5 RTA in electrical and electronics (Note: The size of circle represents the RTA index)

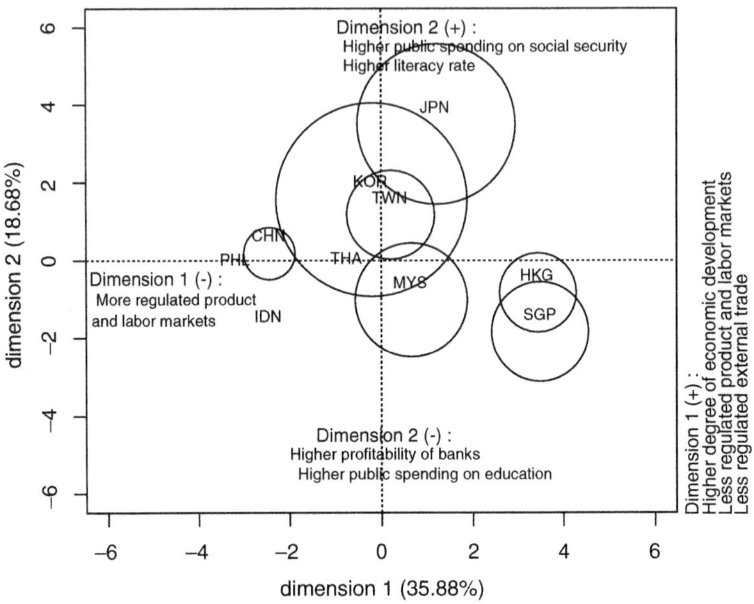

Fig. 12.6 RTA in computers and communications (Note: The size of circle represents RTA index)

RTA index, which is presented by the size of circle where the radius of a circle is given by $\sqrt{RTA/x}$.

Therefore, these figures show the degree to which innovation is concentrated in any of the six technology classes that vary according to whether technological progress in them is typically characterized by the institutional characteristics. Taking these figures and Table 12.2 together, we could understand how the diversity of Asian capitalisms is associated with the national pattern of specialization in innovative activities.

Cluster 1

Firms in cluster 1 can be expected to have stagnated in terms of innovative activities, if we consider the figures and the overall trends of patenting activities in Table 12.1. As the figures show, these economies have common institutional characteristics: more regulated product and labor markets and a closed domestic market. It would be difficult for those economies to attract FDI and for firms embedded in these institutional architectures to assimilate technologies from advanced economies.

Cluster 2

As mentioned above, this group has institutional characteristics similar to those of cluster 1 in terms of *the degree of liberalization of markets*. However, it has relatively higher public expenditure for education (see Column 3 in Table 12.2) and a higher dependence on external trade. These could be considered as the features of an export-oriented welfare capitalism in Asia, where most resources devoted to social policies have been allocated to building human capital through increased spending on education and health (Tohyama 2015). These characteristics might also facilitate the integration of these countries into the world-trade network via a global supply chain. In these economies, the share of IT products has been large, and primary products also account for a larger share of exports. It seems that these institutional characteristics could encourage firms in Malaysia to be specialized in the category of "others," including "agriculture, husbandry, food"; "amusement devices"; "apparel and textile"; "earth working and wells"; "furniture, house fixture"; "heating"; "pipes and joints"; "receptacles"; and "miscellaneous others"(Fig. 12.4).

Cluster 3

Firms in cluster 3, i.e., Hong Kong and Singapore, share similarities in that they are innovative disproportionately in the field of "electrical and electronics." As can be seen in Fig. 12.5 and Column 4 in Table 12.2, these two economies have common institutional characteristics: less regulated product and labor markets, a liberal type of financial market, and open market-oriented characteristics. These institutional architectures could attract massive FDI, as well as with knowledge-intensive workers accompanied by good quality research institutions. As a result, firms in these institutional environments are likely to excel in assimilating technologies from advanced economies, leading to better capacities to advance in high-technology industries such as "electrical and electronics."

Cluster 4

Firms in cluster 4, i.e., Japan, Korea, and Taiwan, have been more active innovators in fields predominantly characterized by high technologies, including "computers and communications" and "electrical and electronics" fields (see Column 4 in Table 12.2, Fig. 12.6). Firms in Taiwan outstandingly innovate in the sector of semiconductor devices. Firms in Japan also innovate in the "mechanical" field, whose subcategories are "metal working," "motors," and "engines and parts." These patterns are consistent with the ones our analysis would expect in MFA and cluster analysis, where we define this cluster as *innovation-led capitalism*.

Cluster 5

Patterns of innovative specialization in China seem to be similar to those of India in that both economies show comparative advantage in "chemical" and "drugs and medical" fields. Yet, fields where firms are innovative are broader in China than in India.[8] More interestingly, it might seem like that the patterns of specialization in China might be irrelevant to its institutional architecture. Rather, it would indicate that rapidly increasing patenting activities could advance before forming a coherent institutional architecture consistent with those activities, in other words, a dominant institutional mechanism that can coordinate individual institutional domains and lead all to the pattern of innovative specialization in China. According to Tohyama

[8]India is not shown in this figure since we focus on how five types of Asian capitalisms in Section 12.2 are associated with cross-national patterns of innovative specialization. As for India, see Tohyama and Harada (2016).

and Harada (2016), where it focused on core institutional domains which directly and indirectly influence an economy's technological specialization, China is distinctive in that the scientific level and innovative capabilities are relatively high, possibly resulting in rapidly increasing patenting activities (see Table 12.1). Furthermore, China has a massive and rapidly growing internal market. It is possible that China's leading firms have developed their capabilities and localized innovations.

However, there could be problems of institutional domains closely associated with innovation and science being isolated from other institutional domains. In addition, the financial system, and institutional domains associated with human capital, and the international regime seem to have less effects on the basic technological style described by such institutional domains as science, technology, and industry (Tohyama and Harada 2016). Institutional domains underlying the technological system might inconsistently interact with each other. In other words, these domains might also be a haphazard assemblage of individual institutional configuration, as we could expect from the previous section, where we define China as a *continental mixed capitalism*.

From these findings by and large, we could argue that the institutional diversity of Asian capitalisms provides firms with better capacities to advance in certain types of technologies, possibly leading to cross-national patterns of specialization in innovative activities.

12.5 Concluding Remarks

This chapter examined the relationship between institutional configuration, industrial specialization, and innovative activities of firms based on several statistical analyses. After presenting five types of Asian capitalism following Harada and Tohyama (2012), and verifying the diversity of institutional configuration in Asian capitalism, we proved that the diversity of industrial specialization in the region is substantially associated with that of institutional configuration, though there exist some significant exceptions. Furthermore, we identified cross-national patterns of specialization in patenting activities and similarity with those of institutional structure as well. Based on these analyses, we verified again the features of the five types of Asian capitalism from the viewpoints of institutional configuration and industrial and innovative specialization.

Insular semi-agrarian capitalism consists of Indonesia and the Philippines, which is characterized by less liberalization of different markets concerning institutional configuration. As for industrial specialization, they have large shares of output and employment in light industries and specialize in agriculture and textiles. It would be difficult for these economies to assimilate technologies from advanced economies due to their institutional characteristics. This result implies that innovative activities in these economies would stagnate. Actually, the number of patents in Indonesia and the Philippines is the lowest among our sample economies (Table 12.1).

Trade-led industrializing capitalism includes Malaysia and Thailand. While its institutional characteristics are similar to those of *insular semi-agrarian capitalism* in terms of the degree of liberalization of markets, this type of capitalism also features relatively higher public expenditure for education, a higher dependence on external trade, and less rigidity vis-à-vis employment and hours worked. As for industrial specialization, it is characterized by the relative importance of not only food but radio machine industries and specialization in electric machine and retail industries. It has similar characteristics in terms of innovative activities: Malaysia has strength in machine industries such as materials processing and handling on the one hand and industries like agriculture and apparel and textile on the other. These contrasting characteristics would result from the opposing institutional characteristics: More regulated markets would prevent firms in the economy from accessing and absorbing the latest technologies from advanced economies. Higher public expenditure for education and higher dependence on external trade might facilitate the integration of these countries into the world-trade network via a global supply chain as can be seen from the fact that Malaysia holds comparative advantage in the "mechanical" industry.

City capitalism comprises Hong Kong and Singapore, which have common institutional features of significant liberalization of markets, higher trade dependence, lower domestic social protection, and high profitability of the banking system. They also share similarities in innovative activities in high-technology industries because their institutional characteristics could allow these economies to excel in assimilating technologies from advanced economies. Nevertheless, what is more interesting is that their industrial specializations are divergent from each other: Singapore has relative importance and specialization in electrical machine, whereas Hong Kong has specificities regarding printing, storage and post, and financial intermediation. This is one of exceptions to a strict correspondence between institutional architecture and industrial specialization.

Innovation-led capitalism, including Japan, South Korea, and Taiwan, is institutionally characterized by higher economic development and barriers to entry into product markets. Its peculiarity regarding industrial specialization is relative importance concerning employment and output, and specialization in machine industries. It also has idiosyncrasy of patent activities in so-called high-technology industries. Economies in this type advance in the latest technologies because their institutional characteristics, such as well-accumulated human capital and full-fledged financial market, would allow firms to create new ideas, transform those ideas into artifacts, and convert them into marketable products. They could make it easy to endogenously develop high technologies.

Continental mixed capitalism, solely consisting of China, has similar institutional characteristics with those of *trade-led industrializing capitalism* on the one hand, and peculiarities, such as less protection of investors, moderate level of dependence on external trade, on the other. The features regarding industrial specialization of China, that are shared with those of India, include the relative importance of basic metal and high value-added ratio in agriculture, business service, retail, and education. China is distinctive in that the scientific level and innovative capabilities are relatively high, resulting in rapidly increasing the number of patents (see Table 12.1). While its comparative advantage can be found in "chemical," "drugs and medical," and "other" industries, this trend cannot be seen in high-technology industries different from *city capitalism* or *innovation-led capitalism*, and it would be less likely to be consistent with its institutional configuration.

This characterization would reveal the coherence of each type of capitalism through institutional environment at the macro level, relative strength and composition of different industries at the meso level, and firm behavior engaging innovation at the micro level. That would make the typology of Asian capitalism more robust. Based on these empirical results, the institutional configurations are likely to provide companies with better capacities to advance in certain types of technologies, resulting in cross-national patterns of innovative specialization and then patterns of industrial specialization. We could argue that technological progress is path dependent because it seems to proceed along the technological and industrial trajectories defined by the diversity of Asian capitalisms. This implies that what matters for Asian economies would be less to close their technological gap with the frontier, rather than to find technological trajectories available for them. There might be multiple pathways for Asian economies to reach the technological frontier and achieve the matured economic structure.

Nonetheless, it is still unclear whether these institutional architectures underlying the technological style are specific to Asian economies, which most developing countries allegedly share. Thus, we need a wide range of comparative analysis, which includes other emerging or developing economies (e.g., Reslinger 2013).

In this chapter, we showed the consistency of diversity at various levels. However, it would be indispensable to analyze deep into the individual linkage among institutions and the cross-national patterns of industrial and innovative specialization in order to fully understand the institutional foundation of firm behavior and industrial structure in Asian economies. This is a future research topic.

Appendix: List of Variables and Industries for the Analysis of Industrial Specialization

Variable	Industries	Source
Employment share in manufacturing	Food and beverages, tobacco products, textiles, wearing apparel, fur, leather, leather products and footwear, wood products (excl. furniture), paper and paper products, printing and publishing, Coke, refined petroleum products, nuclear fuel, chemicals and chemical products, rubber and plastics products, non-metallic mineral products,	United Nations Industrial Development Organization (UNIDO 2011) INDSTAT
Output share in manufacturing		

(continued)

Variable	Industries	Source
	basic metals, fabricated metal products, machinery and equipment n.e.c., office, accounting and computing machinery, electrical machinery and apparatus, radio, television and communication equipment, medical, precision and optical instruments, motor vehicles, trailers, semi-trailers, other transport equipment, furniture; manufacturing n. e.c., recycling	
Employment share in the entire economy Output share in the entire economy	Agriculture, forestry, and fishing, mining and quarrying, manufacturing, electricity, gas, steam and air conditioning supply, construction, wholesale and retail trade; repair of motor vehicles and motorcycles, accommodation and food service activities (hotels and restaurants), transport and storage, information and communication, finance and insurance, real estate, professional and scientific, administrative support, and other business activities, public administration and defense, compulsory social security, other service activities, education	Asian Development Bank Statistical Database
Specialization index of external trade of final product (cf. Amable 2003) Specialization index of external trade of intermediate product (cf. Amable 2003) Domestic value added in exports of final products as a share of total gross exports Domestic value added in exports of intermediate products as a share of total gross exports	Agriculture, hunting, forestry and fishing, food products, beverages and tobacco, textiles, textile products, leather and footwear, wood, paper, paper products, printing and publishing, chemicals and non-metallic mineral products, basic metals and fabricated metal products, machinery and equipment, nec, electrical and optical equipment, transport equipment, manufacturing nec; recycling, electricity, gas and water supply, construction, wholesale and retail trade; hotels and restaurants, transport and storage, post and telecommunication, financial intermediation, real estate, renting and business activities, computer and related activities,	OECD Trade in Value Added (TiVA) database

(continued)

Variable	Industries	Source
	R&D and other business activities, Public administration and defence; compulsory social security, education, health and social work, other community, social and personal services, private households with employed persons	

References

Akamatsu K (1961) A theory of unbalanced growth in the world economy. Weltwirtschaftliches Archiv Rev World Econ 86:3–25

Akamatsu K (1962) A historical pattern of economic growth in developing countries. J Develop Econ 1(1):3–25

Amable B (2003) The diversity of modern capitalism. Oxford University Press, New York

Berthelier P, Desdoigts A, Ould Aoudia J (2003) « Profils Institutionnels » Présentation et analyse d'une base de données originale sur les caractéristiques institutionnelles de pays en développement, en transition et développés', Document de travail de ministère de l'économie des finances et de l'industrie, France

Boyer R (2012) The Chinese growth regime and the world economy. In: Boyer R et al (eds) Diversity and transformation of Asian capitalisms. Routledge, Abingdon

Boyer R (2015) Économie politique des capitalismes: Théorie de la régulation et des crises. La Découverte, Paris

Chowdhury A, Islam I (eds) (2007) Handbook on the northeast and southeast Asian economies. Edward Elgar, Cheltenham

Clark C (1957) Conditions of economic progress, 3rd edn. Macmillan, London

Hall PA, Soskice D (2001) Varieties of Capitalism: Institutional foundation of Comparative Advantage. Oxford University Press, Oxford

Hall BH, Jaffe AB, Trajtenberg M (2001) The NBER patent citation data file: lessons, insights and methodological tools. NBER working paper 8498

Harada Y, Tohyama H (2012) Asian capitalisms: institutional configurations and firm heterogeneity. In: Boyer R et al (eds) Diversity and Transformations of Asian Capitalisms. Routledge, Abingdon

Kasahara S (2004) The flying geese paradigm: a critical study of its application to East Asian regional development. UNCTAD discussion papers, no.169

Kojima K (2000) The flying geese model of Asian economic development: origin, theoretical extensions, and regional policy implication. J Asian Econ 11(4):375–401

Mahmood IP, Singh J (2003) Technological dynamism in Asia. Res Policy 32(4):1031–1054

Pagès J (2014) Multiple factor analysis by example using R. CRC Press, Broken Sound Parkway

Reslinger C (2013) Is there an Asian model of technological emergence? Soc Econ Rev 11 (1):371–408

Tohyama H (2015) Varieties of Asian welfare capitalisms and the influence of globalization. J Int Comp Soc Pol 31(1):51–73

Tohyama H, Harada Y (2016) Diversity of institutional architecture underlying the technological system in Asian economies. Evolut Inst Econ Rev 13(1):239–268

United Nations Industrial Development Organization (2011) INDSTAT2 2011: industrial statistics database. United Nations Industrial Development Organization

Walter A, Zhang X (2012) East Asian capitalism: Diversity, continuity, and change. Oxford University Press, Oxford

Witt MA, Redding G (2013) Asian business systems: Institutional comparison, clusters and implications for varieties of capitalism and business systems theory. Soc Econ Rev 11 (2):265–300

Zhang X, Whitley R (2013) Changing macro-structural varieties of east Asian capitalism. Soc Econ Rev 11(2):301–336

Chapter 13
Dynamics of Chinese-Style Developmentalism as the Mode of Régulation: Formation, Weakening, and Redesign of Flexible Rigidity

Lei Song and Chengnan Yan

13.1 Introduction

In recent years, the Chinese economy has shifted gear from the previous high-speed growth to a medium-to-high speed growth. As the number two largest economies in the world, economic slowing down will not fundamentally weaken China's political and economic positions in the international system. However, changes captured by the term "new normal" have attracted attentions from the academic circles. Against the backdrop of this challenge, scholars are challenged to come up with a new framework, which is both logical and consistent, to explain the Chinese economic growth and adjustment in the whole reform era.[1]

The high growth has covered many conflicts deeply rooted in the Chinese economy. However, conflicts from macro- and microlevels are becoming more and more prominent nowadays. At the macro-level, the national wealth is distributed unevenly, and at the microlevel, Chinese enterprises lack original technical and

[1]As the notion "Beijing Consensus" (Ramo 2004) spread around the world, different from the neoclassical economists who take Chinese experience as nothing but another success of neoclassical economics, some Chinese political economists conducted researches about the so-called Chinese model of economic development. However, in these literatures, theorization of Chinese experience is still at an early stage. With clear and strong influences of economic ideologies, the main body of these literatures is sketchy description of the structural features of Chinese economy (Song and Zhang 2013: 226–227). Furthermore, these studies cannot analyze why the high-growth changes into so-called "new normal" soundly. Put it differently, the advocates of Chinese model of economic development put forward valuable research topic, but they failed to accomplish it.

L. Song (✉)
Peking University, Beijing, China
e-mail: slei@pku.edu.cn

C. Yan
Rikkyo University, Tokyo, Japan

R. Boyer et al. (eds.), *Evolving Diversity and Interdependence of Capitalisms*, Evolutionary Economics and Social Complexity Science 11,
https://doi.org/10.1007/978-4-431-55001-3_13

organizational innovations.[2,3] The emergence of the "new normal" challenges China's mainstream economists, but it also gives us the chance to propose a new consistent logical framework to explain China's economic story.

This chapter aims to provide a self-consistent analytical framework to understand the Chinese previous high-speed growth and the emergence of the "new normal." At the center of this framework is mode of régulation, which we borrowed from the French *régulation* school. We use the term Chinese-style developmentalism to label China's mode of régulation in the reform period. We argue that the Chinese-style developmentalism, on the one hand, provides the Chinese economy with the motive of development and, on the other hand, limits the scope of economic development. In this chapter, we discuss the nature of Chinese-style developmentalism as the mode of régulation through analyzing its configuration, logic, mechanism, limitation, and ongoing adjustment and link Chinese-style developmentalism with the conversion and reconversion of China's growth regime.

In form, the Chinese-style developmentalism is composed of three hierarchical transactions that are (1) transaction between the ruling party and citizens, (2) transaction between the government and capitalist, and (3) transaction within the bureaucratic group. The transaction between the ruling party and citizens stands at a higher level and the other two transactions are at a lower level. Higher-level transaction defines the nature of lower-level transactions, while lower-level transactions are the pillars of higher-level transaction. The Chinese-style developmentalism emerged in the 1980s and matured in the 1990s. The Chinese-style developmentalism ensured economic growth through additional policies which increases investments and enlarges exports, and the economic growth maintained the political stability in turn. Mapping economic growth and political stability into the aforementioned three transactions, we find that economic growth can be taken as the result of transaction between the government and capitalist and transaction within the bureaucratic group and these two kinds of transaction make the exchange of economic growth and political support which is at the very center of transaction between the ruling party and citizens possible.

The Chinese-style developmentalism differs from other kinds of developmentalism. It not only abstractly summarizes the state's economic ideology, national strategy, and political regime but also defines the specific development trajectory as well as growth regime for China in the reform period. Concretely, the investment/export-led development model was established and enhanced under the

[2]For example, China's Gini index is much higher than that of Vietnam, another Asian transition economy.

[3]In the classic studies of late-development advantage, there exists a hypothesis which may be summed up as Gerschenkron-Dore Proposition: in the big successful economic late comers, large enterprises are formed which are liable to undergo paradigm-shift innovation in terms of organizational form (Gerschenkron 1962; Dore 1973: 414). Enterprises in the United States, Germany, and Japan fit well with this proposition, but current enterprises in China deviate from this proposition. In China, we find only size enlargement, not the paradigm-shift kind of organizational innovation (Song 2015).

Chinese-style developmentalism. However, as mode of régulation, the Chinese-style developmentalism also has its limits. On the one hand, the effectiveness of the Chinese-style developmentalism is heavily dependent on the international economic conditions. On the other hand, the Chinese-style developmentalism gives rise to the conflicts between investment and consumption as well as conflicts between private and state capital. In the "new normal" era, changes in international economic conditions raise obstacles for the Chinese investment/export-led development model. Consequently, conflict between investment and consumption as well as conflict between different kinds of capital has been exaggerating in recent years.

The limitation of Chinese-style developmentalism originates from deeper logics. As mode of *régulation* of a transition economy, the Chinese-style developmentalism must balance economic growth and political stability at the same time. While economic growth usually requires a large degree of economic flexibility, political stability requires a great extent of political rigidity. In sum, the Chinese-style developmentalism is the combination of two mutually conflictive component factors that are economic flexibility and political rigidity.

Economic flexibility and political rigidity coexist in the Chinese-style developmentalism, but their relative relationship changes from time to time. The variations of the relationship between economic flexibility and political rigidity shape the dynamics of the Chinese-style developmentalism. Before the second decade of the twenty-first century, Chinese economic development had no obvious confrontations with its political system. In that period, the Chinese-style developmentalism manifested itself as flexible rigidity under which high-speed economic growth was achieved by successive economic reform policies, and economic growth supported political stability in turn. However, as economic reforms entered the deep water zone, political reforms become the prerequisite of sustainable economic development. Seen in this light, the rigid flexibility has been weakened, and the redesign of the relation between economic and political systems is necessary.

13.2 East Asian Developmentalism as Economic Ideology, National Strategy, and Political Regime

In the literature on East Asian economic growth, the developmentalism occupies an important place. However, for researchers from different disciplines, the developmentalism differs in concept.

Firstly, the developmentalism can be understood as the economic ideology different from the laissez-faire approach. For example, the developmentalism can be defined as a set of economic thought and ideology about how a late comer catches up through governmental intervention and nonmarket institutional arrangements (Gao 1997, 2013: 69–70). Similarly, it also can be taken as the economics of industrialization or the renewal of mercantilism German Historical School (Murakami 1992: 6). Generally speaking, in this kind of economic ideology or economic theory, nationalism or national self-esteem figure prominently (Hayami and Godo 2005).

Secondly, for some political economists and developmental economists, the developmentalism is a kind of national strategy toward specific industries. The advocates of the developmental state approach tend to take the developmentalism as industrial policy pursued by the elite bureaucracy (Johnson 1982; Amsden 1989). Be somewhat analogous to these interventionists, some development economists deem the developmentalism to be the approach mobilizing the resources to contribute to the national interest (Suehiro 2010: 21–23).

Thirdly, the developmentalism is seen by some political scientists as a kind of de jure or de facto one-party system. Actually, in the literature on the economic growth of Latin America, the developmentalism is taken as bureaucratic authoritarianism (O'Donnell 1973). To some extent, the East Asian developmentalism is also tinged with soft authoritarianism (Deyo 1987).

Of course, the developmentalism in action normally possesses all the three aforementioned characteristics (Murakami 1992, 5–6). Because the developmentalism relates to economic ideology, national strategy and political regime and economic ideology, national strategy and political regime are all controversial issues, there is long debate about the effects of East Asian developmentalism. However, it is undoubtable that the developmentalism shaped the economic growth in East Asia.

13.3 Chinese–Style Developmentalism as the Mode of *Régulation*: Configuration, Mechanism, Limit, and Logic

Similar to some East Asian economic systems, the path of economic development in China has features: a specific economic ideology, a national development strategy, and a commitment to a one-party system, among other features. In particular, the Chinese model is defined by the fact that economic development has become the singular social goal, collectively agreed upon by policy-makers and the general public alike to overshadow all other possible policy goals. This collective agreement reflects the extent to which all of Chinese society, across social classes, seems to have accepted wholesale Deng Xiaoping's famous assertion: "development is the hard truth."

In general, although the Chinese economic policy does have its unique features, the policies instituted by the Chinese government are similar to policies instituted in other East Asian economic systems: their central focus is directed toward the selective industrial policy (Beeson 2009; Boltho and Weber 2009). Moreover, over the course of economic development, the party-state system has been strengthened. Still, the most important thing to come out of Chinese-style developmentalism goes beyond the dimensions of economic ideology, national strategy, and the one-party system. In fact, the Chinese doctrine of developmentalism is supported by the transactions between (1) the ruling party and citizens, (2) the government and capitalist, and (3) the officers at different levels. Together, these transactions have set in place China's unique set of growth regime.

13.3.1 Configuration and Mechanism of Chinese–Style Developmentalism

13.3.1.1 Configuration of Chinese–Style Developmentalism: Transactions at the Top and Secondary Levels

First, the Chinese-style developmentalism, or the Chinese doctrine of development, is jointly constituted by transactions at both the top level and secondary level within the Chinese political economy. Top-level transaction refers to the compromise between the ruling party and citizens.

In the case of this kind of transaction, the central government (party-in-power) considers promising the reasonable rate of economic growth as necessary to maintain political legitimacy, in the form of tacit consent by the masses. This type of legitimacy is based almost entirely on continued GDP growth. In the case of top-level transaction, the public gives up the right to participate directly in politics, in exchange for reaping employment opportunity and other economic returns. At the same time, the ruling party maintains its own end of the bargain. In order to carry out this top-level transaction, interaction between the government and capitalist and interaction within the bureaucratic group become necessary. Together, these two types of interaction give shape to transactions that occur at the secondary level.[4]

There are two types of transaction that occur between the Chinese government and capitalist class. The first type is basically a political one, while the second type is mainly an economic one. The first type is for central and local governments to confer political status on capitalists, in exchange for the political support of the capitalist class.[5] The second type refers to the transaction between local governments' economic policies and capitalist's investment. Concretely, local governments adopt various forms of preferential policies to incentivize investment by capital holders. In this way, so-called local corporatism is formed (Oi 1992). The downside of this trade-off is that, because the working class gives up political right or is prohibited from exercising political power, they are excluded from participating in the

[4]For more details about the political transaction, see Commons (1959) and North (1992).

[5]Rewards include political appointments to the National People's Congress, the Chinese People's Political Consultative Conference, and other political rewards.

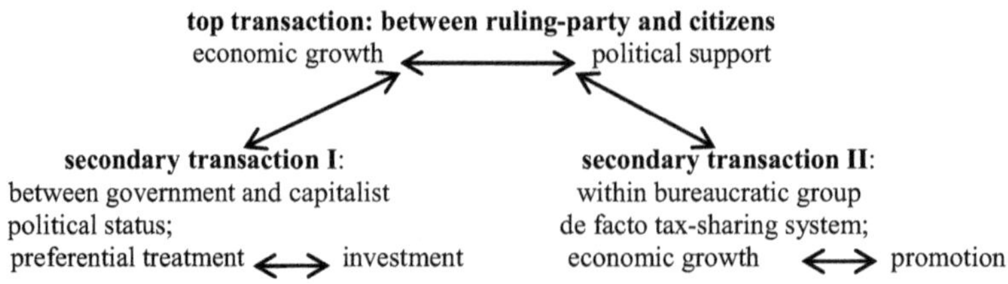

Fig. 13.1 Structure of hierarchical transactions composing Chinese-style developmentalism

transactions between local governments and capital forces. Thus, in reality, China's local corporatism is one deeply lacking in worker participation.[6]

Transaction within China's internal bureaucratic group similarly takes two forms. The first type of transaction occurs between the central government and local governments. In this type of transaction, the central government allows local governments to partake of the increased tax revenue gained from economic growth, in exchange for the efforts of local governments in promoting economic growth. The second type of transaction occurs between government bodies at various levels. To ensure that local bureaucrats work fervently to promote economic growth, governments at various levels across the Chinese political system make economic growth results one of the important criteria to evaluate when considering candidates for career promotion. In this way, the relationships between the Chinese government and individual bureaucrats at all levels are featured by the tight connection between economic performance and individual promotion. This is a key component of China's system of transactions at the secondary level. The structure of the hierarchical transactions can be illustrated in Fig. 13.1.

13.3.1.2 Mechanism of Chinese–Style Developmentalism: Competitive Local Corporatism and Export–Led Growth

Chinese-style developmentalism has led to the formation of specific growth regime. It is important to note, however, that just as the transactions which frame the Chinese-style developmentalism come into being gradually, the effect of Chinese-style developmentalism on growth regime has similarly emerged through a gradual process.

First, the Chinese-style developmentalism first began to take shape during the 1980s and matured during the 1990s.Therefore, it has affected the China's growth regime in varying ways, at different points in time. Simply put, in the 1980s, the top-level transaction discussed above began to take shape through the introduction

[6]Some scholars believe that the main purpose of the alliance between local government and capital is economic development, so that local governments have a tendency to behave as a company would. However, it must be noted that, because the labor force is prohibited from participating in politics, this "company" is not a form of democratic economic decision-making.

of policies associated with reform and opening. The second-level transactions identified above, however, did not begin to emerge until the 1990s. Therefore, in the 1980s, the effect of Chinese-style developmentalism is indirect and limited. Indeed, it was in the 1980s that Chinese economy first began to transition from a planned economy to a market economy. During this time, most major investment came from domestic capital (Huang 2008), and growth was largely consumption-driven (Uni et al. 2004, 5). In this period, there are essentially two reasons for economic growth: the first is the backlash against the planned system; the second is the combined result of a set of policies with social democratic features (Song 2001).

In the 1990s, the top and secondary transactions began to mature and solidify into a predictable and repeated pattern of political and economic actors. In turn, these repeated transactions began to influence the country's pattern of economic growth. Simply put, during this period, each time the economy would face a challenge, the central government would attempt to strengthen the secondary-level transactions in order to resolve the problems. In the process of reform, Deng Xiaoping's southern inspection tour in 1992, entry into the WTO and the large-scale investment projects aiming to soften the shock of financial crisis in 2008 are all important responses of economic policy. The central government implemented these policies to respond different challenges. In practice, meanwhile, the process of instituting these policies has had the effect of strengthening, both directly and indirectly, two important types of secondary transaction. Thus, in the 1990s, once these secondary transactions began to take shape in their distinctive pattern, the Chinese-style developmentalism began to crystallize into its mature state.

China's unique brand of local corporatism stems from the two types of secondary transaction that have emerged during China's first two decades of reform. Aside from the fact that workers are excluded from all decisions, the key defining feature of this kind of corporatism is the competition among local governments, and the center issue of the competition is capital resource or investment. It is important to stress that, at the beginning of the 1990s, with the expansion of global supply chains, international capital began to actively seek new avenues for investment (Harvey 2007). As the result of the combination of competitively preferential policies from local governments, and the eagerness of international capital to invest, the speed of foreign direct investment in China began to increase rapidly. In this way, the Chinese economy began to enter its export-led growth period (Uni et al. 2004, 2005).

13.3.2 Limits and Logic of Chinese–Style Developmentalism

Chinese-style developmentalism is comprised of transactions at various levels. As a whole, the system is defined by economic flexibility, combined with political rigidity. This so-called economic flexibility points to the fact that the Chinese government continuously implements new policies in its efforts to maintain high growth rates. The political rigidity points to the system through which the central government maintains its hold on power. It is important to note that the relationship between China's economic flexibility and political rigidity changes at different moments in time: if, for a period of time, economic flexibility helps to consolidate the political system, then these two aspects work in harmony; if political rigidity becomes too strong, however, this can become a major constraint on economic flexibility; thus, these two aspects can be in tension. Simply put, Chinese-style developmentalism has brought about economic growth, yet inherent contradictions between top-level and secondary-level transactions or conflicts between economic flexibility and political rigidity mean that, over time, the following three types of tensions have begun to emerge.

First, the continued development of secondary transactions depends on the freedom of capital; meanwhile, the party-state system depends on the continued existence of huge state-owned enterprises. At the beginning of reforms, there was a relative abundance of opportunity for capital investment with high returns. Thanks to the ongoing process of incremental reforms, the public enjoyed increasing access to capital for entrepreneurship. Thus, the abovementioned tension did not emerge. Thirty years into China's development, however, there are fewer opportunities for high-return investments. Moreover, the less efficient SOEs occupy a monopoly position in the high-profit industries. Thus, in recent years, the tension between private capital and state-owned enterprises has begun to show.

Second, transactions among government bureaucrats have brought forth the system of local corporatism. This creates competition between localities and is generally useful for promoting growth. Thus, it seems that the second-level transactions work in harmony with first-level transactions. In reality, however, the local corporatism lacks worker participation and limits the rise of local purchasing power for the following reasons. Firstly, local corporatism has caused the cost of housing to rise continuously. At the same time, in the realm of public policy, there is a tendency to lean toward economic liberalism in an effort to increase economic growth. As the state unloads entitlements, the costs to the individual for health care and education have remained high. These high costs for housing, health care, and education limit the rise of real purchasing power for the masses. Under these conditions, it is very difficult for the Chinese economy to transition to domestic demand-led growth. Thus, in recent years, the effect of local corporatism has been to effectively limit the possibility of change of growth regime and weaken the masses' support for government. Therefore, despite the fact that the demands of the changing international economy require that China transitions its engine of growth away from exports and toward domestic demand, this transition will be both slow and difficult to achieve.

Third, unlike Japan and Korea, Chinese-style developmentalism depends to a large extent on the global division of labor. In Japan, the process of catching up has occurred mostly under domestic demand-led growth (Uni 1995). In Korea, the process of catching up has been guided primarily by local capital (Amsden 1989). In China, however, the process of catching up has depended largely on the expansion of export, and the multinational corporations have played a huge role in facilitating China's development. This reliance on the global division of labor and multinational corporations means that domestic private capital is in a dependent position. It also means that domestic Chinese companies have historically had difficulty promoting new technology innovation and creating new organizational forms (Song 2008, 2015). Since 2006, China has responded to this challenge by initiating a new economic ideology that prioritizes the development of domestic enterprises and so-called indigenous innovation. Of course, the very emergence of this new strategy reflects the fact that, at least prior to 2006, China's success in promoting the expansion of large-scale manufacturing was achieved without necessarily upgrading technological capabilities in many industries (Song and Ge 2013).

As this analysis has demonstrated, China faces many challenges as it seeks to adjust growth regime. Section 13.4 will further discuss how the logic underlying Chinese-style developmentalism has evolved as the country struggles to transform itself.

13.4 Change of Growth Regime and Development of Chinese-Style Developmentalism

As the mode of régulation, the development of Chinese-style developmentalism can be divided into three stages: the primary stage from the early years of the reform from 1978 to the end of 1980s, the maturity stage from the early 1990s to the first decade of the twenty-first century, and the transformational stage in the second decade of the twenty-first century. With the development of Chinese-style developmentalism, China's growth regime underwent continuous changes accordingly. To be specific, it has gone through two changes during the last 30 years. The first change was the transition from domestic demand-led growth to export-led growth in the early 1990s, and the second change is the transition that Chinese economy has been undergoing in recent years. By briefly introducing the changes of China's growth regime, this section discusses the relationship between Chinese-style developmentalism as a mode of régulation and the formation and transformation of the growth regimes.

13.4.1 Change of Growth Regime

13.4.1.1 Appearance of Domestic Demand-led Growth

China's reform began with the agricultural sector. Under the household responsibility system, the income growth of peasants was associated with the agricultural output or the growth rate of labor productivity in the agricultural sector (Lin 1991). Because of this kind of institutional arrangement, peasants' income increased with the rise of the agricultural output provided a broad market for industrial products. At the same time as the household responsibility system was introduced, the township enterprise with collective ownership features was widely developed. As the result, industrialization of rural areas was launched. In the early 1980s, the reform experiences of agricultural sector were brought into the industrial sector, whereupon state-owned enterprises and collectively owned enterprises began to implement the contract responsibility system and dual-track price system. The contract responsibility system, quite like the household responsibility system in agricultural sector, institutionalized a connection between the income growth of the employees and the enterprise output or the growth rate of labor productivity. The dual-track price system signified that if the enterprises fulfilled their planned production quotas, they then are given the right to sell the surplus output at market price which is higher than planned price. Therefore, the enterprises had the motivation to increase their output. Under these institutional arrangements, the employees' income increased with the growth of enterprise output, and the shortage problem (Kornai 1980) suffered Chinese economy was alleviated gradually. With the surge in surplus output, the influence of the planned price was gradually diminished, and Chinese economy progressively began to realize the transition from planned economy to market economy. Along with the advance of domestic reform, Chinese government set up several special economic zones, Shenzhen, Zhuhai, Xiamen, etc., and subsequently foreign capital, mainly overseas Chinese capital in the 1980s and capital from western countries in the 1990s, began to enter the China market.

According to the quantitative studies, in the 1980s, there was a positive correlation between the growth rate of labor income and the labor productivity both in the agricultural sector and the industrial sector, and the labor productivity of domestic consumer goods grew faster than that of the export commodities (Song 2001, 72, 73,75; Uni et al. 2004, 2005). In this sense, the growth in this period, primarily focused on the domestic market, had the feature of domestic demand-led growth.

13.4.1.2 Formation of Export-Led Growth

From the end of 1980s, the domestic demand-led growth regime began to change. Political crises in 1989 caused international pressure and economically, due to the soft budget constraint of state-owned sector, distressed debt was accumulated, and intermittent inflation continuously occurred. To solve the abovementioned problems, the Chinese-style developmentalism which first appeared in the 1980s was updated. Together with the international division of labor system changed in this period, the updated Chinese-style developmentalism promoted the formation of new growth regime. At that time, the changes of the economic policy are mainly displayed in three aspects: development of the private ownership enterprise, the administrative system reform, and the foreign economic policy reform.

China's economy stagnated after the Tiananmen Square protests in 1989. To restart the reform, Deng Xiaoping made his southern inspection tour in the spring of 1992 and made proposals: "do not discuss whether a reform is socialist or capitalist" and "development is the hard truth." Deng's attitude implied that the ideology of stressing public-owned economy would be weakened, and any policy could be tried provided that Communist Party's ruling status was maintained. Hence, it paved the way to the development of private ownership enterprise. In fact, it was from this time that China's private ownership enterprise began to develop rapidly. The administrative system reform had two main points: the systematization of cadre assessment system and the reform of fiscal system. Firstly, the importance of economic development soared in the new cadre assessment system. Since the end of 1980s, there has been an assessment system for Chinese local cadres, in which economic development occupied an important position. However, after Deng's southern inspection tour, the role of economic development was further enhanced in the new cadre assessment system which began to be systematized.[7] Secondly, in the 1980s, China's fiscal system has demonstrated a tendency of decentralization. Indeed, there existed a financial contract responsibility system between the central and local governments at that time. Under this system, once the local governments accomplished the central government's allocated quotas, they would be free to dispose the rest of financial revenue. Based on the abovementioned facts, some researchers have regarded the central-local governments relationship as fiscal federalism (Qian and Weingast 1997; Jin et al. 2005). However, although this fiscal system aroused the enthusiasm of local governments to promote their economy, it weakened the central government's control. Due to the impact of the collapse of Soviet Union, in order to avoid the balkanization tendency of local governments, the central government launched the tax-sharing system in 1994. According to this new fiscal system, the consumption tax and customs duty are owned by the central government; the business tax and income tax are owned by local governments. As for the value-added tax—the largest tax category in China, it is shared and split 75–25 between the central and local governments. Thus, the tax-sharing system became a financial tool for the central government to control over the local governments and mitigated their centrifugal tendency. Theoretically, the revenue of the local governments should be reduced under the new system, which would diminish their enthusiasm to develop economy. However, in practice, the tax-sharing system unexpectedly enhanced their motivation to promote economy development. On the one hand, a considerable amount of fiscal revenue was seized by the central government, but the local governments bore the same function of social affairs as usual. Consequently, they had to find some new sources of revenue. On the other hand, although the tax-sharing system changed the relationship between the central and local governments, the cadre assessment system still stressed the economic development. Therefore, even under the new fiscal system, local government officials were still inclined to promote economic development. In this background, from the early 1990s, local government officials began to vigorously develop industrial parks in order to boost investment growth. Because the land is owned by the state, the local governments could expropriate or requisition land for an extremely low

[7]The relationship between local economic development and promotion of government officers was summarized by some researcher as the promotion tournament hypothesis (Li and Zhou 2005).

compensation rates in rural areas. After completing the infrastructure construction through bank loans, the local governments would offer the land to the enterprise on very favorable terms. The local governments promoted the development of industrial parks for two reasons. First, if the local governments successfully attract more investments on manufacturing, then they could gain tax revenue by expanding the industrial scale. Second, in spite of offering a beneficial land price to the enterprise, there was still a gap between the land expropriation price and the supply price, which became the second fiscal revenue of the local governments. In some regions, the second fiscal revenue or the land revenue accounted for as high as 60 percent of the fiscal revenue of local governments.[8]

Encouraged by the opening policy, local government at different levels in this period began to try great efforts to attract foreign capital. In 1994, the central government cut the RMB exchange rate substantially. Consequently, the attraction of China for foreign capital has been increasing. It should be noted that although the policy of Chinese government played a positive role, the growth of international investment should be taken as the result of the joint effect of domestic economic policy and international production regime. As for the latter, the rise of modular production networks played an important role (Sturgeon 2002).

By focusing on the analytical tradition of the régulation school, the principal institutional arrangement in the abovementioned periods can be summarized into Table 13.1.

13.4.2 *Growth Regime and Chinese–Style Developmentalism as Mode of* Régulation

Before entering the second decade of the twenty-first century, the Chinese-style developmentalism has overcome a lot of ideological barriers by continuously adding reform policies, which shaped the growth regime of China in a great extent. In other words, the flexibility in economic realms has overpowered the rigidity in political realms during this period. As the result, the Chinese-style developmentalism took a form of flexible rigidity. However, recently, the further economic reform began to hit the political bottom line.

It is important to note that, as we mentioned above, although the top transaction between the ruling party and the citizens appeared at the early stage of the reform, the two secondary transactions didn't emerge until the 1990s. Therefore, the Chinese-style developmentalism was more influential on the growth regime in the 1990s and 2000s.

[8]Usually the development of industry parks promoted the development of the commercial enterprise in the surrounding areas and drove up the commercial property price. Since the local governments own most of the tax revenue from commercial enterprise, they could reap massive tax revenue from the surge in commercial property price.

Table 13.1 Major institutional forms in the domestic demand-led growth and export-led growth periods

	Domestic demand-led growth period(1980s)	Export-led growth period (1990s-early 2010s)
Monetary regime	Soft budget constraint-based investment;	Land-based public finance;
	Accumulation of bad debt; intermittent inflation;	Increase of direct finance;
	Incremental undervaluation of RMB	Radical undervaluation of RMB(1994)
Wage labor nexus	Reform-without losers;	Reform with losers;
	Quasi-labor-managed firm	Manager-managed firm
Forms of competition	Homogeneous competition	Homogeneous competition in low-rate-of-profit sectors; monopoly of SOE in high-rate-of-profit sectors
Relations of state	Additional policies;	Additional policies;
With the economy	Pragmatic ideology	"State-capitalism" in key industries
Inclusion of the international system	Comparatively independent	Heavily dependent

13.4.2.1 How the Chinese-Style Developmentalism as Mode of *Régulation* Shapes the Formation and Conversion of Growth Regime

In the 1980s, the Chinese-style developmentalism played its role by continuously introducing additional economic policies. In fact, those policies were a series of breakthroughs to the guiding ideology. For example, the household responsibility system broke the faith to the people's commune. The bonus system, dual price system, and the factory director (manager) responsibility system in the industrial sector as well as the fiscal responsibility system between the central and local governments suggested that the cores of the planned economy became loose. Similarly, allowing the overseas Chinese establishing enterprises in China and encouraging the rural collective enterprise (township enterprise) suggested that "exploitation," the key factor of traditional economic ideology, no longer has the overwhelming power. The relationship between Chinese-style developmentalism and domestic demand-led growth during this time can be summarized as Fig. 13.2.

In the early 1990s, China started the reform of the economic system again in order to break the international blockade. In this period, two secondary transactions which supported the deal between the ruling party and the citizens gradually formed, implying the full establishment of Chinese-style developmentalism, which played its role by continuously adding economic policies. Specifically, Deng Xiaoping's speech in his southern inspection tour in 1992 marked the restart of the policy reform, following the institutionalization of economic development indicators into

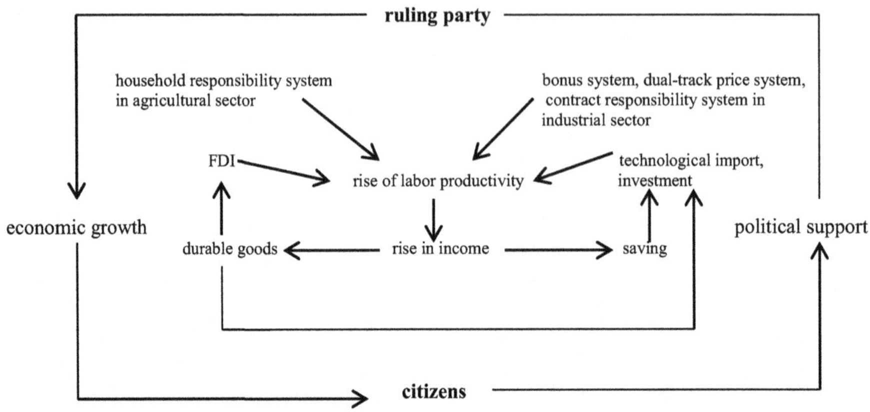

Fig. 13.2 Top transaction, additional polices and domestic demand-led growth under Chinese-style developmentalism in the 1980s

the official assessment system. In 1994, Chinese currency the Renminbi was greatly devalued, creating conditions for foreign companies to enter China. At the same time, as we discussed above, with the fiscal system reform, local governments made great efforts to attract investment and to develop industrial parks. In the late 1990s, responding to the debt crisis of state-owned enterprises, the central government implemented a large-scale layoff project. The market-oriented reform of housing, health care, and education systems started during the same time.[9] In 2001, China joined the WTO, starting to fully integrate its economy into the global economic system. In order to deal with the western financial crisis that occurred in 2008, Chinese government arranged 4 trillion RMB of investment, which further strengthened the previous growth regime. The relationship between the Chinese-style developmentalism and export-led growth in this period can be summarized as Fig. 13.3.

13.4.2.2 How the Chinese-Style Developmentalism as Mode of *Régulation* Impedes the Reconversion of Growth Regime

If the Chinese-style developmentalism has shaped the growth regime by continuously introducing additional economic policies or through a gradual process of reform, neutralizing the rigidity of political system with flexible economic policies, then with the urge to change its growth regime, the rigidity of the political system now has inhibited the flexibility of economic policies, making the Chinese-style developmentalism gradually losing its ability to shape a new growth regime.

[9] In recent years, Beijing tried to adjust its market-oriented social policy (Naughton 2008). However, besides the reform of basic income system, these adjustments are far from fundamental.

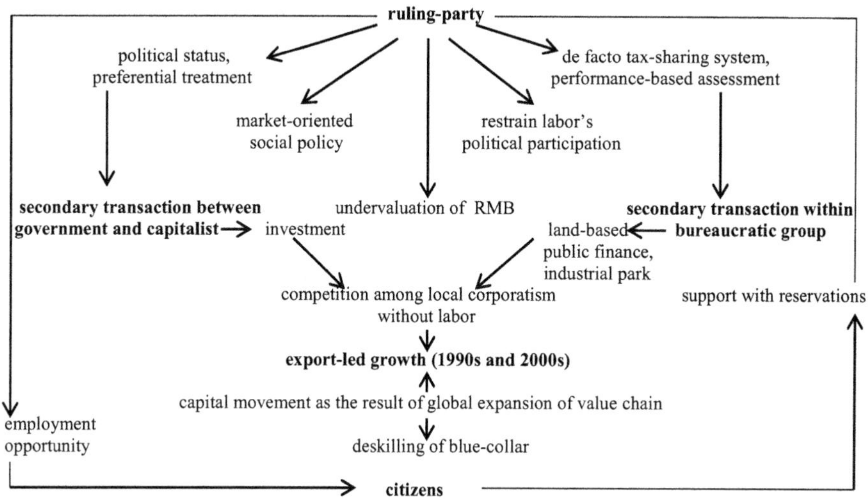

Fig. 13.3 Hierarchical transaction, additional polices and export-led growth under Chinese-style developmentalism in the 1990s and 2000s

In recent years, the change of internal and external environments has made it clear that export-led growth is unsustainable. On one hand, the major western economies such as American, European, and Japanese economies remain in the doldrums, and the external conditions for the export sector to implement massive expansion no longer exist; on the other hand, the export sector is losing its basis of "low human rights advantage," and the environmental pollution and waste of resources are too serious to ignore. Under these circumstances, transforming toward the domestic demand-led growth has become a consensus. However, the labor-wage nexus formed under the export-led growth period, and the neoliberal housing, education, and health-care policies severely restrained the consumption capacity of the citizens, which is the basis of domestic demand-led growth.

Logically, export-led growth means that the benefit of the rise in labor productivity is mainly distributed in the international market, while under the domestic demand-led growth, the benefit of the rise in labor productivity is basically closed in the domestic market (Uni 1995). Seen in this light, achieving the transformation of growth regime is clearly based on fundamental institutional change. As a mode of régulation, the Chinese-style developmentalism did promote the transformation of the growth regime from domestic demand-led to export-led, but it is somewhat difficult for it to complete the task of retransformation of growth regime once again.

As for the current Chinese economy, a potential way to achieve the domestic demand-led growth is to turn to a social democratic policy system. In this system, the wage rise of grassroots laborer will be linked with the rise of the labor productivity, the price of social services such as housing, health care, and education will be under control. However, high wage rise of the grassroots laborer means to further weaken the competitiveness of the export sector, and inhibiting the price of housing, health care, and education means to reduce the government's revenue. More importantly, those policy combinations would undermine the transaction between the government and the capitalist as well as that within bureaucratic group, which are the main parts of the Chinese-style developmentalism.

Another potential way to achieve the domestic demand-led growth is to reduce the proportion of state-owned enterprises and rely more upon private investment. Since the twenty-first century, the wealth of society in China has greatly come into government's possession; the high-profit industry sectors are almost monopolized by the state-owned enterprises. Therefore, there has always been advocacy of reducing the proportion of state-owned enterprises among Chinese academia. Although reducing the proportion of state-owned enterprises may not be able to bring China's economy back to the track of high-speed growth, the policy choices allowing more space for private capital should come within the vision of the authority.

Although what we discussed above are two possible options for Chinese government, either of them would be a strike to the political logic of the Chinese-style developmentalism. The former one means the end of the transaction between the government and the capitalist as well as that within the bureaucratic group. The latter one will directly impact the economic foundation of the ruling party. Therefore, despite the feasibility of the two options, it seems neither of them is politically practicable.[10]

As we have mentioned, the economic flexibility and the political rigidity coexisted in the Chinese-style developmentalism. For a long period of time, the economic flexibility hasn't become a challenge to the political rigidity; actually, it even provided a basis for political rigidity. However, in recent years, the reform of political system, whether it is leftist or rightist, has become the precondition of sustainable economic development. Seen in this light, the ongoing mixed ownership reform which encourages the SOE and private firms to hold each other's stocks and run joint venture is full of meaning. It seems that this reform strengthens the position of SOE and leaves room for the private capital at the same time. If this reform successes, the economic flexibility and political rigidity will coexist once again. It is the very reason why it can be taken as the signal of redesign of flexible rigidity.

13.5 Conclusion

Transforming from a planned economy to a market economy requires reforms both in economic and political realms. In the case of China, policy makers need to balance the subtle relationship between economic growth and political stability. This fact

[10]The One Road One Belt project appeared against the backdrop of this difficult situation. If it goes smoothly, the policy makers will get more policy spaces. However, this project is still an extension of the export-led growth.

determines that the Chinese-style developmentalism includes two features that are economic flexibility and political rigidity. Before the first decade of the twenty-first century, the Chinese-style developmentalism manifested that political stability was enhanced by economic growth, which can be summarized as flexible rigidity. In contrast, in recent years, the Chinese-style developmentalism demonstrated political stability can, on the contrary, restrict economic growth, which can be understood as weakening of flexible rigidity. In order to achieve systematical transformations to maintain sustainable economic growth, China is redesigning the flexible rigidity.

In a fairly long period of time, China's reform strategies are practical and lack of long-term visions. As a result, the Chinese economic development shows the feature of unintended fit. Nonetheless, since the Chinese economy has entered the "new normal" era, we would expect the next phase of Chinese economic growth can only be achieved in accordance with the long-term visions and well-designed reform plans.

References

Amsden A (1989) Asia's next giant: South Korea and late industrialization. Oxford University Press, New York

Beeson M (2009) Developmental states in East Asia: a comparison of Japanese and Chinese experiences. Asian Perspect 33(2):5–39

Boltho A, Weber M (2009) Did China follow the East Asian development model. Eur J Comp Econ 6(2):267–286

Commons J (1959) Institutional economics. The University of Wisconsin University Press, Madison

Deyo F (ed) (1987) The political economy of the new Asian industrialism. Cornell University Press, Ithaca

Dore R (1973) British factory, Japanese factory: the origins of National Diversity in industrial relations. California University Press, Berkeley/Los Angeles

Gao B (1997) Economic ideology and Japanese industrial policy: developmentalism from 1931 to 1965. Cambridge University Press, Cambridge

Gao B (2013) Neoliberal and classical developmentalism: a comparative analysis of the Chinese and Japanese models of economic development. In Huang XM (ed) Modern economic development in Japan and China: developmentalism, capitalism, and the world economic system. Palgrave, London

Gerschenkron A (1962) Economic backwardness in historical perspective. Belknap Press of Harvard University Press, Cambridge

Harvey D (2007) The limits to capitalism. Verso, Brooklyn

Hayami Y, Godo Y (2005) Development economics: from the poverty to the wealth of nations. Oxford University Press, Oxford

Huang YS (2008) Capitalism with Chinese characteristics: entrepreneurship and the state. Cambridge University Press, Cambridge

Jin HH, Qian YY, Weingast B (2005) Regional decentralization and fiscal incentives: federalism, Chinese style. J Pub Econ 89(9–10):1719–1742

Johnson C (1982) MITI and the Japanese miracle: the growth of industrial policy: 1925–1975. Stanford University Press, Stanford

Kornai J (1980) Economics of shortage. North Holland Press, Amsterdam

Li HB, Zhou LA (2005) Political turnover and economic performance: the incentive role of personnel control in China. J Public Econ 89:1743–1762
Lin JYF (1991) The household responsibility system reform and the adoption of hybrid rice in China. J Dev Econ 36(2):353–372
Murakami Y (1992) An anticlassical political-economic analysis (II). Tyuuoukouronnshya, Tokyo (in Japanese)
Naughton B (2008) China's left tilt: pendulum swing or midcourse correction? In: Cheng L (ed) China's changing political landscape: prospects for democracy. Washington, DC: Brookings Institution Press
North D (1992) Transaction costs, institutions and economic performance, occasional papers, no.30. ICEG
O'Donnell G (1973) Modernization and bureaucratic authoritarianism: studies in South American politics. Institute for International Studies, University of California, Berkeley
Oi J (1992) Fiscal decentralization and local state corporatism. World Politics 45(1):99–126
Qian YY, Weingast B (1997) Federalism as a commitment to preserving market incentives. J Econ Perspect 11(4):83–92
Ramo JC (2004) The Beijing consensus. The Foreign Policy Centre, London
Song L (2001) The limits of gradual reform without long-term perspectives: instability of institutional Foundation of Chinese Economy. Keizaikagaku 50(1):65–84 (in Japanese)
Song L (2008) The origin, typology of China's modularization trap and the growth of productivity. Open Times 40(2):88–93 (in Chinese)
Song L (2015) Gerschenkron-Dore proposition and Chinese practices. Open Times 33(5):183–198 (in Chinese)
Song L, Ge DS (2013) Compressed Development and its Impacts on Innovative Activity: Analytical Framework and Evidences from China. In: Hirakawa H et al (eds) Servitization, IT-ization and innovation models: two-stage industrial cluster theory. Routledge, London
Song L, Zhang RB (2013) Beyond ideological and empirical descriptions: theorizing Japanese and Chinese development experiences. In: Huang XM (ed)
Sturgeon T (2002) Modular Production Networks: An American Model of Industrial Organization. Ind Corporate Change 11(3):451–496
Suehiro A (2010) Catch-up industrialization: the trajectory and prospects of East Asian economies. NUS Press, Singapore
Uni H (1995) Japan's export-led growth. Polit Econ Q 32:90–105 (in Japanese)
Uni H, Song L, Yang JH (2004) Export-led growth and exchange rate regime in East Asia (1). Keizaironnsyuu 174(5,6):1–15 (in Japanese)
Uni H, Song L, Yang JH (2005) Export-led growth and exchange rate regime in East Asia (2). *Keizaironnsyuu* 175(1):1–16 (in Japanese)

Chapter 14
Modular Mode of Production, Chinese Style: Origin and Evolution

Lei Song

14.1 Problematic and Structure: Bringing Perspectives of Mode of Production and Diversity Back in

With continued economic growth becoming a reality, China's economy has been all the time stimulating discussion in the arena of economics. In the 1980s and 1990s, the research was basically dominated by mainstream economists, in whose eyes China's economic growth could be considered as another proof of the explanatory force held by mainstream economics. However, since the early 21st century, advocates of the so-called Chinese Economic Model who emphasize the ownership structure and the role of government have stepped into the arena as a new and aggressive army.

With respect to the so-called Chinese Economic Model, we should have an open mind since it is hardly unnatural for a great power that has achieved rapid development to provide driving forces for the advancement of social sciences, as demonstrated through experiences of other great powers such as the USA, Germany, and Japan. However, there exist three obvious problems in the economic theory of the so-called Chinese Economic Model. Firstly, though advocates of Chinese Economic Model tend to regard China's economy as a specialized type of market economy with Chinese features and hence in such a sense we can infer that this kind of research fits into the Diversity of Capitalism Approach (Hall and Soskice 2001; Amable 2003), they barely touch upon this approach. Secondly, although many advocates of Chinese Economic Model are political economists, they seldom pay any attention to the nature and form of mode of production. Yet, the mode of production, namely, the way how production activity is organized or how

L. Song (✉)
Peking University, Beijing, China
e-mail: slei@pku.edu.cn

R. Boyer et al. (eds.), *Evolving Diversity and Interdependence of Capitalisms*, Evolutionary Economics and Social Complexity Science 11,
https://doi.org/10.1007/978-4-431-55001-3_14

organization and technology are combined together (Lazonick 1990), not only figures prominently in the literature of political economics but also remains as a fundamental perspective to understand China's economic growth. Thirdly, even though the insertion in the global economy has a vital impact on China's economy, most theorists of Chinese Economic Model are still likely to attribute the growth of China's economy to domestic factors.

Standing apart from the advocates of Chinese Economic Model, in recent years some scholars start to apply different versions of Diversity of Capitalism Approach into understanding China's economy. Owing to the emergence of this stream of research, our comprehension of China's economy has been extensively deepened. However, some problems inherent in the theory of Chinese Economy Model can also unavoidably be spotted in the research of China's economy based on Diversity of Capitalism Approach to some extent. Firstly, the mode of production remains hardly analyzed in a real sense, and the production activities are left nearly unexamined in a black box. Secondly, the researches based on the perspective of Diversity of Capitalism Approach normally seem to consider China's economy as an integrated unit of analysis, even though diversified modes of production can be identified within China's economy. Besides these two problems, another problem is that scholars approaching to China's economy through Diversity of Capitalism Approach have not paid necessary attention to the influence of the international production network.

With an awareness of the above background, this chapter briefly summarizes the progress and unsolved problems of researches on Chinese economy based on different versions of Diversity of Capitalism Approach. Then, focusing on the complementarity between technology and organization, in this chapter, we will go more deeply into the analysis of the origin and evolution of China's modes of production.

As far as ownership structure is concerned, China's economy is composed of state-owned enterprise (SOE) and non-state-owned enterprise including foreign enterprise and local private enterprise. In terms of technological and organizational forms, which are also key factors of the production activity, the production activity of the three types of enterprises obviously shows their respective features of modular mode. This chapter focuses on the modular modes of production in ICT and automobile industries whose mainstream enterprises are non-state-owned and state-owned, respectively. In these two kinds of industry, the modular modes of production are different from each other yet sharing features in common. The difference mainly lies in the ownership structure, the generating mechanism of modularization, and so on, while the insertion in the international production network and the modularity of product architecture jointly construct a foundation of the common ground. Since 2006, China's innovation policy has changed fundamentally. Accordingly, modes of production in both ICT and automobile industries have been under the adjustment pressure exerted by the central government. However, whatever changes have been made in the innovation policy, China's enterprises cannot be cut off from the global production networks, and fundamental features of mode of production in these industries cannot be easily wiped out in a short period of time. In the foreseeable future, it is somewhat likely that various modular modes of production shall still coexist in China's economy.

14.2 Advances and Issues: Previous Studies of Chinese Economy based on Diversity of Capitalism Approach

As is well known, Diversity of Capitalism Approach has different versions and theoretical sources: *Comparative Institutional Analysis* and *Régulation* School (Aoki 1988, 2001; Boyer 1990; Amable 2003) are the economic versions of Diversity of Capitalism Approach; Comparative Economic Policy and *Comparative Political Economy* (Hall 1986; Hall and Soskice 2001) belong to the version of Diversity of Capitalism Approach with political science background; and Comparative Economic Sociology or Comparative Business System (Dore 1973, 2000; Whitley 1992, 1999; Morgan et al. 2010) can be categorized as the one with economic sociology features.[1]

Though different versions of Diversity of Capitalism Approach have different theoretical sources, scholars from different disciplines share the same theoretical assumption, that is, a country's economic system is made up of institutions that are formed as the result of historical changes, and these institutions shape the economic performances as well as growth trajectories through interconnection/interlock (Whitley 1999: 33; Dore 2000: 45–47) or institutional complementarity (Hall and Soskice 2001: 17–21; Amable 2003; Boyer 2005) to a large extent. In the meanwhile, although early studies of different versions of Diversity of Capitalism Approach differ from each other with regard to their focal points, these studies begin to converge on the institutional arrangements or organizational forms at the enterprise level in recent years.[2]

Originally, the research object of Diversity of Capitalism Approach was western advanced industrial countries, namely, member states of OECD. However, in recent years, different versions of Diversity of Capitalism Approach have successively

[1]Another version of Diversity of Capitalism Approach is Comparative Innovation System (Freeman 1987). However, this version is normally combined with other versions of Diversity of Capitalism Approach. For example, innovation is an important topic in the empirical study of Comparative Institutional Analysis (Aoki 1988, chapter 6); scholar of *Régulation* School puts forward Social System of Innovation and Production (Amable 2000) which synthesizes institution analysis and innovation studies; advocates of Comparative Economic Sociology also pay special attention to innovation activities (Whitley and Zhang 2016).

[2]Comparative Institutional Analysis and Comparative Economic Sociology are originally based on the studies of institutional arrangements or organizational forms at the enterprise level. Similarly, *Régulation* School never rejects this kind of analysis (Boyer and Yamada 2000). In recent years, some theorists of Comparative Political Economy have also changed their research focus to enterprise (Hall and Soskice 2001).

been introduced into studies on developing countries in Asia, and some researches directly refer to China's economy.[3] These researches either conduct analysis on institutional characteristics of Chinese economy and its growth mechanism (Boyer 2012; Yan 2012) or undertake typological comparisons among Asian economies including China (Harada and Tohyama 2012; Witt and Redding 2013; Tohyama and Harada 2014). Benefiting from the sound analytical framework, these researches provide us with new perspectives and analytical framework that are obviously helpful to deepen our understanding of China's economy. In fact, with the era of rapid development coming to an end, the so-called economic theory of Chinese Economic Model is losing its momentum. One of the reasons that led to this situation is that economic theory of Chinese Economic Model lacks an explicit analytical framework. Most of the studies rest on a mere enumeration of phenomena (Song and Zhang 2013). Seen in this light, studies on China' economy based on Diversity of Capitalism Approach can be considered as an antidote or a reference system of economic theory of Chinese Economic Model.

For example, quantitative studies on the relative location of China's economy in the diverse market economies conducted by scholars of Diversity of Capitalism Approach have made it clear that in spite of the differences at the macro and institutional levels, China's economy is nothing but a type of capitalism (Harada and Tohyama 2012: 252). These studies explicitly offer those advocates of the so-called Chinese Economic Model words of caution, warning them not to indulge in the myth that China's economy is too unique to be analyzed by the current economic theories.

However, it is worthy to note that there inevitably exist theoretical issues when the Diversity of Capitalism Approach is applied to the analysis of developing countries. These issues seem especially obvious in the study of China's economy.

First, a root theoretical issue is that the Diversity of Capitalism Approach was originally proposed to analyze the well-developed western economies rather than Asian economies that are either at their initial stages of development or in their processes of regime shift. In other words, although the institutional coherence assumption or the social environment of production coherence assumption is intrinsically embedded in the Diversity of Capitalism Approach, this kind of assumption is not in line with China's conditions.

Institutional coherence assumption or social environment of production coherence assumption refers to the assumption held by the theorists of Diversity of Capitalism Approach that basic economic institutions are coherent within a country and the social environment of different regions within a country has no essential difference. However, as to developing countries, the institutional coherence assumption is not self-evident (Cornelia et al. 2013: 217, 226). For example, in China, institutional incoherence appears to be hardly rare: in different types of enterprise,

[3]Early studies conducted by scholars of Comparative Business System Research offered analysis of East Asian business system. However, in these studies, the economies that have grown into advanced economies, namely, Japan and its followers such as South Korea and Taiwan, were taken as the main research objects, while China was not taken into consideration seriously (Whitley 1992, 1999).

institutional incoherence can be seen not only in the labor relations but also in the financial system such as source of finance and real interest rate level. Besides, concerning a country of a super-large scale such as China, social environments for production apparently vary from one region to another.

Objectively speaking, theorists of the Diversity of Capitalism Approach did not entirely ignore the above issue. For example, Herrigel pointed out that the early development of Germany is quite regional: the regions that were politically, institutionally, and technologically qualified and economically connected with industrial areas within and outside Germany were the ones that finally developed (Herrigel 2000: 6). Similarly, economic sociologist also paid attention to the coherence issue of social environment of production of three regions in Italy (Locke 1994). Whitley mentioned some ideas about the institutional and social environmental differences confronted by different kinds of enterprise in Taiwan (Whitley 1999: 147–152). However, the above issue remains unsolved in the literature of Diversity of Capitalism Approach. It might be proper to keep them untouched in the analysis of advanced industrial countries since this issue seems somewhat only meaningful for studies of economic history. However, as analyzed later, this issue should be taken into account seriously when the Diversity of Capitalism Approach is introduced into the analysis of China's economy.

Another theoretical issue is that previous researches of China's economic system conducted by China's academia were strongly influenced by transaction cost economics which maintains intrinsic connection with mainstream economics. In these researches, the focus was mainly the government-business relationship or the governmental function during the transition process, and the key problem of how the production activities of China's enterprise are organized remains far from being thoroughly discussed. However, the detailed analysis on the production activities of enterprise is one of the bases of the Diversity of Capitalism Approach and should be one of the starting points of research of Chinese economy based on the Diversity of Capitalism Approach.

Actually, due to the insufficient analysis of production activities at firm level, in most cases, the studies of China's economy based on Diversity of Capitalism Approach have to take the form of sheer quantitative research, and its explanatory force is limited.

The third theoretical issue is that the original research object of the Diversity of Capitalism Approach, namely, the formation of economic system and economic growth of western industrial countries, shares different international backgrounds with China. Even though the globalization is not a totally new phenomenon, the impact of the one occurring since the 1990s, which serves as the international background of China's rise, is unprecedented. Therefore, as to the advocates of Diversity of Capitalism Approach, especially the *Régulationists* who emphasize the hierarchy of institutional system, the analysis methods paralleling international background with other institutions might not be applicable to the study of China's economy.

In general, as to researchers aiming to make analysis on China's economy from the point of view of the Diversity of Capitalism Approach, institutional coherence or coherence of social environment of production, China's specific mode of production, and the impact of international regime are all inevitable key issues. It is important to note that during the developing process of China's economy, these three issues are closely related to each other. Therefore, starting from the discussion of the coherence problem, this chapter goes on to describe the specific mode of production in China, with a highlight on the impact of the international regime on the production organization of Chinese enterprises.

14.3 Quantitative Research vs. Case Study: Methods of Understanding of Diversity of the Chinese Economy

Firstly, the incoherence inherent in China's economic systems provides a fundamental perspective for understanding China's economic diversity. Among all the economic institutions, ownership's impact always ranks the most influential. Currently, there are essentially two kinds of important ownership in China, state ownership and private ownership. Actually, enterprises with different ownership may accordingly differ from one another in financial systems, employment systems, and government-business relationship. Therefore, the coherence problem in China's economy can be attributed to ownership differences to a large extent.

Secondly, the regional differences provide the most intuitive perspective to look into the diversity of China's economy. Within China's economy, differences can be witnessed not only between coastal area and inland area but also within coastal areas. Even though the analytical framework provided by the Diversity of Capitalism Approach has not been applied, China's academia has observed and examined these kinds of differences roughly, and a large number of papers about Sunan Model, Zhejiang Model, Guangdong Model, and Chongqing Model have appeared.

Thirdly, the differences among industries provide a technology-based perspective to understand the diversity of China's economy. Studies on the diversity of China's economy from an industrial perspective can be conducted along the following two directions. One is to investigate the differences between traditional industries and modern manufacturing industries; the other is to examine the differences within modern manufacturing industries.

It has to be noted that the above three perspectives overlap to some extent. In different regions and industries, the ownerships of the dominant enterprises are normally different. In inland area and politically important industries, the dominant enterprises are mainly state-owned. In coastal area and industries in full and fierce competition, the dominant enterprises are mainly private enterprises or foreign enterprises.

There are two basic categories of study based on the Diversity of Capitalism Approach: one is the study focusing on one country which emphasizes the effects of specific institutions, organizational forms, and production activities and the other is the typological study of the economic systems of different countries. Somehow these two categories of study are interrelated that the former one lays a foundation for the latter one, as especially revealed in the studies of Japanese economy (Dore 1973; Aoki 1988). As far as the second category of study is concerned, early researches tend to be conducted somewhat subjectively by means of intuitive comparison, while recent researches appear to be much more logical through adopting more quantitative approach (Amable 2003).

Furthermore, in the literature of the Diversity of Capitalism Approach, there exist two major trends of typological study. One trend is to establish causal relationship between institutional configurations and industrial specification through quantitative approaches such as clustering analysis (Hall and Soskice 2001: 39–41; Amable 2000, 2003). The other trend is to make comparison of the features of typical industries or typical enterprises in different countries. The comparative study of American and Japanese economies at the industrial or firm level is an ideal case of the latter trend (Aoki 1988; Lazonick 1990).

Apparently, taking into account the fact that there exist regional and industrial diversities within Chinese economy, both of the above two methods can be applied into the studies on China's economic diversity. The method adopted in the typological studies of Asian capitalism conducted by the *Régulationists* (Tohyama and Harada 2014: 85–89) belongs to the first type. Based on their analytical framework and research methodology, especially through introducing clustering analysis of institutional factors, if the provincial data are available, then perhaps we can break the Chinese economy down into different types through clustering analysis of institutional factors and identify whether the institutional configurations of different regions have given rise to industrial specification or not. However, this method has its own limitations. That is, because of a lack of sound database at province level that is necessary to reflect the provincial institutional environment, it is nearly impossible to conduct clustering analysis. For example, although the function of government is considered as one of the key features in understanding China's economy, the local governments in different regions play different roles. Therefore, even though the extent and mode of local government's involvement ought to be a key configuration in classifying China's economic diversity, it is more like a labyrinth to design meaningful variables to demonstrate the features of local governments' function. Applying the second research method of the advocates of Diversity of Capitalism Approach, in order to understand the diversity of Chinese economy, we need to conduct comparative analysis on the modes of production of the typical enterprise in the typical industry.

We refer to the above two methods as regional/quantitative research and industry/case study, respectively. The former one has the feature of deductive reasoning and normally takes the form of quantitative studies, while the latter one possesses the nature of inductive reasoning and usually appears as case studies. Both the features of methods of typological research of Diversity of Capitalism Approach and their potentialities in studying China's economic diversity are summarized in Table 14.1.

As to China's economic diversity, though regional/quantitative research seems more promising, considering the problem of availability of province-level data may to some extent weaken the plausibility or explanatory force of this approach,

Table 14.1 Diversity of capitalism approach and its potential application to the study of China's economic diversity

		Typological study of diversity of capitalism approach	
		Regional/quantitative analysis	Industry/firm study
Issue of institutional coherence	Not obvious	Clustering analysis-based typological studies (Soskice and Hall 2001; Amable 2003)	Comparative analysis of industry or firm (Dore 1973)
	Obvious	Application of *Régulationists'* method to the study of diversity within Chinese economy.	Comparative analysis of modes of production of China's leading firms in leading industries

industry/firm study should not be ignored. Firstly, industry/firm study is a practical alternative when regional/quantitative research encounters predicament such as the insufficient data issue. Secondly, thorough and comprehensive industry/firm study can help us understand the structural characteristics of the diversity inherent in China's economy and identify the key institutional configurations for the future regional/quantitative research. Based on the above comprehension, in order to pave the way for quantitative analysis of China's economic diversity, in this chapter, we will go on to explore the issue of China's economic diversity on the dimension of mode of production in leading industries.

14.4 Difference and Similarity: China's Modular Modes of Production in Leading Industries

14.4.1 Leading Firms of Leading Industries in the Chinese Economy

According to Schumpeter School's long wave theory, about every 50 years, fundamental technological innovation and leading industry transition occur: cotton spinning industry, railway industry, electric industry, heavy chemical industry, and automobile industry all used to be the leading industries. Seen in this light, ICT industry arose in the 1990s is the leading industry in the era of China's rise (Freeman and Soete 2004: 23–30). Correspondingly, in the literature of political economics, there is a tradition which understands the market economy of a specific period through examining leading enterprise in the leading industry (Aglietta 1979; Aoki 1988; Chandler et al. 1997; Boyer and Freyssenet 2002). Therefore, research on leading enterprise in ICT industry is of great importance to the study of China's economy (Song and Meng 2013).

Meanwhile, as some advocates of comparative economic and social systems pointed out, China's economic development has an obvious feature of the so-called compressed development which means the development process is compressed (Whittaker, et al., 2010). In other words, in the process of China's growth, the leading industries before and after the 1990s all hold prominent positions. Seen in this light, as the automobile industry, which is considered as the leading industry before the 1990s by Schumpeter School, actually becomes a leading industry in the late development state such as Japan in its stage of economic takeoff, ICT industry and automobile industry grew into double leading industries in China, the representative of compressed development states, in its economic takeoff stage.

It is worth noting that, as we mentioned in Sect. 14.3, the ownership structures of China's different industries are different: as to industries of strategic and political significance, such as automobile industry, the dominant ownership is state-owned; as to industries of less strategic and political significance, such as ICT industry, private-owned and foreign-funded firms are of higher proportion. Accordingly, the ownership structure of leading enterprises in automobile industry and ICT industry is apparently different: the representative leading enterprises in automobile industry are six state-owned enterprises, called "three big, three small"; the typical leading enterprises in ICT industry are foreign-funded or private-owned ones such as Foxconn.[4]

Therefore, in the sense of ideal type, in China's two leading industries, in terms of ownership structure, there are two kinds of mode of production represented by two different types of enterprises. Before moving to the comparison of these two kinds of mode of production, one key fact worth noting is that the development of China's two leading industries relates closely to the change of international production system which is partly given rise up by the modularization of product architecture (Steinfeld 2004; Fujimoto and Shinntaku 2004; Whittaker et al. 2010). Therefore, upon analyzing China's modes of production in its leading industries, it is necessary first to have a brief review on the rise and nature of modular mode of production network worldwide.

14.4.2 Modular Mode of Production: American Style vs. Chinese Style

Since the 1990s, the production system has experienced tremendous changes across the world. Confronting these changes, the mainstream literature starts from the analysis of the technological change, focusing on the impact of technological change on the enterprise's organizational structure and describing these changes by terms like Wintelism and modular production network (Borrus and Zysman 1997; Sturgeon 2002). Another kind of analysis is to expend analytical perspective into the

[4]There are two types of leading firms in China's ICT industry. One is represented by Foxconn, and the other is represented by Huawei or ZTE. We believe that Foxconn is of more typical significance. Firstly, compared to Huawei or ZTE, Foxconn is larger in scale and has a higher percentage in China's export share; secondly, Foxconn has a deep connection with Apple Inc., the worldwide leading enterprise of leading industry, and the relation between Foxconn and Apple Inc. provides a chance to understand the relation between China and the western world.

field of finance. It regards modularity in the financial field and modularity of product architecture as two driving forces for the modularity in production system and refers to the new type of production system since the 1990s as the modular mode of production. The so-called modularity in the financial field refers to the prevalence of risk investment (Baldwin and Clark 2000; Aoki and Takizawa 2002) and the rehabilitation of economic ideology maximizing the shareholder value. Compared with indirect financing, risk investment is a new type of direct financing, which tends to invest in different projects and seeks profit within a short period. In other words, if the capital provided through bank financing has the feature of "patient capital," then the risk investment does not stick to specific firms. Similarly, the rehabilitation of the economic ideology maximizing the shareholder value means that enterprise manager began to be under more pressure from the capital market to increase returns to shareholder (Dore 2000). Under this kind of pressure, the enterprise manager naturally tends to select and concentrate in different parts of the value chain. Since maximizing the shareholder value means that the shareholder takes the stock trading as the method to maximize the capital gain, the relationship between the shareholder and the enterprise becomes more floating, and the interface of the two moves to the standard side. In the above sense, the prevalence of risk investment and the rehabilitation of the economic ideology maximizing the shareholder value do change the architecture of the financial system into the direction of modularity. When modularity in the financial field and modularity of product architecture jointly emerge, the modularity in production process begins to come out.

In the field of production, modular production network and modular modes of production refer to almost the same phenomenon. The difference between the two is that the latter one includes changes within the field of finance, involves the root of changes in the field of production, and reflects the hierarchical relations in the new type of production system. Through introducing the term modular mode of production, the deterioration of income distribution in western industrial countries such as the USA (Lazonick 2009) and developing countries such as China can be more reasonably explained.

Though production systems of both the USA and China have been deeply influenced by modularity, modular production networks of the two are obviously different from each other. The difference involves matters of positions that enterprises of the two countries take in modular production systems, respectively, and the degree of modularity of each country's financial system. Basically, the American firms and firms of western country are the designers of design rule who trigger the change of modularity (Baldwin and Clark 2000), while the Chinese firms are the taker of design rule who exploit the opportunity arisen by the modularity.

Despite the above, one of the major differences of the two countries' modular production networks rests on the fact that there are different types in China's modular production network. It is worth noting that this difference is related to the generation mechanism of modularity of product architecture.

14.4.3 Modular Modes of Production: Diversity Within the Chinese Economy

Modularity is usually interpreted as a technical phenomenon. However, there are three kinds of generation mechanism of modularity of product architecture at least. The first is technology-economy-pulled modularity, the second is politics-policy-driven modularity, and the third is socio-regional factor-shaped modularity. Although previous studies analyzed the first kind of generation mechanism thoroughly, the other two kinds of generation mechanism have not been given due attention.

The impact of politics or policy on modularization of product architecture could be either indirect or direct. Basically, the modularity of American ICT industry has been attributed to technical and economic reasons. However, in the USA, modularity of product architecture of ICT industry has been indirectly related to government policy. The US government's antitrust policy prohibits AT&T and IBM from monopolizing key technologies. This policy has led these two major ICT companies to provide key technologies to the emerging and incumbent firms through cross-licensing. These key technologies have become important technological sources of new chip technology companies, and these chip companies have become the driving force of change in the product architecture (Borrus and Zysman 1997: 8–9). In China, the government's policy has more direct impact on the modularization of product architecture. In the automobile industry, since the 1990s, the Chinese government has actively pursued the joint venture policy. Under this policy, foreign enterprises provide their Chinese partners with product conceptual design, architectural design, detailed design, and key components. Furthermore, they are responsible for coordinating the interfaces and relations of the key components. Under such a kind of inter-business relationship, both the complexity embedded in the product design and task of fine-tuning of the relations of key components are outsourced to the foreign enterprise. In the literature of product architecture, the aforementioned complexity defines the degree of modularity of product architecture. Seen in this light, the joint venture policy has shifted the product architecture to the modular side.

Different from the technology-economy-pulled modularity and politics-policy-driven modularity which mainly exist in modern manufacturing industries, the socio-regional factor-shaped modularity mainly exists in the traditional industries. For example, SMEs in China's Zhejiang province are often engaged in the production of specific components or specific processes of production and tend to cooperate closely with each other to complete the production. Under such a trust-based long-term cooperation, the boundaries of firms overlap with the interface of components or processes to a large extent. Seen in this light, the trust-based long-term cooperation changes the product architecture to the modular side.[5]

[5]The product architecture can be defined narrowly and broadly. The narrowly defined product architecture refers to the mapping between a product's function and structure, while the broadly defined product architecture refers to the mapping between a product's function and structure or

In one country, there might be more than one mode of production. In Italy, as competitive modes of production against Fordism, diversified quality production, flexible mass production, and flexible specialization used to coexist in the same period (Regini 1997: 102). Similarly in China, related to the three types of generation mechanism of the modularization, three types of mode of production intrinsically linked with modularization of product architecture coexist after the 1990s. In the ICT and automotive industries, the representatives of modern manufacturing industries, the different generation mechanisms of the modularization shape two kinds of modular mode of production to some extent. The modular mode of production in China's ICT industry can be basically considered as an international extension of the American modular mode of production, with Foxconn, a private firm, as a typical enterprise, while the formation of modular mode of production in China's automobile industry is driven by the joint venture policy and benefited from the emergence of foreign technical services company, represented by large state-owned enterprises. Despite different ownership structures, labor relations in these two kinds of modular mode of production have much in common. In the automobile industry, except for core employees, the labor relation is similar to that of ICT industry in some aspects (Lüthje 2014; Song 2015).

The modular modes of production in ICT and automobile industries are slightly different from each other in the fields of interfirm relationships and possibility of technological advance. In the ICT industry, the relation between western client such as Apple Inc. and Chinese EMS such as Foxconn is quite hierarchical or vertical.[6] In the automobile industry, because foreign firms are forbidden to run the business independently, they have to depend on their Chinese partners. As a result, the relation between foreign and Chinese firms is somewhat horizontal. Furthermore, as to the foreign technological service firm, because Chinese makers are their major clients, the relation between these two kinds of firms is also comparatively horizontal, if not controlled by Chinese makers. Last but not least, although the joint venture policy shifts the product architecture of automobile that Chinese firm made, the degree of modularity of this kind of automobile is not as high as that of ICT product. The comparatively low degree of modularity of product architecture and the comparatively horizontal interfirm relationships leave more rooms for Chinese automobile manufacturers to improve their technological capability than Chinese ICT EMS providers.

Features of American and Chinese modular modes of production are included in Table 14.2, and the results of further comparison of modular modes of production in China's ICT and automobile industries are summarized in Table 14.3.

---

process (Fujimoto 2007: 81–82). The concept of process architecture is important in non-assembly industries. The process-based modularity of product architecture exists both in Japan and China including Taiwan. However, the scale of this kind of modularity in Mainland China is much bigger than that of Japan and Taiwan.

[6]The relation between western client and Chinese EMS is similar to the relation between big manufacturers and SMEs in Japan's high-growth period (Isogai et al. 2000).

Table 14.2 Modular mode of production: American type vs. Chinese type

	American type	Chinese type I	Chinese type II
Typical industry	ICT	ICT	Automobile
Typical enterprises	Apple	Foxconn	SOE
Generation mechanism	Technology-economy pulled	Technology-economy pulled	Political-policy driven
Designer of design rules	American enterprises	American enterprises	Western enterprises
Maker of key components	Western enterprises	Western enterprises	Western enterprises

Table 14.3 Further comparison of modular modes of production in China's ICT and automobile industries

	ICT industry	Automobile industry
Dominant ownership structure	Private	State-owned
Labor relations	Liquid, single-skilled worker	High rate of contract employee
Interfirm relationships	Vertical	Comparatively horizontal
Degree of modularity of product	High	Middle
Possibility of technical advance	Low	Middle

In the next section, we shall choose four representative enterprises from the ICT and automobile industries before and after 2006, respectively, and try to illustrate the features of two kinds of modular mode of production in China through a brief summary of these enterprises' developments. The reason why we focus on 2006 is that after 2006, China's innovation policy changed fundamentally and, after the shift of policy paradigm, new type of enterprise emerges. Therefore, comparing the development of representative enterprises in the ICT and automobile industries before and after the year of 2006 would be helpful to understand the evolution of China's mode of production.

14.5 Change and Consistency: China's Modular Modes of Production Before and After 2006

14.5.1 From Foxconn to Mi: Adjustment of Modular Mode of Production in China's ICT Industry

Foxconn was established in Taiwan in the 1970s. It entered Mainland China in the year of 1988. Foxconn expands rapidly in the twenty-first century. In 2012, its value of export accounts for 4.1% of the total value of export of China, ranking 30th among Fortune 500 companies, higher than all other manufacturers in China. From this perspective, Foxconn can be taken as the symbol of Chinese ICT industry.[7]

As the world's largest electronic manufacturing service (EMS) company, Foxconn mainly provides assembling service for Apple Inc. and other western companies. These western companies provide product design and key components, while Foxconn focuses on assembling process. Due to efficient cost control and quick response to its clients, Foxconn is hailed by these clients. However, for Foxconn, such mode of production leads to not only tense labor relations and low rate of profit but also difficulties in technical advance (Song and Meng 2013). When China started to promote the indigenous innovation in 2006, Foxconn has experienced increasing criticism.

Thus Mi, a rising star in recent years, appears to replace Foxconn as a new symbol of Chinese ICT industry. From 2011 to 2014, its cumulative sales of smartphone, Mi's major product, were 20 million, the selling record among local companies. Mi also began to present serious challenge to Samsung, the second biggest maker of smartphone, in mid-priced market. Excellent cost efficiency and marketing strategy occupy important positions in Mi's business model, in which a considerable portion of profit derives from apps installed in the device. Therefore it is reasonable to believe that Mi and Foxconn have different business models. However, the central problem lies in whether Mi represents one mode of production that is different from that of Foxconn or not. In fact, the design of Mi's smartphone follows the design rule set up by the mainstream western smartphone makers. In addition, its major components are imported from western companies including Samsung, Sharp, LG, and so on, and its assembling process is accomplished by Foxconn, Inventec, and other EMS companies. For the above reasons, although Mi develops a new business model which is different from that of Foxconn, its mode of production is still quite modular and depends heavily on the international production network.[8]

14.5.2 From FAW to Changan: Adjustment of Modular Mode of Production in China's Automobile Industry

FAW is China's first automobile manufacturer and the symbol of Chinese automobile industry. After the 1980s, FAW starts to cooperate with western automobile companies like Volkswagen, Toyota, and Mazda through joint venture project and technical cooperation. Benefiting from the support provided by the aforementioned foreign companies, FAW quickly expands in production scale. However, as we have mentioned before, government policies of joint venture and technical cooperation actually transform the product architecture of automobile from integral side to modular side and facilitate the formation of modular mode of production. Under

[7]Information comes from Foxconn's official website (http://www.foxconn.com.cn).

[8]Information comes from Mi's official website (https://www.mi.com).

this modular mode of production, FAW would only concentrate on the assembling process, and it can hardly accumulate necessary techniques to develop self-owned brands. In fact, the discussion on indigenous innovation strategy within the Chinese academia around 2006 was centered on the performance of indigenous innovation by joint ventures like FAW holds.

As the result of change of innovation policy, a number of automobile companies developing and producing self-owned brands begin to gain more influence after 2006. Among those companies, Changan stands out as the most prominent company. Originally a part of the military industry, Changan started to produce automobiles through its joint venture project with Suzuki, Ford, and Mazda. It has been producing self-branded automobiles since 2006. By 2014, Changan has become the largest manufacturer of self-branded automobile. For Changan, the international production regime is still a significant background. For instance, its designing centers in Turin, Yokohama, Nottingham, and Detroit provide Changan with designs of outlook, interior, engine, gearbox, and chassis. As a matter of fact, professional western designing companies and technique service providers contribute much to the product development of local companies like Changan and other newcomers in the automobile industry, which actively develop its own self-owned brands. The only difference between Changan and other local companies is that Changan sets more research centers directly in western countries in recent years, while other companies tend to purchase services from professional western designing companies and technique service providers. In sum, taking into account the fact that Changan also depends on the collaboration with western automobile design firms, technical service providers, and international production network, although slightly different from that of FAW, Changan's mode of production still falls within the range of modular mode of production.

14.6 Conclusion

The institutional and structural features are the keys to understanding the dynamics of Chinese economy, and studies of these features would enrich our knowledge about modern capitalism. However, the mainstream economists and advocates of the so-called Chinese Economic Model did not undertake in-depth analyses of these features. In the meanwhile, due to the issue of availability of data and absence of detailed case studies at industry or firm level, although the Diversity of Capitalism Approach, which is a promising approach and thus likely to exert great explanatory force in analyzing the institutional and structural features of Chinese economy, has been introduced into the studies of Chinese economy, these features are far from being sufficiently clarified.

From the viewpoint of Diversity of Capitalism Approach including *Régulation* School, the mode of production as well as the diversity of regions and industries can be, respectively, taken as the basic institutional feature and structural feature. Furthermore, considering that there are different kinds of dominant mode of production in different regions and industries, we could draw a conclusion that the mode of production and diversity of regions and industries overlap to a large extent. Moreover, inspired by the tradition of Schumpeter School, in this chapter we investigate the origin and evolution of dominant modes of production in China's two leading industries, by paying special attention to the technology and organization.

The major research finding of this chapter is that in China's modern manufacturing industries, there exist two kinds of mode of production that share similarities yet differ in some respects. Both modes of production of the two leading industries relate to the modularity of product architecture and can be termed modular mode of production. However, these modular modes of production differ from each other in the ownership structure, generation mechanism of modularity, degree of modularity of product architecture, interfirm relationships, and possibility of technical advance. The other research finding of this chapter is that in the foreseeable future, the modes of production of the two leading industries will remain modular although the automobile manufacturers are more likely to upgrade their technological capability than their counterparts in the ICT industry.

References

Aglietta M (1979) A theory of capitalist regulation: the US experience. NLB, London

Amable B (2000) Institutional complementarity and diversity of social systems of innovation and production. Intl Polit Econ Rev 7(4):645–687

Amable B (2003) The diversity of modern capitalism. Oxford University Press, Oxford

Aoki M (1988) Information, incentives, and bargaining in the Japanese economy, Cambridge, Cambridge University Press

Aoki M (2001) Towards a comparative institutional analysis. MIT Press, Cambridge

Aoki M, Takizawa H (2002) Information, incentives, and option value: the Silicon Valley model. J Comp Econ 30(4):759–786

Baldwin C, Clark K (2000) Design rules: the power of modularity. The MIT Press, Cambridge

Borrus M, Zysman J (1997) Wintelism and the changing terms of global competition: prototype of the future? Working paper 96B, BRIE, UC Berkeley

Boyer R (1990) The regulation school. Columbia University Press, New York

Boyer R (2005) Coherence, diversity and evolution of capitalisms: the institutional complementarity hypothesis. Evolut Institut Econ Rev 2(1):43–80

Boyer R (2012) The Chinese growth regime and the world economy. In: Boyer R et al (eds) Diversity and transformation of Asian capitalisms. Routledge, London

Boyer R, Freyssenet M (2002) The productive models: the conditions of profitability. Palgrave Macmillan, New York

Boyer R, Yamada T (eds) (2000) Japanese capitalism in crisis: a Regulationist interpretation. Routledge, London

Chandler A, Amatori F, Hikino T (eds) (1997) Big business and the wealth of nations. Cambridge University Press, Cambridge

Cornelia S, Amable B, Steven C, Lechevalier S (2013) Bringing Asia into the comparative capitalism perspective. Soc Econ Rev 11(2):217–232

Dore R (1973) British factory, Japanese factory: the origins of national diversity in industrial relations. California University Press, Berkeley/Los Angeles

Dore R (2000) Stock capitalism: welfare capitalism: Japan and Germany versus the Anglo-Saxons. Oxford University, Oxford

Freeman C (1987) Technology policy and economic performance: lessons from Japan. Pinter, London

Freeman C, Soete L (2004) The economics of industrial innovation. Penguin Books, London

Fujimoto T (2007) Architecture-based comparative advantage: a design information view of manufacturing. Evolut Institut Econ Rev 4(1):55–112

Fujimoto T, Shinntaku J (eds) (2004) Architecture-base analysis of Chinese manufacturing industries. Toyoukeizaishinnbousya, Tokyo (in Japanese)

Hall P (1986) Governing the economy: the politics of state intervention in Britain and France. Oxford University Press, New York

Hall P, Soskice D (eds) (2001) Varieties of capitalism: the institutional foundation of comparative advantage. Oxford University Press, New York

Harada Y, Tohyama H (2012) Asian capitalisms: institutional configurations and firm heterogeneity. In: Boyer R et al (eds) Diversity and transformation of Asian capitalisms. Routledge, London

Herrigel G (2000) Industrial constructions: the sources of German industrial power. Cambridge University, Cambridge

Isogai A, Ebizuka A, Uemura H (2000) The hierarchical market-firm Nexus as the Japanese mode of regulation. In: Boyer R, Yamada T (eds) Japanese capitalism in crisis: a regulationist interpretation. Routledge, London

Lazonick W (1990) Competitive advantage on the shop floor. Harvard University Press, Cambridge

Lazonick W (2009) Sustainable prosperity in the new economy?: business organization and high-tech employment in the United States. W.E. Upjohn Institute for Employment Research, Kalamazoo

Locke R (1994) Remaking the Italian economy: policy failures and local successes in the contemporary polity. Cornell University Press, Ithaca

Lüthje B (2014) Labour relations, production regimes and labour conflicts in the Chinese automobile industry. Int Labour Rev 153(4):535–560

Morgan G, Campell J, Crouch C, Pedersen O, Whitley R (eds) (2010) The Oxford handbook of comparative institutional analysis. Oxford University Press, Oxford

Regini M (1997) Social Institutions and Production Structure: The Italian Variety of Capitalism in the 1980s. In: Crouch C, Streeck W (eds) Political economy of modern capitalism: mapping convergence and diversity. Sage, London

Song L (2015) The Gerschenkron-Dore proposition and Chinese practice. Open Times 34 (4):183–199 (in Chinese)

Song L, Meng J (2013) Origin and evolution of the Foxconn phenomenon. Open Times 32 (4):125–136 (in Chinese)

Song L, Zhang YB (2013) Beyond ideological and empirical descriptions: theorizing Japanese and Chinese development experiences. In: Huang XM (ed) Modern economic development in Japan and China: developmentalism, capitalism, and the world economic system. Palgrave Macmillan, London

Steinfeld E (2004) China's shallow integration: networked production and the new challenges for late industrialization. World Dev 32(11):1971–1987

Sturgeon, T. 2002. Modular production networks: an American model of industrial Organization. *Industrial and Corporate Change* 11(3): 451–496

Tohyama H, Harada Y (2014) Diversity of Asian capitalism: institutional structure and innovation activities at firm level. In: Uemura H et al (eds) Tennkannki no Ajia Sihonnsyugi. Fujihara Syotenn, Tokyo (in Japanese)

Whitley R (1992) Business systems in East Asia: firms, markets and societies. Sage, London

Whitley R (1999) Divergent capitalisms: the social structuring and change of business systems. Oxford University, Oxford

Whitley R, Zhang XK (eds) (2016) Changing business systems in East Asia: political change, Internationalization and Economic Organization in Northeast and Southeast Asia. Cambridge University Press, Cambridge

Whittaker DH, Zhu TB, Sturgeon T, Tsai MH, Okita T (2010) Compressed development. Stud Comp Intl Develop 45(3):439–467

Witt M, Redding G (2013) Asian business systems: institutional comparison, clusters, and implications for varieties of capitalism and business systems theory. Socio-Econ Rev 11(2):265–300

Yan CN (2012) Analysis of the linkage effects of China's export-led growth: according to the subdivisions of Asian international input-output tables. In: Boyer R et al (eds) Diversity and transformation of Asian capitalisms. Routledge, London

Chapter 15
Structural Change, Sectoral Disparity, and the Economic Growth Process in Japan

Hiroshi Nishi

15.1 Introduction

This study examines the relationship between structural change, sectoral disparity, and economic growth in the Japanese economy. Structural change in this study refers to change in the sectoral composition (share) of an aggregate economy. Sectoral disparity is measured by the sectoral contribution to economic growth and the sectoral difference in the levels of value added and labour productivity. In this study, therefore, we use a disaggregation approach and divide the macroeconomy into sectors based on the Japan Industrial Productivity Database of 2014 (JIP database hereafter) compiled by the Research Institute of Economy, Trade and Industry (RIETI). The disaggregation approach is important because, as we see below, sectoral performances such as growth rates and levels of labour productivity and value added are not always uniform among sectors. Thus, sectoral heterogeneity is evolving in Japan.

This study is based on the growth regime analysis of *régulationists* and post-Keynesians. These authors have analysed the economic growth regime of a country from a macroeconomic perspective (Boyer and Yamada 2000; Boyer et al. 2011; Lavoie and Stockhammer 2013; Hein 2014). In particular, they have reduced the dynamic relationship between productivity growth and demand growth into two equations, namely, the demand regime and the productivity regime, and revealed different constellations for these regimes in terms of country and period.

Since such macroeconomic analysis is conducted at the aggregate level, it assumes no sectorally heterogeneous configuration and structural change. Therefore, these works cannot capture the relationship between macroeconomic performance

H. Nishi (✉)
Hannan University, Matsubara, Japan
e-mail: nishi@hannan-u.ac.jp

R. Boyer et al. (eds.), *Evolving Diversity and Interdependence of Capitalisms*, Evolutionary Economics and Social Complexity Science 11,
https://doi.org/10.1007/978-4-431-55001-3_15

and industrial structure. Uemura and Tahara (2014, 2015) are recent contributions that overcome such issues in aggregate analysis. Their multisectoral approach integrally analyses the growth regime as well as deindustrialization mechanism in Japan, finding that the Japanese economy has undergone both positive and negative deindustrialization depending on the performance of the export-core manufacturing sectors over the past 30 years.

The relationship between structural change and aggregate economic growth has been an important subject in previous studies of this topic. One of the most important research lines originates from Baumol (1967). According to this study, there is negative feedback on economic growth in the process of tertiarization, in what is well known as 'Baumol's disease'. Studies after Baumol attempted to assess whether expansion in a nonprogressive sector has a negative impact on overall economic growth. These studies consider the expansion of the tertiary sector, also classified as a nonprogressive low-productivity sector, to represent structural change.

While some research supports Baumol's prediction (Baumol et al. 1985; Peneder 2003; Nordhaus 2008; Hartwig 2011, 2012), other studies present contrary results (Maroto-Sánchez and Cuadrado-Roura 2009; Dietrich 2012). While the existing literature focuses on the European Union and the United States, recent studies of Japan (Fukao and Miyagawa 2008; Ito and Lechevalier 2009; Fukao 2012; Morikawa 2014) focus on the industrial structure and attempt to find the causes and consequences of differing performance at the industrial and firm levels. They especially focus on the supply side, with the investigation of total factor productivity (TFP) growth the most popular. Fukao and Miyagawa (2008) indicate that the TFP growth rate differs at the industrial and firm levels. Fukao (2012) emphasizes that as the cause of the slowdown in TFP growth, Japan lags behind in ICT investment. Morikawa (2014) intensively investigates the economic performance of the services sector and finds that the firm productivity in this sector is not necessarily low. Ito and Lechevalier (2009) focus on the dispersion of productivity growth across heterogeneous firms, finding evidence that internationalization has a significant and positive impact on productivity dispersion.

Most of these studies point out the heterogeneity of industries and firms. This means that by examining the variables at an average or aggregate level, we cannot correctly understand overall economic performance. Instead, we need to observe the sectoral distribution that creates the aggregate outcomes. However, although the aggregation approach is useful to analyse the growth processes of the 1970s and 1980s, it cannot explain the uneven growth process after the 1990s, as we show in this study. The uneven growth process after the 1990s is not even satisfactorily explained by Uemura and Tahara (2014, 2015), because they do not consider the distribution of the sectors contributing to economic growth.

In this context, we introduce the multisectoral perspective to the economic growth analysis of post-Keynesians and *régulationists*. In their theory, the growth regime is examined by the interaction of growth in output and in labour productivity. The current study does not focus on their interaction but instead empirically explores the industrial foundation that creates growth in output and labour productivity in the Japanese economy.

We believe that such an attempt makes three novel contributions to growth regime analysis. The first contribution is that we shed light on the sectoral distribution and heterogeneity behind economic growth. In other words, we attempt to investigate the industrial foundation of the growth regime. The second contribution is introducing structural change in various sectors to examine Japanese economic growth and stagnation. In doing so, we investigate the change in the sectoral structure of inputs and output in relation to economic growth. To be more precise, the structural change in output means the change in the sectoral composition of value added, which is a proxy for structural change on the demand side. Similarly, the structural change in inputs means the change in the sectoral share of factors of production such as labour and capital, which is a proxy for structural change on the supply side. Thus, we also consider the demand side of sectoral performance, which is inadequately examined in the literature. Hence, the third contribution of this study is that we empirically detect the kind of structural change required to promote economic growth.

The remainder of this paper is organized as follows. Section 15.2 introduces the sectoral classification based on the JIP database. This section also presents the indices used to measure the degree of structural change in this study. Section 15.3 considers sectoral performance and macroeconomic growth in Japan. This section first illustrates the structural change in inputs and output and then examines the sectoral contribution to the growth in Japan over the past 40 years. Section 15.4 presents our econometric analysis. This section reports the impact of structural changes in inputs and output on the growth rates of value added and labour productivity. Finally, Section 15.5 concludes.

15.2 Measurement of Structural Change

15.2.1 JIP Database and Sectoral Classification

We use the JIP database compiled by RIETI throughout our empirical analysis in this study. The JIP database consists of various types of annual data for the period 1970–2011 required to estimate the economic activities in 108 industries covering the Japanese economy. Because investigating structural change requires considering the changes affecting disaggregate units, we require statistical data that can capture multisectoral performance. The JIP database of RIETI is one of the most appropriate databases for this purpose.

This study defines 106 sectors as small classifications and mainly considers their economic performance and relationship with the aggregate economic outcome. The housing sector (JIP classification no. 72) and activities not classified elsewhere (JIP classification no. 108) are excluded, because some important data such as number of workers and man-hours are not available. To analyse structural change, sectoral disparity and economic growth, we aggregate these 106 small classifications into an intermediate classification that consists of 8 main sectors. In this classification, we

Table 15.1 Large, intermediate and small classification based on JIP database

Code in large classification	Code in intermediate classification	Original code in JIP (small classification)
L1 Agriculture	M1 Agriculture	1–6
L2 Industry	M2 Export core manufacturing	42–57
	M3 Other manufacturing	8–41, 58–59, 92
	M4 Other industries	7, 60–66
L3 Service	M5 Financial services	69–70
	M6 Business-related services	67, 73–88, 91, 93, 99, 106
	M7 Consumer services	68, 71, 89–90, 94–97
	M8 Public services	80, 82–84, 98, 100–105, 107

Note: By author on the basis of JIP 2014 and Uemura and Tahara (2015)

follow the criteria employed by Uemura and Tahara (2015). Table 15.1 summarizes the correspondence among the small, intermediate and large classifications.

The large classification is based on the standard classification of agriculture, industry and services sectors. The agriculture sector (L1) directly corresponds to the agriculture sector M1; the industry sector (L2) corresponds to M2, M3 and M4; and the services sector (L3) includes M5, M6, M7 and M8.

15.2.2 JIP Database and Sectoral Classification Indices of Structural Change

This study uses the term 'structural change' to denote the changing sectoral composition (share) of an aggregate economy. Theoretically, structural changes occur on both the demand and the supply sides (Baumol 1967; Pasinetti 1993). A structural change in demand occurs because of a change in relative prices, consumers' preference for higher quality, different income elasticities and the increasing saturation of demand for existing goods. As demand for each sector grows at a different rate during economic growth, this process influences the quantity and composition of the goods demanded from different industries. On the supply side, learning and technological change can lead to productivity improvement, which enables firms to produce the same goods at a lower unit cost or to create new goods frequently and thus attract new effective demand. In the process of economic growth, sectoral productivity grows at different rates. The interaction of these factors leads to sectorally different growth rates of output, inputs and productivity. One of the consequences of structural change is therefore the change in the sectoral share of output and inputs. Deindustrialization is a well-known example of such structural change. According to the literature (e.g. Rowthorn and Wells 1987), deindustrialization means the decreasing share of employment in the industrial (manufacturing) sector.

To investigate the structural change process, we need indices to quantify its magnitude. We use structural change indices to summarize the changes in the sectoral composition of an economy between two points in time. This study adopts the two indices used in Dietrich (2012) because they are based on the sectoral share for an economic variable and are thus appropriate to consider structural change. The first index is the norm of absolute value (*NAV*), the simplest index with which to measure structural change. Let $x_{i,\ t}$ be the share of sector $i = 1, \ldots n$ at time $t = 1, \ldots T - 1$ and $s = 2, \ldots T$. This index can be given by the following calculation:

$$NAV_{s,t} = 0.5\sum_{i=1}^{n} \mid x_{i,s} - x_{i,t} \mid \tag{15.1}$$

The result is a range of *NAV* between zero and unity, simplifying the interpretation of *NAV*. According to Dietrich (2012): 'If the structure remains unchanged, the index is equal to zero, and if the change in all sectors is at its highest—meaning the whole economy undergoes a total change—then the index is equal to unity' (*ibid*, p. 920). The second index to measure the degree of structural change is the modified Lilien index (*MLI*), which is based on Lilien (1982). Dietrich (2012) presents a modified version of the Lilien index that is weighted by the share of sectors in both periods:

$$MLI_{s,t} = \sqrt{\sum_{i=1}^{n} x_{i,s}x_{i,t}\log\left(\frac{x_{i,s}}{x_{i,t}}\right)^2} \tag{15.2}$$

When the *MLI* is low (high), structural change in the economy proceeds slowly (quickly).

From these calculations, we construct the structural change index for value added, labour productivity, capital stock and the capital–labour ratio. The structural change index for value added reflects the rate of change in the sectoral output share. The structural change indices for labour, capital stock and the capital–labour ratio reflect the rate of change in the sectoral inputs share. These are also interpreted as approximations of the structural changes in demand and supply. Labour and capital are the principal factors of production. A change in these inputs can thus lead to changes in output and productivity and may accelerate or decelerate economic growth. In addition, the combination of capital and labour, which reflects the technological level of production, also affects economic growth. Thus, these factors determine the supply side structure. Value added can be determined by not only the supply side but also the demand side. For example, Engel's law predicts that higher income per capita shifts the demand structure. Moreover, an innovation that attracts new effective demand in a sector also contributes to the growth in value added in that sector. Thus, these factors lead to changes in the sectoral composition of value added, meaning that the sectoral composition of value added is not independent of the demand side structure.[1]

15.3 Sectoral Performances and Macroeconomic Growth

15.3.1 Structural Change in Output and Inputs

This section explores the overall trends in the structural change in inputs and output in Japan by examining the annual and 5-year evolution of the structural change indices. These structural change indices are based on the 8-sector intermediate classification. For details of the data sources and construction of the variables introduced in this study, see the panel data analysis in the following section.

Figure 15.1 shows the annual and 5-year structural change index calculations for value added in real terms. The annual variation demonstrates that the structural change in value added was relatively stable from the 1970s to the mid-1990s, except for a hike at the beginning of the 1980s.[2] What is clear from the figure for both calculations is that the structural change in value added began to accelerate gradually in the late 1990s.

Figures 15.2, 15.3, and 15.4 show the results of the structural change indices for labour, capital and the capital–labour ratio for the annual and 5-year terms. From Fig. 15.2, the structural change in labour shows a decreasing trend in the five-year term, with annually cyclical behaviour from the 1970s to the 1990s.[3] After the 1990s, the cyclical behaviour continues, but it is hard to read a clear trend from the figure. Figure 15.3 shows the structural change indices for capital stock for the annual and 5-year terms. In the 1970s, the pace of the structural change in capital stock was high historically. However, these indices show a rather clear trend in the long run. The pace of structural change after the bubble burst decelerated, and it became especially slow during the most recent 10 years. The structural change in the capital–labour ratio reflects the structural change in inputs or production technology. Figure 15.4 shows the structural change indices for the capital–labour ratio for the

[1]Further, the final demand by sector in the JIP database input–output table is also suitable to capture the demand side dynamics. However, since some data on demand components are unavailable, we cannot conduct the statistical analysis smoothly. Therefore, we employ value added to capture the demand side of the economy. For the statistical processing relationship between value added and final demand, see the JIP database website of RIETI.

[2]The original data for value added generates outliers in these indices for 1982 and 1983. This is because the sector of electronic equipment and electric measuring instruments (no. 50) takes a value (6470,7985 million) in 1982 that may be an outlier. Therefore, we changed this value and plotted it by smoothing its value with the 5-year average.

[3]Prasad (1997) also uses the Lilien index to capture the degree of the structural change in labour productivity and documents that the Japanese economy underwent gradual structural change in this term until the beginning of the 1990s.

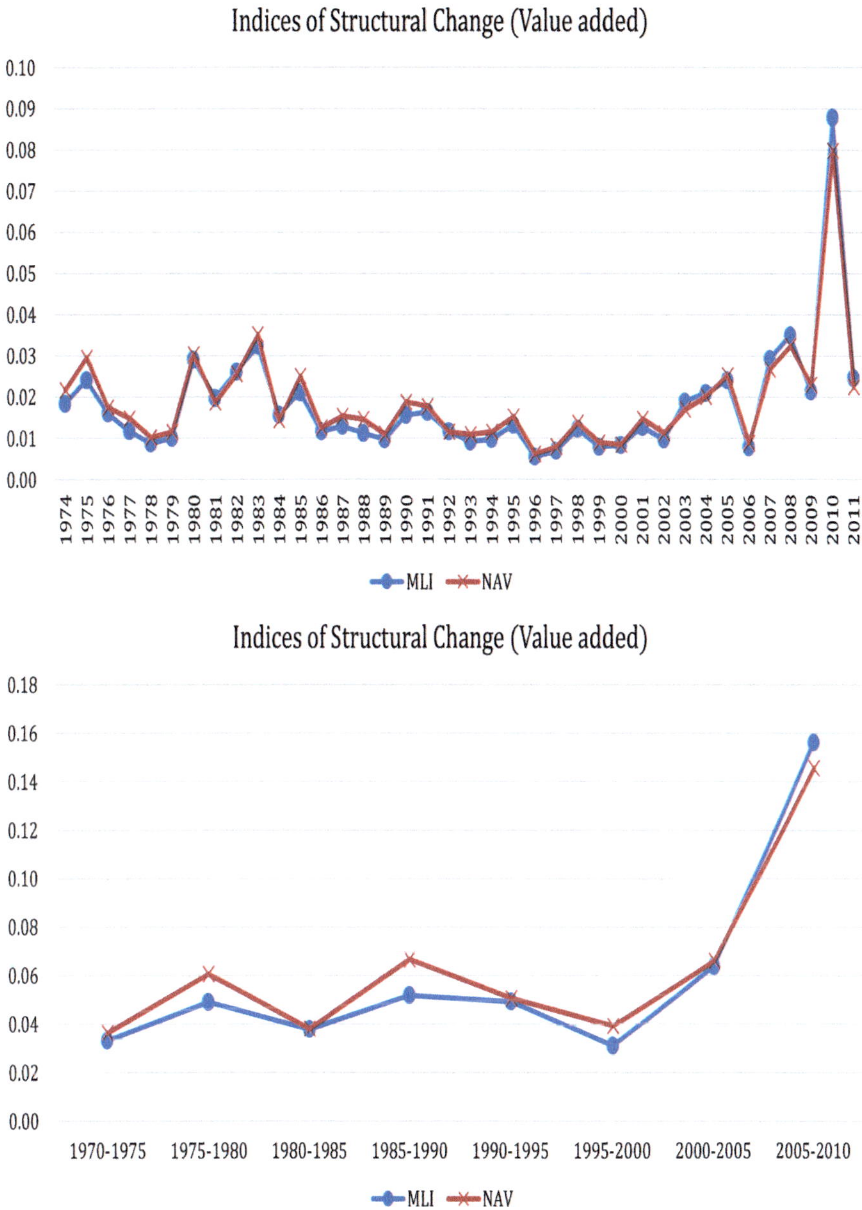

Fig. 15.1 Structural change indices for the annual and five-year terms (value added)
Note: From the author's calculation based on the JIP database

annual and 5-year terms. It is difficult to read a clear trend from the figure on annual change because of its cyclical evolution. For a rough illustration based on the 5-year term, the structural change index for this variable in 1970 was relatively high. Then, the pace of change decelerated during the 1980s, before rising again after 2000.

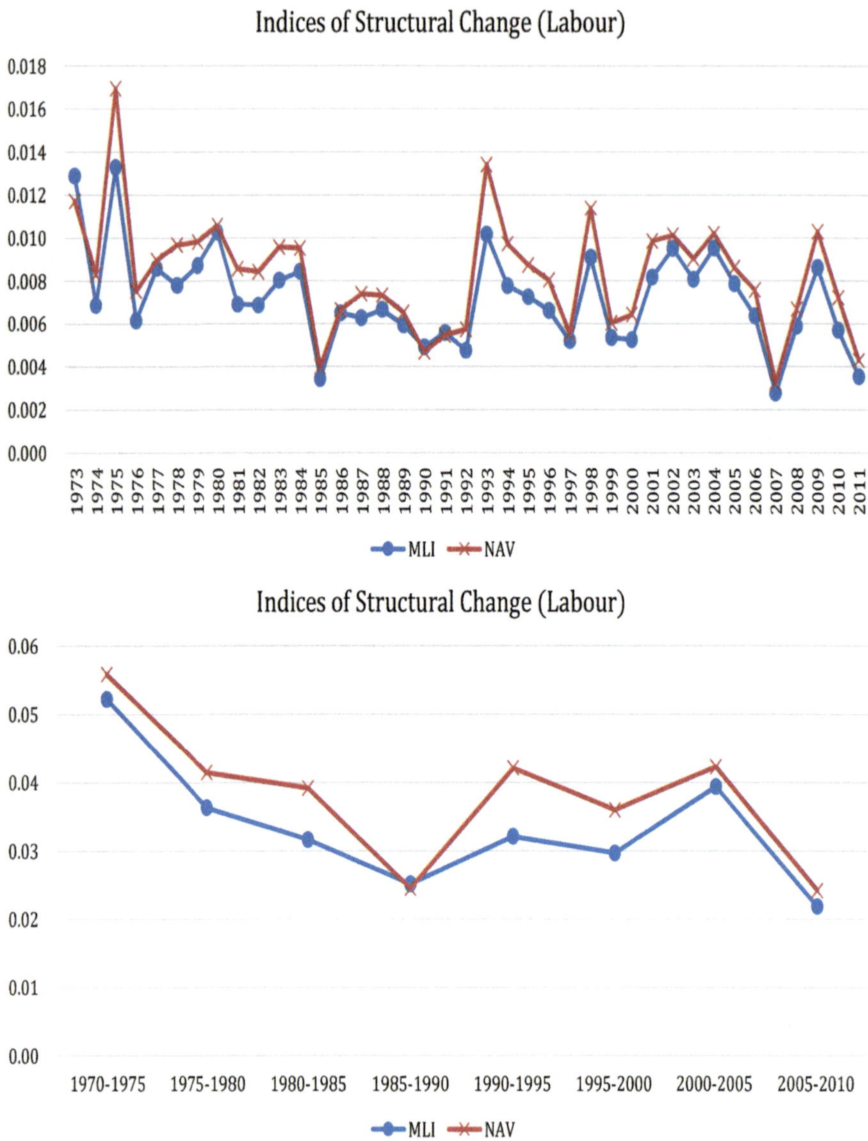

Fig. 15.2 Structural change indices for the annual and five-year terms (labour)
Note: From the author's calculation based on the JIP database

With regard to the pace of structural change, the structural change in value added in the 2000s and the capital–labour ratio generally occurs at a high pace. The indices of these two variables take a relatively high value. On the contrary, each of the recent structural changes in capital and labour generally occurs at a low pace. Those of these two variables therefore take a relatively small value. Hence, a contrast exists

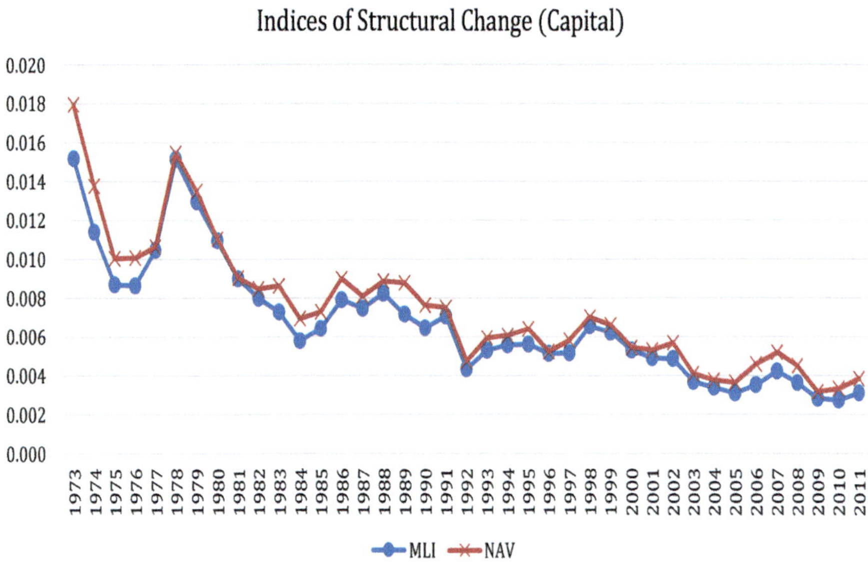

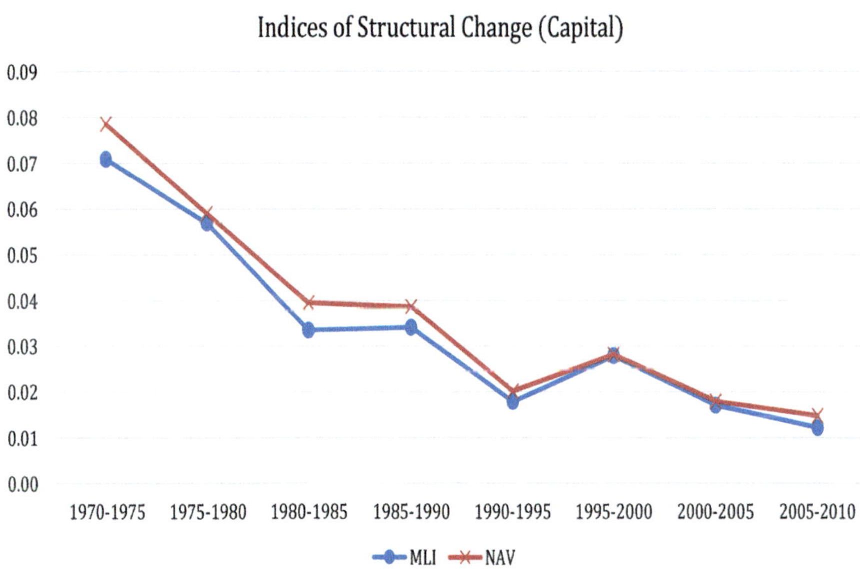

Fig. 15.3 Structural change indices for the annual and five-year terms (capital stock)
Note: From the author's calculation based on the JIP database

between the long-run slowdown of the structural change in capital stock and the recent increase in the rate of the structural change in value added.

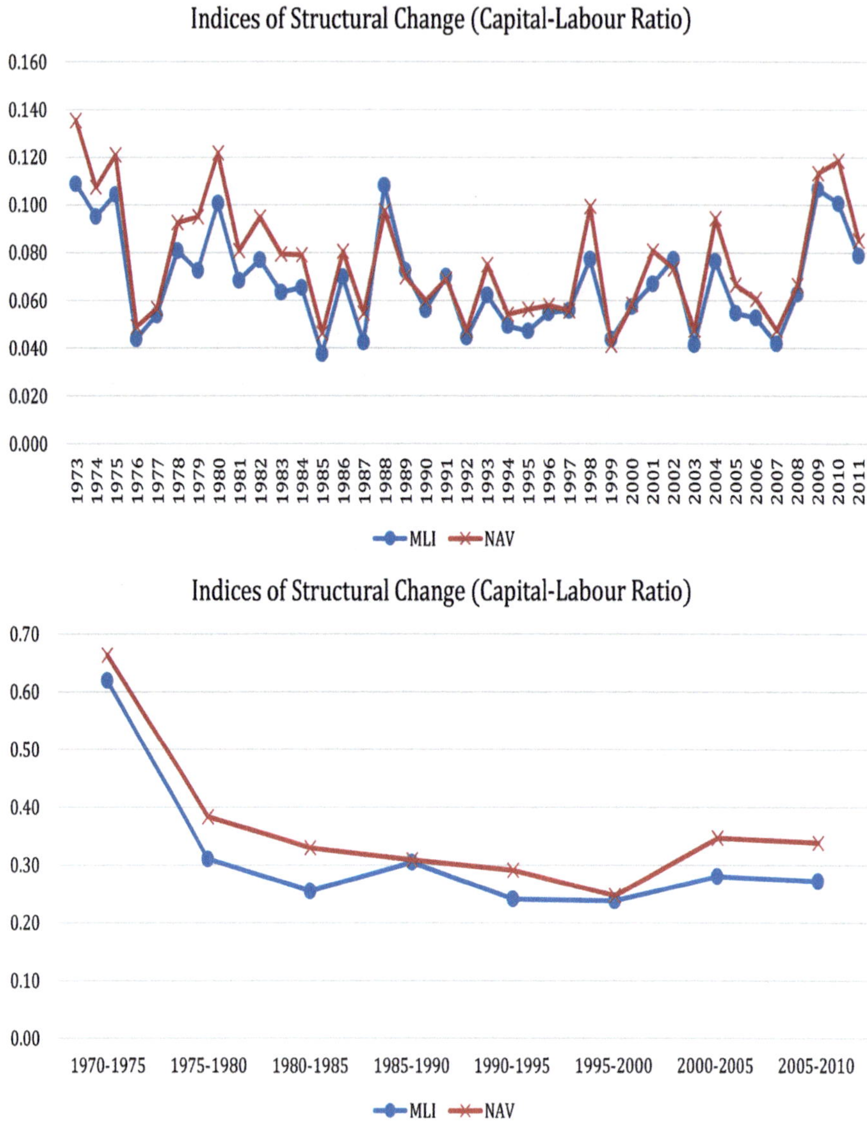

Fig. 15.4 Structural change indices for the annual and five-year terms (capital–labour ratio)
Note: From the author's calculation based on the JIP database

15.3.2 *Changing Dispersion in Sectoral Economic Performance*

Structural change in these terms follows the change in both intra- and inter-sectoral economic performance. Through a decomposition by using the log variance, we measure the change in the sectoral dispersion of the levels of value added and labour productivity for the 8 sectors in the intermediate classification.[4]

The upper part of Fig. 15.5 shows the decomposition of the change in the log variance of value added for the 5-year term. Except for 1985–1990, the change in the log variance takes a negative value from 1970 to 2000, indicating that the sectoral dispersion of economic performance for value added decreases. By contrast, after 2000, the change in the log variance begins to take a positive sign, indicating that the sectoral dispersion of economic performance for the level of value added level increases.

Interestingly, the leading sectoral mechanisms change in the reduction and expansion of dispersion performance. In particular, the industry (L2) sector plays a leading role. Both the within-group and the between-group effects of this sector contributed to reducing dispersion from 1970 to 2000, except for 1985–1990. After 2000, by contrast, these effects began to contribute to expanding dispersion. The services (L3) sector contributes to this in a disturbance manner, which contributes to a large expansion of dispersion in 1985–1990 and a large reduction of dispersion in 1995–2000. In other periods, the services sector does not have a substantial contribution compared with the industry sector. Finally, the contribution of the agriculture (L1) sector is very low.

The lower part of Fig. 15.5 shows the decomposition of the change in the log variance for labour productivity for the 5-year term. From this part of the figure, the change in the log variance for labour productivity takes a negative value from 1970 to 1990. During the next 5 years, the degree of dispersion seems to remain stable. Similar to the case of value added, the value of the change in the log variance takes a positive sign after 2000, which means that the sectoral dispersion of economic performance on the level of labour productivity begins to increase. In this change in labour productivity performance, the industry (L2) sector again plays a principle role. Both the within-group and the between-group effects of this sector constantly and substantially contribute to the reduction of dispersion from 1970 to 1990. These effects of the industry sector, in turn, contribute to the expansion of dispersion after 2000. The contribution of the services (L3) sector is not in a disturbance manner unlike the case of the dispersion in value added. Although the contribution of the services sector is not as large as that of the industry sector, it also contributes to reducing dispersion in 1970–1985 and expanding dispersion after 2000. Finally, the contribution of the agriculture (L1) sector is less apparent.

The figures presented so far show an important hypothesis on the changes in the type of structural change over the past 40 years. The structural change in the Japanese economy until the 1990s accompanies a convergent process of sectoral economic performance with regard to the levels of value added and labour

[4]The log variance measures the degree of inequality in the economic outcomes. This has the advantage of explaining the source of the change in inequality by decomposing it into within-group effects (dispersion effect within each group) and between-group effects (dispersion effect between different groups). A rise (fall) in this variable means that dispersion is increasing (decreasing).

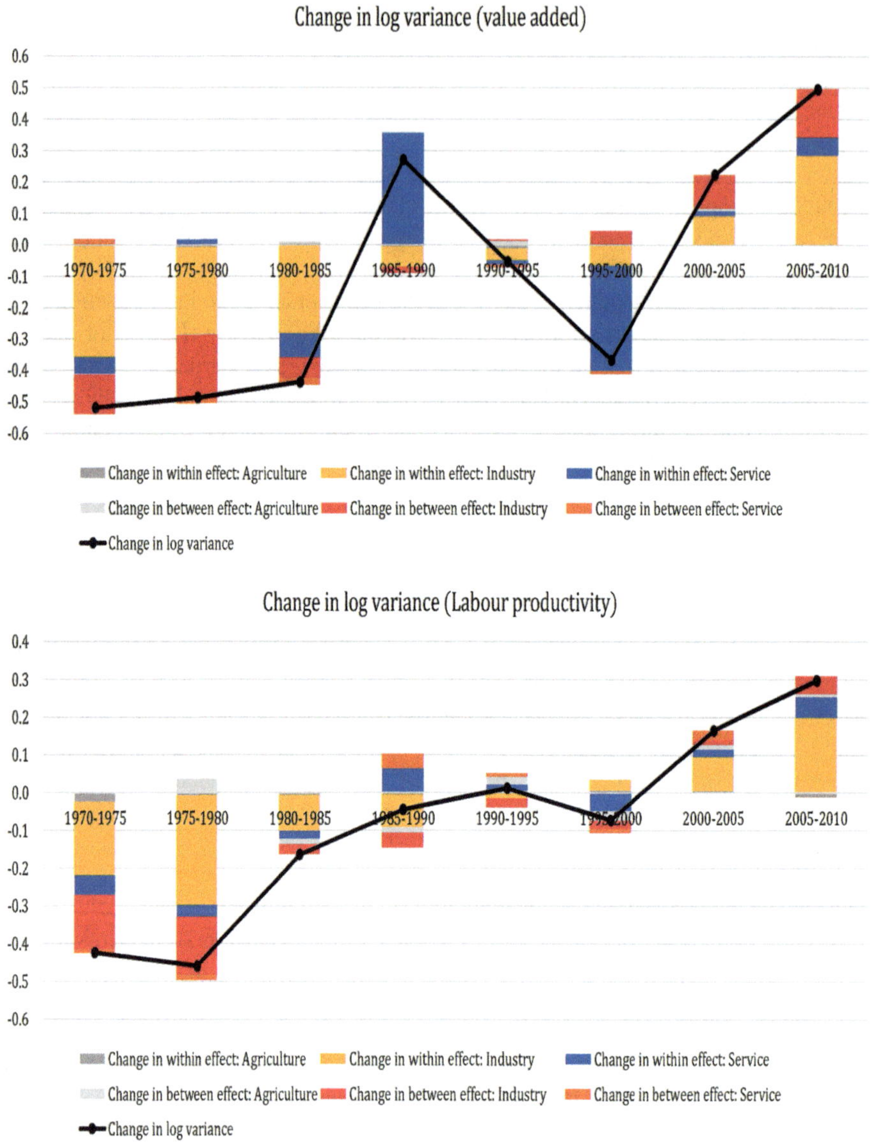

Fig. 15.5 Decomposition of the change in value added and labour productivity dispersion
Note: From the author's calculation based on the JIP database

productivity. The change in the log variance of the levels of labour productivity and value added shows that the negative sign is more dominant until then. However, after 2000, some structural change indices such as those for the capital–labour ratio and value added accelerate following the increasing dispersion of the levels of value added and labour productivity. Sectoral dispersion is especially apparent after 2000 through the lost decade. The hypothesis deduced from this section is that structural change until 1990 might involve an even growth process, whereas the rapid change in the 2000s through the lost decade might involve an uneven growth process. The next section examines this hypothesis in terms of the distribution of the sectoral contribution to economic growth rates.

15.3.3 Economic Growth and the Distribution of the Sectoral Contribution

This section focuses on the relationship between sectoral performance and overall economic growth to show how the performance of each of the 8 intermediate sectors contributes to the aggregate economic growth in value added and labour productivity. Although we focus on the growth rates of value added and labour productivity, we also consider the evolution of employment growth because of the change in the growth in value added and labour productivity. As is well known, the rate of change in employment is equal to the difference between the rate of change in value added and that in labour productivity.

Harberger's (1998) sunrise–sunset diagram is useful to show the distribution of the contribution of the 8 sectors to the economic growth in value added, labour productivity and employment. Such a sunrise–sunset diagram contains four important statistics on the growth in these variables. It shows the sectoral distribution that positively (or negatively) contributes to aggregate growth, which is an indicator of the pervasiveness of growth. It also shows the maximum and aggregate growth rates of these variables. The aggregate rate is shown on the right-hand side of the distribution (i.e. the sum of all contributions), whereas the maximum growth rate is shown at the top of the curve (i.e. the sum of positive contributions). The sectoral contribution is thus the product of each sector's share and each sector's growth rate. Consequently, the slope is steeper for sectors that have high growth rates. Moreover, the relative area under the Harberger diagram is a measure to capture the uniformity of economic growth (the degree of the distortion of overall growth), which is 0 when all industries have equal growth; however, when industry growth rates start to diverge, this value increases (Inklaar and Timmer 2007).

Figures 15.6, 15.7, 15.8, and 15.9 plot the Harberger diagrams for value added, labour productivity and employment growth for each decade divided into the 5-year terms, while Table 15.2 summarizes the four statistics. The upper part of the figures

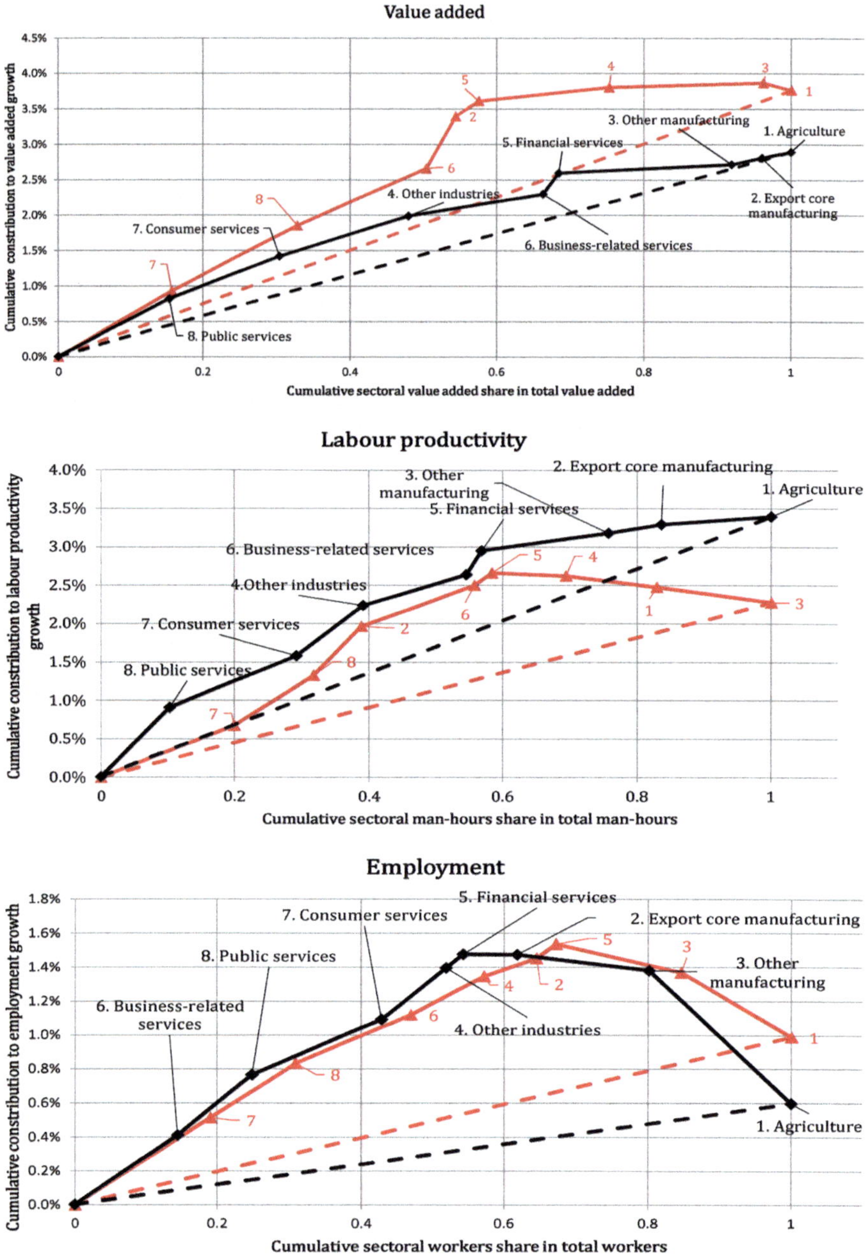

Fig. 15.6 Harberger diagram for value added, labour productivity, and employment growth (1970–1980)

Note: The black solid line with square markers represents the distribution in 1970–1975 (the first half of the period). The red solid line with square markers represents the distribution in 1975–1980 (the second half of the period). This representation is the same for Figs. 15.7, 15.8, and 15.9. VA is value added, LP is labour productivity, and MHS is the share of sectoral man-hours

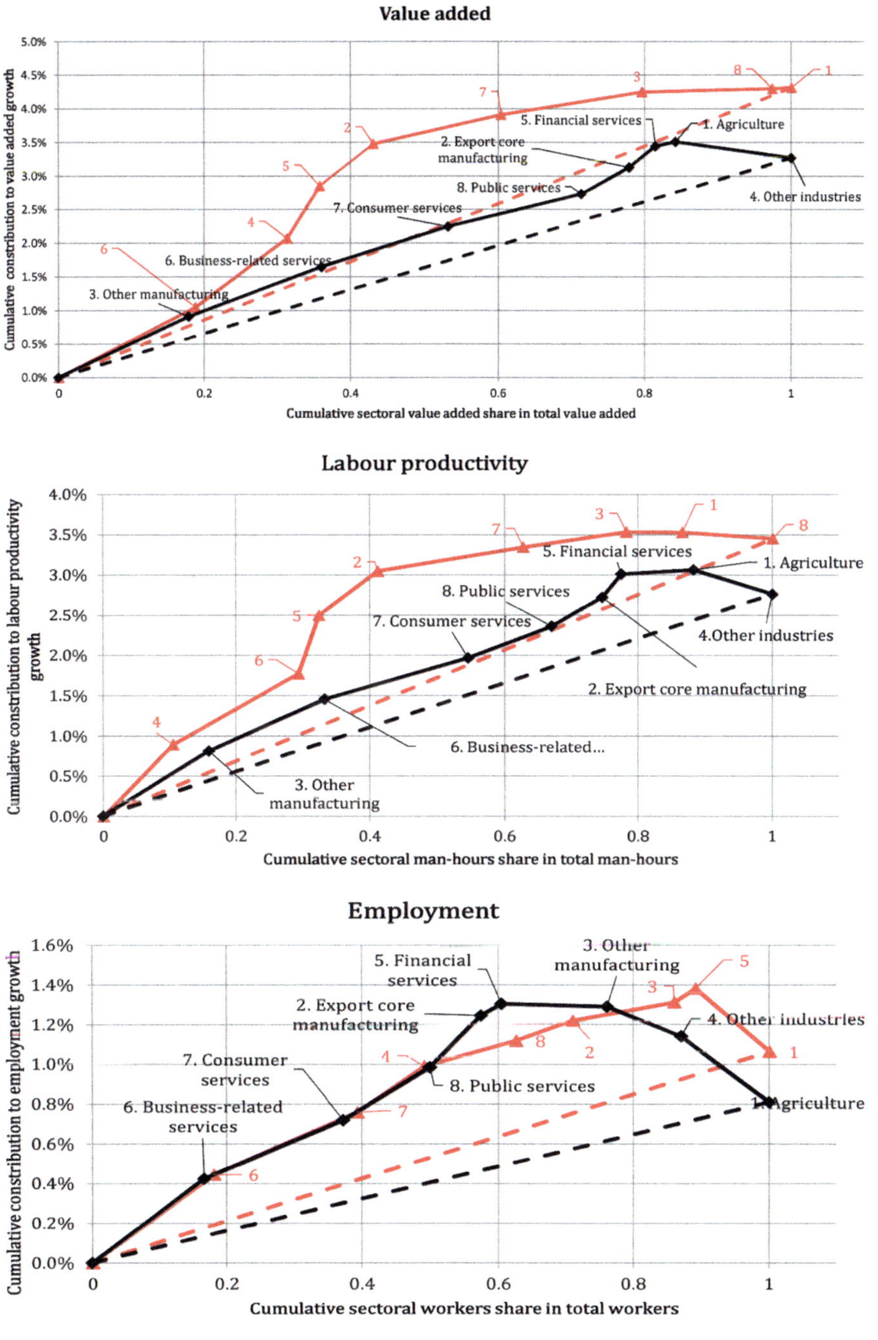

Fig. 15.7 Harberger diagram for value added, labour productivity, and employment growth (1980–1990)

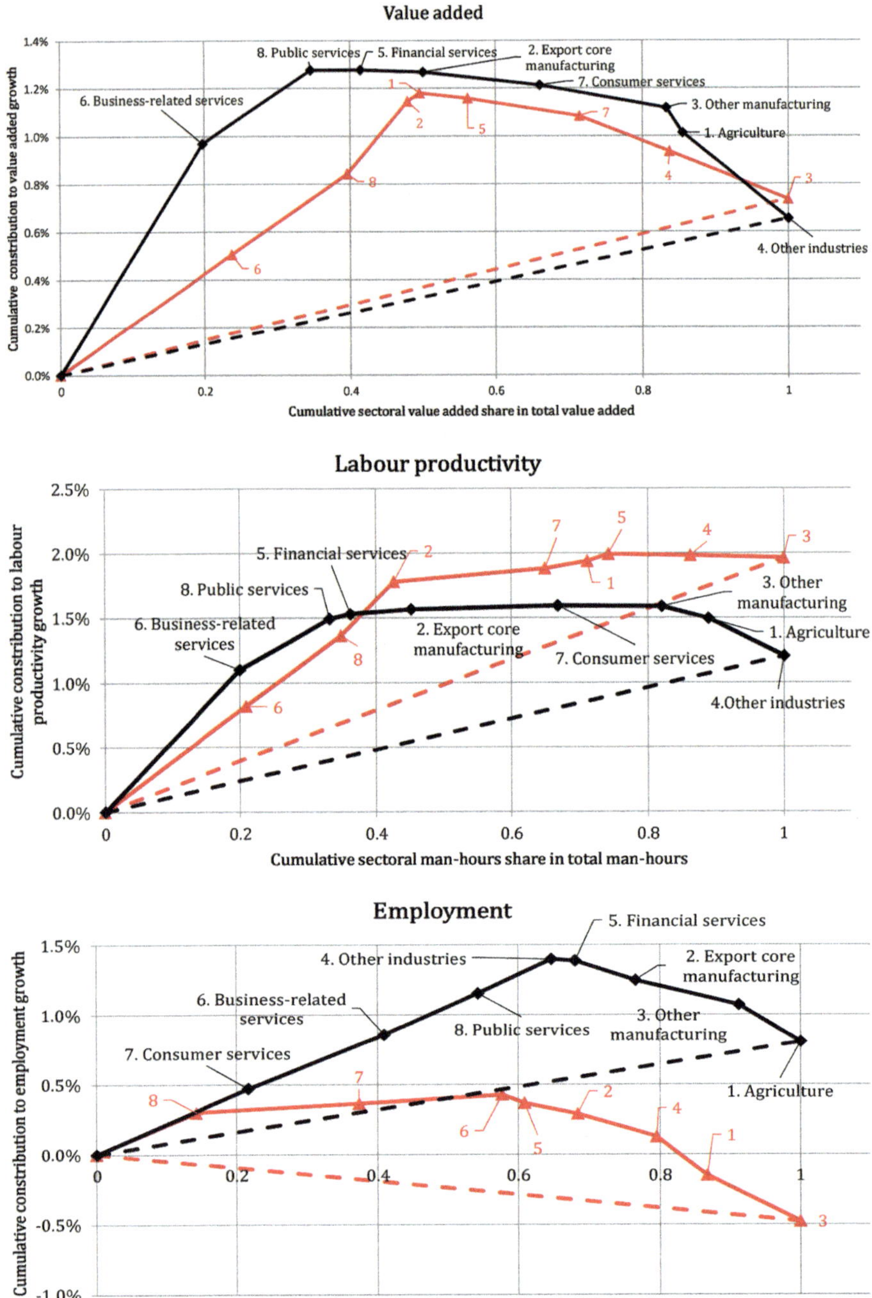

Fig. 15.8 Harberger diagram for value added, labour productivity, and employment growth (1990–2000)

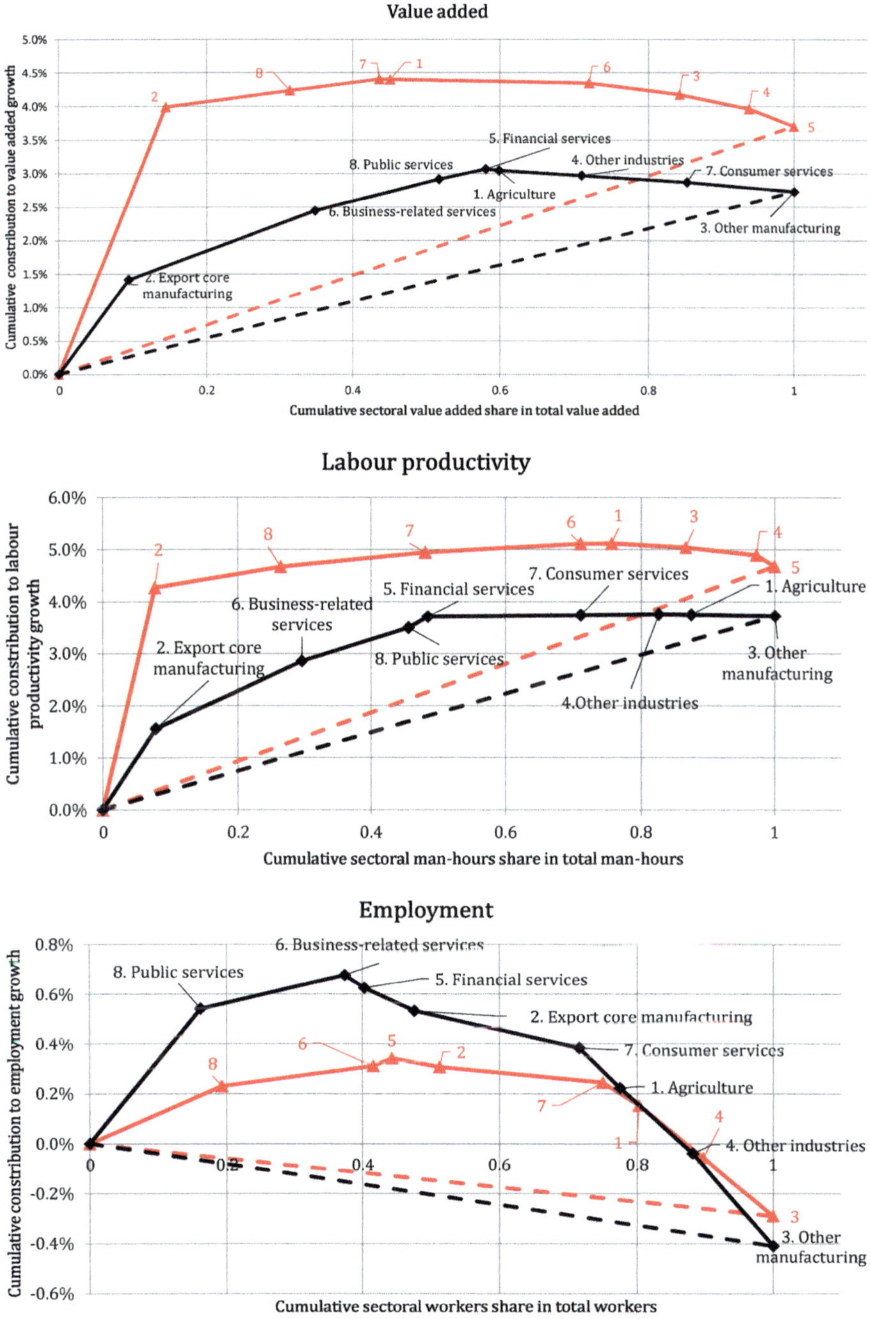

Fig. 15.9 Harberger diagram for value added, labour productivity, and employment growth (2000–2010)

Table 15.2 Summary statistics of Harberger diagram

Value added	Aggregate growth rate (%)	Maximum growth rate (%)	Percentage of industries with positive contribution (%)	Relative area under Harberge diagram
1970–1975	2.89	2.89	100.0	0.21
1975–1980	3.76	3.87	96.2	0.26
1980–1985	3.27	3.50	84.2	0.20
1985–1990	4.31	4.31	100.0	0.26
1990–1995	0.65	1.28	41.4	0.67
1995–2000	0.74	1.18	49.6	0.53
2000–2005	2.73	3.07	58.0	0.44
2005–2010	3.70	4.41	43.6	0.53
Labor productivity				
1970–1975	3.39	3.39	100.0	0.26
1975–1980	2.28	2.66	58.3	0.36
1980–1985	2.76	3.06	88.3	0.25
1985–1990	3.45	3.54	78.2	0.33
1990–1995	1.20	1.59	66.8	0.54
1995–2000	1.96	1.99	74.2	0.33
2000–2005	3.72	3.75	82.6	0.39
2005–2010	4.68	5.12	75.7	0.50
Employment				
1970–1975	0.60	1.47	54.3	0.69
1975–1980	0.99	1.54	67.2	0.50
1980–1985	0.81	1.30	60.5	0.52
1985–1990	1.06	1.38	89.2	0.38
1990–1995	0.80	1.40	64.7	0.53
1995–2000	−0.48	0.43	57.8	1.55
2000–2005	−0.41	0.68	37.4	1.38
2005–2010	−0.29	0.34	44.3	1.51

Note: By author on the basis of JIP 2014

represents the growth in value added. The middle part represents the cumulative contribution to labour productivity growth in relation to the cumulative share of sectoral man-hours in total man-hours.[5] The lower part of the figures represents the growth in employment

[5]With regard to labour productivity decomposition, the current method also follows Syrquin (1988). Aggregate labour productivity per man-hour y is defined as $y = \sum y_i s_{L,\ i}$, where y_i is sectoral labour productivity per man-hour and $s_{L,\ i}$ the sectoral share of man-hours. The increment in labour productivity is as follows:

$$\Delta y = \sum_i \Delta y_i s_{L,i} + \sum_i y_i \Delta s_{L,i}$$

The growth rate of labour productivity at the macroeconomic level is then obtained by dividing both sides by y,

which is

Figure 15.6 shows the sectoral value added, productivity growth and employment contribution in 1970–1975 and 1975–1980. Taking the summary statistics in Table 15.2 into consideration, some observations can be made with regard to the growth in value added. First, most sectors positively contribute to this growth; for example, 100% and 96.2% (in value added share terms) of all sectors positively contribute to the growth in value added in 1970–1975 and 1975–1980, respectively. Consequently, the maximum growth rate in this period is very close to the aggregate growth rate, which is the second observation. Their maximum growth rates reach 2.89% and 3.87%, whereas the aggregate annual growth rates in the economy as a whole are 2.89% and 3.76% in the first and second 5-year periods. The third observation concerns the value of the relative area under the Harberger diagram. The values for the first and second halves of the 1970s are 0.21 and 0.26, respectively, meaning that the growth process of value added is rather even. This point is clearer when we compare it with the two most recent decades.

Figure 15.6 and Table 15.2 also show the distribution of the sectoral contribution to labour productivity growth in this period. First, we see that most sectors positively contribute to the growth in labour productivity: 100% and 58.3% (in man-hours share terms) of all sectors positively contribute to such growth in 1970–1975 and 1975–1980, respectively. However, although the share with a positive contribution in the second half of this period temporally decreased, the negative contribution of this decrease is small. Again, while their maximum growth rates reach 3.39% and 2.66%, the aggregate annual growth rates in the economy as a whole are 3.39% and 2.28% in the first and second 5-year periods, respectively. Finally, the values of the relative area under the Harberger diagram are 0.26 and 0.36 for the first and second halves of the 1970s, respectively. This finding means that the growth process of value added is rather even, which is again clearer when we compare it with the two most recent decades.

Similarly, Figs. 15.7, 15.8, and 15.9 and Table 15.2 show the sectoral contribution to the growth in value added and labour productivity after 1980. A comparison of the diagrams and statistics for the two growth terms over the 40-year period shows the following characteristics in terms of both growth rate and sectoral distribution. The most striking change is the major transformation in the sectoral contribution pattern on the growth terms before and after 1990. The share of positively contributing sectors to value added growth is above 80% during the 1970s and 1980s, but it drastically decreases to 60% in the 1990s. Although both the aggregate and the maximum growth rates of value added recovers in the 2000s, the share of positively contributing sectors remains at 58.0% and 43.6%, lower

$$\frac{\Delta y}{y} = \sum_i s_{L,i}\left(\frac{\Delta y_i}{y} + \frac{\Delta s_{L,i}}{s_L}\cdot\frac{y_i}{y}\right)$$

where the first term in parentheses represents the 'within effect' and the second term represents the 'between effect' (Baily et al. 1992; Krüger 2008). Therefore, aggregate productivity growth can be decomposed into within-sector growth in labour productivity and the sectoral shift in share of man-hours.

than the share of 20 years before. Such a trend means that growth is established by more uneven contributions: while the values of the relative area under the Harberger diagram are below 0.3 during the 1970s and 1980s, they reach 0.67 in 1990–1995 and remain at a relatively high level thereafter. The sectoral distribution of labour productivity follows a similar evolution. The average share in the 1970s and 1980s for the positively contributing sectors to labour productivity growth is 81.2%. However, the share of sectors positively contributing to the growth in labour productivity decreases to 74.8% in the 1990s and 2000s on average. Consequently, the aggregate and maximum growth rates in the 1990s fall below 2.0%. Although both the aggregate and the maximum growth rates of labour productivity recover in the 2000s, labour productivity growth is also characterized by more uneven contributions: while the values of the relative area under the Harberger diagram are below 0.40 during the 1970s and 1980s, they increase to more than 0.50 during the 1990s and 2000s.

Further, the economic growth after 2000 is mostly led by limited sectors. The slope is relatively steep for high-growth sectors. For example, Fig. 15.9 for the 2000s indicates that the top sector has quite steep slopes, which is classified as the export-core sectors (M2) in the intermediate classification. Boyer et al. (2011) and Uemura and Tahara (2014) characterize the Japanese growth regime after 2000 as export-led. It is also possible to understand this character from these sunrise–sunset diagrams.

The rate of change in employment can be calculated by the difference between that of value added and of labour productivity. To be more precise, because labour productivity is defined in terms of man-hour inputs, whereas the employment measure is worker inputs in this study, the calculation can be applied approximately to the growth rate of employment. Some remarks can be made with regard to the change in employment. First, the aggregate and maximum growth rates of employment are generally smaller than those of value added and labour productivity. Second, the share of sectors positively contributing to the growth in employment is also small, meaning that the employment occasion is lost in many sectors. Third, employment growth is established by especially uneven contributions: the values of the relative area under the Harberger diagram are higher after the 1970s compared with those for value added and labour productivity growth, and they increase to more than unity in the late 1990s and 2000s.

Finally, the figure shows the sectors that generate or lose employment in each period (i.e. the services and industry sectors, respectively). Uemura and Tahara (2015) suggest the category of positive deindustrialization, which involves positive growth in value added and labour productivity in the industry sector, while generating employment in the services sector. It is also possible to understand this characteristic from the sunrise–sunset diagrams. For example, the growth in value added and labour productivity in the export-core sector during the 2000s is relatively high. This growth process also decreases employment in this sector but creates employment in the services sectors. Similarly, negative deindustrialization involves negative value added growth and stagnating labour productivity growth in the industry sector, while generating employment in the services sector. Figure 15.9 illustrates that other manufacturing and industry sectors show negative growth in value added and stagnating labour productivity during the 2000s, while employment in the services sector expands. As Uemura and Tahara (2015) indicate, this figure shows that deindustrialization occurs in simultaneous and multiple ways in the Japanese economy.

In sum, the sectoral distribution of the growth in value added and labour productivity is relatively uniform before 1990, generally led by most sectors. However, the distribution shifts leftward after 1990, leading to a sharp overshooting of growth in these terms. According to the Harberger diagram, the growth before 1990 follows a yeast-type process (i.e. overall growth with a relatively large share of positive contribution and a low value of the relative area under the Harberger diagram), whereas that after 1990 follows a mushroom-type process (i.e. uneven growth with a relatively small share of positive contribution and a high value of the relative area under the Harberger diagram). In the mushroom-type growth process, as after 1990, economic growth is intensively led by limited sectors, while others dragged growth downward. Therefore, even if the Japanese economy grows or stagnates on average, the process is uneven among different sectors. The growth process of employment also shows such an uneven characteristic. As in the 2000s, deindustrialization occurs in simultaneous and multiple ways in the Japanese economy.

15.4 Structural Change and Economic Growth

15.4.1 Data and Some Preliminary Processing

The previous sections show both accelerating and decelerating patterns of structural change in the past 40 years in the Japanese economy. Along with the development of structural change, the growth patterns of value added and labour productivity have also changed over time. The previous section showed that while the growth process presents an overall even growth pattern during the 1970s and 1980s, the process becomes uneven in the 1990s and thereafter.

The empirical questions in this section relate to (1) the type of the structural change in output or inputs that significantly influenced the growth in value added and labour productivity and (2) the magnitude of structural changes in growth terms. Moreover, the previous section suggested the possibility of a transformation of growth pattern in value added and labour productivity at the beginning of the 1990s. Taking this into consideration, the next question is (3) whether the impact of the structural change in inputs and output on these variables alters if we divide the whole study period into two subperiods: 1974–1991 and 1991–2011. This division in 1991 is based on the bursting of the bubble in addition to the change in the growth process mentioned above.

To examine these questions, we conduct a panel data analysis at the intermediate classification level and present the results in Table 15.1. All the variables are again constructed based on the JIP database of RIETI. By using real value added, number of workers, man-hours and real net capital stock from this database, we construct the following variables:

- g_{VA} is the growth rate of real value added. Real value added is taken from the growth accounting table (sheet name V), evaluated at 2000 prices. Real value added for the intermediate classification is based on the sum of real value added in the corresponding small classification. The growth rate of value added in each of the 8 sectors is defined as its annual growth rate.
- g_{LP} is the growth rate of labour productivity. Labour productivity is defined as the ratio of real value added to man-hours. The man-hours in the small classification is taken from the labour input table (sheet name 3–8). Man-hours at the intermediate classification is evaluated in the same manner as value added. The growth rate of labour productivity in each of the 8 sectors is defined as its annual growth rate.
- MLI_{VA} and NAV_{VA} are the *MLI* and *NAV* for real value added. By using real value added, we calculate these indices under the intermediate classification from eqs. (15.1) and (15.2).
- MLI_{LBR} and NAV_{LBR} are the *MLI* and *NAV* for the number of workers. We use the number of workers by sector in the labour input table (sheet name 3–7) to calculate these indices. These indices under the intermediate classification are calculated in the manner as stated above.
- MLI_{KPT} and NAV_{KPT} are the *MLI* and *NAV* for capital stock. The capital stock variable is taken from real net capital stock in the growth accounting table (sheet name KT), evaluated at 2000 prices. These indices under the intermediate classification are also calculated in the manner stated above.
- MLI_{KL} and NAV_{KL} are the *MLI* and *NAV* for the capital–labour ratio. The capital–labour ratio is defined as the ratio of real net capital to the number of workers. These indices under the intermediate classification are again calculated in the manner stated above.

Table 15.3 provides the descriptive statistics for the panel data analysis, classified according to the periods examined. A comparison of the 1974–1991 and 1991–2011 results shows that the values of the mean, median and standard deviation of all the variables except for the structural indices for labour are higher in 1974–1991 than in 1991–2011. The values in 1974–2011 range between these two periods. The maximum of all the variables except for MLI_{KPT} is higher in 1974–1991 than in 1991–2011, whereas the minimum of the growth rates in value added and labour productivity is higher in 1991–2011 than in 1974–1991. The minimum of the structural change indices between the two periods is almost equal.

After constructing these variables and indices for each of the 8 sectors, we conduct panel unit root tests to confirm the presence of stationarity. As the panel data include both cross-sectional and time-series items, we need to consider whether these items have common unit root as well as individual unit root processes. Therefore, we conduct four types of panel unit root tests: the Levin, Lin and Chu (LLC) and Breitung tests, which assume common unit roots in panel data, and the Im, Pesaran and Shin (IPS) and Fisher-type augmented Dickey–Fuller (ADF) tests,

Table 15.3 Descriptive statistics for panel data analysis

	g_{VA}	g_{LP}	MLI_{VA}	MLI_{LBR}	MLI_{KPT}	MLI_{KL}	NAV_{VA}	NAV_{LBR}	NAV_{KPT}	NAV_{KL}
1974–2011										
Mean	0.028	0.033	0.030	0.010	0.009	0.017	0.033	0.011	0.010	0.018
Median	0.019	0.019	0.020	0.008	0.008	0.014	0.024	0.010	0.009	0.016
Maximum	2.200	2.240	0.527	0.045	0.037	0.124	0.530	0.037	0.032	0.117
Minimum	−0.695	−0.709	0.000	0.000	0.001	0.001	0.000	0.000	0.001	0.001
Std. Dev.	0.150	0.148	0.045	0.007	0.006	0.015	0.047	0.007	0.006	0.014
1974–1991										
Mean	0.047	0.043	0.034	0.009	0.012	0.019	0.037	0.011	0.013	0.021
Median	0.030	0.022	0.021	0.008	0.011	0.016	0.026	0.009	0.013	0.018
Maximum	2.200	2.240	0.527	0.045	0.030	0.124	0.530	0.037	0.032	0.117
Minimum	−0.695	−0.709	0.000	0.000	0.001	0.001	0.000	0.000	0.001	0.001
Std. Dev.	0.202	0.203	0.062	0.006	0.006	0.018	0.063	0.007	0.006	0.017
1991–2011										
Mean	0.012	0.023	0.026	0.010	0.007	0.015	0.030	0.011	0.007	0.016
Median	0.011	0.017	0.020	0.008	0.006	0.012	0.023	0.010	0.007	0.014
Maximum	0.584	0.451	0.105	0.044	0.037	0.079	0.133	0.036	0.026	0.069
Minimum	−0.162	−0.187	0.000	0.000	0.001	0.002	0.000	0.000	0.001	0.001
Std. Dev.	0.072	0.064	0.021	0.007	0.004	0.011	0.024	0.006	0.004	0.010

Note: By author on the basis of JIP 2014. The computation is based on common samples in each period. The number of observation is 304, 144, and 168 in 1974–2011, 1974–1991 and 1991–2011, respectively

which assume individual unit roots in panel data. All these tests include an individual intercept and trend in the test equation. The lag length in these tests is selected by using the automatic lag length selection based on the Schwarz information criterion.

The results are reported in Table 15.4. With regard to all the variables from 1973 to 2011, most of the tests reject the null hypothesis of both common and individual unit root processes at the 1% significance level. However, MLI_{KPT} at levels between 1974 and 1991 may not be stationary, because neither the LLC and Breitung tests nor the IPS test can reject the null hypothesis of the unit root process at the 10% significance level. In addition, neither the LLC nor the Breitung tests can reject the null hypothesis that NAV_{KL} at levels between 1991 and 2011 has a common unit root process at the 10% significance level. Therefore, NAV_{KL} at levels during this period may not be stationary. Taking these facts into consideration, first, we estimate all the equations for the growth rates of value added and labour productivity and structural change at levels. Second, we estimate the equations with MLI_{KPT} for 1974–1991 and the equations with NAV_{KL} for 1991–2011 by ensuring stationarity for this variable.

Let i stand for the sectoral code and t for time. The equations in a panel data context to be estimated are either

$$g_{it} = F(SCI_{VA,it}, SCI_{LBR,it}, SCI_{KPT,it}) \tag{15.3}$$

or

$$g_{it} = F(SCI_{VA,it}, SCI_{KL,it}) \tag{15.4}$$

where g_{it} is a placeholder for the different variables; this stands for the growth rate of either real value added or labour productivity. $SCI_{VA,it}$, $SCI_{LBR,it}$, $SCI_{KPT,it}$ and $SCI_{KL,it}$ are the structural change indices for value added, labour productivity, capital stock and the capital–labour ratio, respectively. As *SCI*, we employ the *MLI* and *NAV* mentioned above. $SCI_{VA,it}$ represents the structural change in output, and we use $SCI_{LBR,it}$, $SCI_{KPT,it}$ and $SCI_{KL,it}$ to measure the impact of the structural change in inputs. Equations (15.3) and (15.4) are estimated alternatively. While eq. (15.3) presents the role of inputs as a separating type, eq. (15.4) presents the role of inputs as a ratio.

All the estimations are based on balanced panel data. We assume that an equation has an individual effect for both cross-section and period. By controlling for both sectoral and periodical heterogeneity, the estimation here attempts to reveal the economy-wide relationship between growth and structural change. The effects specification follows the Wu–Hausman test. To be more precise, the null hypothesis of the test that cross-section and period effects are random effects cannot be rejected at the 5% significance level for models except for models 4 and 6 for value added growth and model 6 for labour productivity growth. Therefore, first, we estimate all models except models 4 and 6 for value added growth and model 6 for labour productivity growth with random effects. With regard to models 4 and 6 for value added growth and model 6 for labour productivity growth, we estimate the equations with fixed effects. Moreover, for the models for which the null hypothesis cannot be rejected at

Table 15.4 Panel unit root tests

1973–2011	g_{VA}	g_{LP}	MLI_{VA}	MLI_{LBR}	MLI_{KPT}	MLI_{KL}	NAV_{VA}	NAV_{LBR}	NAV_{KPT}	NAV_{KL}
LLC	−9.563***	−8.150***	−11.11***	−5.840***	−2.804***	−6.438***	−10.07***	−4.687***	−1.833**	−5.774***
Breitung	−5.610***	−8.043***	−5.633***	−4.506***	−4.216***	−4.216***	−5.436***	−4.150***	−4.874***	−4.246***
IPS	−10.50***	−10.65***	−9.745***	−7.240***	−3.543***	−4.160***	−9.864***	−6.120***	−3.103***	−4.232***
ADF	125.6***	119.5***	120.4***	82.28***	39.08***	49.17***	113.2***	68.28***	35.48***	50.46***
1974–1991	g_{VA}	g_{LP}	MLI_{VA}	MLI_{LBR}	MLI_{KPT}	MLI_{KL}	NAV_{VA}	NAV_{LBR}	NAV_{KPT}	NAV_{KL}
LLC	−7.445***	−5.157***	−4.783***	−3.582***	0.577	−3.617***	−4.392***	−3.844***	−5.199***	−1.470*
Breitung	−2.053**	−1.994**	−4.491***	0.672	1.800	−3.274***	−4.298***	−0.020	0.590	−2.313**
IPS	−5.721***	−4.001***	−5.106***	−4.203***	−0.801	−3.296***	−4.674***	−4.303***	−3.702***	−2.969***
ADF	58.50***	44.63***	52.45***	49.09***	24.16*	35.83***	48.83***	49.42***	44.93***	33.00***
1991–2011	g_{VA}	g_{LP}	MLI_{VA}	MLI_{LBR}	MLI_{KPT}	MLI_{KL}	NAV_{VA}	NAV_{LBR}	NAV_{KPT}	NAV_{KL}
LLC	−9.173***	−4.591***	−3.764***	−1.740**	−2.385***	−2.386***	−2.330***	−1.647**	−2.484***	−1.116
Breitung	−5.480***	−3.419***	−1.793**	−1.414*	−1.441*	2.689	−2.540***	−1.301*	−1.337*	4.222
IPS	−8.034***	−6.160***	−5.081***	−4.706***	−1.831**	−2.654***	−5.204***	−4.715***	−3.398***	−2.587***
ADF	80.90***	64.42***	55.44***	53.37***	28.53**	39.68***	57.61***	53.34***	41.94***	38.31***

Note: LLC represents Levin, Lin and Chu test. LLC test and Breitung test both assume common unit root process in the panel unit root test. IPS represents Im, Pesaran and Shin test, and ADF represents Fisher type augmented Dickey-Fuller test. The IPS and ADF assumes individual unit root process in the panel unit root test. Significance at 1%, at 5% and at 10% level is denoted by ***, ** and *, respectively

5% but can be rejected at 10% by the Wu–Hausman test, we estimate the equations with random effects and fixed effects. These cases include model 12 and its stationary version of value added growth and model 4 for labour productivity growth.

15.4.2 Results

This section reports and discusses the finding of our empirical analysis. Table 15.5 shows the results for the growth in value added and structural change indices. Models 1 to 6 estimate these relationships using the *MLI*. To be more precise, models 1 and 2 show the results for the past 40 years, models 3 and 5 the results for 1974–1991, and models 4 and 6 the results for 1991–2011. The estimation is conducted alternatively between capital and labour separation and the capital–labour ratio, according to Eqs. (15.3) and (15.4). Table 15.5 also shows the results using the *NAV* in a similar manner. Models 7 and 8 show the results for the past 40 years, models 9 and 11 the results for 1974–1991, and models 10 and 12 the results for 1991–2011. This estimation is also conducted alternatively, according to Eqs. (15.3) and (15.4).

From Table 15.5, the structural change in value added for all the models has a positive impact on the growth in value added and is significant at the 1% level. This finding is true regardless of whether the models use the *MLI* and *NAV* or are conducted separately for labour and capital and the capital–labour ratio. On the contrary, models 1, 3, 7 and 9 show that the structural change in labour has a negative impact on the growth in value added. The coefficients are significant at the 5% or 10% level. This finding means that change in the sectoral composition of labour has a restraining effect on economic growth over the past 40 years and in 1974–1991. In other words, it is a cause of the slow economic growth. Finally, the coefficients of the structural change in capital and capital–labour ratio are not significant in all models. Generally, the structural change in output is more important than that in inputs for promoting growth in value added. The change in magnitude of the impact of the structural change in value added on the growth rate between 1974–1991 and 1991–2011 is also important. The models with the *MLI* indicate that this impact is more than 1 point in 1974–1991 but that this decreases to less than 1 point in 1991–2011. The models with *NAV* show a similar result, indicating that this impact is higher in 1974–1991 than in 1991–2011. In sum, the impact of the structural change in output is positive, but the magnitude of the impact weakens after 1991. By dividing the whole period into two subperiods, we clearly find a change in the impact of the structural change in output on the growth in value added.

Table 15.6 shows the results for the growth in labour productivity and the structural change indices. The table is constructed in the same manner as Table 15.5. The indices of structural change on labour have a negative sign, and the negative impacts are significant at the 10% level only in models 7 and 9. The indices of structural change on capital stock and the capital–labour ratio have both positive and negative signs, but they are not significant. For all the models, the structural change in value added has a positive impact on the growth in labour

Table 15.5 Impact of structural change on growth in value added

Model for g_{VA}	Model 1	Model 2	Model 3	Model 4	Model 5	Model 6
Period	1974–2011	1974–2011	1974–1991	1991–2011	1974–1991	1991–2011
C	−0.0003	−0.014	0.046	−0.018	−0.007	−0.006
	(−0.016)	(−0.900)	(0.969)	(−1.256)	(−0.266)	(−0.493)
MLI_{VA}	1.240***	1.115***	1.264***	0.854***	1.158***	0.841***
	(6.916)	(6.157)	(4.787)	(2.828)	(4.517)	(2.837)
MLI_{LBR}	−2.456**		−4.563*	−0.310		
	(−1.998)		(−1.768)	(−0.374)		
MLI_{KPT}	1.631		0.068	1.472		
	(1.153)		(0.024)	(1.142)		
MLI_{KL}		0.505			0.740	−0.319
		(0.891)			(0.821)	(−0.618)
Cross section	Random	Random	Random	Fixed	Random	Fixed
Period	Random	Random	Random	Fixed	Random	Fixed
No. of obs.	304	304	144	168	144	168
Adj. R_2	0.132	0.109	0.128	0.330	0.120	0.330
Model for g_{VA}	Model 7	Model 8	Model 9	Model 10	Model 11	Model 12
Period	1974–2011	1974–2011	1974–1991	1991–2011	1974–1991	1991–2011
C	0.012	−0.012	0.055	−0.020	0.0004	−0.007
	(0.539)	(−0.710)	(1.311)	(−1.081)	(0.016)	(−0.419)
NAV_{VA}	1.189***	1.031***	1.348***	0.777***	1.055***	0.760***
	(6.201)	(5.662)	(4.791)	(2.830)	(4.095)	(2.784)
NAV_{LBR}	−3.554**		−6.028**	−0.730		
	(−2.442)		(−2.219)	(−0.782)		
NAV_{KPT}	1.438		0.492	2.226		
	(1.016)		(0.188)	(1.622)		
NAV_{KL}		0.310			0.348	−0.255
		(0.513)			(0.374)	(−0.450)
Cross section	Random	Random	Random	Random	Random	Random
Period	Random	Random	Random	Random	Random	Random
No. of obs.	304	304	144	168	144	168
Adj. R_2	0.107	0.094	0.123	0.046	0.099	0.033

Note: Results used by E views 8. t-statistics is in parenthesis. ***, **, and * is statistically different from zero at 1%, 5%, and 10%, respectively. C is a constant term. Random and fixed respectively refer to the random effects and fixed effects in effects specification in panel option

productivity, and this is always significant at the 1% level. Similar to the results for the growth in value added, the structural change in output is generally more important than that in inputs to promote growth in labour productivity.

From Table 15.6, the magnitude of the impact of the structural change in value added on labour productivity growth also changes between 1974–1991 and 1991–2011. These models indicate that this impact is higher in 1974–1991 than in 1991–2011, showing that this impact is more than 1 point in 1974–1991, but that it decreases by about 0.1–0.5 points in 1991–2011. The impact of the structural change in output on labour productivity growth is thus positive for 40-year study period. However, the magnitude of this impact weakens after 1991.

Table 15.6 Impact of structural change on growth in labour productivity

Model for g_{LP}	Model 1	Model 2	Model 3	Model 4	Model 5	Model 6
Period	1974–2011	1974–2011	1974–1991	1991–2011	1974–1991	1991–2011
C	0.006	−0.013	0.029	0.007	−0.011	0.004
	(0.314)	(−0.951)	(0.606)	(0.426)	(−0.446)	(0.338)
MLI_{VA}	1.244***	1.185***	1.266***	0.751***	1.187***	0.855***
	(7.023)	(6.812)	(4.755)	(3.010)	(4.615)	(3.167)
MLI_{LBR}	−1.718		−3.242	−0.830		
	(−1.412)		(−1.245)	(−1.160)		
MLI_{KPT}	0.604		0.076	0.706		
	(0.435)		(0.026)	(0.642)		
MLI_{KL}		0.568			0.699	−0.178
		(1.051)			(0.773)	(−0.378)
Cross section	Random	Random	Random	Random	Random	Fixed
Period	Random	Random	Random	Random	Random	Fixed
No. of obs.	304	304	144	168	144	168
Adj. R_2	0.133	0.133	0.124	0.038	0.124	0.300
Model for g_{LP}	Model 7	Model 8	Model 9	Model 10	Model 11	Model 12
Period	1974–2011	1974–2011	1974–1991	1991–2011	1974–1991	1991–2011
C	0.012	−0.009	0.046	−0.011	−0.003	−0.006
	(0.608)	(−0.691)	(1.086)	(−0.775)	(−0.126)	(−0.530)
NAV_{VA}	1.246***	1.105***	1.333***	0.989***	1.084***	0.950***
	(6.791)	(6.402)	(4.696)	(4.302)	(4.193)	(4.170)
NAV_{LBR}	−2.423*		−5.106*	−0.498		
	(−1.833)		(−1.864)	(−0.614)		
NAV_{KPT}	0.533		0.149	1.430		
	(0.394)		(0.057)	(1.209)		
NAV_{KL}		0.295			0.268	0.107
		(0.527)			(0.286)	(0.218)
Cross section	Random	Random	Random	Random	Random	Random
Period	Random	Random	Random	Random	Random	Random
No. of obs.	304	304	144	168	144	168
Adj. R_2	0.127	0.122	0.119	0.096	0.103	0.091

Note: Results used by Eviews 8. t-statistics is in parenthesis. ***, ***, and * is statistically different from zero at 1%, 5%, and 10%, respectively. C is a constant term. Random and fixed respectively refer to the random effects and fixed effects in effects specification in panel option

Finally, we conducted additional tests for this analysis. As the LLC, Breitung and IPS unit root tests for MLI_{KPT} at levels between 1974 and 1991 cannot reject the null hypothesis of a unit root process, this variable may be not stationary. In addition, since the Breitung and IPS unit root tests for NAV_{KL} at levels between 1991 and 2011 cannot reject the null hypothesis of a common unit root process, the same possibility remains. As models 3 and 12 include nonstationary variables for both value added and labour productivity growth in such a case, they may involve the so-called spurious regression problem. Therefore, we re-estimate these models ensuring stationarity for all the variables. The four panel unit root tests indicate that MLI_{KPT} for 1974 and 1991 and NAV_{KL} for 1991–2011 are stationary in its first differenced form, although we do not report the results of these tests in a table.

Table 15.7 shows the results of this estimation. Models 3′ and 12″ for value added growth and models 3′ and 12′ for labour productivity growth are the estimations that ensure the stationarity of the included variables. Similar to the original models 3 and 12 in Tables 15.5 and 15.6, the structural change in output is positive. While the positive coefficient of the structural change in output is significant at the 1% level to explain the growth rates of both value added and labour productivity, the negative coefficient of MLI_{LBR} is significant at 10% only in model 3′ for the growth rate of value added. In addition, the structural changes in capital and in the capital–labour ratio are not significant in all the models. Moreover, as with the original models, the magnitude of the impact of the structural change in output on these growth rates is lower in 1991–2011 than in 1974–1991.

The Wu–Hausman test indicates that the null hypothesis cannot be rejected at 5% but can be at the 10% significance level for model 12 for value added growth and its stationary version and model 4 for labour productivity growth. Therefore, we also estimate these models with fixed effects (models 12′ and 12‴ for value added growth and model 4′ for labour productivity growth). In these models, the coefficients of MLI_{VA} and NAV_{VA} are always significant at the 1% level, but the magnitude of this impact on the growth rate in this period is still lower than in 1974–1991. On the contrary, the structural change in inputs is not significant for these growth terms. In these cases, the structural change in output is more important than that in inputs for promoting economic growth.

In sum, we find evidence that in general a structural change in output rather than in inputs causes growth in value added and labour productivity. However, the positive impact of a structural change in output has not always been strong. The magnitude of its impact on growth in both value added and labour productivity weakens after the 1990s. As for the structural change in inputs, only that in labour is significant. However, its impact is negative when it is significant, meaning that the structural change in labour does not induce economic growth; rather, it is a stagnating factor for it.

15.5 Conclusion

It is important to consider the industrial structure in economic growth analysis because sectoral heterogeneity matters in the Japanese economy, especially after the 1990s, as the current study showed. The current study investigated the structural change in inputs and output in the Japanese economy for the past 40 years as well as the sectoral and macroeconomic growth processes in value added and labour productivity. By way of panel data analysis, we found evidence of a relationship between structural change and economic growth.

The main findings of this study are as follows. First, the pace of the structural change in value added was relatively stable until the 1990s and then sped up in the late 1990s, while the pace of the structural change in capital stock decreased constantly after the 1970s. It is difficult to read a clear trend for labour productivity

Table 15.7 Impact of structural change on growth terms (additional test)

Dependent variable	g_{VA}				g_{LP}		
Model	Model 3′	Model 12′	Model 12″	Model 12‴	Model 3′	Model 4′	Model 12′
Period	1974–1991	1991–2011	1991–2011	1991–2011	1974–1991	1991–2011	1991–2011
C	0.046	−0.007	−0.013	−0.014	0.029	−0.002	−0.006
	(1.596)	(−0.525)	(−1.074)	(−1.425)	(0.996)	(−0.160)	(−0.652)
MLI_{VA}	1.258***				1.259***	0.883***	
	(4.826)				(4.792)	(3.212)	
MLI_{LBR}	−4.514*				−3.187	−0.468	
	(−1.758)				(−1.231)	(−0.621)	
MLI_{KPT}						1.021	
						(0.870)	
d(MLI_{KPT})	−2.324				−2.618		
	(−0.709)				(−0.792)		
MLI_{KL}							
NAV_{VA}		0.916***	0.843***	0.876***			1.011***
		(2.998)	(3.314)	(2.889)			(4.648)
NAV_{LBR}							
NAV_{KPT}							
NAV_{KL}		−0.554					
		(−0.931)					
d(NAV_{KL})			−0.061	−0.226			0.400
			(−0.121)	(−0.440)			(0.893)
Cross section	Random	Fixed	Random	Fixed	Random	Fixed	Random
Period	Random	Fixed	Random	Fixed	Random	Fixed	Random
No. of obs.	144	168	168	168	144	168	168
Adj. R_2	0.131	0.334	0.051	0.331	0.128	0.300	0.109

Note: Results used by Eviews 8. *t*-statistics is in parenthesis. ***, **, and * is statistically different from zero at 1%, 5%, and 10%, respectively. C is a constant term. Random and fixed respectively refer to the random effects and fixed effects in effects specification in panel option

and the capital–labour ratio because of its cyclical evolution. Second, the sectoral dispersion in the levels of value added and labour productivity clearly reduced until the 1990s, but it increased after the 2000s. Third, the sectoral contribution to the growth in value added and labour productivity showed a different pattern before and after 1990. There was overall growth in the 1970s and 1980s but an uneven growth process in the 1990s and 2000s. We also found that the growth process of employment was more uneven, showing that deindustrialization occurred in simultaneous and multiple ways in the Japanese economy. Finally, the structural change in output was more important than that in inputs for promoting economic growth. However, its positive impact on growth weakened after the 1990s. The structural change in labour inputs was significant among the inputs but did not play a positive role in stimulating economic growth. Rather, it was a cause of slowing economic growth in Japan.

How do we characterize the growth process in the Japanese economy in terms of its industrial foundation? The results of the current study suggest that there was a break in the growth process in the 1990s. As mentioned earlier, the growth process in value added and labour productivity was relatively uniform before the 1990s. Most sectors in the economy positively contributed to that growth during the 1970s and 1980s, while the relative area under the Harberger diagram was not large. In addition, this process accompanied a decrease in sectoral dispersion in the levels of value added and labour productivity. On the contrary, the growth in value added and labour productivity after the 1990s was uneven. The sectoral share that positively contributed to that growth then decreased after the 1990s, and the relative area under the Harberger diagram increased from that in the previous periods. Moreover, this process accompanied an increase in sectoral dispersion in the levels of value added and labour productivity, especially in the 2000s.

Taking these findings into consideration, the growth process before the 1990s can be characterized as a heterogeneity decreased one with overall growth process. The sectoral contribution to value added and labour productivity growth was relatively uniform, sectoral dispersion in these levels was decreasing and the degree of distortion of overall growth was small. To use Harberger (1998)'s metaphor, this corresponds to a yeast-type growth process, in which most sectors positively contribute to economic growth. By contrast, the growth process after the 1990s can be characterized as a heterogeneity increased process with uneven growth process. The sectoral contribution to value added and labour productivity growth was relatively uneven, sectoral dispersion in these levels was increasing and the degree of distortion of overall growth was large. Using Harberger (1998)'s metaphor, this corresponds to a mushroom-type growth process, which only limited sectors positively contribute to economic growth. As a result of this heterogeneous structure, the recent growth regime in the Japanese economy cannot be sufficiently established. The leading sector in the 2000s was the export-core sector, a rather externally dependent sector. In a heterogeneity increased process in which only limited contribute to growth, the stagnation of leading sectors may accelerate the depression of the overall economy. This fact means that the economy would simply lose its leading pillars, leaving only stagnating sectors remaining. On the contrary, a heterogeneity decreased process is not as vulnerable, because most sectors positively contribute to growth. Even if some leading sectors stagnate, the other positive contributors may compensate for such stagnation, and growth can still be sustained. The distorted relation between industrial structure and economic growth should thus be rebalanced for the Japanese economy to grow sustainably.

In addition to the change in industrial structure, the impact of structural change should also be enhanced. As the panel data analysis in the current study showed, even with structural change in inputs, this does not contribute to economic growth significantly. Rather, structural change in output can have a positive impact on economic growth. However, the problem is that such impacts have weakened since the 1990s compared with earlier periods. Structural change in output is related to innovation that improves sectors' product quality and attracts new consumer preferences. The importance of innovation that creates new effective demand in existing and new sectors has been emphasized by Pasinetti (1993) and Yoshikawa (2003). Demand-creating innovation can induce or shift new demand between sectors and cause structural change in value added. Our empirical results therefore suggest that such innovations are necessary to sustain economic growth in Japan.

References

Baily M, Hulten C, Campbell D (1992) Productivity dynamics in manufacturing plants. In: Brookings papers on economic activity: microeconomics. The Brookings Institution, Washington, DC, pp 187–267

Baumol W (1967) Macroeconomics of unbalanced growth: the anatomy of urban crisis. Am Econ Rev 57(3):415–426

Baumol W, Blackman S, Wolff E (1985) Unbalanced growth revisited: asymptotic stagnancy and new evidence. Am Econ Rev 75(4):806–817

Boyer R, Yamada T (eds) (2000) Japanese capitalism in crisis: a Régulationist interpretation. Routledge, London

Boyer R, Uemura H, Isogai A (eds) (2011) Diversity and transformations of Asian capitalisms: a de facto regional integration. Routledge, London

Dietrich A (2012) Does growth cause structural change, or is it the other way around? A dynamic panel data analysis for seven OECD countries. Empir Econ 43(3):915–944

Fukao K (2012) Lost two decades and Japanese economy. Nihonkeiazi Shinbunsha, Tokyo (in Japanese)

Fukao K, Miyagawa T (eds) (2008) Productivity and Japanese economic growth: empirical analysis at industrial and firm level using JIP database. Tokyo University Press, Tokyo (in Japanese)

Harberger A (1998) A vision of the growth process. Am Econ Rev 88(1):1–32

Hartwig J (2011) Testing the Baumol-Nordhaus model with EU KLEMS data. Rev Income Wealth 57(3):471–489

Hartwig J (2012) Testing the growth effects of structural change. Struct Chang Econ Dyn 23 (1):11–24

Hein E (2014) Distribution and growth after Keynes. Edward Elgar, Cheltenham

Inklaar R, Timmer M (2007) Of yeast and mushrooms: patterns of industry-level productivity growth. Ger Econ Rev 8(2):174–187

Ito K, Lechevalier S (2009) The evolution of the productivity dispersion of firms: a reevaluation of its determinants in the case of Japan. Rev World Econ 145(3):405–429

Krüger J (2008) The sources of aggregate productivity growth: US manufacturing industries, 1958-1996. Bull Econ Res 60(4):405–427
Lavoie M, Stockhammer E (eds) (2013) Wage-led growth: an equitable strategy for economic recovery. Palgrave Macmillan, New York
Lilien D (1982) Sectoral shifts and cyclical unemployment. J Polit Econ 90(4):777–793
Maroto-Sánchez A, Cuadrado-Roura JR (2009) Is growth of services an obstacle to productivity growth? A comparative analysis. Struct Chang Econ Dyn 20(4):254–265
Morikawa M (2014) Productivity analysis in service industries: an empirical analysis using microdata. Nihon hyorosha, Tokyo (in Japanese)
Nordhaus W (2008) Baumol's diseases: a macroeconomics perspective. B.E J Macroecon 8 (1):1–37
Pasinetti L (1993) Structural economic dynamics: a theory of the economic consequences of human learning. Cambridge University Press, Cambridge
Peneder M (2003) Industrial structure and aggregate growth. Struct Chang Econ Dyn 14 (4):427–448
Prasad E (1997) Sectoral shifts and structural change in the Japanese economy: evidence and interpretation. Jpn World Econ 9(3):293–313
Rowthorn RE, Wells JR (1987) De-industrialization and foreign trade. Cambridge University Press, Cambridge
Syrquin, M. 1988. Patterns of structural change. In Chenery, H. and T. Srinivasan eds. 1988. Handbook of development economics, 1 Amsterdam: North Holland
Uemura H, Tahara S (2014) The transformation of growth regime and deindustrialization in Japan. Revue de la Régulation 15(1)
Uemura H, Tahara S (2015) The theory of De-industrialization and realities in advanced countries: structural change and diversity. Polit Econ Q 51(4):18–33
Yoshikawa H (2003) Role of demand in macroeconomics. Japn Econ Rev 54(1):1–27

Chapter 16
Multinationalization of Japanese Firms and Dysfunction of Companyist *Régulation*

Yasuro Hirano and Toshio Yamada

16.1 Introduction

Over the last 20–30 years, Japanese main firms have actively developed their overseas business sectors—especially in Asian countries—and have thus become multinational firms. As is well known, this has played an important role in establishing an international division of labor in the East Asian zone. However, what impacts has this multinationalization had on the Japanese economy and its mode of *régulation*[1]? In short, what relationship can we find between the multinationalization of Japanese firms and structural transformations within the Japanese economy? This study approaches this question while bearing in mind our concept of "companyist *régulation*." Let us first explain the concept of "companyism" or "companyist *régulation*."

"Companyism" is a concept that characterizes a mode of *régulation* that supported Japan's postwar economic growth. This mode of *régulation* is propped up by two main pillars: labor–management compromise on employment security and company–bank compromise on management security (security of firm's continuation). In short, companyism rests on both employment compromise and finance compromise.

[1]This spelling relates to French régulation theory that analyzes the dynamic processes that channel capital accumulation and the long-term evolution and present diversity of capitalism.

Y. Hirano (✉)
Fukuoka Prefectural University, Tagawa, Japan
e-mail: yytalkyastock@kub.biglobe.ne.jp

T. Yamada
Nagoya University, Nagoya, Japan
e-mail: tyamada@rainbow.plala.or.jp

R. Boyer et al. (eds.), *Evolving Diversity and Interdependence of Capitalisms*, Evolutionary Economics and Social Complexity Science 11,
https://doi.org/10.1007/978-4-431-55001-3_16

The employment compromise, the first pillar of companyism, contrasts markedly from the US case. In the case of postwar American Fordism, a wage compromise formulated as <the acceptance of Taylorism (limited job) by workers vs. the provision of productivity-indexed wages by management> led a growth regime typically seen as "mass production–mass consumption." In contrast, what led Japan's postwar growth was an employment compromise defined as <the acceptance of unlimited duties by workers vs. the provision of employment security by management>. In return for the workers' devotion and loyalty to their company (in the form of accepting unlimited duties), Japanese workers—especially regular male employees employed by large companies—mostly wanted employment security, rather than wage hikes; more precisely, they wanted employment continuation in the company in which they were currently employed. After a trial-and-error period, this demand by workers was accepted by the management, and so-called lifetime employment and seniority-based wages became the "rule of the game" in Japan, or social norms between management and workers.

To bring about a steadier realization of a wage–labor nexus that centers on employment security, it is essential to secure firm continuation (i.e., management security). In postwar Japan, where an indirect finance system was prevailing, a firm would want in the time of managerial hardship to obtain for this purpose various relief measures (e.g., additional finance, favorable interest rates, and dispatched executives from banks). In exchange for the possibility of receiving relief measures, the company would fix a particular bank as its preferential business partner and shareholder. This finance compromise, the second pillar of companyism, leads to corporate governance by a main bank, and in this way, firm continuation is secured. This is the so-called main-bank system. The main-bank system thus represents a core compromise between the firm and the bank for the purpose of the management security of the firm. This company–bank compromise, together with cross-shareholding and convoy systems, has helped ensure the stability and continuation of Japanese companies.

Employment security in the wage–labor nexus and management security in the finance and interfirm relations—two elements that make one another an institutional complementarity—have formed the kernel of companyist *régulation*. It resulted in high levels of productivity among core workers who engaged in meritocratic competition under employment security, and each company aimed to maximize sales or market share. Companyist *régulation* thus supported an investment- and export-led growth regime in postwar Japan, which in turn led to a high economic growth in Japan and its status in the world as an "economic power."

However, especially after the 1990s, under certain pressures—such as financial globalization and problems with nonperforming loans in post-bubble Japan—the main-bank system fell into dysfunction, the rate of cross-shareholding among firms decreased, and so the conventional measure of enterprise continuation broke down. Additionally, employment security largely contracted, due to a drastic increase in the number and proportion of nonregular workers. As a result, since the late 1990s, both employment security and management security fell into a crisis and thus led to a crisis of the companyist *régulation*.

Such is the concept of companyist *régulation* and its contemporary transformations in Japan, which we have hitherto discussed (Yamada 2000; Yamada and Hirano 2012). Given the aforementioned background, the current study focuses on the relationship between Asian deployments of Japanese firms (especially manufacturers) and their effects on companyist *régulation*. What does the multinationalization of Japanese firms mean for the firms themselves, and what does it bring to the Japanese economy as a whole? First, we outline the international division of labor in East Asia and the role and position of Japanese firms therein (Sect. 16.2). Then, we clarify how the multinationalization of Japanese firms has taken place, by analyzing corporate finance and behavior (Sect. 16.3). In addition, by provisionally naming "post-companyism" the increasingly changed and paralyzed state of affairs of companyism through the multinationalization of Japanese firms, we discuss problematic post-companyist circumstances that are now affecting the Japanese socioeconomic configuration (Sect. 16.4). Finally, this paper closes with some conclusions and prospects (Sect. 16.5).

16.2 Japan and the International Division of Labor in East Asia

In this section, we confirm some basic facts concerning the international division of labor in East Asia; this division of labor has formed in tandem with the multinationalization of Japanese firms.

16.2.1 Development and Characteristics of the East Asian Production Network

The trade structure from the 1990s until the early 2010s is roughly envisioned as a triangle with the following poles: "United States and Europe," "China and the ASEAN," and "Japan and the NIEs," as shown in Fig. 16.1. This triangular structure has gradually formed since the 1990s, around the machinery industry (transportation equipment, general machinery, electrical machinery, etc.), in which East Asia[2] has comparative advantages. The position and role of each pole are as follows:

[2]Here, we use the word "East Asia" to denote Asian newly industrializing economies (NIEs) (i.e., South Korea, Taiwan, Hong Kong, and Singapore), Association of Southeast Asian Nations (ASEAN) members (the five original members of Thailand, Indonesia, the Philippines, Malaysia, and Singapore and the five new members of Brunei, Vietnam, Laos, Cambodia, and Myanmar), China, and Japan. Singapore is both an NIE and an ASEAN member. In the ASEAN statistics that follows, some countries may be omitted.

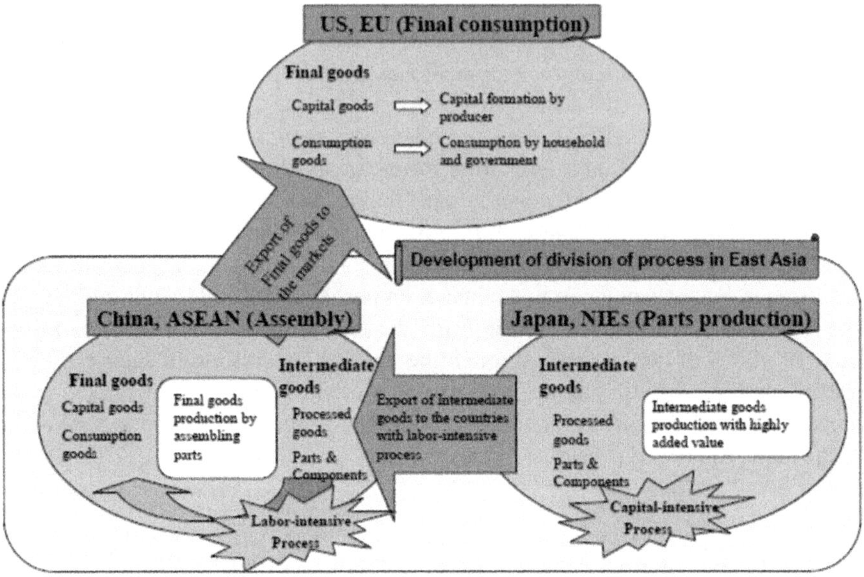

Fig. 16.1 Model of triangular trade structure. (Source: METI 2005)

1. Japan and the NIEs produce intermediate goods (parts, components, and processed goods) in a capital-intensive process and export them to China and ASEAN.
2. China and ASEAN assemble the imported intermediate goods in a labor-intensive manner into final goods (consumption goods and capital goods); they then export them to the United States and Europe. From the 2010s on, however, China has strengthened its industrial abilities and can no longer be characterized as either a simple importer of intermediate goods or a simple exporter of final goods.
3. The United States and Europe consume the imported final goods.
4. In short, a trade structure has become established worldwide, containing the following roles: parts production (Japan and the NIEs), assembly production (China and ASEAN), and final consumption (the United States and Europe).

The presence of East Asia in the world economy has been rapidly enhanced, by virtue of this triangular trade structure. In 1985, the nominal gross domestic production (GDP) of East Asia was about one-half that of the United States; however, in 2010, the GDP of East Asia surpassed that of the United States and is now poised to surpass even that of the European Union (EU) (Hirakawa 2014: Figure 1-1).

While export goods from East Asia to other regions have mainly involved final goods, intra-regional trade within East Asia has considerably consisted of intermediate goods. This constitutes the most salient trade-related feature of the East Asian zone, and it is abundantly clear when we compare intra-regional trade goods with those of other international economic zones (e.g., those comprising the EU and the North American Free Trade Agreement [NAFTA]), as seen in Fig. 16.2.

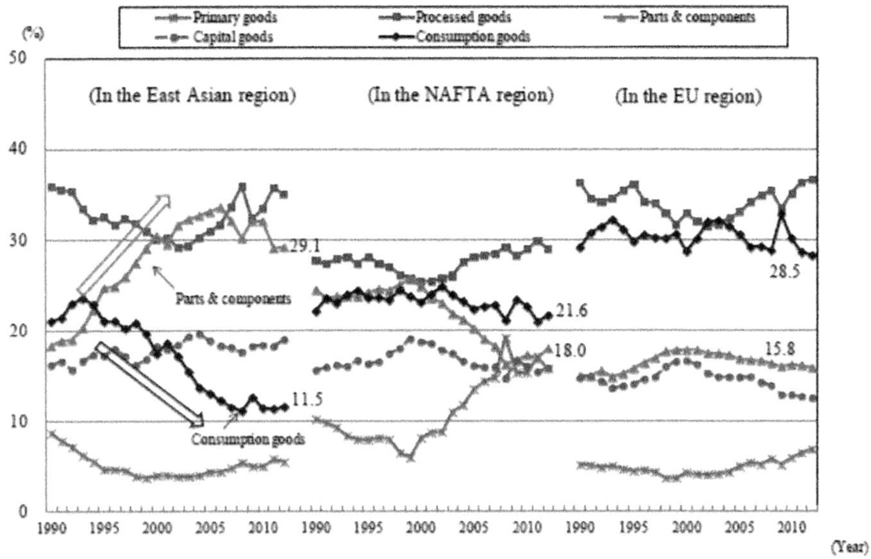

Fig. 16.2 Trends in the value of intra-regional trade (composition of goods). (Source: METI 2014a)

In Fig. 16.2, although it is common in all three economic regions (i.e., East Asia, NAFTA, and EU) that the proportion of trade in processed products is the highest, East Asia shows two particular characteristics. First, East Asia shows a high proportion of parts and components trade that has recently undergone rapid growth (i.e., over 30%). Second, East Asia's proportion of consumption goods trade is not only low but has also tended to decline drastically (i.e., recently about 10%). In contrast, in the case of both NAFTA and EU members, the proportion of parts and components trade has been low and dropping (i.e., recently about 15%), and the relatively high proportion of consumption goods trade has been stable (i.e., over 20% in NAFTA and 30% in EU).

The high proportion of intra-regional trade in intermediate goods suggests the high weight of intraindustrial trade, rather than of interindustrial trade. The presence of both exports and imports within the same industry indicates the existence of a division of process, where intra-regional countries take charge of different processes in order to produce final goods. In short, there has been established in East Asia an international network of process division that centers on the machinery industry. By tightening this production network or supply chain, de facto economic integration has developed in East Asia, leading to the formation of a large cross-border production base.

16.2.2 Business Activities of Japanese Firms in East Asia

Foreign direct investment (FDI) by Japanese firms, especially manufacturers, has played an important role in the development of this international division of production processes. Although companies from the United States, Europe, South Korea, and Taiwan have also established overseas affiliates in East Asia, the presence of Japan-affiliated companies is much more considerable.

In the late 1980s—that is, in a period of rapid yen appreciation, following the Plaza Accord of 1985—Japanese firms embarked for the first time on large-scale FDI. Consequently, Japan's FDI position amounted to JPY 30 trillion in 2000 and JPY 70 trillion in 2011 (METI 2013: Figure III-3-3-10). Although at first FDI was principally destined for North America and mainly from nonmanufacturing industries, manufacturers started to actively establish overseas affiliates mostly in East Asia. Since the 1990s and until 2012, the exchange rate has shown a general trend of yen appreciation, albeit with volatile ups and downs in the yen rate. In this context, Japan has increased its weight of investment in Asia, in both the manufacturing industry and overall.

Especially in the manufacturing industry, the number of Japanese overseas affiliates in Asia has tripled, from fewer than 2000 (about one-half of all Japanese FDI) in 1990 to more than 6000 (more than 70%) in 2010 (METI 2012: Figure 2-2-2-1). The number and percentage of Japanese overseas affiliates in Asia have almost constantly increased, with little correlation with exchange-rate fluctuations. This means that, in terms of Japanese manufacturers' incentives for overseas development, market factors that project potentially greater demand within newly emerging Asian areas have become more important than cost factors, including wage hikes or measures of yen appreciation.

As a result, as of 1997, the total overseas production by Japanese manufacturers already exceeded that of export; thereafter, the gap widened. In 2012, the overseas production rate of manufacturers amounted for 20%, based on all domestic companies, and 35%, based on those developing their business overseas (METI 2014a: Figure II-3-2-32). Especially, the overseas production rate of the transportation machinery sector was 40%. Following the Lehman Brothers shock of 2008, Japanese firms' investments in the plants and equipment has continuously increased abroad, but domestic investment has stagnated (Fig. 16.3). This stagnation in domestic investment is a very serious problem, and among the main capitalist countries, it can be seen only in Japan.

What has been the state of Japanese manufacturing affiliates' business activities in Asia? In terms of sales, although there was a considerable decline on account of the Lehman Brothers shock, figures have steadily grown over the last 20 years, from JPY 20 trillion in 2000 to JPY 50 trillion in 2012. The ratio of local sales has also grown, from 50% in 2000 to 60% in 2011 (Fig. 16.4). The increase in local sales ratio confirms that Japanese firms have, in recent years, placed more importance on market incentives.

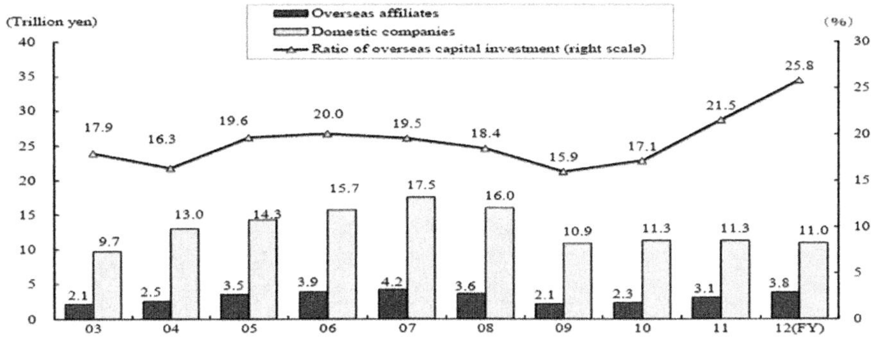

Fig. 16.3 Trends in capital investment in overseas affiliates and domestic companies (manufacturing industries). (Source: METI 2014b)

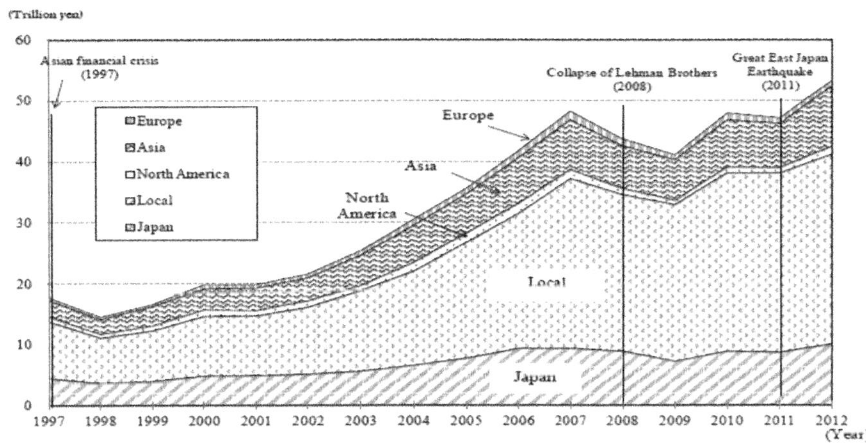

Fig. 16.4 Sales trends of overseas affiliates of Japanese manufacturers in Asia. (Source: METI 2014a)

In line with the increase in production and sales, procurement has also increased, from JPY 15 trillion in 2002 to JPY 35 trillion in 2010. The ratio of local procurement has also increased, from 40% in 2000 to 60% in 2010. On the other hand, total procurement from Japan (i.e., exports from Japan to overseas affiliates) has stagnated since the Lehman Brothers shock, although it did increase favorably prior to that time (METI 2014a: Figure II-3-2-17). The share of procurement from Japan by

Table 16.1 Japan's share of major export items among world exports

Rank	Items	Export amount (Billion dolar)	Share (%)	Share in the world exports (%)		
				1995	2000	2011
1	General machinery	171	21.9	15.2	11.5	8.5
2	Motor vehicles	148	18.9	18	16.1	11.9
3	Electric machinery	129	16.5	17.2	12.8	6.5
4	Precision machinery	46	5.8	19.4	17.7	9.1
5	Iron and steel	42	5.4	11.8	10.7	9.4
6	Plastics	30	3.9	6.3	6	6
7	Organic Chemicals	25	3.1	10.1	8	6.2
8	Precious stone, precious metal	17	2.2	1.4	1.7	3.2
9	Mineral fuels	16	2.1	1	0.3	0.8
10	Rubber	15	1.9	11.8	11.1	6.8
–	Total export amount	784	100	9.5	7.8	4.9

Source: METI (2013)

overseas affiliates of Japanese manufacturers also decreased, from 40% in 1990–1996 to less than 30% in 2012.[3]

16.2.3 *Japan's Reduced Export Competitiveness*

As evidenced in the reduced share of procurement in Japan by Japanese overseas affiliates, the Japanese economy has possibly experienced a decline in its export-related competitiveness. Special attention must be paid to the fact that, despite positive expectations of export increase and economic growth since the recent phase of yen depreciation (starting from 2012), Japan is still seeing export stagnation and an expansion in its trade deficits. As Japan's main export items comprise general machinery, electrical machinery, and motor vehicles (which together account for about 60% of all exports), it will be worthwhile to confirm changes in export competitiveness while focusing on these three categories of export items.

For example, when we measure Japan's export competitiveness in terms of Japan's share of major export items among all world exports, we see that Japan's total export share has reduced by about 50%, from 9.5% in 1995 to 4.9% in 2011 (Table 16.1). Concerning the three aforementioned main export items, we can see a decline in the share of each: from 15.2% to 8.5% in general machinery, from 18.0%

[3]However, the percentage of procurement from the Japanese overseas affiliates within each country accounts for one-third in all local procurement. So, if one were to combine this figure with that of procurement from Japan (i.e., imports from Japan), the procurement ratio from Japan would be, in a broad sense, about 50% (See METI 2014b: Figure II-3-2-20).

to 11.9% in motor vehicles, and, in particular, from 17.2% to 6.5% in electrical machinery.

16.3 Multinationalization of Japanese Firms: Their Mode of Behavior and Its Result

16.3.1 New Platform: Improvement in Firms' Finances at Their Workers' Expense

The low yen exchange rate—caused by the monetary easing in 2013—led to an increase in the values seen in the Japanese stock market in anticipation of an economic recovery. However, while the change in monetary policy did bolster the economic recovery, the platform for the change began much earlier, when Japanese firms began improving their financial health. In particular, two important changes took place as follows:

(1) A decrease in liabilities and an increase in net assets: Since the late 1990s, Japanese firms have been reducing their liabilities and increasing their net assets, although sales stagnated (Iwase and Sato 2014: Figure 2).
(2) Profits generated by reducing labor costs while sales stagnated: An increase in net assets occurred because firms were able to increase their profits each year (ibid.: Figure 6).

These changes were brought about by reducing labor costs. The labor's relative share had a tendency to decline especially from the late 1990s to 2008; this suggests that improvements in firm finances came at the workers' expense. Figure 16.5 shows this tendency: increases in the profit rate came about by reducing labor costs.

On the whole, workers' lives became more difficult and domestic demand stagnated: the latter of these conditions restricted domestic production and investment.

However an increase in profit share and a decrease in liabilities prepared Japan for economic growth, as the growth regime of the Japanese economy from the late 1990s to the 2000s was complex and comprised of profit-led and debt-burdened regime (Nishi 2012, 2014).

16.3.2 Increases in Internal Reserves and Foreign Direct Investment

Firms can use profits in various ways, including stock dividends, capital investment, wage increases in the next period, or internal reserves. However, given the long

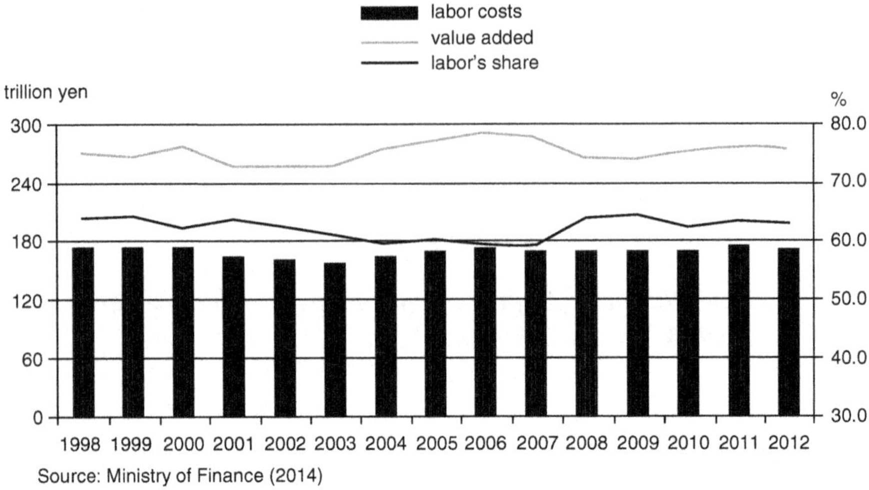

Fig. 16.5 Labor's share, value added and labor costs. (Source: Ministry of Finance 2014)

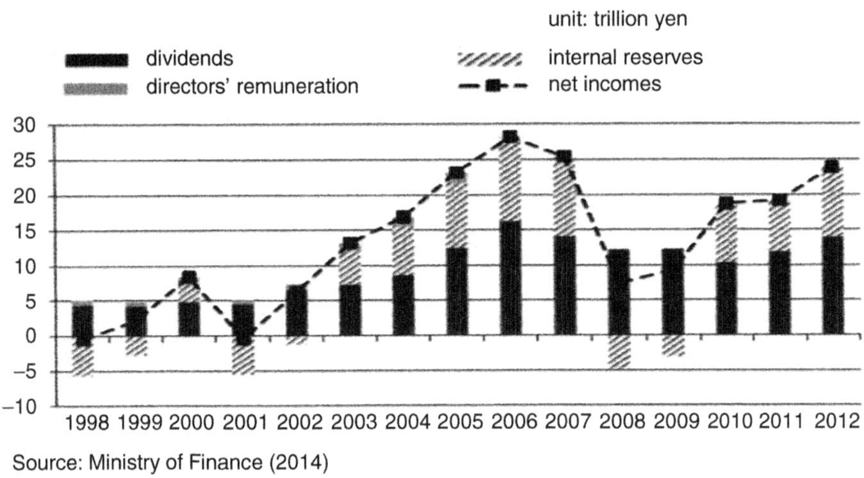

Fig. 16.6 Net income, dividends, internal reserves, and directors' remuneration. (Source: Ministry of Finance 2014)

period of wage stagnation and the decline in the labor's relative share, it is clear that these profits have not been invested in wage increases.

In Japan dividends have not been fluctuating in proportion to profits: after having increased since 2002, they have rather remained constant and have not in any way fluctuated as internal reserves have (Fig. 16.6). This suggests that managers may be paying close attention to valuations of their firms on the stock market.

Finally, changes to capital investment fell to an extent less than depreciation (Fig. 16.7).

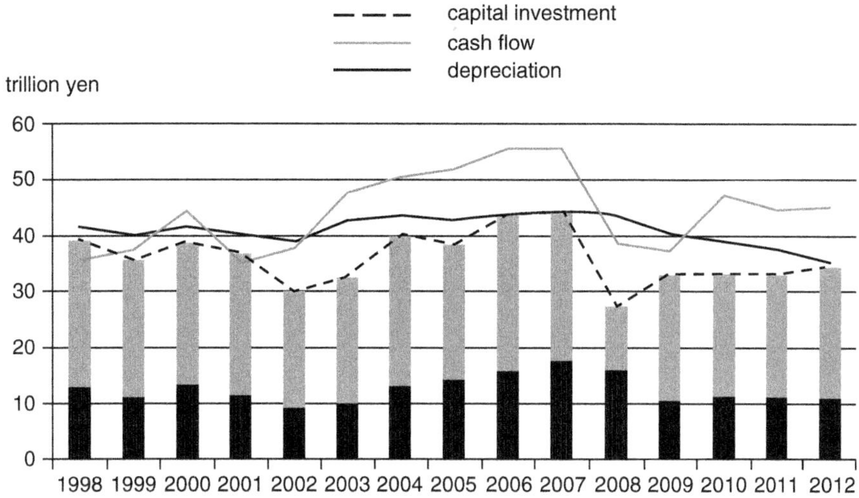

Fig. 16.7 Changes in capital investment, depreciation and cash flow
Source: Ministry of Finance (2014)
Note: Cash flow = internal reserves + depreciation

Thus, a considerable sum of firms' profits was stored as internal reserves.

To recognize forms of these internal reserves, we need to examine variations in firms' assets and liabilities.

According to Table 16.2, there was a JPY 133.6 trillion decrease in liabilities between 1998 and 2008, when the subprime crisis occurred. On the other hand, there was a JPY 232.5 trillion increase in net assets. The retained earnings within net assets almost certainly refer to internal reserves. They amount to about JPY 150 trillion: enormous amount. The assets that grew the most were investments in securities (e.g. stocks and bonds).

After the subprime crisis—namely, between 2009 and 2015—we see a tendency similar to that seen before the crisis. In that period, the retained earnings amounted to JPY 108.9 trillion (Table 16.3). The assets that grew the most were, again, investments in securities (e.g. stocks and bonds).

These investments included the purchase of stocks in related companies—as a part of the traditional relationship among Japanese firms—as well as direct investments in overseas affiliates (Fig. 16.8).

Japanese FDI has grown although the yearly amount has fluctuated. Growth is clearly seen in the overall balance of FDI by Japanese firms. A regional breakdown of Japanese FDI (Table 16.4) indicates that most of it targets North America, with Asia trailing second.

Table 16.2 Variations in assets, liabilities and net assets, and their degree of contribution between 1998 and 2008

unit: trillion yen, %

Assets		Variation	Degree of contribution	Liabilities and net assets		Variation	Degree of contribution
Current assets	Cash and deposit	9.7	0.7	Current liabilities	Notes payable	−32.9	−2.5
	Bills receivable	-20.2	-1.5		Accounts payable	−13.5	−1.0
	Accounts receivable	3.0	0.2		Short-term debt	−56.7	−4.3
	Securities	-8.2	-0.6		Allowances	−0.1	0.0
	Inventory	-19.1	-1.5		Others	10.9	0.8
	Others	18.4	1.4	Fixed liabilities	Bonds	−5.3	−0.4
Fixed assets	Land	15.0	1.1		Long-term debts	−51.9	−4.0
	Construction account	3.1	0.2		Allowances	6.8	0.5
	Tangible fixed assets	-59.0	-4.5		Others	9.3	0.7
	Intangible fixed assets	0.8	0.1	Net assets	Capital stock	20.4	1.6
	Investment in securities	117.7	9.0		Capital surplus	63.4	4.0
	Others	28.7	2.2		Retained earnings	155.9	12.0
Deferred assets		0.1	0.0	Others		−8.9	−0.7
Total assets		90.0	6.9	Liabilities and net assets		90.0	6.9

Source: Ministry of Finance (2017)

Table 16.3 Variations in assets, liabilities and net assets, and their degree of contribution between 2009 and 2015

						Unit trillion yen, %	
Assets		Variation	Degree of contribution	Liabilities and net assets		Variation	Degree of contribution
Current assets	Cash and deposit	42.5	3.0	Current liabilities	Notes payable	−0.1	0.0
	Bills receivable	1.2	0.1		Accounts payable	8.1	0.6
	Accounts receivable	18.2	1.3		Short-term debt	−24.1	−1.7
	Securities	−1.7	−0.1		Allowances	4.1	0.3
	Inventory	−4.1	−0.3		Others	25.9	1.8
	Others	26.7	1.9	Fixed liabilities	Bonds	−2.4	−0.2
Fixed assets	Land	−4.2	−0.3		Long-term debts	13.0	0.9
	Construction account	0.5	0.0		Allowances	−1.3	−0.1
	Tangible fixed assets	2.3	0.2		Others	−9.0	−0.6
				Net assets	Capital stock	−1.3	−0.1
	Intangible fixed assets	−3.4	−0.2		Capital surplus	25.7	1.8
	Investment in securities	70.0	4.7		Retained earnings	108.9	7.6
	Others	10.5	0.7				
Deferred assets		−0.5	0.0	Others		10.6	0.7
Total assets		155.0	10.8	Liabilities and net assets		155.0	10.8

Source: Ministry of Finance (2017)

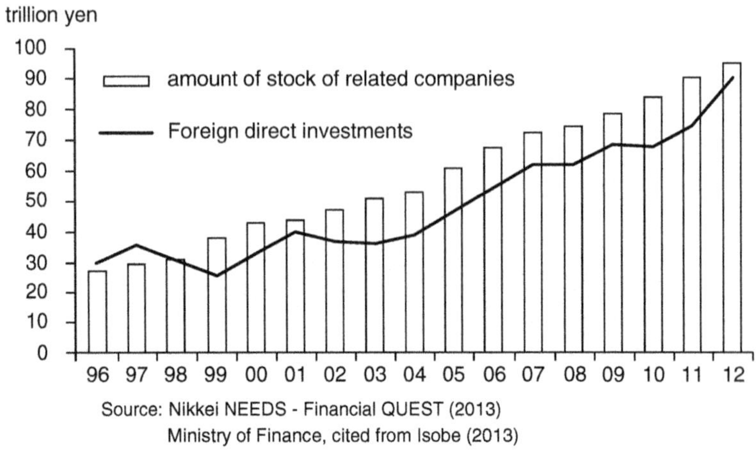

Fig. 16.8 Foreign direct investment and related and stock of related companies
Source: Nikkei NEEDS – Financial QUEST (2013), Ministry of Finance, cited from Isobe (2013)

However, in terms of the number of overseas affiliates, Asia accounts for more than 90% of the increase over from 2000 to 2015 (Table 16.5).

These figures show that Japanese firms have augmented their investment in stocks and bonds by directing much of their internal reserves toward FDI especially in Asia.

This multinationalization of Japanese firms allows them to allocate their resources worldwide in an efficient manner. In fact, both the local sales ratio and local procurement ratio in overseas affiliates have been on the rise over the last 10 years as shown above: this has led to an increase in their competitiveness.

16.3.3 Three Problems for the Japanese Economy

Nevertheless there are three problems that relate to the aforementioned changes.

The first is that a recovery in firm performance does not necessarily mean a recovery in the Japanese economy. While multinationals have improved their finances, Japan's trade balance had recently fallen down into a deficit situation and has turned back into a surplus but very slightly (Fig. 16.9). This indicates Japan's weakening of exports, which can in turn indicate a decoupling of Japanese firms from the Japanese economy.

The second problem is that changes in corporate governance can result in a change in the distribution of profits. The labor's relative share was decreasing till 2007, and after that time, it remained rather constant (Fig. 16.5). This means that the firms' recovery of competitiveness came at their workers' expense. It also means that workers' position vis-à-vis managers became weaker than it was before. It appears that managers' position in the stock market became more fragile than before on account of a loss of management security otherwise inherent in companyist

Table 16.4 Overall balance of foreign direct investment from Japan

(unit: millions of U.S. dollars)

		2000	2001	2002	2003	2004	2005	2006	2007	2008	2009	2010	2011	2012	2013
Asia		49,311	53,230	58,421	64,267	76,416	88,187	107,653	132,986	159,570	175,645	212,708	257,755	288,923	310,283
	China	8699	10,043	12,408	15,296	20,208	24,655	30,316	37,797	49,002	55,045	66,478	83,379	93,215	98,132
	NIES4	23,153	23,733	24,923	24,934	29,506	32,708	39,042	46,560	52,237	58,607	68,438	78,577	93,373	98,026
	Hong Kong	6543	5506	5471	5686	6275	6715	7776	9129	11,716	13,048	15,542	17,127	18,383	19,820
	Taiwan	3565	3646	3779	4348	5455	5932	6328	7742	8830	9349	10,351	11,778	13,333	11,808
	South Korea	4192	4391	5245	5074	6602	8251	10,669	12,103	12,180	12,603	15,043	17,968	25,594	29,850
	Singapore	8853	10,190	10,428	9826	11,175	11,810	14,270	17,586	19,511	23,608	27,502	31,703	36,063	36,549
	ASEAN4	15,568	17,546	18,782	21,507	23,806	27,657	34,313	42,055	44,600	48,441	58,394	72,431	77,159	88,324
	Thailand	4767	6113	6287	7650	9909	11,677	14,839	19,776	20,529	22,748	27,789	35,178	35,040	44,581
	Indonesia	4765	5029	5589	6738	6520	7681	7457	8315	8528	9491	11,946	15,816	18,427	19,787
	Malaysia	4003	4316	3936	3959	4080	4803	7763	8184	7743	8017	9972	11,211	13,312	13,204
	the Philippines	2033	2088	2971	3161	3296	3496	4253	5780	7800	8186	8687	10,225	10,379	10,752
North America		138,455	144,876	140,982	143,385	146,967	156,189	163,230	183,776	234,957	240,246	262,339	286,176	301,042	348,222
	United States	132,222	140,651	136,190	139,195	142,302	150,152	156,411	174,199	226,611	230,948	251,805	275,504	286,529	331,439
South America		21,020	20,700	18,167	21,975	26,588	33,064	39,291	54,749	90,794	99,056	106,978	122,223	119,162	109,325
Oceania		10,151	8119	11,852	13,632	15,091	12,961	13,794	19,617	21,624	36,175	43,865	54,114	66,492	59,022
Europe		56,789	71,044	73,136	88,715	103,437	94,277	120,972	148,748	165,435	179,052	193,499	231,001	252,884	273,039

(continued)

Table 16.4 (continued)

		2000	2001	2002	2003	2004	2005	2006	2007	2008	2009	2010	2011	2012	2013 (unit: millions of U.S. dollars)
EU		54,795	68,721	70,531	85,791	101,417	92,140	118,852	145,280	161,783	174,881	182,194	215,484	237,800	259,153
	West Europe	56,447	70,607	72,404	87,573	101,886	92,453	118,657	145,884	161,649	174,939	188,861	225,482	246,152	267,006
	East Europe	341	437	732	1142	1551	1824	2315	2864	3786	4112	4638	5519	6732	6033
Middle East		793	885	893	900	1022	1685	2038	3066	4164	4453	4928	5298	5065	5298
Africa		758	625	1232	2052	1628	1332	2701	3895	7325	5734	6145	8081	6892	12,077
Worldwide		278,445	300,868	305,585	335,911	371,755	388,197	449,680	546,839	683,872	740,364	830,464	957,703	1,040,463	1,117,267

Source: JETRO.(2014)

Table 16.5 Variations in numbers of corporations by region between 2000 and 2015

					unit::number,%
			Variation (number)	Variation (%)	Contribution rate (%)
Worldwide			10,242	68.0	100.0
North America			−48	−1.0	−0.5
	United States		−25	−1.0	−0.2
South America			355	37.0	3.5
Asia			9587	132.0	93.6
	China		5370	212.0	52.4
		Hong Kong	412.0	50.0	4.0
	ASEAN4		2015.0	81.0	19.7
	NIEs3		913.0	48.0	8.9
Middle East			62.0	81.0	0.6
Europe			260.0	10.0	2.5
	EU		256.0	11.0	2.5
Oceania			−5.0	−1.0	0.0
Africa			31.0	23.0	0.3

Notes
ASEAN 4: Indonesia, Thailand, the Philippines and Malaysia
NIEs 3: South Korea, Taiwan and Singapore
Source: Calculated from METI (2003, 2016)

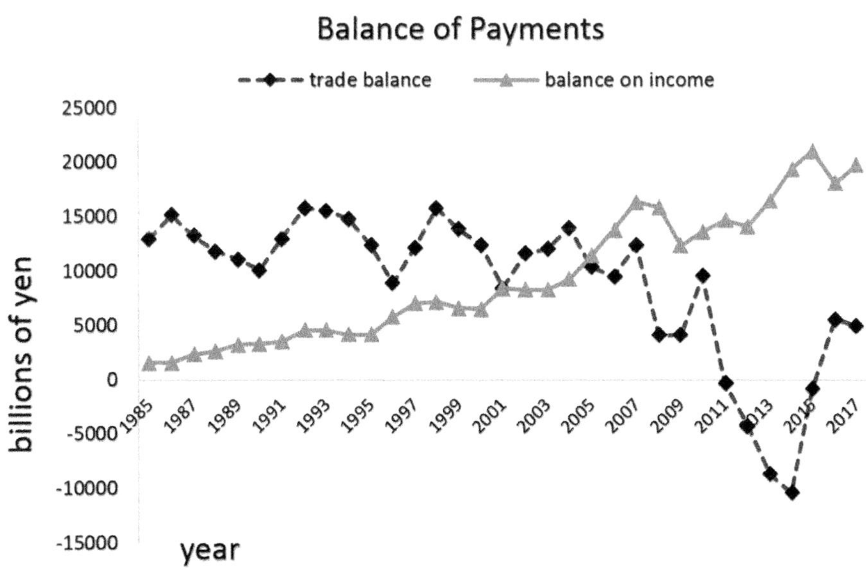

Fig. 16.9 Balance of Payments. Source: Bank of Japan (2017)

régulation. Overall, the relationships among shareholders (or investors), managers, and workers are different from how they were before.

The third is that not every Japanese firm invests abroad. There are multinational firms and national firms. And while the former can allocate their resources worldwide, the latter generally cannot. Additionally it is easier for the former to respond immediately to growing needs vis-à-vis newly emerging markets than the latter, because of the proximity to the market. These circumstances give rise to a new FDI differential between these firm types.

It seems that these three problems, taken together, have brought about a collapse in companyist *regulation*—something by which the Japanese socioeconomy has been controlled even in the presence of some confrontations.

16.4 Problems in Post-companyism

In what follows, we clarify the three aforementioned problems—namely, the decoupling of Japanese firms from the Japanese economy; changes to the relationships among shareholders, managers, and workers; and the differential between multinationals and nationals.

16.4.1 Changes to the Relationships Among Shareholders, Managers, and Workers

Let's begin with the second problem, namely, changes to the relationships among shareholders (or investors), managers, and workers.

Managers are valued by investors in the stock market given the loss of management security caused by the collapse of the main-bank system. It was at this point that changes to the relationships among shareholders, managers, and workers started.

Japanese firms burdened with debt that had been created by the burst of the economic bubble in the early 1990s have been, since the late 1990s, reducing their liabilities and increasing their internal reserves. In this course, managers derived profits by reducing wages on one hand, while on the other hand, they made dividends larger than before to cope with stock market pressures (Fig. 16.6). We find here a change in the relationships among investors (or shareholders), managers, and workers under companyist *régulation*, where managers usually negotiated with workers given management security. Therefore, the relationship between workers and managers was primary and that between shareholders and managers was secondary. Furthermore cross-shareholdings stabilized the relationship between shareholders and managers. In other words, the wage–labor nexus occurred prior to the financial nexus. However, under post-companyism—in which some new elements emerged that led to the dysfunction of companyist *régulation*—with a lack of management security otherwise provided by the main-bank system, managers cannot be allowed to remain in the absence of a positive vote of confidence at the shareholder general meeting. Therefore they cannot neglect valuations in the stock market in advance. As a result, while managers can reduce labor's relative share, they cannot avoid increasing dividends. In fact firms have maintained their dividends since 2001 even in the absence of internal reserves (Fig. 16.6). We find here a transformation of the institutional hierarchy: from superiority of the wage–labor nexus to that of the financial nexus.

A similar transformation can be seen in Germany.

As Streeck (2013) has pointed out, in the postwar era, large German firms formed a dense network of multiple ties to avoid falling victim to the vagaries of the market. Organized by a small number of leading financial institutions such as Deutsche Bank and Allianz, it was fortified by cross-shareholdings and interlocking directorates. It offered firms collective protection against a variety of political and economic risks, including pressure from potential takeovers by foreign firms. Within the network, firms pursued low but steady return on investment.

Their collective system of mutual protection was also useful in relation to the unions. Having to live with them, large firms preferred collective bargaining at the national and sectoral levels, as it shielded them from their workforces claiming a share in excess profits.

The disintegration of the German company network began in the mid-1980s when large German banks, led by Deutsche Bank, gradually abandoned their traditional role as providers of cheap credit and *Hausbanken* (principal bank) of German firms. The main motive behind this seems the higher profit made by Anglo-American banks in international banking. It induced and maybe also constrained German banks to move on to a new business strategy. Gradually they sold their shares with low return they held in them and withdrew from their boards.

This in turn led managers in industrial firms to change their mode of behavior. With the banks no longer willing to protect them from takeover, German managers began to worry about undervalued stock, taking account of shareholder value. They began to divest themselves of their cross-shareholdings to put their capital to more profitable use. As a result, the network between large firms has shrunken. Seeking more profits, German large industrial firms moved from stable national market to unstable global market.

This change of managers' behavior leads to modification of wage–labor nexus. The way industrial relations are affected by the new, more market-driven corporate governance regime is formed, in path-dependent way, by past experiences. The dominant strategy of German firms was to build alliances with the elected representatives of workers and negotiate modifications to industrial agreements allowing for participation in collective bargaining. Workplace alliances disorganize old-fashioned negotiation not by replacing cooperative relations between managers and workers with adversarial ones but by reorganizing and realigning at the firm level. In fact work councils have understood in recent years that defending the firm that employs them is in their interest as well as in that of management, leading them to support "shareholder value" strategy. But the coverage of alliances is declining as workers are confined within core workers. It is called as dualization (Thelen 2014).

On the contrary, the superiority of the financial nexus seen in the United States is not the same as that seen in Japan. While there is a negative correlation between financial income (dividends, capital gain, etc.) and capital accumulation among large US firms in the manufacturing sector, there is a positive correlation between them in the Japanese manufacturing sector (Orhangazi 2008; Nishi 2014). Therefore it appears that forms of institutional hierarchy vary by country.

In brief, under post-companyism, the continuation of a firm is brought about by managers' efforts and without the aid of the banks. In the transition from companyism to post-companyism, on one hand, shareholders became stronger than before in their relationship with managers; managers became stronger than before in their relation with workers on the other hand. These changes are indicated by the increase in internal reserves, the maintenance of dividends, and the reduction in labor's relative share.

Nevertheless traditional employment compromise has not necessarily disappeared from the manager–worker relationship in Japan. Employment security has endured among regular workers. Nonetheless the nature of the compromise therein is likely subject to change, as suggested by changes in managerial objectives. According to data captured through questionnaire surveys executed by Research Institute of Economy, Trade, and Industry in 2011 and Small-Medium Enterprise Agency in 1998, while the old managerial objective was to increase sales, the new one is to increase profits (Morikawa 2012: Table 16.2).

Increased sales can be connected to employment, in that workers are involved in pursuing the objective. On the other hand, increased profits cannot be connected to employment as management can dismiss employees in order to bolster profits. Nevertheless, as the continuation of firms would give regular workers in long-term employment some advantage in terms of employment security, it is possible that some compromise exists, related to an increase in profits between regular workers and managers. They could compromise all the more as it is nonregular workers who are first exposed to unemployment risk. Regular workers take employment security in exchange for bringing about productivity gain through long-term skill formation. Besides, increased profits provide a basis for compromise between investors and managers, as more dividends could be paid out to investors and more internal reserves to managers. Therefore compromise among investors, managers, and workers in post-companyism would focus on increasing profits. It is here that we see the germination of a new compromise that has not yet fully taken hold.

16.4.2 Decoupling of Japanese Firms from the Japanese Economy

Next, we will clarify the decoupling of Japanese firms from the Japanese economy.

As mentioned, since the late 1990s, Japanese firms have been reducing their liabilities and increasing their net assets; nonetheless, Japan has since 2011 been accumulating a trade deficit. Japan's exports have not increased in quantity, in spite of a low yen exchange rate since 2012. This has mainly resulted from the industrial hollowing out in Japan's export goods—a reduction caused by the transfer of production to foreign countries (Furukane 2014). The factories which have already been transferred in foreign countries would not easily come back, even if the exchange rate were to fall. A platform by which they could increase production has not been prepared, as capital investment in Japan has not generally increased. On the other hand, overseas affiliates can send higher remittances to their headquarters than before, given the devaluation of the yen. As a result, the income balance has increased, and the income account surplus has grown. It may seem that there is no decoupling of Japanese firms from the Japanese economy, but it is indeed occurring. A chronic trade deficit translates into a loss of employment opportunities. Besides, investment income—one of the components of the income balance—belongs to companies or investors, and if they do not combine it with real investment or consumption in the domestic market, it will not drive economic growth forward.

When we compare variations in GDP, consumption, fixed capital, FDI, and income balance, it is clear that GDP, consumption, and investment have stagnated, while FDI and income balance have, on average, grown to high levels (Table 16.6). This suggests that there is little correlation among them. In addition to stagnation in the export industry, neither FDI nor an increase in foreign-source income has brought about greater consumption or investment, until now. This means that Japan's export-led growth regime is nearing its end and that there is a decoupling of the activities of multinational firms from the Japanese economy. The influence of the decoupling on companyist *régulation* is too much.

Companyist *régulation* centered on the compromise between management and regular workers at the firm level, but it was simultaneously complemented by a hierarchical labor market and interfirm relationships on a national scale (Isogai et al. 2000). There was a ripple effect of growth from firm to firm, so the overall economy grew. However, the spillover effect has almost stopped, as multinationals rarely transact with domestic firms; therefore, its dysfunction is much more enhanced by the decoupling of multinational firms from the Japanese economy, in addition to the considerable increase in the proportion of nonregular workers. Even if workers and managers were to reach some compromise at the firm level under such post-companyist circumstances, it would be very difficult to bring about relevant *régulation* in the Japanese economy. In this sense, the influence of the multinationalization of firms on companyist *régulation* is overly large.

Nevertheless, if the wages of workers in multinational firms increase and they are expended within the domestic market, Japan might see economic growth. Is this probable, in reality? To answer this question, it is essential that we analyze the third aforementioned problem: a new differential between multinationals and nationals.

Table 16.6 Variations in GDP, consumption, capital formation, FDI and income balance

	Economic growth rate	Variation in consumption	Variation in gross fixed capital formation	Variation in foreign direct investment	Variation in income balance
1997	2.2	2.1	0.1	5.1	21.1
1998	−2.1	−1.0	−8.3	−0.4	1.5
1999	−1.5	0.3	−2.7	−8.1	−8
2000	1.0	−0.1	−0.1	11.8	−1
2001	−0.9	0.5	−4.4	8.1	29.1
2002	−1.3	−0.2	−7	1.6	−1.6
2003	−0.1	−0.6	−1.7	9.9	0.2
2004	1.0	0.4	−0.4	10.7	12
2005	0.0	0.8	0.7	4.4	22.7
2006	0.6	0.7	2.1	15.8	20.8
2007	1.2	0.3	0.8	21.6	18.8
2008	−2.3	−0.7	−2.9	25.1	−3
2009	−6.0	−3.2	−12.9	8.3	−22.2
2010	2.4	0.9	−1.6	12.2	10.5
2011	−2.3	−0.8	0.7	15.3	7.4
2012	0.8	1.2	3	8.6	−3.3
2013	1.1	1.8	4.3	7.4	16.6
Mean value	−0.4	0.1	−1.8	9.3	7.2

Source: Cabinet Office (2014), JETRO (2014) and Bank of Japan (2014)

16.4.3 Differential Between Multinationals and Nationals

Do wages increase in multinational firms? In Japan, under the condition of a low yen exchange rate, they probably increase on account of the products of multinationals entering the international market. In 2012, the overseas production rate among manufacturers was 35% based on all the companies developing their business overseas; especially, the rate of the transportation machinery sector was 40%, as mentioned. Under such circumstances, their products can compete in the international market, where the price is decided in the key currency—namely, the US dollar. Therefore, if the yen were devalued, product prices could be reduced; additionally, the wages of Japanese workers could decrease in US dollars, in the case of yen devaluation. If multinational firms do not reduce their prices to the same extent to which the yen is devalued, they could accept a wage increase for Japanese workers. An indication of change vis-à-vis wage increases began during collective bargaining in the Japanese style "Spring Offensive" of 2015.[4] Almost all Japanese carmakers (e.g., Toyota and Nissan) have accepted considerable wage increases; other multinational companies (e.g., Hitachi, NTT, and Fuji Film) have followed the lead of these automobile manufacturers (The Nikkei 2015).

However, not every firm can accept wage increases. For firms whose products are sold solely on the domestic market, it would be very difficult to accept wage increases, as the competition is severe. As a result, the wage differential would expand between multinationals and nationals, and if the amount and scale of wage increases were limited, the expansion of consumption demand would also be limited. Under such circumstances, it would be very difficult for the macroeconomy to be socioeconomically coordinated at the company level.

We have analyzed three problems—namely, changes to the relationships among shareholders, managers, and workers; the decoupling of Japanese firms from the Japanese economy; and the differential between multinationals and nationals. These problems can likely paralyze companyist *régulation*. In some multinational firms, it seems that a new compromise is being formed among shareholders, managers, and workers, but it is difficult to predict whether or not such a compromise will spread nationwide.

16.5 Conclusion

We examined above how conventional companyist *régulation* fell into dysfunction through the multinationalization of Japanese firms, as represented by large exporting manufacturers. We also examined the problems that the Japanese economy currently faces. We refer to the actual situation in Japan as "post-companyism," where companyism is paralyzed and in flux. However, the post-companyism means not a new mode of *régulation* that supplants companyism but only a certain transition within contemporary Japan.

The post-companyist transformation process is marked not by rapid changes or tipping point but by a series of gradual institutional changes (Thelen 2004). In other words, in today's Japan, on one hand, some elements of companyism—such as employment security for regular workers in large enterprises, in spite of its reduced range of application—have survived by virtue of the effect of path dependence; on the other, we can see the expansion of new post-companyist elements: the breakdown of the main-bank system, an increase in shareholders' pressure, the augmentation of nonregular workers, and increased FDI gains, inter alia (Table 16.7).

[4]Collective bargaining is generally held at the firm level in Japan. "Spring Offensive" was introduced as platform for which labor unions would surpass individual negotiations. It is a united campaign by labor unions, led by Industrial Unions. It is launched every year between March and April, the main aim of negotiations being higher wages.

Table 16.7 Companyism and post-companyism in Japan

	Companyism	Post-companyism
(1) Period	1960s–1980s	Definitively since 2000s
(2) Superior institution	Wage–labor nexus	Financial and international relations
(3) Labor-management compromise	Employment security vs. acceptance of unlimited duties	Higher profitability vs. employment security for limited regular workers on the basis of firm's continuation
(4) Management-finance compromise	Management-main-bank compromise on firm's continuation	Management-shareholder compromise on more dividends vs. management autonomy
(5) Principal business objectives	Sales amount (market share, growth of the firm)	Profitability (return on assets, value of the firm)
(6) Response to foreign market and its consequences	Export to the United States	FDI to East Asia
	Surplus in balance on goods	Deficit in balance on goods Surplus in balance on income
(7) Effects on growth regime	Supporting the investment- and export-led growth regime	Not leading to a new growth regime

Source: Authors

More precisely, as shown in Table 16.7 (1), post-companyism has appeared definitively since the beginning of the twenty-first century, and (2) financial and international relations have taken a dominant institutional domain position and supplanted the wage–labor nexus, which has fallen into a subordinate position in the institutional hierarchy (3). This has resulted in an increase in the number and proportion of nonregular and precarious workers, given the reduced coverage of employees guaranteed by employment security and the imposition on workers of expenses such as declines in wages and labor's share (4). Behind these transformations in the wage–labor nexus, there has existed a collapse in the management security system by way of the main banks and cross-shareholdings, and this has led instead to increased stock market pressures on the firms. To shareholder pressure, management has responded by providing greater dividends and increased their own internal reserves precisely in order to maintain relative autonomy of management from shareholders. In short, firms have realized increases in both dividends and internal reserves, at the expense of workers.

As for principal business objectives (5), Japanese firms have come to attach importance to profitability (e.g., return on assets) rather than to sales amounts (e.g., market share) to ensure their continuation by virtue of their own efforts and responsibilities. Japanese firms have come to pursue firm value rather than firm growth. A narrow compromise around profitability may be virtually established among shareholders, managers, and only a few workers, while a great percentage of them are excluded (6). Given the contraction of Japan's domestic market due to long-term deflation and an increase in emerging markets in East Asia, Japan's principal firms—which hold ample internal reserves–have embarked on full-scale FDI in Asia. Consequently, while the Japanese economy is experiencing a large surplus in terms of balance on income, following a gradual decline in trade surplus, it now has concerns about serious trade deficits (7). We can no longer call the Japanese economy an "export-led growth regime." The new paradigm of the Japanese economy which would supplant the conventional regime remains to be seen.

Under the post-companyist state of affairs, the Japanese economy is now suffering from stagnation, in terms of both exports and wages–or from a slump in both external and domestic demand. How can these difficulties be overcome, so as to "heal" the Japanese economy under a new growth regime and mode of *régulation*? We make here a few suggestions.

First, Japan should promote new domestic demand. Japan, whose society is rapidly aging, needs to substantially expand its medical and social services. Concurrently, expansion in education and training services is essential to enhancing skills among youth and forming a wide-ranging middle class and thus also to halting growth in the number and proportion of nonregular workers and widening inequality. Mechanisms in Japan such as active labor market policy are needed to link education and training to employment. In any case, a new system that copes with these new and urgent domestic demands is needed, in addition to traditional consumption demands.

Second, Japan needs to open itself to meeting a more diversified set of external demands. Although Japan's main export items have comprised products from the machinery industry, Japan's competitive decline in this industry will be inevitable, given how emerging industrial countries are swiftly "catching up." It is true that the export of high value-added products–such as industrial machinery for multipurpose processing–remains at the core of Japan's exports and economy; this alone cannot bring about recovery in the Japanese economy. New export industries must be explored, such as the cultural industry (e.g., animated film, *manga*, Japanese cuisine), infrastructure industry (e.g., high-speed railroad, waterworks, gas services), and a tourist industry that accepts more foreigners.

Third, Japan needs to focus more on a domestic-oriented return of any surplus in balance on income. Overseas affiliates of Japanese multinationals register large surpluses, and if they were to be reinvested in countries other than Japan, then they will not contribute to Japan's economic revitalization. What will be important in Japan will be to forward the surplus in balance on income toward both research and development investment and plant and equipment investments. To bring foreign-source incomes back to Japan, the enactment of policies that remove obstacles within taxation system (e.g., those for more flexible application of "the extraterritorial income exclusion system") could be a positive move (METI 2008; Shimizu and Sato 2014). However, such a taxation system would not automatically translate foreign-source income into domestic expenditures; given that a certain proportion of the earners of foreign-source income comprises affluent individuals, the domestic return of surplus must be generated by imposing a high tax rate on their incomes.

Of course, companyist *régulation* cannot cope with the above tasks–and companyist *régulation* itself is already in dysfunction in Japan anyway. The most serious problem in contemporary Japanese economy consists in the absence of a new mode of *régulation* that will supplant companyism. The first step to a new Japan will be achieving the "political will" on the part of central and local governments to bring about the aforementioned policies, as well as "associative activities" on the part of companies, groups, organizations, and regions to cooperate with such government.

In particular, it is on the ground of the associative activities that we can carefully cope with new domestic demands such as medical services, social services, and education, on the one hand, and with a new creation of original ideas to promote foreign demands such as cultural and tourist industries on the other. We understand the medical services, social services, education, culture, and tourism as an "anthropogenetic" activity and industry. In addition, the ultimate sources to create new innovations in high-tech industries lie in free, equal, and anthropogenetic exchanges among citizens. Japan after the dysfunction of companyism must head toward anthropogenetic society by means of bringing up the "associative activities" in civil society as well as achieving the "political will" on the part of central and local governments. A new mode of *régulation* must respond to these tasks.

We have analyzed the relations between behaviors of Japanese firms and Japanese economy so far. These behaviors of Japanese multinationals form the production network in East Asia at the same time. Therefore, we give lastly an overview of future relations between Japan and East Asia.

Japan has strengthened economic relation with East Asia through trade and foreign investment. And the more economic relation is strengthened, the more interdependence between them may also be strengthened on the social, political, and cultural side. If it be so, what is Japan's role in contributing to the cooperative development? Three matters should be pointed out.

First, there would have to be trust between economic actors resulted from continuous transactions in long term. Japanese firms used to repeat continuous transactions in their own country. They establish trust especially in the case of investments in long term (infrastructures, etc.) rather than in that of spot trading. If Japanese multinational firms established the same relationship in foreign countries where they invest, they would also build reciprocity relations based on trust with local firms.

Second, Japan would be able to contribute by providing technologies to developing countries. It would be better to provide technologies organized in formulation of systems: water purification equipment in waterworks system, railway vehicle manufacturing in railway traffic control system, frozen storage technology in the perishable market, etc.

Third, Japan would be able to contribute to establishing democracy in East Asia. Democracy is an institution suitable for guaranteeing people freedom, independence, and peace. Japan began to democratize her political system first in Asia. As a result, Japanese society is anyhow more civilized than other Asian countries. But in her history, industrialization preceded democracy as well as in almost other Asian countries at present. Therefore, Japan's historical experience could come in helpful for their democratization. It might be necessary for responding to the people's needs for democratization to use not only social and economic power brought by nongovernmental organizations and enterprises but also political and diplomatic power, considering of geopolitical changes in this area: decreasing American influence and increasing China's one.

References

Bank of Japan (2017) Balance of payment (in Japanese). https://www.boj.or.jp/statistics/br/bop_06/index.htm/#p0201
Cabinet Office (2014.) National accounts (in Japanese) http://www.esri.cao.go.jp/en/sna/data/kakuhou/files/2013/27annual_report_e.html
Furukane Y (2014) On the recent export trend. Kyosai Sogo Kenkyu 69:152–165 (in Japanese) http://www.jkri.or.jp/PDF/2014/sogo_69_furukane.pdf
Hirakawa H (2014) World economy in a structural transformation and the institutionalization of East Asian Region. In: Uemura H et al (eds) Asian capitalisms in transition. Fujiwara Shoten Publishing, Tokyo (in Japanese)
Isobe S (2013) Transformation of financial structure in Japanese firms between 1980 and 2012. Finance, December, pp.63–71 (in Japanese)
Isogai A, Ebizuka A, Uemura H (2000) The hierarchical market-firm nexus as Japanese mode of *Régulation*. In Boyer and Yamada (eds) (2000)
Iwase T, Sato M (2014) Internal reserves and distribution of profits in Japanese firms with analysis on financial statement statistics of corporations. Finance, .July, pp 86–95 (in Japanese)
JETRO (Japan External Trade Organization) (2014.) Japan's FDI (in Japanese). https://www.jetro.go.jp/world/japan/stats/fdi/
METI (2005, 2008, 2012, 2013, 2014a) White paper on international economy and trade, each year. http://www.meti.go.jp/english/report/index_whitepaper.html#trade
METI (2016.) The 43rd basic survey of overseas business activities (in Japanese). http://www.meti.go.jp/statistics/tyo/kaigaizi/result-2.html http://www.meti.go.jp/english/statistics/tyo/kaigaizi/pdf/h2c406je.pdf
METI (Ministry of Economy, Trade and Industry, Japan) (2003) The 31st basic survey of overseas business activities (in Japanese). http://www.meti.go.jp/statistics/tyo/kaigaizi/result-2.html
Ministry of Finance (2017) Financial statements statistics of corporations. http://www.mof.go.jp/english/pri/reference/ssc/historical.htm
Morikawa M (2012.) Structural change in Japanese firms: business strategy, internal organization and firms' behavior, RIETI discussion paper series 12-J-017 (in Japanese). http://www.rieti.go.jp/jp/publications/dp/12j017.pdf
Nikkei NEEDS-FinancialQUEST (2013) Data-base
Nishi H (2012) Structural VAR Analysis of Debt, Capital Accumulation, and Income Distribution in the Japanese Economy: A Post-Keynesian Perspective. J Post Keynesian Econ 34 (4):685–712
Nishi H (2014) Income distribution. In: Finance and economic growth. Nihon Keizai Hyoronsha Publishing, Tokyo (in Japanese)
Orhangazi O (2008) Financialisation and Capital Accumulation in the Non-Financial Corporate Sector: A Theoretical and Empirical Investigation on the US Economy: 1972-2003. Camb J Econ 32(6):863
Shimizu J, Sato K (2014.) Abenomics, Yen depreciation, trade deficit and export competitiveness, RIETI discussion paper series 14-J-022 (in Japanese). http://www.rieti.go.jp/en/publications/nts/14j022.html
Streeck W (2013) Re-forming capitalism. Oxford University Press, Oxford

The Nikkei (2015) Major Japanese Companies to Raise Pay Scales as Requested by Abe, March 18. http://asia.nikkei.com/Politics-Economy/Economy/Major-Japanese-companies-to-raise-pay-scales-as-requested-by-Abe

Thelen K (2004) How Institutions Evolve. Cambridge University Press, Cambridge

Thelen K (2014) Varieties of Liberalization and the New Politics of Social Solidarity. Cambridge University Press

Yamada T (2000) Japanese capitalism and the companyist compromise. In: Boyer, Yamada (eds) (2000)

Yamada T, Hirano Y (2012) How has the Japanese mode of *Régulation* changed?: the whereabouts of companyism, In Boyer, Uemura, Isogai (eds) (2012)

Chapter 17
Conclusion: The Evolving Diversity and Interdependence of Capitalisms and Conditions for Regional Integration

Robert Boyer, Hiroyasu Uemura, Toshio Yamada, and Lei Song

17.1 Introduction

Back in 1989, the collapse of the Berlin Wall had been interpreted as an entry into a new epoch: market and democracy would irreversibly replace planning and the concentration of power with a single party. The sting of international competition was supposed to bring converging trends toward a canonical socioeconomic regime, quite similar to the US model built upon the synergy between innovation capitalism and representative democracy. The globalization process governing national economies was perceived as the equivalent of competition among firms: inefficient regimes would be eliminated, and thus, a canonical form of modernity would become the norm.

Three decades later, this diagnosis has proven largely erroneous. The hegemony of the USA is challenged by the rise of China, still ruled by a powerful communist party, but especially dynamic in terms of productive modernization, improvement in living standards, innovation capabilities, and the ability to shape international

R. Boyer (✉)
Institut des Amériques, Vanves, France
e-mail: r.boyer2@orange.fr

H. Uemura (✉)
Yokohama National University, Yokohama, Japan
e-mail: huemura@ynu.ac.jp

T. Yamada
Nagoya University, Nagoya, Japan
e-mail: tyamada@rainbow.plala.or.jp

L. Song
Peking University, Beijing, China
e-mail: slei@pku.edu.cn

R. Boyer et al. (eds.), *Evolving Diversity and Interdependence of Capitalisms*, Evolutionary Economics and Social Complexity Science 11,
https://doi.org/10.1007/978-4-431-55001-3_17

relations. By contrast, the European Union (EU) experienced major difficulties in overcoming the Euro crisis and making compatible fairly diverse brands of capitalism, conceptions of national sovereignty, and democratic control over governments' strategic decisions. The issues are still different in Latin America where most countries suffer the curse of rentier regimes built upon the extraction and export of natural resources. The African continent displays a mosaic of weak states, torn by recurring civil wars that are quite detrimental to the emergence of viable development strategies.

The present book has developed a series of comparative and historical analyses between Europe and East Asia that conclude the rejection of the post-1989 thesis: globalization does not imply economic and political convergence. This conclusion emphasizes three major lessons.

- First, this unprecedented phase of internationalization of trade, direct investment, financial portfolio management, and, to some extent, migration has allowed a remarkable and *renewed diversity of socioeconomic regimes* and growth strategies. This epoch has even allowed the emergence of a serious competitor and alternative to the USA's emblematic finance-led capitalism, built upon a surprising synergy between political objectives and economic dynamism (Sect. 17.2).
- Second, the concept of globalization misrepresents the structural transformation of the contemporary world system. In fact, from favoring the emergence of a single form of capitalism, having the features of the US finance-led regime, intense internationalization has brought about an *unprecedented long-range interdependency* among very diverse and, sometimes, complementary socioeconomic regimes. Of course, the dynamism of international trade and the rise of powerful multinational firms have challenged the domestic coherence of the National Systems of Innovation. Nevertheless, the innovative capabilities continue to be closely related to the nature of the wage-labor nexus, the type of financial system based mainly on commercial banks, or via sophisticated and large financial markets. In spite of reduced transportation costs, international trade has essentially developed among geographically close economies, and in fact, economic regionalization has been a driving force both in Europe and East Asia. Long-distance trade has organized complementary specialization between the four pillars of the world economy (Sect. 17.3).
- Third, *regional economic integration displays contrasting configurations* in Europe, Asia, and Latin America. A careful comparison stresses the reversal of fortune between the EU and ASEAN: the EU was frequently seen as a benchmark for other regional integrations, but the Euro crisis has triggered a reassessment. An irreversible adoption of a single currency has the perverse effect of strengthening macroeconomic divergence among member states and puts at risk a six-decade-long process of supranational institution building. By contrast, the pragmatic and business-driven ASEAN integration has fared better during the 2010s because exchange rate adjustments are easier than political deliberation among heterogeneous national objectives. Thus, it is possible to express the general condition under which regional integration is viable in the long run (Sect. 17.4).

A brief conclusion derives prospective views for this historical and theoretical retrospective. The internationalization pattern followed since the 1980s has probably come to an end because its economic returns are decreasing and many societies manifest growing social and political oppositions from the losers in terms of income distribution and welfare. The functionalist vision of the European regional integration has been challenged by the Euro crisis: political breakthroughs in the direction of full-fledged federalism are not the mechanical spillovers of growing economic interdependencies. A reconsideration of regional integration is urgently needed. Are nationalism and protectionism the only alternatives available for reconciling democracy and capitalism, or should one expect the invention of new strategies and socioeconomic regimes?

17.2 The Renewed Diversity of Capitalisms

After the collapse of the Berlin Wall, the progressive and long-lasting opening of national economies to world trade and foreign investment was naively assumed by many policymakers to bring convergence toward a common economic and political organization, built upon the synergy between market mechanism reliance and representative democracy. At the end of the 2010s, this process of globalization has nurtured a large variety of socioeconomic regimes at odds with the hypothesis that USA's capitalism would define the canonical form of modernity for both Europe and Asia.

17.2.1 East Asia: The rise of Contrasting and Genuine Configurations

In a previous analysis (Boyer et al. 2012), we revealed that the primary factors that determine the institutional diversity of East Asia and advanced capitalisms for the period of 2004–2007 are the degree of liberalization of different markets and the contrast between trade dependence and domestic social protection. We identified five types of Asian capitalism clearly distinct from advanced capitalisms (Harada and Tohyama 2012).

The analysis by Tohyama and Harada in this volume has been considered for the extended period of 2004–2011 (Chap. 12). While it reconfirmed the rather similar determining factors of institutional diversity, the groups (clusters) of targeted economies resulting from the analysis are slightly different from the result of the previous analysis. With regard to advanced countries, three clusters were identified: advanced liberal capitalism, welfare capitalism, and European mixed capitalism as in the previous analysis. The difference here from the result of the previous analysis is the fact that Japan is included in advanced liberal capitalism. As for Asian

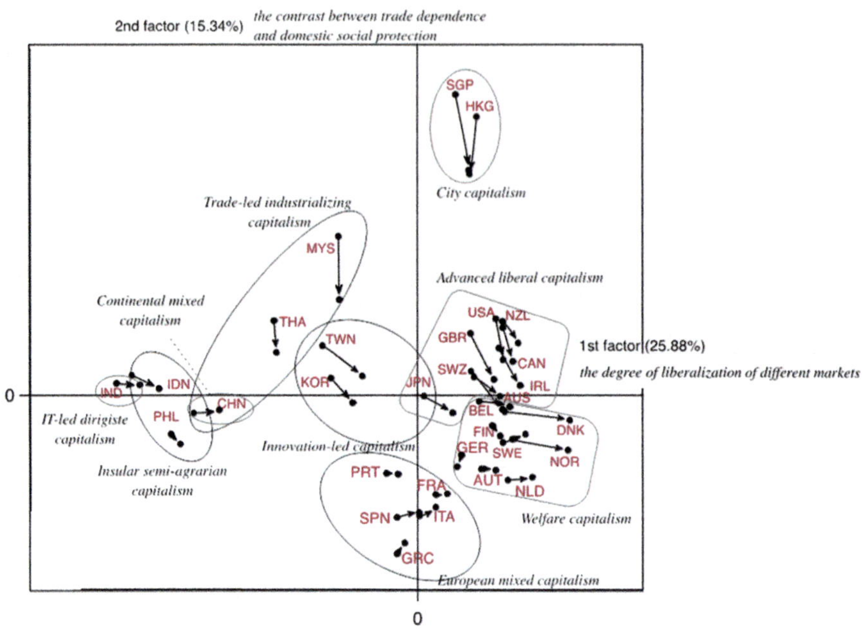

Fig. 17.1 Transformation of institutional diversity of advanced and Asian capitalism from the mid-2000s (2004-2007) to the late-2000s (2007–2011)

economies, despite Japan's separation from innovation-led capitalism, South Korea and Taiwan comprise a group with countries having trade-led industrializing capitalism, such as Malaysia and Thailand, and insular semi-agrarian capitalism (Indonesia and the Philippines) and continental mixed capitalism (China) also continue to exist.

Nevertheless, considering the socioeconomic context of each economy in addition to the result of the statistical analyses comprising institutional configuration and industrial and innovative specialization, it would still be reasonable that we could retain the hypothesis of the five types of Asian capitalism. This is because the relative positions of the most targeted economies can be regarded as more or less unchanged from the mid-2000s to the late 2000s in Fig. 17.1. Further, each economy would be deeply embedded in a specific socioeconomic context in a region from the long historical perspective and patterns of innovative behavior of firms and industrial specialization in an economy in that a specific institutional environment could be affected by the force of inertia (Fig. 17.1).

17.2.2 The Emergence of a New Form of Capitalism: China

Taking the size of its economy and the features of its political system into account, we have sound reasons to say that Chinese capitalism is an unprecedented new brand of capitalism. In concrete terms, the scale of the Chinese economy surpasses the sum of other Asian economies; however, the Chinese political system is quite unique, and the existence of the party-state system means that any institutional adjustment cannot threaten the political system. The structure and logic of this new capitalism brand are complicated and are in the process of evolution, and the changing complexity means the effect of the Chinese economy upon the East Asian regional integration would be complicated and changing through time (Chaps. 13 and 14).

Because the Chinese economy is full of conflicts, it is quite difficult to summarize its institutional features. First, although China has approached state capitalism in recent years, competition in many Chinese industries has been quite fierce. Second, there exist obvious differences among different regions and sectors. Third, regarding the aforementioned issues, the different institutional configurations that are composed of labor-wage nexus, financial institutions, and interfirm relations came into being around different ownership structures. Defining this new capitalism brand as a mixed continental capitalism is appropriate at the present stage (Fig. 17.2).

What makes the issue more complicated is that the Chinese economy has experienced changes and is in the process of a new change. From the end of the 1970s to the early era of the 1990s, China's economic growth has had some features of domestic demand-led growth. Since the middle of the 1990s, the Chinese economy had entered the export–/investment-led growth period. However, from 2006, especially after the 2008 world financial crisis, the Chinese government has attempted to change the mode of growth once again by promoting the indigenous innovation policy and expanding domestic demand. About 10 years later, we notice that China made progress in the field of technological capability, although the progress has not always been balanced across different industries. However, because the real estate industry has become the main source of the local government's income and the price of real estate has lowered the citizen's capacity to consume, the transition of the mode of growth is not easy and is one reason why Beijing began to initiate Asian Infrastructure Investment Bank (AIIB) and the Belt and Road project.

The transition of China's mode of growth exerts twofold effects on the East Asian regional integration. On the one hand, if China transitions to the domestic demand-led growth proceedes smoothly, the other East Asian economies would gain a bigger export market. On the other hand, if the indigenous innovation policy improves the technological capability successfully, the foundation of the international division of labor between China and other East Asian economies would be eroded. Actually, some scholars tend to believe that because Beijing has turned to the Belt and Road project, the importance of East Asian economic integration would weaken for China. However, considering the following two facts, perhaps, we should keep distance from the above judgment. First, the intensity of the linkage between China and other

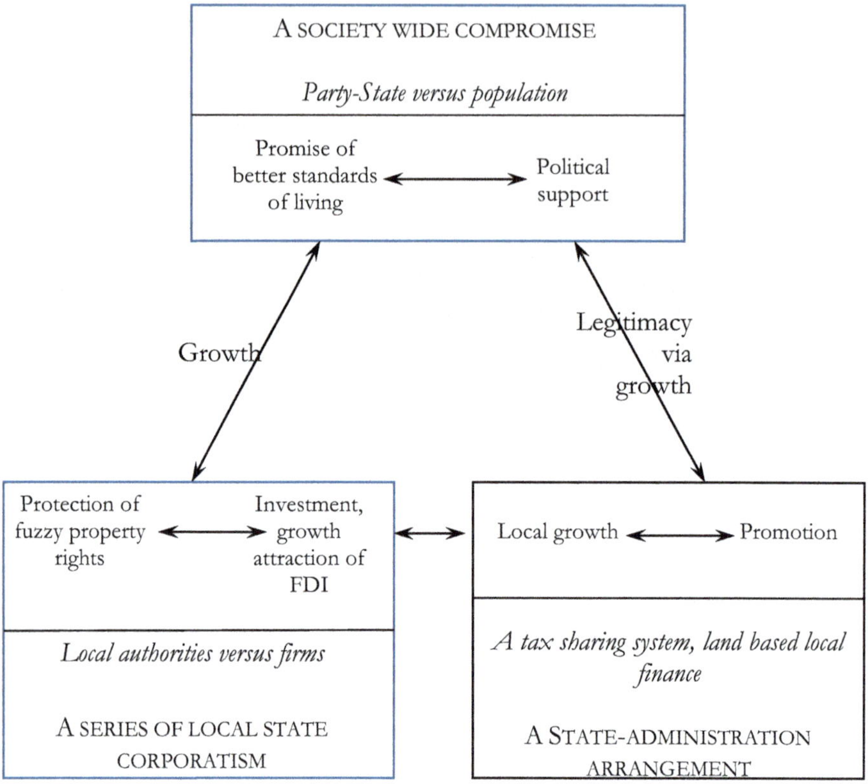

Fig. 17.2 China: a unique mix of institutional arrangements. (Source: Adapted from Lei Song and Chengnan Yan, Chap. 13)

East Asian economies varies, and the possibility of a technical upgrade of China's industries also varies across industries. Second, although there exist complicated political issues between China and other East Asian economies, China's major international rival is the USA. Considering the possibility of restarting the US-led Trans-Pacific Partnership (TPP), maintaining the economic and political linkages with other East Asian economies would bolster China's position in the big game with the USA. Therefore, engaging in East Asian regional integration is still a realistic choice.

As a new brand of capitalism, the formation and expansion of Chinese capitalism not only illustrate that divergence rather than convergence is still one of the main characteristics of modern capitalism but also reveals the mutually enhancing relationship between the progress of regional integration and the rise of the huge capitalist economy.

17.2.3 Six Decades of European Integration and Yet Contrasting Capitalism Brands

Frequently, foreign analysts for the EU consider that the old continent explores a common form of capitalism, labeled as welfare capitalism, opposing the market-led and finance-led US capitalism. Nevertheless, seen from within the old continent, the major differences in institutional architectures and economic policy conceptions persist between two of the nation-states that launched the European integration: Germany and France (Chap. 7). This absence of convergence is more remarkable, the longer the period of regional integration. Furthermore, owing to the Euro crisis, the innovation and export-led German growth model, and consumption-led French model, there is contrasting macroeconomic evolution. Thus, Germany and France are emblematic of a north/south opposition of two types of capitalism: far from converging, they have become complementary (Chap. 2).

Systematic institutional analyses (Amable 2003) had long ago confirmed the coexistence of at least three types of capitalism within the EU: state-led capitalism in Southern Europe, social democratic capitalism in the northern countries with Germany being close to this configuration, and a variant of market-dominated capitalism in the UK. The stability of this taxonomy has been widely confirmed (Harada and Tohyama 2012). Thus, competing in the same single market does not imply the progressive homogeneity of typical European capitalism. This finding is quite general indeed. When the Berlin Wall collapsed, the former soviet-type Central and Eastern European economies have been progressively admitted to the process of continental integration under the same rules of the game, the *acquis communautaire*. A common prognosis has been that all these new members would soon resemble their western counterparts. In fact, they have developed largely original economic institutions and political alliances, partially shaped by their post-World War II trajectories (Myant and Drahokoupil 2010; Baccaro and Pontusson 2016). Poland, Czech Republic, and Hungary have been integrated into the value chain of Western Europe, and these countries have become part of a variant of dependent capitalism, the growth of which is led by foreign investments (Chap. 2) (Fig. 17.3).

In other words, the diversity of capitalisms is not a legacy of the past due to strong inertia but is evidence of the permanent recreation of capitalism. This feature has been enhanced and not at all blurred by the opening of all national economies to the world and/or regional integrations in Europe and Asia.

17.2.4 Why Persistent Diversity Is a Key Feature of Capitalisms and Rentier Regimes?

A more theoretical approach is welcome because most mainstream economists and several experts continue to consider that a canonical form of capitalism should emerge out of a trial and error process and a disciplined force of completion. A

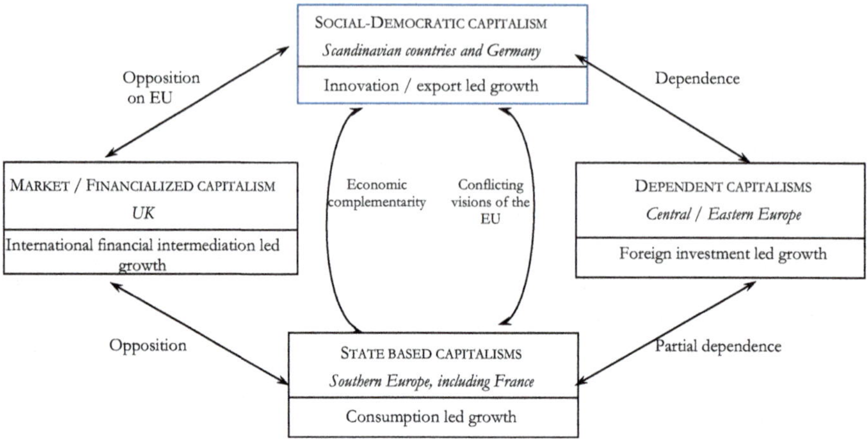

Fig. 17.3 The European Union: coexistence and tensions between four brands of capitalism

first objection states that some countries are given abundant natural resources, while others are not so lucky. The former is likely to explore typical *rentier regimes*, while the latter is induced to innovate in the production of manufactured goods or services to firms and households, which leads to the origin of *capitalism*. Through time, these two broad systems have become more complementary than competing, as evidenced by economic history. This dividing line is frequently forgotten by grand economic theories. The emergence of capitalism launches a dialectical process between scientific and technical innovation on one side and the invention of institutions and organizations on the other side. This a priori historical process implies the exploration of a unique trajectory because four mechanisms are operating (Fig. 17.4).

Under the impact of sunk costs, increasing returns to scale, and learning by doing and by using, any technological system exhibits *path dependency*, that is, persistence, even when the reasons of its emergence and performance have disappeared. Technologies call for *complementary institutions* in terms of education, training, public infrastructure, and market organization, and this is a second and crucial source of inertia: core institutional forms that codify basic social relations cannot be easily copied and imported from one successful country to another. The very functioning of each socioeconomic regime generates *a particular informational system* via prices, national statistics, and surveys, which, in turn, helps make decisions for private and public actors: this reinforces the possible lock-in into a rather specific socioeconomic regime, because the full information required by pure and perfect competition via markets is practically out of reach. Last but not the least, any national economy is embedded into *a dense web of values, beliefs, and objectives* that cannot be transposed from one society to another. When combined in various proportions, these mechanisms generate a significant diversity of capitalisms and rentier regimes as well. The larger their complementarity, the higher is the inertia and resilience of these regimes.

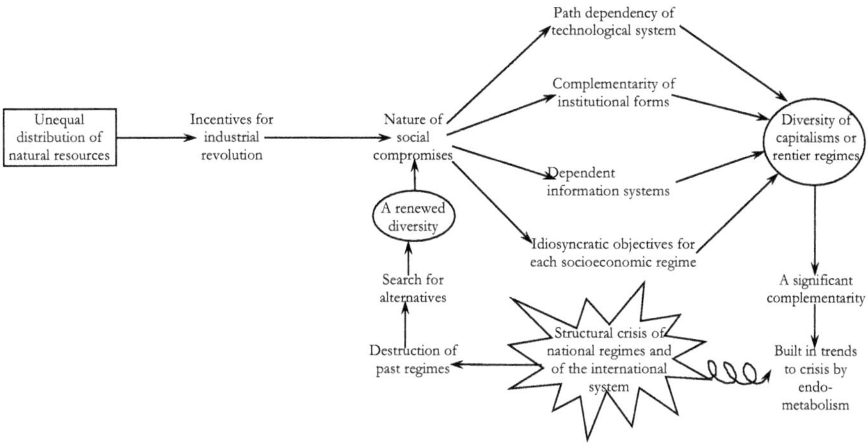

Fig. 17.4 The resilient diversity of socioeconomic regimes

Are structural crises not crucial episodes when all the socioeconomic regimes are challenged in their core foundations? Do actors not search for a better and more resilient configuration? This would mean a dramatic reduction in past diversity. On the contrary, the previous empirical analyses show that some configurations are regressing but most are transformed and some new forms of capitalism have emerged calling for the attention of analysts. From a theoretical standpoint, most crises are endogenous and originate from the very success of a socioeconomic regime. They manifest the regime's limit but simultaneously open opportunities for innovations that recreate diversity (see Fig. 17.3).

17.3 An Alternative Conceptualization of Globalization

This term is largely diffused all over the academic and business world. It refers to a wide range of phenomena. The world market becomes a horizon for all firms. Capital flows without any barrier from one country to another. An unprecedented international division of labor organizes global value chains. Large mega cities become the actors of internationalization and tend to divorce from their domestic territory. Some leading nations or firms can impose their technological and organizational norms. Finally, the only viable growth regime seems to have been based on innovation and export growth, but it could not last if protectionist and nationalist policies diffuse from the USA to the rest of the world. The empirical analyses of the present book suggest another panorama and point out three major features of the contemporary world.

First, far from converging to a common and one best way for all socioeconomic regimes, an intensification of *interdependence between quite distinct configurations* is simultaneously moving all economies.

Table 17.1 An alternative to the concept of globalization

	Globalization	Growing interdependence of diverse capitalisms
1. Definition	A complete set of complementary transformations	An idiosyncratic mix of trade opening, free capital flows, migrations, international property rights rules
2. General vision	An already existing system	A process in the making
3. Conception of time	Self-sustained convergence to a steady configuration	An historical succession of broad periods of opening and regressions of free trade
4. Evolution of nation-states	Dramatically challenged	Some are enhanced, other constrained by the internationalization
5. Convergence/divergence of socioeconomic regimes	Basically convergence	Evolving but resilient heterogeneity
6. Links polity/economy	A purely economic phenomenon, a quasi-natural law	The expression of social compromises including the degree of integration into the world economy
7. Sources of crises	Opposition of badly informed social groups	The loser groups protest and endogenous erosion of any regime

Second, *far from equalizing the status of nation-states* regardless of their size, specialization or geographical localization and the ability to master innovation and to create new oligopolistic markets have generated a clear hierarchy among societies. Internationalization is a profitable opportunity for leaders but a severe constraint for all other nations that have to react to the vagaries of the world economy created by the leading economies. For instance, the EU entered a major crisis when the US real estate bubble bursts, and similarly, Chinese FDI in many Latin American countries is the expression of unbalanced power between trading partners.

Third, one has to mitigate the implicit vision associated with globalization: today, with the hegemony of ICT, any country can trade with any other partner regardless of the distance. In fact, according to the teachings of new economic geography, geographical proximity remains important, agglomeration effects still govern innovation, and e-commerce has to ally with low logistic costs. Paradoxically, we still live in *the epoch of economic regionalization*. This is an intermediate level between the world and nations, now too small to influence the course of internationalization. The regions (North America, Europe, East Asia, Latin America) can try to efficiently organize the division of labor, wealth creation, and distribution and have a say in the renegotiation of international institutions in charge of preserving old and new global commons (Table 17.1).

17.3.1 Interdependence of Diverse Capitalisms in EU and East Asia

Different types of capitalism are interdependent on each other through the trade of final and intermediate goods and services in the process of regional integration in both Europe and East Asia. In particular, the structural characteristics of interdependence of capitalisms in different regions are analyzed by examining the "input coefficient matrix" and the "trade matrix of final goods and services" that are derived from the World Input-Output Database (WIOD).

According to the tables of the input coefficient matrix and the trade matrix of final goods and services (Tables 17.2 and 17.3), shifts in two different and independent patterns of regional integration can be seen in Europe and East Asia (as for the shift in the interdependence in detail, see Table 5.2 in Chap. 5).

In Europe, the pattern of interdependence of capitalisms has been relatively stable among EU member countries in the last 20 years. In 1995 and 2014, Germany was continuously a key player in final and intermediate goods trade in the single European market. Furthermore, after the Euro was introduced in most EU member countries, Germany created stronger ties of final goods trade with other EU member countries in the process of European integration, and this caused more trade imbalance between Germany and Southern European countries (Chap. 4).

In East Asia, interdependence in intermediate goods trade has become stronger among major Asian economies in the last 20 years. Furthermore, the pattern of

Table 17.2 Changes in input coefficient matrix, 1995–2014

Input Coefficient Matrix, 1995 — Cells with a value ≧0.005 are shadowed.

Supply\Demand	Japan	Korea	China	Taiwan	Indonesia	India	US	UK	France	Germany	Italy	Other EU countries
Japan	■	■	■	■	■							
Korea		■	■	■	■							
China		■	■									
Taiwan			■	■								
Indonesia					■							
India						■						
US		■	■	■	■		■	■	■	■	■	■
UK								■	■	■		■
France								■	■	■	■	■
Germany				■	■			■	■	■	■	■
Italy									■	■	■	■
Other EU countries		■		■	■	■		■	■	■	■	■

Input Coefficient Matrix, 2014 — Cells with a value ≧0.005 are shadowed.

Supply\Demand	Japan	Korea	China	Taiwan	Indonesia	India	US	UK	France	Germany	Italy	Other EU countries
Japan	■	■		■	■							
Korea		■		■	■							
China	■	■	■	■	■	■				■		■
Taiwan				■								
Indonesia				■	■							
India						■						
US	■	■		■			■	■	■	■		■
UK								■	■	■		■
France								■	■	■	■	■
Germany				■				■	■	■	■	■
Italy									■	■	■	■
Other EU countries				■				■	■	■	■	■

Table 17.3 Changes in trade matrix of final goods/services, 1995–2014

Trade Matrix of Final Goods/Services, 1995 Cells with a value ≧1.0% are shadowed.

Supply\Demand	Japan	Korea	China	Taiwan	Indonesia	India	US	UK	France	Germany	Italy	Other EU countries
Japan	■						■					
Korea	■	■					■					
China	■		■				■					
Taiwan	■		■	■			■					■
Indonesia	■				■		■					
India						■	■					
US							■					
UK							■	■		■		■
France									■	■		■
Germany										■		■
Italy							■		■	■	■	■
Other EU countries								■	■	■		■

Trade Matrix of Final Goods/Services, 2014 Cells with a value ≧1.0% are shadowed.

Supply\Demand	Japan	Korea	China	Taiwan	Indonesia	India	US	UK	France	Germany	Italy	Other EU countries
Japan	■		■				■					
Korea	■	■	■				■					■
China	■		■				■					
Taiwan	■		■	■			■					
Indonesia					■		■					
India						■						
US							■					
UK							■	■				■
France									■	■		■
Germany			■				■	■	■	■		■
Italy							■		■	■	■	■
Other EU countries							■	■	■	■		■

Source: WIOD2016

international division of labor has changed drastically with the rapidly growing Chinese economy. In 1995, Japan was a key supplier in intermediate goods trade with other Asian countries. In 2014, however, China was exporting not only final goods but also intermediate goods to other Asian countries and was importing final goods from other countries. Therefore, China with the growing market has become the center of Asian economic integration, and this may strongly influence the growth regimes and industrial structure changes, especially de-induatrialization, in Japan and South Korea (Chaps. 5, 15 and 16).

Furthermore, looking closely at the interdependence among the EU, East Asia, and the USA, East Asian economies have established their own international division of labor and have become relatively independent of the EU member countries in the last 20 years. However, despite these transformations of regional interdependence in EU and East Asia, the trade of both intermediate and final goods has been stronger between China and Germany. This imposes competitive pressure on the German economy and, in turn, may influence the economies of other EU member countries such as France, Italy, Spain, etc.

17.3.2 Comparative Institutional Advantage, Economic Specialization, and the Hierarchy Among Social Innovation Systems

Both in the EU and Asia, the institutional diversity of capitalisms and trade specialization are closely correlated, which explains their long-term coexistence. This is the key contribution of the theory of international trade based on comparative institutional advantage built along a national trajectory. Within each region, some economies are able to innovate and, thus, reap oligopolistic rents, whereas others have to rely on the import of these products to sustain their competitiveness in more traditional sectors. The polarization of innovative capabilities is the source of the hierarchy observed in most regional integrations.

This characterization reveals the coherence of each type of capitalism through the institutional environment at the macro level, the relative strength and composition of different industries at the meso-intermediate level, and firm behavior engaging innovation at the micro level. For instance, the institutional diversity in Asian capitalisms provides firms with better capacities to advance in certain types of technologies, possibly leading to cross-national patterns of specialization in innovative activities (Chap. 12). In the EU, an equivalent polarization prevails between the concentration of globally competitive manufacturing in the North and of sheltered services and traditional goods in the South.

What was the pertinent level of social systems of innovation in the 2010s? After World War II, the relevant territory was national; however, after three decades of internationalization of value chains under the aegis of large multinationals, the configuration became more complex. In some sectors—pharmaceutical products and information and communication technologies—some powerful firms exploited, for their benefit, the opportunities provided by national trajectories that have formed human capabilities and public infrastructure. However, some continental economies are able to care about the preservation of a national coherence of their innovation system. This is specially so for China and, to some extent, India: active government policies aim at mastering the knowledge and techniques of the next productive paradigm.

The challenges faced by Europeans and Asians are rather different. The European programs of the 2000s that aimed to transform the old continent into the most competitive in the world while preserving a high welfare level have not been successful. Only Nordic countries have been able to convert the human resources nurtured by extended welfare into the catalysts for demand- and user-driven innovations, partially induced by public policy procurement (Chap. 9). However, neither have European firms conquered key positions in the sunrise industries nor have they been able to build the intra-European synergies that would sustain a coherent and dynamic innovation system at the continental level. For Asian economies, the dynamism of innovation can benefit from the legacy of Japanese and Korean trajectories and the ambition of the Chinese authorities to build an autonomous innovation system. The other economies' objectives would be less inclined to close their technological gap with the frontier but rather to find technological trajectories available to them.

17.3.3 Regional Economic Integration: Distance Matters

A third objection to the concept of globalization challenges the implicit vision of a homogenous distribution of trade among equally important partners. The rapid rise of digital goods and electronic platforms gives the impression of the abolition of the physical distance that defines localized markets. Nevertheless, the different segments of the value chains that deliver these products are localized according to specific competitive advantages of localities, and the wealth created tends to be concentrated in precise financial hubs. A clear hierarchy is shaping the distribution of these benefits of the internationalization of e-commerce.

Furthermore, some industries remain strictly attached to domestic spaces: mining, agriculture, infrastructure, housing, public services of education, and health and administration. These markets are localized, and distance continues to matter. Therefore, the gravity model of international trade continues to hold and explain why trade is more intense among neighbors than distant partners, assuming an equal competitiveness in terms of prices or quality. This is one rationale for regional integration, and statistical data confirm the density of intraregional trade: high but stagnant in the EU, rapidly growing in East Asia, moderate but significant in North America, and small and stagnating in Latin America. Finally, the defenders of Brexit had to recognize that the distant markets of Commonwealth would not compensate for the loss incurred on abandoning the single European market. Similarly, the UK territory was attractive for Japanese multinationals and Chinese investors because it was an entry point to the EU (Chap. 10).

Regionalization is a fairly general trend because geography still matters for sustaining domestic standards of living, and the shift from national to regional markets exceeds the benefits of increasing returns to scale. With the high growth of international trade, medium-sized economies that used to enjoy domestic consumption-led regimes ended up constrained to play the game of export-led growth because only continental economies can contemplate the possibility of an inward-looking development. If their governments want to have a say in geopolitical matters concerning the rules governing trade, intellectual property rights, and the redesign of the international financial system, they have to accept pooling a part of their national sovereignty. This is precisely the path followed by European nation-states.

Economic regionalization is, thus, quite general; however, this does not imply the existence of a unique pattern. First, competitive advantages may differ: the benefits are far more modest among rentier regimes but quite important when the issue at stake is the redeployment of productive chains. Hence, integration in Latin America is far slower than in Asia. A second factor stresses the degree of path dependence and inertia in the reaction to major transformation in the productive paradigm: the rather slow adoption in the EU and far more dynamism in East Asia. The third one is probably the most important: different political compromises shape contrasting integration trajectories.

17.4 European and East Asian Regional Integrations Compared

Until the 2010s, the European Union was frequently taken as the benchmark and/or the model of economic regional integration. With the dramatic, and for many experts, surprising crisis of the Euro, a more balanced approach is required. Regional integrations are long-term processes and include the simple transition from a rather closed economy to an open one, where division of labor is translated to a wider territory. New rules of the game are to be searched for and implemented, and they cannot be governed by a pure economic logic because major political issues are involved. The complex interactions between economic processes and political deliberation and intermediation do lead to path-dependent configurations organizing multilevel governance, if not fully fledged supranational governments. Therefore, the governments have reacted quite differently to the 2008 world financial and economic crisis and revealed deep oppositions in the conception and implementation of institutionalization of regional integrations. A comparison of East Asia and Europe is quite instructive indeed and points out some conditions for a viable and successful adaptation to the structural transformations of the world economy.

17.4.1 Two Contrasting Trajectories

Both Europe and East Asia came out of World War II largely economically destroyed, poor, and fragmented. In this context, the USA played a determinant role in their economic reconstruction and the adoption of new political institutions: these interventions drastically changed the future of Germany, Japan, and many other countries. Nevertheless, different initial political polarizations deliver contrasting evolutions (Fig. 17.5).

In the old continent, in the 1950s, the administrative and political elites were convinced that the two world wars originated from the economic rivalry between Germany and France. Thus, their task was to organize this competition by the enactment of rules of the game imposed by an agreement among national governments. This seminal conception has reasonably inspired all the steps of the six-decade-long European integration. The construction of a coal and steel market was the first step in the progressive construction of an integrated European market for goods, services, and capital that implies citizens' mobility across the continent. The enactment of norms and rules feeds an institutionalization process of economic

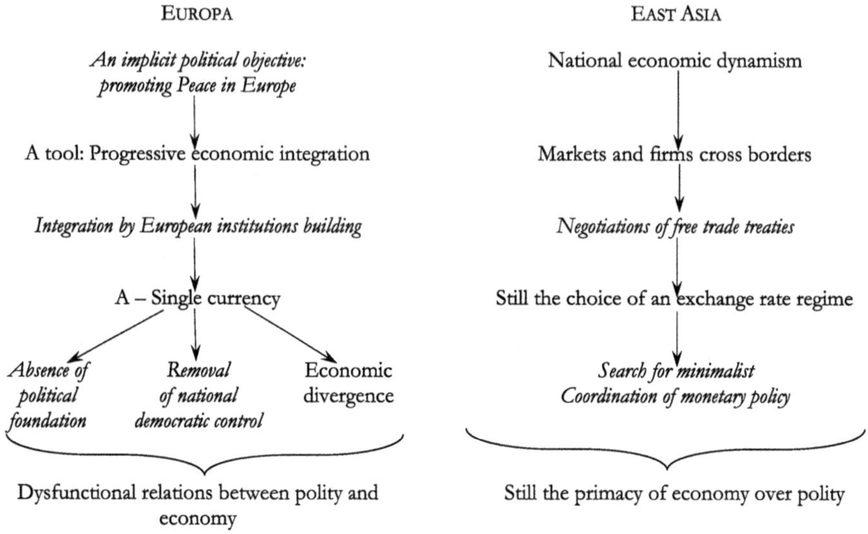

Fig. 17.5 How polity and economy interact in European and Asian integrations

activity. In a sense, the Euro was conceived as a necessary tool for preserving the single market achievement.

Nevertheless, in the early 2000s, most governments did not perceive that a common currency is more than a technical device because it required political foundations, which is a sense of solidarity between members and the democratic control of citizens to get their adhesion. The functionalist conception of regional integration turned polity to a servant of the economy. Its limits have been brutally revealed by the Eurozone crisis in 2010s and the inflow of migrants: the imposition of unpopular austerity programs and the rebuttal of a common migratory policy mean the end of an epoch. Economic efficiency and responses to citizens' political demands resulted in an open conflict. Parties defending national sovereignty against further steps toward a federal Europe fairly bloomed and prospered in different forms in all member states.

The situation in East Asia is different: the absence of a peaceful political integration between all former adversaries, in particular, China, Japan and South Korea, is a serious obstacle to the search for economic cooperation. Instead, the post-World War II era implied political and economic reconstruction on a national basis until the 1970s. Later, the internal technological and political modernization was so dynamic that firms decided to extend their productive networks through international trade. In the 1990s, their growing interdependence made attractive the negotiation of the ASEAN free trade agreement, the rationale of which is typically economic. Other nations wanted to join the agreement owing to the fast growth of the region (Chap. 3).

The political concerns were secondary and manifested themselves only after the 1997 Asian crisis: the volatility of exchange rates was perceived as a danger and possible source of dislocation of trade relations, but the outcome was an initiative for coordinating monetary policy and not the launch of a common currency. The trust among ASEAN members is not high enough to justify such a bold decision. Therefore, the 2000s experienced a growing number of members but only a soft coordination to foster the productive networks among them. The treaties exerted a few limitations to national sovereignty, and in any case, the objective did not imply a convergence toward any fixed exchange rate regime. Rapid growth smoothed the redeployment of national productive systems within a positive and steadily increasing sum game with China, Japan, South Korea and Taiwan.

Only in 2015 did the governments consider a possible common market. Despite intense geopolitical rivalries, the free trade zone was not at risk, and Asian dynamism helped Asian countries' out of the 2008 world crisis. The contrast between the EU and ASEAN is clear. In the EU, political motives pretend to monitor the economy but finally lead to a dysfunctional supranational construction. In ASEAN, business objectives are leading a prudent and limited political coordination. The outcome is finally the coexistence of two fairly different regional integrations.

17.4.2 The Primacy of Business Over Political Objectives: East Asian Integration

This book is built upon the analyses of the interactions between polity and economy and defends the thesis that they explain the present configurations of regional integration in EU and East Asia. Polity can be seen in three major areas: polity in a narrow sense, that is, juridical-political order, policies, and politics. The economy consists of two major areas: production and trade, and money and finance.

East Asia is deeply embedded in the international economy via trade, direct investment, and financial flows, and until recently, most countries rely on the US dollar as settlement currency. This could be perceived as a drawback compared to the emergence of the Euro, seen as a potential rival to the dollar. Nevertheless, the absence of a common currency allows an independent monetary policy adapted to each nation's conditions, and exchange rate adjustment allows one to react to the vagaries of the world economy and the evolution of competitiveness. In fact, multinational firms are key actors involved in organizing the international division of labor, and their strategies are embedded in national policies concerning taxation, regulations, and infrastructure (Table 17.4).

From this viewpoint, the policies of China and Japan as well as small- and medium-sized economies tend to be respectful of the demands from business, irrespective of whether the demand is domestic or international. Of course, the citizens' demands cannot be ignored, but income redistribution via welfare systems tends to be limited because the priority is to extend productive capacities. This is an important distinction with respect to the EU, seen globally by Asians as an alliance of welfare states. The continental Chinese economy acquires an increasingly large

Table 17.4 The links between polity and economy: East Asia. *The primacy of business over political objectives*

	Polity			Economy	
	Polity (Juridical-political order)	**Policies**	**Politics**	**Production and Trade**	**Money and Finance**
Global	UN IMF WTO ICJ	EPA with third countries	Each state as an independent political actor	Economic dependence on the US	Strong influence by the international financial market
Supernational/ Regional	ASEAN ADB No super-national institution among China, Japan and Korea	Few common policies Chiang Mai Initiative	Political conflicts and cooperation among East Asian countries	Multinationals' activities International production networks Growing China as the core of economic interdependence	No monetary union National currencies US Dollar as the settlement currency
	Heterogenous national modes of régulation,			**National growth regimes**	
National.	Sovereign states Domestic laws National foreign affairs	National fiscal policies National labor and welfare policies (weak) National migration policies	Conflicts of interests among domestic actors Preferences of the ruling party and social groups	The national production system The national standard of workers Large differentials in productivity and competitiveness	Domestic monetary control by the central bank National exchange rate policies

influence upon the rest of the world, and its dynamics set the pace of East Asian integration. Such asymmetry becomes the source of an implicit or explicit hegemonic position, more powerful than the one exerted in Europe by Germany. A key difference must be stressed upon: formally, all the Asian partners of China maintain their independence in terms of exchange rate, taxation, and public spending. This soft and pragmatic integration is quite distinct from the complex nexus of supranational rules that intend to govern the EU national economies and imply clear constraints upon the degrees of freedom of the EU member states.

17.4.3 Polity and Supranational Institutions Building at the Cost of Economic Dynamism: The EU

The interlocking of national and European polities is the distinctive feature of the EU. A complete juridical and political order is now ruling the everyday functioning of societies. The European Court of Justice deals with conflicts between European and domestic legislations. The Schengen agreement was implemented to facilitate free internal mobility of citizens. The European Commission is the executive branch of the European Council, and a Parliament is given a large number of rights to control European policies and voting regulations and to decide on a common but rather limited budget.

This has a direct counterpart in the economy. The enforcement of competition is given to Brussels' authorities; the national public budget must respect limits in terms of deficit and total debt. The European Commission is in charge of negotiating external tariffs and free trade treaties that are binding for all member states. The Open Coordination Method (OCM) has been invented to favor the voluntary convergence of many domestic policies regarding labor laws, welfare, and social rights (Table 17.5).

Table 17.5 The links between polity and economy: the EU. *Polity and supranational institutions building over the economies*

	Polity			Economy	
	Polity (Juridical-political order)	**Policies**	**Politics**	**Production and Trade**	**Money and Finance**
Global	UN IMF WTO ICJ	EPA with third countries Externalization of migration policies	EU as a global political actor	Relatively large intra-regional trade	Iinfluence by the international financial market
Supernational/ Regional	EU European Commission ECB ECJ OCM Shengen agreement	Common monetary policies Common industrial policies Migration policies	Coordination of interests between European Commission and member states	The single market Immigrant workers Trade imbalance between the North and the South Production networks with Eastern Europe	Euro as the single currency Monerary control by ECB The lack of fiscal federalism
	National (and regional) modes of régulation,			**National growth regimes**	
National.	Sovereign states Domestic laws National foreign affairs	National fiscal policies National labor and welfare policies National migration policies	Conflicts of interests among domestic actors Preferences of the ruling party and social groups	The national productiion system Large differentials in productivity and competitiveness	The lack of autonomy of monetary and exchange rate policies

A new and crucial step has been decided by the governments that joined the Euro when they abolished their domestic currency in the 2000s. The European Central Bank is in charge of setting a common monetary policy that maintains inflation around 2% per year, with the possible unexpected outcome that the policy does necessarily fit in with the specific conditions of each national economy, given the fact that at least three different *régulation* modes must coexist within the same supranational rules. The Euro has thus generated an unprecedented divergence in macroeconomic evolutions in terms of productivity, growth, employment, and remunerations (Chap. 2). For the founders of European integration, economic factors were supposed to drive real convergence and make an increasingly close interdependence necessary, finally leading to political integration. Alas in the 2010s, adverse and diverging trends across European societies threatened the very existence of the EU. Institutional rigidities have hurt the economic dynamism, the coherence of the division of labor, and the political legitimacy of the EU. The EU is no longer a model of regional integration to be emulated elsewhere. By contrast, East Asia seems to explore a more promising path and anticipate the next shift in capitalism and the world from the North to the East. Last but not the least, other regional integrations such as NAFTA or MERCOSUR have not been successful either, and they cannot define an alternative for European policymakers.

Two general lessons can be drawn from the present book.

17.4.4 The Exchange Rate Regime Matters for the Viability of Contrasting Growth Regimes: The Euro Crisis Revisited

The choice of an exchange rate regime is one of the more difficult challenges addressed by contemporary macroeconomics. Under the post-World War II international system, fixed but adjustable exchange rates were the common choice by public authorities: this system would stabilize expectations, and differential unitary costs could be adjusted in case of divergence via revaluation or devaluation. With the explosion of international financial flows, the determinants of exchange rates have drastically changed: basically, they tend to equalize the rate of returns of financial assets. These essential financial determinants can durably be far away from the exchange rate, warranting a trade balance equilibrium. The consequence is usually a form of de-industrialization in case of overvaluation or, on the contrary, a stimulus with an undervaluation of the domestic currency. Consequently, the exchange rate is a crucial variable affecting the growth regime (Chaps. 4 and 5).

Within the *régulation* theory, the function of the exchange rate should be *to make compatible a national régulation mode* with the requirement either of an international regime or the viability of a regional integration. This is the central message a various chapters in this book. There is no optimum monetary regime valid at any period and for any country. For instance, a dollar-pegged regime and a hybrid and more flexible one have been experienced in East Asia from the 1990s to the 2010s (Chap. 6). In the future, many other regimes could emerge and have a definite impact on the evolution of regional integration and the distribution of its benefits across countries (Chap. 6). In the EU, a flexible exchange rate could have compensated for the absence of active redistribution among the Eurozone countries (Chap. 11). The absence of such mechanisms explains the *tipping point* from a relatively smooth and successful economic integration until the end of the 1990s to the brutal perception of the dysfunctionalities generated by the European treaties. One notes the divergence of real economic variables, the absence of devices warranting a modicum solidarity among members, the infringement of national sovereignty, and the lack of anticipation of the issue of migrants and refugees entering the EU (Chap. 8) (Fig. 17.6).

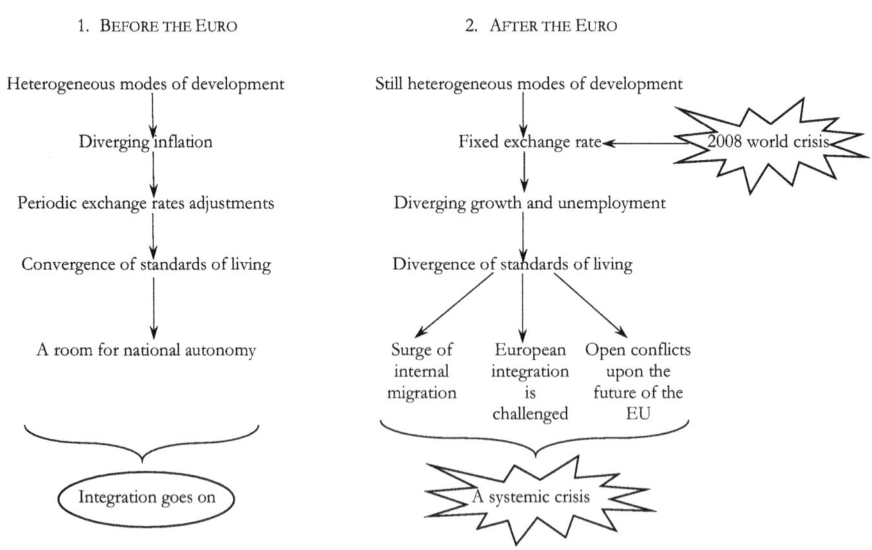

Fig. 17.6 How important is the choice of an exchange rate regime?

17.4.5 Some Structural Conditions Have to Be Fulfilled for a Successful Regional Integration

A more general result emerges from the analyses presented by various Chap. (2, 3, 4, 5, 6, 10, and 11). This book proposes one synthetic criterion concerning the dividing line between the success and failure of a regional integration project: everything is up to *the compatibility of various and more or less heterogeneous national régulation modes and growth regimes within the rules of the game that result from intergovernmental bargaining*. Therefore, a dynamic process is set in motion with uncertain outcomes: either a self-sustaining deepening of labor division along with permanent supranational institutional innovations to sustain the momentum or a dead end and/or open crisis with the risk of abandoning regional integration (Fig.17.7).

- An *asymmetry of supranational rules* in favor of a dominant economy that implicitly bets on the convergence toward its own model is bound to fail in the *absence of redistribution* toward other members and if *a common currency* is blocking the competitiveness adjustments of the weaker economies.
- A dynamic compatibility must prevail between *political objectives and economic dynamism* and not the systematic domination of one rationale over another.

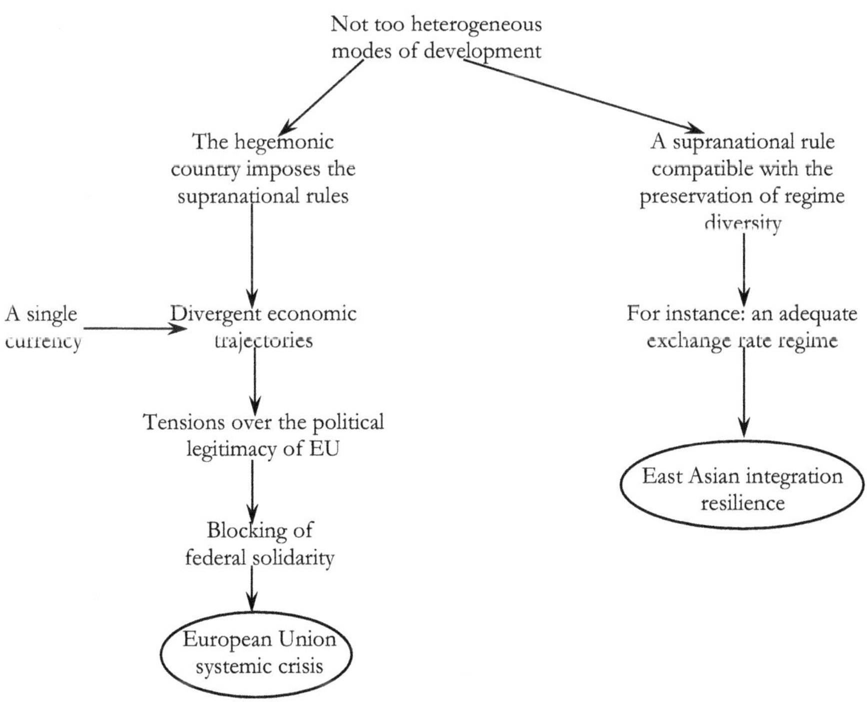

Fig. 17.7 Under which conditions can a regional integration succeed?

- There exists *no optimum strategy for regional integration* that would be relevant in any epoch and for all societies. There exist as many trajectories as historical experiences and abilities to negotiate innovative supranational compromises.

17.5 Conclusion: A Bifurcation in the Relations Between the National, the Regional, and the International

This book provides reasonable evidence on the entry into a new phase of capitalisms and international relations.

All growth regimes encounter structural limits: innovation- and export-led ones breed overcapacities that trigger trade war, finance-dominated capitalisms only thrive via the succession of speculative bubbles that generate an unprecedented social and economic polarization, and state-based capitalisms lack the economic dynamism that would sustain extended welfare, whereas social democratic capitalisms fare better but cannot be transplanted in adversarial and individualistic societies.

International relations are in turmoil. The post-World War II system of international institutions has been losing effectiveness and legitimacy. An emerging rivalry between the USA and China makes the future of the monetary and financial international system quite uncertain. The protection of national interests is blocking the emergence of new global commons concerning the ecological sustainability, public health, development, and eradication of poverty. Regional integration was explored as an alternative to globalization because it seemed possible to reconcile economic dynamism and the democratic expression of citizens in their will to monitor the internationalization process and share its benefits. The open and then creeping crisis of the EU is a dramatic blow against this belief. Finally, Asia seems to explore the future of capitalism and the move toward a dynamic economic regional integration; however, the growing power and multifaceted initiatives of China put at risk the cooperation of relatively weaker partners, in particular, Japan, South Korea, and Taiwan.

What will be the relevant level for building a new order: the world, regions, or nation-states? (Table 17.6).

17.5.1 Is a Revival of Globalization Possible?

The many obstacles to the present form of globalization prevent it to be prolonged into the 2020s. In 2018, a trade war was launched by the foreign policy of American presidency, and tariffs are more likely to increase than to be totally abandoned. The champions of the new e-economy, such as Google, Amazon, Facebook, and Apple, are facing for the first time the will of governments to challenge their monopolistic or

Table 17.6 One global world, few regional integrations, and a myriad of economic nationalisms

	One global world	Regional integration	Competing nationalisms
Economic conditions	No more tariffs and nontariff barriers	Single market generates significant economies	Primacy of national sovereignty does not bear large economic costs
	Immaterial goods abolish distances	Still sheltered sectors	A coherent productive system
Political configurations	Need for strong and unified world institutions	Acceptation of partial pooling of national sovereignty	A strong state defending national interest
Viability	Problematic self-regulation	A distribution of integration gains supporting legitimacy by social groups at the national level	An admissible trade-off between autonomy and well-being
Type of crisis	Incapacity to sustain global commons/public goods	National economic divergence and inability to redefine new rules of the game	Tensions upon standards of living, rising costs of economic nationalism

oligopolistic rents, and they demand to localize their centers. Intangible goods that were running at the forefront of the abolition of frontiers are now required to be re-embedded into national territories in terms of labor laws, product regulations, and taxation.

Financial globalization is shrinking because governments intend to be the rescuers of last resort only for domestic banks to prevent the costly bailing out post the 2008 crisis. Nevertheless, some constraints introduced by financial regulations have been removed in the USA because the message that unleashed competition leads to systemic instability has been forgotten. IMF and WTO have lost their influence and authority, and this puts at risk the defense of two basic global public goods: world financial stability and the defense of fairness in international trade. The preservation of environment should have become the next global common, defended and monitored by a new and strong World Environment Agency. Instead, a harsh bargaining among nations makes success quite problematic, and public opinions ask for the equivalent of "America First." Globalization seems to belong to the past because the losers now have a voice via the rise of nationalist movements.

17.5.2 Can a New Balance Between Polity and Economy Sustain Regionalism?

This intermediate level could again well be a promising avenue to follow. On the one hand, regions are still sufficiently large territories for reaping increasing returns to scale that domestic markets of most medium-sized countries do not deliver anymore. On the other hand, policymakers should have learnt from Brexit and the impressive rise of populist movements in Europe that regional integration has to rely upon the explicit adhesion of a majority of citizens. Pedagogy is not sufficient because the potential losers have to be promised that they will have a share of the benefits: this cannot be the case if progressive taxation of personal income is abandoned, public services are cut, and wages become the adjustment variable for sustaining competitiveness.

The Nordic social democratic societies show that this solidarity can be implemented on a national basis. Nevertheless, Southern European countries do not enjoy the benefits of a dynamic innovation and productive system, and thus, they ask for a form of redistribution and/or a common industrial policy to overcome their weak productive basis. The incapacity to work out such a compromise is precisely one of the origins of the EU 2010 crisis. Political innovation is thus required to restore an adequate mix between economy and polity.

Where are the politicians who will dare to state that they will defend the common good for the region and not the interest of their homeland? Will international financiers be patient enough to give a chance to renewed regionalism? Will national public opinion and specially the euro-sceptic citizens trust the seriousness of this aggiornamento?

17.5.3 The Specter of a Nationalist Backlash

A negative answer to these questions would make rather likely a general move toward political nationalism and economic protectionism.

First, the costs are not very large for continental economies, rich of talents and natural resources, such as the USA. Second, in medium-sized economies, such as the UK, a fraction of the Brexiters does accept lower well-being in exchange of the recovery of a full and unconstrained British identity. The flaw of a purely economic approach to internationalization is to totally put aside any other motive, be it ethical, social, or political. Nevertheless, if the domestic production system is weak and not diversified enough, a dramatic decline in the standard of living might prove to citizens that economic dynamics cannot be the mechanical outcome of political voluntarism applied to the economy.

The perils of a nationalist withdrawal are acute in the EU. The promises of internationalization have not been fulfilled for low-skilled workers, welfare dependents, farmers, and small entrepreneurs. Traditional left-wing parties seem to have abandoned the representation of the "somewhere," who belong to the fraction of the population who defend local roots and identity, in favor of expressing the demands of the "everywhere," who prosper in the new productive paradigm because they can develop their talents abroad as well as at home. Conversely, some right or extreme right parties that used to be the voice of entrepreneurs and free trade have recently captured the votes of the numerous left behind. The inflow of a new generation of migrants, not anticipated by the European treaties, grants a growing audience to nationalist political programs. Finally, the fairly distant and indirect democratic control of EU institutions and policies confirms the feeling that effective democracy can only be exerted at local and national levels.

Finding new ways for reconciling polity and economy is the key challenge that needs to be addressed by all governments. It sets an ambitious research agenda for the *régulation* theory, socioeconomics, and almost all social sciences.

References

Amable B (2003) The diversity of capitalisms. Oxford University Press, Oxford

Baccaro L, Pontusson HJ (2016) Rethinking comparative political economy: the growth model perspective. Polit Soc 44(2):175

Boyer R, Uemura H, Isogai A (eds) (2012) Diversity and transformations of Asian capitalisms. Routledge, London

Harada Y, Tohyama H (2012) Asian capitalisms: institutional configurations and firm heterogeneity. In Boyer R, Uemura H, Isogai. A (eds) (2012)

Myant M, Drahokoupil J (2010) Transition Economies: Political Economy in Russia, Eastern Europe, and Central Asia. Wiley, New York

Index

R. Boyer et al. (eds.), *Evolving Diversity and Interdependence of Capitalisms*, Evolutionary Economics and Social Complexity Science 11,
https://doi.org/10.1007/978-4-431-55001-3

Printed by Printforce, the Netherlands